ACTIVE
Sociology
FOR GCSE

JONATHAN BLUNDELL
Adviser: Janis Griffiths

Longman

Pearson Education Limited
Edinburgh Gate
Harlow
Essex CM20 2JE
England, and associated companies throughout the World

First published 2001
ISBN 0 582 43443 2

Printed in Great Britain by Scotprint, Haddington

The publishers' policy is to use paper manufactured from
sustainable forests.

Acknowledgements

The publishers would like to thank the following for permission to reproduce copyright material:

p3 *Sociology* by A. Giddens and p206 *Women and Poverty in Britain in the 1990s* edited by J.Millar and C. Glendinning, © Blackwell
Publishers; p20 by David Ward, p62 by David Hencke, Larry Elliott and Ruth Kelly, p79, p85 by Dea Birkett, p90 by Adrienne
Katz, p91 by Peter Lennon, p95 by Kamal Ahmed, p105 by Gary Yonge, p109 by Amelia Gentleman and Jamie Wilson, p112 by
Jon Henley, p127 by Nick Hopkins, p141, p146 by David Brindle, p150, p153, p190 by John Carvel, p182 by Rebecca Smithers,
p183 by Donald MacLeod, p190 by Victoria Brittain and Larry Elliott, p191 by Will Woodward and Lucy Ward, p213 by Tessa
Mayes and Angus Stickler, p214 *Images of Deviance* edited by Stanley Cohen © The Penguin Group UK, p219 by Lisa Buckingham,
p221 by Sarah Boseley, p247, p264, p269 by Andrew Pudephatt, p279, p280 by Martin Kettle and Owen Bowcott, p280 by Chris
Reed, p281 by Alan Travis, p282 by Philip Willan, p312, p316 by Kamal Ahmed, p316–7, p343 by Larry Elliott and Victoria
Brittain, p370b by David Brindle, p370c by James Meikle, p392 by Stephen Bates, p400 by Madeleine Bunting, © Guardian; p23
The Forest People by Colin Turnbell © HarperCollins Publishers Ltd; p29 *Sociology Review*, Philip Allan Updates, (February 1998)
and p128 *Sociology Review*, Philip Allan Updates, (September 1995); pp39, 40 and 342 from *Sociology Update 2000*, p56 from
Sociology Update 1998, p81, 223, 258, 340, 341, p399 from *Sociology Update 1997*, by Martyn Denscombe (Olympus Books);
Crown copyright material is reproduced under Class Licence number C01W0000039 with the permission of the Controller of
HMSO and the Queen's Printer for Scotland; p41 reproduced with kind permission of Joseph Rowntree Foundation; p66–7, pp89
and 93 by Barry Hugill, p279, © *Observer*; p76 © *Sunday Express*, 14/4/1996; p78 by Paul Barker © *The Independent*, 6/9/1989;
p112 *Roots of the Future* by M. Frow, with kind permission of Commission for Racial Equality; p239 © Ruaridh Nicoll, 1998; p250
Reproduced with kind permission of Operation Black Vote; p327 by R. Cohen from *Hardship Britain*, with kind permission of Child
Poverty Action Group; p 370 © New Internationalist www.newint.org; p397 © Crosswalk.com at http://movies.crosswalk.com
quoted in *The Guardian Editor*, 23/7/1999; p302 © News International Newspapers Limited 1993.

Age Concern p126, All-Sport pp100, 102, Andes Press pp23, 152, 236, 240, 242 (right), 290, 322, 392, 394, Art Directors &
Trip pp6, 14, 68, 72, 76, 218, 228, 334, 366, 368, 382, BBC Picture Library p58, Greg Evans p129, 166, 376, Mary Evans
p260, Format Photographers pp64, 124,184, 196, 216, 244, 336, Granada Media p44, Hulton Getty Images pp54, 56, 148,
168, 212, 292, 319, 326, 328, Jeffrey Morgan p106, Julian Nieman p140, Network Photographers pp12, 120, 172, 178, 186,
238, 242 (left), 304, 338, Rex Features: pp16, 69, 90, 122, 214, 266, 280, 308, 310, 312, 386, 398, Ronald Grant Archive
p300, Tony Stone, p8, Sporting Pictures p110, The Tate Gallery p198, University of Kent, p332, John Walmsley pp26, 46, Janine
Wiedel pp34 86, 200, 246, 348, 354, 384, 388.

The publishers have made every effort to trace copyright holders. However, if any material has been incorrectly acknowledged, we
would be pleased to correct this at the earliest opportunity.

Contents

8 Education   165

9 Work   195

10 Politics   225

11 Crime   255

12 Media   287

Introduction

To the student

Sociology is an interesting subject but one that can be confusing and difficult at times. This is because of the nature of what it studies; there are no easy answers when it comes to crime, poverty and so on. Our lives are complicated. *Active Sociology for GCSE* has been designed to guide you through GCSE Sociology in ways that will I hope help you see just how important and interesting sociology is. Enjoy the journey.

Find out for yourself

These activities are intended to get you doing some sociology yourself. With some adaptation, many of these activities could be the basis of your coursework project. Talk to your teacher about this.

Key terms and important terms

Sociology involves a lot of words and phrases that may seem complicated at first. Sometimes, rather unfairly, these are called 'jargon'. In fact, they are usually a short way of expressing complicated ideas, and are therefore very helpful. To help you, each chapter has a list of ten key terms at the beginning, and then explanations of all important terms in an alphabetical list at the end. You do need to learn the important terms. When you look at the exam-style questions, you will see that questions often ask you to explain or use these terms.

Vocabulary box

The important terms lists are for sociological words. Any other words that you may not be familiar with are explained in the vocabulary boxes at the end of each section. You are likely to know at least some of these words, but occasionally the box may help you. I hope you won't feel patronised when the words are familiar to you – just ignore the box!

Web sites

This book recommends many web sites. Unfortunately, the content, and even the address, of a web site can change. I hope you will find what you want, but I cannot guarantee this.

Further research

You will find suggestions for further reading throughout this book, and at the end of each chapter you will find a list of web sites which you could visit. Few of these are specifically for students of GCSE Sociology, but you should be able to find something of use at each of them.

To the teacher

Active Sociology for GCSE is designed to be accessible to all students taking GCSE Sociology. The questions in each section progress through levels of difficulty, from simple identification of facts or definitions through interpretation of material to comparison and evaluation.

The sociology in practice sections have two purposes:

- Consolidation of learning – where possible the questions require students to look back at sections of that chapter. The questions will stretch most students.
- Extension of learning – by providing new material.

At least one part of each sociology in practice section will provide an international or global angle on the subject of that chapter.

Key skills

Sociology presents many opportunities to demonstrate key skills. The find out for yourself activities will enhance key skills where appropriate. The following symbols are used to identify the relevant key skills:

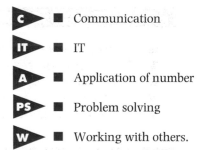

- Communication
- IT
- Application of number
- Problem solving
- Working with others.

Improving own learning and performance may be applied to any activity as required. The activities can often be adapted to cover other key skills. They can also often be adapted to form the basis of a coursework project.

Web sites

The URLs and content of the recommended web sites were checked during the final stages of preparing this book. Unfortunately, web sites change frequently and it cannot be guaranteed that there will not have been changes. This is why the suggestions to students are not more specific. You are advised to check the URL and content of a site before students access it. You may also find that some sites' content will cause them to be blocked by your centre's web filtering systems. You may want to set specific questions for students visiting the site, depending on the site's content at that time.

1 The Individual and Society

KEY TERMS

conflict
consensus
culture
identity
norms
roles
social control
socialisation
status
values

What makes us human? We are not meant to live totally alone. Individuals who grew up without any contact with other people would never learn to be fully human. They would not speak or understand language. They would not learn all the things that help us get on with others and live as members of a society. This chapter explores how we learn – through the process of socialisation – and the things that we have to learn. You will see that this helps us live as members of a society by giving us a culture that we share with others.

Yet this process of learning, while it helps us live with others, places limits on what we can do. If we do not do as society wants, we face punishments. Social control is the other face of socialisation.

The chapter goes on to explore some of the other ideas and debates that concern sociologists. We ask to what extent people's behaviour is decided by their genes and to what extent by the society that they live in. We ask what societies are like – is the most important thing about them that all kinds of people get along and agree on the basic things most of the time, or is it that there are deep conflicts based on unequal distribution of power and wealth?

You will come across these questions later as you study different topics within sociology.

IN THIS CHAPTER YOU WILL LEARN ABOUT:

- what cultures are, what they have in common and how they differ
- how people learn norms, values and roles and so become members of a culture
- how the processes of socialisation and social control go together
- the debate as to what extent biology and genes shape human behaviour
- different opinions sociologists have about the nature of society

CHAPTER CONTENTS

Culture

KEY FOCUS

We are all born into and live in a culture. A culture is the whole way of life of a group of people. Having a culture makes us fully human – this can be seen from the examples of children who have not belonged to a culture.

Shocking truth of the puppy boy

Puppy boy Horst is three years old – and just beginning his life as a human being.

He is the child raised by a devoted pet Alsatian called Asta while his parents went out drinking.

He became so like a dog that he didn't know how to use a toilet – and cocked his leg against a bush instead.

Now, as Horst gradually learns the behaviour of a normal little boy, the full shocking story of his lost babyhood is being unravelled.

Alsatian Asta had a litter of eight puppies just before Horst was born and they were taken from her. Pining for her brood, the dog turned her affection to the new baby. Asta nuzzled him, licked his hands, face and bottom clean, kept him warm in a furry blanket under her tummy.

Horst and Asta were confined to one room. When they were discovered there, sharing a raw chicken, Horst's extraordinary existence came to light. The wallpaper was clawed to tatters.

Now Horst is in a clinic in Wuppertal being reborn. He can keep down hot food – which he had never had – and he has added weight to his feeble frame, a third underweight. The staff are talking to him, slowly teaching him to accept and enjoy cuddles, smiling at him, showing him toys and encouraging him to explore his new world.

And he's learning that humans can be loving too.

Adapted from the *Daily Mirror*, 24 March 1988.

Can someone be truly human if they grow up without human contact?

People and society

Human beings are social animals. We share our lives with other humans – in families, in schools, in workplaces and so on. The groups we live in and with are social groups. We behave in similar ways to other people. Most of the time we can understand and predict what other people are thinking and doing. This is the basis of society – the 'socio' that you are studying in sociology.

Culture

A term very closely related to society is **culture**. Sometimes culture is used to mean the very best achievements in art, music, literature and so on. In sociology, however, it has a broader meaning. Culture refers to the things that are shared by the members of a society, the things that make it possible to understand other people. It includes behaviour that we have learned, that is, shared ways of doing things. These are different in different cultures. For example, in some cultures it is normal to eat with your hands, in others with chopsticks and in yet others with a knife and fork. It includes language because we have to be able to communicate with the other members of our society.

Socialisation

Culture has to be learned. We are not born knowing that we should eat with a knife and fork; we have to learn this, usually from our parents. We don't even know at first what we can and can't eat. Babies often experiment with eating things that horrify their parents, or mix foods up in a way older people find unpleasant. This is because babies have not yet learned the cultural rules about eating. The process of learning is called **socialisation**.

We belong to one culture. While other cultures will also have a language, ideas about what, how and when to eat, what to wear and so on, these may well be different from our own. Differences between cultures are referred to as **cultural diversity**. Culture then gives us something we share with some other people, but is also something that makes us different from many people. We learn who we are not only through what we are like, but through what we are not like.

Other animals can be described as social because they live in complex societies with animals carrying out different **roles**. Ants and bees, for example, have societies that work because different types of insects – queen, drones, workers and so on –

are doing different work, all contributing to the overall survival of the nest or hive. But other animals have little if any culture. Most of what they do is by instinct. A worker ant never had the choice of doing anything else.

Humans have very few instincts. We have reflexes – we blink or duck, without thinking about it, if we see an object coming towards us – but not instincts, which are patterns of behaviour that are inherited, not learned. The ability of birds to migrate to places they have never been before is an instinct, and there is no equivalent in humans. Human babies are in fact helpless compared to the young of other animals – we have to be taught how to do almost everything. Our behaviour is learned, not inherited, and is part of our culture.

Unsocialised children

Very occasionally, children are not socialised, and therefore do not learn a culture. There are legends about human babies raised by animals, such as the twins Romulus and Remus who in Roman stories were raised by wolves. More recent and well-documented cases suggest that children who do not grow up with other humans cannot make up for this later. The early years are vital – little children learn languages, and many other things, very quickly, but this becomes harder as they grow older.

One such case is 'The Wild Boy of Aveyron', a boy of about 11 or 12 found in France in 1800.

'On 9 January 1800 a strange creature emerged from the woods near the village of Saint-Serin in southern France. In spite of walking erect, he looked more animal than human, although he was soon identified as a boy of about 11 or 12. He spoke only in shrill, strange-sounding cries. The boy apparently had no sense of personal hygiene and relieved himself where and when he chose ... He refused to wear clothes, tearing them off as soon as they were put on him ... Later the boy was moved to Paris and a systematic attempt was made to change him from beast to human. The endeavour was only partly successful. He was toilet-trained, accepted wearing clothes and learned to dress himself. Yet he was uninterested in toys and games, and was never able to master more than a few words. So far as we can tell, on the basis of detailed descriptions of his behaviour and reactions, this was not because he was mentally retarded. He seemed either unwilling or unable fully to master human speech.'

Sociology by A. Giddens, 3rd edition, Polity, 1999.

It seems that by not being with other people, this boy had missed out on some of the important things we learn through socialisation. What were these things?

What makes us human?

Was the wild boy of Aveyron a human being? Yes, of course, in the sense that he was a member of the same species as us. Yet in many ways he missed out on some of the important things that make us human. He never really learned to communicate at more than a basic level with other people. He did not belong to French society or to any society, because he could only join in to a very limited extent.

To many sociologists, it is possession of a culture shared with others that makes us human. We do not and are not meant to live completely alone. All of human progress, all aspects of social life today, are built on the relationships of people with other people. As was said at the start of this section, we are social animals – yet this is exactly what makes us distinctively human.

QUESTIONS

1 What is meant in sociology by 'culture'?

2 What is the difference between an instinct and a reflex?

3 Some animals are social, but they do not have a culture. Explain what this means.

ROUND-UP

Culture is the whole way of life of a group of people. It is learned through the process of socialisation, and shared with others. Human beings who never come to have a culture, through being isolated from other humans when they are young, are not able to fully acquire a culture.

VOCABULARY

Well documented: plenty of written evidence is available
Shrill: very high-pitched
Mentally retarded: having low mental ability

Norms, mores, values and roles

KEY FOCUS

Norms, values, mores and roles are learned during the process of socialisation. They make up the culture of a society, and they vary enormously between societies and over time.

Social life is full of rules – some written, some not.

Norms, mores, rules

Norms are the unspoken and unwritten rules of behaviour in everyday life. We learn them during socialisation, and they tell us what we should and shouldn't do in particular situations. Sometimes they may be explicitly taught to children by their parents or others, but often they are learned through observation, and also by trial and error – by seeing what the reaction of others is.

Mores (pronounced 'more rays') are a stronger form of norms, referring to ways of behaving which most people in a society believe are essential to maintain standards of decency. There is a moral aspect to mores which is not always present in norms. The term is less widely used in sociology than norms.

Even stronger than mores are rules, regulations and laws. Organisations like schools and places of work have rules, and are able to punish those who break the rules. Laws apply to the whole of a society. Rules and laws are usually written

down, and those who break them know as they do so what the likely punishment will be if they are caught.

QUESTIONS

What norms apply in the following situations?

(a) The waiting room of a doctor's surgery. (Where should you sit? Can you talk to other people? Where should you look? etc.)

(b) At a party for teenagers. (You may be tempted to say there are no norms – but think of what behaviour would be approved or disapproved of.)

Values

Values are the beliefs that lie behind social norms. For example, one norm is that if you get on a bus on which there is only one passenger, you do not sit next to that person! (How might the passenger react if you did?) This is not simply a norm, because it reflects the underlying values of privacy and personal space. In our society, we assume the passenger would prefer not to have the company of a stranger. It is possible, however, to imagine a society where to fail to sit by and talk to the passenger would be seen as being unfriendly, and would be disapproved of.

The majority in any society shares values, in this sense. They are not the same as attitudes, on which people can differ enormously within a society. In politics, for example, people disagree as to which party has the best policies (a difference in attitude) but most people feel that the political system of having parties, with voting and elections, is preferable to having a dictator.

Values that you may think of as your own personal values are in fact shared with many others. You have learned them from other people (although you may have chosen them from among several possibilities). Some of the basic values in Britain can be traced back to Christianity. Although religion is not as strong as it once was, it still guides many people's ideas about what is right and wrong behaviour.

We are often in new social situations where we have no experience of the norms required. Knowing the values of our society helps us work out what the norms are likely to be.

Values differ enormously between societies. Western societies place a high value on materialism, the possession of money and consumer goods. In other societies in the past, such as the Cheyenne of North America, possessions were considered worthless except for the prestige that could be acquired by giving them away. A Cheyenne who gave away everything he owned would be highly respected; someone who did that in Britain today would be considered eccentric or even mad.

Role and status

Status refers to the position someone has in society. For example, being a pupil in school is a status, as is being a son or daughter. In sociology a distinction is often made between **ascribed status** and **achieved status**.

Ascribed status is decided by social characteristics fixed at birth, and cannot be changed easily, for example an individual's gender and ethnicity.

Achieved status is the result of a person's own efforts, for example in getting educational qualifications or entering a professional career.

Norms tend to go with statuses. For example, there are norms expected of a pupil in a classroom, or of a teacher. The set of norms that goes with a status is called a role. Just like a part in a play, a role gives us a script to follow, but allows room for us to perform it in our own way.

Everyone has many roles, which we switch between quite easily, sometimes having several roles at the same time. Here is a list of some of my roles:

- Family roles: father, husband, son, uncle, brother, godfather.
- Work-related roles: teacher, head of department, lecturer, writer, trade union member.
- Social and leisure roles: football supporter.

There are also many roles I play only occasionally, or for short periods: a patient for my doctor and dentist, a customer for various shops and my bank, a passenger for bus and train companies and so on. Each of these roles gives me a shared interest with others, and puts me in a relationship with others.

When we know and understand each other's roles, social life becomes orderly and predictable. Even if I have never seen a particular doctor before, I know what to expect when I go to his or her surgery. The doctor's role is to be sympathetic, to listen and to offer some explanation and advice or treatment. I also know how I should behave – there is a patient's role – and the doctor will expect me to behave like a patient.

FIND OUT FOR YOURSELF

Now work out your own roles, using the categories of family roles, work-related roles (you may need to separate school roles from those in any part-time work you have) and social and leisure roles.

Roles do not always fit together well. Your role as a pupil may well clash with your other roles. You are expected to spend a considerable amount of time studying, and this may make it difficult to find time for your roles as a best friend or a part-time worker. This is called **role conflict**.

QUESTIONS

Write a one-sentence definition in your own words of each of the following:

norms, mores, rules, values, status, ascribed status, achieved status, roles, role conflict.

ROUND-UP

Social life is usually orderly and predictable because people behave according to roles, sets of norms attached to their statuses. The norms are derived from values, which are shared by most people in a society but can vary a lot between societies.

VOCABULARY

Moral: concerned with issues of right and wrong
Prestige: high status, respect

Cultural diversity

Human cultures around the world, and throughout history, have some shared features, but there are also huge differences.

Far from being old fashioned and irrelevant, traditional culture can be essential to a modern tourism industry.

What cultures share

Forms of behaviour that are found in all cultures are sometimes called **cultural universals**. These are some cultural universals:

- Language. Children have to learn to speak their language in order to participate fully in their society. Although languages are very complicated (as you will know if you are studying a modern foreign language) young children are able to learn their language relatively quickly. Language enables us to talk to others, to communicate our feelings and to be aware of ourselves and of the past and future. Languages vary enormously (for example in how many tenses they have, or in whether nouns have a gender or not) but share a basic structure that makes it easier for children to learn languages.

- Marriage and the family. All cultures have arrangements by which one or more men form a socially approved relationship with one or more women for the purpose of having and raising children. Our society, of course, only allows one man and one woman, and we approve the relationship through the wedding ceremony. These ideas are examined in more detail in the chapter on families (see page 135).

- Religion. Belief in a god or gods, or in some form of supernatural or magical power, seems to be a universal feature of human cultures, as are rituals and other practices involving these beliefs. For some people, these beliefs are proof that there is a god who is so vast and unknowable that different cultures inevitably worship god in different ways.

- Property. All cultures have rules that allow an individual or family to claim things as their own.

- A ban on incest. The one thing which all cultures ban is not, as you might at first think, killing people (in fact, depending on the circumstances and who the victim is, this is sometimes approved of; for example, killing an enemy soldier in wartime). Nor is it cannibalism; there have been societies where eating people was acceptable in some situations. Incest, that is sexual relationships between close relatives such as brothers and sisters, and parents and their children, is the one thing that is almost universally banned. There have been exceptions when royal families, such as the Pharaohs of Ancient Egypt, are seen as divine, because it was thought unacceptable for gods to marry or have children with ordinary people. Pharaohs therefore had to marry very close relatives, such as a sister.

Even within these cultural universals, there are wide differences between cultures. For example, while all cultures have some kind of religious belief, what exactly people believe in and how they show this varies considerably. There may be belief in a single god (as in Christianity), or in many gods, or in natural spirits. There may be formal institutions such as churches, or none at all.

How cultures differ

Cultural diversity or difference is striking. We will look here at only two types of difference:

- Food. We all have to eat, but what is eaten, when and

how varies. In Britain we do not normally eat insects, or certain animals such as cats and dogs, but these may be considered delicacies elsewhere. Pork and beef are eaten in Britain, but pork is not eaten by Jews while Hindus do not eat beef. We eat many foods with a knife, fork and spoon (although for some foods and some occasions eating with your fingers is acceptable); in other cultures, chopsticks or fingers may be the norm. Even when we eat reflects cultural diversity; if you have visited southern Europe you will know that people tend to eat their evening meal much later than is normal in Britain.

■ Clothing. Some protection from the weather is common but not universal; some peoples go without clothing (though decorating the body seems to be almost universal). Clothing norms tend to be different for the two sexes. Trousers are a western tradition (though not everywhere in the west; Roman men wore tunics and togas and Scotsmen wore kilts). Men's clothing from other parts of the world, such as the Malaysian sarong, would look odd on a British man in most situations. In Islamic countries norms require females to cover their legs, arms and sometimes their faces and heads.

In studying other cultures it is important not to assume that your own way of doing things is necessarily better than anyone else's. Each culture must be understood on its own terms; its norms and values will be different, but not better or worse. Avoiding making judgements in this way is called **cultural relativism**.

An end to diversity?

Western (or more precisely, American) consumer culture has spread rapidly around the world in the last few years. This means that in many countries people can (if they can afford it), for example, drink Coca Cola or eat at McDonald's or wear a baseball cap. Hollywood films (such as *Titanic*) and some pop music are also popular all around the world, although in most countries people also like and listen to artists from that country. English is the most important global language, spoken and understood all around the world. Does this mean that cultural diversity will eventually disappear, and everyone will have American or western culture?

The answer is probably not. The response of many cultures is to try to keep their traditional practices; this can even be a way of making money out of tourists, who will pay to see traditional dances or buy carvings. Being seen as different from other places is essential to attract tourists.

It seems likely that people will choose to keep the elements of their culture they value most, and combine them with the aspects of western culture they want. People in western countries will also borrow from elsewhere. 'Ethnic' clothing and jewellery are popular, and we eat food prepared in the

styles of many different cooking traditions. British food culture has changed so much that curry (originally from India) is now a national dish. Since the possible combinations of the west and the rest are endless, you could argue that cultural diversity will even increase.

FIND OUT FOR YOURSELF

Two examples of diversity, food and clothing, are discussed here.

Write your own similar account of cultural diversity in drinks. You could start with the British cup of tea – hard to find in France or the USA, which prefer different types of coffee. Then you could go on to alcoholic drinks. Which countries do not allow alcohol at all? What drinks are popular in which countries?

Are there any differences between drinks considered appropriate for men and for women?

QUESTIONS

1 What is meant by a cultural universal? Explain using two examples.

2 What one practice is forbidden in almost all cultures?

3 What is meant by cultural relativism?

4 What is meant by consumer culture?

5 Is the spread of western culture likely to wipe out local cultures around the world? Give reasons for your answer.

ROUND-UP

All cultures have a number of features, which are referred to as cultural universals. However, even these take very different forms in different cultures; this is evidence of cultural diversity. This diversity may be threatened by the spread of American culture, but many cultures find that the things that make them different are useful, interesting and worth keeping.

VOCABULARY

Rituals: set ways of doing things
Cultural diversity: the exact form that culture takes varies enormously in different times and places

Socialisation

KEY FOCUS

The process of socialisation is most important in early childhood, but continues throughout life. In early childhood the main agency of socialisation is the family, but later the media, schools, **peer groups** and other **agencies of socialisation** become important.

We learn our culture from others through socialisation.

Primary socialisation

Sociologists refer to the process of socialisation in early childhood as **primary socialisation**. This takes place mainly within the family and home. Children learn, from their parents especially but also other family members, the most basic norms, values and roles of their culture.

They also, of course, are learning a lot more, and it is difficult to draw a line between what is part of culture and what are other skills. For example, children learn what can and cannot be eaten. While all children may learn that you cannot eat stones, there may be cultural differences when it comes to eating other things. In western societies we tend not to eat insects, but in some parts of the world termites and grubs are considered tasty snacks.

How does socialisation actually take place? Children are constantly watching their parents and others, and learn a lot by copying. What they do will be praised or corrected by their parents, so they learn, for example, that they can get approval for eating without making a mess. Socialisation is not simply a one-way process, with children passively taking in what goes on. Children try out different behaviour to see what the reactions of others will be. They work out for themselves, on

past experience, what is expected in different situations. They also, of course, reject some of what they are being taught, behaving at times in ways that are disapproved.

Secondary socialisation

From quite an early age, **secondary socialisation**, carried out by secondary agencies of socialisation, is also important. Children have now learned the basic attitudes and skills necessary to mix socially with others, and move on to learning less general skills and attitudes. Secondary agencies are all those institutions or groups from which children learn their society's culture. The main ones are the mass media (television, radio, books, newspapers and magazines and so on), pre-school education such as play groups and nurseries, school, religion and peer groups.

Mass media

Even from a very early age, children today are aware of the mass media. There are books, magazines, music, television programmes and so on aimed at even pre-school children. Sometimes these have an openly educational or socialising intention; they are meant to help children learn more about their culture and about what is expected of them. Even when this intention is not there, children will take in messages from the media, for example, from the different things they see boys and girls doing in a book or television programme.

Schools

Schools, where formal education takes place, are set up specifically to carry out socialisation. Children have to learn how to get on both with other children and with adults, and are expected to conform to rules and regulations about behaviour, uniform and so on. They also learn some of the requirements for adult life; for example, having to turn up at a set time and not leave until a set time can be seen as training for work. Children learn to be independent from their parents, and the peer group becomes very important. They also learn knowledge and skills that the society thinks it is desirable for them to have. At school, as in the family, children do not passively accept rules and authority; some challenge them and risk getting into trouble.

Peer groups

Peer groups are people in the same social position whom we are with regularly, for example a class at school or a particular group of friends. Peer groups can exert very strong pressures on individuals, especially when they are young. There is growing evidence that peer groups are very important from an early age. Even young children observe other children closely, trying to learn how they should behave – and they may pick up messages that their parents would rather they didn't! At school, conforming to the norms and values of a peer group may bring the individual into conflict with the school's rules and requirements.

Religion

Religions provide strong guidelines for behaviour, and threats of punishment for wrong behaviour. Christianity has the Ten Commandments, and the example of Jesus's teachings and behaviour in the New Testament; Islam has its five pillars and so on. Most children learn about religion both at home from their family and at school, and many also practise a religion, attending a church or other religious institution.

Socialisation throughout life

Socialisation never reaches a full stop. Children learn how to live in their own society, but during their lives they will face new situations and move on from one role to another. Learning what is needed for the new situation can be called **resocialisation**.

Some situations in which resocialisation can happen are:

- leaving the family home
- starting a new job
- being sent to prison or to a mental hospital (and later, being released)
- getting married
- becoming a father or mother
- for a parent, when children grow up and leave home
- retirement
- sudden changes of fortune such as winning the lottery.

Socialisation in the past and in other societies

In the section above, most of the discussion has been about socialisation into modern western society. Socialisation, however, must happen in all societies; it is essential, because without it there is no continuity from one generation to the next.

Two of the agencies of socialisation above were far less important in history: schools and the mass media.

Before the rise of these modern agencies of socialisation, the family and community must have been even more important.

Religion and peer groups have also always been important. In the case of peer groups, for example, in many traditional societies people of the same age go through rituals and ceremonies together, and feel a strong attachment to their age group.

FIND OUT FOR YOURSELF

How important are the Ten Commandments as guides for behaviour? Conduct research to find out how many of your class, or of another class, know what the Ten Commandments are (first you may need to find out yourself what they are). Find out if they know what they mean, and whether they agree with them. What do your findings tell you about how important religion is in socialisation and in shaping people's values? Present your findings to the class.

QUESTIONS

1. What is primary socialisation?

2. Identify two agencies of secondary socialisation and explain how they play a part in socialisation.

3. Why might a person being released from prison after serving a long sentence experience difficulties? In what ways would the individual need to be resocialised?

4. Is socialisation a one-way process of taking in ideas? Explain your answer.

5. Think of two social groups you belong to. They can be formal groups with a recognised membership, such as a class at school, a church, club or society, or informal such as a group of friends. In what ways do these groups influence the way you think and behave?

ROUND-UP

Primary socialisation takes place in the family. Secondary socialisation takes place through other agencies such as the mass media, schools, religion and peer groups. Socialisation continues throughout life.

VOCABULARY

Passively: accepting without question
Pre-school: before starting school, which in Britain is usually at age 5

Socialisation into gender roles

KEY FOCUS   Here we look at one particular example of two ideas you have been studying, socialisation and roles. How are boys and girls socialised into the different roles society gives them?

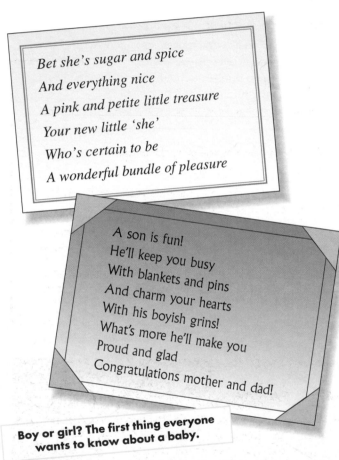

Bet she's sugar and spice
And everything nice
A pink and petite little treasure
Your new little 'she'
Who's certain to be
A wonderful bundle of pleasure

A son is fun!
He'll keep you busy
With blankets and pins
And charm your hearts
With his boyish grins!
What's more he'll make you
Proud and glad
Congratulations mother and dad!

Boy or girl? The first thing everyone wants to know about a baby.

The importance of gender

The first thing that we usually ask about a newborn baby is whether it is a girl or a boy. This indicates the importance of a person's sex. In fact, it is possible to predict certain things about a baby's future by knowing its sex; for example, a girl is likely to live several years longer than a boy.

The social role that goes with someone's sex is referred to as gender. Gender is a very important aspect of a person's **identity**. Gender is to some extent shaped by the biological differences between males and females, but there are also gender differences that come from particular societies.

Gender roles are different in different places and times. For example, a hundred years ago many people accepted that 'a woman's place is in the home'. Women were expected to spend most of their time and energy being housewives and mothers and not to compete with men in employment. There has been a dramatic change since then. It is now seen as acceptable, even a good thing, for girls to gain high qualifications and take up highflying careers.

In spite of these changes, there are still considerable differences between the gender roles of boys and girls, men and women. These can be called stereotypes. Stereotypes are one-sided, exaggerated ideas. The stereotypical teenage girl is interested in romance and her appearance. The stereotypical teenage boy is mainly interested in football, and far less concerned (or at least claims he is) with his looks.

The family and primary socialisation

Parents treat boys and girls differently in many ways. A feminist sociologist, Ann Oakley, suggested that there are four ways in which gender socialisation takes place in the first years:

■ Manipulation. Parents encourage behaviour that is seen as normal for the child's sex and discourage the behaviour associated with the other sex. For example, mothers may encourage girls to pay more attention than boys to their hair and appearance.

■ **Canalisation**. Children are 'channelled' by their parents towards toys and activities seen as appropriate for their sex. For example, girls may be given toys such as dolls and miniature kitchens that encourage an interest in being a mother and doing housework. Of course, boys may get these toys as well, but they are more likely to have 'boys' toys' – trains, cars and so on.

■ Verbal appellations. These are the ways we talk to children that tell them at an early age how important gender is – 'good girl', 'naughty boy' and so on.

■ Different activities. Boys and girls are encouraged to get involved in different activities. Girls are expected to help their mother indoors while boys get greater freedom to roam outdoors. As they get older, girls are still expected to help out at home far more than boys.

Many parents are aware of these differences, and decide to try hard to bring children up in non-sexist ways. This is very difficult, because children are soon receiving messages from other agencies of socialisation. We will look at four briefly here. Education and the mass media are both examined in more detail in later chapters.

Agencies of secondary socialisation

Education

At school, socialisation into gender roles continues. Although boys and girls now study the same things, they learn to behave differently, in the classroom and in the playground. Teachers may treat boys and girls differently. The way subjects are taught and the books that are used may reinforce this. For example, older science textbooks are far more likely to show men and boys carrying out experiments. Children learn from this that scientific experiments are an activity that is more appropriate for boys than girls. Later, at A level and degree level, fewer girls than boys choose to study sciences.

Mass media

Gender differences are apparent in the mass media children use. Television programmes, magazines, books and music all carry what sociologists call representations of gender. Although there are now deliberate attempts to avoid gender stereotypes, there are still strong differences. Boys are more likely to be the heroes of stories, to be active and adventurous. Girls are more likely to be shown as less active, more interested in the home, and needing the help of boys and men to do things.

Religion

The teachings of traditional religions such as Christianity and Islam lay out very different roles for men and women. The prophets and other characters in the holy books are mainly men, and God himself is always seen as male. Almost all priests are men. From these messages girls will form the impression that religions consider men to be more important.

Peer groups

Groups of friends of the same age play a very big part in establishing gender roles. From a very young age, both sexes learn from their peers what is appropriate for their sex. They also learn that if they behave too much like the other sex, or play with them too much, they risk name calling and perhaps worse. This applies more to boys than girls. Girls are allowed to be 'tomboys', but boys who like activities seen as feminine face scorn.

 FIND OUT FOR YOURSELF

Is it true that girls are expected to help out more at home? Conduct research to find out. If you are in a mixed school, you can ask questions about housework, tidying up the bedroom and so on to both boys and girls. If you are in a single-sex school, ask about what brothers and sisters are expected to do.

Remember to ask not just about housework, but also jobs such as walking the dog, mowing the lawn, doing shopping – these count as well.

Present your findings to the class.

QUESTIONS

1. What are stereotypes? Explain by referring to gender roles.

2. What does Oakley mean by canalisation? Explain using an example.

3. Identify and explain two other ways in which gender socialisation takes place in the early years.

4. Choose one agency of secondary socialisation and explain how it creates or reinforces gender differences.

5. Which agency of secondary socialisation is the most important for gender differences? Give reasons for your answer.

ROUND-UP

Gender differences have some basis in biological differences between the sexes, but are mainly created by society. Young children are socialised into gender roles during primary socialisation in the family and this is later reinforced by other agencies of socialisation.

VOCABULARY

Feminist: someone who calls for equal rights for women
Appellation: the act of naming

Social control

Social control refers to the ways in which society shapes and controls the way we think and behave. Sometimes social control takes the obvious form of physical force and punishment, but most of the time it involves the groups and institutions we looked at earlier as agencies of socialisation.

Miners' strike, 1984–5 – if all else fails, people can be controlled by force.

Making people conform

Societies have to have ways of making their members conform to norms and values. Everyone learns the culture of their society through socialisation, but knowing norms and values does not mean people will conform to them. Therefore societies develop ways of making people toe the line – do as expected – at least most of the time.

To achieve this it is necessary to have a system of **sanctions**. Sanctions can be either rewards for conforming to society's expectations, or punishments for failing to conform. Failing to conform is called deviance, and is the subject of a later chapter. One particular form of deviance is crime, which involves breaking not just a norm but a law.

Sanctions can be applied by an official institution, such as a court, or by a person in authority. This is referred to as formal **social control**. Sanctions can also be applied by everyone in everyday life; for example, you would probably find a way of letting a friend know if you disapproved of something they had done. Your disapproval, and perhaps the threat of the friendship ending, would be the sanction. This is an example of informal social control.

The range of sanctions that can be used is vast. In everyday life, it might be a 'tut' of disapproval, or a comment if someone pushes ahead of you in a queue. In school, it might be a frown of disapproval from a teacher, or being sent out of the room, or being suspended. In the case of crime it might be a fine, a prison sentence or even in some countries execution.

FIND OUT FOR YOURSELF

Make a list of all the ways in which sanctions can be applied to a student in school, starting with the lightest (probably a look from a teacher, without words) to the heaviest (probably permanent exclusion). You should be able to think of at least ten, although you may not be entirely sure what order to put them in.

When we studied socialisation, we saw that socialisation was necessary for social life to exist at all. The same agencies of socialisation through which we learn culture are also **agencies of social control**, because they can impose sanctions on those who do not conform. Sociologists differ in the way they interpret this. Functionalists see social control as essentially good, and necessary if society is to function well. Others such as Marxists and feminists are interested in how people can be made or persuaded to behave in ways, and to believe in things, that are against their interests. Seen in this way, social control is not positive at all; it suits those who control, not those who are controlled.

We will now look at the agencies of socialisation again, this time drawing out how they make people conform, that is, how they act as agencies of social control as well as socialisation.

Families

We are at our most impressionable when very young, and the strength of the bond between parents and children means that parents are in a uniquely powerful position to influence children. During primary socialisation in the family, children accept norms and values to such an extent that they internalise them; that is, they think of them as their own and they act as a conscience. We come to believe the norms and values are right and proper, and so we are unlikely to deviate from them. If we do, we are likely to feel guilty and express remorse.

Parents have many ways of influencing their children's behaviour. They reward some kinds of behaviour, and make clear their disapproval of others. They act as role models; the constant example set by people that the child would like to be like is a powerful influence.

Schools

Schools exercise control over pupils in many ways. Pupils have to be in school and have to behave in certain ways (for example, working in lessons), and they can be punished if they do not conform to these requirements. Some sociologists argue that this control of behaviour is the real purpose of schools; what is actually taught in lessons, the content of the curriculum, is less important than the acceptance of authority and punctuality. This other side to what is learned in schools is called the 'hidden curriculum'. Pupils who do as they are told will be ideal workers later in life.

Peer groups

Peer groups are powerful agents of social control because people feel a need to belong to groups and fear rejection. They will therefore conform to peer group norms. A group of workers in a factory, for example, may have an unspoken agreement not to work too hard. Anyone who broke this agreement would be subjected to sanctions, for example the other workers might not speak to them, or might insult them.

Religion

To believers, religions offer very powerful rewards for good behaviour and punishments for bad behaviour. In Christianity, sinners face an eternity of hell and damnation, while the righteous will have everlasting peace in heaven. These are, for Christians, far more powerful motivations than any earthly reward or punishment. Other religions also lay down rules for good conduct, and prohibit other behaviour, promising rewards and threatening punishment.

Mass media

Messages in the media can have a strong influence on behaviour. The news constantly tells us who has been punished for which crimes, and police and crime dramas also reinforce the idea that breaking the law is wrong. Television provides powerful role models. Girls may strive to be very thin because the media pushes the message, through advertising and the prominence of models, that this is what attracts boys. This is a form of social control, influencing how girls think and behave, with potentially serious consequences.

Force

If the agencies of social control discussed above fail to control people's behaviour, societies have yet more powerful sanctions. The police are an organisation set up for the explicit purpose of social control, with a range of sanctions, from cautioning to criminal charges. They can use force when they think it necessary. They can use handcuffs, truncheons, and even sometimes guns. Criminals (people who break the law) can be completely removed from the rest of society, by being put in prison.

Sometimes even this is not enough. If the police cannot cope, the army will be used. At times, in Britain and elsewhere, the army has been used to control crowds and demonstrations. In Northern Ireland in 1969, when the police were unable to control the increasingly unstable situation, the army was sent in. It became a more or less permanent presence on the streets; social control was enforced through the threat of immediate armed response.

QUESTIONS

1. What is meant by a sanction?
2. Give an example of an informal sanction in everyday life.
3. Choose two agencies of social control and explain how they control people's behaviour.
4. What is the hidden curriculum?
5. Social control and socialisation are really two sides of the same coin. Explain what this means.

ROUND-UP

The process of socialisation is inevitably accompanied by the reward or punishment of behaviour which deviates from what is acceptable in that culture. All the agencies of socialisation are also agencies of social control.

VOCABULARY

Remorse: feeling sorry for what you have done
Punctuality: being on time

Nature and nurture

KEY FOCUS

In Socialisation into gender roles (pages 10–11), we looked at how far gender differences were the result of biology and how much the result of society. This idea is followed up in this section with the 'nature versus nurture' debate. We look at wider issues about human behaviour, not just gender.

How much can we learn about people by studying animal behaviour?

Nature and nurture

Sex refers in sociology to the biological differences between males and females. These are the physical differences in bodies but also that only women can give birth and breast-feed. Gender refers to the differences between men and women that are derived from the kind of society they live in.

Sociologists, perhaps not surprisingly, often see gender as more important than sex differences. They show how the gender roles of males and females vary enormously between cultures. There are societies where, for example, women go hunting and fishing and where men look after young children (see the section on Sex and gender on pages 84–5).

It seems that gender roles are not natural and inevitable, but can be what we want them to be. So feminists have argued that women can do, and should be able to do, everything that men can do, for example in jobs.

To many people, however, it seems 'unnatural' for women to do things that only men have done in our culture in the past. The word 'unnatural' suggests that they think there are natural differences between the sexes that we cannot and should not avoid.

In the '**nature** versus **nurture**' debate, nature refers to natural, biological differences; nurture to differences arising from culture and socialisation.

All in the genes?

There are other areas of social life too where some people think that the causes of behaviour are biological, not social. In the nineteenth century, as sociology was developing, many theories looked at biological differences for causes of behaviour. Lombroso believed that criminals were 'throwbacks' to an earlier, primitive, type of human, and that they could be recognised by their appearance (see biological and psychological explanations on pages 260–61). Others believed in the existence of different races, with white Europeans 'naturally' superior to everyone else. This belief led to the Nazi killing of six million Jewish people and other 'inferior' peoples.

More recently, such ideas have been based on genes. Genes are said by some scientists to determine not only things like hair and skin colour, but also the way we behave. In recent years there have been claims that scientists have discovered genes for violence, for being gay, for intelligence and so on. Theories that say genes decide how we behave are called **genetic determinism**. These claims are not accepted by everyone, as you will see.

Socio-biology

One kind of genetic determinism is called **socio-biology**. Socio-biologists have argued that much human behaviour can in fact be explained by biological differences, not social differences.

For example, they say that men are naturally suited to be breadwinners and women to be caring and to do domestic work because this is the way the sexes evolved in prehistory. They say that men are more aggressive because they need to compete with other men for mates and to defend their territory.

Both sexes try to ensure their genes survive in the next generation, but have different strategies for doing this. Men have a higher sex drive. Men are also promiscuous, and more likely to commit adultery, because they want to have children by as many women as possible. There is no limit to the number of children a man can have, and the more he has, the better the chance of his genes surviving. Women, on the other hand, can only have a limited number of children. Therefore, say socio-biologists, they have a lower sex drive and will try to find a man who will stay and protect them and the children. This is a woman's best way of ensuring the survival of her genes.

Socio-biologists are saying that people are basically still like other animals. Stags clash antlers, fighting over does. Many male animals mark their territory (for example by spraying urine). These examples from nature seem to back up socio-biology.

The evidence against

Socio-biology seems to justify sexual inequality and to see human life as inevitably involving aggression and competition. Women who want careers and fulfilment beyond housework and childcare are 'unnatural'. Rape can be seen as understandable, normal male behaviour taken too far. And if you can tell who are going to be criminals from their genes, why wait until they have broken the law before locking them up?

In fact, there is plenty of evidence from nature against this view. Males of some animal species mate for life with one partner; so spreading their genes widely is not 'natural' for them. Our nearest relatives, bonobo chimpanzees, cooperate with each other far more than they compete.

There are also problems with the logic of socio-biology. Surely a man would have a better chance of his genes surviving if he protected his children, which would mean staying with a partner and not running off after others. On the other hand, a woman might choose as her children's father a man who had damaged genes; it would make sense for a woman to have children by at least two men to reduce the risk of this. As for the idea that women have a lower sex drive, many cultures have strongly disapproved and punished any signs of female sexuality. In societies that have moved towards greater equality – and among bonobo chimpanzees – females can and do demonstrate a sex drive.

Conclusion

Sociologists do not think that biology is unimportant. But they do not think that it can determine our social behaviour. Humans can think, weigh up alternatives, make decisions. We

have a sex drive – but we can choose to be celibate. Perhaps there is a gene for violent behaviour – but no one is violent all the time. In any situation, anyone, whatever their genes, can decide not to be violent (or to be violent!).

Elsewhere in the book you will come across the idea of social construction. Several things which at first sight appear 'natural' turn out on closer inspection to be 'social'. For example, childhood is in a way 'natural' – we all went through a period of physical immaturity – yet who is thought of as a child, and how societies treat children, varies enormously (see Children and childhood on pages 120–21). The biological and the social are both important.

see Children and childhood on pages 120–21

QUESTIONS

1. What is meant by genetic determinism?
2. Describe Lombroso's biological theory of criminal behaviour.
3. Identify two differences between men and women that are biological, according to socio-biology.
4. Why are examples about the behaviour of animals not helpful in understanding human behaviour?
5. In what ways would sociologists argue against socio-biology?

ROUND UP

The nature-nurture debate is about the extent to which biological factors, such as our genes, influence our behaviour. The argument that most of our behaviour can be attributed to our genes is called genetic determinism. Most sociologists reject genetic determinism because even if our genes push us toward certain kinds of behaviour, we can decide to behave differently.

VOCABULARY

Celibate: abstaining from sexual intercourse
Throwback: a person who has the characteristics of a more primitive type
Strategy: a long-term plan for success

Consensus and conflict

KEY FOCUS This section follows on from earlier sections by asking questions about the nature of society. This is used to introduce you to the main theoretical perspectives in sociology, which you will come across at times throughout the book.

Are clashes like this one outside the World Trade Conference in Seattle in 2000 unusual interruptions in a peaceful society – or inevitable when power and wealth are unequally distributed?

Socialisation and consensus

If we all learn the norms and values of our society, and accept them and keep to them, this will make society predictable and stable. There should not be any great conflicts or civil wars. A society like this would be based on consensus – agreement.

Social control and conflict

If, on the other hand, the norms and values are against our interests, and suit those who are running society, this means there are fundamental conflicts in society. There are groups with different degrees of power. A society like this would be based on conflict, with one group defending its wealth and power against others.

This conflict would not have to be in the form of fighting in the streets. It might take other, less dramatic, forms, like party politics and campaigns.

Which of these descriptions best fits society today? Different sociologists have had different answers to this important question. The answers come from different theoretical perspectives in sociology, which you will come across from time to time in this book. This is the place where they are explained in most detail, so turn back to these pages when you need to.

Functionalism – a consensus theory of society

Functionalists see society as like a human body. The different parts of society are like different organs, each with a part to play that is essential to the health and survival of the whole. Every part of society has a function, a particular job to do. As long as all the parts of society do their job, society is healthy and everything runs smoothly. This is called the **organic analogy** – comparing society to an organism.

Here are some of these functions:

■ Schools – to give young people the skills they need for

work. If schools fail to do this, there is a knock-on effect on industry.

- Families – to socialise children. If families fail to do this, there is a knock-on effect in, for example, rising crime.

Marxism – a conflict theory of society

Marxists see society as divided by class. There is a permanent conflict of interests between classes, which occasionally takes the form of strikes and other protests, and which can lead to a revolution. The two classes are the ruling class (or bourgeoisie, to use the Marxist term) and the working class (or proletariat). The ruling class has almost all the power and wealth, and exploits the working class. The workers are 'wage slaves' – they have to work to survive, but they are never paid the full value of their work. This is because the ruling class takes some of the value of the work in the form of profits.

The agencies of social control are then ways in which the ruling class keeps the workers in their place. For example:

- Schools – children learn to do as they are told and accept their place in life. There are different schools – public schools – for the children of the ruling class.
- Mass media – brainwash people into only being interested in gossip, sport and trivia, and not interested in what is really going on in society.

You will see that **Marxism** is a bit like a conspiracy theory. The ruling class is a shadowy group with immense hidden power. Marxists are in favour of a revolution that would end exploitation and make everyone equal.

Feminism: an alternative conflict theory

Like Marxists, feminists see society as being fundamentally divided, but between the sexes rather than between classes. It is men who rule society and who have the power in most social situations – in relationships, in families, in schools and so on. This situation is called **patriarchy**. Feminists are in favour of equal opportunities for men and women, and of equal relationships in all areas of life.

The New Right

The **New Right** is a reaction against changes in the 1960s and 1970s. The New Right tends to favour a return to traditional values. For example, it is very much in favour of traditional nuclear families, and against recent developments such as the increases in divorce, cohabitation and lone-parent families.

A note of caution

The descriptions above are very brief and cannot take account of the many variations within each theory. For example, there are many different kinds of feminists, who sometimes strongly disagree with each other.

There are other theoretical perspectives in sociology as well. You will come across these if you go on to study Sociology at A level.

As you will have noticed, each theoretical perspective can look at the same thing and interpret it in a different way. Each may seem convincing – until you hear what another perspective has to say. The nature of the ideas and evidence in sociology is that often they can be interpreted in different ways. This is why, throughout the book, you will find explanations of disagreements among sociologists.

This does not mean that anyone's opinion goes in sociology. Rather, it means that social life is very complex and that there are no easy answers. Sociology is about trying to get nearer to understanding why things are the way they are – without expecting ever to reach a final answer, because social life will keep moving on.

QUESTIONS

1. For which perspective is society based on consensus?
2. For which perspective is society based on class conflict?
3. Identify and explain one similarity between Marxism and feminism.
4. In what ways, according to functionalists, is society like a living thing?
5. What is meant by patriarchy?

ROUND-UP

The way in which social control can be seen as the same thing as socialisation, but interpreted differently, points to the difference between seeing society as based on conflict or on consensus. **Functionalism** is a theoretical perspective based on a consensus view of society while Marxism is based on a conflict view.

VOCABULARY

Organism: a living creature
Analogy: a comparison to show similarities
Conspiracy theory: the belief that a secret organisation is behind anything unusual

Individuals and identities

KEY FOCUS

Both socialisation and social control tend to emphasise how much what we believe and do comes from society. So do the theoretical perspectives underlying them, the consensus and conflict approaches respectively. In this section we look at how individuals make choices and can, to some extent, decide their identities.

STANLEY WAS DEEPLY DISAPPOINTED WHEN, HIGH IN THE TIBETAN MOUNTAINS, HE FINALLY FOUND HIS TRUE SELF.

Identity involves asking, 'Who am I?'.

Identity and personality

Your personality is what makes you unique. You may share some of your personality traits – your charm, wit, compassion and so on – with other people, but your particular combination of them belongs to you alone.

Identity is rather different, because it involves identifying with a particular identity or group. It is about whom you want to be

like, and it involves some choice. Choosing whom you want to be like can also mean choosing who you don't want to be like. For example, if you identify with a particular football team, you will not identify with teams against which your team plays.

How would you show that you identify with a football team? Here are some possible answers: by going to matches; joining a supporters' club; wearing a replica shirt, scarf and so on; having a bag, pencil case and so on with the team's name and symbol.

As you can see, what you wear or carry with you can identify you to others as a follower of a particular team. You are making a clear, public statement of identity, using symbols that others can easily recognise. Followers of another team will then see you as different – so there may be times when it would be wise to hide that scarf!

Identities

Supporting a football club is just one aspect of identity. Other aspects that apply to all or to many people are:

- sex and gender identities – male or female?
- ethnic identity
- age
- class
- occupation
- nationality
- role within a family
- belonging to a church or other religious organisation.

All of these identities will be shared with many other people – not necessarily people you know. At a football match, you might feel a strong sense of solidarity with thousands of people you don't know, because you support the same team. Knowing you share this identity can make it easier to, for example, start a conversation with someone.

How much choice?

The identities that we can have all come from the society we live in. Yet there is almost always some degree of choice. How much choice will depend on the particular case.

Supporting a particular football team usually involves a high degree of choice, although some people are socialised into supporting a team by their family, community or peer group. There is also, of course, the choice of not supporting any team.

Nationality for most people involves little choice. For most people, birth gives citizenship of a nation-state and the right to have that nation's passport. Some people, though, have a choice; perhaps because they have been born in a country their parents were not citizens of. Or the choice may be to do with the political and cultural situation in that country. There is also a choice about to what extent to identify with your nationality. People in Scotland, for example, might identify themselves as British or as Scottish. They may feel both, at different times and to different degrees.

Identities today

The world today is changing rapidly. Identities are probably less fixed than they used to be, and there is greater choice. Here are some examples of what this means:

- Girls and women. Once women's main identities were almost inescapable – housewife and mother. Now there is greater freedom to pursue careers that offer different identities.

- Boys and men. For working-class males, occupational identity – being a coal-miner or a steelworker, say – used to be very strong. Many of these jobs have disappeared.

- Minority ethnic groups. Many young members of minority groups are creating new forms of identity. For example, no one until the last few years had ever had the identity of a London Bangladeshi, or a Scottish Sikh. There are new mixes of local British cultures and the cultures of the countries of origin of families who have settled here.

- People have a much wider choice of things they can buy or be interested in. So one aspect of identity might be liking a particular type of music, or wearing clothing with a particular designer label.

Interactionism

The **consensus approaches**, like functionalism, and the **conflict approaches**, like Marxism, which you read about in the last section, all stress how society can shape and influence our behaviour.

In this section, the idea of identity has been used to show that we do have some choice over who we are and what we do. In sociology there is a theoretical perspective that focuses on this more than the other perspectives do – **interactionism**.

Interactionists start not with society but with individuals. They are interested in what happens when small groups of people are together. They try to understand why people do

particular things. When it comes to research methods, they are likely to prefer participant observation and informal interviews, because of the kinds of data these methods produce. They will be less interested in large-scale social surveys.

HINTS AND TIPS

See Chapter 2 for an explanation of participant observation, informal interviews and social surveys.

FIND OUT FOR YOURSELF

Make a chart showing all aspects of your identity. Start with the words 'Who am I?' in the middle and around them place all your identities, and the people you share them with.

QUESTIONS

1. What is meant by identity, and how is it different from personality?
2. What symbols of identity might help you recognise:
   (a) a supporter of the England football team
   (b) a Hell's Angel
   (c) a priest?
3. Identify and explain three aspects of identity.
4. Identify and explain two types of identity that now offer more choice than in the past.
5. Which research methods do interactionists prefer, and why?

ROUND-UP

Identity gives us something in common with a group. We can choose to adopt many identities, such as supporting a football team, but with other identities there is less choice. The interest in choice – in how people shape society rather than being shaped by it – is associated with interactionism.

VOCABULARY

Compassion: showing concern for the misfortunes of others
Symbol: something that stands for something else
Solidarity: unity of interests

The individual and society – sociology in practice

The people of the rainforest

The Baka live in the rain forests of Cameroon in Central Africa.

'THE Baka have no marriage ceremony as such, but certain rules must be observed. Once the match has been agreed by the couple and their respective parents, the man must bring gifts for the father and mother of his future wife: meat from a big animal to prove his hunting ability, axes and spears. He then stays in his wife's village, working and hunting with her family, until the first child is born. This is usually when the couple go to settle at the man's home village, though close contact will be maintained with the woman's and she will often return there for subsequent births.

Within the framework of a marriage men and women have fairly distinct roles although some chores are shared. Women are responsible for building huts, carrying loads and daily tasks, like gathering vegetable foods, cooking, collecting water and firewood. Men have the … job of supplying meat for the group through hunting and trapping, and of collecting honey when in season. However, both men and women work in the plantations … and parents take more or less equal responsibility for bringing up their children. The social life of men and women is also quite disparate – for instance, apart from the main evening meal, they eat separately …

… Within the group as a whole the women are generally politically influential, vociferous and respected. Age is in fact more relevant to status in Baka society than sex: there are no chiefs as such, but elders, whether male or female, are in many ways the mainstay of the group.'

Baka – People of the Rainforest, Channel 4 Publications, 1988.

Questions

1 Look back at the section on Norms, mores, values and roles (pages 4–5). What norms, mores and values of Baka culture can you work out from this passage?

2 Look back at the section on Socialisation into gender roles (pages 10–11). In what ways are Baka gender roles similar to and different from gender roles in Britain today?

3 Do you think there is greater or lesser sex equality in Baka society than in Britain today? Give reasons for your answer.

Colour-coded ribbons

CAMPAIGNERS in the Stephen Lawrence case will this week take delivery of a further 20,000 orange ribbons, orange being the murdered teenager's favourite colour. The success of the ribbon is the latest in a series of colour-coded statements.

'It's a walking petition. You don't have to deliver leaflets, just wear the ribbon. It's even safe for people in authority to wear it. Without any doubt, the ribbon has helped show the strength of the campaign,' said the manager of the campaign.

The Lawrence ribbon is not intended to raise money, unlike the pink ribbon employed by breast cancer charities.

The first and best known ribbon is the red one associated with HIV and AIDS, although its principal function is raising awareness, not cash.

Adapted from 'Causes pin hopes on colour code' by David Ward, *Guardian*, 22 June 1998.

Questions

1 What three ribbons are discussed in the extract? What others do you know of? What other symbols of identity do some people wear?

2 Look back at the section on Individuals and identity (pages 18–19). Wearing a ribbon is a public statement of identity. Explain what this means.

3 'It's even safe for people in authority to wear.' This suggests social control – not everyone is free to show any symbol of identity. What symbols of identity would not be allowed in your school, and why?

Socialisation, social control and choices

Questions

1. Look back at the sections on Socialisation (pages 8–9), Social control (pages 12–13) and Consensus and conflict (pages 16–17). In the left-hand cartoon, how people behave comes from the society they live in. Explain how both socialisation and social control are based on this idea, and how they are different.

2. Look back to the section on Individuals and identities (pages 18–19). In the right-hand cartoon, people are able to make choices. Which theoretical perspective does this suggest to you, and why?

3. (a) Which aspects of your identity are the result of you making choices? In which aspects did you have little or no choice?

   (b) Write a short essay on 'How free are we to decide who we are?'.

VOCABULARY

Disparate: totally different
Vociferous: having a lot to say

The individual and society – important terms

achieved status	a position gained through effort, rather than being born into it
agencies of socialisation and social control	parts of society, such as the education system and families, which play a part in the processes of learning norms and values
ascribed status	a position into which you are born
canalisation	the channelling of children towards toys and activities seen as appropriate for their sex
conflict approach	sociology that emphasises deep divisions in society
consensus approach	sociology that emphasises agreement within society
cultural diversity	the wide range of differences between cultures
cultural relativism	the belief that no culture is superior to another
cultural universals	aspects of culture that are found in all cultures
culture	a shared, learned way of life
feminism	a theoretical perspective that focuses on the situation of women
functionalism	a theoretical perspective that is based on consensus
genetic determinism	the theory that human behaviour is decided by genetic makeup
identity	our sense of who we are in relation to others
interactionism	a theoretical perspective that focuses on individuals and small groups
Marxism	a theoretical and political perspective that sees society as divided by class
mores	a stronger form of norms
nature and nurture	the term given to the debate about how much biology and genes influence our behaviour
New Right	a theoretical and political perspective based on traditions and free choice
norms	guidelines for behaviour in particular situations
organic analogy	comparing society to a living organism; used by functionalists
patriarchy	the domination of social life by men; a term used by feminists
peer group	a group sharing the same social position
primary socialisation	the earliest and most important stage of socialisation
resocialisation	when a new culture has to be learned
role	a set of norms that goes with a status
role conflict	when an individual is faced with competing demands from different roles
sanction	a reward, or punishment for breaking a norm
secondary socialisation	socialisation after the first, primary, stage
social control	the way behaviour is regulated and controlled by society
socialisation	the process of learning a culture
socio-biology	a theoretical perspective based on genetic determinism
status	a position in society
values	beliefs that underlie norms

The individual and society – exam-style questions

Source A

This item describes a group of people living in the rain forest of Central Africa.

'Like children everywhere, pygmy children love to imitate their adult idols ... So a ... father will make a tiny bow for his son, and arrows of soft wood and with blunt points. He may also give him a strip of a hunting net. The mother will delight herself and her daughter by weaving a miniature carrying basket, and soon boys and girls are "playing house".'

Adapted from *The Forest People* by
Colin Turnbull, Paladin, 1984.

Source B

In western culture, most hot foods are eaten with a knife and fork. Children learn from their parents how to eat in the approved manner. In other cultures, children will learn what kinds of things should be eaten, and what should not.

Foundation tier

1 Look at source A and answer these questions
   (a) In what part of the world do the people described live? [1 mark]
   (b) What might a father make for his son? [1 mark]
   (c) What game do boys and girls play together? [1 mark]
   (d) What do sociologists call the process of learning from adults? [2 marks]

2 Look at source B and answer these questions:
   (a) What are two different ways in which hot food can be eaten? [2 marks]
   (b) What is meant by the term 'culture'? [2 marks]
   (c) What is meant by the term 'norm'? [2 marks]

3 In source A, boys and girls are learning different gender roles. Explain what is meant by a gender role. [2 marks]

4 Give one example of different gender roles in Britain today. [2 marks]

5 Explain with examples what is meant by cultural diversity. [5 marks]

Higher tier

1 Look at source A and answer this question:
   What do sociologists call the process of learning from adults? [2 marks]

2 Look at source B and answer these questions:
   (a) What are two different ways in which hot food can be eaten? [2 marks]
   (b) What is meant by the term 'culture'? [2 marks]
   (c) What is meant by the term 'norm'? [2 marks]

3 In source A, boys and girls are learning different gender roles. Explain what is meant by a gender role. [2 marks]

4 Give one example of different gender roles in Britain today. [2 marks]

5 Explain with examples what is meant by cultural diversity. [4 marks]

6 Explain with examples what is meant by social control. [4 marks]

The individual and society – further research

There are a number of sites which will be helpful whatever topic area you are studying. The following are GCSE Sociology sites or have sections for GCSE Sociology:

- www.hewett.norfolk.sch.uk/soc/gcse
- www.hartland64.freeserve.co.uk/gcse
- www.barrycomp.com/bhs/gcse.

Other useful sites include:

- www.hants.gov.uk/school/crofton/socrev (revision summaries on all topics)
- Sociology Central: freespace.virgin.net/chris.livesey/home
- Sociology Learning Support: www.chrisgardner.clara.net
- *Sociology Review* magazine aimed at A level students: www.le.ac.uk/sociology/socrev.

The Association for the Teaching of the Social Sciences has many good links (look for 'good sociology sites'): www.atss.org.uk.

You can reach many social science sites through:

- Yahoo.com/social-science/sociology
- the Social Science Gateway: www.sosig.ac.uk.

You can find out more about the early sociologists at The Dead Sociologists Society: http://ravem.jmu.edu/~ridnelr/DSS/DEADSOC (this is not a world wide web site).

Basic sociological terms and the theories of Marxism and functionalism are explained in the GCSE section of Sociology Arena: www.hartland64.freeserve.co.uk/gcse.

Research Methods

This chapter is all about how sociologists find things out. Much of what you will read in other chapters is based on research that has been done using the methods described here. As you will see, sociologists use a wide variety of methods, suited to what they are studying and the kinds of data they want to produce.

This chapter will be particularly important to you if you are doing a coursework project. You will find ideas on how to go about your project in a way that should help you to impress the examiners! There are opportunities to practise using the different methods that you will have to choose between. You will see that all the methods have both advantages and disadvantages. You will also find some ideas on how to present your findings.

Before undertaking any research, it is important to be aware of what is already known about what you are going to study. This chapter has sections on secondary data, which is data that already exists and can be used by sociologists.

KEY TERMS

interview
participant observation
primary data
qualitative
quantitative
questionnaire
reliability
sampling
secondary data
validity

IN THIS CHAPTER YOU WILL LEARN ABOUT:

■ the main research methods used in sociology
■ the practical and ethical problems that researchers may encounter
■ the secondary sources that can be used
■ how findings can be presented
■ advice on coursework projects

CHAPTER CONTENTS

Research methods: the basics

KEY FOCUS   This section introduces the most important terms and ideas in sociological research methods.

One way of collecting information.

Research

This book is full of sociological descriptions of aspects of social life such as the family, education, crime and the mass media. These descriptions did not suddenly appear; they are based on the findings of sociological research projects over many years.

Research refers to the process of finding out information and analysing and evaluating it. Sociology uses many different ways of researching. Sometimes, as with **experiments**, these

are similar to research methods used in the natural sciences such as physics, chemistry and biology. At other times, like historians, sociologists use documents. They also use the same methods as market research and opinion poll organisations, such as **questionnaires** and **interviews**.

Almost anything that involves people is of interest to sociologists, and almost any way of finding out information is used at some time.

The main types of method discussed in this chapter are:

- experiments
- social **surveys**, including questionnaires
- **informal interviews**
- **participant observation**
- use of **secondary data**.

Testing ideas

Most people have what can be called 'common sense' theories about the things sociologists study. They may, for example, have ideas – a theory – about why some people commit particular crime, perhaps saying it is because of not being brought up properly, or of having a particular kind of personality. In sociology this is only a starting point. Sociologists need to take such theories and examine them thoroughly, using appropriate research methods to see whether they are in fact accurate descriptions of reality.

Whether the findings of a research project are acceptable or not depends on whether they can be said to be valid, or reliable, or both.

Validity

Validity refers to whether the findings accurately reflect the reality they are describing. Findings may be invalid if, for example, in a questionnaire someone gives the answer he or she thinks the researcher would like to get rather than the most truthful one, or if people behave differently because they know they are being observed.

Reliability

Reliability refers to whether the findings can be checked by another researcher. Can someone else, doing the research in the same way, get the same results? If so, the research can be said to be reliable. This is the measure used in science; an experiment should always have the same outcome regardless of who the researcher is. This is more difficult in sociology because it involves people, who can choose how to behave or what answers to give. They may, for example, give different answers to different interviewers.

Both validity and reliability are important, but sociologists do not agree on whether validity or reliability is the more important.

Quantitative and qualitative

Sociological research can produce two different kinds of findings or data. **Quantitative data** refers to numbers and **statistics**, often presented in the form of graphs and tables. A questionnaire given out to many people, for example, produces quantitative data when the returned forms are analysed and the researcher works out how many people gave particular answers.

Qualitative data is descriptive, in the form of words rather than numbers. A recording or transcript of an interview, for example, in which someone explains in detail his or her views or experiences, is a type of qualitative data. If this definition of qualitative data sounds vague, don't worry; it is in fact much easier to say what qualitative data isn't than what it is – it isn't quantitative!

Qualitative data is often very difficult for researchers to analyse. Researchers may well have an enormous amount of notes, observations, interview transcripts and so on to sift through. The process of sifting, of sorting out what is most relevant and useful, is called coding. Researchers try to pick out themes running through their findings, and to make connections between them.

Many research projects produce both types of data, and both are useful. Most questionnaires, for example, contain questions where only certain answers can be given, so that statistics can be calculated, and other questions which allow people to express themselves in their own way.

Putting it all together

The terms we have used so far – the types of method, validity and reliability, quantitative and qualitative – tend to fit together.

The most reliable method, at least in theory, is the experiment. Experiments produce quantitative data. Experiments in sociology, however, have questionable validity. This is because

they create an artificial situation, and measure what happens in it, when sociology is about 'real' life. Sociologists cannot alter the **variables** as easily as scientists can.

Participant observation, on the other hand, has high validity. Reading a good participant observation study, you are likely to feel that this is how it must really be. It shows life as it is really lived by a group of people, and helps us see the world in the way they do. Participant observation produces qualitative data. But some people have argued that participant observation is not very reliable, in the sense that other researchers could attach themselves to the same group and reach different conclusions. The group would have changed over time, and this kind of research is very personal – a lot depends on the personality and skills of the participant observer.

QUESTIONS

1. What is research?
2. Explain the difference between quantitative and qualitative data.
3. What is validity?
4. Why are experiments in science said to be reliable?
5. Why is qualitative data often difficult to analyse?

ROUND-UP

Sociologists choose their research method or methods according to what they are studying and what kind of information they hope to get. They may choose a method which produces mainly quantitative or mainly qualitative data. The findings will be assessed according to how valid or reliable they are.

VOCABULARY

Document: a letter, article or other piece of text that provides evidence
Analyse: to examine in detail
Transcript: a written or printed copy of what someone has said

Experiments

KEY FOCUS

Experiments are the main way of doing research in the natural sciences but their usefulness in sociology is less certain. Experiments involve setting up artificial situations when usually sociologists want to observe 'natural' behaviour. Nevertheless, experiments do have some uses in sociology.

Experiments on people involve problems that do not arise in scientific laboratory experiments.

Experiments and science

In the natural sciences – physics, chemistry and biology – a lot of research is carried out by experiment. Experiments take place in controlled conditions and try to establish a relationship between two or more variables, that is, factors that can be changed. The relationship might be:

- **cause** and effect – one variable causes the other
- a **correlation** – the two variables change together but the researcher cannot prove exactly what the relationship is.

The researcher usually starts with a **hypothesis**, an idea about what will happen, and then tests it. The researcher tries not to affect the outcome in any way, by being as objective as possible. For example, a chemistry student might apply heat (one variable) to a liquid to see if it changes colour (another variable). He or she would also have a control, that is, an identical container of liquid to which heat was not applied. If the heated liquid changed colour and the unheated one did not, the researcher would be able to say that applying heat had caused the change of colour. At the end of an experiment the original hypothesis has either been proved or disproved.

Experiments and sociology

Doing experiments on chemicals is one thing, but doing them on living creatures is another. Experiments on animals are highly controversial, even when there may be medical benefits to people as a result.

Experiments are not common in sociology, but they are the most appropriate method for finding out about some things that sociologists are interested in. Some sociologists believe that sociology should try to be as scientific as possible, and this means using experiments when possible. It also means being objective, not letting your own values and feelings affect the research in any way (because sociologists study people, they are more likely than natural scientists to have strong feelings about what they are studying). This approach is called **positivism**.

Laboratory and field experiments

In **laboratory experiments** the researcher is able to control most aspects of the research. Other experiments take place 'in the field' – in the world outside. **Field experiments** have the advantage of being in the real social world, rather than creating an artificial situation. They tell us more about how people behave. However, the researcher usually loses quite a lot of control over the experiment; once the researcher has started his or her experiment, he or she has to let it run its course.

The Hawthorne Effect

If the people being studied are told or become aware that an experiment is taking place, their behaviour is likely to change. This is known as the **Hawthorne Effect** after a factory in the USA where researchers attempted to find out in what conditions workers were most productive. Whatever they changed – the light, the temperature, number and frequency of breaks and so on – the workers worked harder, because they knew their work was being observed. The term Hawthorne Effect can be used for any situation where people change their behaviour, whatever the method.

Ethical problems

The Hawthorne Effect makes research findings invalid, so a researcher may be tempted to conceal the true purpose of the research. This raises ethical problems, because people have a right to know that they are taking part in research, and the researcher should not manipulate their behaviour. If you tell people you want to carry out an experiment on them, they might well refuse to take part!

The problem of artificiality

Another problem with experiments is that they involve situations that are not natural but have been deliberately created by the researcher. So the findings may not apply to real life. Experiments also tend to be short in duration, and therefore they can only measure short-term changes in behaviour. For example, if a researcher wanted to study the effects of watching violent videos, it would not be very helpful to get a group of people to watch a video in a 'laboratory', then see how they behaved for a hour or so before they went home. Firstly, the effects might only come out much later. Secondly, the researcher would have no control over what the group had watched earlier and watched later; in other words, he or she could not control all the variables.

QUESTIONS

1 What is meant by correlation?

2 What is the Hawthorne Effect?

3 Why are experiments not used much in sociology?

An example of a field experiment

'In this experiment, the researchers visited a San Francisco elementary school; they claimed to have developed a new IQ test which could predict which children were likely to become "high-attainers" in the very near future. Teachers were told that about 20 per cent of a particular age group would come into this category of "very able children" and were invited by the researchers to administer the IQ test. Once this had been done, Rosenthal and Jacobson informed the teachers which pupils the test had identified as most likely to become high-attainers. In fact, the names had been selected at random.

Over a period of 18 months, the researchers visited the school regularly and found that the "named" children had, in fact, improved significantly in their school work – more than could be explained purely by chance. Rosenthal and Jacobson explained this dramatic improvement in performance in terms of increased or raised teacher expectations of the children in question.

So this experiment identified a central variable in pupil attainment – the role of the teacher in shaping the child's self-image.'

'Sociologists in white coats' by Mike Moores, *Sociology Review* 7(3), February 1998.

QUESTIONS

1 Why was this a field experiment rather than a laboratory one?

2 Which two variables were found to be related to each other?

3 What was the hypothesis, the idea that the experiment set out to test?

4 What ethical problems can you see with this experiment? To help you, think about how the pupils (both 'high-attainers' and the others), their parents and the teachers would feel when they realised what had happened?

ROUND-UP

Experiments, especially field experiments, have some uses in sociology although they are more usually associated with the natural sciences. However, because they involve interfering in people's lives in some way they raise ethical problems that do not arise in the natural sciences. They are still worth considering if you are doing a coursework project.

HINTS AND TIPS

Experiments and coursework

Your school situation almost certainly provides opportunities for field experiments, though you may find you have to change your behaviour to see how others react.

VOCABULARY

Controlled conditions: the researcher does not let outside factors influence the research
Manipulated: controlled or influenced
Teacher expectations: how teachers expect a pupil to do in school work

Social surveys: questionnaires

Social surveys are often carried out by using questionnaires. In this section you will learn how good questionnaires are constructed or put together, and some of the problems researchers meet when using questionnaires.

3 How long have you been working in your present job?

Tick one box only

Less than 1 year ☐
1–5 years ☐
More than 5 years ☐

4 Have you applied for promotion while working in this job?

Yes ☐   No ☐

If no, please go to question 7.

5 Have you been promoted while working in this job?

Yes ☐   No ☐

If yes, please write the title of your current post here.

....

....

How useful are questionnaires as a research method in sociology?

What are questionnaires?

A questionnaire is simply a list of questions. The questions are decided in advance and the questionnaire is then carried out with a number of **respondents**. Because everyone answers the same questions in the same order, the results are said to be **comparable**. The researcher decides in advance the wording, order and focus of the questions, and often the range of possible answers too.

The fact that the questionnaire can be carried out by other researchers so that the results can be checked means that questionnaires are **reliable**. However, they may not be **valid** because the researcher is deciding in advance so much and closing off possible answers and issues.

HINTS AND TIPS

Reliability and validity are explained on page 26.

Some people who receive questionnaires will not complete them for various reasons. This means that there may be a low **response rate**.

Two types of questionnaire

- **Self-completion questionnaires** are handed to or posted to the respondent, to be picked up later or posted back when completed.
- In **interview questionnaires** the researcher reads out the questions and records the respondents' answers, usually in writing but sometimes on a laptop computer. Interview questionnaires can be carried out face to face or over the telephone.

Comparing types of questionnaires

Self-completion questionnaire	Interview questionnaire
Low response rate – people may not return questionnaires	Usually has good response rate
Few costs – no interviewers	More expensive – have to pay interviewers
Respondents may not follow the instructions or understand the questions	Interviewer can explain purpose of research and answer questions
	The respondent may be influenced by the interviewer
	More time consuming
Can reach a large number of respondents, who may be far away	

'The object of the research was to obtain facts, and in particular to report on the extent of sexual experiences in the fifteen to nineteen age group. We felt that information could be collected in only two ways: (a) the face to face interview; (b) the self-administered questionnaire. The disadvantages of both methods are magnified when the questions refer to sexual behaviour, but the interview offers clear advantages over the questionnaire. For example in one written questionnaire given to girls the question, "Are you a virgin?" brought the reply, "Not yet". In an interview, by contrast, the researcher is able to persist until he has got the relevant answer.'

The Sexual Behaviour of Young People by M. Schofield.

QUESTIONS

1. Give two possible reasons for the unusual reply given to the question, 'Are you a virgin?'.

2. How does an interview questionnaire, as opposed to a self-completion questionnaire, help to overcome such problems?

Types of questions

There are two main types of questions used in questionnaires; most questionnaires contain examples of both types:

- **Closed questions** – also called fixed-choice questions – ask respondents to choose between a number of given answers. This often involves ticking a box. Closed questions can be two-way (yes/no, male/female) or multiple choice. They can also be scaled, as when the possible answers are strongly agree/agree/disagree/ strongly disagree. It is straightforward for the researcher to analyse the results to such questions and to present the results in the form of a chart or table of statistics. On the other hand, respondents may feel that the answer they want to give is not available.

- **Open-ended questions** allow respondents to answer the question in their own way. The answer is therefore in the respondent's own words and it is much harder to produce statistics. On the other hand, the answers are more likely to reflect truthfully and accurately what respondents want to say.

In practice, many questions are a mixture of these types. For example, a closed question may give a list of possible answers but also have an 'other' category where respondents are allowed to write in their answer.

Getting it right

In order for a questionnaire to be successful, researchers must:

- think very carefully about what they want to find out, and how they want to present the findings
- use questions which respondents will be willing and able to answer
- avoid letting the wording of questions reflect their own ideas and prejudices
- choose the sample (see Sampling on pages 32–3) carefully and try to ensure a good response rate
- understand that respondents are giving their cooperation freely, and that they have a right to understand the purpose of the questions and to refuse to take part.

Often researchers test their questions on a very small number of respondents to see if there are any problems. This is called a **pilot study**. Putting problems right at an early stage saves money, time and effort later.

QUESTIONS

1. What is meant by response rate?

2. What is a pilot study?

3. Draw up a list of tips for researchers headed 'A Beginners' Guide to Successful Questionnaires'. Present your ideas in the form of a poster for display.

▶ FIND OUT FOR YOURSELF

Design and carry out a questionnaire about what subjects members of your class (or another class) study and why, which they like or don't like and why. Include both open and closed questions. Present your findings to the class.

ROUND-UP

Questionnaires are a very popular way of carrying out research. It is possible to get replies from many people, and from people who live far away and it is fairly easy to analyse the data and produce statistics. However, great care has to be taken over the way questions are asked. Successful questionnaires usually contain different types of questions.

VOCABULARY

Magnified: made to seem bigger
Closing off: written so that certain answers cannot be given

Sampling

KEY FOCUS

When carrying out questionnaires or interviews it is very important to select your sample – the people you will actually do the research on – very carefully. This section explains the various ways in which researchers can choose samples.

Sampling – selecting respondents.

Three key terms

- **Population** – this is the whole group that you are studying, for example everyone in your year group.

- **Sampling frame** – this is a list of everyone in the population, for example a registration list with everyone in your year group on it. Some commonly used sampling frames are the electoral register (a list of everyone in an area who is registered to vote in elections) and telephone directories.

- **Sample** – this is the group of people, taken from the sampling frame, with whom you actually do the research; for example, it might be one person in every ten from your year group.

Why have samples?

Samples make research more manageable by making it possible to do research with smaller numbers of respondents. This keeps down the cost and the time spent.

Sometimes samples are not necessary. If you are in a small or medium-sized school, you might find it possible to ask questions of everyone in your year group. The Census, carried out once every ten years, is the government's survey that attempts to get information about every single person in the country, not just a sample.

HINTS AND TIPS

You will find more information on the Census on page 354.

Samples are usually chosen so that they are 'representative' – this means the researcher can say that the results apply to the whole population, not just the sample. The sample has to be a cross-section of the population. Generalisations about the whole population can then be made.

Types of sample

Samples can be chosen in several different ways. Here are four of the most common ones:

- **Random samples**. This is when everyone in the sampling frame has an equal chance of being chosen. This can be done by drawing names from a hat. It is the method used in making draws for sports competitions, and for the National Lottery (you would be annoyed if you chose a number and found later that it was less likely to be chosen than others!). Random samples are not always representative; for example, by chance, a sampling frame containing equal numbers of boys and girls might produce a sample dominated by one sex.

- **Stratified samples**. To overcome this, the sampling frame can be divided (for example into boys and girls) and a random sample is then taken from each. Stratifying samples can be done by sex, age, ethnic group or any other characteristic. In draws for sports competitions, seeding is a way of stratifying the sampling frame and keeping the top players or clubs apart.

- **Systematic samples**. This is when there is a regular pattern, for example every tenth name in the sampling frame is chosen.

- **Cluster samples**. This is used when the population is spread out over a large area, such as the whole of Britain. Certain areas are chosen and random samples taken in those areas, to avoid the expense and time involved in travelling around the country.

There are also types of sample that do not involve a sampling frame:

- **Quota samples**. This is when a researcher is sent out with instructions to find people with certain characteristics, for example ten teenagers taking GCSE Sociology. This is often used in market research; if you are stopped in the street by someone asking questions he or she may well be finding out whether you are a suitable person for the survey.

- **Snowball samples**. This has become well known as a way of contacting people when normal sampling will not work. It involves finding one respondent, and getting the individual to put you in touch with one or several more respondents. It has been used, for example, in interviewing gangsters – for whom there is no sampling frame!

QUESTIONS

1. Name two commonly used sampling frames.
2. Why are samples usually chosen to be representative?
3. What is a quota sample?

QUESTIONS

Interviewing a representative sample?

An interviewer is sent out with instructions to carry out interviews at half of the houses in a street containing eight houses. Six houses are of similar size, but the two at the end, numbers 7 and 8, are much larger. She calls at number 1, but finds they are away on holiday. She goes next door to number 3, and carries out an interview. On leaving, she sees an ice-cream van outside number 4, so she crosses the road and buys an ice-cream. She then carries out interviews at numbers 4 and 6. She then thinks she'd better cross the road 'to even things up' but number 7 has a large, ferocious looking dog in the garden, so she goes to number 5 instead and carries out an interview. She now has four interviews, so, feeling pleased with herself, she goes back to the office.

1. Draw a map of the street. Put in dotted lines with arrows to show the route the interviewer took and then mark in different colours the houses where she did interviews and the houses where she didn't

2. The interviewer had done what she was asked. But was this a representative sample? Give a reason for your answer.

3. The sample – which people actually got interviewed – was really a matter of chance. What would be a better way to get a sample – and to make sure it was representative?

Based on *Issues in Social Research* by Simeon Yates, Open University, 1998.

ROUND-UP

Samples are used to keep research projects at a manageable level. Provided the samples are carefully chosen, the results can be said to apply to a much larger population. There are several different ways of choosing samples.

VOCABULARY

Market research: studying what people buy and consume, and why

Cross-section: a sample which is representative

Interviewing

Interviews are a widely used method in sociology. They need careful planning and interpersonal skills. They can produce valid data, and are especially suitable for sensitive topics, but there are several potential problems interviewers must always be aware of.

Unstructured interviews are like informal conversations, but are guided by skilled, trained interviewers.

Types of interviews

There are two broad types of interview. **Structured interviews** have already been covered on pages 30–31. They are very similar to standard questionnaires except that the interviewer reads out the list of questions to the respondent.

This section looks at the second kind of interview: unstructured interviews. These do not have a predetermined list of questions, as surveys do. Instead, the interviewer will just have some ideas about what he or she wants to ask. The interview is like an informal conversation, which the interviewer will steer towards what he or she wants to find out about. Sometimes the interviewer may follow up interesting lines that crop up in the interview. The interview will probably take place in an informal setting, perhaps over a cup of tea or coffee. The interviewer tries to put the respondent at ease as much as possible, so that the individual feels that he or she can talk freely. The respondent is treated far more like an individual than is the case with surveys.

Usefulness of interviews

Interviews are particularly suitable for asking about things which people feel are in some way personal or private. Respondents may be more willing to talk about such matters to someone they feel they can trust than to write answers on a questionnaire. They also have time to develop their answer, to explain fully what they mean.

The interviewer can explain what he or she wants to find out. If the respondent does not understand a word or question, the interviewer can rephrase it. If the interviewer is not sure what the respondent means, he or she can check.

Unstructured interviews are likely (though not certain) to produce valid data, that is, data which accurately reflects what is being studied. However, because there is no standardised list of questions, they cannot be replicated or repeated exactly with another respondent to check for reliability.

Interview bias

One of the problems with face-to-face interviews is that the respondent may give the answer that he or she thinks the interviewer wants to get. Trying to be helpful or friendly, the respondent may give invalid data! The interviewer also has to beware of influencing the answers given by tone of voice or facial expression.

The way the answers are recorded can also be a problem. It can be off-putting if the interviewer tries to write down answers or if a tape recorder is used; both tend to undermine the informality and trust that the interviewer wants to create. Tape recording doesn't necessarily save time. The interviewer will have to listen to the tape, probably several times, making a transcript of parts or all of it. Transcripts are quite difficult; people don't speak in sentences and paragraphs! On the other hand, trying to write as you listen is very demanding and it becomes difficult to continue to guide the interview in the way you want. Relying on memory and making notes later is also risky. The interviewer will forget some details, and may use his or her own words rather than those of the respondent, so reducing the validity of the data.

Advantages and disadvantages of interviews

Advantages	Disadvantages
Higher response rate than questionnaires	Needs considerable skills in interviewer
Respondents can put answers in own words	Interviewer bias may affect answers
Interviewer can explain and check answers	Problem of how to record answers
Can ask about more personal and difficult topics	Takes a long time, so cannot interview large numbers
High validity	Cannot be checked for reliability

Structured and unstructured

In real-life research, the two types of interview are not always as different as we have shown them here. Any interview can be placed on a 'line' going from the very structured to the completely unstructured. Different kinds of interview are suitable for different research projects. Broadly speaking, if you are counting something, asking how many or how often, a structured approach will be appropriate; if you are trying to find out why people think or behave in a particular way, an unstructured interview will be better.

HINTS AND TIPS

If you decide to carry out interviews as part of your coursework:

- make appointments with your respondents, preferably in writing
- make sure respondents know the date, time and place, and that these are convenient
- explain something about the purpose of the research
- choose a quiet place where you won't be disturbed
- choose a place which is warm, comfortable and perhaps with refreshments available
- decide in advance how to record the answers
- if you decide to tape record, make sure you know how the recorder works and ask the respondent's permission
- even if you are tape recording, keep a written log of basic details – where, when, who, start and finish times.

Focus groups

One special kind of interview which is being used more and more is the **focus group**. This is when a group of people are allowed to discuss something together, with the researcher listening, making notes and if necessary joining in. This kind of research is now used regularly by market researchers, and by political parties who want to find out what voters think.

QUESTIONS

1 What is meant by interviewer bias?

2 Which of the following situations would be suited for a more structured interview, and which for a more unstructured?
  (a) Finding out how much time pupils spend on homework.
  (b) Finding out what pupils think makes a good teacher.
  (c) Finding out why pupils chose particular subjects for GCSE.
  (d) Finding out how many pupils want to go on to do A levels.
  Explain each answer.

3 Discuss the problems interviewers have when it comes to remembering or recording what respondents say.

ROUND-UP

Structured interviews are a way of carrying out social surveys and are similar to questionnaires. Unstructured interviews are more like guided conversations, in which respondents can use their own words. They are suitable for exploring why people think or behave in particular ways, and for sensitive topics. However, they require considerable skill and the results cannot easily be quantified.

VOCABULARY

Interpersonal skills: being good at dealing with people
Predetermined: decided in advance
Standardised questions: everyone answers the same questions
Rephrase: to repeat something using different words, usually to make it easier to understand

Observation and participant observation

KEY FOCUS Observation and participant observation produce qualitative data that describes social life in a valid way. Unlike surveys and interviews, they involve studying social behaviour as it goes on around us.

THIS IS GREAT FOR MY PROJECT...
... KEEP HITTING HIM!

Sometimes the right thing to do is to intervene.

Observation

Research by observation involves two important considerations: the extent to which the researcher is involved in the social group he or she is studying, and the extent to which the group studied is aware that research is taking place.

Observation research can be:

■ **fully non-participant** – the researcher is completely separate from the research situation, for example observing from behind a one-way mirror or using a wall-mounted video camera, *or*

■ **fully participant** – the researcher becomes a member of the group being studied and joins in with the action, *or*

■ it can be at any point on a scale running between these two extremes.

Observation research can also be:

■ fully **covert** – the group is totally unaware that research is taking place, *or*

■ fully **overt** – the researcher fully explains to the group who he or she is and what he or she is doing, *or*

■ it can be at any point on a scale running between these two extremes (for example the group may be aware that the researcher is writing about them in some way, but not know exactly what the focus of the research is).

Ethical issues

Observation research raises more ethical issues than other types of research. People have a right to be told that they are being observed (just as they have the right to refuse to take part in a questionnaire or interview). On the other hand, if they know they are being observed their behaviour may change, making the findings less valid. One of the great strengths of observation is that it is about real life (questionnaires and interviews are artificial situations set up by researchers).

This strength is greatly weakened if the behaviour of the group is changed. Think of how a class behaves differently if a stranger, a school inspector perhaps, is present. A researcher can disturb behaviour in the same way. Sometimes it is not practical to tell everyone they are being observed, for example when the behaviour of a crowd is involved. Observing people in public places often does not and cannot involve asking their permission. Even then, the people involved should not be named.

There may be other ethical problems for the researcher if the group is involved in deviant or criminal behaviour. The researcher may have to take difficult decisions about whether to pass on information to the authorities about, for example, law breaking. To do so may well make it impossible to do further research.

QUESTIONS

1. Describe non-participant observation.
2. Explain the difference between covert and overt participant observation.
3. What is meant by 'ethical issues'?

Covert participant observation: an example

A famous example of this style of research is James Patrick's *A Glasgow Gang Observed*. While a young teacher at an approved school in the 1960s, Patrick (not his real name) was invited by a gang leader to come and see what gang life was like. Although the gang leader knew who he was, no one else did. He had to change his accent (although he was from Glasgow himself, it was from a different area) and learn to dress like the gang. There were problems of gaining entry to the gang.

Because he was researching under cover, Patrick had to concentrate on not giving himself away. He found it very difficult to cope with gang fights (some gang members were suspicious about the way he managed to keep out of the action), carrying weapons and taking drugs. Once the gang 'raided' a library, pushing people and setting fire to newspapers; Patrick shouted that the police were coming, ending quickly a situation he could not allow in a way that did not blow his cover.

Patrick found it difficult to remember and write down everything that happened and what was said. He was often with the gang for many hours at a time, and obviously could not make notes when he was with them. His account therefore relies a lot on memory.

Patrick's account of gang life gives a real feel of life on the streets of Glasgow at the time. But participant research is usually limited. For example, this is an account of just one gang. We do not know whether other gangs in Glasgow or elsewhere were similar. It is also Patrick's personal account; another researcher would have had a different relationship with the gang and written about it differently.

Finally, it is worth noting that although the gang members were violent, future criminals and Patrick strongly disapproved of them, he also got to know and understand them. He became, to some extent, 'on their side'. One of the problems of participant observation is how to get involved but at the same time keep a distance and not 'go native'. It was always possible that Patrick would become a real gang member, and no longer be playing the part of one.

QUESTIONS

1. To what extent was Patrick's research (a) participant or non-participant and (b) covert or overt?

2. Identify and explain three problems Patrick faced and what he did about them.

Advantages and disadvantages of participant observation

Advantages	Disadvantages
Social life is studied in its natural setting, during daily life	May be difficult to gain entry, and to leave
Researcher can get to see group's point of view	If covert, difficult to maintain cover
Valid	Difficult to keep notes – have to rely on memory
	Can get too involved and become biased
	Group may behave differently if members know they are being observed
	Cannot be replicated (repeated identically)

FIND OUT FOR YOURSELF

A GCSE student decides for her coursework to study the behaviour of a group of boys in her year who go to watch football matches together. What kinds of problems would she face? Make a list. Then draw up a list of points of advice you would give her.

ROUND-UP

Observation can be participant or non-participant and overt or covert. It involves studying real life as it goes on around us. Usually people should be told that they are being observed, but this may disturb their behaviour.

VOCABULARY

Go native: to become a member of the group being studied
Consent: permission

Quantitative secondary data: official statistics

KEY FOCUS Official statistics are an important source of information for sociologists, but we often need to treat them with caution. We need to be sure what they are measuring and how they measured it.

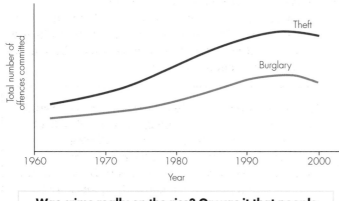

Was crime really on the rise? Or was it that people reported more crime to the police?

Secondary data

The research methods we have looked at so far – surveys, interviews, observation and participant observation and experiments – are ways of producing **primary data**. Sociologists also use secondary data – material that already exists. Secondary data can be either quantitative (see below) or qualitative (see pages 42–3).

The first step in your own research project will be finding out what is already known about what you are studying – that is, looking for relevant secondary data.

Official statistics

The government and other official bodies produce large amounts of quantitative data referred to as official statistics. Types of official statistics include:

- numbers of births, marriages and deaths
- the findings of the Census, carried out every ten years and aiming to collect information on every household in the country
- *Social Trends*, published every year by National Statistics, and containing a wide range of statistical data
- crime rates
- unemployment rates
- school league tables
- the General Household Survey
- the Family Expenditure Survey.

Some of these statistics provide very accurate figures which are not affected much by factors such as decisions taken by those compiling them. These kinds of statistics are sometimes referred to as 'hard statistics'. They include the records of births, marriages and deaths (as far as we know, these miss out very few people), divorce rates and numbers of students with particular exam passes.

Other sets of statistics can be described as 'soft' because the process of being collected affects them much more. The crime rate, for example, only counts crimes that are recorded by the police, and even then the police decide what to count and what to leave out. Laws making previously legal activities illegal can also affect the crime rate; in other words, what is being counted doesn't stay the same so we have to be careful when making comparisons over time.

Uses of official statistics

Official statistics are an invaluable source of material for sociologists. The figures produced cover many areas of social life and have been compiled at great cost, with large samples – in effect a lot of preliminary research has been done for you if you use them. Government surveys are usually well planned and organised and meet the high standards sociologists require. The statistics are fairly easy and cheap to get hold of because most public libraries keep them, and increasingly they are available free on the Internet. They are particularly useful for making comparisons over time – 'before and after' studies.

Some problems

However, official statistics must be treated with caution. They do not always measure exactly what you want in the form you want it; they have been collected by civil servants, not sociologists. Sometimes they have clearly been manipulated for political reasons. Ways of counting crime, unemployment or poverty can be changed to make the government of the day appear in a more favourable light.

For example, between 1979 and 1997 Conservative governments changed the way unemployment was calculated on more than 30 occasions. Most of these changes made unemployment lower than it would otherwise have been. Any comparisons over time became very difficult; governments claimed unemployment had fallen but many people were not convinced.

Similarly, when poverty began to rise in the 1980s the government simply stopped collecting information on poverty. If the findings of a survey are embarrassing or inconvenient, they may not be released to the public. Sociologists then cannot always be sure that official statistics are valid. Statistics may sometimes give a very misleading impression, and we always need to think carefully about what they mean. For example, the sharp rise in the number of divorces after 1970, when a new law made it easier to get divorced, does not mean more people were unhappy with their marriages. There may even have been more couples before then who stayed together in 'empty shell marriages' because there was no alternative.

What statistics don't tell you

Official statistics are only a starting point for sociological research. Sociologists will always want to ask questions about reasons for particular trends, questions which the official statistics on their own will not answer. Look at the table on household spending per week.

Household spending per week, UK average, 1998–99

Leisure goods and services	£59.80
Food and soft drinks	£58.90
Housing	£57.20
Motoring	£51.70
Household goods and services	£48.60
Clothing and footwear	£21.70
Alcoholic drink	£14.00
Personal goods and services	£13.30
Fuel and power	£11.70
Fares and other travel costs	£8.30
Tobacco	£5.30
Miscellaneous	£1.20
Total	**£352.20**

Family Expenditure Survey, 1998–99.

What else might a sociologist want to know?

■ How were the statistics compiled? How many people were asked, who in each household was asked, how did people work out the answers (did they make an informed guess, or keep a record for a week or more)? What exactly is the difference between leisure, household and personal goods and services?

■ What do these statistics show and not show? What were the equivalent figures for five, ten or 50 years earlier? Are we better off than we used to be (do we have more money to spend on things that are not essential)? These figures are averages – did poorer families spend a higher proportion of their money on particular items? If so, what did they spend less on?

IT ► FIND OUT FOR YOURSELF

The government web site for official statistics is at http://statistics.gov.uk. Visit this site to see what statistics are produced. You will find a wealth of information that will also help with your study of other topics in sociology. This is a good site to visit if you want the latest figures.

For his coursework, a student decides to look at whether boys or girls truant lessons more, and why. His school provides him with its statistics on 'unauthorised absences' (no names!), based on the register that is completed every morning and afternoon. These statistics may be a useful starting point, but what problems can you see with assuming that they are accurate counts of what the student wants to study?

QUESTIONS

1 Name three types of official statistics.

2 Explain, using examples, the difference between 'hard' and 'soft' statistics.

3 Identify and explain two reasons why sociologists should treat official statistics with caution.

ROUND-UP

A vast range of statistics on all areas of social life is available. These are of great use to sociologists but it is important to remember to be careful when using them. They are not always produced in the most useful way and may leave out important aspects of a topic.

VOCABULARY

Compiled: brought together in one place
Preliminary: belonging to the first stages of something

Presenting quantitative data

KEY FOCUS This section explains some of the main ways of presenting statistics. This will help you understand data in this book and other sociology that you read, including items in exam questions, and it will also give you ideas for presenting the data that your coursework project produces.

Graphs, tables and charts

Quantitative data means statistics, and that means mathematics. Some students are put off by this, but statistics are unavoidable in sociology, and you will find that the level of understanding you need is probably not too demanding. This is what you will need to be able to do for GCSE Sociology:

■ Work out the meanings of common kinds of graphs, tables and charts. You will probably have one or more of these to study in your exam, and there will be marks for correctly answering questions about them.

■ Produce some tables, charts or graphs to present some of your coursework findings. You may be able to use computer programs to help you do this, but you will still need to work out which way of presenting the data is best. If your research only produces qualitative data you will not need to use graphs, tables and charts.

Graphs

Look at the graph and then answer the questions.

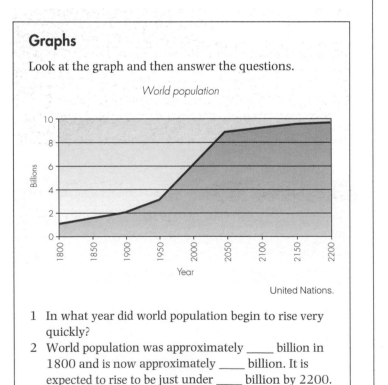

World population

United Nations.

1   In what year did world population begin to rise very quickly?
2   World population was approximately ____ billion in 1800 and is now approximately ____ billion. It is expected to rise to be just under ____ billion by 2200.

Tables

Look at the table and then answer the questions.

Declining population in Europe (selected countries) (in millions)

Country	1998	2050 (predicted)
Belgium	10.1	8.9
Germany	82.1	73.3
Greece	10.6	8.2
Italy	57.4	41.2
Netherlands	15.7	14.2
Russia	147.4	121.3
Spain	39.6	30.2
Ukraine	50.9	39.3
UK	58.6	56.6

United Nations.

1   Which of the countries listed here had the smallest population in 1998?

   Helpful hint: Find the smallest number in the 1998 column, and look for the name of the country.

2   Which country will have the smallest population in 2050?

3   By how much will the population of the United Kingdom fall?

   Helpful hint: Find the UK line, and take away the 2050 total from the 1998 total. The answer will be in millions.

Bar charts

In a bar chart the bars can be either vertical (going up) or horizontal (going across). Look at the bar chart and then answer the questions.

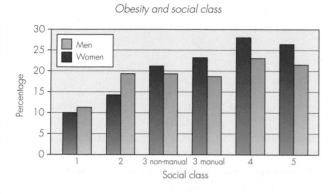

Obesity and social class

Note: obesity means being very overweight.

New Policy Institute, *Monitoring Poverty and Social Exclusion 1999.*

1   In which social classes are men more likely to be obese than women? *Helpful hint:* Find the classes for which the blue box is taller than the green box.
2   What percentage of women in class IV are overweight?

Pie charts

Look at the pie chart and then complete the sentences.

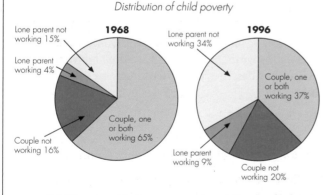

Distribution of child poverty

Child Poverty and its Consequences, Joseph Rowntree Foundation, 1999.

1   In 1968, 19 per cent of children in poverty were in lone parent families. By 1996 this had risen to ____ per cent. *Helpful hint:* You will need to work out where the figure of 19 per cent has come from (clue: two figures have been added).
2   In 1968, ____ per cent of children in poverty lived with a lone parent or a couple who were not working. By 1996 this had risen to ____ per cent.

Your turn

Below are some figures about different types of households in Britain in 1998. Turn them into:

1   a bar chart. It is best to use graph paper. You will need to decide on your scale (how many squares count for what percentage).
2   a pie chart. Make your circle/pie quite big. You will need a calculator to work out how big the slices of pie should be. A circle is 360 degrees, so for the first figure of 28 per cent you need to work out 28 per cent of 360. This will give you a number of degrees. You will then need a protractor to mark this on your pie chart.

Types of households in Britain, 1998

One person living alone	28% of all households
Two or more unrelated adults	3%
Couples without children	28%
Couples with children	30%
Lone parents	10%
Two or more families	1%
Total	**100%**

Family Expenditure Survey, 1998–99.

ROUND-UP

There are several ways of presenting statistical data. The most common are tables, bar charts, pie charts and graphs. You need to be able to work out what these mean, and you may need to be able to produce your own.

HINTS AND TIPS

When you come across charts and graphs in this book or others, practise working out what they mean even if there are no questions attached.

Qualitative secondary data

KEY FOCUS Sociologists make use of a very wide range of qualitative data which already exists. These include personal documents such as diaries and letters, autobiographies, novels and media material such as newspapers and recordings of television programmes.

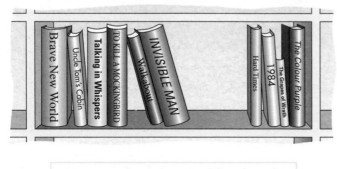

Even novels can be a useful source of data in sociology.

Personal documents

The personal documents used most often by sociologists are letters and diaries. There are other more unusual types of documents which can be useful such as household accounts, wills and even shopping lists. Documents are not necessarily written; photographs and home videos can be useful sources. Some documents such as school reports may also contain quantitative data (in this case, exam or test grades).

Usefulness of personal documents

In deciding how useful such documents are, sociologists have to consider whether the documents were intended to be read by a wide audience. Well-known people have often kept diaries or letters with the intention of their being published at some time. These are likely to be written in a way that gives a good impression of the writer. This makes them very different from diaries and letters which were only ever intended to be read by the writer or the person the letter was written to. More private letters and documents are, of course, less easy to get hold of; they belong to individuals and families who may not make them available to a researcher even if the researcher is able to find out they exist!

Sometimes researchers ask people to keep diaries, which can then be used alongside data from interviews or questionnaires. One of the best known examples of this was the Mass Observation research in the 1930s in which large numbers of people were asked to keep diaries, providing a rich source of information about life at the time.

Using letters: an example

A classic example of the use of letters in sociology was in *The Polish Peasant in Europe and America* by Thomas and Znaniecki. They used letters written between relatives at home in Poland and recently arrived immigrants in the USA as part of a study of the experience of immigration. They obtained these personal letters by placing an advertisement in a newspaper offering to buy letters.

Life history and autobiography

Thomas and Znaniecki also used **life histories**, people's own accounts of their lives. Life histories rely on memory, and so need to be checked against other records just as contemporary reports and newspapers.

Closely related to life histories are **autobiographies.** These are different though because they are not written at the request of a researcher. Autobiographies can provide fascinating insights into social life but they need to be treated with caution. As with letters and diaries intended for publication, the writer may be more concerned with creating a good impression than with the truth. Even if the writer's intentions are good, because autobiographies are usually written many years after the events they describe, the writer's memories may be faulty or incomplete.

Official documents

Just as the government and other official organisations produce statistics, they produce documents of many types. Some of these are available immediately to the public, such as Acts of Parliament and reports by commissions. Others are made available only to particular researchers, not the general public. Yet others remain secret for many years, covered by official secrecy laws. Minutes of cabinet meetings and related papers are only released after 30 years. Census returns – the actual forms filled in by the public, not the statistical summaries compiled from them – are available after 100 years. Most documents that are kept secret are eventually made public when they are no longer seen as confidential or sensitive.

Novels

Many novels explore themes of interest to sociologists. Sometimes novels (and other fictional writing such as plays and short stories) are intended to be accurate descriptions of what life was like in a particular time and place, and can bring that experience to life in a way factual writing cannot. It can be difficult, though, for the sociologist to separate what is based on reality from what comes from the writer's imagination.

FIND OUT FOR YOURSELF

Choose a novel that you have read and know well (perhaps one you have studied for English literature). In what ways might this novel be helpful in sociology? (For example: what society is it set in? what are the social characteristics of the people – their sex, class, age, ethnicity and so on? Does the novel tackle any social or political issues?) In doing this exercise remember that the novel may tell you something about the time and place it was written in.

Mass media

The mass media – newspapers, magazines, television, radio, film, the Internet and so on – provide a vast amount of material of interest to sociologists. The media can be used in two ways. Firstly, they can be a source of information on a topic being researched. Watching a relevant documentary television programme, for example, might be part of the preliminary work done alongside reading printed material, getting to know what is already known about a topic. When using the media in this way the researcher needs to remember that the programme may be biased or may miss out important information.

Secondly, the media can be studied in their own right. Sociologists have, for example, looked at whether the media are biased in favour of one political point of view rather than another, and at how women and ethnic minorities are shown in the media.

Studying the media in a way which produces quantitative data is called content analysis. It involves counting the number of times or for how long particular words or images are used in a media product such as a television programme or a newspaper. A simple content analysis of newspapers, for example, might compare how much space different papers gave to a particular news item and the number and size of accompanying photographs.

Another way of studying the media, often used alongside content analysis, involves looking at the hidden meanings in media products, for example why particular words or colours or camera angles have been chosen, and the impression they give. This is called semiology, and depends more on the interpretation of the researcher than content analysis. It produces qualitative rather than quantitative data.

These two methods of studying the media are examined in more detail on pages 296–7.

These two methods of studying the media are examined in more detail on pages 296–7.

HINTS AND TIPS

As you read this section, you may have wondered whether everything that was discussed was really secondary data. It seems as if the answers people give in an interview count as primary data, but if you ask them for their life history this is secondary data. It is best not to get too concerned about whether a source of data is primary or secondary – what really counts is how useful it is!

QUESTIONS

1. Give five different types of personal documents that might be useful for sociologists.

2. What two kinds of documents were used in the Polish peasant project?

3. How can novels be useful in sociology?

4. What research method is used to study the mass media and which produces quantitative data?

5. Why do autobiographies need to be treated with caution?

ROUND-UP

Sociologists can draw on a very wide range of secondary sources. Virtually any document – and remember documents do not have to be written – can be of interest and use, as long as the origins, accuracy and intentions of the document are borne in mind.

VOCABULARY

Will: the legal document in which individuals say what they want to happen to their possessions when they die
Contemporary: at the same time
Minutes: the official record of what has happened at a meeting

Other aspects of research methods

KEY FOCUS
This section covers some important aspects of research methods which have not yet been considered. These are pilot studies, longitudinal and panel studies, case studies, comparative studies and triangulation.

By following a panel of respondents over a long period, longitudinal research can follow changes in people's lives over time.

Pilot studies

Carrying out a pilot study is a strategy used by researchers to help them spot problems with their research before it is fully under way. For example, a questionnaire can be tested on a few people. If they find it hard to understand some questions, or if the researcher finds it hard to assess their answers, this probably means those questions need to be rewritten or even left out.

Longitudinal and panel studies

One of the best known examples of a **longitudinal study** is the series of television programmes which started in 1964 with *7Up*. This was a 40-minute documentary for ITV about a group of 7-year-old children. Every seven years another programme was made about the children, following them as they grew up, got jobs, got married and so on. *42Up* was shown in 1998. Although the series of programmes is in many ways entertainment as much as sociology, it sheds light on aspects of social life. The filmed informal interviews are fascinating. They demonstrate, among other things, the importance of social class, because the children from privileged

backgrounds became privileged adults while the working-class children have remained working class or moved up the class ladder only a little way, into the lower middle class.

The group of children who have been followed in the programmes are the panel. Following a panel (a **panel study**) enables us to track changes in the lives of individuals over a long period. Because the research takes place at regular intervals over a long period of time it is referred to as longitudinal research. One of the disadvantages is that it is difficult to maintain the original numbers. Some people no longer want to take part, others move away and lose contact with the researchers, some will die. The researchers then have to decide whether to continue with the smaller group or recruit new members.

A much larger and more sociological longitudinal study is the British Household Panel Survey, which has been interviewing a panel involving more than 5000 households since 1991. The research is able to follow what happens to families from year to year. Often in sociology we talk about lone parents, or the poor, or other groups as if they were fixed and unchanging. Longitudinal research has shown that in fact people move quite quickly in and out of these categories: lone parents get married, unemployed people get jobs. This helps us realise that when we talk about such groups we mean constantly changing groups of individuals who often only share their situation for brief periods.

Case studies

A **case study** is simply a detailed, in-depth study of one particular example of a type of group, organisation or event. For example, if a student decided to study social behaviour in schools, but only carried out research in her own school, this would be a case study. Looking back over earlier sections, you will see that James Patrick's *A Glasgow Gang Observed* (see page 37) is a case study of a gang.

It is not usually possible to generalise from the findings of a case study, unless earlier research has shown that the case selected is typical or representative. The student in the example above would not be able to claim that social behaviour was the same in all schools, nor did Patrick claim to have found out anything about gangs in general, only about the 'case' he studied. Case studies can, however, be valuable, and they are often used to develop ideas for testing in further, larger scale research. For students' coursework, case studies are completely acceptable. You do not have the time or money to do research on the scale you might like to!

Comparative studies

Comparative studies involve studying the similarities and differences between two or more groups or institutions. For example, two schools could be compared, in many different ways – their size, the background of their pupils, how pupils do in exams and so on.

Often comparative research involves comparing two different countries or cultures. This is very useful in helping avoid ethnocentrism – assuming that our way of doing things is better than anyone else's. For example, comparing British schools with French schools would help us understand both. We might begin asking questions about things we hadn't noticed before.

Triangulation

Triangulation refers to ways of checking the validity of research findings by carrying out the research in different ways. Triangulation involves using two or more different methods. For example, the findings of a questionnaire could be checked against in-depth interviews with a sample of respondents, or by participant observation.

In practice many research projects involve more than one method. When doing participant observation, researchers often also carry out interviews, or ask respondents to keep diaries.

Using triangulation: the Moonies

A well-known example of using several methods is Eileen Barker's study of the religious sect the Unification Church, popularly known as the Moonies, after their leader, the Reverend Moon. To find out whether Moonies could be said to have been brainwashed into joining the sect, Barker carried out overt participant observation, living with communities of Moonies, but also carried out interviews and sent questionnaires to all Moonies in Britain. She was able to check that the findings from one method were not contradicted by those from another method. Her conclusion, incidentally, was that Moonies were not brainwashed; they were free to join and to leave.

An alternative form of triangulation is to use more than one researcher. In some kinds of research, such as informal interviews, it is possible that the interviewer will, without intending to, influence the answers given. It might make a difference, for example, whether the interviewer is black or white, or male or female. Using different interviewers is a way of checking whether this is happening.

FIND OUT FOR YOURSELF

You may have visited a school in another country on an exchange visit, or have attended a school in another country because you were living there. If so, think and make notes about the similarities and differences you observed, and about what else you would want to ask or find out about.

QUESTIONS

For each of the following, write one sentence that explains what the term means and another sentence giving a way in which it is useful in sociological research:

(a) comparative studies
(b) pilot studies
(c) case studies
(d) longitudinal research
(e) triangulation.

ROUND-UP

This section has introduced a number of new terms which should help you understand the range of ways research can be carried out in sociology, and some of the problems and advantages involved.

VOCABULARY

Brainwashed: to completely change someone's ideas and beliefs
Contradicted: proved wrong

Coursework projects

KEY FOCUS You may have to carry out a research project of your own as part of your studies. This section provides some advice and ideas.

Now it's your turn!

Coursework

The best way to understand sociology is to do it. You have read in this chapter about some of the ways in which sociologists carry out research, and the problems they have to overcome, but this will mean a lot more to you when you have to do research yourself.

What should I do?

The most important thing is to be sure that your proposed project is acceptable to your exam board. Exam boards usually say that you must do a project on something related to topics you have studied. You could look through this book at the chapters you have studied, and ask yourself what you found most interesting.

Your project will have to be sociological, and it will have to be related to some of the sociology you have studied. As with much else, your teacher is the person whose advice you should ask for if you are not sure.

Your project should also be something that interests you. You are going to have to spend quite a lot of time on the project, so make it something you feel worth doing, and that you can get a good mark for.

Don't be too ambitious. You will be studying other GCSEs and will have other calls on your time. There's a limit to how many questionnaires you can analyse or interviews you can carry out. So if you were thinking of say, comparing some aspect of two local primary schools, ask yourself whether a case study of one school might be more manageable and give you just as much chance of getting a high mark.

Don't start by thinking of the method you would like to use. You must choose the best method for what you decide to study.

Your teacher will be able to tell you the sorts of topics that previous students have chosen. Your teacher will also have examples of coursework projects that have been supplied by the exam board. These will give you an idea of the standard and format that is required.

Stages of the research process

All the way through your project it is a good idea to keep a diary, saying what you did and when. This will be very useful when you are finishing writing your project.

Keep everything related to your project in one place, perhaps in a special folder.

Stage 1 is the decision about the area of social life that you want to investigate. For example, you might decide that you want to do some content analysis of television, or look at ways in which boys and girls behave differently in school.

Stage 2 is the refining of this into a specific focus. You may decide to videotape 50 advertisements from television and ook at the ways in which black people are shown, or you may decide to ask your fellow students about their plans for their futures. At this stage you may have a hypothesis, although this is not always appropriate; for example, that black people will be shown in a limited number of stereotypical roles in the adverts, or that boys have clearer career plans than girls.

Stage 3 is when you decide on the most appropriate method. Do you want to use a questionnaire or interview to ask students about their futures – and which kind of questionnaire or interview?

Stage 4 is the actual gathering of data.

Stage 5 is when the data is analysed. You will need to decide in what format to present your findings. If you have quantitative data, you need to decide whether a pie chart, bar chart or other kind of diagram is appropriate.

Stage 6 is the final presentation of your research. All the stages will need to be commented on. If you find you have made a mistake somewhere along the line, for example you realise that interviews would really have been more appropriate than questionnaires, don't be afraid to admit this. You are learning sociology, and you will get credit for showing that you can learn!

Ethical considerations

You will need the cooperation of other people throughout your research. If you ask people to complete a questionnaire, or be interviewed, you are asking them to give you their time. You should be aware that you are asking for something, and offering nothing in return. Remember to say please and thank you to your respondents.

People you approach have a right to know what you are doing and why. They have a right to refuse (without giving a reason), and you must accept this; however, remember that many people may feel they have no real choice about helping you. They may feel uncomfortable about the topic of an interview, but not want to damage your chances of doing well. Be alert to these issues.

You must avoid situations that cause embarrassment and avoid asking for information that is too personal. It is not acceptable, for example, to interview people about the experience of being bereaved, or about criminal or delinquent behaviour.

Your teacher will give you instructions about where and when it is acceptable to do research. If you are outside school, and doing research with anyone other than family or friends, you should carry verifiable identification. You may need to ask permission, for example from a shopping centre manager. Look after yourself if you approach people you don't know. Even when interviewing in the street, for example, you should tell your teacher or parents where you are and what you are doing, and if possible have a friend with you. Do not call on strangers at their homes.

You must respect anonymity and confidentiality. Anonymity means, for example, that you do not ask for names on questionnaires, and that you do not use real names (you can invent alternatives) when describing the behaviour of people you have observed. Confidentiality means that it must not be possible to trace particular comments or pieces of information in your research report back to named individuals.

HINTS AND TIPS

Choosing your research method

Questionnaires

By using questionnaires you can reach more people than with other methods. But because you may not have direct contact with them, there is a risk of a low response rate. You can minimise this risk by explaining clearly on the questionnaire what you are doing and why, by asking politely for help and by making it clear how the questionnaire can be returned to you.

Interviews

Think carefully about where and when you want to interview people. Appointments are best, if you can manage this – but they must suit your respondent as well as you. Choose a place that's convenient for both of you (you may need to ask someone's permission to use a suitable room). Try to make sure you are not disturbed. Think carefully about how you are going to record or make notes of the interview. If you're using a tape recorder, check before the interview that it works!

Observation

This covers such a range of possible situations that it is impossible to cover many of the issues raised. When observing large numbers in public places (for example queuing behaviour at a bus stop, or litter dropping in a shopping centre) it is usually not practical to inform people that they are being observed. In participant observation you need to win the trust of the group but not betray this trust by the way you do your research or write it up.

ROUND-UP

Coursework is your chance to do real sociology. Take it seriously, choose your project well and not only will you go into the exam knowing you've already got a lot of marks, but you'll also have a better understanding of sociology than you would have done otherwise.

VOCABULARY

Bereaved: when someone close to you dies
Verifiable: able to be checked

Research methods – sociology in practice

Types of data

'COMPARE the following reports of a game of soccer:

"Wimbledon 0 Liverpool 0"

"There was more excitement in the Selhurst car park than on the pitch ..."

Here we have both a quantitative result, and a qualitative assessment of the same game. Which do we care more about – the result, or the game? The points, or the passion? Which we find more important or illuminating will depend on what we are interested in. If we are team managers or fanatical fans, we may care more about the result than about how it was achieved. If we are neutral spectators, then we may care more about the quality of the game than about the result – in which case the match report confirms our worst fears of a no scoring draw! In social research, as in everyday life, our assessment of quantitative or qualitative data is likely to reflect the interests we bring to it and the use we want to make of it.'

Qualitative Data Analysis by Ian Dey, Routledge, 1993.

Questions

1 Use the extract to explain the difference between quantitative and qualitative data.

2 Write two short paragraphs about your family. One paragraph should include mainly quantitative data (for example how many people there are); the other paragraph should include mainly qualitative data.

3 'Which kind of data is the more useful will depend on what you are researching and what you want to find out.' Explain what this means using any examples from the sections in this chapter.

Beware of the questionnaire?

IN some research methods, like participant observation, readers are dependent on one researcher's view, but with the questionnaire other researchers can come along and ask the same questions to see if they get the same results. This ability to repeat, or replicate a study is seen as one of the hallmarks of a science. However, in spite of its advantages, some sociologists are very critical of questionnaires. But why? ...

... A major problem with the questionnaire method is that the same word can mean different things to different people. Thus the results may not be valid. Suppose (in a questionnaire asking what they think of their Sociology teacher) two students, Jack and Jill, have ticked the same box. Both said that their Sociology teacher, Dirk Hyam, is 'excellent'. However, later in the day you talk to each of them about their sociology classes. 'Oh, Mr Hyam's really excellent,' says Jill, 'He's made the subject really interesting.' 'Old Dirk,' says Jack, 'yeah, he's excellent. Always making jokes and he doesn't get on your back if you don't do the work.'

Although both students ticked the same box, it's clear that they mean very different – almost opposite – things by 'excellent' and there's no valid reason for them both to be part of the same percentage figure. Thus, critics argue that the statistics from questionnaires aren't really as precise, factual and 'scientific' as many people believe. So next time you read an article telling you that 45% of those questioned believe this, or 33% think that, be sceptical.

... If you're going to use a questionnaire in your coursework, don't rush out and tear it up. Questionnaires are fine and can provide useful data – providing you are aware of their limitations. If (you) want to collect ... basic, 'factual' information, then the questionnaire is the method to use. If you want to go deeper and find out more about people's opinions and personal experiences then the questionnaire on its own won't do.

Adapted from 'Beware of the questionnaire?' by Steve Taylor, *S magazine*, February 1999.

Questions

Look back at the sections on Research methods – the basics (for the meaning of validity and reliability) (pages 26–7) and Social surveys – questionnaires (pages 30–31).

1 What is one of the advantages of using questionnaires, according to the article?

2 How does the article question the validity of questionnaires?

3 According to the article, 'the questionnaire on its own won't do' for some research. What is using more than one method called, and what are the advantages of doing this?

Researching another culture

A film crew spent two years filming the life of a group of Baka people in the rain forest of Central Africa.

'FOR the first six months we did not attempt to film, but concentrated on learning the language, on going with the Baka into the forest to see how they lived, on discovering who was who within the village and so on. In the evenings around the fire we listened to stories, tried to grasp the details of the latest scandal to rock the community, and shared food … In these early days everything we did was a source of fascination and amusement, but gradually the novelty wore off, we began to be accepted as members of the village, and felt we could start to film … Our presence was welcome and our eccentricities often amusing to the Baka, but otherwise it did not much affect the life of the village.'

Baka – People of the Rainforest,
Channel 4 Publications, 1988.

Questions

1 Look back at the section on Observation and participant observation (pages 36–7). How did the film crew try to get accepted by the group?

2 What problems involved in participant observation are shown in the item?

3 'Our presence … did not much affect the life of the village.' Do you think this is likely to be true, and why is this important for the validity of the research?

Research methods – important terms

case study	an in-depth study of one particular case
cause	in a causal relationship, a change in one variable causes another variable to change
closed question	a question with a limited number of answers to choose from
cluster sample	samples chosen to be in limited areas
comparative	comparing different cases
correlation	when two variables are correlated, they change together
covert	hidden; those studied are not aware of being studied
experiment	a method involving testing a hypothesis under controlled conditions
field experiment	an experiment taking place in a 'natural' social situation
focus group	a kind of group interview
Hawthorne Effect	where the presence of researchers affects behaviour
hypothesis	a theory about what will happen that can be tested
informal interview	an interview in which the interviewer does not keep to a prepared list of questions
interview	asking questions directly, face to face or by telephone
laboratory experiment	an experiment taking place in an artificial and controlled environment
longitudinal study	a study taking place over a long period, following changes over time
open-ended question	a question which allows the respondent to answer in his or her own way
overt	open; those studied are aware that they are being studied
panel study	the panel is a group who are researched at intervals over a long period
participant observation	joining in the activities of a group in order to study it
personal documents	any documents giving information about someone's life from the person's point of view
pilot study	a small-scale testing of a survey
positivism	the scientific approach
primary data	data collected by the researcher
qualitative data	data in the form of description rather than numbers
quantitative data	data in the form of numbers and statistics
questionnaire	a list of questions
quota sample	a sample without a sampling frame, involving finding respondents meeting set criteria
random sample	a sample in which everyone in the sampling frame has an equal chance of being chosen
reliability	data is reliable if it can be repeated and the same results obtained
respondent	someone providing information in a questionnaire or survey
response rate	the percentage of a sample who provide data
sampling	procedures for selecting respondents
sampling frame	a list from which a sample is selected
secondary data	data which already exists
self-completion questionnaire	a questionnaire sent to or handed to respondents for them to complete themselves
snowball sample	a sample in which one respondent puts the researcher in touch with other potential respondents
statistics	sets of quantitative data
stratified sample	a sample in which the sampling frame is divided, for example by age and sex
structured interview	the interviewer reads out questions and records the answers
survey	systematic collection of data, usually by questionnaire
systematic sample	a sample in which respondents are chosen according to a system, for example every tenth name on a list
triangulation	combining several methods or using several researchers
validity	data are valid if they accurately measure or describe reality
variable	a factor which varies and can be measured

Research methods – exam-style questions

Source A

The research was based on in-depth interviews with 14 women of Nigerian origin. I did a pilot study first and this helped me a lot in working out what I'd be able to actually do … My interviewees were of different ages. My hypothesis became this: The crucial factors affecting identity are (a) the age at which the women came to London and (b) the length of time they had lived in London. I found that the women in my survey tended to lose their Nigerian identity after 15 years.

'An account of a student's coursework project' by Helen Isibar, *S magazine*, February 1999.

Source B

1 Please tick the daily newspapers that you regularly read:

☐ Daily Express   ☐ Guardian
☐ Daily Mail   ☐ Independent
☐ Daily Mirror   ☐ The Star
☐ Daily Telegraph   ☐ The Sun
☐ Financial Times   ☐ The Times

2 On average, how many hours of TV do you watch in a day?

☐ 0–1   ☐ 1–2   ☐ 2–3   ☐ 3–4   ☐ 4+

Foundation tier

1 Look at source A and answer these questions:
   (a) How many people did this student interview? [1 mark]
   (b) What was her main research method? [1 mark]
   (c) What was the country of origin of the women she studied? [1 mark]
   (d) What is meant by a pilot study? [2 marks]
   (e) What is meant by a hypothesis? [2 marks]
   (f) What was this student's hypothesis? [2 marks]

2 Look at source B and answer these questions:
   (a) What research method is being used here? [1 mark]
   (b) What type of questions are being asked? [2 marks]

3 What is meant by quantitative data? [2 marks]

4 What is meant by a sample? [2 marks]

5 Give two advantages and two disadvantages of one of the methods discussed in the sources. [4 marks]

Higher tier

1 Look at source A and answer these questions:
   (a) What is meant by a pilot study? [2 marks]
   (b) What is meant by a hypothesis? [2 marks]
   (c) What was this student's hypothesis? [2 marks]

2 Look at source B. What types of questions are being asked? [2 marks]

3 What is meant by quantitative data? [2 marks]

4 What is meant by a sample? [2 marks]

5 Name one type of sample and explain how this type of sample is chosen. [2 marks]

6 Discuss the advantages and disadvantages of one of the methods discussed in the sources. [6 marks]

Research methods – further research

There are revision quizzes on research methods at Sociology Learning Support: www.chrisgardner.clara.net.

The main site for British official statistics: www.statistics.gov.uk.

The site of the British Household Panel Survey, using longitudinal research: www.irc.essex.ac.uk/bhps.

3 Class

KEY TERMS

caste
class
estates
income
life chances
meritocracy
mobility
occupational scales
slavery
wealth

This chapter introduces not only class, but also social stratification more widely. In the first section, you will find out that societies have been divided into different groups, with different levels of power and wealth, in several different ways. Class is put into perspective by considering caste, the estates system and slavery. The next three chapters go on to look at three other aspects of stratification today, three other influences on life chances: gender, ethnicity and age. These, and class, are ideas that you will find you keep returning to as you study later chapters. You will find that it is very difficult to separate class, gender, ethnicity and age in people's lives.

Class is a difficult idea to pin down. You usually cannot tell someone's class easily. Yet a lot of sociological evidence shows that class still has an enormous impact on our lives. The aim of this chapter is to show you that, however difficult it is to measure class, it is a very important idea which is still essential if you want to understand how society works.

IN THIS CHAPTER YOU WILL LEARN ABOUT:

- different types of stratification, compared to class
- how class affects people's lives through life chances
- how class can be measured, by wealth, income and occupation
- the different classes in Britain today
- how much movement there is between classes

CHAPTER CONTENTS

Class as a system of stratification

The system of stratification found today in Britain and other developed countries is the class system. To help understand what class is, it helps to compare it to other types of stratification.

An extreme form of stratification – slave owners and slaves.

What is stratification?

The term stratification refers to the way different groups of people are placed at different levels in society. The levels are strata – a term borrowed from geology, the study of rocks. In geology, there are different strata of rocks formed at different times in history. In our case, the strata are classes, and classes will be the main type of stratification we consider here. Gender, ethnicity and age, which are considered elsewhere in the book, are also aspects of stratification. The remainder of this section, however, looks at some different types of stratification.

Feudal estates

The type of stratification that we had in the Middle Ages is called the **estates** system (also known as **feudalism**). At the top of this system was the king; below him the noble lords, then knights and finally the great majority of the population, the serfs or peasants. There were also monks and scholars. Each of these was an estate, rather than a **class**.

Estates were different from classes in that it was almost impossible to move up or down. If you were born a serf, then you would always be a serf, and you could not marry someone born to a higher estate. So people's destinies were decided at birth; their social position was ascribed (given) to them.

Another difference is that the feudal estates had strong obligations to each other. Nobles were given land by the king, but in return had to pledge allegiance to him and fight for him when needed. The nobles in turn gave land to knights, who had to pledge allegiance to them and fight when needed. The serfs were allowed to use small pieces of land but had to give some of their produce to their lord and serve in his army when required.

Caste

The **caste** system was found in India (it still survives, but is less strong than it used to be). It is based on Hindu religious beliefs about reincarnation; that is, people are believed to be reborn into a new life after death. The caste you are born into will be the result of your behaviour in your past lives. Those who are at the bottom therefore deserve to be looked down on.

As in the feudal estates system, caste is ascribed – a person's social position is decided at birth. People accept this because it is seen as the will of god; rather than try to change the caste system, they will try to live virtuous lives so as to be reborn in a higher caste.

Slavery

Slavery was found in the ancient civilisations of Greece and Rome, and more recently in Europe and America until the nineteenth century. Slavery is a very strong form of stratification. It divides people into slave owners and slaves, and often allows slaves to be treated very badly. Unlike serfs in the feudal system, slaves can be bought and sold; the owner does not have a strong personal obligation to his or her slave.

The presence of black people in the West Indies and North America is a direct result of the slave trade. Their ancestors were brought over on slave ships from Africa, usually chained below decks in appalling conditions, to be bought by slave owners to work on plantations.

A more recent form of stratification that has some similarities to slavery was the apartheid system in South Africa. There was a strict racial divide between white people and black people, with white people running society and having better health, education, housing and employment. This system was also like the caste system, in that people's social position was decided at birth, by their skin colour.

▶ FIND OUT FOR YOURSELF

Slavery is not just history – it still exists in some parts of the world. Find out about this by visiting the web site of Anti-Slavery International at http://www.antislavery.org.

How class is different

You will have noticed that in each of these systems of stratification, it is very hard if not impossible to move out of the layer of society you are born into. This is where class is different. The class system allows for social **mobility**; that is, people can move up and down. People achieve a position in society, rather than this being decided for them by their birth. Their position is said to be **achieved status**, not **ascribed status**.

Societies that have stratification systems like caste, slavery and feudal estates are said to be closed, because movement up and down is not possible. Societies that have the class system are said to be more open.

QUESTIONS

1. What is meant by stratification?

2. Name three forms of stratification other than class.

3. Identify and explain two ways in which the caste system is different from the class system

4. What is the difference between closed and open systems of stratification? Explain your answer by giving examples.

5. What aspects of your social position are ascribed and which are achieved?

ROUND-UP

The class system in Britain today can be contrasted with other stratification systems, such as the feudal estates system, caste and slavery. Class is found in open societies where social position can be achieved rather than being ascribed.

VOCABULARY

Geology: the study of the earth and of rocks in particular

Serf: an unfree person, tied to his land (if the land was sold, the serf belonged to the new landlord)

Plantation: a big farm, especially in tropical countries, on which cash crops like cotton, bananas, sugar and rubber are grown

Class and life chances

KEY FOCUS

Class background has many effects on almost all areas of our lives. This section outlines some life chances affected by class, then looks in more detail at life expectancy and health.

The *Titanic* sinks – most of the first-class passengers were saved; the poorer people in third class drowned: a dramatic example of life chances.

The *Titanic*

'"Women and children first" was the cry when a ship was sinking and the lifeboats were launched. But this was not the whole story. When the giant liner *Titanic* sank after hitting an iceberg in the North Atlantic in 1912, it was also "first class first". All passengers travelling first class had the chance to abandon ship, but third class passengers had to remain below deck and were kept there at gunpoint. The result was that those travelling first class had a much better chance of survival. 45% of women travelling third class died, 16% of those travelling second class and only 3% of those travelling first class.'

Sociology: An Introduction by Alexander Thio, 2nd edition, Harper Row, 1989.

The extract above partly reflects how strong ideas about class were at the time. You may even think it strange that there were first, second and third classes. Class distinctions do however survive, in trains and aeroplanes, although today different names are found ('economy' sounds better than 'third class'!).

The story also has a more general message: that many things in our lives are directly associated with our class position. Among the '**life chances**' affected by class are:

- how long people live (life expectancy)
- how healthy people are
- how much and what they eat

- the kind of housing they live in
- the level of education they reach and the qualifications they achieve
- how likely they are to be unemployed, or to be made redundant
- their chances of being killed or injured at work
- the money they can spend on both necessities and luxuries
- how often they can take a holiday, and what kind of holiday
- their chances of being the victims of crime.

HINTS AND TIPS

Life chances are the statistical chances of particular things happening to different groups in society. Life chances apply to groups; they do not tell us about particular individuals.

With all of these life chances, the **working class** is at a disadvantage compared to the **middle class**. It is reasonable to assume that upper class people have even better life chances, although this class is very small and data is hard to come by.

Class is, of course, not the only factor connected to life chances. Other factors include ethnicity and gender (for example in the *Titanic* disaster, women had a better chance of surviving than men, and you probably know also that females live longer than males on average).

Life chances concerned with education and work are discussed in other chapters. The remainder of this section will look at health inequalities, which are not covered elsewhere.

Health and class

Life expectancy

Life expectancy at birth, 1987–91

Socio-economic group	Men	Women
Classes 1 and 2 (professional and managerial occupations	74.9 years	80.2 years
Classes 4 and 5 (semi-skilled and unskilled workers)	69.7 years	76.8 years

Health inequalities 1997, in *Sociology Update 1998*.

You can see from the life expectancy table that working-class people have shorter lives on average than middle-class people.

Working-class babies have a higher risk of being stillborn, of being underweight and of dying in infancy.

Illness

General health problems and more specific ones such as tooth decay affect manual workers more than professionals. Almost all serious diseases are more common lower down the class scale.

Health-related habits

Diet   Eating plenty of fresh fruit and vegetables is known to be essential for good health. Those in the higher classes eat more fresh fruit and vegetables than those on lower incomes. Children in social classes 1 and 2 eat more fruit and vegetables, and have sweets and fizzy drinks less often ('Health of Young People 1995–1997', Department of Health 1998).

Smoking   Those in the working class are more likely to smoke than those in the middle class. Smoking is known to cause several illnesses, including fatal ones.

Cigarette smoking by gender and socio-economic group, 1996–97

Socio-economic group	Males (%)	Females (%)
Professional	12	11
Employers and managers	20	18
Intermediate and junior non-manual	24	28
Skilled manual	32	30
Semi-skilled manual	41	36
Unskilled manual	41	36
All aged 16 and over	29	28

Social Trends Pocketbook 1998.

The poorer diet and higher rates of smoking and other unhealthy habits are part of the explanation for health inequalities. Other factors include:

- environment – the area people live in – for example the quality of the air, and how close they are to threats to health such as pollution and busy roads
- housing – the quality of dwelling, for example whether it is adequately heated in cold weather and free of damp.

Health inequalities reflect the lower incomes of the working class. They are less able to afford a good diet, less able to avoid threats to health, less able to afford health care for which they have to pay, such as visits to the dentist.

PS C   FIND OUT FOR YOURSELF

Investigate class differences in one of the following:

- ownership of new technology such as computers, mobile telephones and digital television
- holidays
- transport (ownership of cars, use of public transport).

You will need to track down statistics using *Social Trends* (government statistics, available in book form and on CD-ROM), the official statistics web site at www.statistics.org.uk, or other reference sources. Present your findings to the class.

QUESTIONS

1   What is meant by the term life chances? Give three examples.

2   Look at the table on life expectancy.
(a) How much longer do men in classes 1 and 2 live on average than men in classes 4 and 5?
(b) How much longer do women in classes 1 and 2 live on average than women in classes 4 and 5?

3   Look at the table on cigarette smoking.
(a) In which class do a higher percentage of women smoke than men?
(b) Suggest two reasons why more working-class people smoke than middle-class people.

4   What could be done to try to make life chances related to health more equal between the classes?

ROUND-UP

Class makes a fundamental difference to our lives – even to how long we can expect to live. In a wide range of ways, from success at school to our health, class influences our life chances.

VOCABULARY

Redundant: workers are made redundant when their employer no longer requires them
Stillborn: when a baby is born dead
Damp: moisture in a house, for example as damp patches on walls

Measuring class

Class is difficult to measure – unlike, for example, gender and age. This section looks at some of the ways sociologists and government statisticians have tried to measure class. This has been done by basing it on people's occupations, but as you will see this causes some problems.

Unfortunately, people don't fit easily into stereotypes – it's not easy to decide what class someone is in.

How do we know what class someone is in?

The most common way of deciding someone's class is by his or her occupation or job. Occupation is associated with a range of other factors such as income, status, lifestyle, educational background and life chances. All of these can be described as indicators of class. Other indicators include the area where someone lives, the type of house the person lives in, his or her accent and the way the individual spends his or her leisure time. There are differences between classes on all these indicators.

Occupational scales

Having decided to use occupation as an indicator of class, researchers still have to put those occupations in groups and rank them. Some use the pay and other benefits of work (such as pensions and use of company cars) to rank occupations;

others look at the status or prestige that goes with an occupation while others look at the skills an occupation involves.

Sociologists use a number of different **occupational scales** to measure class. The scale tells you which occupation is in which class.

Occupations are usually divided into the following:

- Manual occupations – those that involve a fair amount of physical effort. These are also known as blue collar occupations and are seen as working class.
- Non-manual occupations – those that involve more mental effort, such as professions and office work. These are also known as white collar occupations and are seen as middle class.

The distinction between these two types of occupations is very important in scales like the **Registrar General's Scale**.

Registrar General's Scale

The Registrar General's Scale

Social class	Examples of occupation
I Professional and managerial	Accountant, doctor
II Intermediate	Teacher, farmer
III Non-manual – skilled occupations	Police officer, sales representative
III Manual – skilled occupations	Electrician, bus driver
IV Semi-skilled manual	Farm worker, postman/woman
V Unskilled manual	Labourer, cleaner

This scale has for many years been the most common, but it is increasingly seen as rather old-fashioned. It covers hundreds of occupations. It is based mainly on 'the general standing in the community of the occupations concerned'. Not everyone, though, agrees with where all the occupations have been put, and some have had to be moved as the status has changed over the years. For example, the first aeroplane pilots were put in class 3, but this occupation was later moved to class 1. The distinction between manual and non-manual occupations is now less important than it used to be. There are fewer manual workers, so there is a big bulge in the middle of this scale, with few people at the bottom now.

Underlying the Registrar General's Scale are the terms we usually apply to class – the middle class and the working class. Classes 1, 2, and 3 non-manual are middle class while classes 3 manual, 4 and 5 are working class. Notice that the **upper class** is missing from the scale.

Market researchers working for companies selling products to the public use a variation on the Registrar General's Scale which uses letters instead of numbers: classes A, B, C1, C2, D and E. Often these are simplified into just four classes: AB, C1, C2, DE.

The new classification system

Because of the problems of the Registrar General's Scale, the government decided to introduce a new occupational scale, devised by a team of sociologists.

Unlike the old scale, it has eight classes. One of these is a completely new category, the long-term unemployed and those who cannot work because they are sick. This means that for the first time the official scale includes at least some of the 60 per cent of the population who do not have jobs. It is important to include these people so that we can get an understanding of how not having a job can affect people's life chances and those of their children.

New occupational scale – first used 2001

1　Higher managerial and professional occupations, e.g. company director, doctor, teacher
2　Lower managerial and professional occupations, e.g. nurse, police officer, soldier
3　Intermediate occupations, e.g. secretary, driving instructor, computer operator
4　Small employers and own account workers, e.g. publican, farmer, taxi driver
5　Lower supervisory, craft and related occupations, e.g. plumber, train driver, butcher
6　Semi-routine occupations, e.g. shop assistant, hairdresser, bus driver
7　Routine occupations, e.g. waiter, cleaner, building labourer
8　Never employed and long-term unemployed

The problems of occupational scales

Although the new scale is seen as a big improvement on the Registrar General's Scale, it is based on the same idea, that people can be put in classes by their occupations. Any scale based on occupation has some problems:

■　The very rich, who do not need to work, are missed out.
■　How much people own – their **wealth** – is missed out.

■　There are many other people who do not work. Some are covered by class 8 of the new scale. Groups not covered include retired people and students.
■　The older scale was based on the occupation of the 'head of the household' – which always used to mean the man. His wife was assumed to be in the same class. But today many couples work in occupations that are in different classes. Some women are in higher occupations than their husbands.
■　The scales may work for people who live alone, but what about families? How well off a family is depends on how many people work, as well as in what jobs.

Women and the class scales

A very high proportion of women are in class 3 non-manual of the Registrar General's Scale, working in offices and shops. Should married women who work be given a class according to their own occupation or their husband's occupation? Whichever is chosen, the fact that the couple will almost certainly share their income is missed out. This suggests that in working out the class position of a family we should look at both the man's and the woman's occupations.

QUESTIONS

1　What is meant by 'head of household'?

2　Identify two problems with using occupation as the main indicator of class.

3　Give two reasons why the new class scale can be seen as an improvement on the Registrar General's Scale.

4　Why is it important to include people who do not work in a class scale?

5　What, in your opinion, is the best way to decide a married woman's class position? Give reasons for your answer.

ROUND-UP

The usual way of deciding someone's class is by their occupation. There are several scales that rank occupations according to income, skill, prestige or a combination of these. All of these scales raise some problems for sociologists.

VOCABULARY

Occupational: based on people's occupations (jobs)
Prestige: high status or reputation

The distribution of wealth

KEY FOCUS   Like income, wealth is an indicator of class differences and like income, wealth, as you will see, is very unequally distributed.

The distribution of wealth is very unequal.

Wealth

Wealth refers to the ownership of financial savings and of things that can be bought and sold to generate or make income.

There are many different forms of wealth. Some of the most important are:

- ownership of stocks and shares in companies
- ownership of land
- ownership of houses and other buildings
- ownership of works of art, jewellery and other valuable items.

Having these forms of wealth is an important indicator of social class position. The very wealthy do not need to work.

Inheritance of wealth

Wealth is often inherited; that is, the wealthy have not earned their wealth themselves, but have had it passed down to them by their parents or other relatives. For example, the Royal Family has inherited much of its wealth in this way. However, having wealth tends to create more wealth; shares produce dividends, land and buildings can be rented, works of art grow in value and so on. A growing number of extremely wealthy people have made their own money through business or entertainment.

Distribution of wealth

In 1994 the percentage of wealth owned by:

the most wealthy 1 per cent = 19 per cent
the most wealthy 5 per cent = 38 per cent
the most wealthy 10 per cent = 51 per cent
the most wealthy 25 per cent = 73 per cent
the most wealthy 50 per cent = 93 per cent.

Over the past 25 years, these figures have not changed much. The wealthiest 1 per cent of adults own about 20 per cent of the wealth while the poorer half of the population own only 7 per cent.

These figures have to be treated with caution. They probably underestimate the wealth owned by the wealthiest. This is because wealthy people may employ tax advisers to help them appear less wealthy than they are, so that they pay less tax.

The distribution of wealth in Britain is therefore very unequal.

Housing, pensions, shares

Despite this strikingly unequal distribution of wealth, there are several forms of wealth that are now owned by large numbers of people. About 80 per cent of adults have a current bank account and more than half have a building society account. Smaller numbers have premium bonds and personal investments such as TESSAs and PEPs (*Social Trends Pocketbook 1999*). Most households also own consumer durables that could be sold to generate small incomes, for example televisions, washing machines, cars and so on.

The three forms of wealth owned by many people are housing, pensions and shares.

Housing

About two-thirds of homes are now owned by their occupiers (the people who live in them). This is a big increase from the days when many people lived in housing rented privately or from the local council. In the 1980s, many people renting council housing were able to buy their homes at low prices, so home ownership increased considerably. During the late 1980s, house prices went up considerably. People who had bought their homes several years earlier found that their homes were worth a lot more – their wealth had increased.

However, this is not quite as straightforward as it may seem. Housing is not like other forms of wealth, because people have to live somewhere! If you sell your home, you can turn this form of wealth into money, but you still have to find somewhere to live. This almost certainly means buying another property, and if the prices of all housing have gone up you may not be any better off. It is different if someone owns two or more properties, because if one is rented or sold this really does produce money that does not have to be spent on more housing.

Pensions

Many people now have occupational or individual private pensions, so that when they retire they will have a reasonable **income**. The money saved in this way, and invested by a pension fund while people work, is a form of wealth. However, it cannot usually be used before retirement, and using it would mean losing income after retirement. Like housing, pensions can't be turned into money without being replaced.

Shares

When people buy shares in a company, they own a part of that company and can take part in some decisions the company makes. There was a big increase in share ownership in the 1980s and 1990s. This was the result of the policies of the Conservative governments at the time. They privatised many industries that had previously been publicly owned (such as gas, electricity, telephones, water and the railways) and shares were sold to the public. For the first time, many people who were by no means well off owned a form of wealth previously only owned by the wealthy.

As with the spread of housing and pensions, this doesn't necessarily mean that wealth is being spread more equally. This is because the people who bought shares for the first time bought only a few, and some sold them later. The vast majority of shares are still owned by a relatively small number of people.

FIND OUT FOR YOURSELF

What forms of wealth does your family own? Make a list. (Many people consider this kind of information to be personal, so you do not have to share what you find out with your fellow students.)

QUESTIONS

1 State three types of wealth.

2 Why was there a big increase in the number of people owning shares in the 1980s and 1990s?

Looking again at the distribution of wealth

Here are the figures on the distribution of wealth in 1994 again – but this time they leave out the value of the housing people own.

Percentage of wealth owned by:

the most wealthy 1 per cent = 28 per cent
the most wealthy 5 per cent = 52 per cent
the most wealthy 10 per cent = 65 per cent
the most wealthy 25 per cent = 82 per cent
the most wealthy 50 per cent = 94 per cent (*Social Trends Pocketbook 1998*).

QUESTIONS

1 What percentage of wealth, excluding the value of housing, was owned by the poorer half of the population in 1994.

2 What percentage of wealth was owned by the richest 1 per cent in 1994 (a) including the value of housing and (b) excluding the value of housing?

3 What are the main differences between the two sets of data? How can these differences be explained?

ROUND-UP

The distribution of wealth in Britain is very unequal. A small percentage of the population own most of the wealth. More people own their own homes and shares and belong to pension schemes than before, but there are reasons why these need to be considered differently.

VOCABULARY

Stocks and shares: the stock of a company is divided into shares; a shareholder is entitled to part of the company's profits
Inheritance: passing on from one generation to the next
Privatised industries: those which were once owned by the government on behalf of the nation, but were then sold and became private companies

The distribution of income

KEY FOCUS

Income is an important part of stratification, because people's position in society is related to their income. By looking at income we can study how equal, or unequal, Britain is – how big the gap is between the highest and lowest incomes.

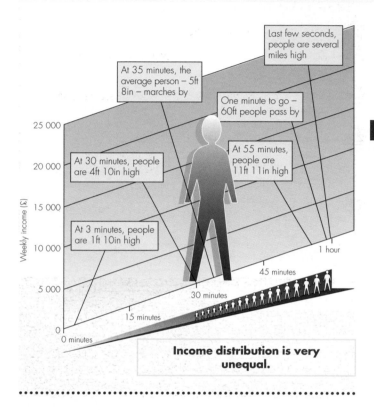

At 35 minutes, the average person – 5ft 8in – marches by

Last few seconds, people are several miles high

One minute to go – 60ft people pass by

At 30 minutes, people are 4ft 10in high

At 55 minutes, people are 11ft 11in high

At 3 minutes, people are 1ft 10in high

Weekly income (£)

25 000

20 000

15 000

10 000

5 000

0

0 minutes   15 minutes   30 minutes   45 minutes   1 hour

Income distribution is very unequal.

Defining income

Income means the amount of money coming into a household. For most households, this will be mainly in the form of pay for work, but other types of income include:

- social security and other state benefits
- pensions
- interest on building society and bank accounts
- dividends on shares.

Tax has to be paid on most income, and there may be other deductions such as National Insurance and pension contributions. People's wage slips show two incomes: the amount before tax and other deductions, or original income, and the amount after deductions, or disposable income. Disposable income is the amount of money that people directly get and can spend – although in practice a lot of the pay packet will be used to pay for such items as mortgage and rent payments.

Income is important because it has huge consequences for people's life chances. For example, those on high incomes will be able to live in a larger house, pay for private health care and education and so on.

The average weekly earnings in 1998 were £427 for a man, £310 for a woman (New Earnings Survey).

HINTS AND TIPS

People buying their home have to 'pay the mortgage' every month. Those who are renting someone else's property to live in pay rent.

The income parade

Income is unequally distributed; that is, some people have bigger incomes than others. But how unequal is the distribution of income in Britain today?

A striking way of explaining the distribution of income is the 'income parade', which gives a height to each household according to its income and then imagines the people walking past a fixed point.

A household on average income is said to be 5 feet 8 inches tall. Someone who has a lower income than average will be shorter, someone who has a larger income will be taller. The incomes are adjusted to take into account the costs of supporting children and the number of adults. All the people then walk past us in the income parade, the shortest first, and the whole parade takes one hour.

At first, the people going past are tiny. After three minutes a single unemployed mother with two children living on income support goes past; she is 1 foot 10 inches tall. After half an hour, the people going past are still only 4 feet 10 inches, well below average. Only after 62 per cent of the households have gone past do we see the household on average income.

With nine minutes to go, a single woman aged 45 without children who is a personnel officer goes past. A little later come a couple in their 50s whose children have left home; he is a self-employed journalist, she runs a day centre for elderly people part time. They are 11 feet 11 inches high. In the last minute, a company chief executive and his non-working wife pass by; they are about 60 feet tall.

The really striking transformation is in the last few seconds. We cannot be sure of the exact incomes of the very rich, but the final people to pass us by are several miles high!

If you were puzzled as to why the average household did not pass us after half an hour, but much later, the answer lies in those final fabulously rich households. There are far fewer rich people than poor, and the richest are very rich indeed.

Growing inequality

The income parade tells us that the distribution of income in Britain is very unequal, but it does not tell us how this is changing and has changed in the recent past. There have in fact been two distinct periods – 1961–79 and 1979–94/95, as shown in the graph. This divides the population into tenths, and then shows how the income of each tenth changed over the period. The higher the bar, the more a tenth's income increased:

■ Between 1961 and 1979, the income of every tenth increased, but the poorest tenth did better than everyone else. In terms of the income parade, the tiny people at the beginning got a bit bigger.

■ Between 1979 and 1994–95, the movement was very different. The poorest tenth got the smallest increase. The richest tenth got the biggest increase, then the next tenth, then the next and so on.

Change in real after-tax income by tenths of the population, 1961–94/5

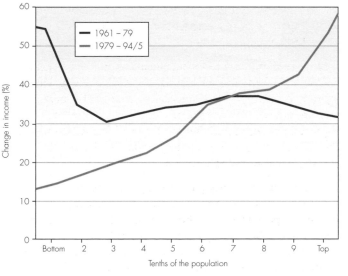

Tenths of the population

Questioning identity edited by Kath Woodward, Routledge, 2000;
Department of Social Security, 1997.

The figures show that the gap between the lowest and highest incomes has been rising dramatically, more so than in most other countries. The progress that was being made towards reducing income inequality has been reversed. One result of this has been a big increase in the numbers of people living in poverty.

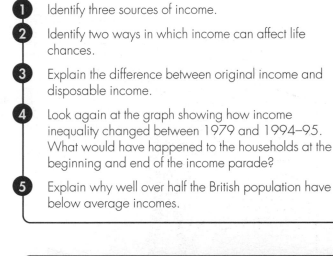

QUESTIONS

1 Identify three sources of income.

2 Identify two ways in which income can affect life chances.

3 Explain the difference between original income and disposable income.

4 Look again at the graph showing how income inequality changed between 1979 and 1994–95. What would have happened to the households at the beginning and end of the income parade?

5 Explain why well over half the British population have below average incomes.

ROUND-UP

The distribution of income in Britain is very unequal and has been becoming more unequal. A very small number of people have extremely high incomes while a much larger number have very low incomes.

VOCABULARY

Dividends: the share of a company's profits paid out to shareholders
Mortgage: the agreement by which people agree to borrow money, usually from a bank or building society, to buy a house, repaying it over many years
Rent: a payment made to property owners by someone living in or using their property

Two views of class: Marx and Weber

KEY FOCUS

This section looks at the theories of class developed by two early social theorists, Karl Marx and Max Weber. These two very different theories have had a big influence on thinking about class.

For Marx, class conflict between the workers and the bosses; for Weber, an attempt to keep up with other workers.

Karl Marx

The German thinker and writer Karl Marx argued in the nineteenth century that societies were divided into two main classes. What made them different was whether or not the members of the classes owned property or not.

Those who owned property such as factories, mines, farms and buildings would be able to make money simply through having these. They did not even need to work themselves; they could pay somebody to be the manager or supervisor. Marx called them the **bourgeoisie** or **ruling class**.

Those who did not own property had to work for a living. All they owned was their ability to work, so they had to sell this to the bourgeoisie by working in factories, mines and so on. Marx called them the **proletariat** or working class.

According to Marx, the bourgeoisie would always pay the proletariat as little as possible for their work. This would increase the profits the bourgeoisie made. It was exploitation of

the workers, because they were not getting paid the full value of their work. There was always a conflict of interest between bourgeoisie and proletariat: **class conflict**. So the bourgeoisie would get richer, and the proletariat would get poorer. Society would eventually be made up of a small number of extremely rich people and a huge number of poor people.

Marx thought that this situation would be so unstable that there would be a revolution. The workers would come to realise how they were being exploited. They would realise that they all belonged to the same class; Marx called this **class consciousness**. The revolution would begin a new stage of history and a new type of society, in which everyone would be equal. This classless society would be communism and would replace the current capitalist society.

At the time Marx was writing, there were clearly at least two other classes: the middle class and the criminals, vagrants and others at the bottom end of society who did not work (Marx called them the *lumpenproletariat*). At the time many European countries also still had large numbers of peasants. Marx realised that these groups existed, but did not see them as an essential part of capitalism. People in the middle class would be pulled up into the bourgeoisie or pushed down into the proletariat as the revolution came nearer.

Max Weber

Weber, who was also German, was writing in the early twentieth century, after Marx had died. He and Marx agreed that class was about economic factors such as money and work, and that classes were in conflict with each other. Beyond this, though, they disagreed.

Weber recognised Marx's division of society into two, but also saw divisions within the two classes. For example, people in professional occupations on high salaries were in a very different situation to unskilled and low paid workers. Weber though that these divisions were so important that it could not be said that all workers belonged to the same class because they were workers.

Weber saw society as made up of many small groups competing with each other. In deciding someone's class position, said Weber, we need to consider the person's status as well as his or her economic situation. For example, nurses do not earn very high wages but they have high status because their work is seen as very important. Someone on similar pay but in less important work would have lower status.

Weber also, unlike Marx, took into account other aspects of stratification such as gender and ethnicity. For example, individuals in the same occupation might have different status depending on whether they were male or female, black or white. The social position of groups can also be affected by how they organise themselves (for example through a trade union) to pursue their interests.

This leads to a much more complicated view of stratification. While Marx saw just two classes, for Weber there were large numbers of different layers in society, each competing with those around them for power and wealth.

Comparing Marx and Weber in action

Imagine a strike at a factory. The workers demand a pay rise and refuse to work until they get it. How would Marx and Weber make sense of this?

For Marx, the strike would demonstrate the class conflict that is always present in capitalist societies. A section of the proletariat, the factory workers, tries to get a fairer share of the company's profits from the owners who are part of the bourgeoisie.

For Weber, however, the strike would not be about class conflict on such a big scale. The workers at the factory might

well be comparing themselves with workers at another factory close by who had just had a pay rise. They would be trying to catch up with another group on roughly the same level as them. They would be pursuing their own interests, not those of the whole proletariat.

FIND OUT FOR YOURSELF

Marx and Weber, along with the Frenchman Emile Durkheim, are often referred to as the 'founding fathers' of sociology; that is, as the most important thinkers in establishing the subject of sociology.

Choose one of these three and research his life and ideas using Microsoft Encarta and other reference works. Try to find photographs. Then design a poster about your chosen sociologist for wall display.

QUESTIONS

1. What are the two classes in Marx's view of capitalist society?

2. What does Marx mean by class consciousness?

3. Identify two differences between Marx's and Weber's views of class, and write a sentence explaining each.

4. Give an example of (a) an occupation that is not well paid but has high status and (b) an occupation which is well paid but has low status.

5. Which do you think is the more useful way of thinking about class, Marx's or Weber's? Give reasons for your answer.

ROUND-UP

Marx argued that there were only two classes, the bourgeoisie and the proletariat, who were in conflict with each other. For Weber, there were many classes, based on status as well as occupation.

VOCABULARY

Lumpenproletariat: Marx's term for the people at the bottom of society, below the working class
Revolution: a dramatic change in the economic and political system

Meet the classes

Here, in their own words, are people from each of the main social classes in Britain. Bear in mind that each is an individual, and so cannot be assumed to be representative of his or her class – it does not tell us about other individuals in that class, who may be very different. Yet what we learn about them, and what they say, may also be very revealing.

Upper class: Andrew Cavendish

Andrew Cavendish is 73. His family home is Chatsworth in Derbyshire. It has 175 rooms and is set in a garden of 100 acres and an estate of 11 000 acres. 175 people work there. It is open to the public seven months a year.

'A lot of people do try and pigeonhole people by class. I take a passionate interest in Association Football, but there was nothing I could say in an interview when I completely failed to convince a woman from *The Times* that this wasn't an affectation on my part.

'Class is like beauty. It's all in the mind's eye, isn't it? I think the system is breaking down ... for better or for worse, the **aristocracy** has ceased to be any force in the country.

'I have just had a hip operation done and there was to begin with some embarrassment about what the staff should call me, but we settled on my Christian name which was very good. I wouldn't want anyone to be embarrassed because of what I am.

'... I am a patron of the Polite Society, manners are so important. But in too many people's minds they get muddled between servility and civility.'

Upper middle class: Charles Mavor

Charles Mavor is a banking director at a merchant bank and is 37. He lives with his wife in an old rectory in Cornwall, commuting every week to his London flat. He went to a private school and to Exeter University.

'I would say I am upper middle class. Class is a combination of values, your approach to life, employment as well as how you have been brought up. But above all else, education conditions attitudes that last a long time.

'My job is lending money to medium-sized companies and the people running those are not upper middle class. I deal with a broad cross-section and after 15 years or so of working the view you form of people is far more meritocratic than based on class – are they people you respect, trust, find interesting? But I do feel embarrassed at times. If I'm in a room full of industrialists the way I speak could be a disadvantage. It could be taken as seen as projecting a form of arrogance.

'Someone in my job could earn between £60 000 and £150 000 depending on the institution, experience and precise responsibility ... I think I have only ever voted on one occasion, though I am essentially conservative with a small "c" by nature. And if I felt my children could be well educated in the state system, backed up by what we could give them as parents, I wouldn't educate them privately.'

Middle class: Anna Woodthorpe Brown

Anna Woodthorpe Brown is 31 and lives in a village in Norfolk with her husband and two young children. She works as a gardener and for her husband's computer consultancy.

'Both my parents are Irish and working class. I think other people define me as middle class but I think deep down I like to consider myself working class, part of it is wanting more street cred, and you don't want to be associated with the toff types. I do sound middle class and I spoke better than other children on the estate, but I was at a good Roman Catholic girls' comprehensive, where my accent was influenced I suppose.

'I think the upper class like to control other people, and I think the majority of the working class like to be controlled. It might sound snotty but ... we have three dogs, they like to know where the boundaries are, where they can tread. They are not actually able to think for themselves that much and when they do things go terribly wrong.

'Most working class people are pretty decent people but they like to know where the boundaries are. They want to be told this is acceptable and this isn't, and work between those two lines.'

Working class: Ned Leary

Ned Leary, 44, works on the production line in the car assembly plant at Ford Dagenham, where he has been for 16 years. He lives in south London and is married with two children.

'In our plant there really is a class society, you've got the management canteen and car park, workers' canteen and car park, and we know our place.

'I left school straight away. I was a bit of a fool to myself because I could have gone on. I would like to have been an artist, and I still sketch now if I've got an hour to spare and nothing to read. Now I can't afford to re-educate myself and try something entirely different and I haven't got the time.

'We earn £6.50 an hour, in fact you get paid by the minute. If you're five minutes late you miss five minutes' pay. It's a 39-hour week so we earn about £14 000 a year.

'It's enough for a mortgage, we live in a nice little house in a cul-de-sac. I'm happy where I live, but as far as I'm concerned the Halifax Building Society owns my house, it's the curse on my household.'

Underclass: Judith Gardam

Judith Gardam is a 28-year-old single mother with two children. She separated from her husband and has been living on about £70 a week state benefits. She lives in a council house in Bootle, Liverpool.

'It's just not fair being branded as a scrounger. My children were born in wedlock and the marriage was going nowhere basically ... so I've got to depend on state benefits in order to survive.

'It is a class war, they've got the money, they've got the education, they've got the jobs and don't have the backgrounds most single mums have, so they simply do not, with a capital N, understand. Who are they to judge single parents?

'I go to college twice a week doing English and Maths GCSE ... I want something better for the kids but at the moment I feel I am lower than lower class. I am a single parent, a nobody.'

Adapted from *The Observer*, 12 December 1993.

QUESTIONS

1 For each of the five people, pick out three things about their lives, backgrounds or ideas which you think say something about the class they belong to.

2 Compare what the five people say about (a) class, (b) education, (c) work. Note: not all of them comment on all of these things, but you should find enough to work on.

ROUND-UP

From these brief accounts of the lives of these people, we can begin to appreciate the importance of class differences.

VOCABULARY

Affectation: something done only for show, to make an impression on others

Meritocratic: when success is a result of talent and ability, not background

Patron: someone who helps an organisation by giving it support

The upper class

KEY FOCUS

For all its wealth and power, Britain's upper class tends not to get noticed a lot. For example, it doesn't appear as a class in the Registrar General's Scale or on other occupational scales. It is a very small group – look back at the sections on the distribution of income and wealth – but it deserves particular attention.

The ownership of ancient property can lead to new ways of making money.

The main owners of wealth and income

The upper class is the main owner of wealth and income, which, as we have seen, are very unequally distributed. Upper class people's income usually comes not, as it does for most people, mainly in the form of wages for work, but from their wealth. Shares pay out dividends, investments give interest and so on. Ownership of wealth produces high incomes.

Who belongs to the upper class?

There are three fairly distinct groups within the upper class.

The landowning aristocracy

The landowning aristocracy has inherited titles (such as duke, earl, marquis, viscount and lord) and inherited wealth. At the

very top of this group is the Royal Family. You have already met a member of this group in Meet the classes on page 66. The wealth of the aristocracy has been reduced in the last hundred years by estate duties, and some have had to open their houses ('stately homes'), or parts of them, to the public to raise money. A continuing source of wealth for many is the ownership of antiques and 'old master' paintings. The aristocracy also has less political power than in the past, after it lost the automatic right to seats in the House of Lords. However, it undoubtedly still has considerable influence behind the scenes.

The 'pop aristocracy'

'Pop aristocrats' made their money in sport, the media and entertainment, and often come from working-class origins. Their ability to earn income tends to be unpredictable; for example, in football and other sports, stars make lots of money in their 20s, but they will retire in their 30s (their career may be ended earlier by injury). The top pop stars tend to make more money and continuing sales of their recordings will bring in income in years to come. Among the richest people in this category are Paul McCartney, Phil Collins, Liam and Noel Gallagher of Oasis and the Spice Girls. A new group that belongs here are those who have won millions on the National Lottery.

The entrepreneurs

Entrepreneurs have made their money from business. They have usually started with some money or a family business behind them, but have built up much more successful businesses and become very rich. The best-known member of this group is probably Richard Branson who started the Virgin group of companies. The richest of all in 1997 was Joseph Lewis, who was born in a pub in the East End of London, made a fortune in the restaurant business and now speculates on world currency markets from his villa in the Bahamas. He is thought to be worth about £3 billion (*Guardian*, 7 April 1997).

The Royal Family

The Queen and the Royal Family, while undoubtedly belonging to the upper class, are no longer thought to be at the very top of the list of the wealthiest. This is because much of what the Queen 'owns' is technically owned not by her as a person but by 'The Crown'. The Queen does not own Buckingham Palace, Windsor Castle, St James's Palace and Kensington Palace or the Crown Jewels. Her exact wealth is unknown.

The Old Boys' Network

The people who have the most important and well-paid positions in British society tend to be drawn from a very small minority. They have been to one of the top public schools and to Oxford or Cambridge Universities. They often know each other socially, for example through membership of exclusive gentlemen's clubs in the West End of London, and through attending events such as hunt balls, the Henley Regatta and Royal Ascot. They marry someone from the same social level. The network of contacts that this creates, is popularly known as the **Old Boys' Network**. It enables the ruling class to ensure that its children are able to move into positions of power and influence.

The word boys in Old Boys' Network is important. The network mainly involves men; it also mainly involves white men, excluding members of minority ethnic groups. Among the top positions that seem to draw their members from this network are politicians, judges, top civil servants, senior officers in the armed forces and company directors.

Those whose wealth is new, especially from the pop aristocracy, may find it hard to break into this group. 'Old money' looks down with distaste on 'new money' and its often lowly origins. To try to gain acceptance, the newly wealthy may, for example, send their children to the top public schools.

How large is the upper class?

Sociologists do not agree on exactly where the boundary between the upper class and the middle class is, and particularly on where the managers of the largest companies should be placed.

However, the people listed in the three groups above together make up less than 2 per cent of the British population. This makes it much smaller than any other class.

FIND OUT FOR YOURSELF

There are probably stately homes, castles or similar properties not far from where you live. These were once probably, and

may still be, the homes of members of the landowning aristocracy. Find out more about such properties. Your local library or tourist information centre will probably have leaflets for any that are run by the National Trust or are open to the public. Find out about when they were built and the families who lived or live there. If you can, visit one.

QUESTIONS

1. Which three groups make up the richest people in Britain? Give a named example from each group.

2. What is meant by the Old Boys' Network?

3. Identify and describe two kinds of links between people in the Old Boys' Network.

4. Why do people with 'new money' find it hard to get accepted by those with 'old money'?

5. 'The upper class is far more important than its size suggests.' Do you agree? Give reasons for your answer.

ROUND-UP

The upper class is so small that it could pass unnoticed – except for its huge wealth and income, and the power and influence this gives it. The old landed aristocracy remains important, but successful businesspeople and others also belong to the upper class.

VOCABULARY

Estate duties (also called death duties): taxes on inheritance

Entrepreneurs: company owners who are willing to take risks

Hunt ball: a social occasion with dancing connected to a meeting of fox hunters

The middle class

The middle class is the largest class, but this is partly because it is a rather imprecise term that covers lots of people in very different situations. This section looks at who belongs to the middle class and how it has grown.

The middle class includes people in a wide range of jobs.

The largest class

Marx, writing more than a hundred years ago, expected the middle class of his day to disappear as conflict between the bourgeoisie and proletariat increased. In fact, the middle class seems to be bigger than ever. On the Registrar General's Scale, classes 1, 2 and 3 non-manual are middle class, and at the 1991 Census these classes accounted for just over half the population. So the middle class is now bigger than the working class.

The middle class has grown enormously since the beginning of the twentieth century. At that time, most jobs were working class; the three middle-class groups on the Registrar General's Scale made up only a quarter of the population.

Why has the middle class grown?

After World War II (1939–45), there was a big growth in the number of people in middle-class occupations in the public sector. There were a lot more teachers, social workers, health workers, civil servants and so on. The newly created jobs were often taken by people from working-class families, so that they moved up the social class ladder.

More recently, the nature of jobs available has changed again. In the 1980s and 1990s, a lot of traditional working-class jobs, such as working in coalmines, steel works and shipyards, declined. New jobs that replaced them were often, though not always, middle class, for example computer programming and some jobs in travel and tourism.

Another reason for the growth of the middle class is that more people were getting higher qualifications, staying on at school and going to university. There were plenty of people qualified to take new middle-class jobs (although some highly qualified people have to settle for jobs below what they are able to do).

Who belongs to the middle class?

The middle class is big and contains people in many different situations and with different life chances – so much so that some sociologists have said we should refer to the middle classes, not just the middle class. Different writers have suggested dividing the middle class in different ways. The one used here is a common and widely accepted division.

The upper middle class

These are the managers and the professionals. Professionals

are people who have specialised knowledge and qualifications that are gained only after a long period of training. They include lawyers, architects, lecturers, teachers, social workers, doctors and nurses. Managers are less likely to have qualifications related to their job; their class situation depends much more on the position they have in an organisation.

The lower middle class

This includes occupations such as clerks, office workers, telephone sales and shop workers. These kinds of jobs count as middle class because they are non-manual, but the distinction between manual and non-manual work is less important than it used to be. Some of these jobs used to be seen as much more important, and more skilled, than they are now. Being a clerk was once a highly thought of job. We can see this still in titles like 'town clerk' for the person responsible for local authority administration, but clerk today tends to imply routine office work such as filing.

Lower middle-class jobs today are often not very well paid and do not require high qualifications. In some ways, however, they are still different from working-class jobs. Working conditions are usually cleaner and safer (compare an office to a factory) and there may be more opportunities to get promotion or to go on training courses. Women hold a high proportion of lower middle-class jobs.

The petty bourgeoisie

These are the owners of small businesses (the **'petty'** is from the French *petit*, meaning small, while you already know the term **bourgeoisie**). They may own a shop or workshop employing a small number of people, or be self-employed as a plumber, electrician and so on, or be a landlord or small farmer. Marx expected this group to disappear, to be swallowed up by one of the two bigger classes, but this has not happened. Although running a small business is very risky, more people are always willing to have a go. They are attracted by the idea of working for themselves rather than for a boss, and there is usually help available to get started. Most small businesses last less than two years; only 20 per cent of those set up in any one year survive for five years.

The divided middle class

The people at the top of the middle class, such as professors and doctors, have a lot in common with the upper class. However, other members of the upper middle class, such as teachers and nurses, are not as well paid and have lower status. Those in the lower middle class earn little, if any, more than the working class and have a lot in common with them. The middle class is clearly divided and it doesn't make a lot of sense to treat, say, a top consultant in a hospital and a hotel receptionist as being in the same class. Perhaps then it is better to think of there being several middle classes, rather than one middle class.

Higher up the middle class, people enjoy many advantages in life chances: decent salaries, good health and education and long lives. Towards the bottom, life chances are similar to those of the working class.

QUESTIONS

1. Which classes on the Registrar General's Scale are middle class?

2. Why did Marx expect the middle class to disappear? (You may need to look back at the section on Marx and Weber on class on pages 64–5.)

3. List the three main groups within the middle class, and give three examples of jobs within each group.

4. Why have the number and proportion of middle-class jobs grown in the last 50 years or so?

5. Is there one middle class – or is it better to talk about several middle classes? Give reasons for your answer.

ROUND-UP

The middle class contains at least three groups with different levels of income and status. The middle class has grown considerably as a result of changes in the economy and the expansion of education.

VOCABULARY

Consultant: a doctor holding the highest position in a branch of medicine in a hospital

Professional: someone who is expert and qualified in a responsible job

The working class

KEY FOCUS   The working class has a special place in Marxist accounts of class, because it was the working class that was supposed to unite and overthrow capitalism. This has not happened, and the working class has in fact got smaller. However, it remains distinct from the middle class.

Many traditional working-class jobs have been lost.

Working class or lower class?

Americans tend to use the term 'lower class' rather than working class, but in Britain lower class is seen as being rather negative. Working class, on the other hand, is something a person can be proud of, to be working to earn a living and support a family. Working class will be the term used here.

The working class

Like the middle class, the working class contains several different groups. On the Registrar General's Scale, classes 3 manual, 4 and 5 are working class. These are, respectively, the skilled, semi-skilled and unskilled workers.

The number of people in the working class has fallen over the last hundred years or so, at the same time as the number of people in middle-class occupations has grown. The biggest fall has been in unskilled manual work; there are far fewer jobs than in the past for which no skills or training are needed. But, especially in the 1980s and 1990s, many traditional working-class jobs in industries such as shipbuilding, coalmining and heavy industry were lost as the economy changed and as a result of government policies.

The impact of these changes on working-class communities is shown in films like *The Full Monty* and *Brassed Off*. The men made unemployed struggle to find a purpose to their lives and hope for the future as their families and communities fall apart.

The communities affected – even destroyed – by these changes had been united by a powerful sense of identity. The work was difficult, but the men took pride in this. There were powerful local loyalties, to football clubs, trade unions, even brass bands and choirs. Society was seen very much in terms of 'us' and 'them' – the workers and the bosses. For Marxists, these powerful loyalties, spread through the rest of the working class, would be the basis for a better future. The working class was seen as the proletariat, the victim of capitalism who would one day rise up and overthrow it. The defeat of the miners' strike of 1984–85 is often seen as the ending of this way of life and these hopes.

Embourgeoisement

Living standards for everyone have risen in the last century. For example, life expectancy – how long people live – has grown enormously. The working class today is better off than in the past. Most have secure incomes, own televisions, washing machines, cars, even houses. Does this mean that there are no real differences between the working class and the middle classes? Are we all middle class now? The idea that such differences have disappeared is called **embourgeoisement**.

The evidence for this is not only the higher incomes and ownership of consumer durables, but also in how the classes vote. Traditionally, the Conservative Party has been seen as the party of the middle and upper class, and the Labour Party as the party of the working class. The improvement in working-class living standards – affluence – should have meant that more working-class people voted Conservative. This did happen, in both the 1950s to early 1960s (when the Conservatives won three general elections in a row) and again from 1979 to 1992 (when they won four in a row). It was thought in both periods that Labour could never win again, because it had lost its traditional voters. Affluent workers had, it was said, rejected the old working-class ways and were behaving like the middle class, less involved in their communities and more interested in being consumers.

In fact, Labour won its biggest ever victory in 1997, attracting many middle-class voters as well as working-class ones. When sociologists looked more closely at the affluent working class, they found that in other ways they still behaved like the working class. They did not mix with the middle class, and were willing to strike when they had a grievance. They had little loyalty to the company and did not expect job satisfaction. This seems to prove that, although workers had changed, embourgeoisement has not happened.

Here are some other ways in which working-class jobs remain different from middle-class ones:

■ The working environment is less likely to be clean and safe.
■ The work is more physically demanding and even dangerous.
■ The work is less likely to require qualifications such as exam passes.
■ There are fewer benefits (such as pension schemes, perks like company cars).

The working class has had to change, and is smaller than it used to be, but it has not disappeared.

Has embourgeoisement happened?

Yes	No
Workers earned wages nearly as high as the middle class	Workers continued to have different attitudes to work, such as little loyalty to the company
They wanted to buy consumer durables	Still differences between working- and middle-class jobs
Some voted Conservative	Affluent workers voted Labour again in 1997

The underclass

While the majority of the working class now have reasonably healthy, prosperous lives (compared to the past, if not to today's upper class), a minority do not. Those who cannot work, such as the long-term unemployed and the disabled and chronically ill, are in effect shut out of much of what most people take for granted. These groups are sometimes referred to as the **underclass**, a term which means people at the very bottom of society but not fully a part of society.

FIND OUT FOR YOURSELF

Find a video of the film *The Full Monty* and watch it. Make a list of the ways in which it shows the impact of changes on working-class communities, on gender roles and on other themes you have studied in sociology.

QUESTIONS

1. Which classes in the Registrar General's Scale are working class?
2. Which three groups make up the working class? Give an example of an occupation for each group.
3. What is meant by embourgeoisement?
4. What was the significance of the 1984–85 miners' strike for ideas about the working class?
5. Are we all middle class now? Explain your answer.

ROUND-UP

The working class is smaller than it used to be, and like the middle class can be divided into several different groups. The theory that the higher paid members of the working class have become like the middle class is called embourgeoisement; there is evidence on both sides.

VOCABULARY

Consumer durables: goods you can buy which have a long useful life, such as a car or television
Affluent workers: members of the working class earning high wages
Chronically ill: continuously ill for a long time or permanently; different from acutely ill, which means very ill but for a limited time

Social mobility

Class, unlike caste, is not fixed at birth. This section looks at how many people move away from their class background into another class.

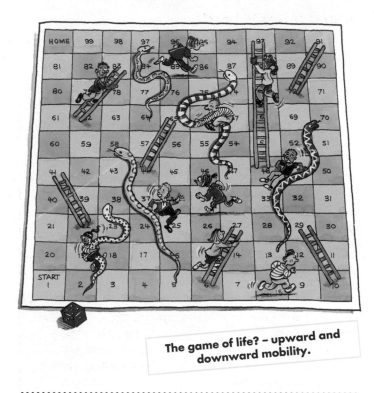

The game of life? – upward and downward mobility.

What is social mobility?

Social mobility means movement up or down the class system. Unlike other systems of stratification, such as caste, class position is not determined for life at birth – people can move up and down. But how much mobility is there? Do people rise to the position their abilities and qualifications deserve? Or are they held back by a class system which favours those who are already well off?

During the twentieth century, upward mobility was much more common than downward mobility. This was because of changes in the numbers and proportions of different kinds of jobs. Unskilled manual jobs became less common, while the number of middle-class jobs grew, so there was more 'room at the top'. Many people born into the working class were able to move up into the expanding middle class, helped by qualifications that were now available to people of their background.

Most mobility is over a short distance, for example from the top of the working class to the bottom of the middle class. It is

possible to move from one end of the class system to the other, but this is unusual.

The discussion here is about the middle class and working class only. This is because there is very little movement in or out of the upper class.

Measuring mobility

There are two ways of measuring mobility:

- **Intergenerational mobility** – between generations, for example the child of working-class parents who is successful in education and moves up into a middle-class profession.
- **Intragenerational mobility** – within one generation, for example a man whose first job is a working-class one but who moves up to become a manager.

Societies with a lot of mobility are called open societies; those with very little or none are called closed societies.

Absolute and relative mobility

Absolute mobility refers to the total numbers of people moving up and down. When this type of social mobility is measured, it is clear that Britain is an open society because many people have been upwardly mobile from the working class to the middle class.

Some sociologists, however, argue that **relative mobility** is much more important. Relative mobility looks at the chances of an individual from one class being mobile compared to an individual from another class being mobile. When this type of mobility is studied, a very different picture emerges.

It is true that during the second half of the twentieth century many working-class people were upwardly mobile. However, the chances of someone born into the working class getting a middle-class job were much less than those of someone born into a middle-class family. Because of the growing number of middle-class positions, the majority of middle-class children got middle-class jobs, joined by only a small proportion of the total number of working-class children.

Seen in this way, it appears that the only reason for the upward mobility of some working-class people was the increase in middle-class jobs. If it had not been for this, they would have been stuck in the working class. If middle-class people had had more children, perhaps there wouldn't have been any upward movement at all! So it seems the 'normal' situation is that Britain is a closed society, with upward movement only possible in particular economic circumstances. Class inequalities have not been reduced.

Is this unfair?

Many sociologists see the low level of relative mobility as unfair, and a waste of the talent of working-class people. The privileged middle class is seen as giving its children a flying start in life, while the children of the working class do not have such advantages. Both John Major and Tony Blair, Prime Ministers from different political parties, wanted Britain to be a **meritocracy**; that is, that those with ability who put in effort should be able to rise to the level they deserved. This does not seem to have happened.

An alternative view is that children from middle-class backgrounds succeed in greater numbers because they deserve to. It is said to be natural that those in the middle class are more likely to have inherited ability and talent, because they or their ancestors must have had these to reach the middle class. It is then natural that middle-class children take most of the best jobs, because their greater ability leads to higher qualifications. This assumes that intelligence is largely inherited, which is a controversial idea (see Measuring intelligence and ability on page 176). To those who believe ability and intelligence are spread equally across the classes, our present system wastes a lot of talent.

Is Britain a meritocracy?

Yes: Talented people from all backgrounds can reach the top.
Those from middle-class backgrounds are likely to be more intelligent.

No: The privileged buy their children a start in life.
Talented working-class children find it difficult to reach the top.

What about girls?

Like other areas of the sociology of class, gender raises problems for social mobility. Most research on social mobility assumes that you can work out the class of a household from the head of household's occupation. A woman's class then depends on her husband or father's occupation. These assumptions are increasingly unrealistic because more women work, reach high positions and support families – they can be socially mobile through their own work.

In the past, women have been able to be upwardly mobile

through marrying a man of a higher class. Many novels, such as those of Jane Austen, are about girls seeking a 'good match' to improve their own and their family's fortunes.

Today, large numbers of women work in offices, shops and other routine non-manual work; there is downward mobility to these occupations from higher classes and upward mobility from the working class.

FIND OUT FOR YOURSELF

How much social mobility has there been in your family? Find out from your parents and grandparents about their working lives. Ask them also about other members of your family, including those in earlier generations. You may find your family has been geographically mobile – that is, moved between countries or from one part of the country to another – as well as socially mobile.

QUESTIONS

1. What is meant by social mobility?

2. Explain the difference between intergenerational and intragenerational mobility.

3. What is meant by a meritocracy?

4. Why was there considerable upward mobility from the working class to the middle class in the second half of the twentieth century? Why in the same period was there little downward mobility from the middle class to the working class?

5. Would you describe Britain as an open or a closed society? Give reasons for your answer.

ROUND-UP

While there has been considerable upward mobility in Britain, sociologists do not agree on what this means. The working class has less chance of reaching the middle class than the middle class do of staying there.

VOCABULARY

Expanding: getting bigger
Assumptions: ideas that are taken for granted without being tested

Is class still important?

This section examines several claims that have been made about how class has allegedly become less important in Britain. These include ideas about the importance of consumption (the things we buy) and about the 'classless society'.

Henley regatta: one of the forms class differences take today?

The end of class?

Britain is often thought by British people and by those from other countries to be a country obsessed with class. While other countries also, of course, have rich and poor, in Britain the distinctions have in the past seemed to be particularly clear.

This has been shown in, for example, how often class is a theme in British television dramas and situation comedies.

However, in recent years several claims have been made that class is no longer as important as it used to be.

Consumers, not producers

Class is based on occupation and the money people earn from their occupations. One claim made about class today is that it is now less important what occupation you have, and more important how you spend your money. Class is said to be no longer about producing things, as workers do in factories; it is about buying things.

The mass media today tend to ignore class or claim it is no longer important, but when they do recognise it, it is often in

the form of ideas about consumption. They give the impression that to be upwardly mobile all you need to do is to acquire more sophisticated tastes and cultural habits.

An example of this approach is a book called *Class – Where Do You Stand?* By answering questions such as these the authors claim to be able to tell you your class:

'Where are you most likely to do your main food shopping?
Asda, Co-op, Costco or other discount clubs, Delicatessen, Fortnum and Mason, Happy Shopper, Marks & Spencer, Safeway, Sainsbury, Tesco, Waitrose, corner shop, other stores.

Do you – or are you likely to – attend, watch or take part in:
ballet, bingo, casino gambling, greyhound racing, Rugby League, Rugby Union, sailing, scuba-diving, snooker, soccer, none of these?'

Quoted in the *Sunday Express*, 14 April 1996.

Can you work out which of the answers above would put you highest on the class scale, and which lowest?

Answers to questions such as these depend to a large extent on how much money people have, and therefore on their occupations. This directs us back to the 'older' way of looking at class; perhaps the new stress on consumption does not make all that much difference. Low incomes limit what people can choose to consume!

FIND OUT FOR YOURSELF

Try writing some questions (with possible answers) along the same lines as the ones above. Here are some ideas:

- Holidays
- Shopping for clothes and fashion
- Buying hot food (restaurants, take-aways, etc.)

A classless society?

The idea of a classless society goes back to Karl Marx, who hoped that future communist societies would be classless because everyone would be equal.

When ex-Prime Minister John Major talked about a classless society, he meant something different: a meritocracy. Everyone would have an equal opportunity to succeed, neither helped nor hindered by his or her class background. Those who succeeded in reaching the higher positions would do so because of their abilities and effort. The outcome would of course be a very unequal society, quite different to Marx's vision.

As we have seen in the section on social mobility, the claim that Britain is becoming a meritocracy is a very questionable one. The odds still seem to be stacked in favour of those at the top; there is not yet equality of opportunity. The continued existence of independent fee paying schools plays a big part in this, because those with money can buy advantages for their children.

Other inequalities

The third set of claims about class becoming less important is that other aspects of inequality, such as gender and ethnicity, have become as important as or more important than class. These aspects of our identities have more impact in our daily lives than class, which can seem to be a background factor.

Feminists have played a big part in changing thinking about class by showing that the old assumptions, such as that you could decide a woman's class position by her husband's job, were no longer acceptable. It is no longer taken for granted that class is more important than gender.

These aspects of inequality are not new, but it is only fairly

recently that some sociologists have accepted their importance. Class is now often seen as one important aspect of stratification alongside and cross cutting others.

What do people think about class?

Perhaps the question of the continuing importance of class can be settled by asking British people what they think. Research shows that many people see Britain as a society of sharp class divisions and think that class has a big impact on the opportunities people have. Two-thirds agree that 'there is one law for the rich and one for the poor' and 'ordinary people do not get their fair share of the nation's wealth' (Adonis and Pollard, *A Class Act*, Penguin, 1998). An almost Marxist sense of 'us' against 'them' remains strong. Most people can clearly identify themselves as belonging to a particular class.

QUESTIONS

1. What is meant by consumption?

2. What three types of claims about the decline of class are discussed here? Write a sentence explaining each.

3. What did Marx mean by a 'classless society', and how is this different from a meritocracy?

4. Approximately what percentage of people identify themselves as middle class?

5. Given that the middle class is now bigger than the working class, why do you think so many people think of themselves as working class?

ROUND-UP

Media, politicians and even sociologists have suggested that class is dead or dying. The importance of consumption and the recognition of other aspects of stratification have changed the way sociologists think about class, but there is strong evidence that it remains very important.

VOCABULARY

Hinder: to be in the way of
Obsessed: to be completely preoccupied by

Class – sociology in practice

Caste

Although caste-like structures are common to most societies, including Britain, caste in its original form is unique to India. Castes are based on occupation and have a strict hierarchy. Caste members make friends with their own caste. They marry within their caste, and even eat only with members of their caste.

Caste is based on the religion of Hinduism. There is a key difference between caste and class. A class system can be said to be related to ownership of wealth. This is not so for the caste system. Brahmins (one of the highest castes), being spiritually superior, were expected to give up worldly pleasures. Other castes had to provide the Brahmins with food and other material requirements.

After independence from Britain in 1947, many high caste Indians felt shame about how the lower castes had been treated. A series of measures was brought in to help the Scheduled Castes (once called 'untouchables'). However, in some areas there is still discrimination and violence. The Scheduled Castes find it hard to get an education and a decent job.

Questions

1 Look back at the section on Class as a system of stratification for more information about caste (pages 54–5). Is caste based on ascribed or achieved status? Explain your answer.

2 What are the similarities and differences between caste and class?

3 Look back at the section on Social mobility (pages 74–5). Compare and contrast the chances of social mobility under the caste and class systems .

The working class

YOU no longer, thankfully, see signs outside pubs that say 'no blacks' … But what you do see, more and more, are little cardboard notices, propped in the bar window, which say, 'We regret we are unable to serve persons in working clothes'.

… If (those persons) are lucky, and it isn't raining too hard, you find them clustered around the doorway, on the pavement, drinking the pints that someone has been condescending enough to bring out to them.

They are in jeans. Their arms are vividly tattooed. Their heavy boots still bear the mud of the construction site they have just come from …

The persons these pubs don't want to see, among their potted palms and mock-Edwardian upholstery, are working men, bearing the stigmata of their trade.

Why is it socially offensive to dis-criminate overtly against the black and brown citizens of Britain (about 4.5 per cent of the population) – but not against the working class (about 57 per cent) … What matters most is whether you are working class or middle class, not black or white.

Adapted from 'The social barricades which still face the working masses' by Paul Barker, *Independent*, 6 September 1989.

Questions

1 Look back at the sections on Class and life chances (pages 56–7) and The working class (pages 72–3). In what ways are the life chances of working-class people different from other classes? Use examples from at least two areas of social life (such as work, education, health and so on).

2 What other forms of discrimination – being treated differently because of their class – might working-class people face?

3 Do you agree that class matters more than race and ethnicity? Explain your answer. (You may want to look ahead to Chapter 5 on Ethnicity for ideas.)

The middle class

DOMESTIC servants are being employed in ever increasing numbers by the English middle classes ... Most of the jobs are not declared, as many 'servants' also draw benefits, and both employer and employee are happy not to tell the state.

The author of the research, Rosie Cox from Coventry University, said, 'Servants are thought of as part of the Victorian past, but the fact is that in the 1990s the richest 10 per cent can now afford to buy leisure time by employing the poorest 10 per cent to do their domestic chores.'

Some were employed as child minders so that the employer could go out to work, but many did chores so that employers could have more leisure time.

'In general (in London) the servants are women whose English is not good enough to get a job outside the domestic sector. Outside London, where there are fewer available immigrants, the women are more likely to be poor English.'

Although some of the work was well paid and enjoyable, most was not and the pay and conditions were worse than the legitimate sector.

'There are particular reasons why women are likely to take these jobs, particularly women who already have a large burden of childcare responsibilities or are vulnerable in some other way, such as immigration status or language difficulties,' Ms Cox said.

Adapted from 'Middle classes hiring more servants for domestic chores', *Guardian*, 9 January 1997.

Questions

1. Look back at the sections on The distribution of wealth (pages 60–61) and The distribution of income (pages 62–3). In what ways is the situation described in this article related to changes in the distribution of income and wealth?

2. (a) Look back at the section on The middle class (pages 70–71). From which part of the middle class are the employers of servants likely to come from? Explain your answer.

   (b) Look back at the section on The working class (pages 72–3). Do you think the servants described here belong to the working class, or to the underclass? Give reasons for your answer.

3. How does this article show how difficult it is to separate class from other aspects of stratification such as gender and ethnicity?

VOCABULARY

Condescending: patronizing – helping someone, but in a way that makes the person aware that he or she has lower status

Stigmata: distinguishing marks of social disgrace

Class – important terms

absolute mobility	the total numbers of people moving up and down the class scale
achieved status	status based on achievement or merit
aristocracy	part of the upper class; those with titles such as lord, duke, etc.
ascribed status	status based on origin – family background
bourgeoisie	(Marxism) the owners of factories, farms, mines, etc.
caste	the stratification system which used to be widespread in India
class	large groups at different levels in society, based on wealth, income, occupation
class conflict	(Marxism) there is always a conflict of interests between the two main classes
class consciousness	(Marxism) when the proletariat becomes aware that it is being exploited by the ruling class
embourgeoisement	when the affluent working class becomes part of the middle class
estates	the different levels of society in the feudal system
feudalism	the economic system of the Middle Ages
income	money coming in, to a family or an individual
intergenerational mobility	social mobility between one generation and the next
intragenerational mobility	social mobility within one generation
life chances	how position in the stratification system affects the lives of individuals and groups
meritocracy	when those with talent and ability, and who put in effort, get the highest positions in society, regardless of background
middle class	those in the middle of the class system, in non-manual occupations
mobility	movement between classes
occupational scales	ways of ranking occupations to decide someone's class position
Old Boys' Network	the connections between privileged people, one of the ways in which they can pass on their position to their children
petty bourgeoisie	owners of small businesses, the self-employed, etc.
professionals	members of the middle class who have occupations based on high qualifications and responsibilities
proletariat	(Marxism) the working class
Registrar General's Scale	a widely used occupational scale
relative mobility	the chances of an individual from one class being mobile compared to an individual from another class being mobile
ruling class	the upper class is a ruling class if it has political power as well as great wealth
slavery	a form of stratification in which the basic division is between slaves and slave owners
status	the type of role held in society
underclass	a group with life chances below those of the working class
upper class	those at the top of the class system
wealth	money and goods owned by an individual, which can be sold to bring in income
working class	those who work in manual occupations

Class – exam-style questions

Source A

Changes in social class between 1984 and 1997

Bar chart: Percentage of all in employment (y-axis, 0 to 35) by class category (x-axis): Professional, Managerial and technical, Skilled non-manual, Skilled manual, Partly skilled, Unskilled. Legend: 1984, 1997.

Labour Market Trends, March 1998.

Source B

Some writers have argued that a process of embourgeoisement has taken place. However, there are several ways in which working-class occupations are still clearly different from middle-class ones. Non-manual workers are far more likely to work in a clean and safe environment, to have extra benefits such as a company car and a pension scheme. They are also likely to need to have formal qualifications such as exam passes and professional training.

Foundation tier

1 Look at source A and answer these questions:
   (a) What percentage of workers in 1997 was professional? [1 mark]
   (b) What percentage of workers in 1997 was unskilled? [1 mark]
   (c) In 1997, were there more workers in non-manual occupations or in manual occupations? [1 mark]
   (d) Identify which two classes increased in size between 1984 and 1997 [2 marks]
   (e) Identify two classes that decreased in size between 1984 and 1997 [2 marks]
   (f) What is the name of the class scale being used in this chart? [2 marks]

2 Look at source B and answer these questions:
   (a) Identify one way in which the working conditions of non-manual workers are likely to be better than those of manual workers. [1 mark]
   (b) What is meant by embourgeoisement? [2 marks]

3 Identify and explain one reason for the fall in the percentage of the population who are working class. [2 marks]

4 The table in source A uses occupation to measure class. Name two other indicators of class. [2 marks]

5 Identify and explain two other forms of stratification other than class. [4 marks]

Higher tier

1 Look at source A and answer these questions:
   (a) Identify which two classes increased in size between 1984 and 1997. [2 marks]
   (b) Identify two classes that decreased in size between 1984 and 1997. [2 marks]
   (c) What is the name of the class scale being used in this chart? [2 marks]

2 Look at source B. What is meant by embourgeoisement? [2 marks]

3 Identify and explain one reason for the fall in the percentage of the population who are working class. [2 marks]

4 The table in source A uses occupation to measure class. Name two other indicators of class. [2 marks]

5 Identify and explain two other forms of stratification other than class [4 marks]

6 'We are all middle class now.' Do you agree? Give sociological reasons for your answer. [4 marks]

Class – further research

There are revision questions on class at the Hewett School site. Follow the topic areas links to social class and stratification: www.hewett.norfolk.sch.uk/curric/soc.

4 Gender

KEY TERMS

femininity
feminism
gender
gender roles
masculinity
patriarchy
sex
sex discrimination
sex equality
sexism

Gender is one of the four aspects of stratification that we look at. As with the other three – class, ethnicity and age – it has a chapter of its own, but it is also a theme running through the entire book. So you will find sections on gender in most of the other chapters, and you will need to read some of them to get a good idea of this topic.

This chapter begins by looking at what is meant by sex and gender. Our sex identity – whether we are male or female – is perhaps the most basic aspect of our identity. The first thing people want to know about a new-born baby is whether it's a boy or a girl. Yet sex is so important partly because of what a society or culture adds to it – the idea that there are different roles for males and females. This chapter explores some of the differences.

This involves looking at, among other things, the campaign for women's equality with men, known as feminism. It also involves recognising that there are ways in which men, not just women, face disadvantages.

IN THIS CHAPTER YOU WILL LEARN ABOUT:

- the differences between 'sex' and 'gender'
- the history of feminism
- how males and females have gender roles, and how these vary between societies
- how there have been advances towards greater equality
- how men as well as women suffer some disadvantages

CHAPTER CONTENTS

Sex and gender

KEY FOCUS This section looks at the correct use of the terms sex and gender, and at how gender differences between cultures suggest that gender does not have to depend on sex.

Is it a boy or a girl?

Sex difference

For some sociologists, the most basic division in society is between men and women rather than between different classes. Feminists in particular are interested in the position of women in society compared to that of men.

Sex difference is basic to our identity and to how others see us. The first question asked about a baby is, 'Is it a boy or a girl?'. We use the terms 'girl' and 'boy' all the time. Boys and girls are socialised into different interests and ways of behaving. There is a continuing argument about to what extent these differences are natural and to what extent they are shaped by the social environment children grow up in, the way they are socialised.

The argument is often called the 'nature versus nurture debate'. The nature side is the biological view that gender differences are natural and inevitable, and are based on sex differences. The nurture side is the sociological view that gender does not have to be connected to sex, but that it usually is.

Sex and gender

The word **sex** refers to the biological differences between men and women. Your sex is either male or female.

The word **gender** refers to cultural and social differences between men and women. Your gender is either masculine or feminine.

A new born baby has a sex but no gender. The baby will acquire gender as it grows up and is socialised. A transsexual may be of male sex but feminine gender (or the other way around).

The belief that it is natural for men and women to behave differently is very common, but there is not necessarily a connection between being a male and behaving in a masculine way, or between being female and behaving in a feminine way. This is partly because what is meant by 'masculine' and 'feminine' is different in different societies at different times.

Sex and gender around the world

G. P. Murdock, an anthropologist, collected information on more than 200 different societies around the world, ranging from 'traditional' hunting and gathering societies to modern industrial ones. He argued that in almost all societies men and women had different roles that were based on their biological differences. Because women gave birth to and looked after children, they did light work near the home, while men, because they were stronger did heavier and more dangerous work further from home, for example hunting, clearing land and quarrying. In modern terms, this meant the role of the woman was to be a mother and housewife, and the role of the man to be the 'breadwinner'.

If Murdock were right, it would mean that the move towards greater equality for women in, for example, going out to work was going against nature. It would be especially wrong for a mother of young children to go out to work; she should be at home looking after the children.

There is a problem with this though. The pattern Murdock found did not apply in all societies. Other anthropologists have found cultures where:

■ both men and women behave in what we would see as a 'masculine' way, being aggressive and competitive

- both men and women behave in what we would see as a 'feminine' way, being gentle and submissive
- men behave in a 'feminine' way and women behave in a 'masculine' way, for example the men may look after babies and young children while the women work
- there seem to be no set rules – everyone joins in with whatever needs to be done. This happens with the Mbuti 'pygmies' of the Central African rain forests.

In each of these cases, of course, the ways men and women behaved would be thought of as natural and right. While there are only a few cultures which do not follow what we think of as 'natural', their existence suggests that it is up to a society to decide what is appropriate for men and women. Feminists argue that the pattern that is found nearly everywhere reflects the domination of most societies by men – and so we can change it if we want to. Perhaps everyone could belong to one gender.

Back to biology?

There are clearly biological differences between women and men. The question is how significant are they, and how much society makes them more important than they might be. Women carry foetuses, give birth and breastfeed; men cannot do these things. Just about everything else is possible for both women and men.

HINTS AND TIPS

The phrase opposite sex is in common use. However men and women have a lot in common – arguably far more than the differences between them. Because of this the term the other sex will be used here rather than the opposite sex.

Strength and speed

One area where there seems to be big differences between men and women is in physical sports. Men are seen as stronger and faster, and it would be seen as unfair for men to compete against women in, say, athletics events or tennis.

The differences however are between averages. The strongest and fastest women are stronger and faster than most men – but not as strong and fast as the strongest and fastest men. Could this change?

Women have been catching up quickly in athletics events, but women's world records are about 10 per cent slower than men's. It is not very long since it was not socially acceptable for women to exercise and since women were held back by heavy clothing while exercising. Women professional athletes are proving that women can be faster and stronger than would once have been thought possible – although their prize money is still much lower than men's ('Running standing still' by Dea Birkett in the *Guardian*, 23 July 1992).

Men are, on average, physically stronger than women. However, this is not necessarily very important. Very few jobs depend on strength today; it is engines and machine tools that provide the strength, not people. Whether individuals can fly an aeroplane, or operate a crane, or repair machinery depends on their skills and training, not on their sex.

FIND OUT FOR YOURSELF

One of the ways in which we learn about gender is from the mass media. Children learn what is seen as appropriate for their sex, and what is appropriate for the other sex. Watch several children's television programmes and make a note of how the male and female characters are shown (how they are dressed, what they do, how they talk and so on). What do you think children would learn about **gender roles** from these programmes?

QUESTIONS

1. What is the difference between sex and gender?
2. Describe the 'traditional' roles for men and women that Murdock found in most of the societies he considered.
3. Why does a new born baby have a sex but not a gender?
4. What evidence can be used against the 'nature' argument that differences between male and female gender roles are natural and inevitable?
5. In many countries women are not allowed to take an active part in fighting as members of the armed forces. Do you think this is because of biological or social reasons or both? Give reasons for your answer.

ROUND-UP

Gender refers to the different roles a society has for men and women. Gender is based on sex differences but societies can have very different gender roles.

VOCABULARY

Transsexual: a person who acts as if he or she belongs to the other sex, or who has had surgery altering his or her external sexual characteristics to those of the other sex
Anthropologist: someone who studies human cultures
Foetus: an unborn baby, carried in the womb

Feminism

This section considers the history of the movements for women's rights and equality, and at how feminism has influenced sociology.

The improvements in women's lives could not have happened without protest.

What is feminism?

Feminism in sociology is about considering society and social institutions from the point of view of women. Feminist sociology is part of a much wider social movement about equality for women.

Feminism covers a very wide range of ideas, so much so that it is better to talk about 'feminisms' than about there being just one feminism.

A history of feminism

■ Mary Wollstonecraft (1759–97) was one of the first writers to argue that men and women should be equal. 'Equality' was a fashionable idea at the time, connected with the French Revolution, but men tended to assume it meant that men should be equal, not women.

■ From the middle of the nineteenth century, feminists were campaigning for the right to vote and for better education for girls (for example being able to go to university). This was the first wave of feminism. The **Suffragettes** demanded votes for women and were prepared to attract attention in any way they could, even to get sent to prison. All women over 21 finally won the right to vote in 1928.

■ During World War II, many women worked, for example in factories, and this changed what they expected out of life. But after the war, most had to go back to being housewives and mothers, or doing traditional women's jobs.

■ The second wave of feminism began in the late 1950s and became the **Women's Liberation Movement** of the 1960s and 1970s. It was concerned with equal pay, equal education and opportunities, better childcare and free contraception and abortion, and with raising women's awareness of the ways in which men dominated their lives ('consciousness raising').

■ At the beginning of the twenty-first century, some of the demands of second-wave feminism have been met and the situation of women has improved in many ways. For example, Britain has an Equal Pay Act and a **Sex Discrimination Act**. However, feminists feel that these are limited and that there is still some way to go before women are really equal.

Equality

If feminists want equality between men and women, what does this mean?

It doesn't necessarily mean being the same as men. Some feminists see men as being too aggressive – towards each other, women and the environment. They see men as naturally hunters and killers, and responsible for many of the world's problems. They would not want to be the same as men, but would rather men changed and adopted more 'feminine' qualities. Underlying this is, of course, an idea that men and women really are different, and not just in the obvious physical ways.

Equality doesn't have to mean doing the same as men by working full time either. For those influenced by Marxism, working involves being exploited by capitalists. Why should women want to be exploited even more by going out to work, and still have the housework to do as well? A better answer would be for society to recognise properly the value of the unpaid work women do, for example by paying women for it.

Equality may turn out to be complicated, because it will still involve being different – contributing equally but differently to society and having that contribution valued equally.

Patriarchy

A key word used by feminists is **patriarchy**. It refers to the domination of society and of institutions within it (such as the family) by men. All societies that we know of have been patriarchies; even when women have been the rulers (such as Cleopatra in Ancient Egypt, or Queen Elizabeth I in England) men have had higher status and more power than women.

The usefulness of the term is, however, limited because it doesn't allow us to see how the position of women can be different in different societies. Women in Britain today have much more freedom and greater opportunities than, say, a hundred years ago, or than women in other countries such as Afghanistan (where females cannot work or go to school). Describing these very different situations simply as 'patriarchies' is misleading.

The negative stereotype of the feminist

Feminists are often shown in very negative ways in the media. The popular stereotype of the feminist is of the man-hating, dungaree-wearing, cropped-haired lesbian. Like most stereotypes, there is a core of truth in this. Some feminists did decide that spending a lot of effort making themselves look attractive for men was a waste of time, and stopped using makeup and wearing 'feminine' clothes. However, the stereotype owes much more to attempts by men in the media to discredit feminism and its ideas. Feminism was and is a challenge to men's control of society, so it is not surprising that some men react strongly against it. Ridiculing and making fun of feminism is a way of avoiding taking it seriously.

Such has been the strength of this stereotype that many women who agree with many feminist ideas don't see themselves as feminists. In fact, some feminist ideas have become so widely accepted that we don't realise how radical they seemed a generation or two ago (for example the idea that women should be paid the same as men for the same work). Young women who are benefiting from the changes feminism has brought and who see their future in terms of independence and a career often do not realise how much they owe to feminism.

Feminism and sociology

Because sociology is about how people live, feminism has had a strong influence on it, especially since the 1970s. Sociologists, whether male or female themselves, now have to take full account of women in their research and theories. They study areas of social life that, before feminism, were not considered important enough to study, such as housework and motherhood. Feminism has also changed the way sociology is done; feminists tend to prefer methods that produce qualitative data, such as informal interviews, rather than surveys.

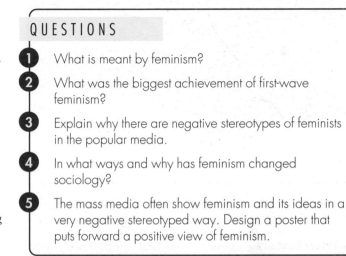 **FIND OUT FOR YOURSELF**

Work in a small group. Each of you should interview an older woman (perhaps your mother or grandmother) about the changes in the roles and status of women that have happened over her lifetime. Ask about housework and looking after children, school, work opportunities and the freedom she had to choose what to do. Read about interviews in the chapter on Research Methods first (pages 34–5). Make notes about what the woman you interview tells you and compare them to those of other members of your group. Present the findings of your group to your class.

QUESTIONS

1. What is meant by feminism?
2. What was the biggest achievement of first-wave feminism?
3. Explain why there are negative stereotypes of feminists in the popular media.
4. In what ways and why has feminism changed sociology?
5. The mass media often show feminism and its ideas in a very negative stereotyped way. Design a poster that puts forward a positive view of feminism.

ROUND-UP

Feminism has a long history, with some remarkable achievements. Its ideas have become so widely accepted that some are no longer even thought of as feminist. However, women are not yet equal and feminists continue to look for ways in which men and women can be different but equal.

VOCABULARY

Suffragettes: women who campaigned for the right to vote (the right to vote is also called suffrage)
Lesbian: a female homosexual, attracted to other women

Gender and life chances

KEY FOCUS

Although men do not live as long as women, in most areas of social life women continue to be at a disadvantage. This section looks at some life chances which are related to sex and gender; for some of them, you will need to look elsewhere in the book for more detail.

Women today: still under some man's thumb?

Life and death

In the section Class and life chances, you read about the chances of survival of those on the *Titanic* when it sank in 1912 (pages 56–7). We concentrated then on class, but gender was also clearly a factor. When a ship sinks, it's 'Women and children first'.

This draws attention to perhaps the most striking difference in life chances between the sexes. Men's lives have always been seen as more expendable. It has almost always been men who have been expected to fight and be willing to die in wars, and men who have been expected to risk their lives in a disaster or emergency.

With sex and gender, life chances are much less clear-cut than they are with class stratification. Although men have greater power and status, they face some disadvantages – unlike the upper class. This is partly a reflection of class, for, of course, it is not usually upper-class men whose lives are expendable, but of those much lower down the scale.

Sexism

Systematic discrimination against people because of their sex is known as **sexism**. In the past sexism has almost always been directed by men against women. Sexist beliefs and practices have often been based on religious ideas that have been used to justify them (for example by quoting a passage from the Bible or another holy book which seems to show that god approves of male superiority).

Life chances

The relationship between gender and some life chances is examined in greater detail elsewhere in this book.

Women and discrimination

Both sexes are protected from discrimination on the grounds of sex by the Sex Discrimination Act 1975. This Act bans discrimination at work (for example in recruitment, training, promotion and redundancy), in education, accommodation, transport, entertainment and the provision of goods and services. However, discrimination is often difficult to prove, and it can be difficult for people to take cases to tribunals. Discrimination has not been eliminated.

Women and work

There are still 'men's jobs' and 'women's jobs'. It is still difficult for women to break into some traditionally male occupations, and difficult for women to reach the top in any occupation – they reach a '**glass ceiling**'. Women earn less than men on average. Women are more likely to work part time, to be in temporary or casual work and not to work continuously through their lives. (See also Gender and work on pages 208–9.)

Women and class mobility

Women have less chance of being upwardly mobile than men do, and more chance of being downwardly mobile. This is partly because women often have time off work to have children, which interrupts careers. (See also Mobility on pages 74–5.)

Women and housework

Even women who work full time are expected to take the main responsibility for childcare and housework. This means that many women work a '**double shift**'. It also limits how much time to themselves women have. Many men help more than they used to with housework and childcare. (See also Husbands and wives on pages 154–5.)

Women and education

Girls do better than boys at GCSE (more girls get five or more passes at grade C or above) and (just) at A level. However, boys do better at degree level. The National Curriculum has reduced differences in subject choice, but there are still significant differences in the subjects boys and girls choose when they are able to (as at A level and higher), and this has an effect on occupations in later life. (See also Gender and education on pages 180–81.)

Women and crime

Women are less likely to be convicted of offences than men, and they probably do commit fewer offences. They are more likely than men to be victims of some crimes such as rape and sexual assaults. (See also Gender and crime on pages 274–5.)

Women and health

Men live shorter lives than women and are more likely at any age to die than women. However, women suffer more ill health, especially chronic diseases. Women are more likely to have been in hospital, including mental hospitals.

Women and welfare

Women are more likely than men to take on the care of elderly, disabled or ill people as informal, unpaid carers.

Teenage girls and sex

Pregnancy while still a teenager changes a girl's life; it is likely to be less of a momentous event for the father, even if he is of the same age. Britain has higher rates of teenage pregnancy than most other countries: 30 pregnancies for every 1000 girls aged 15 to 19 each year compared to 17 in Ireland, seven in France and four in the Netherlands ('Population Trends 95', 1999, in *Sociology Update 2000*). One reason that has been suggested for this is that sex education in British schools is not very good.

Sexual behaviour among teenagers seems to be one area of life about which girls still think and behave as traditionally expected. One researcher, Janet Holland, found that 'Young women spoke of having unprotected sex; of not using condoms, even when they were to hand; of making no protest at rape; of accepting violence; of coming under pressure to have unwanted vaginal intercourse rather than non-penetrative sex' ('Teenage sex in the nineties' by Barry Hugill in the *Observer*, 26 April 1998). In other words, they did what boys wanted, even when they didn't want to.

IT ▶ FIND OUT FOR YOURSELF

Visit the web site of the Equal Opportunities Commission, the official organisation campaigning for **sex equality**, at www.eoc.org.uk.

If you are doing a coursework project, you should look at the 'Checklist for Gender Proofing Research' for advice on avoiding sexism in your research.

QUESTIONS

1 What is meant by life chances?

2 Identify and explain three ways in which women are disadvantaged in employment compared to men.

3 What is meant by a 'double shift' (see Women and housework above)?

4 Identify and explain one reason why Britain has a high rate of teenage pregnancies compared to other countries. Can you think of any other possible reasons?

5 In which of the areas of social life considered in the life chances section above do females seem to be doing best? Why might this be a hopeful sign for greater equality in the future?

ROUND-UP

Sex and gender differences have a major influence on our life chances in all areas of social life. Legislation and changing attitudes have reduced the impact of sexism and discrimination but there are still many inequalities.

VOCABULARY

Expendable: able to be sacrificed, not considered worth saving

Redundancy: losing a job because you are no longer needed

Tribunal: a special court

'Genderquake'? The rise of girls

KEY FOCUS

There is a new confidence and brashness about young women in Britain. Does this mean a different future – a more female one, with women in positions of power and taking their share of highly paid and high status occupations?

Is 'Girl Power' changing relations between the sexes?

Changing aspirations

There has been a huge change in the ways in which girls and young women see their lives. As recently as the mid 1970s, Sue Sharpe's research on girls at school found that most of them saw their futures in terms of marriage and children. They were not aspiring to careers. They expected to work, but not in well-paid occupations, only to supplement their future husbands' incomes. Work would be fitted in around domestic commitments. Their main interests were falling in love,

settling down and having children. They didn't work hard at school because they felt they didn't need qualifications.

By the mid-1990s, it was claimed that there had been a big change in women's aspirations. Work and career had become more important than family commitments. As a result, women were putting off starting a family until they were established in careers. Girls were doing better at school; their attitudes were said to have changed because they needed qualifications for good careers. One survey, based on interviews with 18–34-year-olds and looking at changes like these, claimed they amounted to a '**genderquake**' – a basic shift in gender relations (*No Turning Back – Generations and the Genderquake* by Helen Wilkinson, Demos, 1994).

Changes at work

The following changes at work can be seen as contributing to a 'genderquake':

- women's earnings increasing in relation to men's earnings (but still lower)
- women taking more posts in professions
- women earning a larger share of household income in many households
- most of the new jobs being created being taken by women
- businesses and workplaces changing in ways that seemed to suit women – more team work, more flexibility.

Other changes

Young women have become more prepared to be adventurous in ways that young men have always been – taking risks, taking part in adventure sports and travelling abroad. They also show a much more open interest in sex. '**Ladettes**' – young women who behave like lads, drinking beer, ogling the other sex and generally having fun – provide a new kind of role model. There are now plenty of young and successful women to try to copy.

One of the biggest changes, although difficult to measure, seems to be in confidence. One research project described the 13–19-year-old girls it interviewed as 'The Can-Do Girls'. The girls were optimistic, enthusiastic and confident, setting themselves high standards. They were ambitious and aimed to be financially independent – always able to support themselves.

Syreeta, aged 15

> Men will be coming to women for answers in the workplace. There'll be fewer receptionists and secretaries; women will go straight in at the managerial level – not tea ladies.

> It's a big change for men to be in control and suddenly women have power. They haven't quite grasped the fact … a lot of men do feel un-needed when women don't want men to do everything for them.

A 13-year-old

Sarah, aged 13

> You have to fight to change things bit by bit. Girls our age are aware that nothing happens at the click of a finger, you have to work at it – a slow process. We're the ones who can do it.

Adapted from 'All about new Eve' by Adrienne Katz, *Guardian*, 8 October 1997.

The changes even seem to affect primary school girls. Boys used to dominate school playgrounds with football; now girls simply refuse to let them. The girls' confidence is even encouraging some boys to abandon the football and join them in clapping and dancing games. The influence of the Spice Girls and other role models in popular culture seems to have created a feeling of 'Girl Power' ('When the girls come out to play ... boys fall in' by Martin Wainwright, *Guardian*, 17 April 1998).

How much has really changed?

What is most noticeable to sociologists about talk about the 'genderquake', 'Can-Do Girls' and 'Girl Power' is that they tend to be about the young generation and about what they might achieve in the future – but have not achieved yet.

Values and attitudes do seem to have changed fundamentally. Sexual equality seems to be taken for granted among young people, by boys as well as girls. But it is by no means certain that the confidence and even the success in school exams of girls today will lead to high paid, high powered jobs in years to come. There are still many barriers in the way. Confidence may not survive setbacks as the girls inevitably encounter sexism and pressures to conform to 'traditional' gender roles.

Teenage girls also face problems that undermine their new confidence. The media continue to push the idea of thin as attractive, leading many girls to worry unnecessarily about their weight and appearance. Girls know they are being manipulated by media images, but this doesn't make the pressure to be thin any easier to deal with. Moreover, there are plenty of girls who are not 'Can-Do Girls', who lack self-esteem and belief in their ability to succeed.

The verdict on the 'genderquake' then has to be – wait and see.

 FIND OUT FOR YOURSELF

Sue Sharpe's research asked teenage girls about what they imagined their future would be like. In a small group, design and carry out a questionnaire for teenage girls today asking the same sorts of questions. Do they see their futures more in terms of work, or family? Present your answers to the class.

QUESTIONS

1. What is meant by the 'genderquake'?

2. What were the plans for their futures that girls used to have (as found in Sue Sharpe's research)?

3. How does a 'ladette' behave? Name some women in the media who behave in this way.

4. Identify and explain three ways in which women's situation with regard to work has improved.

5. Explain why the idea of a 'genderquake' is not yet accepted by most sociologists.

ROUND-UP

There have been improvements in women's situation in British society, and big changes in the aspirations and confidence of young women. This has led to predictions of fundamental changes towards sex equality, but it is too early to tell whether changes in values and attitudes will really lead to a different kind of society.

VOCABULARY

Aspiring: having an ambitious plan to reach
Manipulated: to be controlled by
Ogling: looking at with lust

What about men?

KEY FOCUS The impact of feminism has led to considerable interest in the position of women in society and to, for example, women's studies courses at universities. Until very recently there has been much less interest in men and masculinity. This section looks at some recent sociological thinking about men.

Can men be different?

Men and gender

Studying gender doesn't just mean studying women; it has to mean studying men as well. Most older sociology was always about men, because it didn't pay much attention to women. Now, however, there is a growing interest in men and **masculinity**.

Men's disadvantages

- Men do not live as long on average as women.
- Men are more than three times as likely to kill themselves than women.
- Men are pushed by society into being breadwinners, working hard to support a family and suffering stress, and sometimes early death, as a result.

- Boys do not do as well at school as girls.
- Men are not allowed to show their feelings in public (except anger).
- Men are expected to fight and be ready to die in wars or to save others: their lives are less valued than women's.
- Men seem to find it harder to have close, intimate relationships, for example with their children, than women do.
- While it has become easier for women to do jobs traditionally done by men (such as being a car mechanic) it is still hard for men to do work seen as women's work.
- Men are not valued as parents; they get little if any paternity leave when their children are born, and if they separate or divorce they are unlikely to get custody.

There are also a number of ways in which it has been said it is becoming harder to be a man in the traditional way:

- There is more unemployment, and there are fewer secure jobs; it is harder than it used to be for a man to be sure he'll be able to support a family.
- Feminism has drawn attention to the amount of violence and abuse by men against women and children, so that all men are more under suspicion than before.
- Children are being brought up successfully in families where there is no father; perhaps men are not essential.

All this makes it appear that it must be very difficult to be a man. It seems a very long way from the feminist view that men oppress women. Are men to be pitied? There are, of course, advantages to being a man. These include power and status, especially for successful men, at levels women can rarely reach even today.

Masculine roles

Boys are socialised into masculine roles. These tend to emphasise:

- being tough and adventurous
- competing and winning
- being good at sport
- being aggressive
- not being 'weak'.

Although there is more awareness today of gender issues, the above are still strong aspects of masculine roles. Girls today can be encouraged to be tougher and more adventurous than in the past. It is acceptable for a girl to be a 'tomboy', or later to enjoy dangerous sports, for example. But if boys start to behave more like girls, this is often still seen as something that should be discouraged. Girls can be more like boys and still be girls, but it does not seem to work in the same way for boys. While there may be biological differences, society then encourages some aspects of boy's natures and discourages others.

The pressure to conform to what is expected of boys comes not only from parents but, perhaps even more strongly, from peers. The risk of being labelled as effeminate by other boys is a very powerful factor. It is one of the factors behind the lower success of boys at school, because studying hard is not seen as masculine.

Changing gender roles

Just as feminine roles have changed, masculine ones have too. Not all men can be or want to be macho he-men. Men also have to come to terms with the way feminism has changed society.

There are more fashion products and cosmetics for men; it is no longer thought effeminate for men to be interested in their appearance and attractiveness. Men can now show emotions more than before. The footballer Paul Gascoigne – in all other ways, very much a 'lad' – was filmed crying at the end of a match. This doesn't have to mean becoming feminine. Masculinity is different in different cultures, and in some cultures more expression of emotion has always been allowed.

One new role for men that has been much discussed in the media is '**New Man**'. New Man has listened to feminists and is anti-sexist and non-aggressive. He is willing to do his fair share of the housework and childcare as well as working full time. He is more faithful and considerate to his partner than men used to be. Research has suggested, however, that while many couples try to make more equal relationships work, the pressures on men to work long hours make it difficult to keep to this.

On the other hand, in complete contrast to New Man, there is the '**New Lad**', catered for by magazines such as *Loaded*. New Lads leer at 'babes', make sexist remarks about them, drink too much beer and are very much like men supposedly used to be. Feminism has passed them by completely.

If men have a choice of ways of being men, what do women want them to be? Men often complain that the messages they get are confusing. Women seem to want men who are caring and sensitive, yet who can also take charge and be assertive.

> **A** UK man said, 'Women like to hold these positions of authority, but they also want you to carry this box for them. They want to able to shout and holler at you like a man but they also want to use their feminine ways'. Or to put it another way, 'They want equality but they also want chivalry'.
>
> 'I'd be a real man if only she'd let me' by Barry Hugill, *Observer*, 16 August 1998.

FIND OUT FOR YOURSELF

Find and watch the film *Billy Elliott*, released in 2000. This film shows the difficulties faced by a boy from a working-class family who wants to be a ballet dancer. After watching the film, write a short essay about how this film illustrates some of the ideas you have read about here.

QUESTIONS

1 Identify three ways in which men can be said to be disadvantaged compared to women?

2 Identify and explain two ways in which men's lives are becoming harder than in the past.

3 In what ways are boys encouraged to conform to masculine roles?

4 Identify and explain one reason why New Man is a role which men find difficult to live up to.

5 Which sex is the more disadvantaged in Britain today? Explain your answer.

ROUND-UP

Gender studies means studying men and masculinity, as well as women and **femininity**. Boys still tend to be brought up to conform to masculine roles, but these roles are a little more flexible than they used to be.

VOCABULARY

Effeminate: when a man or boy shows characteristics regarded as feminine

Macho: showing typically masculine characteristics, such as physical strength and sexual appetite

Chivalry: courteous behaviour by men towards women

Gender – sociology in practice

Men and their children

Among the Aka 'pygmies' of Central Africa, men look after the babies.
What does a pygmy baby call its Mum? Daddy!

Before World War Two: Changing nappies and feeding baby was not a man's job and it would be a disgrace to be seen pushing a pram. This created a real dilemma for men who wished to have a genuine relationship with their children. Men who liked taking care of babies were considered effeminate. Many men actually rebelled against these restrictions, but paid a price for it. Their relationship with their friends in the pub, or even with their own brothers, would be soured if it were known they did 'women's work'. The alienation of fathers and children was further increased by the father having to be the disciplinarian, inflicting punishment.

'The men we used to be' by Peter Lennon, *Guardian*, 6 March 1996.

Questions

 Look back at the section on Sex and gender (pages 84–5). What does the example of the Aka pygmies suggest about masculine gender roles?

2 What was the traditional role of the father in Britain?

3 In what ways has the role of men towards their children changed in the last 50 years. (You could start by thinking about: Is it still fathers who are responsible for discipline? Is it now more acceptable for men to look after babies?)

Women in the developing world

In many countries in Africa and Asia, women are the main farmers. They till the land, sow seeds and harvest the crops. They also do most of the housework, such as cooking and cleaning. The work they do is often physically harder than men's work. It can require considerable stamina, for example in carrying heavy loads over long distances.

In the developed west, there has been considerable progress towards sex equality. Women in 2000 are able to do almost any jobs, although they are still campaigning to remove some obstacles that are in the way of their path to the highest positions. Women demand and expect equality. In the developing world, however, equality is often lacking. Around the world, girls are far less likely to get an education than boys. Pregnancy and childbirth are still dangerous, and cost many women their lives. The men often insist on traditional cultural practices that limit women's opportunities.

'In many countries if there has to be a choice about who goes to school, parents may often send sons rather than daughters as the rewards from boys' future prospects are deemed greater than for girls – who may marry and settle elsewhere' (*The A–Z of World Development*, by A. Crump, New Internationalist Publications, 1998).

Percentages of primary school age boys and girls not attending school

	Boys (%)	Girls (%)
Sub-Saharan Africa	44	50
Middle East and North Africa	13	22
Asia and Pacific	15	22

The A–Z of World Development by A. Crump, New Internationalist Publications, 1998.

Questions

1 What are the differences between the main concerns of feminists in the developing world (poorer countries) and feminists in the developed world (richer countries)?

2 Why are there more girls missing school than boys? (Note that in most countries parents have to pay school fees.)

3 How does missing school reduce the opportunities women have?

Ladies nights are sexist?

LADIES' nights at nightclubs are against the law if women pay less than men. The Equal Opportunities Commission has sent nightclubs a letter explaining that such nights break the Sex Discrimination Act and should stop.

Many nightclubs offer women discounts on admission prices and on drinks. The EOC has ruled that it is discrimination if men have to pay more.

Typical of those affected were the Gass Club in Leicester ('Ladies free B4 11 pm Gents £10') and Legends nightclub in Essex ('Admission £5, ladies half price'). Both advertisements have now been dropped.

The EOC said it had received over 100 complaints from men angry about having to pay more than women.

Tony O'Neill manager of Golds nightclub in Leicester said, 'These are a load of middle-aged stuffed shirts who have probably never been in a nightclub in their lives.' He said he was still planning women-only evenings once a month, with a male stripper going 'the full monty'.

Adapted from 'Club ladies' nights ruled sexist' by Kamal Ahmed, *Guardian*, 2 April 1998.

Questions

1 It is often assumed that the Equal Opportunities Commission acts for women, helping make them equal with men. What does this article suggest the EOC's role is?

2 Do you agree that charging men and women different prices is wrong? Explain your answer.

3 Think of other areas of life where discrimination of this kind is happening (the discrimination can be against men or against women). What could be done to prevent such discrimination?

Gender – important terms

double shift	when a woman who works full time is still expected to do housework and childcare
femininity	the gender role of a woman; traditionally being soft and gentle
feminism	the campaign for equality for women
gender	social and cultural differences between the two sexes
gender roles	what society expects of a gender
genderquake	the idea that there has recently been a big shift in gender relationships, with women achieving more
glass ceiling	women in organisations often seem to get promoted to a point quite high up but not be able to get any further
ladette	a new role for women, at least in the media, behaving as badly as men
masculinity	the gender role of a man; traditionally being strong and assertive
New Lad	a new role for men, but involving behaving in the same old ways
New Man	a new role for men, involving treating women as equals
patriarchy	any society or organisation controlled by men
sex	biological differences between men and women
sexism	the belief that men are superior to women, and behaviour arising from this
sex discrimination	when someone is disadvantaged or treated differently because of their sex
sex equality	when the two sexes are equal
Suffragettes	early feminists who campaigned mainly for the right to vote
Women's Liberation Movement	feminists in the 1960s and 1970s, sometimes shortened to 'women's lib'

Gender – exam-style questions

Source A

Although many more women are working outside the home, and some are reaching the top in their chosen careers, they still face problems. Even when they work full time, women are still often also expected to be housewives and mothers. The traditional gender role for women is still very strong.

At work, women may experience problems such as sex discrimination, or even sexual harassment.

Foundation tier

1. What is meant by the term sex discrimination? [2 marks]

2. Describe the traditional gender role for women. [3 marks]

3. Using source A and sociological knowledge, identify two problems that women still face when trying to have a career. [4 marks]

4. Using sociological knowledge, give two reasons why women are now taking some of the highest paid jobs. [5 marks]

5. Do you agree that men, as well as women, face problems because of their sex? Give two sociological reasons to explain your views. [6 marks]

Higher tier

1. Describe the traditional gender role for women. [2 marks]

2. Using source A and sociological knowledge, identify two problems that women still face when trying to have a career. [2 marks]

3. Using sociological knowledge, give three reasons why women are now taking some of the highest paid jobs. [6 marks]

4. Do you agree that men, as well as women, face problems because of their sex? Give sociological reasons for your views. You may choose to refer to several different areas of social life. [10 marks]

Gender – further research

Two American feminist sites:

- www.feminist.com
- www.estronet.com.

Estronet also has a section for teenagers: www.missclick.chickclick.

The Equal Opportunities Commission: www.eoc.org.uk.

5 Ethnicity

KEY TERMS

ethnicity
race
racism
racial discrimination
racial prejudice
institutional racism
minority ethnic group
stereotype
nationality
nationalism

You might at first be tempted to think that this section is not about you. It is. Everyone has an ethnic identity, everyone belongs to one or more ethnic groups. Ethnicity is not just about ethnic groups that are small compared to the majority, or those who arrived as immigrants in the recent past, or those whose skin colour is different.

The term race is still as much used as ethnicity. This chapter will show you why sociologists prefer the term ethnicity. The word race does still have its uses though, because many people still behave as if there were different races. Racism, racial prejudice and racial discrimination are the appropriate terms for these thoughts and actions.

Britain is a nation containing many different ethnic groups. Along with class and gender, ethnicity is one of the ways in which groups are stratified in society.

There are still many problems facing minority ethnic groups. You can read about these throughout the book, because ethnicity is a theme that runs right through your course.

IN THIS CHAPTER YOU WILL LEARN ABOUT:

- how to talk and write about this topic without giving offence
- the idea of 'races', and how this has been discredited
- the history of black and other minority groups in Britain
- the different ethnic groups in Britain today
- nations, nation-states and nationalism

CHAPTER CONTENTS

Talking about ethnicity and race

KEY FOCUS Sociologists now use the term ethnicity much more than race. This section considers both these terms and a number of others, giving advice on how best to think and write about this controversial area.

Is Tiger Woods black? He describes himself as 'Cablinasian' – Caucasian, black, Indian and Asian. He says he is a quarter Thai, a quarter Chinese, a quarter black, one-eighth white, one-eighth American Indian (*Guardian*, 24 April 1997).

Race and ethnicity

Most sociologists prefer not to use the term race. This is because 'races' do not exist. When the word is used, it is often put in inverted commas, as has been done here, to indicate that it is a doubtful term.

The word often used instead of race in sociology is **ethnicity**. This refers not to supposed biological, natural differences, as race does, but to cultural differences. An **ethnic group** will be culturally different from other ethnic groups. These cultural differences may include:

- religion
- language
- customs and traditions
- style of dress
- identification with a country or region
- identification with the group and its history.

Ethnic groups in Britain today

Using this idea of ethnicity, it is possible to identify different ethnic groups in Britain today. These are often thought of as white, **black** (**Afro-Caribbean**) and Asian. This is in fact far too simple, as you will see; each of these categories contains many ethnic groups, and there are others who do not fit easily into any of the three groups. This is considered in the section, Ethnic groups in Britain today (see pages 104–5).

Before looking at the situation in Britain, we need to spend some more time making clearer the terms that are often used.

Terminology

Each of the terms below has a symbol attached to it to guide you as to which terms you should use and which to avoid:

- **◉** – acceptable
- **Ⓝ** – do not use
- **Ⓤ** – use with caution.

◉ Minority ethnic group

An **ethnic minority** is an ethnic group that does not make up the majority of the population in a society. Afro-Caribbean and Asian groups are **minority ethnic groups** in Britain today while whites are the majority ethnic group.

Note: the word ethnic applies to all distinct cultural groups, including the majority. British fashion styles or jewellery are as ethnic as anything from Africa or Asia! Do not use the word ethnics to refer to members of minority ethnic groups.

Ⓤ Black

This term was once considered an insult. It became acceptable when it was adopted by black Americans campaigning for their rights in the 1960s and 1970s. They used slogans such as 'Black is beautiful'.

The term is misleading though because it implies all black people have something in common. An African and a West Indian in Britain today, for example, have little in common. It is also misleading in that no one is actually black – we are all shades of brown, and many supposedly 'black' people have quite light coloured skin.

Sometimes, even more confusingly, 'black' is used to mean 'non-white', thus including Asians as well.

Black (and white) are very strong words that can make people's individuality seem less important than their skin colour. If you do use this term, it is better to refer to 'black people' not just 'blacks'. People are people before they are black or white.

(N) Coloured

This term is no longer used much. It used to mean anyone who was not white (so apparently white isn't a colour, but black is). It therefore ignored the many ethnic differences among black and Asian people.

(N) Negro

This term goes back to the old racial classifications and today sounds old-fashioned and is insulting.

(N) Nigger

A term of racist abuse – but one taken over and hurled back at the racists in a statement of ethnic pride by some black Americans, as in the rap group NWA – Niggers with Attitude. Used by a person who is not black, it is racist and very offensive.

(N) Half-caste

What has caste got to do with it? The term refers to people whose parents are from different racial or ethnic groups; so mixed race or mixed background is better. Mixed race is also a very vague term – there are so many possible mixtures!

(U) Immigrant

This refers to people moving from one country to another. It is not appropriate for black and Asian people in Britain today who were born here. Their parents or grandparents may have been immigrants, but they are not. Oddly, when white Europeans went to live in the Americas, Asia, Africa and Australia, they were referred to not as immigrants (invaders might have been a better term) but as settlers.

(U) Afro-Caribbean

This is used for black British people whose families came to Britain from the West Indies, which are islands in the Caribbean Sea. Their ancestors would have been taken from Africa to the West Indies as slaves, so they were originally African. The term ignores the differences between the islands of the West Indies (for example Jamaica, Trinidad and Barbados have different histories and cultures). It also leaves out the fact that Britain is now their home.

(U) Asian

This is used to refer to people in Britain who migrated here from the Indian sub-continent: India, Pakistan, Bangladesh and also Sri Lanka. It tends not to mean people from other Asian countries, such as China and Japan, although logically it ought to. As with Afro-Caribbean, the term ignores the many differences between people from different countries and regions and the fact that most 'Asian' people in Britain are British.

As you can see, many of the terms are misleading. It is impossible not to simplify the situation, but important to use terms that help our understanding and which are not insulting. If you are in doubt over the latter, what counts is not whether the speaker or writer thinks the term is insulting, but whether the people being talked or written about do. Terms like black (for all non-whites) and coloured can be acceptable when they are used to discuss **racism**, because that is when the many differences between non-white ethnic groups become less important. They share being the victims of racism.

QUESTIONS

1. What is an ethnic group?

2. Write one sentence to explain the best use of the following terms: (a) immigrant, (b) black.

3. Explain the difference between race and ethnicity.

4. When Tiger Woods called himself 'Cablinasian', which parts of his background did this draw attention to and which did it play down? (The point is not that there could be a better word, but that any chosen word will have particular implications.)

5. Look at the list of cultural differences under the heading Race and ethnicity. Use this list to describe the culture of your own ethnic group (you will have to decide what this is).

ROUND-UP

Ethnicity, which refers to what makes a group culturally distinct, is a term sociologists now use more often than race. A number of other terms are used in discussing this area; some should be avoided, others used with caution only for their specific meanings.

VOCABULARY

Doubtful term: this means that the term is misleading or refers to something which is false

Ethnic pride: being proud of your ethnic group

The myth of 'race'

This chapter is about ethnicity, not race. However, it is important to spend some time looking at the idea of 'race', because it is so misleading and has been so influential.

Why do so many black people make outstanding sports players? The answers are complex, and as much to do with social environment and individual determination and skill as to do with supposed 'racial' differences.

The idea of race

It was once believed – and still is believed, by some people – that humans were divided up into biologically distinct 'races'. Each **race**, it was thought, had its own unique physical appearance and its own distinctive abilities and ways of behaving.

One of the most common ways of dividing people up into races was into:

- Caucasian – white
- Negro – black African
- Mongolian – Asian.

In the nineteenth century some scientists went to quite extreme lengths to prove that there were races. These scientists were white Europeans and Americans, and not surprisingly they felt that white people were superior. Various schemes of classifying 'races' 'proved' that white people were more civilised and more intelligent than anyone else. Taken to their logical extreme, these ideas were the justification for Hitler's attempts to exterminate 'lesser peoples', and for many other racist atrocities.

The opinion of most scientists today is that there are no races. The attempt to categorise people into races was based on a few physical features – especially, the most noticeable feature of all, skin colour. In fact, when we look at other features, a very different picture emerges. Blood groups, for example, have nothing to do with skin colour. There are no clear-cut 'races'.

Although the older and cruder kinds of racism are no longer considered acceptable, a variety of beliefs based on ideas about racial difference survive. One of the most enduring is about sporting ability.

Only 20 years ago, people 'knew' that black footballers could never be successful in Britain. They couldn't stand the cold, and in any case their natural talent was only useful in flashy wing play; they didn't have the grit and determination to play in other positions. These ideas now sound ridiculous.

White men can't jump?

Black people make up around 10 per cent of the population of the USA, but they dominate professional basketball, making up about 70 per cent of the top players. More widely, it is noticeable how many top athletes are black. Does this mean that, because of biological differences, black people are better at sport?

The reasons why American black people are successful in basketball are at least as much to do with environment and opportunity. Sport is part of society, so we need to look for sociological explanations as well as biological ones. It has been suggested that while white teenagers practise basketball in their suburban driveways, black teenagers play on overcrowded inner city courts where competition for space and possession improves their skills much more. Sports are also a way out of poverty when other routes, such as careers in business or as doctors or lawyers, may be blocked or made difficult by discrimination.

The film *White Men Can't Jump* in fact disproves its own title. The white character played by Woody Harrelson is able to impress Wesley Snipes and the other street-tough black players, proving that those who are determined can cross racial barriers (*The Race Gallery* by Marek Kohn, Vintage, 1996).

Black men can't swim?

There is a very widespread belief that black people can't swim as well as white people. As with basketball, this may be partly to do with the social environment; black people may be less likely to live near swimming pools, or to feel these are places they can go to without facing abuse.

On the other hand, biology does seem to play a part. Many black people do have denser bones than average, which makes swimming harder. This makes little difference to swimming as leisure, but it may matter when it comes to top international competitions. Determination and intensive coaching, though, probably make a bigger difference (Kohn, 1996).

A place for biology?

This last example, about swimming, suggests that there may be a small place for biology in explaining differences between human groups (which we should not refer to as races). These differences will be strongest where a group has not mixed with other groups; in scientific terms, where the gene pool has not been made bigger by having new genes added. In today's world, this applies to very few peoples.

Finally, to go back to the basketball example, it is true that some of the tallest people in the world are Africans (remembering that the USA's black population is descended from Africans brought over as slaves). But Africa also has the world's shortest people (the so-called 'pygmies' of the Central African rain forests). The old **stereotype** of the Negro included thick lips. Africa does indeed have some peoples with thick lips – and also some with thin lips. Africa is made up of a vast range of different peoples; to label them all as 'Negro' or 'black' is absurd.

This point can be made more generally about all ways of classifying 'races'. They involve picking on relatively insignificant differences and ignoring the much greater similarities – what we all have in common that make us members of the human race.

But you can't ignore race

Although races do not exist, many people continue to behave as if they do. They hold prejudiced opinions and may discriminate against people they believe belong to other 'races'. Racism is still a very strong force in the world today, even if the ideas behind it are known to be wrong. The idea of race therefore has very serious consequences for our lives.

FIND OUT FOR YOURSELF

Investigate 'racial' differences in sport. Why are minority ethnic groups more successful in some sports than in others? Sort out sports into those in which minority groups seem to do well and those in which they don't. Try to find sociological reasons for this. You should also try to distinguish different minorities; for example, why are there few British Asian footballers compared to black ones?

QUESTIONS

1. What were the three main races according to some early race theories?

2. Which physical feature did race theories assume was the most important? Why do you think they did this?

3. Here are two possible explanations for the success of black sports players.
   (a) All blacks have natural abilities which whites don't have.
   (b) Sport offers a route to success when other routes are blocked by racism.
   Which of these explanations is racist? Which is sociological?

4. There are few black and Asian MPs in Britain. What sociological reasons can you suggest for this?

5. Why does race continue to be important?

ROUND-UP

Race is an outdated and discredited concept. We now know that differences between groups are insignificant compared to what all members of our species share. However, racist ideas survive and continue to have a big impact on people's lives.

VOCABULARY

Species: the biological term for a group of animals who are able to interbreed – all people belong to the species Homo sapiens

Categorise: to sort into categories

Exterminate: wipe out

Ethnic groups in Britain today

KEY FOCUS This section looks at statistics on the bigger ethnic groups in Britain today, and explores the wide variety of groups that now exist.

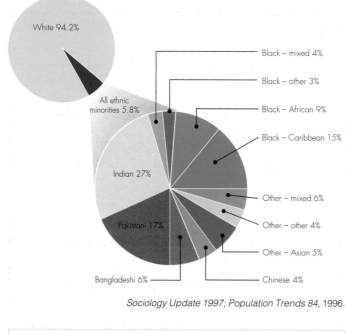

Sociology Update 1997; Population Trends 84, 1996.

According to the 1991 Census, the British population is made up of these ethnic groups.

Census information

This provides some basic information. We can see that non-whites make up about 5 per cent of the population. The largest minority ethnic group is the Indian population, followed by the Pakistani population. The Census provides other information not shown here; for example, 41 per cent of Indian people were born in Britain, 34 per cent in India and 17.5 per cent in East Africa.

However, in other ways, the information here is less helpful to sociologists. This is a result of the way that the information was asked for and the choices of answer people were given. The captions on the two pie charts tell you what answers people could give.

The 'white' category is huge. It is made up of many different ethnic groups, but the Census data do not tell us about this. The 'white' category is not broken down into European, American, Australian or Irish (to name only some of the largest possible groups), nor does it consider Welsh or Scottish

people. Other research has suggested that if 'Irish' were included on the Census as a minority ethnic group, it would be the largest.

For non-whites, some of the categories are about skin colour ('black') while the Asian ones are about country of origin. Many people would have felt unhappy about saying they belonged to any of these categories.

On the other hand, a Census question that gave anything like a full range of possible answers would be huge!

Breaking down 'black' and 'Asian'

The following are some of the more important differences within these categories.

■ The area of origin of black (Afro-Caribbean) people (or their parents or grandparents) will probably be either the West Indies (also known as the Caribbean) or Africa. The West Indies is made up of many islands, each with its own culture and history. The best known are probably Jamaica, Trinidad, Barbados and the Leeward and Windward Islands. Africa is a vast continent; former British colonies (from which African people in Britain are likely to be from) are in all different regions of Africa.

■ The Indian subcontinent, where most of the people in Britain referred to as Asians are from, is made up of three countries: India, Pakistan and Bangladesh. Each country has many ethnic groups with different languages and religions. For example, from the state of Gujerat in India, there are both Muslims and Hindus, and members of both of these religions may speak Gujerati or Kitchi.

Ethnic diversity

Britain is much more ethnically diverse than the Census figures show. Other minority ethnic groups not already mentioned on these pages include those from parts of Asia other than the Indian sub-continent (for example Thailand, Malaysia and Japan), from the Middle East, from Europe (such as Greek Cypriots, and recently different groups fleeing the wars in the former Yugoslavia) and traveller gypsies. There are also Jewish people with distinctive religious beliefs (and a history of being persecuted).

Not everyone in an ethnic group follows to the same extent the cultural practices of their group. For example, some immigrants from the West Indies have lost any distinctive cultural traits from their original home. Members of minorities may, however, feel their culture and traditions are under threat because they are a minority, and react by following their culture even more strongly.

Cultures also change all the time. Often today, the situation is quite new. For example, there have never been children of Bangladeshi Muslim families growing up in London before. These children will have a lot in common with other London children of all backgrounds but also something in common with Bangladeshi children in Bangladesh. In creating a blend of Bangladeshi Muslim and British culture, they are creating a new ethnic identity for themselves.

Who are we?

SEBASTIAN Naidoo's father is a South African born Indian and his mother is white and British. He is a 26-year-old student at the City University in London. When presented with racial classifications in the past he has ticked either 'Indian' or 'other', but once he scrawled 'human' over the whole lot. 'I wanted to make fun of their questions and to show them how arbitrary their racial categories were,' he said.

He said he would not describe himself as 'Asian British' because he felt this term mixed up race, ethnicity, culture and **nationality**.

CHRIS'S mother is Spanish and her father is from Grenada in the Caribbean. She is a 23-year-old legal clerk. She has usually ticked 'black other' on forms. She does not feel 'black Caribbean' because her father did not bring her up, and she does not like the term 'mixed race' because there is no mixed race community or clear identity. She said she wouldn't want to describe herself as Black British because so much of British society rejects Black people.

Adapted from 'Row over plan for Census race labels' by Gary Yonge, *Guardian*, 9 December 1996.

Where minorities live

Most of Britain's minority ethnic groups are concentrated in Greater London and in the larger cities and conurbations, such as Birmingham, Greater Manchester, Liverpool and in West Yorkshire. There are relatively few members of ethnic minorities in country areas, and in South West England, Wales and Scotland (apart from the big cities) (Tony Champion *et al.*, *The Population of Britain in the 1990s*, Oxford University Press, 1996).

This is a result partly of where jobs were available, and where people could find members of the same group to live near (for example so that they could worship with followers of the same religion). It also reflects a need to keep together in self-defence against racism.

C ▷ FIND OUT FOR YOURSELF

Britain is not the only **nation** to have many different ethnic groups. Find out about ethnic groups in the USA by researching in an encyclopaedia or other source. (If you have access to a computer with Microsoft Encarta, look under USA, Population, Ethnic Composition.) Present your findings to your class.

QUESTIONS

1. What is the largest minority ethnic group in Britain?

2. Look at the pie charts.
   (a) What percentage of Britain's population is non-white?
   (b) What percentage of Britain's minorities described themselves as belonging to one of the four 'Black' categories?

3. Identify and explain two reasons why minority ethnic groups in Britain are concentrated in cities.

4. Give two reasons why the categories used in the Census could be improved upon.

5. Explain what you think Sebastian Naidoo means when he describes the racial categories on the Census and similar forms as 'arbitrary'.

ROUND-UP

Non-white minority ethnic groups make up around 6 per cent of the British population. The main source of information, the Census returns, uses categories that are far from satisfactory. The 'black' and 'Asian' groups need to be thought of as made up of many smaller groups of people from different areas, with different religions, languages and cultural traditions.

VOCABULARY

Arbitrary: based on prejudice or whim
Conurbation: an urban area where two or more cities or towns merge into each other
Traits: characteristic features

Migration into Britain

The peoples of the British Isles are the result of many different peoples coming to settle here. We are a nation of immigrants. This section looks at the history of immigration up to the present day, and the many different peoples and cultures who have contributed to what we know today as Britain.

Walter Tull, the grandson of a slave in Barbados, was one of Britain's first black football stars, playing in midfield and on the wing for Tottenham Hotspur and Northampton Town. He was also the first player to suffer racist abuse. When World War I broke out he became the first black army officer. He was killed in the second battle of the Somme in 1918.

Before 1945

When the Romans invaded Britain in 43 CE, the population was made up of many small 'tribes' of 'Ancient Britons'. Many 'Britons' were in fact quite recent arrivals from the mainland of Europe. With the Romans came probably Britain's first black inhabitants. Rome recruited its army from all over its Empire, which included North Africa, so black Roman soldiers would, for example, have been stationed on Hadrian's Wall, and would undoubtedly have married and had children here.

After the Romans withdrew in the fifth century, there was settlement by peoples from what is now Germany (the Angles, from whom the word 'England' comes, the Saxons and the Jutes) and from Scandinavia (the Vikings and the Danes). In 1066, the successful invasion by William the Conqueror brought Normans to England, and made French the language of the 'English' upper class.

England had a substantial black population by the time of Queen Elizabeth I, who in 1596 attempted to expel all 'Blackmoores', on the grounds that they caused economic problems. By the eighteenth century there were around 20 000 black people in England. Many were Africans brought here as slaves; it was at one time fashionable to have a black servant or slave, usually a young boy. There were also Indian sailors.

From the eighteenth century onwards, Britain had a large empire overseas. British people went to Britain's colonies to work in government, as soldiers and as merchants. The British economy depended on slavery overseas. To justify slavery, racist ideas that black people were inferior developed. The colonies were exploited by Britain and, not surprisingly, some people in the colonies saw moving to Britain as a way to improve their situation. Britain, however, placed restrictions on entry. Britain's black and Asian populations were concentrated in London and the main ports, such as Liverpool, Cardiff, Glasgow and Bristol.

During the nineteenth century, a lot of Irish people emigrated to Britain (and to the USA), fleeing poverty and famine. Although white, they faced racism that survives in aspects of popular culture such as the stereotype of the unintelligent Irishman (used in Irish jokes).

In the twentieth century, immigrants to Britain included Poles and others from eastern Europe, and Jews fleeing persecution (although, even just before World War II began, some Jews were being turned away).

Black in Britain before 1945: some examples

Olaudah Equiano	writer and campaigner who helped to bring about the abolition of the slave trade in Britain and the colonies in 1807
Ignatius Sancho	born on a slave ship, became a best selling writer and composer in the eighteenth century
Sir Dadabhai Naoji	elected Liberal MP for Finsbury in 1892 – Britain's first Asian MP
Mary Seacole	a black nurse whose work was copied by Florence Nightingale
Samuel Coleridge Taylor	born in Sierra Leone, a composer and music professor in London in the late nineteenth century
Arthur Wharton	Britain's first black professional footballer, signed for Preston North End as a goalkeeper in 1896

Taken together, these lives give us a glimpse of an aspect of British history that is often forgotten.

After 1945

The recent period of immigration from the West Indies began in 1948. Britain, recovering from the war, had a shortage of workers and West Indians – citizens of the British Empire – were invited to come and work, as bus and underground train drivers and in other manual work. The period of immigration from India and the Indian subcontinent (Pakistan and later Bangladesh) began a bit later.

From the early 1960s, British governments placed restrictions on immigration of black people. The right to settle in Britain was taken away from many people in Britain's colonies and ex-colonies, even from those who held British passports. Acts of Parliament were worded so that the result was to continue to allow in people thought of as 'white' while keeping out those seen as 'black'. Laws seemed to give the message that it was acceptable to treat people differently because of their skin colour. This probably encouraged prejudice and discrimination.

At the same time as the racist immigration laws, there was a series of laws to establish and protect rights for black and Asian people, for example making **racial discrimination** illegal.

Since the 1970s, the numbers of people immigrating to Britain have been very small and slightly lower than the numbers of people emigrating. Britain still accepts close relatives of those settled here. However, **refugees** and **asylum seekers** now find it very difficult to get permission to be allowed to stay.

FIND OUT FOR YOURSELF

This activity will be particularly useful if you study art. Using books of eighteenth- and nineteenth-century paintings, find black and Asian people in scenes of British or European life and in family groups (where there may be a black servant). Note the name of the painting, the artist and the year. One to get you started: look for Henrietta of Lorraine by van Dyck.

QUESTIONS

1. Who were the first black people in Britain?

2. Draw a time-line for the last 2000 years showing approximately the main periods of arrival of different groups of immigrants in Britain.

3. Name one group of immigrants who arrived in Britain in the twentieth century. What was the main reason for their moving to Britain?

4. Name another group which came to Britain for another reason, and give the reason.

5. What two types of laws have affected immigrants to Britain in recent years? In what way can these types of laws be seen as contradictory?

ROUND-UP

Britain has been settled by many groups of immigrants over thousands of years. There are no 'original' British or English people. The history of black people in Britain is often overlooked. The recent period of immigration began in 1948 and ended by the mid-1970s.

VOCABULARY

Refugees: people trying to escape from some danger or problem in their own country
Asylum: safety, protection

Prejudice and discrimination

KEY FOCUS This section looks at the disadvantages ethnic groups can suffer, and at the attitudes and practices that cause them.

> We cannot be a beacon to the world unless the talents of all the people shine through. Not one black high court judge; not one black chief constable or permanent secretary; not one black army officer above the rank of colonel. Not one Asian either. Not a record of pride for the British establishment.

Tony Blair, Prime Minister, speech to the Labour Party Conference, 1997

Prejudice and discrimination make it hard for members of ethnic minorities to get top jobs.

Prejudice

The word prejudice literally means judging first – that is, without any knowledge of what you are judging. **Racial prejudice** means jumping to conclusions about somebody, based on assumptions about race. Prejudices are irrational: they are not based on reason or fact, and indeed people tend to hang on to them even after it has been proved to them that they are wrong.

Prejudice can be negative or positive. Negative prejudices tend to be about how different people are from us – they are directed against other ethnic groups. Positive prejudices are about us, and how we are better than others. Most people accept that white people in Britain can be prejudiced against minority ethnic groups, but minorities can also be prejudiced against the majority ethnic group and against other minorities.

Stereotypes

A set of prejudices can combine to form a stereotype. There have been stereotypes held about most ethnic groups, based on ignorance or on exaggeration. For example, there has been a widespread stereotype in Britain of Irish people being not very intelligent. It is easy to produce evidence against stereotypes – for example the enormous contribution of Irish people to literature and the arts – but stereotypes tend to be rigidly held.

Racism

Racism is the belief that one racial group is naturally superior or inferior to another. It is not a recent phenomenon; throughout history many peoples have regarded others as inferior. Racism has been used to justify slavery and genocide. Genocide is the mass killing of a people, such as Hitler's attempted extermination of Jews and gypsies. More recent examples have included 'ethnic cleansing' in the former Yugoslavia in the 1990s and the mass killing of Tutsis by Hutus in Rwanda in Central Africa.

Scapegoating

Prejudice and stereotyping are often a way of pinning the blame on a minority for troubles that are nothing to do with them. Hitler, for example, blamed Germany's economic problems on Jewish people, without any justification. The Jews were being used as **scapegoats**.

Racial discrimination

Racial discrimination happens when people in positions of authority act upon their prejudices. It is when people from different groups are treated differently. Sometimes prejudice can have little effect, but if an employer, manager, judge, police officer or someone else in a position of authority is prejudiced, he or she can act in a discriminatory way. For example, an employer can decide not to employ black or Asian people, or a judge might impose a harsher sentence because of someone's ethnicity. These would be examples of negative discrimination.

Discrimination can also be positive, when some special advantage is given to a minority, usually to make up for past negative discrimination. For example, in the USA, some colleges have reserved a certain number of places for students from minority ethnic groups, even if they are less qualified than others. This is called affirmative action.

Discrimination is against the law in Britain today, as a result of the Race Relations Act of 1976. This does not mean it does not happen. Open discrimination – for example signs in pub windows saying, 'No blacks' – have disappeared because they are illegal now. However, a black person may be turned down for a job because of discrimination. If the individual protests, he or she may, for example, be told that he or she did not do as well in the interview as another candidate. In this kind of situation it is very difficult to prove that there has been discrimination.

Overt and covert racism

Overt racism is an openly racist act or statement by an individual.

Covert (hidden) racism is part of the way an organisation or group of people deals with minorities. It is less obvious and harder to tackle.

Institutional racism

There are two types of racism: the racism of individuals and that practised by organisations or institutions (such as the health service, schools, the police, the armed forces and the media). The latter is called **institutional racism**. It is a controversial idea because it is sometimes mistakenly taken to mean that everyone in an organisation is racist. This is not the case. In fact, institutional racism is possible even if no one intends to be racist. Institutional racism can be the outcome of an organisation following its normal rules and procedures without taking into account minority ethnic groups.

Definition of institutional racism used by the Macpherson Inquiry's report into the police investigation of the murder of black teenager Stephen Lawrence:

'The collective failure of an organisation to provide an appropriate and professional service to people because of their colour, culture or ethnic origin. It can be seen or detected in processes, attitudes and behaviour which amounts to discrimination through unwitting prejudice, ignorance, thoughtlessness and racist stereotyping which disadvantages minority ethnic people.'

Quoted in 'How racist are our institutions?' by Amelia Gentleman and Jamie Wilson, Guardian 24 February 1999.

Racism and discrimination in practice

Some of the possible outcomes of racism and discrimination are:

- verbal abuse and name-calling
- racial attacks and harassment (see Minority ethnic groups and crime on pages 278–9)
- minority ethnic groups having higher rates of unemployment, and being in jobs that do not match their qualifications
- minority ethnic group families being more likely to live in housing which lacks amenities such as central heating
- minority ethnic group children finishing their education

with fewer and lower qualifications than the majority (see Ethnic groups and education on pages 182–3).

These disadvantages do not affect all minority groups equally. For example, Indian people are more likely than Pakistani and Bangladeshi people to get good educational qualifications and then middle-class occupations.

⏵ FIND OUT FOR YOURSELF

The **Commission for Racial Equality** (CRE) was set up to work towards the elimination of racial discrimination, to promote equal opportunities and to ensure that the law was enforced. Find out about the CRE's work by visiting its web site at www.cre.gov.uk. If you have been a victim of racism or racial harassment or discrimination, the area of the site called 'Your Rights' will give you advice.

QUESTIONS

1. What is meant by scapegoating?
2. What is the difference between prejudice and discrimination?
3. What positive prejudices do white British people tend to have about themselves? List as many as you can think of.
4. What is meant by institutional racism?
5. Why do laws against racial discrimination fail to solve the problem completely?

ROUND-UP

Minority ethnic groups can be the victims of prejudice and discrimination, stereotyping and scapegoating. Racism can be both by individuals and by institutions, and in the case of institutions it is not necessary for any individual to be intentionally racist for the outcome to be racist.

VOCABULARY

Irrational: not based on reason or fact
Unwitting: without being conscious of it
Genocide: the deliberate killing of an ethnic group or nationality

Nations and nationalism

KEY FOCUS

The earlier sections have touched on but not explored an area related to race and ethnicity, but rather different – the question of nationality. This section explores the ideas of nation and nationalism and looks at what the future of Britain might be.

English no longer always means white.

The nations of the British Isles

Which of the following, if any, are nations and which are **nation-states**?

- Britain
- England
- Wales
- Scotland
- Northern Ireland
- the United Kingdom (UK)
- Ireland
- the Republic of Ireland.

Answer: the United Kingdom and the Republic of Ireland are nation-states. They have their own governments and issue passports to their citizens. The British Isles is a geographical term referring to the two large islands, Britain and Ireland, that in politics form these nation-states, together with many much smaller islands.

England, Wales and Scotland are often thought of as nations. For example, they have international teams in some (but not all) sports. Wales and Scotland have assemblies that take political decisions; England does not. For all three, the most important decision-making body is the British government.

The full name of the United Kingdom is the United Kingdom of Great Britain and Northern Ireland. Great Britain, or Britain, is therefore made up of England, Scotland and Wales, but not Northern Ireland.

Northern Ireland is a part of the United Kingdom, but not often thought of as a nation, although it has international teams in some sports. Some Northern Irish people consider themselves British, others consider themselves Irish. The Republic of Ireland is a nation-state, while the island of Ireland is divided into two nation-states.

In the end there are few fixed answers to questions like these. The situation is very complex. Britain is not unique in this; many other nation-states contain several ethnic groups and have areas with separate languages and cultures which can be thought of as nations. (Britain is though unique in being represented by four teams in some international sports.)

What are nations?

Nations are communities of people who feel they have a strong identity through having a shared culture (language, religion and so on), sense of history and a homeland. They can be thought of as a stronger version of ethnic groups.

A nation-state is what we think of as a country – a geographical area, with clear borders and a single government. Nation-states are not always the same as nations. Some Scots and Welsh people, for example, would like Scotland and Wales to be nation-states, free of rule by the British government in London, issuing their own passports and so on. Scotland and Wales can be described as nations but not nation-states.

Nationalism

Nationalism is the strong emotional identification with a nation, giving a sense of belonging. It is often in evidence at sporting events, but can also be the cause of wars. The sense of belonging is strengthened by:

- national flags
- national anthems
- uniforms
- styles of dress
- monuments
- special occasions, etc.

These are national symbols. Nationalism creates a sense of belonging among people who do not know each other (we can only ever meet a very few of the people who belong to our nation). Nations have been described as 'imagined communities'.

Federal Europe

British passports used to say, 'The United Kingdom of Great Britain and Her Colonies'. Today, above 'United Kingdom', appear the words, 'European Community'. This is an indication of changing times. At the same time as power has devolved (moved down) to smaller political units like the Scottish and Welsh assemblies, it has also moved up to much bigger ones, such as the European Union. Nation-states are being squeezed between the two. Governments like the British government have lost some of their powers in both directions.

Britain today – and the future of England?

Britain today is a nation-state that is multi-ethnic. It contains many different groups, religions and languages. Most members of minority ethnic groups are British citizens and passport holders. This is partly the result of the British Empire, now long gone, when the countries these families came from belonged to Britain.

The growth of Scottish and Welsh nationalism is one sign in recent years that British national identity is not as strong as it used to be. For English people, England and Britain tended to mean the same thing in the past, but we are becoming more aware of the differences there have always been within the nation-state of Britain. For example, English is not the only language; other languages that have been spoken in the British Isles for so long they can be said to be native include Gaelic and Welsh. Unlike Wales and Scotland, England has very few national symbols of its own, because most of England's symbols are British ones too.

After the creation of the Welsh and Scottish assemblies, there is a question mark over Britain's future. Should England have its own assembly too? If Scotland and Wales break away, what would England as a nation-state be like? English national identity is being discussed and argued about, having gone almost unnoticed at times in the past.

There are racist political parties who would like English nationalism to be exclusively white and find it hard to accept that black and Asian people can be British or English. Because of history there are deep racist attitudes in white English culture, and some black and Asian people are even reluctant to describe themselves as British because they associate the word with the British Empire.

England's **ethnic diversity** – shown, for example, in the national football team, and in popular music – makes a white

nationalist culture which dominates other cultures less likely. A multi-cultural England, celebrating its rich diversity, is a possibility and a hope for the future.

⚑ FIND OUT FOR YOURSELF

You can find out about the nation-states of the world by visiting the web site of the United Nations at www.un.org. Follow the link 'About the United Nations' to find out about UN members. When this book was written, the UN had 189 members. You will find some quizzes and games by going to UN CyberSchoolBus. Test your knowledge of the flags of the world.

QUESTIONS

1 Which nation-state do you live in?

2 What is the difference between a nation and a nation-state?

3 Make a list of occasions when you feel strongly that you belong to a particular nationality.

4 Make a list of some of the symbols of your nation and of one other nation of your choice.

5 Write a short essay explaining why 'Britain and England are not the same'.

ROUND-UP

Ethnic and racial identities are closely connected to national identities. The United Kingdom is a nation-state containing several nations, and many ethnic groups. It has changed as a result of the end of the British Empire and of economic decline, and the creation of assemblies in Wales and Scotland opens up the possibility of further changes.

VOCABULARY

Diversity: when there are lots of differences and variations

Devolved (from the noun 'devolution'): moving powers usually held by central government to regional assemblies

Ethnicity – sociology in practice

France United?

IN 1998, the French national football team won the World Cup, and in 2000 the European Championship.

Like Britain, France has minority ethnic groups who have experienced prejudice and discrimination; as with Britain, this is partly the result of having had colonies around the world in the past. There is also a racist political party, the National Front, which has had much greater success than any racist party in Britain. In 1998, before the World Cup, the National Front won 15 per cent of the votes in regional elections; it was calling for the repatriation (sending back to country of origin) of thousands of immigrants.

The team that won the World Cup was multi-racial. Among the top players were:

- Zinedine Zidane – son of an Algerian night watchman in a poor area of Marseilles
- Lilian Thuram – a Black Frenchman from Guadeloupe in the Caribbean
- Marcel Desailly and Thierry Henry – both with origins in the French Antilles
- Youri Djorkaeff – descendant of Armenian refugees.

Winning the World Cup seemed to create a new sense of French nationality – one which definitely included the minorities. The popularity of the National Front plunged.

'We've seen people of all colours, of all origins, singing the *Marseillaise* (the French national song). This French team has done more for integration than decades of government policy.' Michéle Tribalat, sociologist

'OK, everyone's happy and singing now. But how many blacks and Arabs are there in big business and politics? Sport and music, that's where we always end up.' Malik, aged 18

Adapted from 'France united by a team of all colours' by Jon Henley, *Guardian*, 11 July 1998.

Questions

1 In what ways does the success of the French football team seem to have reduced racism?

2 Some newspapers noted that some of France's black and Arab stars were reluctant to sing the national anthem. Midfielder Christian Karemeu, from French New Caledonia, publicly refused. Why might the players feel like this?

3 Malik says that minority ethnic groups in France are successful in sport and music, but not much else. Is this true of Britain as well? Give examples of people from minority groups. Why do you think these are areas people from minorities can succeed in, and what stops them succeeding elsewhere?

Roots of the future

'... 27 per cent of London Underground's staff and over two thirds of independently-owned local shops belong to ethnic minorities. About 23 per cent of Britain's doctors, 15 per cent of pharmacists, 13 per cent of physiotherapists, 10 per cent of nurses, 16 per cent of university professors, 13 per cent of travel agents, 10 per cent of textile employees, 9 per cent of hotel employees, 10 per cent of domestic employees, 13 per cent of service industry managers and 24 per cent of restaurant employees were born overseas. The influence ethnic majority musicians have had on British popular music is out of all proportion to their numbers in the population ...

Yet this small, hard-working and highly productive population is still sometimes regarded as a "problem", and the positive role it plays is either ignored or taken for granted. It is still claimed that "they take our jobs", or that "they are a drain on the economy", or "a threat to British culture". Not all immigrants inspire such concerns, however, just the ones who appear "different", because of their race or colour, or the way they dress, or the fact that they speak other languages as well as English.'

'Roots of the future', Commission for Racial Equality, 1996.

Questions

1. Look at the section Migration into Britain (pages 106–7). What contributions have immigrants made to British life?

2. 'Britain is and has always been a nation of immigrants.' What is the evidence for this view?

3. Look back to the account of ethnicity in the section Talking about ethnicity and race on pages 100–1. In what ways are the racist myths about immigrants related to ethnicity?

The mixed generation

APPARENTLY, something like 40 per cent of young Black men in Britain are either married to or live with a White partner ... For many years, celebrities like Frank Bruno, Lenny Henry and Paul Ince have been the public face of this development and have, accordingly, borne the brunt of criticisms which have been thrown out.

In popular street talk, one of the criticisms is that the reason they have White partners is because these men are successful and want a 'trophy' or because they lack self-esteem etc., etc.

But the figures reveal a much more fundamental shift in attitudes toward mixed relationships ...The figure is not as high for Black women, but never-theless one in five young Black women is in a mixed relationship ... Further-more, a one in five pre-school Black child is from a mixed race background ... In fifty years time [blackness will be] an increasingly mixed race experience.

Adapted from 'The mixed generation' by Onyekachi Wambu, *The Voice*, 7 May 1996.

Questions

1. Which change in relationships between black and white people does this article focus on?

2. Why do you think this article (and many other writings on race and ethnicity) describe people with only one black parent as black?

3. One of the implications of this article is that more and more people will have some relatives who belong to different 'races' and ethnic groups. What are the possible consequences of more mixed relationships for racist beliefs and practices?

Ethnicity – important terms

Afro-Caribbean	a black British person with family origins in the Caribbean (West Indies)
asylum seeker	someone who enters a country and asks for protection from persecution in the country they have come from
black	used to refer to people from dark-skinned 'races'
Commission for Racial Equality	an official organisation that watches over issues of racial equality
ethnic group	a group sharing a culture and sense of identity
ethnic minority	an ethnic group that is smaller than and usually in an inferior position to a larger ethnic group
ethnic diversity	when there are many ethnic groups existing alongside each other
ethnicity	the classification of people into ethnic groups
institutional racism	when the way an organisation works has the effect, possibly unintentional, of discriminating against an ethnic group
minority ethnic group	see ethnic minority
nation	a group of people sharing a strong sense of ethnicity
nation-state	an independent country, with its own government
nationality	being a citizen of a nation-state
nationalism	strong feeling of belonging to a nation
'race'	outdated way of classifying people into groups
racism	the belief that some 'races' are superior to others, and behaviour arising from this
racial discrimination	when someone is disadvantaged or treated differently because of their 'race'
racial equality	when all 'races' are treated equally
racial prejudice	when an individual believes that some 'races' are superior to others
refugee	someone trying to escape from persecution or misfortune
scapegoat	when a person or group is blamed for problems that are not their fault
stereotype	a misleading set of ideas about what a type of person is like

Ethnicity – exam-style questions

Source A

Ethnic minorities in Britain, 1998 (thousands)

White (ethnic majority)	53 066
Black – Caribbean	509
Black – African	351
Black – other (non-mixed)	298
Indian	948
Pakistani	557
Bangladeshi	222
Chinese	171
Other – Asian non-mixed	202
Other – other	395
Total all groups	56 731

Labour Market Trends, Office for National Statistics, September 1999.

A total of 3.7 million people belong to minority ethnic groups.

Nearly half of all Britain's ethnic minority populations live in Greater London. Other areas with high concentrations are Greater Manchester, West Yorkshire and the West Midlands.

Foundation tier

1 Using the table in source A, identify the largest ethnic minority in Britain in 1998. [2 marks]

2 What is the meaning of the term ethnic minority? Use two examples to illustrate your answer. [3 marks]

3 Using sociological knowledge, give two ways in which an ethnic minority's culture may be different from the culture of the majority of the population. [4 marks]

4 Using sociological knowledge, give two reasons why so many members of minority ethnic groups live in city areas. [5 marks]

5 Ethnic minorities often face racism. Explain what this means, using examples from two different areas of social life. [6 marks]

Higher tier

1 What is the meaning of the term ethnic minority? Use two examples to illustrate your answer. [2 marks]

2 Using sociological knowledge, give three ways in which an ethnic minority's culture may be different from the culture of the majority of the population. [3 marks]

3 Using sociological knowledge, give two reasons why so many members of minority ethnic groups live in city areas. [5 marks]

4 Ethnic minorities often face racism. Explain what this means, using examples from several different areas of social life. [10 marks]

Ethnicity – further research

Two sites covering news and current issues from an Afro-Caribbean perspective:

- www.blink.org.uk
- www.blacknet.co.uk.

The Commission for Racial Equality: www.cre.gov.uk.

The Runnymede Trust: www.runnymedetrust.org.

The story of West Indian immigrants to Britain after World War II is told at: www.bbc.co.uk/education/archive/windrush.

6 Age

KEY TERMS

adolescence
age
ageism
childhood
cohort
generation
life course
old age
social construction
youth culture and youth
   subcultures

Age is one of the four aspects of stratification that are considered in this book. It has a chapter to itself here, but you will also find references to age in many of the other chapters. Like class, ethnicity and gender, age is a theme that runs through all of your sociology course.

Age is an inescapable fact of social life. You are probably looking forward to future birthdays, when you will acquire new rights and opportunities. This shows how important age is; when you are a teenager, exactly how old you are is very important. Later on, age becomes important in other ways. Older people would sometimes like to forget how old they are!

Age is also one of the areas of life where it is very difficult to sort out what is natural and what is social. Is a 15-year-old a child? The law in Britain today says 'yes'. In a different kind of society, being 15 might be far less important than having passed a test or ritual to become an adult. And biologically, what is important is whether the person has passed through puberty and is able to have children.

IN THIS CHAPTER YOU WILL LEARN ABOUT:

- different ways of thinking about age
- children and childhood
- growing up – the transition to adulthood
- youth culture and youth subcultures
- older people.

CHAPTER CONTENTS

Age and generation

Another aspect of stratification in society is by age. Different age groups are treated differently. This section introduces the topic of age before we go on to look in some detail at childhood, adolescence and old age.

Our lives pass through several stages.

What is age?

In western societies such as our own, individuals know how old they are. We measure age from the day a person is born up to the present time. This way of measuring age is called **chronological age**.

Chronological age decides many aspects of our lives today. Many things depend upon how old you are. Whether you can get married, leave home, leave school or learn to drive, for example, depends on your chronological age.

Chronological age is particularly important for children. Children's lives are very closely regulated by society; that is, there are many things that are decided for children. This can only be done because children are defined by society as not old enough to decide for themselves.

There has probably been an occasion when you were frustrated by your chronological age. You may have felt old enough to do something – but society said you weren't old enough. Many societies in the past did not have an idea of chronological age. The passing of time is more likely to be

measured by an important event, such as the death of a leader or a natural event such as an earthquake. Some cultures do not celebrate birthdays, and are more interested in **biological age** than chronological age.

Biological age

Just as we get older chronologically, we get older biologically. We inevitably change over time.

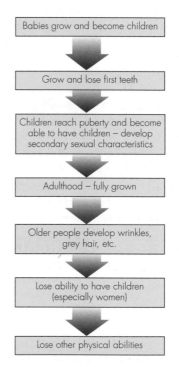

Biological age is not necessarily the same as chronological age. For example, some people reach puberty before others; some people develop signs of ageing, such as grey hair, before others of the same age.

The life course

This term refers to an individual's life and to all the changes he or she passes through. Some of these changes are biological, others are social, but it is very difficult to separate them in this way. **Childhood**, for example, is both biological (a child is physically immature) and social (a child is someone under 16,

because our society has decided childhood ends at 16). We all pass through different stages of life, from childhood to adulthood into middle age and eventually old age.
(You can find out more about the **life course** in the section The life course and families on pages 136–7.)

'The Seven Ages of Man'

Here is a famous speech from one of Shakespeare's plays. In it, the character describes seven ages through which men live.

'And one man in his time plays many parts,
His acts being seven ages. As, first the infant,
Mewling and puking in the nurse's arms.
And then the whining schoolboy, with his satchel
And shining morning face, creeping like a snail
Unwillingly to school. And then the lover,
Sighing like a furnace, with a woeful ballad
Made to his mistress' eyebrow. Then the soldier,
Full of strange oaths, and bearded like the pard,
Jealous in honour, sudden and quick in quarrel,
Seeking the bubble reputation
Even in the cannon's mouth. And then the justice,
In fair round belly with good capon lined,
With eyes severe and beard of formal cut,
Full of wise saws and modern instances;
... The sixth age shifts
Into the lean and slipper'd pantaloon,
With spectacles on nose and pouch on side;
His youthful hose, well saved, a world too wide
For his shrunk shank; and his big manly voice,
Turning again toward childish treble, pipes
and whistles in his sound. Last scene of all,
That ends this strange eventful history,
Is second childishness and mere oblivion,
Sans teeth, sans eyes, sans taste, sans every thing.'

As You Like it by William Shakespeare.

1 List the seven ages of man according to Shakespeare.
2 Write your own list of the ages of woman today. You can have more or less than seven if you think this is right.
3 Shakespeare's final age is 'second childhood'. Is this an accurate description of old age? Give reasons for your answer.

Our lives in history

Another aspect of age is that we live at a particular time in history. This makes a big difference to the experience of life. A woman living in the nineteenth century, for example, would have a very different experience of life from a woman living in the late twentieth century.

The people born at roughly the same time and living through the same historical period are called a **cohort**. For example, the cohort of men who lived through World War II are now elderly.

Cohort is the idea that we use when we talk about 'my **generation**' or 'the 90s generation'.

QUESTIONS

1 What is meant by a cohort?
2 What is meant by the life course?
3 Explain the difference between chronological age and biological age.
4 Your cohort has lived through particular events, and this will have affected your experience of life. What are the most important events your cohort has lived through?

ROUND-UP

There are two different ways of thinking about age: chronological age, starting from birth; and biological age, based on changes in our bodies. We also live at a particular period of history, and belong to a cohort with others of the same age. Our lives pass through several stages. The remaining sections of this chapter look at three of these: childhood, adolescence and old age.

VOCABULARY

Chronological: about time
Puberty: the start of growing up, when the sex glands start to work
Secondary sexual characteristics: characteristics that distinguish males from females but are not related directly to reproduction, for example beards in men

Children and childhood

What is meant by children and childhood is not as obvious as it may seem because they vary between cultures and over time. This section looks at what childhood means in Britain today, and at how it can be different elsewhere.

Forced to become a consumer: growing up too soon?

Who is a child?

This is not as silly a question as it may sound, because there is no clear answer. One answer is a biological one – that children are humans who are not yet physically mature. Yet some people still at primary school, who we would think of as children, may have reached puberty (become capable of reproduction) and have acquired secondary sexual characteristics such as body hair. If we still treat them as children, then being a child is social as well as biological.

In Britain today, people become adults at the age of 18 – the 'coming of age' – but in fact many adult rights and responsibilities have already been acquired. For example, you can leave school and work full time at 16, and drive (if you have passed the test) at 17. Despite the design of eighteenth birthday cards, most people already have keys to their homes before then!

Not all rights and responsibilities come at a given age. Some can arrive very early; for example, the teenage girl who becomes a mother. Others may be very late; for example, a student may not be financially independent until well into his or her 20s because he or she needs support from parents.

Childhood in the past

What it means to be a child, and what is expected of children, has changed enormously over time. Childhood is different in different cultures and at different times in history. So we can say that childhood is socially constructed.

Some historians have argued that, in the past, the experience that children had of life was so different that childhood was very short. In the Middle Ages, it is said, children were

Some rights and responsibilities: 5–21 years

Age	Rights and responsibilities
5 years	Compulsory schooling begins You have to pay child's fare on trains and buses You can drink alcohol in private
10 years	You can be convicted of a criminal offence if it can be proved that you knew what you were doing was wrong
12 years	You can buy a pet
13 years	You can have a part-time job, subject to restrictions
14 years	You can go into a pub but not drink alcohol
16 years	You can leave school You can marry with your parents' consent A girl can consent to heterosexual intercourse You can hold a licence to drive a moped You can have beer or cider with a restaurant meal, and can buy liqueur chocolates
17 years	You can hold a licence to drive most vehicles You can buy or hire a gun or ammunition
18 years	You can vote You can buy alcohol You can serve on a jury You can get married without your parents' consent You can be tattooed
21 years	You can become an MP You can adopt a child

'miniature adults' from about the age of seven. They dressed like adults, were expected to work and look after themselves, and they joined in games and outdoor activities with adults. There were no schools, and no ages at which rights and responsibilities were acquired. They might even marry very young, and be treated as criminals if they committed crimes.

The big change to this very different idea of childhood was probably the gradually growing importance of education and schools, first for the upper class but eventually for everyone. Children became people who were still at school, who had not yet learned what they needed for adult life.

Childhood in other cultures

Another way of looking at the **social construction** of childhood is to look at other cultures. 'Traditional' societies do not see childhood as ending at a particular age, but rather as ending with a ceremony or ritual, a **rite of passage**. The child leaves his or her family home for a period to undergo a series of rites of initiation into adult life. Before this, the individual is a child; afterwards, an adult with, depending on the society, the right to carry weapons, to marry and to take part in decision-making. For boys the rites often involve circumcision, during which they must not flinch. For girls there is sometimes the mutilation of the genitals (euphemistically known as female circumcision). For both sexes, there may be scarring, special clothing, fasting and feasting.

In comparison, the end of childhood in Britain is a long, drawn-out process of gradually acquiring rights and responsibilities.

Concerns about children today

Compared to a generation ago, parents tend to be more protective of their children. For example, the freedom children have to roam around their home area has been restricted because of fears about traffic and 'stranger danger'. One in three children is now driven to school. Parents also control the time their children spend on activities more. In many ways, children have less freedom.

On the other hand, children are much more exposed to some aspects of the adult world than they used to be. Television images, including ones before the 'watershed', mean that children know about violence, death, sex and tragedy at a younger age than they used to. They are also exposed to advertising from an early age, and to the pressures to buy (or get their parents to buy) the latest toys and games. In these ways childhood is no longer a period of innocence.

FIND OUT FOR YOURSELF

Interview an older person (perhaps one of your parents or grandparents) about what childhood was like when they were young. Ask a range of questions about family, play and games, work, helping at home and so on.

QUESTIONS

1. Identify and explain three ways in which childhood in the Middle Ages was different from childhood today.

2. What is the importance of schools in explaining what we mean by a child today?

3. Identify two concerns that parents have about their children that are stronger today than in the past.

4. Explain what is meant by saying that childhood is socially constructed.

5. 'Childhood is a time of innocence.' Write an essay discussing whether this is still true or not.

ROUND-UP

Childhood is partly based on biology, in that children are physically immature, but it is also social because who is thought of as a child, what is expected of children and when childhood ends are different in different cultures. Children in Britain today acquire rights and responsibilities gradually; in some ways they are more protected from the adult world than in the past yet in other ways more exposed to it.

VOCABULARY

Circumcision: the cutting off of the foreskin (outer skin of the penis)
Initiation: a ceremony admitting new members to an organisation
Euphemistically: a way of saying something which disguises the reality of what has happened; for example, saying 'passed away' instead of 'died'

Adolescence

Bridging the gap between childhood and adulthood is adolescence, a period which is long and drawn out in modern western societies. Youth cultures and subcultures can be seen as helping young people adapt to adult life, but they can also be rebellious and anti-authority.

The 1950s: a new generation of teenage rebels against the establishment.

Transition to adulthood

As you have seen in the section on Children and childhood, many traditional societies initiate individuals into adulthood by a rite or ceremony. Before this, the individual is a child, afterwards an adult. In western societies today the situation is rather different. There is a drawn-out period in which people are neither children nor adults, and in which their situation has some of the aspects of both. They can be described as adolescents, or **teenagers**, or youth.

Adolescence is a period of transition; individuals have to learn to move out of the comfort of their parents' home and into the world of work. At home they are valued as individuals, but at work they will have to compete and be successful. Functionalist sociologists saw membership of a strong peer group in adolescence as a way of easing the

transition; by belonging to such a group adolescents had support in growing more independent.

Teenagers

Teenagers are a recent phenomenon. Of course, there have always been people whose chronological age was in their teens, but teenagers as a distinct, identifiable group go back to the 1950s. As economies recovered from World War II, there was growing affluence. Young people were able to work and earn good wages, and because they were often living at home they could spend some of their money on their leisure activities.

This led to the rapid growth of new industries aimed at this new market. The biggest and most successful of all was pop music, beginning with rock and roll in the mid-1950s. With the music went new styles and fashions, marketed through new boutiques specialising in clothes for teenagers, films and other media products. The newly affluent teenagers bought records and record players, socialised in coffee and milk bars and went to dance halls and later discotheques. They adopted new slang words; in the 1960s, 'groovy', 'fab' and 'far out' entered the language as terms of enthusiastic approval.

Many people assumed that all teenagers shared a similar way of life and set of attitudes. This was called **youth culture**. One aspect of it seemed to be a rebellious spirit among teenagers. Much of the imagery in the music and styles was about being a rebel against the stifling conformity of adult society. Sometimes the rebellion took forms that many adults strongly disapproved of, such as drug taking. To some, age seemed to have become the most important division in society. Being young seemed more significant than class or sex identity. 'Hope I die before I get old,' sang The Who in 'My Generation'; 'Don't trust anyone over 30' was a hippy saying. The generation gap seemed wider than ever before.

The idea of youth culture, however, misses out the many different groups within a generation – of class, sex and ethnicity. Many teenagers did not share in the growing affluence, and did not have the time or money to participate in youth culture.

Sometimes the music and styles gelled into what are called **youth subcultures**, such as the mods and rockers of the early 1960s, and later the punks. These are examined in more detail in the section Youth subcultures (see pages 124–5). These subcultures were predominantly male, and usually working class. The majority of teenagers, however, then as now, did not belong to youth subcultures, although they may have enjoyed the music. The majority conformed most of the time to the norms and roles laid down by society.

The end of affluence

The affluence did not last. In the 1970s, the economy went into decline. Young people had less money to spend because of unemployment and lower wages. More of them stayed in education or training, which became more necessary in order to get jobs, but this made them less independent than those who worked.

As a result of these changes, youth subcultures based on pleasure and leisure – sociologists have called them 'spectacular youth subcultures' – became less noticeable; the last to make a huge impact were the punks of the late 1970s. Instead, in sociological discussions of youth the focus moved to unemployment and how young people were pushed to the fringes of society.

Today young people have access to a wide range of styles and tastes in music, fashion and so on. They can combine these in new and innovative ways, sometimes drawing on ideas from the old 'spectacular' youth subcultures. This involves using the old subcultures in ways that were never intended. Teenage rebel imagery has been taken over by advertising companies. A song by The Clash, a punk band with strongly anti-establishment views in its lyrics, can be used to sell jeans ('Should I stay or should I go now'). Teenage rebellion seemed once to be about changing society; now we can look back in nostalgia.

QUESTIONS

1. Why did teenagers become a distinct age group in the 1950s?

2. Which industries benefited most from the arrival of teenagers as consumers in the 1950s and 1960s? Explain your answer.

3. In what way can youth culture be seen as making the transition to adulthood smoother?

4. Identify and explain one reason why 'spectacular' youth subcultures ended in the 1970s.

5. Why are peer groups so important for teenagers? Explain your answer.

ROUND-UP

Adolescence is a difficult period, in which it helps individuals to be supported by distinctive youth cultures or subcultures. The spectacular youth subcultures of the 1950s to 1970s have been replaced by a wide range of styles.

VOCABULARY

Affluence: being well off
Transition: changing from one stage to another
Innovative: introducing something original and new

Youth subcultures

This section looks briefly at a range of youth subcultures and their relationship to broader youth cultures, considering class, ethnicity, and sex and gender differences between the different subcultures. As you read this section, remember that youth subcultures involved only a small proportion of adolescents at the time.

Youth culture goes mainstream – rave in the 1990s.

everything that was going wrong with British society. British society and its values were indeed going through a period of change, and many older people opposed the changes. The youth subcultures were, however, more a symptom than a cause. They were treated as scapegoats.

Condemnation in the media and by politicians put pressure on the police and courts to deal firmly with offenders.

> Teddy boys are … all of unsound mind in the sense they are all suffering from a form of psychosis. Apart from the birch or the rope, depending on the gravity of their crimes, what they need is rehabilitation in a psychopathic institution …

Family Doctor, *Evening Standard*, 12 May 1954.

> 'Rock 'n Roll, often known now as rock, roll and riot, is sexy music. It can make the blood race. It has something of the African tomtom and voodoo dance.' The *Daily Mail* went on to call for compulsory military service for teenagers, '… to knock the rock 'n roll out of these babies, and to knock a bit of sense into them'.

Daily Mail, 4 and 5 September 1956.

The adult reaction

There was widespread media concern and condemnation of these subcultures. The media contributed to the creation of 'moral panics', in which the youths were seen as symbols of

Some spectacular youth subcultures

Period	Name	Style/dress	Music	Other features
1950s	Teddy Boys	Based on upper-class Edwardian – long jackets, narrow trousers, fancy waistcoats Quiffed hair	Rock and roll	Working class
1960s	Mods	Smart dress – 'dedicated followers of fashion' – parkas, suede shoes	The Who	Working class Amphetamines (speed) Mopeds with as many wing mirrors as possible
1960s	Rockers	Black leather jackets and long hair	Rock and roll	Working class Motorbikes
1960s–70s	Skinheads	Braces, rolled-up jeans, heavy 'bovver' boots Very short hair	Ska and bluebeat	Working class Aggressively territorial Linked to racist and fascist politics
Late 1970s	Punks	Bin liners Safety pins as jewellery Spiked hair	Sex Pistols, Clash, Damned	Unemployed working class

HINTS AND TIPS

Find out more about the mass media's reaction to young people in the section on Effects of the media (see pages 300–1).

Girls and youth subcultures

The spectacular youth subcultures were mainly male. The girls were there as girlfriends of the subculture boys. Punk was a partial exception; girls are more noticeable in punk images and were among the successful singers and bands.

Girls have, however, always fully participated in youth culture. There are usually strong friendship groups among teenage girls, and part of their shared interest is likely to be in, for example, chart music and the latest dances. Girls have been less noticeable because their leisure time is, or at least was, less likely to be spent in public. One sociologist, Angela McRobbie, wrote about girls sharing a **'bedroom culture'**, exchanging news and gossip about favourite stars and so on in each other's bedrooms.

Middle-class subcultures

In the 1960s and 1970s many middle-class adolescents were part of a very broad and loose subculture or movement. It was based on a pleasure-seeking (bohemian) lifestyle (which for some included the drugs LSD and cannabis), rock music and an interest in some social and political issues (such as the anti-Vietnam war movement). Those who took this most seriously were described as hippies. As with the working-class subcultures, there was a distinctive style. Clothing was loose, colourful and often 'ethnic', with beads and jewellery. Both girls and boys grew their hair long. Having long hair became a sign of protest and rebellion.

Dropping out of work for a few years was not a possibility for the working class, but middle-class hippies were able to. The hippie lifestyle became more difficult with economic recession in the 1970s.

Minority ethnic groups and subcultures

Both the working-class subcultures and the hippies were mainly white. It is possible to distinguish some black subcultures. Rude boys in the 1960s were black youths who rejected regular work and made a living 'hustling' – gambling, drugs and petty stealing.

Later came the religious subculture of Rastafarianism, which appealed to older people as well. The soundtrack to this subculture was provided by Bob Marley and the Wailers and other reggae stars; it preached escape from white 'Babylon' to the supposed homeland of all black people, in Ethiopia.

Rave culture

In the late 1980s and early 1990s what has been called rave culture attracted widespread media attention. It was a revival, in a way, of the earlier spectacular subcultures. Acid house music developed into rave, with all-night dances, often at 'secret' locations in the countryside. Unlike earlier subcultures, some of the media coverage was positive, because rave culture involved both boys and girls, and all ethnic groups, and was non-violent. Another difference was that rave quickly became mainstream youth culture; the music and style were not confined to a small minority. The media turned against rave culture when it became associated with the taking of the drug ecstasy.

FIND OUT FOR YOURSELF

Choose one of the subcultures mentioned in this section. Try to find out more about it, using reference books and the Internet. Try to find and record some of the music favoured by the subculture. Present your findings to the class.

QUESTIONS

1. Why were girls less involved in spectacular subcultures?
2. Identify two subcultures among British black people.
3. Identify and explain a way in which rave culture was different from earlier subcultures.
4. What did Angela McRobbie mean by bedroom culture? Is this still a way in which teenage girls socialise?
5. Why was there such a strong reaction from many older people towards youth subcultures?

ROUND-UP

Teddy boys, mods and rockers, skinheads and punks were mainly working-class male subcultures. However, middle-class, female and ethnic minority adolescents also took part in subcultures and broader youth cultures. Each subculture is distinguished by dress and style, favoured music and sometimes by favoured drug.

VOCABULARY

Partial: not complete
The birch: corporal punishment (beating with a stick)
Bohemian: living an unconventional lifestyle

Older people

Britain's population is getting older. In the future, a higher proportion of the population will be old. The old face negative stereotypes of having 'one foot in the grave' and being 'past it'. This section looks at some of the realities of being old.

OLD CODGER.

HOW LONG BEFORE PEOPLE CALL YOU NAMES?

Fighting back against ageism.

How many old people?

There are many more older people than there used to be. This is because life expectancy has increased dramatically; it has more than doubled in the last 150 years:

- 1901 (people aged 65 and over): 1.7 million, less than 5 per cent of population
- 1997 (people over **retirement** age – 65 for men, 60 for women): 12 million, 18.2 per cent of population ('Sociology Update 1998' from *Regional Trends*, National Statistics).

In the future old people will make up an even higher percentage of the population.

Because people live longer, old age covers a wide span of ages. Sociologists and others often find it helpful to divide older people into different age groups:

- 65 to 74: the young elderly
- 75 to 84: the old elderly
- 85 and over: very elderly.

This helps us recognise the differences between, for example, those just retired and those in advanced old age.

By 1997 there were thought to be about 8000 people aged 100 and over. A million people are aged 85 and over. More of the old are women than men, because women have a higher life expectancy.

Retirement

The idea of retirement only really began with the introduction of old age pensions in 1908. Until then people worked as long as they could, and then relied on relatives (or the workhouse, if they had none) to support them. Work ended because it became impossible, not because a set age had been reached.

Retirement can be a very difficult period for people. They need to plan ahead and decide how to use their time if they are not to feel a sense of helplessness and of not knowing what to do with their time. Retirement tends to be harder for men, because they will probably have been working continuously for many years, and because work gives men status. Women will probably have had some periods in their adult lives when they have not been in paid employment (for example when they had children), and their status depends less on their job.

Both men and women often take up new hobbies and activities when they retire, or spend more time on those they did not have time for until then. It can be a time to do things they always wanted to but had no time for, such as taking a degree with the Open University, cruising around the world, raising money for a charity. They may spend a lot of time helping their children bring up their children, especially now that many mothers work. Many retired people make an important contribution to family and community life, making old age a time of active challenges and fulfilment.

Stereotypes and ageism

Despite the contributions older people make to society, there are common stereotypes of older people as 'fogies', 'old codgers', 'wrinklies' and so on. Many people see old age as a time of loneliness, declining health and waiting to die. While these may have some truth (as stereotypes often do) they are gross generalisations and do not apply to the majority. Most old people reject the stereotypes.

Ageism is the treatment of older people as different and inferior because of their age, not because of any qualities an individual has. Older people can be discriminated against through ageism, just as others can through sexism and racism. Compulsory retirement is one form of ageism; another would be a job advertisement which sets limits on which ages can apply. Sometimes older people are also refused some medical treatments on the grounds of their age.

Ageism is a significant feature of British society. Other cultures have different attitudes. In traditional cultures, those who survive to old age are treated with great respect, and their opinions sought because of the wisdom they will have acquired. Being an elder is a fulfilling final development in life, not a loss of roles and of purpose. Older people in many cultures are highly valued as family members; the modern western idea of old people's homes causes horror among people from some parts of the world, because it is unthinkable that old people should not be with their families.

There are, however, also some positive representations of older people. One of the first US astronauts, John Glenn, went back to space in old age. Politicians such as ex-Prime Minister Edward Heath and showbiz personalities like Jimmy Savile show what can be achieved. Even some employers see old as good.

> B&Q prefer older workers. Peter Cook, aged 67, began to work as a DIY adviser after he had retired from a lifetime of work in construction. 'I was retired and frankly I was bored … I knew I could do the job. And they wanted someone with experience who would be trusted by the customers. I hope I have more to offer than a spotty teenager who has just started a career.'
>
> 'Older workers mean happier customers' by Nick Hopkins, *Guardian*, 17 November 1998.

Older people make up a growing proportion of the total population. Many have money to spend from investments and occupational pensions. They are therefore becoming a sought-after market; more companies are making and selling products aimed at old people. The media too have to cater for an audience containing many older people, and politicians know they need older people's votes to win elections. Because of this shift in the makeup of the population, it is possible that ageism will decline in the future. Old people will be too important to be patronised or insulted.

Security in old age

In the past, one reason people had children was to make sure there was someone to look after them when they got old. This has become less important because more people have pensions and money saved or invested for retirement. Many older people still rely on their children, and especially on daughters. This affects women more than men, because women are less likely to have an occupational pension and so receive only the basic state pension.

IT ▶ **FIND OUT FOR YOURSELF**

The leading charitable organisation working on behalf of older people and on ageing issues is Age Concern. Visit its web site at www.ace.org.uk. You will find the section of the site called 'Ageing Issues' particularly helpful.

QUESTIONS

1. About how many people in Britain are aged 85 and over (there are about 58 million people altogether)?

2. Identify and explain one reason why retirement tends to have a greater impact on men than women.

3. What is meant by ageism?

4. Why might an employer such as the home improvements chain B&Q prefer older workers?

5. In what ways can old age be said to be socially constructed? (Look back at the explanation of social construction in the section on Children and childhood if you need to (see pages 120–21).)

ROUND-UP

Older people make up a growing proportion of the population and as numbers continue to grow will have even more economic and political influence in the future. There are negative stereotypes of old age and ageist practices. Retirement is a big step in older people's lives, especially for men.

VOCABULARY

Patronise: behave in a condescending way
Investment: money put into an enterprise, expecting a profit

Age – sociology in practice

Growing old with pride and pleasure

'IN contemporary British society, older people are encouraged to conceal grey hair, wrinkles and other signs of ageing. In other cultural traditions, however, less negative interpretations are placed upon physiological aspects of old age. For the Sherbro people of Sierra Leone, incoherent or incomprehensible speech by an aged person is perceived as a positive sign. Their incoherence indicates their close communication with ancestors, who are regarded as important arbiters of destiny. Similarly, for the Venda speaking people of Southern Africa, old age is regarded as a "pleasure". Signs of old age, such as greying hair or the birth of a grandchild, are welcomed as indicators of a person's approaching contact with the "real" world of the spirits. In cultures where the afterlife is accorded great significance, old people's proximity to death enhances rather than reduces their status.'

'Growing up and growing older' by Jane Pilcher, *Sociology Review*, September 1995.

Questions

 Why do older people in the cultures discussed in the article have more status than older people in the developed world?

2 Look back to the section on Children and childhood (pages 120–21) for the idea of social construction. In what ways does this article suggest that old age is socially constructed?

3 Design a poster that celebrates the positive aspects of old age.

Sunny Delight

'IT came from nowhere. Last year, no one had heard of Sunny Delight. This year it's all the rage among children.

Question: How has Sunny Delight become Britain's third best-selling drink in such a short period?
Answer: Simple. It's done with the cunning use of advertising.

The advertising of Sunny Delight is a classic example of "pester power". It was linked to a healthy lifestyle for children and putting parents at ease. Since it contained vitamins A, B (1 and 6) and C, parents thought it was healthier than conventional brands such as Coke and Pepsi. Sunny Delight also sponsored the English Basketball Association and blitzed schools with balls sporting the drink's logo.

Kids across Britain went glassy-eyed with desire for Sunny D and pestered their parents for it in the supermarkets. Mums complied and packed the drink in their children's lunch boxes.

But the Food Commission, an independent watchdog, has now declared Sunny Delight to be no better than conventional carbonated drinks. Its main ingredient is refined white sugar.

Food Commission spokesman: "Sunny Delight is full of thickeners, colours and flavourings to make it look like a fruit juice, when it is basically just a very sugary drink. It is just a marketing con."

Younger and younger children are being targeted (by advertising). Many children's cartoons are little more than full length commercials ... Advertising for multinational products like McDonald's hamburgers, computer games and football T shirts are specifically directed towards children.'

Adapted from Introducing Media Studies by Ziauddin Sardar and Borin van Loon, Icon Books, 2000.

Questions

 Sunny Delight became a successful product by appealing to two different age groups. What were they, and how did the product appeal to them?

2 Should there be restrictions on advertising aimed at children, and aimed at getting them to use 'pester power'? Give reasons for your answer.

3 Some people argue that advertising like this is one of the things that makes children grow up too quickly. Look back to Concerns about children today in the section on Children and childhood (see pages 120–21). Is childhood still a period of innocence when children are protected from some aspects of the adult world?

A youth subculture

Questions

1 Study the photograph carefully. Describe the punk style – clothing, hair, jewellery and anything else you notice.

2 In what ways does punk represent a rebellion by young people against respectable adult norms and values? (It may help to look back at the section on Adolescence (pages 122–3).)
  (a) Why have youth subcultures such as punk had such a strong appeal to teenagers?
  (b) However, the majority of teenagers never belonged to such subcultures. Why was this?

Age – important terms

adolescence	the period between the start of puberty and adulthood
ageism	when someone is disadvantaged or treated differently because of their age
bedroom culture	the youth culture of girls, based on socialising in each other's bedrooms
biological age	age measured by changes in the body
childhood	the time of being a child
chronological age	age measured from date of birth or other point
cohort	the people born at about the same time, sharing similar experiences, such as your year group at school
generation	all members of a society born at around the same time
life course	the stages of life, such as childhood, adulthood and so on
retirement	stopping work because of age; sometimes taken as the beginning of old age
rite of passage	a ceremony to mark the transition from one stage of life to another
social construction	an idea that seems to be natural (such as childhood) can often be shown to vary enormously in different cultures so that what it means can be said to be socially constructed
teenager	someone between the ages of 13 and 19 inclusive
youth culture	the general culture of young people
youth subculture	a group of young people with distinct style, music, etc., such as mods, skinheads

Age – exam-style questions

Source A

Old age is sometimes thought of as starting at retirement. Older people in Britain today are often not valued as much as they might be. Some traditional societies treat older people with great respect, yet in Britain older people often face ageism. This can take many forms. For example, there are negative stereotypes of old people in television programmes. Older people are thought of as 'old codgers' or 'wrinklies'. They may also face discrimination in other ways.

Foundation tier

1 What is meant by a stereotype? [2 marks]

2 What is meant by the term ageism? Use an example to illustrate your answer. [3 marks]

3 Why is retirement often a more difficult experience for men than for women? Give one reason. [4 marks]

4 Using sociological knowledge, give two ways in which older people may be discriminated against. [5 marks]

5 Older people have less status in Britain than in some 'traditional societies'. Do you agree with this view? Explain your answer by referring to at least two factors that affect the status of older people. [6 marks]

Higher tier

1 What is meant by the term ageism? Use an example to illustrate your answer. [2 marks]

2 Why is retirement often a more difficult experience for men than for women? Give one reason. [3 marks]

3 Using sociological knowledge, give two ways in which older people may be discriminated against. [5 marks]

4 Older people have less status in Britain than in some 'traditional societies'. Do you agree with this view? Explain your answer by referring to several factors that affect the status of older people. [10 marks]

Age – further research

On children's rights, the Child Rights Information Network: www.crin.org.

United Nations Children's Organisation: www.unicef.org.

On older people, see Age Concern's site: www.ace.org.uk.

7 Families

The family is an area of social life that we all feel we know about; after all, most of us live in a family. But over a lifetime, one person will probably live in several types of family, made up of different people. Births, marriages, deaths, divorces, separations, remarriages and adoptions all change families. So there are many different types of families.

Families are different around the world, and they have also changed in British history too. Roles within families – that is, what we expect a mother or father, say, or a grandparent to do – have also changed.

Its importance in our lives makes the family a fascinating area to study. You can learn a lot from finding out about your own family; throughout this chapter there will be several opportunities to ask members of your family about their lives. You must remember though to keep facts about families separate from your opinions, which may well be strong ones. Even sociologists find this difficult. You will come across, for example, sharp divisions of opinion between those who are in favour of traditional nuclear families, where the man is the breadwinner, and those who think that such families can have a very dark side.

IN THIS CHAPTER YOU WILL LEARN ABOUT:

- different types of families in Britain, around the world and in the past
- changes such as the increase in divorces and in lone-parent families
- the roles of husbands and wives, children and grandparents
- alternatives to families, such as communes
- how families may change in the future

CHAPTER CONTENTS

Different kinds of families

The traditional nuclear family of mum, dad and the kids is still often thought of as normal, but there are many different types of families.

Families can be very different from each other.

What is a family?

Who belongs to your family? Write a list of all those people you consider belong to the same family as you, and beside each put their relationship to you. This is not an easy question! Here are some of the problems you may have had to think about when drawing up your list:

■ Sometimes 'family' means relatives we live with – that is, that we share a **household** with; but at other times it means all relatives, including those who live elsewhere.

■ Sometimes 'family' means close relatives; at other times it means anyone we are related to. Do you include cousins? What about second, third and fourth cousins?

■ 'Family' usually means people we are related to by blood or by marriage. Sometimes however people extend this to include others. There may be children who are adopted or fostered, or friends of your parents whom you call aunt or uncle, or you may have godparents.

■ You probably only included in your list people who are still alive, but if you were asked about your family tree there would be many more people you could list (though you might not know their names without a lot of research). Many people are fascinated by their ancestry and many families keep some record of their family tree. Is there one for your family?

Households

A household is the people who share a house or other living place. Many households are families, but households are not the same as families. Families don't always live together, and a household may contain people who belong to different families, for example a group of students sharing a house. Sociologists are interested in the different living arrangements people have, so this part of the course could be called 'families and households', not just 'families'.

Nuclear and extended families

There are two basic types of family: nuclear and extended.

A **nuclear family** is one made up of an adult man, an adult woman and their dependent children. Traditionally, the man was the '**breadwinner**', responsible for providing what the family needed to survive and prosper, while the woman was responsible for home and family. This kind of family has often been thought of as the 'normal' or 'typical' family.

An **extended family** contains a nuclear family, but added to it are other relatives. If there are three **generations** living together (grandparents, parents and children) this is a vertically extended family. If there are other relatives of the same generation, such as two brothers, their wives and children living together, this is a **horizontally extended family**. This kind of family has often been thought of as having been more common in the past than today, and more common in poorer countries.

Almost everyone has extended family; nowadays though we are less likely to live with members of our extended family.

Other types of family

These include the following:

■ **Lone-parent** families – one parent and his or her dependent children. Today lone-parent families are usually the result of separation or **divorce**, but some people decide to bring up children alone. In the past lone parents were more likely to be the result of the death of one parent. Women often died in childbirth, men in wars and both sexes from diseases.

- Reconstituted families – when a new family is created after a divorce through a second marriage, there are **stepparents** and stepchildren.

- **Empty nest** families – originally nuclear families, but the children have grown up and left home. Because people live longer on average than in the past, the parents are now likely to have many more years of life ahead of them.

Types of marriage

The law in Britain and in other western countries only allows someone to be married to one other person at a time – this is called **monogamy**. Having more than one marriage partner at the same time, **bigamy**, is a criminal offence. Today many people do have two or more husbands or wives in their lifetime, but not at the same time. They are divorced or widowed, and then remarry. Some show-business personalities and film stars are well-known for the number of marriage partners they have had. Having several marriage partners one after the other (not at the same time) is called **serial monogamy**.

In other countries, both today and in the past, **polygamy** has been allowed; that is, people have been allowed more than one marriage partner.

Polygyny, a man having several wives, is allowed by law in most of Africa and the Middle East and parts of southern Asia. Even in these countries most marriages are monogamous, because it is expensive to support several wives and their children. Having several wives indicates that a man is wealthy and important. The first wife is usually regarded as senior to the other wives.

Polyandry, a woman having several husbands, is rare. Where it does happen, it often involves a woman marrying two or more brothers. It can also happen when there are fewer women than men as a result of female infanticide, the killing of girl babies.

Changing times

In later sections of this chapter we will look at recent changes to families, such as the increases in lone-parent and reconstituted families and in serial monogamy. These and other changes have contributed to what sociologists call the growing diversity of families today.

▶ FIND OUT FOR YOURSELF

Ask three friends to tell you who lives in their household and their relationship with them. Write these down, then work out:

- how many adults and how many children there are in these households
- which type of family this is.

If you find the second part difficult in some cases, this shows how diverse families have become; the definitions we have been using cannot match all the many different living arrangements people may have. Present your findings to the class.

QUESTIONS

1. List four different kinds of families, then write an explanation of each one.

2. What is meant by the term nuclear family?

3. Write one sentence on each of the following to explain the differences between them:
   (a) families and households
   (b) vertically extended families and horizontally extended families
   (c) monogamy and polygamy
   (d) polygyny and polyandry.

4. (a) What is the main cause of lone-parent families today?
   (b) What was the main cause in the past?

5. Look back to find the meaning of the term serial monogamy. Can you think of any examples of famous people who have practised serial monogamy?

ROUND-UP

The basic types of family are the nuclear and extended family. Other kinds of family include lone-parent families, reconstituted (step) families and empty nest families. The nuclear family is usually thought of as the most common, but this may be changing. The nuclear family is based on monogamous marriage, but in other cultures men (and less often women) may be allowed to have several marriage partners at the same time.

VOCABULARY

Ancestry: people from whom you are descended – your father and mother, grandparents, great grandparents and so on

Notorious: well known for something bad

The life course and families

KEY FOCUS It is easier to understand the different types of family and household when we realise that each individual will have several different living arrangements over their lifetime.

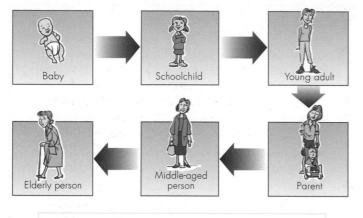

We all go through many changes in our lives.

Life course

The **life course** refers to an individual's life, to all the changes (and continuities) they experience. Here we will be concentrating on how looking at the life course can help us understand families, but of course it is also helpful in understanding other areas of social life. Sometimes, as with education and work, these affect family life a lot. The life course is a longitudinal approach.

Most people's life courses have four stages:

- First age – childhood when we are dependent on others and socialisation takes place.
- Second age – full-time employment and adult responsibilities; marriage and children.
- Third age – about ages 50–74. Children are grown up so less parental responsibility but may increasingly care for own parents. Active, independent life continues past retirement age.
- Fourth age – old age, dependence on others.

There is nothing fixed about most of these stages. For example, the first age for some people extends well into their 20s because they are still supported by their parents.

Generations

Generation refers to age differences within families. Children and their cousins are one generation within a family; their parents and aunts and uncles form another generation, grandparents and great aunts and great uncles another and so on.

A life course

Here is the life course of a (fictional) man:

0 years	Born. He is the first child. His mother is 23; she has been working in an office. His father is 26 and works in a factory. They have been married 2 years. All his grandparents are alive and live nearby.
3 years	Sister is born.
5 years	Starts school. Brother born.
18 years	Finishes education. Starts work, but still lives at home. Mother returns to work part time.
24 years	Sister gets married; she and her husband buy a house together. Father's parents have died.
25 years	Moves into a flat shared with two friends.
27 years	Sister and brother-in-law have a son – becomes an uncle. Maternal grandmother, now a widow, moves in with parents.
29 years	Gets married and buys a house with his wife.
31 years	Has a daughter. Sister divorces and has custody of her son.
33 years	Has a son. Sister remarries, to a widower with a daughter.
38 years	Father retires. Brother still lives at home with parents.
45 years	Children at school. Wife working full time. Father dies.
47 years	Daughter leaves school and starts work but still lives at home. Mother comes to live with family.
54 years	Daughter leaves home and marries. Son finishing a college course, living away from home. Mother dies.
57 years	Daughter has twins – becomes a grandfather.
65 years	Retirement.
70 years	Wife dies. Living alone.
75 years	Dies.

QUESTIONS

1. Work out the different types of family and household that this man lived in, when and for how long. You should also keep track of the ages of his closest relatives.

2. This man was born into a nuclear family, and then was the father in another nuclear family. Notice that he did not spend all his life in a nuclear family.
   (a) When did he live alone?
   (b) When did he live with friends?
   (c) When did he live with his wife but without children (there were two periods)?
   (d) When was he part of a vertically extended family household (two periods again)?

The man described in the box is a fictional person and not intended to be representative. It is also, perhaps, a rather simplified version of a life course. For many people today, there are more frequent changes and a wider range of types of families and household.

You are probably left with many questions about the man. You'd probably like him to have a name, but a lot more is left out. When was he happiest? Why did he marry his wife? Why did they have two children (why not none, or one, or more than two)? How close was he to relatives he did not live with? Being able to describe a living arrangement as, for example, 'a nuclear family' does not tell us much about how it is actually experienced by the people involved.

Cohorts

The experience of the life course is also different for different **cohorts**. Cohort refers to those born in a particular period; we use the idea when we talk about 'my generation' or the '90s generation'. Different cohorts have different experiences that shape their family lives. In the last century these experiences included the introduction of pensions and lowering the retirement age, the world wars, more women working, equality for women and mass unemployment – all of which affected different cohorts differently.

▷ FIND OUT FOR YOURSELF

Ask a grandparent or older relative about his or her life course. Try to write down what kind of family he or she was living in at different times. Present your findings to the class.

QUESTIONS

1. Explain in your own words what is meant by a generation.

2. Why is the life course described as a longitudinal approach?

3. Suggest three events in their lives that lead to people living in different kinds of families.

4. Draw a time-line which shows changes in your family since you were born.

5. Draw up a life course for a woman which includes the following (in any order you choose): single person household, marriage, divorce, lone parenthood, **remarriage**, **reconstituted family**, full- and part-time work, adoption. Make up the details but keep it reasonably realistic. What different ways are there to present what you have done to the class? Choose a way to present your ideas.

6. Think of your own generation and those who are 20 years older. What generational differences are there? Start with these: the older generation are more likely to be raising children and to be working …

   Now think of that older generation as a cohort – put to one side the differences that come from the fact that they are at the stage in life of adult responsibility while you are probably not. What differences are there that are to do with having been a particular age at a particular time? Start by thinking about these: what political, sporting and cultural events would have made the biggest impact on each group (you may need to ask older people about their experiences); are there different attitudes to work, or education or drugs?

ROUND-UP

To understand families, it is necessary to look at how they change over time as individuals move into and out of different living arrangements. Different generations and cohorts have different experiences of family life.

VOCABULARY

Continuities: things that do not change but rather stay the same
Longitudinal: over a long period of time
Fictional: imaginary, made up; as in books which are 'fiction'

The conventional nuclear family

KEY FOCUS The conventional nuclear family is often taken to be the best or the only 'real' family. Functionalist sociologists have argued that it is ideally suited to modern life, while the New Right are concerned about the growth of other kinds of families.

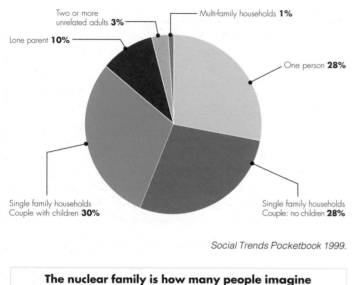

Two or more unrelated adults **3%**

Lone parent **10%**

Multi-family households **1%**

One person **28%**

Single family households Couple with children **30%**

Single family households Couple: no children **28%**

Social Trends Pocketbook 1999.

The nuclear family is how many people imagine families – but there are several other kinds.

Is the nuclear family changing?

Less than a quarter of households in Britain are now couples with dependent children. This percentage has been falling slowly for many years; in 1961 it was 38 per cent. This suggests that the nuclear family is in decline.

A growing proportion of couples living together are not married, and a growing number of families are reconstituted – that is, they are created from one or two families breaking up through separation or divorce.

As we saw in the last section, however, many people do spend parts of their lives in nuclear families still. If we add to the households we count as nuclear families couples before they have children, and couples after the children have grown up and are independent, then more than half of households are based on nuclear family relationships.

Another way of looking at the figures is to ask how many people are living in nuclear families at any particular time. The answer is about 40 per cent (if you are wondering how this can be so different from the figure of percentage of households, remember that nuclear family households on average contain more people).

Families in media and politics

Although there have been so many changes in British family life, the nuclear family is still the type of family most often seen on television dramas and in soap operas. Advertisements also make use of the nuclear family.

FIND OUT FOR YOURSELF

Test these claims for yourself by researching the mass media:

- Soap operas. Choose a soap opera and list the main families or households. How many of them are nuclear families and how many are other types?
- Advertisements. As you watch advertisements on television, watch out for those that show families. How often do you see families made up of mum, dad and the kids, rather than other types of family?

As well as the media, politicians of all parties also talk a lot about 'the family'. Political parties are keen to be seen as 'the party of the family'. The kind of family they mean is the conventional nuclear family of the father and husband who is the main breadwinner, the mother and wife who cares for home and family (although these days she may do some paid work as well) and one or two (but not too many) children. In advertisements the two children in this family are usually one boy and one girl, healthy, happy and white.

Sociologists argue that the media and politicians are in effect showing one particular kind of family as better than all other types of family. They show a **stereotype**, based in truth but misleading because it exaggerates the good features while not acknowledging the negative side (what in the next section we call 'the dark side' of the nuclear family).

The stereotype contains two ideas:

- that a family should be made up of father, mother and children
- that the father and mother should have different roles. It is assumed that men are naturally better suited for the world of work, and that women are better at doing domestic work, looking after the home and family.

Functionalism

These ideas about the family are connected to a particular view within sociology, that of functionalism. For functionalists, the conventional nuclear family is the ideal family for modern society because it fits the needs of society so well, and makes the best use of men's and women's different natural abilities.

In the past, people had to rely on their families for many needs, for example to care for them when they were sick or old, to lend or give money, to teach them. An extended family then was more useful; a large family meant that there were more people to turn to. Today these functions have been taken over by, for example, doctors and hospitals, banks, schools and so on. We no longer need to be able to turn to large extended families. Modern industry also needs people who can move to where there are jobs available. It is much easier to move a nuclear family to a new area than an extended one.

Although the family has lost many of its functions, it still has two important functions according to a functionalist sociologist, Talcott Parsons:

- The **primary socialisation** of children. Parents still need to teach their children the norms and values of their society, how to tell right from wrong and so on.
- The stabilisation of adult personalities. The family also provides comfort and security for its adult members as well as children. This second function has sometimes been called the 'warm bath' – the family as a warm, loving environment where the cares of the world can be washed away.

The New Right

Functionalists like Parsons were writing some years ago when the nuclear family still clearly seemed to be normal. This was also before the rise of feminism, and you may be able to see this in Parsons' views. For example, there are assumptions that women should not go out to work, and that it is the **housewife** who should ensure that the home is a comforting place for her husband.

More recently, a new set of ideas has arisen and has been behind many government policies. This New Right view is concerned by what it sees as the decline of the nuclear family. The stable environment children need, it is argued, has been undermined by a whole series of changes beginning in the 1960s. These include:

- easier abortion and contraception
- more divorce and **cohabitation**
- the rise of lone parents
- more illegitimate births
- women going out to work in greater numbers – they are seen as taking men's jobs and making it harder for men to be breadwinners.

All these changes are seen as evidence of collapsing morals and a crisis in the family, and as leading to other problems such as growing crime and drug abuse. We need, say the New Right, to return to traditional family values.

QUESTIONS

1. What are the two main ideas that make up the stereotype of the nuclear family?

2. Look at the pie chart at the beginning of this section. What percentage of households in Britain are couples with dependent children (that is, nuclear families)?

3. Write one sentence to explain why the extended family 'fitted' pre-industrial societies and one sentence to explain why the nuclear family 'fits' modern industrial society

4. Identify and explain the two important functions that functionalists say the nuclear family still has.

5. The New Right's position is based on moral values, that is, on ideas about how people should behave. Below is a list of changes in family life of which the New Right disapprove. For each state what the New Right would argue people should do (use the word 'should' in your answers). The first one is done for you as an example:
   (a) Abortion – women who get pregnant should have the baby and take responsibility for raising it.
   (b) Illegitimate births.
   (c) Cohabitation.
   (d) Divorce.
   (e) Lone-parent families.
   (f) Mothers working full time.

ROUND-UP

The conventional nuclear family is seen as the best type of family for modern life by functionalists and the New Right. It is seen as having been undermined by recent changes and the New Right argues for a return to traditional values.

VOCABULARY

Pre-industrial: before the Industrial Revolution; that is, before about 1750

Moral: about what is right and wrong, and what people should and should not do

Illegitimate births: when the parents are not married

The dark side of the family

KEY FOCUS

While some sociologists (as well as politicians and the media) have seen the conventional nuclear family as normal and natural, others have pointed out that nuclear families can be very negative for their members. In this section we look at some of these ideas.

Every week, another two women escape domestic violence.

According to the Home Office, two wom...

A lot of violence and abuse takes place within families.

What is meant by the dark side of the family?

Nuclear families put small numbers of people together in a confined space, the modern family home. Arguments and conflicts are perhaps inevitable sometimes in all families. Emotional conflicts can lead to stress and even to mental health problems. Violence and abuse take place within some families.

Violence

A high proportion of violent offences and even murders take place within families. Violence within families can be physical, sexual or emotional. Women and children are more likely to be the victims, and men are more likely to be the aggressors than women. There can also be violence between brothers and sisters, and the elderly can be victims of abuse and neglect.

We are much more aware of these kinds of problems than was the case in the recent past. There have been many highly publicised cases of neglect, abuse and violence within families. Is there more domestic violence than in the past? The New Right (see the previous section on the nuclear family) would argue that there is; that the growth of abuse is caused by the breakdown of family values which they believe has happened. There are, however, two other possible explanations:

- That we count as violence and abuse today behaviour which was acceptable in the past. For example, since 1991 the law has recognised that rape can take place within marriage (the previous view was that the man had a right to sex with his wife whenever he chose). Smacking of children is currently controversial. Parents are becoming less likely to smack their children, at least in public, as more people disapprove than used to be the case.

- That there is no more violence and abuse than in the past, but more comes to public attention. For example, Childline and similar initiatives have encouraged children who are victims to talk about what has happened to them; in an earlier period, abused children may have kept quiet because they had no one to talk to.

▶ FIND OUT FOR YOURSELF

Visit these web sites to find out what help and advice is offered to victims of abuse:

- Women's Aid Federation for England: www.womensaid.org.uk
- The charity Childline: www.childline.org.uk.

Collect information about one of these organisations or any other organisation doing similar work. Design a poster to publicise the organisation's work.

The truth may well be a combination of all three explanations.

Much but not all violence within families is by men. Men were for many centuries legally allowed to beat their wives and children; indeed, some felt they had to in order to assert their authority. Although the law now provides some protection, there is still a feeling that the law should not intervene in what is seen as 'a private matter'. As a result of greater awareness, refuges for women to escape from violent men exist in many towns, but it is still difficult for a woman to walk out of the family home. Many try to keep the relationship going, believing they can change the man, or because they have no other way of supporting themselves.

Abuse of children

Children, being smaller and weaker than adults, are at risk of neglect and injury because adults have more power than they do. Social work departments keep a close watch over children they have reason to believe are 'at risk'. Many abused children do not report what is done to them, and may even believe it is their own fault or that all children are treated like that. The combination of being abused and feeling guilty leaves deep emotional scars.

Abuse of men

Recent research has revealed that men can be victims of abuse by women; there are battered husbands as well as battered wives. There is a popular stereotype of the 'hen-pecked husband', but this is misleadingly light-hearted. Men find it much harder than women to admit to being abused; they fear being laughed at or not being believed even by friends. Men stay in abusive relationships for the same reasons as women. Although men are more likely to be able to support themselves if they walk out, they will probably have to continue to support the family so may be worse off. They may also stay to try to protect the children from their mother. They know that they are unlikely to get custody if there is a separation or divorce.

The exploitation of women

'I have broken the silence on my marriage to Paul Gascoigne to help bring domestic violence out into the open. I never told anyone about the real horror and extent of it ... Although everyone knew what went on, nobody wanted to help and nobody wanted to talk about it. Everybody thinks domestic violence is a private thing – something that goes on between husband and wife in the privacy of their own home. Well, it is not and that is why I have spoken about the eight years of physical and emotional abuse I experienced.' Sheryl Gascoigne, wife of the footballer Paul Gascoigne

Quoted in the *Guardian*, 25 November 1999.

Feminists see violence against women and children as the inevitable outcome of men dominating families. The nuclear family is, they say, designed to suit men's interests. When they marry, men get a domestic servant and sexual slave for nothing. Women are expected by men to carry out a whole range of domestic tasks – cooking, cleaning, washing up, the laundry, care of children and so on – without any payment, except perhaps a 'housekeeping allowance'.

Feminists do not agree about the solutions they suggest to these problems. Persuading men to do more housework may help without changing the basic nature of the relationship. Men today are often prepared to do more than used to be the case, but it is usually still seen as 'helping' rather than an equal sharing of tasks, even when both work full time. Both men and women learn what to expect from marriage during socialisation. So part of the solution may be to change the way children are brought up.

The most radical feminists are sceptical of the possibility of changing the nature of the nuclear family, which has existed for so long. The only solution is for women to stop living with men.

Despite the evidence that the family can often be a site of abuse and exploitation, most women still seem to be attracted by marriage, motherhood and family life. Today they may try more to shape the marriage, for example by insisting on their husbands doing more domestic chores. It does seem though that women as well as men gain considerable satisfaction and fulfilment from marriage. Even when marriages fail and end in divorce many are prepared to try again with someone else.

QUESTIONS

1 What is meant by domestic violence?

2 Some people think that there may be a lot of violence by women against their boyfriends or husbands that we don't know about. Why might men keep quiet if this was happening to them?

3 How could victims of domestic violence be encouraged to report what has happened to them? Think of different answers for the different groups of victims – men, women and children.

4 Sheryl Gascoigne says that 'Everybody thinks domestic violence is a private thing'. Why do you think she decided to talk about what happened to her, rather than keeping it private?

5 Do you think smacking children is a kind of abuse? Give reasons for your answer.

ROUND-UP

Much violence and abuse takes place within families, though it is impossible to measure exactly how much. Women and children are usually the victims, but men can be as well. Feminists draw attention to the less dramatic but also exploitative nature of everyday family life, such as who does housework.

VOCABULARY

Chores: routine jobs that have to be done regularly, like washing up and vacuum cleaning
Fulfilment: a feeling of having done something worthwhile
Sceptical: tending not to believe something

Cohabitation and the decline of marriage

KEY FOCUS   Is marriage in decline? There are fewer marriages each year, and more people live together without getting married.

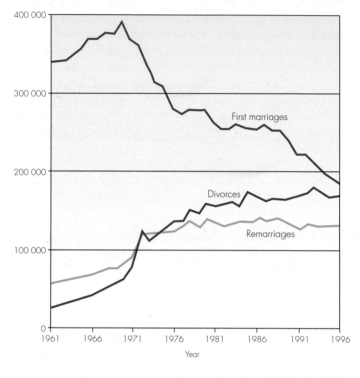

Social Trends Pocketbook 1999.

> **Marriage is changing – but is it on the way out altogether?**

The decline of marriage

The graph shows that the number of first marriages, that is, between people who have not been married before, has been declining fairly steadily since 1971. In 1996 there were 185 000 first marriages – less than half the number in 1970. Remarriages, where one or both partners have been married before, now account for about 40 per cent of all marriages, whereas they were only about 20 per cent of marriages in 1970. Divorces have more than doubled over the same period, although the rise seems to have levelled off in the last ten years shown on the graph.

As a result of these changes, a smaller proportion of the British population is married (although most adults are married). More people are getting married later in life, or not marrying at all, or divorcing and not remarrying.

Church weddings

The decline of marriage also involves a decline in the traditional white church wedding. Traditional weddings in Britain are:

- expensive
- formal
- religious.

More than half of all weddings now do not take place in church; many are in registry offices but the law now also allows weddings in some other places. Many people feel that remarriages should be kept small and low-key.

Why is marriage less popular?

Feminists would argue that the decline of marriage is a result of women being more aware that they are exploited in the nuclear family. Fewer women are willing to tie themselves down to one man, and more are willing to look for more fulfilling alternatives. However, the number of women who remarry suggests that marriage continues to attract women; perhaps many see the problem more as finding the right partner rather than the nature of marriage itself.

Another reason is the expense of the traditional church wedding. The average cost is now about £7000. A registry office wedding with fewer guests may be cheaper, but many people will feel they have missed out if they do not have a 'proper' wedding.

FIND OUT FOR YOURSELF

Make a list of all the things that people expect for a 'proper' wedding such as flowers, photographer and so on. Then try to work out roughly how much these might cost (ask an older person if you get stuck). You will see how the cost can mount up! Now consider which of these items it would be acceptable not to have without risking upsetting or offending friends and relatives.

A third reason for the decline of marriage is the dramatic increase in the number of couples who live together without getting married – cohabitation.

Cohabitation

Cohabiting used to be unacceptable and was called 'living in sin'. Children born to cohabiting couples were treated as different and inferior because they were illegitimate. But by the mid-1990s a quarter of all single women were cohabiting. There had been a huge shift in public opinion so that people no longer feared strong disapproval.

There are different types of cohabitation:

- The commonest one in Britain seems to be the 'trial marriage'; a couple live together to see if they would be able to live together permanently. The intention is eventually to marry unless things go wrong.
- Another type is virtually the same as marriage except that no ceremony has taken place. The couple are committed to a permanent relationship; private promises to each other take the place of the traditional vows.
- Some cohabitation involves short-term relationships without commitment.

A lot of cohabiting relationships eventually lead to a marriage. This suggests that marriage as such is not being rejected, but delayed. This can be for economic reasons – it gives time to save up, for the wedding or for a house. More people are still in higher education in their 20s and may not feel financially independent enough for marriage for years.

How to save marriage?

Here are some ideas from Helen Wilkinson, of the think-tank Demos, on how marriage could be changed to make it more relevant and popular:

- The ceremony should be performed by a friend or family member given a licence to perform that wedding only.
- The couple should write their own vows – ones they think they can keep. This will make couples discuss their relationship seriously, and may make it easier for them to sort out problems that arise later.
- Marriages should be initially for a set period of, say, ten years, with the option of renegotiation.

What do you think?

Births outside marriage

Social disapproval of 'illegitimate' births was so strong that even in the twentieth century pregnant girls were sometimes committed to asylums so that the family's shame could be hidden from the community. 'Bastard' remains a strong term of abuse (even though many members of our aristocracy are descended from the illegitimate children of kings).

The number of children born outside marriage has been increasing dramatically, so that they now account for about a third of all births. Most are born to parents who are not married but are living together in a stable relationship. This situation is arguably not all that different from the nuclear family.

However, about 40 per cent of births outside marriage are to parents who do not live together. Sometimes a relationship has broken down during pregnancy and some births are to girls who are too young to marry or live with the father. There are also women who decide to raise children alone, or with the support of a father who does not live with the family. This has become possible because women are more likely than in the past to be able to support themselves and children, and because being a lone parent is no longer as disapproved of as it once was. They may also be influenced by feminist ideas about the exploitative nature of marriage, and want to have children without having a permanent male partner.

Divorce and remarriage

KEY FOCUS

There are many more divorces than before the law changed in 1971. Divorces result in lone-parent families and often in reconstituted families. The rise in divorces is the result of a number of factors including changes in public opinion and the greater ability of women to support themselves.

Michael

> Helen and I were sitting and doing something and Mum came in and said Dad didn't love her any more. Then everything changed.

> I find it very difficult when I see children in television ads where there are two parents and the children are obviously happy. I cried a lot in the weeks after Dad left.

Helen

'Helen and I ...' by Angela Neustatter, *Guardian*, 5 February 1998.

A high divorce rate

There are about 170 000 divorces a year. This is about three times the number just before the Divorce Act of 1971 made it easier to get divorced. Britain has one of the highest divorce rates in Europe (though it also has one of the highest marriage rates).

About 40 per cent of marriages taking place now will end in divorce. Usually it is women who start divorce proceedings; about two and a half times as many divorces are given to women than men.

Wives for sale

Before divorce was available to most people, the practice of wife-selling was common. If a man or woman wanted to split up, they arranged for another man to 'buy' the wife. This was done in public. The husband took his wife to market and the second man made a bid. The sale was recorded by a clerk of the market who might be paid a toll – a commission – for his part in the sale. Some early wife sales involved the price of the wife being decided by how much she weighed.

HINTS AND TIPS

If you enjoy English literature, try reading the first chapter of *The Mayor of Casterbridge* by Thomas Hardy, which describes a wife sale.

Why are there more divorces?

The simple answer to this question is that it has become much easier to get divorced. Until the twentieth century, divorce was a long, difficult and expensive procedure. Before 1971, the partner who wanted to divorce had to provide evidence of grounds for divorce, such as cruelty, desertion or adultery. People could not get divorced simply because they wanted to or because they felt the marriage had failed.

This changed in 1971, when it became possible to divorce because of 'irretrievable breakdown' of the marriage, after a period of separation. It is no longer necessary to provide evidence of irretrievable breakdown.

However, the fact that divorce is easier does not necessarily mean that people will want to take advantage of it. When divorces increased after 1971, this may have been because there were lots of marriages that had broken down – **'empty shell marriages'** – and couples waiting for the opportunity to divorce.

Why are there still many divorces now? Here are some answers to this question:

- There has been a big change in attitudes to divorce. It is now seen as acceptable, and sometimes as the best thing to do for the children. Divorce no longer means shame and social disapproval. High profile divorces have helped this change in public opinion.

- This in turn may be part of a wider change in moral attitudes. Individuals put their own happiness first and no longer feel tied to their spouse 'till death us do part'.

- Feminists say that women now realise they do not have to put up with a marriage which does not live up to what they expect and want. Women today are more likely to be able to support themselves after divorce, so there is an escape route from empty shell marriages.

- Divorce has become much cheaper. It is now within everyone's reach. The lower figures in the past were partly because only the rich could afford divorce.

Effects of divorce

For husband and wife

Divorce is not just a legal process. It is emotionally stressful, usually accompanied by arguments and tension. Decisions have to be made about:

- how to divide possessions
- who will live in the family home and who will move out
- custody of children
- rights to see children for the parent who does not have custody.

Friends may take sides and lose contact with one partner.

For children

Custody of children is usually given to the mother, although courts now consider each case on its own merits before making a decision. Research has found that children whose parents are divorced or separated are more likely than other children to:

- live in poverty
- as children, behave in anti-social ways
- do less well at school
- as adults, have a low paid job
- become a parent at a young age
- use drugs and smoke and drink a lot.

Boys and girls seem to be affected in the same ways.

At first sight this seems to prove that divorce is bad for the children. However, most children of divorced parents are not affected in these ways, and do not suffer any disadvantage. It is not simply being a child of divorced parents that matters. What seem to count most are these factors:

- How well off the family is after divorce. As with lone parents, the problems may be as much to do with poverty as with the family.
- How much conflict there is before, during and after the divorce.
- How well parents cope with their new lives affects how well children adapt.
- Whether the divorce involves other changes such as moving in with a stepfamily.
- How much contact children have with the parent they are not living with.

Remarriage

Many divorced people remarry. This suggests that divorce is more about dissatisfaction with a particular partner than with marriage itself. Having more than one marriage partner over a lifetime is called serial monogamy. Men are more likely to remarry than women.

Reconstituted or blended families

There are now more than half a million families in Britain that have been put together from other families that have broken up. There are many different kinds of reconstituted families depending on whether one or both parents have been married before, how many children each has (if any) and so on.

The term reconstituted family is preferable to stepfamily, because stepfamily can seem to suggest that somehow these are not 'real' families. Another acceptable term is blended family.

QUESTIONS

1. What is meant by an empty shell marriage?

2. What 'high profile divorces' do you know of? Write a list of famous people who are divorced.

3. Find four reasons for the rise in the number of divorces since 1971.

4. Why do you think women are more likely to divorce a man than the other way around?

5. Write a paragraph arguing for or against the statement that 'divorce does not have to have negative effects on children'.

ROUND-UP

For growing numbers of people, marriage is no longer 'till death us do part'. Many marriages end in divorce. This is partly because divorce is much easier than it used to be. However, many divorced people, especially men, remarry, which suggests that marriage is still seen as a good thing.

VOCABULARY

Desertion: running away from a responsibility, such as a man running away from looking after his family

Adultery: when a married person has a sexual relationship with someone other than their partner

Custody: keeping safe or looking after; after a divorce, one parent will have custody of the children

Lone-parent families

KEY FOCUS There are a growing number of lone-parent families, in which only one parent brings up children. Usually the parent is the mother. There is a continuing argument about whether children are better off in two-parent families.

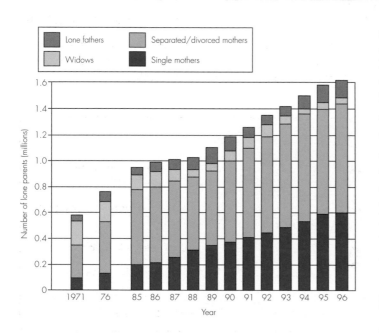

Guardian, 15 May 1998.

> **One in four families with children now have only one parent (*Social Trends*, 1999).**

Some facts

There are about 1.6 million lone-parent families. About 20 per cent of children live in lone-parent families; this has increased from less than 10 per cent in 1972. Britain has a much higher proportion of lone-parent families than other European countries.

There have always been lone-parent families. In the past both fathers and mothers were often left to raise children alone because of the death of their partner. As happens today, many remarried. The difference today is that most lone-parent families are the result of separation and divorce rather than death. Some are also the result of a conscious decision to raise children alone.

Many children who are being cared for by one parent today will have been born into a two-parent family. Both parents will have brought up the children for some time before the

separation or divorce. Many lone parents go on to remarry, and start reconstituted families. The children will then be living with one parent and one stepparent, and perhaps with stepbrothers and stepsisters. This shows how lone-parent families are sometimes a temporary stage in the life course.

The mother heads most lone-parent families. This is because the mother is more likely to have custody of the children after a separation or divorce. It is still usually assumed that the children are better off with their mother.

Unlike many children in lone-parent families in the past, who had only one living parent, children in lone-parent families today often see both parents. They will live with one parent but see the other. How often varies a lot; it may be a regular arrangement (such as every weekend) or far less frequent.

Do children need two parents?

Those in favour

Several writers have argued that lone-parent families are bad for children. This way of thinking can be traced back to functionalism. According to functionalists it was essential to have a father and a mother, since both had different skills and roles that together made a successful family. Any other form of family would be dysfunctional – it would create problems.

Some of the negative effects on children of having only one parent have been said to be:

- underachieving in school
- being more likely to be unemployed
- becoming dependent on welfare payments, unable to support themselves
- more likely to turn to delinquency and crime or to drug and alcohol abuse.

In sociological language, the argument in favour of a two-parent family is that lone-parent families fail to socialise children properly or to act as effective agents of social control.

A particular concern is often the lack of a father figure to act as a role model, showing boys how adult men should behave (going out to work, supporting a family, loyal and committed to wife and children). Boys who do not see men behaving as they should will be unable to become good husbands and fathers themselves, it is said. Like their fathers, they will get a girl pregnant and then, scared of the responsibility and probably unable to support her and the child, abandon her. The damaging pattern is passed on to the next generation.

Those against

To other writers, the criticisms of lone-parent families described above sound too much like moralising and preaching, and seem out of touch with the realities of life today.

Firstly, is it necessary to have two parents? Lone parents may be supported by other family members (including the father, even if he is not living with the family). A lone parent may well be able both to support the family economically and provide a warm, loving family environment. This may be better than staying with the other parent in an empty shell marriage where there are lots of arguments. Children may even suffer more from such a situation than from one parent leaving. Bringing up children alone may be the way a parent protects his or her children from the abusive behaviour of the other parent.

Secondly, do children from lone-parent families really have more problems? Many children from lone-parent families experience no problems at all, while plenty of children from two-parent families do badly at school, turn to delinquency and drugs and so on. It is just as likely that the problems arise from living on a low income. Lone-parent families are more likely than other types of family to be living in poverty. The problems that have been associated with lone parents are those associated with poverty.

FIND OUT FOR YOURSELF

It may be possible to invite a lone parent into school to talk to you about his or her experiences. Discuss this with your teacher.

Making dad pay: the Child Support Agency

One of the reasons behind the arguments about lone-parent families is the cost to the government. Because it is difficult to work full time with young children, many lone parents need to be supported by welfare payments; this would not happen if there was a second parent able to earn money. The job of the Child Support Agency (CSA) is to make absent parents (usually fathers) pay money to the parent who has custody of the children, so reducing welfare dependency. The Prime Minister at the time it was created, Margaret Thatcher, said, 'Nearly four out of five lone mothers claiming income support receive no maintenance from the fathers. No father should be able to escape from his responsibility'.

The CSA has been very controversial. It has had only limited success, with delays and errors being common:

- Many lone mothers do not want to be dependent on men who they see as belonging to their past. Some refuse to reveal the name of their ex-partner, saying they are afraid of violence.
- Many 'absent' fathers become responsible for new families as they find new partners. Having to support two families can become a great burden.

IT ▶ FIND OUT FOR YOURSELF

Visit the Child Support Agency's web site: www.dss.gov.uk/csa.

For a different point of view, visit the web site of Families Need Fathers, which helps fathers stay in touch with children when the mother has custody: www.fnf.org.uk.

QUESTIONS

1. Approximately what percentage of children in Britain lives with only one parent?
2. State two ways in which lone-parent families today are different from those in the past.
3. Why are there more lone mothers than lone fathers?
4. Explain what the CSA does and why it was set up.
5. Write a paragraph arguing that 'lone-parent families can work just as well as two-parent families'.

ROUND-UP

There are more lone-parent families than there used to be, and most today are the result of separation and divorce. Lone-parent families vary a lot; from those where the parent really is alone to those where the 'absent' parent plays an important part in bringing up the children. Sociologists disagree as to whether lone-parent families can bring up children as well as two-parent families.

VOCABULARY

Temporary: only for a short time
Conscious decision: a decision made after careful thought
Maintenance: the money an absent parent has to pay to a former partner to help him or her with regular expenses

The family in history

Families and households in Britain have changed a lot over the centuries. This was not a simple change from extended to nuclear families, but was rather more complicated, as this section shows.

Is this the way families always used to be?

Before the Industrial Revolution

Functionalist sociologists, you will remember, argued that just as the nuclear family 'fitted' modern society, so the extended family was ideally suited to pre-industrial society. The argument was that people needed to have lots of relatives with them to share the family's work (such as running a farm) and to support them in sickness and old age. Today we have hospitals, schools and so on. We do not need to have around us an extended family that we can turn to for help (and who can turn to us for help). The big change came with the Industrial Revolution, when the nuclear family became the norm.

Most sociologists now reject this argument, because historical research has shown a rather different picture.

The historian Peter Laslett, studying parish registers and census data (see the section on the Census on pages 354–5) found that the average size of households changed very little during the period he studied, 1564 to 1821. The average size of households was about 4.75 people. He concluded that nuclear families were common, and extended families unusual, before and during the Industrial Revolution. People married late and started a family late; this, together with low life expectancy (on average, people died in their 30s), meant that three generations living together (the vertically extended family) was unusual. There were some important differences

from modern families. Lords and noblemen had servants, and so they had large households. People probably also lived closer to many of their relatives than they do today, with brothers and sisters and their families living nearby.

After the Industrial Revolution

The period of the Industrial Revolution (1750 to 1850) was when modern industry based on factories developed, and people moved in large numbers from country areas to the new industrial cities like Manchester. According to functionalists, the nuclear family should take over from the extended family at this time.

Anderson studied the Census records for 1851 in Preston, an industrial area. He found that in this early industrial period the extended family actually became more common. Extended family relationships were useful when people moved to cities. They provided someone to stay with, help in finding a job and help in sickness and poverty. The extended family made it easier to move from the close-knit supportive village community to the impersonal city.

It seems then that there was far more continuity than the functionalists suggested. Nuclear families have always been common, and extended family links were at least as useful in the new cities as they had been in villages.

The Industrial Revolution did, however, change family life in important ways. Before then, it was difficult to separate home life and work. People lived where they worked, and the whole family worked together. The Industrial Revolution led to the idea of 'going out to work', at a factory. As time went on, it was men who went out to work and women who stayed at home to do cooking and cleaning. So it was the Industrial Revolution and its consequences that made many women housewives.

The mid-twentieth century

Young and Willmott carried out a series of important studies of working-class families in London in the 1950s and 1960s. Their findings have added to our understanding of how families changed and developed.

Studying working-class families in Bethnal Green in the East End of London in the 1950s, they found strong extended family networks. The extended family, built on strong relationships between married women and their mothers, was alive and well. Women lived in the same street as or very close to their mothers, and relied on them for help and advice. The extended families were part of a strong local community.

When the East End was redeveloped, many of these families moved out to new housing estates in Essex. This broke up the extended family relationships. Women had less contact with their mothers because they lived further away and it was difficult to keep in touch. A new kind of family, the privatised nuclear family, based on a stronger bond between husband and wife, took over.

The increase in telephone and car ownership now helps people keep in touch with their relatives even if they live some distance away. There are grounds for thinking that extended family links remain strong. Extended families may live apart, but they get together for important occasions, such as Christmas, weddings and funerals. Moreover life expectancy has increased, and relatives care for many elderly people who live with them or nearby.

Up to the present

What can we add to the table below to describe British families at the start of the new century?

What happened in history

Date	Typical family	Evidence	Writer
1500	Small household – nuclear	Parish records	Laslett
1700	Small household – nuclear	Parish records	Laslett
1850	Extended in cities	Census returns	Anderson
1950	Extended in cities but in decline	Survey	Young and Willmott
1970	Nuclear, privatised	Survey	Young and Willmott

The most striking characteristic of British families today is their diversity – that is, that there are many different types of families. Nuclear families remain important, and extended families living together are unusual. There are also large and growing numbers of lone-parent families, reconstituted families and people living alone. The presence of minority ethnic groups has also contributed to the diversity of Britain's families.

FIND OUT FOR YOURSELF

Does your family have a family tree? Many people are interested in their ancestry, so it is possible one of your family has done some research and produced a family tree. If so, study it and see if you can find signs of how things have changed. Look for example at how long people lived, the age at which they got married (if they did) and how many children they had.

QUESTIONS

1. When was the Industrial Revolution?

2. Identify and explain two changes that the Industrial Revolution made to people's lives.

3. State two ways in which extended families could help people who moved into cities during the Industrial Revolution.

4. Many people have extended family in other countries. What changes in the last 50 years have made it easier to keep in touch with them?

5. Write two paragraphs (a) one explaining the development of the family according to functionalists and (b) one explaining what probably did happen according to available evidence.

ROUND-UP

The British family has changed in many ways over the centuries, but in more complicated and less clear ways than a simple change from extended to nuclear families at the time of the Industrial Revolution.

VOCABULARY

Parish registers: the records kept by churches of christenings, weddings and funerals
Census: the big national social survey carried out by the government every ten years; see pages 354–5
Impersonal: unfriendly

Family diversity

In this section we pull together several ideas from earlier sections about the growing diversity of families in Britain today, and look at families in minority ethnic groups.

Mother: 'I ... was called in and saw him for about five minutes; we weren't allowed to talk, but in those days that was quite a revolutionary thing to do – most of my friends only got to see their husbands on their wedding days ... I had confidence in my family's choice. They knew what sort of man would be good for me and I trusted them. Children can't be controlled any more, they want freedom.' Pushpa Pabla, aged 60

Daughter: 'I was introduced to quite a few boys because my mum would have loved me to have an arranged marriage. I didn't like any of them ... Even though I was brought up with many Indian values I still wanted to have a career and be an individual ... In the end I think my mum was just relieved he was Asian, because it means at least I'm keeping some part of my culture ... Just because I married the man of my choice doesn't mean I am rejecting Asian culture.' Kiran Bajaj, aged 34

Quoted in the *Guardian*, 25 June 1994.

Minority ethnic group families change and adapt to life in Britain.

Many different family types

There no longer seems to be one form of family that is by far the most popular. The conventional nuclear family, as we have seen, has been in decline though this can be exaggerated. A wide range of family and household types now exists in Britain, and the disapproval that used to be attached to some types – cohabitation, lone-parent families, same sex couples – is now less strong than it used to be even a few decades ago. The existence of many different types of family is called diversity.

Diversity also exists in the roles people take within families, as well as in the types of family. Even within nuclear families, women may work full time, part time or not at all; men may choose to stay at home as **househusbands**, or to attempt an equal relationship as 'New Men'. Others may juggle different responsibilities, as parents and stepparents to children who may or may not live with them.

Minority ethnic groups

Due to immigration in the 1950s and 1960s, Britain now has significant Afro-Caribbean and Asian populations. These have added to the diversity of family life. The minority ethnic groups all contain within them a diversity of family forms. Family forms that existed in the countries of origin have been modified to meet the new situation of living in Britain.

Afro-Caribbean families

The common pattern in the West Indies (the Caribbean) was for men to play little part in family life. Women were often economically independent, working to support their children, often with the help of their own mothers. This kind of family is described as **matrifocal** – centred on the mother. The lesser importance of men in the family may be due to the history of slavery. Male slaves could not be breadwinners for their families. High unemployment also makes it difficult for men to fulfil the breadwinner role.

Afro-Caribbean women in Britain are far more likely than white or Asian women to be lone mothers, a continuation of the pattern in the Caribbean. Men, however, are more likely to be involved in family life than in the Caribbean. To the New Right, as you have seen earlier, lone-parent families are 'broken' families and the lack of a breadwinner father is seen as leading to problems especially for boys. However, this kind of family may for the mother be the best adaptation to a situation in which men cannot be relied on as breadwinners.

Asian families

Britain's Asian population is made up of people from many different cultures, following different religions and speaking different languages. Many, though not all, came to Britain from country areas where extended families were strong, with three generations often living together. Marriages were seen as forming strong bonds between families not just between individuals.

The extended family networks played a part in making the process of migrating to Britain easier. Men often came to Britain first, staying with male relatives and bringing their families over only when they had work and homes. For women who for cultural reasons were unable to work outside the home, immigration to Britain disrupted family networks

Ethnicity and household composition, 1991 (percentage)

Household composition	Black	Indian	Pakistani/ Bangladeshi	Other ethnic minorities	White
One person	27	10	7	22	27
Two or more unrelated adults	6	3	3	7	3
One family: Couple:					
No children	13	14	7	16	28
Dependent children	20	50	60	37	24
Non-dependent children only	6	8	4	5	9
Lone parent:					
Dependent children	21	4	7	8	5
Non-dependent children only	6	3	2	3	4
Two or more families	1	9	9	2	1
All households (000s)	**328**	**226**	**132**	**185**	**21 027**

Social Focus on Ethnic Minorities, 1996.

QUESTIONS

Study the table, then complete the following:

The highest proportion of lone parents with children is among ..... families.
..... and ..... people are the least likely to live on their own.
The highest proportions of nuclear families with dependent children are among ..... and ..... families.
..... people are the most likely to be living as couples without children.

and made them feel isolated and unsupported. Where there are other families from the same region, community networks have now been rebuilt. There is still a stronger sense of loyalty to family than is found in western culture.

Young Asian people often find themselves torn between a tradition of arranged marriage and the British practice of allowing almost complete individual choice. They have found ways of combining the cultures. For example, they may let their parents draw up a shortlist of several possible marriage partners, then make the final choice themselves from this list. Sometimes, however, there has been conflict between generations. Young Asians reject their parents' plans for them and choose their own partners while their families try to preserve traditions they see as under threat in the new environment.

In the case of both Afro-Caribbean and Asian families, the types of family common in the countries of origin have changed and adapted to British life.

Geographical diversity

There are areas of Britain where particular types of family are more common than elsewhere. Cities often have high proportions of people living alone. Parts of the south coast of England have large numbers of elderly people who have settled there in retirement.

QUESTIONS

1. What is meant by a matrifocal family?

2. Why is there sometimes disagreement between British Asian parents and their children about marriage?

3. Identify and explain two ways in which extended family networks help recently arrived immigrants?

4. In what ways have families in Britain become more diverse?

ROUND-UP

The growing diversity of British families is shown in the many different types of families and in the different roles people can have within families. Britain's minority ethnic groups have contributed to this diversity.

VOCABULARY

Exaggerated: made to seem bigger or more important than it really is

Alternatives

The last section showed how diverse people's living arrangements can be. Some of these are not so much families as alternatives to families. We are going to look here at three types of alternatives to families: communes, shared households and people living alone.

A kibbutz – an alternative to family life.

Communes

A **commune** is a group of people who live together and who agree to share at least some of their property. Communes have existed at different times throughout history. People have often tried to find a better way of life, spurred on by idealism. Some communes have been based on political beliefs such as socialism, others on religious beliefs.

On a commune people usually share out domestic work, taking turns at cooking, looking after children and so on, and share the work that supports the commune, such as agriculture. Children will know who their parents are, but often everyone shares the responsibility of bringing them up as children of the commune.

A well-known example of communes is the kibbutz (plural: kibbutzim) of Israel. When the state of Israel was set up in 1948, many Jewish people who went to live there were attracted by the idea of living on these agricultural communes. The adults shared the work and the proceeds. Couples had their own living accommodation, but their children spent most of the time with other children, sleeping in dormitories and being cared for by nominated kibbutz members.

This seems a long way from what we think of as 'families'. However, the kibbutzim do what families do; they socialise children into the norms and values of their society. In some ways, the kibbutzim are like very large extended families. Unrelated children brought up together on communes feel strong bonds, seeing each other as like brothers and sisters.

FIND OUT FOR YOURSELF

Another well-known commune was the Oneida community in New York in the nineteenth century. Use an encyclopaedia or Microsoft Encarta to find out about this commune.

Shared households

Probably the most common form of household today shared by people who are not related is the group of college students or other unmarried young adults sharing a flat or house. This type of living arrangement has been shown in several television situation comedies and dramas, such as *The Young Ones.*

Shared households differ from communes in that they are smaller and are not usually motivated by religious beliefs. They are also usually temporary arrangements that end when one or more people move out or get married. Many people live in a shared household at some time in their lives, but only for fairly short periods.

'Singlehood'

Over a quarter of all households in Britain now contain just one person. There are three main types of people living alone:

- Elderly people, often widows and widowers. The rise in average life expectancy has led to more people living longer.
- Divorced and separated people, for example men whose ex-wives have custody of their children. Many such men go on to remarry.
- Young adults living alone. In the past, many people moved away from their parents' home when they got married; today, growing numbers live alone for several years before marriage. Reasons for this include the following:

- More young people go to college or university. Some choose to live with their parents still, if the college is near enough, but for many this means moving to a new town or city. Even if they do not live alone at college, they become more independent, used to looking after themselves.
- The average age at which people get married has been going up. More young people are single and earning a wage which enables them to live alone.

Many young people of course cannot afford to leave home. At the same time as those with good jobs and money are buying houses on their own, others have to rely on their parents to carry on supporting them.

The increase in '**singlehood**' has led to the government planning to build many new houses in the next ten or twenty years. The total population will only go up a little, but we will need a lot more houses. Companies are beginning to produce

more goods aimed at people who live alone, from chilled meals for one to mini-dishwashers. But it is important to remember that people living alone do have families, and may see them and rely on or help them a lot. The young adult will have parents and brothers and sisters, the divorced person may have children to see at arranged times and the elderly may have children and grandchildren. And as with shared households, living alone is likely to be a temporary stage in someone's life.

Living as one: one-person households as a percentage of all households, England

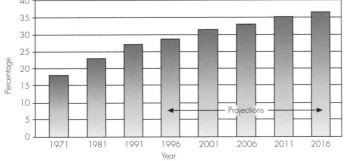

Guardian, 20 January 1998; Mintel surveys, 1994.

Average age at first marriage, England and Wales

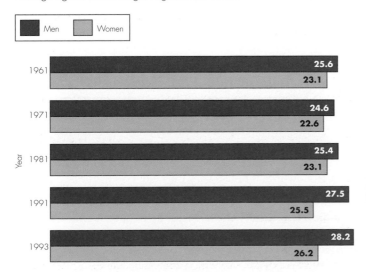

Guardian, 20 January 1998; Mintel surveys, 1994.

QUESTIONS

1. What is meant by a commune?

2. What is meant by 'singlehood'?

3. Look at the diagram Living as one. What percentage of all households will be single person households in 2016 according to this?

4. Look at the diagram Average age at first marriage.
   (a) What is the increase in the ages at which men and women marry from 1961 to 1993?
   (b) What reasons can you think of to explain why men marry at a later age than women?
   (c) What reasons can you think of for why the average age at which both men and women marry has been going up?

5. What advantages and disadvantages are there to living on a kibbutz?

ROUND-UP

As well as living arrangements we can confidently say are families, there are others which are less clear. We have looked here at communes, shared households and single-person households. Apart from communes, these tend to be temporary stages in people's lives; that is, people spend parts of their lives in family households and parts in other types of living arrangement.

VOCABULARY

Idealism: believing that life can be better
Dormitories: large rooms containing several beds
Temporary: only lasting for a limited time

Husbands and wives

KEY FOCUS

This section looks at what has been called the domestic labour debate: are men helping more with housework and childcare? These have been traditionally seen as women's work, but today most women work outside the home as well. How have male and female roles within the family changed?

How couples divide the household tasks, Britain, 1994 (percentage)

	Always the woman	Usually the woman	About equal or both together	Usually the man	Always the man
Washing and ironing	47	32	18	1	1
Deciding what to have for dinner	27	32	35	3	1
Looking after sick family members	22	26	45	–	–
Shopping for groceries	20	21	52	4	1
Small repairs around the house	2	3	18	49	25

Sociology by A. Giddens, 3rd edition, Polity Press, 1999; *Social Trends*, 1996.

Are men helping more with housework than they used to?

QUESTIONS

Look at the table above.

1. Which task(s) are mainly done by women?

2. Which task(s) are mainly done by men?

3. Which task(s) are roughly shared equally?

The domestic division of labour

Until the middle of the twentieth century there was a clear **division of labour** between the sexes. The man's role was to go out to work and provide for the family, the woman's role was to be a housewife and mother, looking after home and family. These have been called **segregated conjugal roles**; that is, very clearly different expectations of men and women. In fact, it was always more complicated than this. Men have always done some types of work associated with the home, such as house repairs, gardening and looking after a car. These are not usually thought of as part of 'housework' in the way that we think of, for example cooking and cleaning which have always been seen as women's work. Moreover, women did often do paid work, though this was seen as less important than their domestic duties.

Today most women go out to work. If they are still expected to do most of the housework, this would mean they carried a double burden. They would also experience role conflict between the role of worker and the role of mother and housewife (for example having doubts about whether it was right to leave children with a nanny or childminder).

The symmetrical family?

In the 1970s Young and Willmott believed they had evidence of a new type of sharing of domestic roles that was more equal. This new division of labour was based on **joint**, not segregated, **conjugal roles**. While there were still clear ideas about what was men's work and what was women's work, both husband and wife were contributing equally to the family. They called this new kind of family 'symmetrical' to emphasise the equal importance of the man's and woman's work. Their evidence was based on asking both men and women how much housework they did.

Feminists and others have challenged Young and Willmott's **symmetrical family** theory. They point out that although men do help more, this is still seen as helping – the main responsibility is still the woman's, even if she works full time. Men also usually choose which tasks they will do, and not surprisingly choose the ones that are less dull and repetitive. For example, a man may cook a special meal for guests (and get praise and appreciation for it) rather than taking on the daily responsibility of getting the children fed. The work men do, such as home improvements, often gives a sense of satisfaction that women's domestic work does not.

Women who work full time still spend about eight hours a week more on housework, cooking and shopping. As a result, women have less free time, even at weekends, than their husbands. They are also 'on call' more of the time, for example when a child wakes during the night.

Men may want to help more, but may not be able to. Young and Willmott themselves noted how in some types of well-paid jobs men were being expected to work very long hours. Other writers have suggested that in some businesses we now have a situation where people feel that they must work late if they want promotion or to keep their job. This 'long hours culture' may prevent some men from playing as much of a part in family life as they would like. (See page 218 for more on the long hours culture.)

New machines and devices to help with housework should, at least in theory, reduce the amount of work but they may affect men and women unequally. For example, washing up is one chore that men often took on, but in many households this has now been replaced by loading a dishwasher. New types of housework also emerge. Barbecues have become popular and although this is a form of cooking it is seen as men's work.

Housework is only one aspect of what happens between husbands and wives. Other areas that can be studied include how money is managed and how decisions (such as whether to move house, or where to go on holiday) get made.

New Man?

While on average men have only begun to help with housework a little bit more, some men in recent years have chosen a complete role reversal. There are men who are househusbands, staying at home, usually to look after small children, while their wife, if they have one, works, usually in a highly paid job. Here the traditional role expectations for men and women are reversed.

New Man has a different meaning from househusband. A New Man shares housework and childcare equally with his partner, but does not necessarily stay at home full time to do this. The idea of New Man is associated with a desire to make men and women more equal, and to change negative aspects of men's behaviour. New Man would be caring and cooperative, would share his emotions and abandon the old masculine aggressiveness and competitiveness. Although the idea of New Man attracted a lot of media attention in the 1990s there do not seem to be many of them around.

QUESTIONS

1. What is meant by women's 'double burden'?

2. What did Young and Willmott mean by 'the symmetrical family'?

3. Explain the difference between separate conjugal roles and joint conjugal roles.

4. What problems and difficulties might a househusband meet? (For example, think about what his mates might say.)

5. Do you think that when a man and woman both work full time they should share all the housework (including looking after children)? Give reasons for your answer.

▶ FIND OUT FOR YOURSELF

This section has only considered domestic labour by husbands and wives. How much housework in your home is done by children (including you!)? Which tasks do children do? How long do they take? Are they paid or rewarded in any way? Are they a source of disagreements or even arguments? Keep a record over the next week. Write up your findings and share them with other members of your class.

ROUND-UP

Women in the past were expected to see home and family as their priority, while for men it was their job. This has begun to change as more women work and have careers. But women who work are still often expected to do most of the housework and many relationships are still far from equal.

VOCABULARY

Segregated: separate
Role reversal: when the expected roles are reversed, for example when a teacher learns something from a student
Priority: the most important thing

Grandparents and children

Having looked at the roles husbands and wives take within families, we now look at grandparents and children.

Grandparents – what is the reality today?

Grandparents

Because people live longer than they used to, more people today know their grandparents than used to be the case in the past. Grandparents used to be unusual because few people lived long enough to be grandparents. However, people are getting married later than they used to, so the average age at which women have children has been going up. This may mean that in the future it will become normal to become a grandparent in your 80s if you have had children late and your children do too.

Having three or even four generations of a family alive at the same time makes possible relationships and support that did not exist before. Grandparents can help their children and grandchildren, but also need help and support themselves. The kinds of help include:

- economic support – giving and lending money, gifts
- accommodation – some older people live with their children
- personal care – older people may need help from their children, usually daughters

- looking after children – nearly a quarter of pre-school children with working parents are looked after by their grandparents
- emotional and moral support – listening, talking and giving advice; mothers often ask their own mothers for advice about childcare.

Many grandparents are active and able to play a significant part in the lives of their children and grandchildren. In many families grandparents have a role to play in bringing up their grandchildren. Grandparents are allowed to spoil children in a way parents cannot, because grandparents do not have the main responsibility for socialisation and social control. They can also be important because they are adults children can talk to when they feel they cannot talk to their parents.

It is often grandmothers who take a more active role than grandfathers. Some grandparents live close to their children and their families and help daily (for example being an unpaid childminder while the mother works), but some live too far away for this. Both parents and children tend to lead full, active lives today and time with grandparents may need to be planned and involve specific activities.

▶ FIND OUT FOR YOURSELF

Interview someone who is a grandparent. Ask him or her about his or her grandchildren – how many he or she has, how often he or she sees them, what things they do together and so on. Write out a list of questions first and make a note of the answers. Share your findings with the class.

Children in families

Children are at the heart of families; many people would say they are the main reason we have families.

People in Britain today have fewer children than in the past, and than in less developed countries. The average number of children has been falling for many years and is now about 1.75 (the television programme *2.4 Children* is a little out of date!). In some countries, such as Italy and Japan, there is growing concern that not enough children are being born to replace the numbers of people who die. The population of these countries will fall (unless they accept immigrants from other countries). This is potentially very serious, because a growing proportion of the population will be elderly. There will be fewer people working and paying taxes to provide the services that the elderly need.

In the past and in less developed countries today, people had more children because children were an economic benefit. There were several reasons for this:

- As soon as they were able, children would contribute to the work the family did.
- They would be able to support their parents in old age and ill health, so having children was a sort of insurance.
- There was also a high risk of a child dying, so it made sense to have several children to ensure some survived.

These reasons no longer apply in Britain, so it is not surprising that people have fewer children. We now expect babies to survive to adulthood; it is considered tragic if a child dies. We no longer rely so much on our children in old age; there are pensions, savings and a health service. Finally, and perhaps most importantly, children have become an economic cost, not an economic benefit.

What is meant by being an economic cost? The Joseph Rowntree Foundation has estimated that by his or her seventeenth birthday, a child in Britain today will have had an average of £50 000 spent on 'regular' items. About 90 per cent of this comes from parents, with the remaining 10 per cent from grandparents, other relatives and family friends. The government provides a small amount in Child Benefit (to all families) and Income Support (to those on low incomes) but these cover only a small part of the total cost of bringing up a child. Parents will also have to support most children beyond the age of 17 (for example while they are at college or university) so the total costs are even higher. So it is now very expensive to have children.

HINTS AND TIPS

The Joseph Rowntree Foundation carries out research on many aspects of family life. Visit their website at www.jrf.org.uk.

Why then – since they could be so much better off without – do people still have children? One reason for having children has always been the desire to have an heir. This has applied more to fathers than mothers, and they have wanted boys rather than girls. The wealthier a man was, the more important this was. In the sixteenth century King Henry VIII had six wives in quick succession in an increasingly desperate attempt to father a male heir to the throne.

Having children changes the status of both parents. The birth of a child is always seen as a cause for celebration, and a sign of hope for the future. A woman who becomes a mother is seen as having fulfilled her destiny and confirmed her status as a 'real' woman.

So far we have been assuming that having children is a matter of choice. There have always been forms of contraception, but for many married women in the past children arrived regularly and often (and each time with a risk of death in pregnancy and childbirth). The contraceptive pill, widely available since the 1970s, has changed this since it allows women to decide whether and when to have children.

QUESTIONS

1 Look again at the list of ways in which grandparents can help and are helped by their younger relatives.
(a) Which are the most important kinds of help grandparents can give?
(b) What kinds of help are they most likely to need themselves?

2 Name two countries where the population may fall because people are having fewer children.

3 How much is spent on a child in Britain on average by his or her seventeenth birthday, according to the Joseph Rowntree Foundation?

4 What does it mean to say that children are now an economic cost to their parents rather than an economic benefit?

5 How many reasons can you find above for people continuing to have children despite the cost and although they are less important as insurance for old age? Write a sentence on each. Can you think of any other possible reasons?

ROUND-UP

Many people's grandparents now live long enough for them to get to know them, and there is a developing role for grandparents in families. Children are now an economic cost to their parents, and people are choosing to have fewer children than in the past.

VOCABULARY

Pre-school children: children who are not yet old enough to go to school
Contraception: ways of avoiding getting pregnant, such as condoms and contraceptive pills
Insurance: protection against a risk

What is the future of the family?

KEY FOCUS   In this section you will be reminded of some trends associated with the family. You will learn about some recent developments that seem to make it possible for different types of family to exist in the future. Alternatively, the nuclear family may remain most people's choice of family.

60-year-old woman gives birth

Should we use our growing knowledge of science in ways that will change the family?

Some trends

Already in this chapter you have come across a lot of information and ideas about family life at the start of the new millennium:

- Fewer people live in nuclear families.
- There are more divorces and remarriages, creating reconstituted families.
- There are more lone-parent families, usually headed by a woman.
- Women are having fewer children, and having them later.
- More children are born to parents who are not married.

These changes – and others, such as the number of teenage pregnancies and the apparent increase in child abuse – have led some writers to suggest that the family is dying. Most of them think this is a bad thing, and that because the family will not be able to act as an effective agency of social control over young people there will be more crime and anti-social behaviour.

Remember though, that most people are still born into nuclear families and spend a great deal of their lives in a nuclear family. People who get divorced are not usually rejecting the whole idea of marriage, because most of them get married again; they are just rejecting one partner.

Medical advances

In recent years there have been new advances in medical science that have already begun to change the family. You will know about some of these; they have been covered in the media because they are new and sometimes exciting or shocking.

FIND OUT FOR YOURSELF

Watch out for the latest news stories along these lines. Cut out any articles you find in newspapers and bring them into class.

Beating the menopause

Middle-aged and even elderly men have always been able to father children. Now it is becoming possible for women in their 50s and 60s to have children. New drugs can halt the effects of the menopause. Alternatively, eggs taken from a young woman can be stored until she is ready to have children. Women may use these to start a family after a successful career, or to start a second family after a divorce and remarriage.

Surrogate mothers

A couple can have a baby with the help of a surrogate mother who bears the child for them. The egg can be from the surrogate mother, fertilised by the other woman's partner, or taken from the other woman and implanted in the surrogate mother's womb. It is also possible for eggs to be taken from an aborted foetus.

Choosing a baby

Improved testing means that couples will know very early in the development of a foetus what sex it is and what genetic characteristics it will have. They may have some choice over whether to continue the pregnancy, and perhaps over some of the baby's characteristics.

Other developments which are less related to scientific advances but should be mentioned here are as follows:

■ Same sex couples. More homosexual and lesbian couples live together in long-term relationships. It is likely that in the future more children will be brought up by such couples.
■ Teenage mothers. At the same time as it becomes possible for older women to have children more safely, there is concern about the number of teenage mothers. More girls under 16 become pregnant and have babies in Britain than in most other countries. Sometimes the fathers are also very young.

These developments raise a number of possibilities that were unthinkable even a few years ago:

■ A woman may have a baby who is younger than her grandchildren.
■ A mother may be as old or older then grandmothers today when she gives birth.
■ A mother may have a baby at the end of a long career.
■ A baby's mother may have died a long time before the birth.
■ Parents may be able to choose the sex and other characteristics of their baby.
■ A baby may have both a genetic mother from whose fertilised egg he or she developed, and a mother who gave birth to him or her.

None of this is inevitable, because people may not want to make these choices, or if they do they may be prevented by the cost or by new laws.

Will the family change beyond recognition? Two views

No

Many people may feel these developments are wrong, perhaps for religious reasons. The techniques may prove to be expensive or dangerous. The nuclear family remains popular today. It is possible there will be a reaction against the high divorce rates of recent years; perhaps more couples will stay together for life. Fear of Aids may lead to a return to monogamy.

Yes

Even if these developments are only taken up by a few people in the early stages, they are likely to become more common. People already control when they have babies through contraception, and many take advantage of screening of foetuses to find out if there are defects, with the possibility of an abortion if there are. So we can already choose to have some babies and not others.

QUESTIONS

1 What is meant by a surrogate mother?

2 People sometimes say the nuclear family is dying. Find two reasons for thinking this is not the case.

3 List three important changes in family life in recent years. For each change, suggest a reason why this has happened.

4 What effects could the changes you have written about in question 1 have on people's attitudes towards the nuclear family?

5 Should parents be able to choose their children's characteristics (such as eye and hair colour)? Explain your answer.

ROUND-UP

The British family has changed throughout history. At the start of the millennium, the nuclear family is still the most popular kind of family although fewer people live in one then ever before. Recent medical advances and social changes mean that the family may well change in dramatic and perhaps unexpected ways.

VOCABULARY

Surrogate: a substitute; a surrogate mother carries another woman's baby in her womb
Menopause: the 'change of life', when women stop having monthly periods, usually between the ages of 45 and 50

Families – sociology in practice

Extracts from the Christian marriage service

'THE priest says:
Marriage is given that husband and wife may comfort and help each other, living faithfully together in need and plenty, in sorrow and in joy. It is given that with delight and tenderness they may know each other in love, and through the joy of their bodily union may strengthen the union of their hearts and lives. It is given that they may have children, and be blessed in caring for them and bringing them up in accordance with God's will, to his praise and glory.

Groom, and then bride, say:
I, ….., take you, …..
To be my wife/husband

To have and to hold
From this day forward,
For better, for worse,
For richer, for poorer,
In sickness and in health,
To love and to cherish,
Till death us do part,
According to God's holy law;
And this is my solemn vow.'

Questions

1 Can you find connections between what is said in the Christian marriage service and the view of the functions of the family put forward by functionalists like Parsons (see the Conventional nuclear family on pages 138–9).

2 In another, older, version of the service, the bride promises to obey her husband (but the husband does not promise to obey his wife). How does this support the feminist view of the family?

3 Look back at the box How to save marriage in the section on Cohabitation and the decline of marriage (pages 142–3). How would you rewrite the marriage service in order to make it more relevant to today and to attract more people to the idea of getting married?

Domestic violence: break the chain

'IF you are being physically or sexually assaulted by someone you live with, or are being threatened by them, that is domestic violence. Domestic violence is controlling behaviour and includes all kinds of physical, sexual and emotional abuse within all kinds of intimate relationships. It harms women and men. It wrecks thousands of lives.
Domestic violence is rarely a one-off event. Physical and sexual abuse tends to increase in frequency and severity over time, sometimes only ending when one person actually kills the other. Other forms of abusive or controlling behaviour may be ongoing. This chain of events needs to be broken.
A lot of people can help to break the chain ... But individuals also have an important part to play. For people experiencing violence, the support of a trusted friend can be invaluable. Breaking the chain is a job for everyone.
Domestic violence is much more common than most people realise. Even if you are not experiencing it yourself, you may well know someone who is … We must not let domestic violence beat us. Together we can break the chain.'

'Domestic violence: break the chain', Home Office, 1999.

Questions

1 What is domestic violence? Does it have to involve violence in the sense of someone being physically hurt?

2 The extract says that domestic violence is more common than most people realise. Why don't we realise how much there is? (Look back at the section on The Dark side of the family (pages 140–41)).

3 Why is domestic violence 'rarely a one-off event'?

China's one-child policy

When China became a communist country in 1949, its population was 500 million. The leader, Mao Zedong, encouraged Chinese people to have lots of children. His idea was that if there was a nuclear war China would be more able to survive if it had a bigger population. He saw every new child as a worker of the future, helping to make China a great country. Despite famines and disasters, the Chinese population did grow – so much that it was later seen as a problem.

The Chinese government was so worried in the 1970s by the 'population explosion' that it introduced a series of measures to try to stop people having so many children. The best known policy was to allow only one child per family. There were heavy fines for those who had a second child. There were posters everywhere. Some women were forced to have abortions. Many couples particularly wanted a male child, to be the heir. If the first-born child was a girl this was not possible. It is believed that many girl children were given away for adoption, or sold, or even allowed to die. The couple could then have a second child.

The policy was not enforced as strongly in the countryside as in cities. Many couples were allowed to pay a fine and have a second child, or even a third. The average number of children came down from six per family to two per family. The policy created some big problems:

- There is an imbalance in the population – more boys than girls.
- Because education was better in the cities, and most children were in the countryside, China was producing fewer educated people.
- A single child may one day have to support four grandparents.

The policy has now been relaxed and China is trying to hold down population growth by encouragement rather than force.

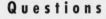
Questions

1 Look back at the section on Different kinds of families for information about extended families (pages 134–5), and the section on The family in history (pages 148–9). The Chinese policy made families smaller.
(a) Why would many couples still want more than one child even if they faced fines and other punishments?
(b) Why was it so important to have a boy child?

2 The Chinese policy is now widely seen as a mistake. Why do you think this is?

3 In what ways could a country with a population explosion try to reduce its population without being as heavy-handed as the Chinese were?

Families – important terms

bigamy	having two marriage partners at the same time; a criminal offence
blended family	see reconstituted family
breadwinner	the traditional man's role of providing for his wife and children
cohabitation	a man and woman living together without being married
cohort	all the people born at about the same time, for example your year group at school
commune	a large group of people living together; an alternative to the family
conjugal roles	the expected behaviour of husbands and wives
division of labour	how the work that has to be done is divided up, for example between husband and wife
divorce	the legal procedure by which a marriage is ended
domestic division of labour	how work in the home such as housework and childcare is divided up
empty nest	the situation of a married couple whose children have grown up and left home
empty shell marriage	when love between a married couple has ended and there is no real reason to stay married
extended family	a family consisting of more people than one or two parents and their children
generation	those who were born at approximately the same time
horizontal extended family	an extended family containing other relatives of the same generation
household	the people living in a house
househusband	a man whose main responsibility is housework and childcare rather than going out to work
housewife	a woman whose main responsibilities are looking after the home and children
joint conjugal roles	when husband and wife both work, do housework, etc.
life course	the different stages in our lives
lone-parent family (also single-parent family)	one parent bringing up children alone
matrifocal family	a family which is based on the mother
monogamy	a husband and wife without other partners
nuclear family	a family consisting of two parents and their children
polyandry	when a woman has more than one husband
polygamy	having more than one marriage partner
polygyny	when a man has more than one wife
primary socialisation	the most important period of socialisation, almost always taking place within the family
reconstituted family	a family which is formed when people who have been divorced remarry
remarriage	when someone marries again, having been divorced or widowed
separated conjugal roles	when a husband and wife have different roles within the family, for example the husband goes out to work while the wife is a housewife
serial monogamy	when over their lifetime individuals have several marriage partners, one at a time
singlehood	when an adult does not live with a partner
socialisation	the process by which we learn the norms, values and roles expected of us
stepparent	when the mother or father of children remarries after divorce or being widowed, the new partner is a stepparent (stepmother or stepfather) to the children
stereotype	a misleading and exaggerated idea about something, but usually with some basis
symmetrical family	when responsibilities and tasks within a marriage are shared equally between husband and wife
vertical extended family	an extended family containing more than two generations, for example grandparents, parents and children living together

Families – exam-style questions

Source A

Only about a quarter of all households in Britain now contain traditional nuclear families with dependent children. The number of lone-parent families, on the other hand, has been growing quickly. This, and the increase in other types of family, means that there is more diversity of family types.

Not all of the couples with children are married. More people are cohabiting.

Foundation tier

1. What is the meaning of the term nuclear family? [2 marks]

2. Using source A, identify one change that is taking place in families in Britain today. [3 marks]

3. What is meant by the term lone-parent family? Use an example to illustrate your answer. [4 marks]

4. Using sociological knowledge, give two reasons why more couples are cohabiting (living together without being married). [5 marks]

5. Do you agree that there is more diversity in types of family in Britain today? Give two sociological reasons to explain your views. [6 marks]

Higher tier

1. Using source A, identify one change that is taking place in families in Britain. [2 marks]

2. What is meant by the term lone-parent family? Use an example to illustrate your answer. [3 marks]

3. Using sociological knowledge, give two reasons why more couples are cohabiting (living together without being married). [5 marks]

4. Do you agree that there is more diversity in types of family in Britain today than in the past? Use a variety of sociological reasons to explain your views. [10 marks]

Families – further research

Summaries of research on families at the Family Policy Studies Centre: www.fpsc.org.uk.

The Joseph Rowntree Foundation: www.jrf.org.uk.

The views of the New Right in the USA: www.frc.org.

For an alternative, feminist view: www.feminist.com.

There are revision activities on families at Sociology Learning Support: www.chrisgardner.clara.net.

There is a section on families at the Sociology Arena site: www.hartland64.freeserve.co.uk.

8 Education

KEY TERMS

comprehensive schools
grammar schools
hidden curriculum
independent schools
labelling
school subcultures
secondary modern schools
setting
streaming
vocational education

Education is an area of social life that you cannot help being involved in; after all, reading this book is part of your education. Education does not always happen in schools and other institutions such as colleges, although in this chapter we will be concentrating on schools. Much of your life is part of your education; we never stop learning.

Britain's education system has an interesting history. It only gradually became open to everybody, and it has been through many changes. These changes are not yet over; even in the time you have been in school there have been important reforms. You need to be familiar with these.

Because you are in a school, there are many opportunities to find out about this topic. You can learn a lot from studying and thinking about your own school and about other schools you have been to. You can find out a lot from asking teachers, governors and others about schools and education. You should also use your parents and other family members as a resource; they will be able to tell you a lot about how education has changed.

IN THIS CHAPTER YOU WILL LEARN ABOUT:

- different stages of education and different types of schools
- how the British school system has developed including recent changes
- the roles of teachers, other education workers and students
- how different groups of students do in the school system
- alternatives to schools

CHAPTER CONTENTS

What is education for?

Why do we have schools? This section looks at some of the suggested explanations. Schools are part of secondary socialisation and they provide the skills and knowledge people need for the world of work.

Preparing for the world of work?

Informal and formal education

Education in its broadest sense happens all the time for everyone. The development of skills, knowledge and values through socialisation does not only happen at school; it is part of everyday life. In traditional societies, children are educated through being with and learning from their parents and other adults. This is informal education.

In modern industrial societies we have special institutions, called schools and colleges, to provide formal education. There used to be a clear divide in most children's lives. They were at home with their mother until they started school at the age of 5. This has changed; children now often receive some 'pre-school' learning at nurseries and playgroups.

This chapter concentrates on what happens in schools and colleges. This will include some consideration of informal education, because through the **'hidden curriculum'** (explained in the section What happens in schools) this takes place in schools alongside formal education.

Why do we have schools?

Education, at least informal education through socialisation, is necessary for the survival of a society. But why do we need to have schools? There are several possible answers.

Skills for work

Schools and colleges teach the things that people need to know in order to work:

- literacy (reading and writing)
- numeracy
- computer skills.

Children also learn how to behave in ways that will be necessary in the ways of work, such as taking orders and being punctual.

Selecting people for jobs

Schools are a way of sorting out which people should be able to get which jobs. Those who do well in tests and get good qualifications are seen as more suited for occupations that are highly paid and have high status. For some jobs, you have to get a particular qualification.

Secondary socialisation

Schools act as agents of secondary socialisation, not only through what is taught but also in the ways children learn. For example, children learn to get on with other children from different backgrounds and with different abilities.

Schools can help create a feeling of belonging to a society. In some countries this is done more openly and more often than in Britain, for example singing the national anthem and having the national flag in every classroom.

'Keeping them off the streets'

Perhaps one of the functions of schools is simply to keep children in one place for most of the day. Schools act as childminders – they make it possible for parents to go out to work knowing that their children are safe and looked after.

Summerhill: an example of a 'free' school

IMAGINE A SCHOOL …

… where children only attend the lessons that interest them.

… where climbing trees and building dens are considered as important as decimal fractions.

… with small informal classes, allowing every child to progress at their own rate.

… where living away from home is a positive, enriching experience.

… where children learn lessons for life; self-confidence, tolerance and consideration for others.

… where the whole school deals democratically with issues such as bullying and racism, with each individual having an equal right to be heard.

… where creativity is not stifled by pressure and self-expression is not curtailed by conformity.

… which produces young people who, having lived life fully as children, go on to be contented, self-assured adults.

Imagine such a school!

A.S. NEILL'S

SUMMERHILL

GIVING CHILDREN BACK THEIR CHILDHOOD

A negative view

Functionalists have suggested the purposes of schools above. These sociologists stress the role of schools in creating societies in which everyone agrees on the basic values and in which everyone accepts their place.

Marxists, who see society as based on conflict between classes, put forward an alternative interpretation of the same purposes. They would say that the way the school system works is that working-class children get the qualifications and skills that will lead them into low paid, low status occupations, while children from the higher classes will get the qualifications needed for higher occupations. From this point of view, schools do not provide equal opportunities. Some students start the race ahead of others, for example those whose parents can afford to send them to independent schools (see the section on Independent schools on pages 186–7).

Marxists say that students are taught in schools to accept the values of the ruling capitalist class. They are taught to accept hard work, conformity to rules and obedience to authority – and that they will be punished if they do not behave as they are told. All of this is preparation for the world of work and for later life.

Can we do without schools?

Many people believe, wrongly, that going to school is compulsory. In fact, it is education that is compulsory. This education can be at home by parents or by tutors appointed by parents. It is thought that about 5000 children are taught at home; this is called 'home-based education'.

There is also a 'deschooling' movement, based on the writings in the 1970s of Ivan Illich. Illich argued that by forcing students to learn things they didn't want to know in places they'd rather not be in, schools were not educating them. Education could take place much more effectively outside schools, in the community, where people could learn what they wanted to and what was appropriate to their situation – throughout their lives, not just before adulthood.

FIND OUT FOR YOURSELF

Find out more about Summerhill by referring to an encyclopaedia. Look under Summerhill or under the name of its founder, A. S. Neill. You will also find more about Summerhill in the sociology in practice section at the end of this chapter.

QUESTIONS

1. What is meant by the term home-based education?
2. What is the difference between informal and formal education?
3. Identify three purposes of schools, according to the positive view taken by functionalists.
4. How would Marxists see these same three purposes?
5. Do you think school should be compulsory? Give reasons for your answer.

ROUND-UP

Both formal and informal education takes place in schools. Schools prepare students for the world of work, and the qualifications students get decide the kind of job they will be able to get. Functionalists see this as necessary and desirable, while Marxists see it as exploitation of the working class. The school system is questioned by the supporters of home-based education, deschooling and free schools.

VOCABULARY

Institution: an organisation, or a building where an organisation is situated
Compulsory: the law says you have to do it
Interpretation: a way of making sense of something, an explanation

British education before 1988

KEY FOCUS

To understand British education today, it is helpful to know about how the education system developed, from education for the few to education for all, the different kinds of schools and the thinking behind them.

British education has come a long way in a hundred years.

There have been schools in Britain for hundreds of years, but until the nineteenth century there was no nationally organised system of education. This meant that there were schools in some places, but not others, and that there were different kinds of schools:

- **Primary** – charity and church schools provided very basic education for some of the children of the poor, while for those who could afford it there were **private schools** which charged parents.
- **Secondary** – **public schools** (not for the public, despite the name, but for the well off) and some **grammar schools**.
- Higher – the only universities in England were Oxford and Cambridge. Scotland at this time had more publicly funded schools and five universities.

In the nineteenth century demands for more and better education grew. The government gradually began to provide money to build new schools, and to pay to keep them running. A lot of today's primary schools were built towards the end of the nineteenth century. By the end of the century the state provided free, compulsory education for all children up to the age of 12.

The nineteenth century education system was based on class; each class received a different type of education:

- Working class – elementary education only; it was thought dangerous to allow them to learn too much. Elementary schools stressed obedience, punctuality and hard work and taught reading, writing and arithmetic.

- Middle class – grammar schools tried to provide a similar education to public schools but had a lower status and were not usually boarding schools.
- Upper class – public schools, which taught boys how to be gentlemen and to be the future leaders of society. They were usually boarding schools and charged fees.

The twentieth century

The age at which children could leave school gradually went up, and more subjects were taught. Systems for inspecting schools and checking standards gradually developed. During World War II (1939–45) there was a lot of discussion about how to build a better society after the war. It was felt that Britain needed an education system that would allow all children to develop their talents fully. The 1944 Butler Act reorganised education into three stages and created a new national system of secondary education with three types of school.

The three stages

- Primary – up to age 11. Subdivided into nursery, infant and junior stages.
- Secondary – from 11 to 15 (raised to 16 in 1973).
- Further/higher – non-compulsory education beyond the school leaving age.

The three types of secondary school

- Grammar – for about the top 20 per cent by ability, the 'bright' children. Studying classics, maths, science and other 'difficult' subjects for GCE O level exams.
- **Technical** – for children suited to technical subjects, emphasising training for jobs; for about 5 per cent of children.
- **Secondary modern** – for the majority – a basic education with, from the 1960s, opportunities to take lower level exams called CSEs (a top grade CSE was equivalent to the lowest pass grade GCE O level).

Independent, fee paying schools existed alongside these three types of state school, for children from families who could afford to pay.

Selection

The three types of secondary school were intended to give everyone a good education, but it was assumed that there were different types of children who needed different types of education. In practice, grammar schools were, not surprisingly, seen as better than the other types.

In order to get a place in a grammar school, children took the eleven plus intelligence test (see pages 176–7). At the age of 11, children either passed and went to a grammar school, or failed and went to a secondary modern. Going to a secondary modern, which was seen as an inferior type of school, could affect children's self-esteem. They might think they were not clever, and so not try hard. For **'late developers'** – children who failed the eleven plus, but then did well – it was difficult to move schools and to get entered for exams.

In practice, grammar schools turned out to be for the middle class, and secondary moderns for the working class. An unequal start in life was made worse by unequal education.

◄ FIND OUT FOR YOURSELF

Ask an older relative about his or her experiences of the grammar/secondary modern system. Ask whether he or she took the eleven plus exam, and if so what he or she thought about it. If your relative was educated under a different system, perhaps even in another country, find out about this. Present your findings to your class.

Comprehensive schools

Comprehensive schools are based on the idea of one type of school for everyone; that everyone living in the area served by a school (its **'catchment area'**) will go to the school, whatever their ability or background, and without an entrance exam. In 1965 the Labour government began to encourage local authorities to make their secondary schools comprehensive. By the end of the 1970s about 80 per cent of secondary school pupils were in comprehensive schools.

Did comprehensives succeed?

The move from the old selective system to comprehensives was very controversial, and some local authorities have kept the old grammar and secondary modern system. In a sense, comprehensives never could be really comprehensive, because a small number of pupils living in the catchment area would go to independent schools. Where grammar schools still exist, they often 'cream' the brightest pupils from neighbouring comprehensives.

It was hoped that comprehensives would enable children from all social classes to succeed. In fact, as before, middle-class children did better than working-class children. Part of the reason for this was that schools continued to use **streaming**

and **setting**, and that middle-class pupils tended to be in the higher sets and streams (see pages 172–3). It was also hoped that children would mix with children from all sorts of backgrounds, so breaking down barriers between the classes. In fact, many comprehensives had catchment areas dominated by one class of people, so there was not as much mixing as hoped.

One concern about comprehensives has been whether bright children do as well in them as in grammar schools. This is difficult to measure – you cannot know how someone would have done in a different school. Research tends to show that bright children do just as well in comprehensives as in grammars, while those of lower ability do slightly better in comprehensives than they would in secondary moderns.

QUESTIONS

1. What are the three stages of education?

2. What three types of secondary school were created by the 1944 Education Act?

3. Identify two criticisms that were made of the selective system of grammar, technical and secondary modern schools. How were comprehensives intended to improve on this system?

4. Identify two ways in which comprehensive schools could not be fully comprehensive.

5. Do you think that comprehensive schools were better than the previous grammar and secondary modern school system? Give reasons for your answer.

ROUND-UP

Education for all is a relatively new idea; it is only since the end of World War II that everyone has gone to secondary school. The selective system of grammar, technical and secondary modern schools was gradually replaced by the comprehensive system.

VOCABULARY

Local authorities: councils, such as city councils and county councils. Councillors are elected by people living in the area

Punctuality: being on time, for example for lessons

Elementary: simple, basic

1988 and after

The Education Reform Act of 1988 brought in by Margaret Thatcher's Conservative government introduced several very important changes in British education. This section also looks at several other developments since 1988.

	Pupils aged 15	GCSE/GNVQ Results			
	Total	5+ A*–C	5+ A*–G	No passes	Average point score
St Augustine of Canterbury RC	150	33%	90%	6%	33.5
Iffley Mead School	19	0%	0%	63%	0.4
Oxford School	146	34%	84%	10%	30.2
Peers School	185	35%	77%	11%	29.6

Performance Tables 2000.

Performance tables – making schools compete, and making some winners and some losers.

The reforms described below did not apply to independent schools, to which many middle- and upper-class parents send their children.

The National Curriculum

The 1988 Act divided compulsory schooling into four Key Stages:

■ Key Stage 1: ages 5–7 – reception and years 1 and 2.
■ Key Stage 2: ages 8–11 – years 3, 4, 5 and 6.
■ Key Stage 3: ages 12–14 – years 7, 8 and 9.
■ Key Stage 4: ages 15–16 – years 10 and 11.

The **National Curriculum** introduced in 1989 was made up of three core subjects – English, mathematics and science – and seven foundation subjects. This was later felt to be too restrictive, and the curriculum was changed. Schools now have some lesson time to use as they choose. For Key Stage 4 now only the three core subjects, physical education, short courses in technology and a modern foreign language, religious education and sex education are compulsory. This means some schools even have room for subjects like sociology!

There are tests at the end of the first three Key Stages in the core subjects, and GCSEs are taken at the end of Key Stage 4.

The main aim of the National Curriculum is to ensure that all students take the most important subjects. For example, when there was a choice, science was always chosen more by boys than girls, but now everyone has to study it to GCSE level. Most countries have a national curriculum; Britain was unusual in deciding to have one so late. The British National Curriculum was also imposed from above rather than, as in other countries, being agreed upon by government and schools, and sets out in more detail what must be taught, when and how.

Some teachers did not like the changes. For example, English teachers used to be able to choose which books their classes read, now the choice is only a very narrow one. Teachers may feel that they are no longer allowed to judge what is best for their classes.

Local management of schools

Before the Act, **local education authorities** (**LEAs**) played a big part in running schools. The Act gave schools greater control, allowing schools to make more decisions about staffing and how to spend their budgets. This weakened the role of LEAs.

New types of school

Schools were allowed to **'opt out'** of local authority control completely, receiving grants directly from the government. These **grant maintained schools** were allowed to select their students through entry exams. Many people saw this as the government's way of bringing back grammar schools without actually saying so.

City technology colleges (**CTCs**) were a new kind of school specialising in technical and scientific education. They were an attempt to make education more suited to the needs of the economy. They received generous grants from the government.

Training for jobs was also strengthened through a number of changes including the introduction of General National Vocational Qualifications (GNVQs). These changes are sometimes called the 'new vocationalism' and are considered in a separate section, Vocational education (see pages 184–5).

Competition and choice

These are the two themes that run through many of the changes in 1988 and after. The government wanted to make schools compete against each other, and it wanted to give parents more choice, not just between schools but between different types of school. To help parents choose, schools must:

- publish prospectuses
- publish GCSE and National Curriculum test results; these are published as **league tables**
- be inspected regularly, with the report being published.

FIND OUT FOR YOURSELF

- Find and read your own school's prospectus. Do you think it gives an accurate picture of the school?
- Find out when your school was last inspected, and what was said about it.

League tables have been very controversial. Critics of them say that they are misleading unless the kind of students at each school is taken into account. Schools with a largely middle-class catchment area will probably do better than those with a largely working-class catchment area.

However, the tables have been widely taken as proving how good or bad a school is. Middle-class parents rush to try to get their children into a school that does well in the tables, while other schools get a bad reputation and find it hard to keep up their student numbers. This is important because schools are funded according to the number of students they have – more students, more money. If the critics of league tables are right, some of these supposedly 'failing' schools are actually doing very well.

FIND OUT FOR YOURSELF

Ask your parents or other people of their generation whether they think education in schools is better than when they were at school. Ask them what changes they like and what changes they don't like.

1997 and after

The new Labour government elected in 1997 saw education as a priority. However, many of its policies were similar to the Conservative policies. There have been some changes: Labour

is less keen on selection, and schools cannot now 'opt out' (although those that did do not have to change back).

The following changes, however, are probably here to stay:

- the National Curriculum (although its content may be revised)
- the principle of competition, and pressure to meet higher standards, as measured by testing at each Key Stage and publication of league tables
- the principle of parents selecting schools – the Labour government has even created new types of school through allowing schools to specialise in certain subjects
- while many schools remain comprehensive in name, the principle behind comprehensives has been buried beneath the newer values of competition and choice.

QUESTIONS

1. Since when has there been a National Curriculum?

2. What are the three core subjects of the National Curriculum?

3. Why do you think these subjects were chosen? Are there any other subjects you think should be core subjects? Give a reason.

4. Why are league tables controversial?

5. Using your answer to 4, discuss whether league tables are likely to improve education or not.

ROUND-UP

Schools have undergone many far-reaching changes since 1988. The guiding principles of the changes have been competition between schools, and parental choice.

VOCABULARY

Vocational: related to jobs and work
Compulsory: no choice
Budget: a plan of how money will come in and how it will be spent

What happens in schools?

This section looks at several sociological ideas which describe what goes on in schools. We will use these ideas later when we look at why different groups achieve at different levels.

Who is on which table, and why?

The hidden curriculum

Formal education in schools takes place through the official curriculum of time-tabled lessons in particular subjects. Informal education takes place outside particular subjects and lessons, as a general part of school life; this is called the hidden curriculum. Students may not realise that they are learning through the hidden curriculum.

Some of what is learned through the hidden curriculum:

■ Competition. Like wider society, schools encourage students to compete against each other, in teams or as individuals – in sports and exams.

■ Obeying rules and authority. Students learn to accept even the rules they don't agree with, and to accept punishment for breaking them as fair.

■ Hierarchy. Through the example of the school, students learn that people are on different levels. At the top of the school is the head teacher, then there are senior teachers and heads of department, then classroom teachers and finally, at the bottom, students.

■ Different roles and expectations for boys and girls.

■ Boredom. Students often feel that quite a lot of what they

do in school is pointless or boring. They have to learn to accept this.

Streaming and setting

Schools have different ways of putting students into classes:

■ Streaming is when students are with the same class in all subjects on the basis of their general ability. This means that there will be top and bottom streams, and streams in between. Moving between streams is not common. This assumes that students can be divided into those who are 'bright', who are 'less able' and so on – and assumes that those who are bright, for example, are bright in all subjects.

■ Setting is when students are in different classes in different subjects on the basis of their ability. So, for example, a student might be in a top set for mathematics, but in a lower set, with different classmates, for English. Unlike streaming, this recognises that students achieve different levels in different subjects.

■ **Mixed ability** classes are when students are put in classes on the basis of factors other than ability.

Streaming and setting are becoming more common, especially in Key Stage 4. This is because GCSEs have tiers. It makes sense to teach students who are going to be entered for the higher tier in a different class from those who are going to be entered for the lower tier.

Labelling

Applying labels to people is an inevitable part of life; when we meet people, we often make assumptions about the kind of people they are on the basis of little information. In schools (and elsewhere) **labelling** can have important consequences.

Teachers label students as 'bright' or 'lazy' or as a 'troublemaker', for example. Once labelled, it can be very hard to shake off the label. When something happens, the 'troublemaker' will be the first suspect. There is a tendency for the label to become a **self-fulfilling prophecy**, that is, the student will act in the way that he or she has been labelled – the 'bright' student will gain confidence, the 'troublemaker' will get into trouble and so on.

In secondary schools, students have many different teachers and so it is quite possible for teachers to have different impressions of the same student and to apply different labels. **Peer groups** are very important for teenagers, so the labels applied by peers may be just as important as those applied by teachers. For the teacher, 'bright' is a positive label, but other students may see the same behaviour differently and label the student as a 'swot' or 'licker'. Equally, the 'troublemaker' may be popular and respected among his or her peers.

Students label teachers too, usually on the basis of strictness or approachability, how strongly the teacher enforces rules, what punishments they give and how often and how hard students are made to work.

Labels can be negotiated. This means that the individuals labelled can try to change how others think of them. The 'troublemaker' may decide to stay out of trouble, the strict teacher to relax more as he or she gets to know the class. In fact, a lot of what goes on in classrooms is negotiated. Although teachers are in formal control, students have many ways of influencing what happens. Most teachers and classes, rather than being in confrontation, achieve what Hargreaves called a 'working consensus'. Teachers offer incentives – 'If you work quietly I'll let you off homework' – while students appeal to fairness – 'You let your other class go early' or 'Our other teacher lets us do that'.

Subcultures

A group of students who develop a clear set of norms and values can be referred to as a **school subculture**. Usually subcultures are based on opposition to the school – they are about breaking the rules and not working hard.

An anti-school subculture was found by Paul Willis in his study of 'the lads' (their names for themselves) in a Midlands secondary school. These working-class boys knew they would

work in local factories, and that they did not need qualifications for this. They had to stay at school until old enough to leave, so they passed the time 'having a laugh', at the expense of teachers. There was at least one group with very different values in the school as well – the 'ear'oles' – so called because they always listened to teachers. These were the boys who worked hard and kept the rules.

◀ⒸⓌ FIND OUT FOR YOURSELF

Work in a small group. Does your school or college have streaming, setting or mixed ability classes (it may be different for different subjects)? If you're not sure, ask a senior teacher. Then think about how this affects teaching and learning in your school or college? Would you rather have a different system for any of your subjects? Why? Your group should then present its findings and views to the class.

QUESTIONS

① What is meant by a subculture?

② What is meant by the hidden curriculum?

③ Identify and explain three things that children learn through the hidden curriculum.

④ Give two labels that might be given to a student by teachers, and for each say what behaviour might lead to those labels being given.

⑤ Look back at the information on Summerhill, the free school, in the section on What is education for? (see pages 166–7). What is the hidden curriculum at Summerhill?

ROUND-UP

Some of the features of school life identified by sociologists are the hidden curriculum, the importance of how students are grouped into classes, labelling, self-fulfilling prophecies and negotiation, and the existence of student subcultures.

VOCABULARY

Hierarchy: people or things arranged at different levels
Consensus: when everyone agrees
Tier: a layer or level; there are different tiers for GCSE exams

Teachers, teaching and schools

KEY FOCUS This section looks at some of the people, other than students, involved in education, and the part they play in education: teachers, head teachers, governors and others.

What is the reality of teaching today?

can be taken together, in the Bachelor of Education (BEd) courses which last four years, or one after the other, by taking a three- or four-year degree followed by a postgraduate certificate of education (PGCE). Training as a teacher involves some study at a university or college, and time spent in schools. In schools student teachers observe at first and then teach. The time they spend in schools is known as teaching practice. You may well have had lessons taught by 'students' or 'interns'.

Schools are hierarchies; that is, there are people at different levels or rankings. The head teacher is at the top; below him or her are one or more deputy heads; then, depending on the size and type of school, probably heads of department or heads of year; then classroom teachers without other responsibilities. There are also other people employed in or by the school.

The majority of teachers are women, but most head teachers and senior teachers are men. There are more female heads in primary schools than in secondary schools. Head teachers are paid according to the size of the school, and most primary schools are much smaller than secondary schools, so the people earning the most money tend to be men.

In terms of social class, teaching is definitely a middle-class occupation. It has, however, lost status over the last hundred years or so; that is, teachers are no longer held in such respect. Teachers are also less well paid relative to other occupations than they were in the past. Many people who work as teachers could, because they have degrees, work for more money in other occupations. They choose teaching because they believe in the importance of education and in making a contribution to society.

Teachers

There are about 400 000 full-time teachers in Britain. It is difficult to get an exact figure because as well as full-time teachers, many work part time and there are also supply teachers who go into schools to cover for teachers who are absent. There are also teachers working outside schools. The numbers are very nearly the same for primary and secondary teaching.

To qualify as a teacher, it is necessary to have a degree and a teaching qualification. You have to have A levels before you can start these courses. The degree and teaching qualification

Teaching styles

Teachers have different styles of teaching. Sometimes these are related to the subject, sometimes to requirements made of teachers, but sometimes also there is some choice. The styles can be thought of as two extremes, with many possibilities in between.

One extreme is the teacher who teaches from the front of the classroom to the whole class, with everyone sitting in rows and working on their own on the same tasks which the teacher has set. This is usually thought of as 'traditional education'.

At the other extreme, pupils can decide to some extent what they work on and how, with groups of students working at different speeds on different projects. The teacher moves around and helps. The students may sit in groups around tables, not always facing the front. This is a more 'progressive' teaching style.

In recent years governments have tried to push for more 'traditional' teaching. They have seen this as more likely to lead to most students working hard to acquire skills and knowledge. Critics say that students who are taught like this become passive – they are being 'spoon-fed', not learning to think for themselves. The pressure of exams and tests, and the publication of league tables of school performances, is making it harder for teachers to justify 'progressive' styles of teaching.

The school as a community

So far we have considered the teaching staff of a school. There are many others who make up the community of the school – including, of course, the students.

Other staff often employed in schools:

- administration staff such as secretaries and receptionists
- site staff such as caretakers and cleaners
- kitchen staff
- assistants to teachers, such as those supporting students with learning difficulties
- librarians
- technical assistants, in science laboratories.

The school's community also extends outside the school itself. Parents will be invited to the school several times a year for events such as parents' evenings, and there will be a parent-teacher association to discuss school matters and raise money. Local businesses and organisations such as churches and charities often also have close links to schools.

Governors

One important group has been left out so far – the governors. Head teachers are in control of the day-to-day running of schools, but governors take the important decisions. The governing body of a school is responsible for:

- the school's aims
- how the school's budget is spent
- appointing (and dismissing) staff
- the curriculum (what is taught) and collective worship
- pupil behaviour and discipline.

Governing bodies of schools must include representatives of the local authority, of parents and of teachers. Depending on the size of the school, there are usually between nine and 19 governors. Governors all have other work and commitments; being a governor takes up only a small part of their time and they are not paid for it.

FIND OUT FOR YOURSELF

As a class, invite one of your school governors to come and talk to you about what he or she does. Prepare a list of questions to ask before the governor comes.

QUESTIONS

1   (a) Who is responsible for the day-to-day running of a school?
    (b) Who is responsible for a school's aims and policies?

2   What qualifications are needed to become a teacher?

3   What is meant by a hierarchy? In what ways are schools hierarchies?

4   Identify and explain two reasons why there is a growing shortage of teachers.

5   Look back at the explanations of traditional and progressive teaching styles. Which do you think is better, and why?

ROUND-UP

Schools are often at the centre of a community, involving many people in many different ways. Governors, who are volunteers, and head teachers take the most important decisions. Most people employed in schools are teachers.

VOCABULARY

Occupation: job
Passive: not taking an active part
Collective worship: in a school, when in an assembly or other gathering pupils say prayers or practise their religion in some other way

Measuring intelligence and ability

KEY FOCUS

A part of education you cannot avoid is assessment – through tests and exams, your ability and progress are measured. But what exactly is being measured – and are exams the best way of doing this?

Years of schooling – all over in a couple of hours?

Example of an intelligence test: in what ways might different students (for example, from different cultural backgrounds) find these questions easier or more difficult?

> 1 Underline the odd one out:
>   house   igloo   bungalow   office   hut
> 2 Insert the word missing from the brackets:
>   fee (tip) end
>   dance (…) sphere

- Intelligence is seen as something fixed and unchanging. In fact, many believe it is affected by social conditions – so it can be increased.

- The content of IQ tests has been said to be based on what white middle-class people are likely to know. It is not surprising that black and working-class people do not do as well.

- The results seem to depend on where the test takes place, how confident the student feels and so on.

- We are not sure what 'intelligence' means anyway. It is not the same thing as having a very good memory. Perhaps IQ tests measure not intelligence, but how good people are at IQ tests.

The eleven plus exam

As you have learned, in order to get into a grammar school, students had to pass the eleven plus exam. Today, the eleven plus still exists in some areas while other **selective schools** often set their own exams.

The eleven plus was based on intelligence testing. Intelligence tests produce a score known as the intelligence quotient (**IQ**), which relates the student's mental ability to his or her age. The idea that there were different types of students with different levels of intelligence (as measured by IQ scores) lay behind the creation of grammar, technical and secondary modern schools by the 1944 Education Act.

The eleven plus exam resulted in grammar schools being full of middle-class students and secondary modern schools full of working-class ones. To some, this proved that intelligence ran in families – successful parents were more likely to have bright children. To others, it suggested that the tests were being used as a way of condemning many children to failure. Girls did better than boys in eleven plus exams, so much so that to keep the numbers in grammar schools equal boys had to be allowed in with lower scores than girls.

IQ tests, and the ideas behind them, have been very controversial:

Assessment in schools

It must be said first of all that there is much more assessment than a few years ago. Pupils now take national standardised (everyone takes the same test) tests at the end of each Key Stage, as well as the assessments teachers have always made by setting and marking work and tests. Schools and parents (and students themselves) can now compare how students are doing against national expectations at that age. This is part of the growth of competition in schools.

The main form of assessment is exams (the tests at the end of each stage are a kind of exam). Alternative methods of assessment include continuous assessment, where the student is assessed on assignments set regularly throughout a course and coursework projects, which at GCSE and A level are often options with a small number of marks available. At university level, continuous assessment, usually with a final exam as well, is common, and at postgraduate level exams are rare –

doctorates are awarded for an extended project called a thesis or dissertation.

Examinations

Many people dread exams. After months or years of study, everything depends on a few hours in a room full of other worried people. In the room with you will be people who couldn't sleep the night before, people with colds or hay fever (exams are usually at the peak of the hay fever season), and people who are terrified by exams. If the questions are about things you didn't revise (however thoroughly you revised everything else), or if you answer the wrong number of questions by mistake, then failure looms. Why do we have exams?

Exams are thought by many to be the best way of assessing what has been learned. This assumes that what has been learned can easily be assessed by an exam (practical exams in science, music and so on are necessary because of this). Although many exams try to test skills, such as the ability to evaluate different arguments, the nature of exams is that they mainly test how much you remember. Perhaps those with good memories have an advantage.

Coursework

When the National Curriculum was first introduced, there was no final exam in some subjects at GCSE, such as English. At the end of the course students were assessed on a folder containing their best work.

There has been a move away from coursework and continuous assessment and towards exams at the end of courses. While you will be doing coursework projects in several of your GCSE subjects (including, probably, sociology), these account for only a small percentage of the marks (usually 20–30 per cent). The majority of marks are for the final exams.

The advantages of coursework are as follows:

■ It allows students to work on a project which to some extent they have chosen.
■ Because it is chosen, students should feel committed to the project and this will help them reach a high standard.
■ The project can be worked on over a long period.
■ The project may involve skills which cannot be examined but are important.

▶ FIND OUT FOR YOURSELF

Make a list of all your GCSE subjects. For each one, find out how many of the final marks are for coursework (ask your teachers if you don't know). Present the results as a bar chart. Which subject has the most marks, and which the least? Would you prefer to have more or less coursework? Why?

However, despite these advantages, limits are set on the amount of marks available for coursework. There are several reasons for this:

■ There is a possibility of cheating – a project may not be the student's own work. There is also the grey area of how much help a teacher or parent is allowed to give.
■ Coursework is harder to mark and grade than many exams, because in exams answers can be compared to other answers more easily. Many coursework projects are unique.
■ Above all, there is a feeling that coursework is an easy option. Those of you struggling with coursework may well not agree!

QUESTIONS

1 What does IQ stand for?

2 Identify two criticisms of continuous assessment (coursework) as a way of assessing students.

3 Identify and explain three reasons why IQ tests have been controversial.

4 At the end of Key Stage 3 (Year 9) you will have taken standardised tests in some subjects (SATs). Do you think these tests allowed you to show what you could do in those subjects?

5 Write a paragraph for or against the statement, 'Exams are a fairer test of students' abilities than continuous assessment'.

ROUND-UP

Intelligence testing is controversial, not least because of differences of opinion about what they actually measure. Assessment throughout schooling is based on examinations; alternative methods such as coursework are out of favour at the moment.

VOCABULARY

Standardised: the same for everyone
Continuous assessment: when a student's work throughout a course counts towards the final grade or mark
Doctorate: the highest level of degree; available in many subjects, not just medicine

Class and education

Research has consistently shown that children from working-class backgrounds do not on average do as well in school as those from middle-class backgrounds. They are also less likely to go on to further and higher education. Why is this?

Does class background make a difference?

Working-class underachievement

Working-class pupils do not do as well on average as middle-class pupils. Some of the arguments about underachievement by working-class pupils go back to the 1970s and earlier. When most working-class pupils went to secondary modern schools, the underachievement was linked to this type of school. This is no longer the case. Moreover, state education is free, so the fact that working-class families are less well off should not make a difference.

The explanations for underachievement by working-class students can be divided into two groups: those that emphasise home environment, and those that look at what happens within schools.

Home environment

Although schooling is in theory free, parents are asked to pay for quite a lot – uniforms, sports kit, materials for art and design and so on. Middle-class parents are more likely to be able to afford extras – a place on an optional school trip, extra books for exam courses, even a tutor to give extra help if a student is finding a subject difficult. For children from working-class families struggling to get by, there may not even

be a proper breakfast, which will make it difficult to concentrate in class.

Living conditions at home may help middle-class students to study. They are more likely to have a quiet place to do homework, for example. Crowded, unhealthy living conditions not only stop children studying but are likely to lead to more absence through illness.

Middle-class parents are also more likely to be able to provide what has been called **'cultural capital'**. For example, there may be:

- more books in the home
- educational toys
- a computer to use
- visits to museums and art galleries
- other people in the family who have done well in education.

This may be a matter of money, but it can also reflect differences in values. Middle-class children are more likely to have been socialised into ideas about how it is important to do well, and how it is worth studying hard to get a good job in the future (this is known as deferred gratification). This is important at age 16, when those who go to work will have more money to spend than those who stay on – but will be worse off years later.

Working-class children may even find the way they speak holds up their achievement. Success in school requires being able to speak and write in what is seen as 'correct' English; middle-class children are likely to find this easier because they have come across it more often.

Working-class parents may be less confident than middle-class parents in attending parents' evenings, asking for information and help from the school and so on. They are also less likely to take full advantage of the choice of different schools.

Schools: labelling – low expectations

Teachers inevitably label students and it has been suggested that working-class students are more likely to get negative labels. Schools are by their nature middle class – teachers are middle class because of their profession – so working-class students do not fit in as easily. If their behaviour is seen as bad, they are likely to be labelled not only as badly behaved but also as not bright. Equally, well-behaved children are thought of as bright – and are usually middle class.

Teachers' expectations can have a real effect on how students achieve. This is called a self-fulfilling prophecy. Students who have been told they are not good at a subject are more likely to stop trying than to set out to prove the teacher wrong. Teachers give more time and attention to those students who they think will do better as a result.

Streaming and setting

Streaming in particular is linked to social class. Middle-class students are more likely to be in higher streams, working-class students in lower streams. Those in bottom streams, knowing they are seen as failures, are likely to have little confidence or interest in school work.

Subcultures

Anti-school subcultures like 'the lads' as described by Paul Willis (see page 173) are likely to be made up of working-class students. In reaction to a school that seems not to value them, and to make it difficult for them to succeed, working-class students can reject school and its values. They win prestige in the eyes of their peers by misbehaving, truanting and being seen to do very little work.

Individual schools

The nature of a school can make a big difference. Many head teachers and teachers are well aware of the kinds of problems discussed here, and try to change the atmosphere and organisation of the school in ways that will help give working-class students an equal chance. Some of the characteristics of schools that manage high achievement compared to schools with similar intakes are:

- strong leadership (the head teacher)
- dedicated, well-prepared teachers
- emphasis on academic achievement
- students encouraged and praised rather than continually criticised.

Higher education

In spite of these disadvantages, many students from working-class backgrounds are successful and go on to study in **higher education**. The big expansion in numbers created more places for the working class. However, going into higher education has become much more expensive because of the freezing of the grant at a low level and the charging of fees in England. Students can get special loans but many working-class students miss out on the financial support that middle-class parents can provide.

(see page 173)

QUESTIONS

1 What is meant by cultural capital?

2 What is meant by a self-fulfilling prophecy? Explain by using an example.

3 Identify three characteristics of schools which help working-class pupils achieve well.

4 Make a table with two columns. On one side list the home environment factors, on the other school factors.

5 Are home factors or school factors more important in deciding how students do at school? Write a paragraph considering both sets of factors.

FIND OUT FOR YOURSELF

What extra payments have you or your parents had to make to your education in the past year? Ask your parents – there may be some you have forgotten or don't know about. For which ones was there some choice? Would some parents be less able to make these payments than others?

ROUND-UP

The spread of comprehensive schools did not end the difference in achievement between students from different class backgrounds. A range of factors involving home environment and the school that may prevent working-class children doing as well as middle-class children have been identified.

VOCABULARY

Loans: when someone borrows money but has to repay it later

Underachievement: not doing as well as expected

Prestige: being looked up to

Gender and education

KEY FOCUS Both boys and girls are doing better at school than was the case a few years ago, but girls have improved much more rapidly than boys. Girls do better at GCSE, are overtaking boys at 16–19 and catching up fast at degree level. The gap has led to government concern about why boys underachieve.

Pupils achieving GCSE grades A*–C by selected subject and gender

| | Percentages | | | | | |
| | Males | | | Females | | |
	1988/89	1992/93	1995/96	1988/89	1992/93	1995/96
English	38	44	43	53	61	61
Any science	35	41	45	33	41	46
Mathematics	36	39	42	32	40	43
Any modern lauguage	19	24	28	30	37	43
French	17	20	20	27	31	32
History	16	17	17	18	22	22
Geography	21	22	24	18	20	23

Social Trends Pocketbook 1999.

Do both boys and girls do better if they don't learn together?

....

QUESTIONS

Look at the table above.

1 In which subject in 1995–96 did girls most outperform boys and by how much?

2 In which subjects did boys do better than girls in 1988–89? In which of these did they still do better in 1995–96?

Boys and girls

Girls

In the 1970s and 1980s there was a great deal of concern, among feminists in particular, about the education girls received. Girls took different subjects, and got jobs that were lower paid and had lower status. Girls found it difficult to get the same opportunities as boys. For example, there was systematic discrimination to ensure as many boys as girls went to grammar schools.

Feminists tended to attribute this discrimination to the ideas men held about girls:

- that girls do not need a good education, because they will be mothers and housewives
- that too much education will spoil their feminine nature
- that women have lower intelligence than men.

These ideas suited men because they provided reasons for keeping the best education and the best jobs for males only. Research showed that:

- girls got less attention from teachers than boys
- teachers did not expect girls to do as well as boys
- teachers did not think careers were as important for girls
- many older textbooks and teaching materials are sexist; for example, when older science books showed pupils doing experiments, it was always boys.

The rise in girls' achievement in the last few years can be contributed to the following:

- Awareness of gender issues in schools – schools and teachers being much more aware of these issues, and trying to treat boys and girls the same to ensure equal opportunities.
- Changes in employment and expectations of employment – girls and their parents having much higher expectations, aiming for qualifications and careers. This is a big change from a few years ago when most girls thought of their future in terms of getting married young and having children. Many girls do, however, as they used to, go into routine clerical or shop work combined with domestic work.

Boys

In the past few years the concern has been with boys underachieving rather than with girls. In fact, boys today are doing better than a few years ago, but their performance has not risen as quickly as that of girls.

The biggest factor involved is probably changes in employment. There are fewer traditional men's jobs (in manufacturing, engineering and so on) than there used to be, and more jobs in service industries, which have been seen as women's jobs. Although there are new opportunities for boys, in computing and technology, for example, it has been said that boys face a far more uncertain future than boys like Paul Willis's 'lads' did in the past. Boys worry about their futures (though they may not like to talk about it) while girls are far more confident.

Other factors which have been suggested:

- A 'laddish anti-learning culture' – boys do not work as hard because they will be criticised by other boys.
- For boys' lower levels of literacy (reading and writing) – mothers read more to their children and are seen reading for pleasure themselves, so boys associate reading with females.
- There is a shortage of male teachers at primary level to act as role models.

There are also related differences in attitudes to school and work:

- Girls work more consistently; boys are more easily distracted from their work.
- Girls can work steadily at long projects like coursework; boys find it harder to be organised.
- Girls are willing to spend more time doing homework, not rushing it.

Subject choice

The subjects that boys and girls were taught a hundred years ago were very different. Girls spent a lot of their school time on practical work that was seen as related to their future role as housewives, such as needlework. Exams were considered inappropriate for girls at one time.

From the 1970s onwards, the division between girls doing sewing and cookery while boys did woodwork and metalwork began to break down. When there was a choice, though, boys and girls still tended to do different subjects. Girls, for example, were less likely to do sciences. The National Curriculum changed this, ensuring that all students, girls and boys, took the core and foundation subjects. There is now very little choice before the end of Key Stage 4.

At A level and beyond, boys and girls do still make different choices. Boys tend to do sciences, girls arts and social science subjects. These choices are important, because they decide what careers people are likely to follow. It seems that girls are less likely than boys to choose courses that will lead into the highest paid, highest status careers.

Single- and mixed-sex schools and classes

There are still many single-sex schools. In the past, even in mixed schools, boys and girls were kept apart a lot: there were separate entrances, separate playgrounds and boys and girls sat on different sides of the classroom. Most comprehensives today, however, mix girls and boys as much as possible.

Girls only schools have been thought to raise girls' level of achievement. Girls' progress is not held up by boys' disruptive behaviour or demands on teachers' time. Boys cannot dominate the use of equipment, for example in laboratory experiments in science.

It has also been suggested that boys do better without girls. Boys often say girls distract them, and some of their disruptive behaviour may be showing off intended to impress girls.

Some mixed schools have experimented with single-sex classes.

QUESTIONS

1. What is meant by the term single-sex school?

2. What is meant by discrimination?

3. Identify two reasons that have been put forward to explain why girls began to do better than boys in the 1990s.

4. Identify three reasons put forward to explain why boys no longer do as well as girls. Which if any of these could schools or teachers take action about?

5. Would you like to be taught in a single-sex class for some subjects? Give reasons for your answer.

W C FIND OUT FOR YOURSELF

Do you think coursework (rather than exams at the end of a course) helps girls more than boys? In a small group, design and carry out a short questionnaire asking which method of assessment students prefer; do girls say they prefer coursework? Also ask teachers their opinion.

ROUND-UP

There has been a complete turnaround in thinking about gender in schools, from concern about discrimination against girls to concern about boys underachieving. There are still clear differences in the subjects boys and girls choose, although up to age 16 there is now only limited choice.

VOCABULARY

Discrimination: when someone is not treated fairly, for example because of his or her sex or race
Truculent: always arguing, not cooperative

Ethnic groups and education

KEY FOCUS Some minority groups achieve well above national averages, some below. The explanations lie in a combination of home and cultural and school factors.

Battle won as Sikh school joins state sector

Britain's first state-funded Sikh school will be officially opened this week marking the successful end of a two-year local campaign.

The Guru Nanak Sikh primary and secondary school in Hayes in the west London borough of Hillingdon ... is the first of the Sikh religion to have obtained approval to enter the maintained sector, allowing them state funding and voluntary aided status similar to Roman Catholic and Anglican church schools.

Adapted from 'Battle won as Sikh school joins state sector' by Rebecca Smithers, *Guardian* Weekly, 2 December 1999.

Encouraging diversity – the way to end underachievement?

Ethnicity and educational attainment

Examination results by ethnicity, England and Wales, 1994

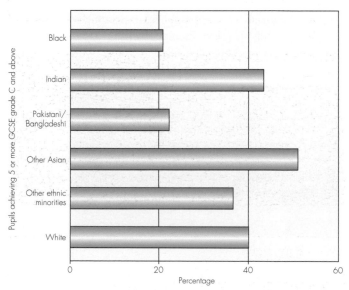

Social Focus on Ethnic Minorities edited by J. Church and C. Summerfield, Office for National Statistics, 1996.

The chart shows that educational attainment by ethnic group is not straightforward. Some minorities do better than both the national average and than white students (these figures are very close, since whites are the vast majority of the population). Others, notably Pakistani, Bangladeshi and black students do significantly worse. Within the black category, there is a huge difference between Africans, who do even better than Indians, and Afro-Caribbeans. There are also significant differences between boys and girls that are not shown here. The 'other ethnic minorities' category includes many different groups. All this makes it difficult to make statements that apply to all minority ethnic groups.

As with class, explanations of the relationship between ethnicity and educational attainment can be divided between those that look at the home and background, and those that look at school factors.

Home, background and culture

The minorities who do least well – Bangladeshi, Pakistani and Afro-Caribbean – have the highest proportions of students from working-class backgrounds. All of the factors you studied under class may play a part in the underachievement of these minorities. In other words, their lack of success may be much more about class than about ethnicity.

Just as working-class children may find it hard to adapt to the kind of English required in schools, language can be a factor for students from minority ethnic groups. British Asian children are likely to be bilingual. Afro-Caribbean children may at home speak a Creole language which teachers may see as 'bad' English. Language problems may lead to a lack of confidence.

Encouragement by parents can be important. There is evidence that many parents from minority ethnic groups place a very high value on education and on hard work. This has been said to be important in the success of British Indian children. Afro-Caribbean parents have established special Saturday schools to boost their children's education. The problem then becomes explaining why this does not lead to higher achievement.

Schools

Some schools in working-class areas of cities have high numbers of minority ethnic students. Where these schools are short of resources or of good teachers, the type of school may well play a part in underachievement. In other words, it may be that minority ethnic group students are more likely to be in schools where many students fail (or rather, are failed by the school).

Labelling

Some teachers may have stereotyped views of different ethnic groups. Afro-Caribbeans, boys in particular, may be thought of as loud and disruptive, while Asians are more likely to be seen as capable and hard working – and perhaps be ignored because it is felt they do not need help. As noted before, labels can be resisted but can also lead to a self-fulfilling prophecy.

Ethnocentrism

Ethnocentrism refers to the way that what is taught in lessons may seem irrelevant to minority ethnic students. Text books may rarely show members of ethnic minorities, History for example, may seem to be all about Britain and Europe – and ignore the role of other cultures and peoples. There have been attempts to counter this by introducing multicultural education. For example, an English lesson may include poetry from the Caribbean or a story from India, and children now often learn about religions other than Christianity.

Racism

Ethnic minority students do sometimes encounter racism from teachers and other students. Most schools recognise this as very serious and deal with it quickly. Some racism, though, is unintentional and harder to tackle. For example, it has been argued that when teachers put students in sets and streams, they are influenced by behaviour as well as ability. So an Afro-Caribbean boy who would be able to succeed in a top set may be put in a lower set if it is thought his behaviour will affect those in the top set.

Teachers

There are very low numbers of teachers from minority ethnic groups. This may influence students to feel school is a very 'white' experience (even if a lot of pupils are not white), and it also means there is a lack of successful, well-educated role models in the school.

Exclusions

There is particular concern that very high numbers of Afro-Caribbean boys are excluded from schools; **Ofsted**, the school inspection office, says the figure is six times the average for all students. Most exclusions are not for violent behaviour or bullying, but for refusing to obey school rules, verbal abuse or insolence – in other words, their attitude ('Crisis over black pupils' exclusion' by Donald MacLeod, *Guardian*, 11 October 1996).

QUESTIONS

1. Name three minority ethnic groups.
2. What is meant by ethnocentrism?
3. What reasons can you think of for the lack of teachers from minority ethnic groups?
4. Identify and explain three factors within schools which could contribute to lack of achievement by Afro-Caribbean students.
5. Why do you think Sikh parents established the Guru Nanak school? What do they hope it will achieve for their children?

ROUND-UP

Although it is clear that members of some minority ethnic groups underachieve, the picture is far from clear, especially when class and gender are also taken into account. There is racism in British schools, but some children achieve very highly despite this, often with strong support from parents and community.

VOCABULARY

Bilingual: able to speak two languages fluently
Exclusion: not being allowed to attend school as a punishment
Attainment: the level that people reach, for example how well they do in a school subject

Vocational education

This section looks at the relationship between education and the world of work. There has been an increasing emphasis in education on training people for work and providing them with the skills they will need.

Preparing for the world of work.

What is vocational education?

Vocational education is the teaching of skills that are directly related to particular occupations or types of occupations. There has in the past been a big difference between vocational education and academic education, which has had far less connection to the world of work. This difference is becoming blurred.

Vocational education in schools today

Some connections between schools and the world of work today include the following:

■ Many students have the chance to do work experience – spending a week or longer at a place of work and doing some work (without being paid). They may also follow one person around, learning what his or her job involves; this is called work shadowing.

■ Schools offer advice and ideas about occupations. Students can talk to careers advisers and use the resources in a careers library to find out about what different occupations are suitable for someone with their interests and qualifications.

■ The content and skills taught in some lessons are relevant to preparing for work.

■ In some schools there are vocational courses available. General National Vocational Qualifications (GNVQs) are available at foundation, intermediate and advanced levels. They give training in areas of work such as health and social care, and travel and tourism.

■ Key skills, which are discussed further below, are intended to provide students with skills necessary for work and also to help them continue learning throughout their lives.

■ It has also been said that the hidden curriculum in schools prepares students for work. For example, they have to arrive at a certain time, and have to learn to do as they are told by those in authority.

Vocational education beyond schools

Education does not end when you leave school and start work. Many places of work offer their workers opportunities for education. Someone might go to college for one day a week (day release) or take courses provided by the company itself. One qualification available is the NVQ (National Vocational Qualification) which is specific to a particular job.

Educational institutions such as colleges of **further education** offer vocational courses such as GNVQs. Many professions require people to obtain extra qualifications.

Changing times

Before the Industrial Revolution, many jobs were passed from father to son. For example, the son of a blacksmith would learn the skills of the trade from his father. Sometimes craftsmen took on apprentices to train.

During the Industrial Revolution, many people left traditional crafts and went to work in new factories in towns and cities. Many of the new jobs required few skills, so any training was done on the job.

Recently, the world of work has changed and there are fewer unskilled jobs. It has become necessary for people to have more skills and training. There has been a growing emphasis on vocational education. The main reason for this has been the government's concern about the economy. British industry has to compete with other countries' industries in the global market. To make sure British industry is successful, it is argued, we need a highly trained and adaptable workforce.

Some of the changes that have resulted from this concern include the following:

- Subjects changed their names and style to match new employment needs. Until the 1960s, vocational education meant woodwork and metalwork for boys and needlework and cooking for girls. Children in higher streams often did not take these because it was assumed they needed a more academic education. The differences in who took what subjects show old attitudes about gender and class. Then woodwork and metalwork lessons became (with other content) design and technology. Cooking and needlework became domestic science, home economics and then textiles and food technology.

- The introduction of new qualifications such as GNVQs. The government hoped that GNVQs would be one way of ending the old divide between academic and vocational education. They offer an alternative route to jobs and higher education for older students. An advanced GNVQ is equivalent to A levels; this makes it clear that vocational education is seen as just as good as academic education. However, most people who get what they need to to do A levels choose A levels rather than GNVQs. GNVQs are awarded mainly through continuous assessment.

- The introduction of the teaching of key skills across all subjects. The three main key skills are: communication; application of number; information technology (IT). There are also three other key skills: working with others; improving own learning and performance; problem solving.

For and against GNVQs

For:
- GNVQs provide a non-academic alternative for students.
- They encourage more students to stay on and get qualifications.

Against:
- Are they really as demanding and the same standard as A levels?
- A lot of people do not complete them; continuous assessment is very stressful.

Information and communications technology

The arrival of computers and information and communications technology (ICT) has changed the nature of work, and therefore the nature of the vocational education needed. Because many jobs now involve using ICT, both government and schools see it as a priority to have lots of computers in schools. ICT has now become one of the key skills.

The development of the Internet is bringing in further changes in how people work and the skills they need. Communicating and exchanging information across national frontiers and cultures has become easy. It is not clear yet what this will lead to. However, it is fairly certain that as the world of work changes, vocational education will change as well.

FIND OUT FOR YOURSELF

Find the address or telephone number of a further education college near to you. Ask for a prospectus and details of courses. Make a list of vocational courses, listing the type of job and the qualification offered.

QUESTIONS

1. What does GNVQ stand for?

2. Give two examples of areas of work which can be studied for GNVQs.

3. Why has vocational education been seen as increasingly important in recent years?

4. Identify and explain three ways in which vocational education has changed in recent years.

5. Why do many people still see A levels as better than advanced vocational qualifications such as GNVQs?

ROUND-UP

In the past vocational education and academic education were seen as separate. Recent changes in the world of work have led to an increasing emphasis on vocational education.

VOCABULARY

Information and communications technology: the use of computers and microelectronics to produce, store and communicate information
Specific: relating to a particular thing

Independent schools

KEY FOCUS   Many parents choose to send their children to schools outside the state sector, for which they have to pay fees. They do this because they believe their children will receive a better education, but this can be seen as the well off buying an unfair advantage.

Eton College – a top boys' public school for those who can afford it.

What are independent schools?

Independent schools are those that are not part of the state sector; they are not funded by the government and instead raise money mainly through the fees they charge.

There are two types of independent school. Despite their names (they sound like opposites!) they are very similar:

- Public schools – the older and more famous independent schools such as Eton, Harrow and Westminster. Schools that belong to the Headmasters' Conference (HMC) are public schools. There are about 230 of these.
- Private schools – all other fee-charging schools.

There are independent schools that are boys only, girls only and mixed. The public schools are mostly boys only, but some such as Eton now admit some girls. There are equivalent top schools for girls such as Roedean. There is roughly the same number of girls in independent schools as boys. Other independent schools are for particular ethnic or religious groups.

Some independent schools are boarding schools or have boarders as well as 'day pupils'. Independent schools for primary school-aged children are called preparatory (prep) schools.

There are about 2000 independent schools. In 1995–96 there were 603 000 students in independent schools, of which 268 000 were aged 10 and under and 335 000 were aged 11 and over. This is about 7 per cent of all school-aged children.

The independence of independent schools means that they are not subject to most of the restrictions placed on schools in the state sector. For example, they do not have to teach the National Curriculum, nor do their teachers have to have qualifications to teach.

The high fees that independent schools charge mean that they are only available to the children of the better off. Eton charges about £12 500 a year.

This means that the education system has two tiers – independent schools for those who can afford them, and state schools for everyone else. Many public school pupils go on to leading universities (about 50 per cent of students at Oxford and Cambridge universities are from public schools) and on to highly paid and often powerful positions. Public schools in particular play a big part in allowing parents to pass on their privileges to their children.

For independent schools

Why some parents choose independent schools:
- They have a lower teacher-pupil ratio than state schools; in 1995–96 there was one teacher for every ten pupils, compared to one for every 19 in the state sector.
- Independent schools are thought to have an academic culture that fosters learning. Parents feel that their children are less likely to be influenced by the anti-school subcultures that are often found in state schools. Parents believe discipline is stricter. Exam pass rates and university entrance rates are usually high.
- Resources and facilities are often much better than state schools can afford.
- Boarding schools are seen as helping children learn to be independent of their parents. Staff and students both have to be fully involved in school life.

Against independent schools

Why some parents prefer state schools:

- Independent schools are seen as unfair because they allow a minority to buy an advantage. State schools are free, and are not based on the ability of parents to pay.
- State schools usually have a wide mix of students, so children learn to get on with others. Independent schools are seen as elitist, only for students from a particular background.
- State schools are usually close to where students live, and are part of a local community. For independent schools, students may have to travel a long way or even abroad, and so see their parents less often.

Among the wealthy and powerful people who can send their children to independent schools are politicians. So ministers in a government responsible for running state schools can and sometimes do decide to send their children to independent schools – which would seem to indicate that they do not think they are making a good job of running state schools!

When the Labour government of the 1960s introduced comprehensive education, it was recognised that schools could not be truly comprehensive if the wealthy were able to send their children to different schools. Independent schools were seen as divisive, unfair and out of place in a modern society. A government report recommended that half of all places in independent schools be given to students from state schools, who would not pay fees, but this was never done.

The idea of parental choice has now become one of the central ideas in education. Any attempt to get rid of or reduce the number of independent schools would be seen as interfering with parental choice, and so is now very unlikely.

In fact, parents who buy independent schooling for their children are paying twice, since the taxes that they pay fund state-sector education.

Assisted places

In the 1980s the Conservative government introduced a scheme to pay for a limited number of able children whose parents could not afford the fees to attend independent schools. This was highly controversial, as it seemed to be an admission that state schools (which the government was responsible for) were not good enough for the most able children. The government saw the scheme was more effective in helping bright children achieve than investing in the state sector would be.

The effect of the assisted places scheme was to take out of comprehensive schools and put into independent schools some of the most able children. So, as with grammar schools in some areas, comprehensive schools had some of their brightest pupils creamed off.

The assisted places scheme was ended in 1998.

FIND OUT FOR YOURSELF

Find the names and addresses of some independent schools by looking in the relevant jobs section of the *Times Educational Supplement* (*TES*). Your teacher will probably be able to get a copy of the *TES* for you. Then write to ask for a prospectus. Compare the prospectuses you receive with your own school's prospectus.

QUESTIONS

1. (a) About how many independent schools are there?
   (b) What percentage of children goes to independent schools?
2. Name three independent schools.
3. What is the assisted places scheme? Why was it introduced?
4. Identify and explain two reasons why some parents send their children to independent schools.
5. What have been the effects of the continued existence of independent schools on comprehensive schools?

ROUND-UP

A significant number of British students still attend independent, fee-paying schools. To their critics, they help to maintain an unfair system; to their supporters they offer greater parental choice and the quality of education the state sector too often fails to provide.

VOCABULARY

Boarding schools: schools at which the students (called boarders) stay overnight, only going home at holidays and perhaps weekends

Elitist: only designed for a small number of people; seen as special

Divisive: creating divisions and conflicts between different groups

Education after 16

Students are allowed to finish their schooling at the end of Key Stage 4. However, many stay on, and even among those who leave many return to education, one way or another later. At ages 16–19 students take A levels or vocational qualifications; beyond that there are degrees and diplomas.

Students in higher education, Britain, 1961–95

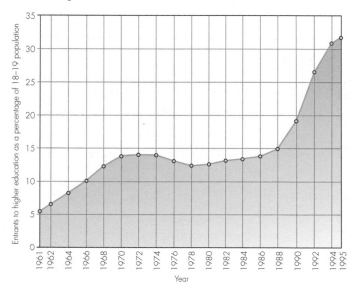

National Committee of Inquiry into Higher Education, 1997.

> **Whatever the choice you make, education continues after you leave school.**

The choice at 16

After Key Stage 4 (the GCSE years) about two-thirds of students stay on at their school or go to a sixth form or further education college to take A levels or vocational qualifications. This is a much higher proportion than in the past. A number of factors are involved, including:

■ the lack of attractive jobs
■ the abolition of social security payments to school leavers
■ as more people have qualifications, it becomes essential to have qualifications to compete.

AS and A levels

The A stands for Advanced, the AS for Advanced Subsidiary. An AS is half of an A level (three modules instead of six) and is often taken at the end of year 12. Normally, to study AS and A

levels students need to have done reasonably well at GCSE, getting five passes at grade C and above. Some subjects are taught at A level which are not normally taught at GCSE, for example psychology, economics and philosophy.

GNVQ

General National Vocational Qualifications (GNVQ) prepare students for areas of work, such as health or the media, but not for particular jobs. They can be studied at different levels: foundation, intermediate and advanced. Advanced GNVQs are equivalent to A levels.

NVQs

Those young people who go into work at 16 will also receive training and opportunities for education. These include National Vocational Qualifications (NVQs), which are focused more on specific jobs than GNVQS, and are also available at different levels.

Universities and higher education

The first universities in England were Oxford and Cambridge – and for centuries they were the only ones. New universities were built around the turn of the century, especially in the industrial cities. However, England had fewer universities and fewer people attending them than other countries. University education was only for the privileged few.

In the 1960s there were new universities and the start of a big growth in student numbers. This was seen as necessary to ensure Britain had highly trained people who could help the economy be successful. Also in the 1960s a new kind of college called a polytechnic was opened. Polytechnics offered mainly vocational courses. Although they were supposed to be equal to universities, they were widely seen as inferior so Britain had a two-tier higher education system: universities and polytechnics. Since 1991 polytechnics have been allowed to call themselves universities, and both they and the old universities now offer similar courses.

Universities offer a very wide range of courses. Most courses lead, at the end of three or four years of full-time study, to the award of a degree. The most common degrees are the Bachelor of Arts (BA) and Bachelor of Science (BSc). The sexist assumption that only men (bachelors are men) get degrees tells us something about the history of higher education! Universities also offer further qualifications after a degree, such as master's degrees and doctorates, and training for professions, such as the Postgraduate Certificate of Education (PGCE) for those wanting to be teachers.

There was a big rise in the number of higher education students after 1988 (see graph).

The government was keen to increase numbers but provided little extra money. This has had the following results:

- The number of students per lecturer has risen.
- Universities have tried to find new income, for example by sponsorship, more foreign students (who pay higher fees).
- The numbers of staff have been reduced, and there are now more temporary and part-time staff.
- Fewer repairs are made to buildings and equipment.
- There is less money for library and other resources.

This has made things harder for both students and staff. Students also get a grant worth less than in the past, so most work part time, or take out a loan, or both. It is likely that some potential students now decide not to go to university because of the cost. They are likely to be from less well-off backgrounds. The principle that everyone who has the ability should be able to go to university has been undermined.

Universities have also begun to be subject to the same kinds of controls as schools. For example, teaching and research are inspected and graded, and league tables are published.

Adult education

'School' and 'education' are seen as mainly for young people. In fact, millions of adults are involved in learning. Some study full time, returning to education after working. Others take a vast range of courses, from degrees to those that do not lead to any qualifications, in a wide variety of settings – schools, universities, adult education centres and so on. They do this for many reasons, from advancing their careers to pursuing an interest. As well as this formal education, many adults are of course also learning informally, through small local groups, through the media, using libraries and so on.

For adults who cannot get to a place of education, such as a school or university, there are growing opportunities for distance learning, where the student studies at home. The Open University pioneered this style of learning and many other universities and institutions now offer distance learning courses, some by Internet and e-mail.

▶ FIND OUT FOR YOURSELF

Find out about the distance learning courses offered by the Open University by visiting its web site at www.open.ac.uk.

Because of new technology and changes in the economy, many people need to acquire new skills to advance in their careers, or to move into new careers. The government is committed to creating opportunities for adults to continue learning throughout their lives – lifelong learning.

FIND OUT FOR YOURSELF

Your school's careers library will probably have some university and college prospectuses. Look through some of these to see what courses are offered and what qualifications students can get. If these prospectuses are not available in school, you can write directly to the colleges and universities.

QUESTIONS

1. What is meant by the term adult education?

2. What was meant by the two-tier (or binary) system of higher education? When did it end?

3. What kinds of courses can students who stay in education after GCSEs choose to do?

4. Identify two results of the reduced government funding of universities.

5. Why do you think the government is so keen on lifelong learning?

ROUND-UP

At age 16, most students who stay in full-time education take A levels or GNVQs; those who start work receive job-based training. The higher education sector has grown rapidly in recent years but the funding has not matched the rate of expansion.

VOCABULARY

Degree: a qualification awarded by universities and other higher education institutions

Grant: a sum of money given, not needing to be repaid (a loan has to be repaid)

Distance learning: when a student does not attend a school or college, receiving the course materials by post or Internet and studying at home

Education – sociology in practice

Extracts from *Summerhill* by A. S. Neill

'NO pupil is compelled to attend lessons. But if Jimmy comes to English on Monday and does not make an appearance again until Friday, the others quite rightly object that he is holding back the work, and they may throw him out for impeding progress.

Afternoons are completely free for everyone. What they all do in the afternoons I do not know ... Tea is served at four. At five, various activities begin. The juniors like to be read to. The middle group likes work in the Art Room – painting, linoleum cuts, leather work, basket making. There is usually a busy group in the pottery.'

'My view is that a child is innately wise and realistic. If left to himself without adult suggestion of any kind, he will develop so far as he is capable of developing.'

'... We set out to make a school in which we should allow children freedom to be themselves. In order to do this, we had to renounce all discipline, all direction, all suggestions, all moral training, all religious instruction. We have been called brave, but it did not require courage. All it required was what we had – a complete belief in the child as a good, not an evil, being.'

Questions

1. What beliefs led A. S. Neill to set up Summerhill?

2. What would Neill's opinion of tests and examinations be?

3. Summerhill is one example of a 'free' school, that is, free in giving children freedom. Do you think such schools can be successful in educating children? Give reasons for your answer.

Basic education for all

MORE than 130 million children of primary school age in developing countries are growing up without access to basic education, the United Nations organisation for children, UNICEF, warned yesterday.

It said it would cost an extra £4.2 billion a year to extend the benefits of elementary schooling to all children – less than the annual spending on cosmetics in the United States, or on ice cream in Europe, and only 10 per cent of the world's military budget.

Without the investment, increasing numbers of people will be ill-equipped to make decent lives for themselves in the twenty-first century, threatening not only their health, nutrition and child-raising abilities, but also damaging democracy, social progress and international peace.

Girls suffered disproportionately from lack of education, comprising about 70 per cent of the children denied basic primary schooling.

'Lack of schools blights hope' by John Carvel, *Guardian*, 9 December 1998.

ALL the evidence shows that taking girls out of the fields and homes, and putting them behind desks raises economic productivity, lowers infant and maternal mortality, reduces fertility rates and improves environmental management. Countries that have pursued gender equality over the past three or four decades have grown faster and become more equal societies.

'Educating girls is a real lifesaver' by Victoria Brittain and Larry Elliott, *Guardian Weekly*, 9 March 2000.

Questions

1. Why is it important that all the world's children receive at least primary school education?

2. Why is it particularly important that girls go to school?

3. Find out about education in developing countries and campaigns for more education by visiting these web sites: www.actionaid.org.uk and www.oxfam.org.uk. Gather information from these sites and design a poster that will explain the situation to younger students.

Who makes the top 13?

EACH year more than 1000 students from the poorer social classes, making up 50 per cent of the population, do not win a place at a top 13 university to which their grades entitle them ... according to the report by the Sutton Trust, an education charity.

The trust examined the intake of the students at what are, according to unofficial league tables, the top 13 universities in Britain ... Even when their grades are the same, public school students are still much more likely to win places at the 13.

Independent schools have 7 per cent of students. These students get a third of the top grades but even allowing for this they get more places than they should.

There is particular concern about Oxford and Cambridge universities. Oxford University takes nearly half of its students from independent schools.

In 2000, Oxford rejected an application to study medicine from Laura Spence, who was at a comprehensive school in Tyneside. Laura had 10 A* GCSEs. She won a £65 000 bursary to study at Harvard, a top university in the United States.

'End bias elite universities told' by Will Woodward and Lucy Ward, *Guardian Weekly*, 8 June 2000.

Questions

1. Look back at the section on Independent schools (pages 186–7). What advantages does the information above suggest that independent schools give to their pupils?

2. Look back at the section on Class and education (pages 178–9) and also at the increasing cost of university education for students (page 189). Write an essay explaining some of the problems facing bright children from poor backgrounds.

Education – important terms

catchment area	children living in a school's catchment area will normally go to that school unless they choose otherwise
CTC (city technology college)	a new type of school specialising in training for work and computers
comprehensive school	a school taking students of all abilities and backgrounds from a local area
cultural capital	interest and knowledge that can help you do well in education
curriculum	the time-tabled subjects at school
ethnocentrism	when the content of lessons and courses concentrates on one country or ethnic group
exclusion	when a student cannot attend school as a punishment; being expelled is permanent, being excluded is usually for a set time
further education	education from ages 16 to 19
grammar school	a school that selects its pupils by ability
grant maintained school	a school which has opted out of local authority control
hidden curriculum	what students learn in school apart from the content of lessons, for example being on time and doing what they are told
higher education	education for adults at an advanced level, for example at universities and colleges
independent school	a school that is outside the state sector
IQ (intelligence quotient)	a way of measuring intelligence; IQ tests were used in entrance exams for grammar schools
labelling	thinking of someone or something in terms of a label, for example when teachers label a student as 'bright'
late developers	students who do not learn much in school at first but then do much better
league tables	published statistics on each school's exam passes and other information
LEAs (local education authorities)	local bodies with responsibilities for running schools.
lifelong learning	people should continue to learn throughout their lives
LMS (local management of schools)	when schools have some of the powers LEAs used to have, for example control of their budgets
mixed ability	when students are put in classes at random or for other reasons than their ability
National Curriculum	the government's rules about what must be taught in schools
Ofsted	the body responsible for inspection of schools
opting out	schools that opt out of local authority control become grant maintained schools
peer group	people of your own age group
primary	the first stage of schooling, from ages 5 to 11, Key Stages 1 and 2
public school	one of the older independent schools, such as Eton
private school	an independent school
school subculture	a group of students with a set of norms and ways of behaving that mark them out as different from other students
secondary	the second stage of schooling, from ages 11 to 16, Key Stages 3 and 4
secondary modern school	a school taking students who did not pass the entrance test for grammar school
selective school	any school which chooses some or all students on their ability
self-fulfilling prophecy	when assumptions lead to that situation happening; for example, when students told by teachers they will fail, then do fail because they do not think it worth trying
setting	when students are in different classes in different subjects according to their ability
streaming	when students are with the same class in all their subjects, based on ability
technical school	a school emphasising training for jobs and technical subjects
vocational education	education related to the world of work and jobs

Education – exam-style questions

Source A

'THE hidden curriculum can be found in the way that a school is organised. Most schools are organised in a hierarchy of authority. There is not much doubt about who is in charge or about how decisions are made. The more the school hierarchy is taken for granted, the less likely it is that pupils will question it. Yet progressive schools such as Summerhill have always tried to involve pupils in taking decisions.'

Adapted from 'School secrets' by Pat McNeill, *New Statesman and Society*, 5 January 1990.

Foundation tier

1. Who is in charge of a school? [2 marks]

2. What is meant by the term hierarchy of authority? [3 marks]

3. Using an example, explain what is meant by the hidden curriculum. [4 marks]

4. State two ways in which 'progressive schools such as Summerhill' would be different from most other schools. [5 marks]

5. The hidden curriculum is a way in which schools try to control pupils. Can school subcultures resist this control? Give two reasons for your views. [6 marks]

Higher tier

1. What is meant by the term hierarchy of authority? [2 marks]

2. Using an example, explain what is meant by the hidden curriculum. [3 marks]

3. State two ways in which 'progressive schools such as Summerhill' would be different from most other schools. [5 marks]

4. The hidden curriculum is a way in which schools try to control pupils. Can school subcultures resist this control? Use a variety of reasons and examples to support your views. [10 marks]

Education – further research

A good site for statistics is the Curriculum, Evaluation and Management site at Durham University: http://cem.dur.ac.uk (this is not a world wide web site). You can follow a link here to the site of YELLIS, the Year 11 Information System – your school may be using its testing system to produce statistics.

On education in Britain: www.eng.umu.se/eduation.

The main government site for education is: www.dfee.gov.uk.

For the latest news, read the *Times Educational Supplement*, a weekly newspaper for teachers and others working in education at: www.tes.co.uk; and the *Guardian* newspaper's education system, published as a supplement to the newspaper on Tuesdays and at: www.guardianunlimited.co.uk/education.

There is a section on education at the Sociology Arena web site: www.hartland64.freeserve.co.uk.

9 Work

KEY TERMS

alienation
discrimination
industrial relations
Industrial Revolution
leisure
non-work
strikes
trade unions
unemployment
work

Work is a difficult term to define – and an inescapable fact of life. Most of this chapter is about jobs (or the lack of them), but it's important to see the word work in a wider way. You are working when you are doing school work, or helping with chores at home, as well as when you do a paper round. Work in this wider sense is different from leisure and from non-work.

You will almost certainly have some experience of work by the time you finish your school education, either through a work experience placement or a part-time job or both. This chapter will tell you more about the world of adult work, about industrial relations and about the problems faced by particular groups, such as women, young and old people and minority ethnic groups. You will find that the idea of 'going to work' is quite recent. In the Middle Ages and earlier, most people lived where they worked; perhaps we are returning to this situation, as more people work from home, using computers and telephones.

The future of work is uncertain, but you would do well to note some recent trends. It looks likely that the ability to learn new skills is going to be essential. The key skills you will have noticed in Chapter 8 on Education (under Find out for yourself) are the government's way of acknowledging that education now has to be about making sure people have the skills to carry on learning throughout their lives.

IN THIS CHAPTER YOU WILL LEARN ABOUT:

- the differences between work, leisure and non-work, and different kinds of work
- how the nature of work has changed and continues to change
- unemployment and its consequences for society, families and individuals
- the problems faced at work by particular groups, such as women and minority ethnic groups
- industrial relations, industrial conflict and trade unions

CHAPTER CONTENTS

Work and leisure: terminology

KEY FOCUS   We begin this chapter by thinking about the basic terms we use. The word work is used in a variety of ways. The rest of the chapter is mostly about paid employment, but it is important to realise that the term work covers other things as well, and that it is not always easy to separate work from leisure and non-work.

Work or leisure? Growing vegetables might be a hobby (trying to win a prize for the biggest marrow!) or a way to save or make money.

What is work?

Work is a word we use a lot, and you might think it would be straightforward to define it. As with other ideas you have encountered in sociology, however, work turns out to be a quite complicated idea.

One way of defining work is as paid employment. This fits what we mean when we ask, for example, what line of work someone is in, or when we talk about going out to work.

However, this definition does not fit all senses of the word work. You do school work and homework, but you are not paid for it. People do **housework**, but are not paid for it. These kinds of work are as difficult as much paid work but the rewards (if any!) are very different.

An alternative way of defining work is to say that it is what we do when we are not at leisure or relaxing. This way, housework and homework count as work; after all, we do call them work! Remember, though, that laws and regulations (such as those about how many hours a 15- or 16-year-old may work) are about paid work!

So playing sport is not working – unless you are being paid for it! The problem here is that many people's leisure activities are related to their paid work. A teacher may stop marking to watch a television programme, but be thinking about using the programme in a lesson. A businessperson might relax by reading the financial pages of a newspaper. Are these work or leisure? What is work for one person might be leisure for another, and vice versa. Taking photographs, for example, can be a leisure pursuit or a profession.

So:

- work is difficult to define
- it is difficult to decide whether unpaid 'work' such as housework is work
- people's leisure activities are not always separate from their paid work
- what is leisure for some is work for others, and vice versa.

Formal and informal economy

One way in which sociologists have tried to solve these difficulties is by distinguishing between the formal and the informal economy.

Formal economy

The **formal economy** is the world of official, paid work. It includes employees and the self-employed. Employees work for an employer, who pays them, probably weekly or monthly. Tax and National Insurance contributions are deducted from the pay before the employee gets it. Self-employed people receive payments from their customers, and have to pay tax and National Insurance out of this.

Occupations are usually thought of as being divided into non-manual and manual. Manual means using your hands (rather than your brain) but of course both non-manual and manual work usually involve using both physical and mental skills.

Non-manual work is referred to as white collar work, manual work as blue collar work.

Informal economy

The **informal economy** is work that is not officially recorded. It can be divided into three areas:

- The **hidden economy**. This is work done for someone else, usually paid for in cash, so avoiding tax. It is sometimes called the black economy. The person doing the work might be working in the formal economy and doing this work as an 'extra', or might be unemployed and claiming benefits at the same time as, for example, cleaning someone's house.

- The **domestic economy** includes:
  - housework
  - childcare
  - do it yourself
  - home repairs and maintenance
  - gardening

  and any other 'work' people do for themselves or their family without money being involved. It is work which people do for themselves but which they might have paid someone to do. For example, you could repair a broken window yourself (domestic economy), or you might call a company whose name you find in a directory like Yellow Pages (formal economy) or you might ask an acquaintance who you know is handy and offer to pay in cash (informal economy).

- **Communal economy** is unpaid voluntary work. Many people work without pay for a local group or a charity, or helping out friends and neighbours. Examples include running a scout or guide group or youth club, or raising money for charity, or doing odd jobs to help an elderly or disabled person.

All of the three areas of the informal economy are closely related and overlap with each other and with leisure. Gardening has been included above as part of the domestic economy, but you could argue that for many people it is purely **leisure**. Yet gardening is also full-time work for some people!

Leisure

As we have been discussing what work is, it has been impossible not to talk also about what leisure is. The two terms, work and leisure, go closely together.

Leisure isn't all of the time when we are not doing work. Leisure means doing something, as in 'leisure activities' or 'leisure pursuits'. Leisure involves some freedom and choice, more so than work. You might exercise, or read, or pursue a hobby. Some activities are much less active than others; do watching television and listening to music count as leisure?

Non-work

Work and leisure do not take up all of our time; there are other things that just have to be done. We have to eat, sleep, keep clean, travel to and from school or work and so on. The sociologist Stanley Parker suggested that these activities could be called **non-work**. Sometimes non-work is hard to separate from work and leisure. Is walking the dog non-work or housework?

So our time can be divided up into work, non-work and leisure. Work takes up less time for most people than you might think. Most people who work full time (and many work part time) work for 35 to 45 hours a week. Work out how many hours there are in a week, and then what percentage is spent working. Then remember that most people have several weeks of holidays a year, as well as days off for public holidays. Although we often refer to people by the jobs they do ('He's a teacher' or 'She's a doctor'), most of the time, and even most of their waking hours, they are not in these roles.

FIND OUT FOR YOURSELF

Test the ideas about work, non-work and leisure by making a chart showing how you use your time. Do this for one school day and one weekend or holiday day. Write what you were doing, for how long, and decide whether it counts as work, non-work or leisure. For work, decide whether it was in the formal or informal economy.

The history of work

KEY FOCUS

Today, for most people, work means going out to work, in a place that is different from the place where they live with their family, and working for a set number of hours. Even those whose work is based in their home – in a room converted into an office, for example – tend to keep work and home life separate. It was not always like this.

Work as it used to be for many. Until the middle of the twentieth century, working-class men needed to live close to their place of work.

Before the Industrial Revolution

The **Industrial Revolution**, from roughly 1750 to 1850, was the big turning point in the history of work, and of many other aspects of life.

Before the Industrial Revolution many people worked where they lived. A blacksmith, for example, had his forge as part of or next to the house where he and his family slept. Moreover, his whole family would help with tasks that supported his work, fetching water, keeping the fire going and so on. If the family were farmers, then everyone helped out in that too; the man might do the heavier work, such as ploughing, but his wife and children could help with looking after livestock, scaring birds off the crops and so on. The family was the unit of production.

People did not work for a set number of hours (such as 9 to 5) and then stop, as many do now. Before watches and clocks, it was difficult to tell the time accurately in any case. People worked when there was work to be done, and stopped when it was finished. At some times of year there might be a lot of work (at ploughing and harvesting, for example) and at other times very little to do. Without artificial light, the hours of daylight in winter reduced the hours that could be worked.

After the Industrial Revolution

The Industrial Revolution and all the social and technological changes that went with it changed the nature of work. Many people left the villages and local communities they had grown up in and moved to the new, rapidly growing, industrial towns. Here they worked in workshops, mills or factories, alongside people they did not know at first, for an employer. They worked for set hours (usually much longer than today, with time off only on Sundays), and the practice of 'clocking on' and 'clocking off' at the start and end of the day began. People were paid at the end of the week or month. Artificial light and heat meant that they could be made to work after dark or in winter. People usually lived very close to their place of work, because they had to walk (or, later on, ride a bicycle) to work. This is why there used to be (and are still some) areas of closely packed housing for working-class people near to the sites of factories and other places of work.

Men, women and children in the Industrial Revolution

Increasingly, it was men who worked, while women stayed at home looking after children. In the nineteenth century, new laws were brought in that stopped women and children doing work which was seen as too dangerous or inappropriate, such as working in coal-mines. Many women became housewives, staying at home, and with the whole family depending on the man earning a wage.

The world of work became mainly a man's world; men became 'breadwinners'. The home and family became the main responsibility of women, although many women did work, in jobs that were considered suitable. These were often related to the new role of women as **housewives**; women worked as maids or cooks, or took in other people's washing and ironing. Overall, however, we can say that the public world of work became separate from the private world of family and home.

Children too were kept out of the world of work. By the end of the nineteenth century, all children under 11 had to attend primary school. Many still helped their families in the older style of work when needed; children from farming families might skip school at harvest time so they could help out. Gradually, however, the school leaving age rose, and restrictions were placed on what jobs children could do and when while still of school age.

Work as exploitation

Karl Marx, writing in the nineteenth century after the Industrial Revolution had transformed work, saw work as exploitation. The bosses of the factories and mills, whom he called the capitalist ruling class, were exploiting those who worked for them, he argued. The bosses wanted to make as much profit as possible, and to do that they would make their workers work hard for very long hours and little pay.

Workers were not working for themselves but for their bosses. Workers took no pride in their work; they did not feel any sense of 'owning' the goods they made in the way a craftsman would. Marx described this as alienation.

Marx believed that work did not have to be like this; in a better society, people would be able to take satisfaction in using their skills to the benefit of everyone. The working class needed to organise itself and take over, creating a new system which Marx called communism.

Working conditions in many jobs at the time were appalling by today's standards. So were living conditions; remember that workers lived close to the factories and so were affected by

pollution at home as well as at work. Workers began to protest and demand better pay and conditions, or even a complete change in the economic system. So emerged the political movements of socialism and communism (see Chapter 10 Politics) and **trade unions** whose purpose was to try to establish rights for workers and then defend those rights (see the section on Trade unionism on pages 216–17).

FIND OUT FOR YOURSELF

Find out more about the Industrial Revolution's effects on work by using reference books and CD-ROMs such as Microsoft Encarta. Use your findings to design a poster showing work 'before' and 'after'.

QUESTIONS

1. What is meant by the Industrial Revolution?

2. Comparing before and after the Industrial Revolution, what changes were there (a) in the hours and seasons people worked, and (b) in the places where they worked?

3. Explain why the term housewife is not appropriate for describing women before the Industrial Revolution.

4. The Industrial Revolution led to a separation between home and work. Explain what this means.

5. Why did Karl Marx object to the situation in factories and other workplaces at the time he was writing?

ROUND-UP

The nature of work has changed dramatically over the centuries. Before the Industrial Revolution, families often worked together, at or near home, and only worked as long as they wanted or needed. The Industrial Revolution separated the world of work from the world of the home, with men going out to work and women and children not.

VOCABULARY

Clocking on/off: registering on arriving and leaving work

Breadwinner: a man's traditional role, providing food and money for his family

The meaning of work

This section looks at some of the reasons why people work, and the meaning that their work has for them. Many jobs are satisfying; people feel a sense of pride in their achievement, and may be admired by others. However, other jobs are experienced as boring and frustrating.

Different jobs give different levels of satisfaction; money is not the only important factor.

Reasons for working

Why do people go to work? What does work mean to them? There are four important answers. Most people work for a mixture of these motives.

- Money. Without doubt, being paid is the most important thing for many people. The money earned may only be enough for the basic necessities of life, or it may go towards leisure activities, holidays and savings. The kind of **job satisfaction** people experience not because of the job but because it enables them to enjoy life outside work is called extrinsic satisfaction.

- Job satisfaction. For many people, work is about more than just money. They also get some enjoyment or satisfaction from using their skills, from the opportunity to be creative and from knowing that a job has been well done. Some jobs make this possible far more than others. Those that allow people to be creative and use their abilities are more satisfying. This kind of job satisfaction is called intrinsic job satisfaction, which means that satisfaction is found in the job itself.

- Social life. We make friends with work colleagues; working in a team with people you know and like can be a main motive in working. Many people socialise outside work with their work colleagues.

- Status and a sense of identity. Work is important in helping us form our ideas about ourselves and others. People may be respected and looked up to because of their work. Many people develop a sense of self-esteem from work, whether from the nature of the work itself, or what it makes possible, such as supporting a family.

These four motives are not easy to separate in real life, and they overlap a lot. Thinking about work in this way can help us understand why some people do unpaid voluntary work, or, on the other hand, why someone may be willing to put up with a dull and repetitive job.

Alienation

One of Karl Marx's ideas about work in capitalist society was that workers were alienated from their work. By this he meant that workers did not get much, if any, satisfaction from their work. They worked because they had to earn money in order to survive, and not for any other reason; they were 'wage slaves'. For most people, work did not use their talents and abilities, or if it did, it did so in a twisted way to make the bosses rich, rather than improving everyone's lives. Work was boring, meaningless, a waste of time and ability.

Marx did not believe work had to be like this. In a different kind of society – a communist one – he believed people's work would enable them to gain satisfaction by using their skills and abilities to everyone's benefit.

Many other writers have taken up the idea of **alienation**. It applies far more to some jobs rather than others. Workers on an assembly line in a factory might have high levels of alienation; they would feel no sense of ownership in what they were making, since they worked on only a small part of it. On the other hand, people in professions they had chosen – for example doctors believing strongly in using their skills to save people's lives – might not feel alienated at all.

Aspects of alienation

- Powerlessness – workers feel they have no say in or influence over their work.
- Meaninglessness – the job may seem pointless.
- Waste of ability – workers may feel they have the skills and ability to do much more rewarding work.
- Isolation – feeling cut off from others.

The experience of alienation

'I stand in one spot, about two- or three-feet area, all night. The only time a person stops is when the line stops. We do about thirty-two jobs per car, per unit. Forty-eight units an hour, eight hours a day. Thirty-two times forty-eight times eight. Figure it out. That's how many times I push that button.

The noise, oh, it's tremendous. You open your mouth and you're liable to get a mouthful of sparks ... You don't compete against the noise ... You pretty much stay to yourself ... It don't stop. It just goes and goes and goes. I bet there's men who have lived and died out there and never seen the end of that line.'

Phil Stallings, a worker on an American car assembly line, interviewed by Studs Turkel in *Working*, Penguin, 1977.

In what ways does this extract illustrate some of the features of alienation?

Reducing alienation

There are a number of ways in which alienation can be reduced. Workers find ways of making work more satisfying, or of breaking the boredom, for example, through building up a sense of working together, or by sabotaging the machinery (see page 214).

Most ways of reducing alienation depend on employers taking action:

- By breaking down barriers between managers and workers. For example, everyone uses the same car parks and lunch facilities. This makes workers feel more valued.
- By changing work practices. For example, the assembly line way of making cars can be replaced by a small team building a whole car together, and feeling a greater sense of achievement.
- By allowing workers more opportunities to learn different jobs within the same company, or to have training opportunities.

- By creating a more pleasant working environment, and better conditions, so that workers feel they are looked after.

▶ FIND OUT FOR YOURSELF

Some members of your class probably have part-time jobs, for example babysitting, working in a shop or delivering newspapers. Why do they work? Design a questionnaire asking about this. Present your findings in the form of a table or chart showing which reasons were important and for how many people.

QUESTIONS

1. From the list of reasons why people work, choose two which you think are particularly important and explain why you have chosen them.

2. What is the difference between intrinsic and extrinsic job satisfaction?

3. What is meant by alienation?

4. Give three feelings that might be experienced by a worker who is alienated.

5. Identify and explain three ways in which employers can reduce alienation.

ROUND-UP

People work for many reasons; to earn money is perhaps the most obvious one, but not always the most important. While many people experience job satisfaction, others experience alienation. There are several ways in which employers can try to reduce the alienation their workers may feel.

VOCABULARY

Socialise: mix with, in a friendly way
Repetitive: repeated many times
Sabotage: deliberate damage of equipment

How work has changed

Work in Britain today is very different to the past; we have already looked at some of the history of work. Here we consider different sectors of the economy, the shift towards a service economy and the effects of changes in technology.

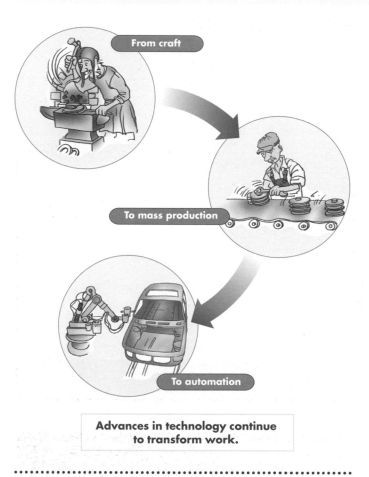

From craft

To mass production

To automation

Advances in technology continue to transform work.

The three sectors of the economy

The types of jobs that people do are normally divided into three kinds:

- The **primary sector**. Jobs in this sector involve collecting or extracting raw materials and natural resources, for example coal-mining, farming and fishing.
- The **secondary sector**. Jobs in this sector involve turning the raw materials into a product and processing them into goods that can be sold. For example, wood cut down by lumberjacks (primary sector) can be made into furniture and other goods made of wood in a factory (secondary sector).
- The **tertiary sector**. This is also referred to as the **service sector**. Jobs here involve dealing with other

people providing a service for them. Salespeople, teachers, doctors and nurses and office workers are employed in this sector.

Before the Industrial Revolution, most people worked in the primary sector, and some in the secondary sector as craftsmen making goods for sale. With the Industrial Revolution, there was a lot more manufacturing (secondary sector), in factories rather than in craft workshops as had happened before.

In recent years, both the primary and secondary sectors have come to employ far fewer people in Britain than they used to. This is partly because they are less important than they used to be, but also because workers in these sectors can often be replaced by machines. Britain's economy has moved towards the tertiary or service sector. Industries that used to employ a lot of people, such as coal-mining (primary sector) and making steel and ships (secondary sector) have declined. The new jobs that have replaced them are often in the service sector, such as tourism and the media.

The primary and secondary sectors remain important; what has changed is that the work is now often done in other countries rather than in Britain. The manufactured goods we buy are often imported from other countries; even a lot of the food we eat is imported. You can check this by looking for the country of origin on goods in a supermarket, or on the labels of clothes, toys and so on.

Mechanisation and mass production

There have also been big changes in the technologies used at work, in all three sectors.

Machines were used more and more in factories after the Industrial Revolution; instead of craftsmen doing all the work by hand, some of it could be done by machines. This reduced the number of workers required, and also reduced the skills they needed. It also made the goods that were produced cheaper, thus benefiting consumers. The process of replacing some workers by machines is called **mechanisation**.

As mechanisation spread with the invention of new machines in the nineteenth century, it led to **mass production**. This means that a product could be manufactured in large quantities in a factory, using an assembly line. Each worker had a particular task to carry out and had endlessly to repeat it (see Phil Stallings' description of his work in the section The meaning of work for an example (page 201)). There was a very strong **division of labour**; workers only had to know their own particular small task, and might know nothing of what other workers in the same factory did.

The early manufacture of motorcars by the Ford Company is a good example of mass production. Henry Ford revolutionised car production with factories that turned out large numbers of Model T Fords, at (for the first time) prices many people could afford. The cars were identical; Ford even said that his customers could have any colour they liked, as long as it was black. The workers' experience was of boring, repetitive work, likely to lead to feelings of alienation. At the same time managers were adopting new ways of closely monitoring what their workers did every minute of the shift. This method of production is called Fordism, and the style of management Taylorist.

Mass production: for and against

For:
- Mass-produced goods much cheaper so more people could afford them.
- Leading to rising standards of living.

Against:
- Boring, repetitive work leading to alienation, absenteeism and unrest.
- The disappearance of traditional skills of making things by hand.

Automation

Mass production revolutionised work in the first half of the twentieth century; today, equally far reaching changes are taking place. **Automation** refers to how machines or robots are now completely taking over from people in some areas of work. For example, parts of the manufacture of cars, such as painting them, are now completely automated. This means fewer workers are needed, and also reduces costs.

Another aspect of this is the rapid spread of new information and communication technology. Computers contribute to the process of automation because they are able to do some of the work previously done by people. Increasingly, for example, telephone calls about routine matters do not require anyone's involvement. An automated telephone answer system can deal with most enquiries.

Although automation has led to the loss of some jobs, it has also improved working conditions. Some dangerous or unpleasant jobs can be automated. Automation also has huge benefits for consumers. Making a withdrawal from a bank account used to involve being able to get to a bank during

(very restricted) opening hours and queuing. Today, automatic cash machines have made this transaction possible more quickly, in more places and at any time.

New technologies have also made it possible for more people to work at home, conducting business by e-mail or telephone and using a computer. We will look at some of the implications of these continuing developments in the section The future of work (see pages 218–19).

FIND OUT FOR YOURSELF

Interview several older people (such as your parents and grandparents) about places where they worked or used to work. Ask if they can tell you about any changes to the work people did (for example new machines being introduced) and what the workers thought about them.

QUESTIONS

1. Briefly explain each of the three sectors of employment, and give an example (not taken from these pages) of an occupation in each sector.

2. What is meant by mechanisation?

3. What is meant by the Fordist method of production?

4. Identify one advantage and one disadvantage of automation.

5. List examples that you know of where people have been replaced by machines or computers (for example booking tickets by telephone or via the Internet).

ROUND-UP

There has been a long-term shift in Britain away from the secondary sector being the most important towards more people working in the service sector. There have been several developments in technology: from craft to mechanised production, then to mass production and finally towards automation of work.

VOCABULARY

Absenteeism: people missing work without good reason
Assembly line: in a factory, when machines and workers are arranged so that a different process is carried out at each stage

Unemployment

KEY FOCUS   We have looked at work; we will now look at the lack of work. There are many people who want to work but cannot find jobs. This section looks at unemployment: who is unemployed and why.

Work closure costs 500 jobs

Dole beckons for car workers

The number of people unemployed changes as companies are affected by economic changes.

Without work

As you have seen in this chapter, work is a vital part of social life. Yet there are many people who do not work, for example children and retired people. This section deals with those people who want or need to work but can't: the unemployed.

How many people are unemployed?

In 1998 about 1.8 million people in Britain were unemployed. There are, however, different ways of counting **unemployment**, and many people argue that the real figure is much higher.

The official figures count how many people receive benefits from the government because they are unemployed; the total is called the claimant count. The main benefit is the Jobseeker's Allowance. However, many people are not eligible for these benefits so do not get included in the official total of unemployed people.

The International Labour Office uses a different method of counting unemployed people. This counts the number of people who are actively looking for work; that is, those who want to work but cannot find work. This produces a much higher figure.

Groups not included in the claimant count

- Young people living at home with their parents.
- Women whose husbands are in work.
- People looking for part-time work (for example so that they can continue to study, or to look after children).
- People who have nearly reached retirement age.

Who is unemployed?

Some groups are more likely to be unemployed than others. These include the following:

- Young people, especially those who have left school with few qualifications.

- Older workers. As people get older, they are more likely to experience long-term unemployment. This is because if they lose a job it becomes harder to get another one. Many companies are less likely to employ an older person. Some people who lose their jobs when they are in their 40s or 50s may never be able to find another job, unless they get new skills or qualifications, or take a job that is below what they are used to.

- Members of minority ethnic groups, especially Afro-Caribbeans and those from Pakistani and Bangladeshi backgrounds.

- Those living in particular parts of the country. There may be a shortage of jobs where older industries closed down and were not replaced by new ones. In the last 30 years or so many jobs have been lost in coal-mining and in heavy industries, and many men have not been able to find new jobs. This has affected mainly Wales, Scotland and the north of England. Most of the south east of England, by contrast, has very little unemployment.

For all of these groups, having skills and qualifications increases the chances of getting a job, as does being able to move to areas where there are jobs.

What causes unemployment?

An individual may be unemployed because, for example, he or she does not have the skills employers want. But looking at the whole country, there are more people wanting to work than there are jobs, so some people are bound to be unemployed. How has this situation come about?

After World War II governments saw unemployment as a huge problem, and tried very hard to keep unemployment low. It was thought that any government that allowed unemployment to rise would be so unpopular that it would lose the next general election. There had been a lot of unemployment and hardship in the 1930s, during the Depression. Full employment, along with the welfare state and the expansion of education and health, was one way of making sure there would be no return to those bad old days.

For many years there was full employment – everybody who wanted to work could do so. At times there were even more vacancies for particular jobs than people willing to take them. This was the reason why many West Indian and Asian people settled in Britain in the 1950s and 1960s – to do work that otherwise would not be done.

HINTS AND TIPS

See Chapter 5 Ethnicity for more information on how immigration was related to employment.

But from the 1970s, the situation began to change:

- Firstly, many manufacturing industries have closed down. There is now less manual work for working-class men. The manufactured goods that British people buy are now often made in other countries, especially those where workers can be paid less and working conditions are often poor.

- Secondly, jobs have been lost through the introduction of automation and new technology. This has affected both manual work, for example where robots take over factory production, and non-manual work such as in banks and offices.

- At the same time, for big multinational corporations, it has become cheaper to employ people in poorer countries rather than in Europe or North America. For example, many items of clothing sold in Britain are made in South East Asia, because this is cheaper than paying workers in a British factory would be. Unemployment today is then partly a result of globalisation.

New jobs

The new jobs that have been created are often in the service sector, for example in shops, hotels and leisure. Many of them are the types of jobs that have been traditionally seen as suitable for women. Many are also part time or temporary. Some of the difficulties men can experience in adapting to the way work has changed are shown in the film *The Full Monty*. A group of redundant steel workers try to make money in the expanding service sector – as strippers.

Unemployment has then been increased by changes in the British and the world economy. While there are many new opportunities for enterprising young people, the kinds of jobs that in the past many would have done have gone forever. Teenagers now do not expect to follow their parents by

working in a local factory or mine. It has become essential to get skills and qualifications.

Governments no longer hope to get rid of unemployment altogether. Some unemployment is caused by forces that governments cannot control. Governments can try to persuade multinational corporations to create jobs in Britain, but they cannot make them.

FIND OUT FOR YOURSELF

There are several excellent films about unemployment. Try to find and watch *Raining Stones* (certificate 15), about a man without regular work who needs to find money to pay for his daughter's confirmation.

QUESTIONS

1. What is unemployment?

2. What is meant by full employment?

3. Identify two groups of people who are more likely to be unemployed than others and explain why this is.

4. Identify and explain three reasons why unemployment has increased since the early 1970s.

5. Why do the new kinds of jobs being created now often not suit those who used to work in industries such as coal and steel?

ROUND-UP

Many people want to work but are unable to find jobs. Not all of them appear in the government's statistics on unemployment. Some kinds of people are more likely to be unemployed than others: the young, the old and members of minority ethnic groups. Some parts of Britain also have higher unemployment than others.

VOCABULARY

Depression: the economic slump of the 1930s, which caused great unemployment and hardship

Multinational corporations: business organisations that operate in many different countries

The effects of unemployment

KEY FOCUS

The previous section looked at unemployment in general; in this section we look at what it actually means to the individuals and families who experience it, and at its effects on British society.

'You tell the kids they can't have this and they can't have that. And they want to know why ... cos the other children have got them ... it's hard, it's really hard on them. The children would come in, perhaps their friends are going to the pictures, and sometimes I'd cry because I know mine can't go. Whereas before, when I was working, I could give it to them. But not now and they don't understand.'

'Redundancy, unemployment and poverty' by C. Callender, in *Women and Poverty in Britain in the 1990s* edited by J. Millar and C. Glendenning, Harvester Wheatsheaf, 1992.

The loss of a job can be devastating.

Effects on people

Some of the effects of unemployment apply to almost all unemployed people, while others affect particular groups more than others.

General effects

The following are possible consequences of unemployment for all unemployed people:

- Less income and a lower standard of living, possibly leading to poverty.
- Loss of status and a feeling of failure and of not being 'normal'.
- Boredom – having whole days to fill and nothing to do – and no money to spend on activities that might fill the time.
- Changed relationships – losing touch with former workmates, tension within families and marriage difficulties.
- Disapproval from others, who see unemployed people as 'scroungers'. This arises from the strong 'work ethic' in Britain, which says that everyone who is able to work should work.

All of the general effects listed in the box are closely connected. For example, unemployment often means that it becomes very difficult to afford leisure activities that might relieve the boredom.

In a small number of cases, unemployment can be a catastrophic blow. It can lead to mental problems, to poor health and even to suicide.

Effects on particular groups

- Young people – unemployment means having little money, and stops young people doing what they feel they should be doing. It can be hard to socialise, and very hard to do the things that are expected of young adults, such as moving away from home and getting married.

- Men – unemployment means that a man is unable to be the traditional breadwinner, supporting a family. This can damage self-esteem and lead to feelings of worthlessness, of not being a 'real man'.

- Women – women are also strongly affected by unemployment. Many women's wages are essential to their families, and unemployment can also mean losing friends from work.

- Minority ethnic groups – as well as unemployment, members of minority groups may face **discrimination**.

- People with disabilities – may lose an important part of their social life; not working can increase feelings of isolation and not belonging.

For a small number of people, not working is a positive choice. Many people find work boring or unpleasant, and long to get out of the 'rat race', or to spend time with family and friends and on activities they enjoy. Some people in high-powered professional jobs have chosen to 'downsize' – to move to less stressful, less well paid jobs, accepting less money in order to get a better quality of life. For those who stop working altogether, the term not employed may be more appropriate than unemployed. They are likely to be working in some sense – trying to be self-sufficient, or doing voluntary or community work.

For most people, however, the experience of **redundancy** and unemployment is a negative one. Work is often unpleasant, but it is necessary to earn money so as to be able to play a full part in society.

Effects on society

Government and unemployment

High unemployment is expensive to governments, because they pay unemployment and social security benefits. Although fewer people get these than in the past, it is still money that could otherwise be spent on education, health and so on. Moreover, unemployed people cannot contribute to the economy by working or by paying taxes.

Unemployed people are also a concern to governments because they are on the fringes of society. Although many move quickly back into work, the long-term unemployed are left out of much of what the rest of society takes for granted. They are one of the groups that make up what has been called the underclass.

Unemployed people are a very diverse group. Exactly who is unemployed changes all the time as people find or lose jobs. This, and the lack of resources, makes it very difficult for the unemployed to organise and campaign for changes in government policy. Their voices tend to be unheard. This is perhaps one of the reasons why governments and people seem to feel that little can be done to greatly reduce unemployment.

Racism and unemployment

As you have seen in the previous section, social scientists explain unemployment in terms of changes in the economy. However, some people, including politicians, have tried to put the blame on minority ethnic groups. The argument is that if black and Asian people were not in Britain, there would be more jobs for white British people. This argument is made particularly in areas of high unemployment. Minority groups are made into scapegoats, blamed for the problem of unemployment. The result can be an increase in racial harassment and violence against blacks and Asians.

The argument is wrong. Black and Asian people came to Britain to take jobs when no one could be found to do them. They contributed to the economy by working hard, paying taxes and so on. They – and now their children and even grandchildren – are more likely to become unemployed when the economic situation changes and are, of course, as entitled to government support as anyone else.

Trade unions and workers

High unemployment makes trade unions weaker. It is easier for employers to pay low wages if there are no other jobs for people to go to. It is also easier for them to offer only part-time or temporary contracts, or not to improve working conditions. The task of trade unions, which is to improve their members' situation, then becomes harder.

⏵ FIND OUT FOR YOURSELF

Find out what financial help is available to unemployed people. Visit the web site http://www.dss.gov.uk and use the A to Z index or search facility to find this.

QUESTIONS

1. Identify three effects unemployment might have on an unemployed person.

2. Why do unemployed people sometimes (usually wrongly) get accused of being 'scroungers'?

3. What does 'downsizing' mean, and why do some people choose to do it?

4. In what ways is unemployment damaging to the economy?

5. Why does unemployment weaken the position of trade unions?

ROUND-UP

Unemployment has serious negative consequences for both individuals and society. Unemployment is associated with poverty, and so with other problems such as poor health and depression.

VOCABULARY

Catastrophic: disastrous
Self-esteem: respect for yourself
Rat race: hectic competitive work, always trying to do better than everyone else

Gender and work

KEY FOCUS The experience of work is different for men and women. They tend to do different kinds of work, and to be treated differently despite laws designed to prevent this.

> Women have to work harder for recognition, because men assume men are better.

> When I told them I was pregnant, they began planning to replace me.

> The boss hires girls in short skirts, but the men get promoted faster.

> Sometimes women get promoted too fast to make it look like they're treated equally.

> When I get home, I've still got the cooking and housework to do.

> There's no point employing a woman – she'll leave to have children before long.

Men and women have different experiences of work.

Men's work, women's work

Some kinds of jobs are dominated by one sex or the other.

Which of the following would you say are men's jobs, which women's jobs and which are likely to be done by either? Judge; nursery school teacher; secretary; merchant banker; sailor; shop assistant; librarian; secondary school teacher; nurse, fire-fighter.

About half of all women work in just three types of job: sales, secretarial and office work and personal services, such as hairdressing. Men are less likely to be doing this kind of work.

Why are there such differences? These are some of the reasons suggested by sociologists:

- Socialisation – boys and girls are brought up to have different expectations, learning that some work is more appropriate for one sex or the other. This happens through different agencies of socialisation (see page 8). For example, children learn through the toys they are

given and the games they play some of what is expected of them as adults.

- Educational opportunities – the skills and qualifications boys and girls acquire through their education can steer them towards some jobs and away from others. For example, more boys than girls take subjects at A level and beyond which are needed for working as engineers.

- Discrimination – men and women are not always treated equally. In particular, women trying to break into male-dominated areas of work may face suspicion and hostility. Women who reach positions of authority where they have to make decisions and give orders are likely to be thought of as 'bossy'. They may also be judged by physical appearance rather than ability.

FIND OUT FOR YOURSELF

If you are in a school which has a programme of work experience for students, try to compare the work experience placements boys and girls are given. Do girls tend to get 'feminine' jobs for work experience? If so, is this because this is what they want, or would they have preferred something else? To do this you will need to interview, or give a questionnaire to, students who have done work experience or who are about to and know what they are going to do.

Women and work

The number of women working has been going up steadily for many years, and there are now as many women working as men. However, many more women than men work part time.

In the past, it was common for young women to work until they were expecting their first child, then to stop working until the children had grown up and left home. Today, having children still has a big effect on women's work but usually for a much shorter period. Women spend fewer years not working while looking after children. More than half of all mothers with children under 5 are now working (*Social Trends Pocketbook*, 1999) and most of those not working say they would like to if they had the choice (*Social Trends Pocketbook*, 1999).

Having even a short time off work, for maternity leave, can damage a woman's chances of promotion. She may be seen as having missed important changes at work.

Inequality at work

Men and women are in unequal situations at work:

- As you have seen, men and women tend to do different jobs. Women's work tends to have lower pay and status than men's work.
- When men and women are working together in the same occupations or in the same organisation, women are less likely to be in the senior posts. For example, although the majority of teachers are women, most head teachers (even of primary schools) are men. Women find it harder to reach the posts at the very top; they encounter the 'glass ceiling', an invisible barrier.

Women's inequality takes the form of lower pay, lower status and other disadvantages.

The law makes discrimination at work on gender grounds illegal. The most important laws are the Sex Discrimination Act and the Equal Pay Act. However, these are sometimes difficult to enforce. For example, it is very difficult for a woman who did not get a promotion to prove that the reason was because she was a woman.

Unequal pay

Women working full time earn on average only about 80 per cent of what men working full time earn (New Earnings Survey, 1997).

Many more women than men work part time, and if they are included there is an even bigger gap between men's pay and women's pay.

There are two possible reasons for this:

- Discrimination against women by men. It is usually men who are in charge of recruitment and promotion, so men who believe women are less capable can favour men. This is direct discrimination and is illegal. Discrimination can also be indirect, when it is not intended by anyone but happens because of the way things are done. For example, a company might say that to get promotion a worker had to go away on a residential training course. This would be difficult or impossible for women with young children, so would have the effect of unintentionally discriminating against women.
- The division of labour in families. Because men have traditionally been seen as the 'breadwinners' it has been acceptable to pay men more than women. They are seen as needing the money to support their families. Married women who worked were seen as only doing so to earn a little extra money, perhaps to pay for luxuries like a holiday. Women's domestic commitments – looking after home, husband, children and elderly relatives – are seen as preventing them from working long hours, or spending time training to get skills and qualifications. Because women are less able to earn good wages, even women often see their husband's work as more important than their own.

Other inequalities

Because more women are in part-time or temporary work, and spend parts of their adult lives not working, they are more likely than men to miss out on some of these advantages:

- occupational pensions
- opportunities for training and for promotions
- redundancy pay.

QUESTIONS

1. What is the 'glass ceiling'?
2. Identify and explain two reasons why men and women tend to do different kinds of work.
3. What is the likely effect on a woman's career of having 'time off' to have children?
4. Identify two reasons why women are on average paid less than men.
5. 'Women no longer face discrimination in the world of work.' Do you agree? Give reasons for your answer.

ROUND-UP

Men and women tend to have different kinds of jobs, and when they do work together men dominate the higher levels. Women are still paid less and often face discrimination.

VOCABULARY

Maternity: motherhood
Unintentionally: without meaning to
Redundancy pay: a one-off payment when someone's job is ended by his or her employer

Minority ethnic groups and work

KEY FOCUS Black and Asian people are more likely to be unemployed than white British people, and more likely to be in low paid or low status jobs. This section looks at this situation in detail and at some of the reasons for it.

Unequal prospects for black academics

Race barrier remains in jobs market

Minorities face job bias from leading firms

Black and Asian people face problems at work.

Inequality at work

Many members of minority ethnic groups are at a disadvantage in work compared to the white majority population. The situation is different, however, for different groups, and for men and women. It is far more complicated than a simple black/white division.

Inequalities faced by minority ethnic groups include the following:

- Higher rates of unemployment.
- They are more likely to be in low paid, insecure jobs.
- They are less likely to reach high status, high pay occupations (as with women, there is evidence of a 'glass ceiling' blocking the way to the very top).

Some minority ethnic groups have low levels of qualifications (see the section Ethnic groups and education on pages 182–3), but in fact these disadvantages apply regardless of qualifications; that is, a member of a minority group has less chance of getting a job than a British white person with the same qualifications.

Different minorities

The most disadvantaged groups are those with Pakistani and Bangladeshi origins. In 1998 unemployment for both men and women from these groups was over 20 per cent, when the national figure was around 5 per cent (*Labour Market Trends*, September 1998). Bangladeshis and Pakistanis also earn on average about £2 less per hour than whites ('Black women lead the way in pay stakes' by Charlotte Denny, *Guardian*, 15 July 1998). Unemployment and low pay mean that many Pakistani and Bangladeshi families live in poverty (see the section Who are the poor? on pages 322–3). The situation is made worse by the larger average size of families and by the fact that large numbers of women choose not to work. This means that a wage earner is likely to be supporting more people than is the average for the whole population.

The situation of Indian and Chinese people, and Asians from Africa, is very different. Indians and Chinese are more likely than white people to be in top (social class 1) occupations. Despite this, Indian people are more likely to be unemployed. Many Indians and African-Asians run businesses, from corner shops and restaurants to large companies like Shami Ahmed's Joe Bloggs jeans. Often these families had been successful in business before moving to Britain, and were well educated.

The greater success of these groups can be explained partly by their class; many are from middle-class backgrounds and by their higher educational qualifications.

Afro-Caribbean people, especially men, have high rates of unemployment and are underrepresented in the higher class occupations. Black women, however, have recently begun to outstrip other groups; black women earned an average of £6.10 per hour in 1997 compared to £5.19 for white women (*Guardian*, 15 July 1998). Possible reasons for this are:

■ that black women face less discrimination than black men because they are seen as less threatening
■ that because black men have always faced low pay and unemployment, black women have always had to work. Young black mothers expect to work as well as care for children.

Successful black women in Britain include:

■ MPs Oonagh King and Diane Abbott
■ TV cook Dorinda Hafner
■ leading barrister Lady (Patricia) Scotland
■ newscaster Moira Stewart
■ singer Mica Paris.

Explanations

The disadvantages faced by minority ethnic groups, after taking into account educational qualifications, indicate racism and racial discrimination. This is when people are treated unfavourably because of their ethnicity. This can happen both in blocking access to jobs and in how people are treated at work.

Discrimination is against the law, but as with sex discrimination, it can be very difficult for the victim to prove that it has happened.

There have been several attempts to discover racial discrimination in the way job applications are handled. Researchers have replied to real job advertisements using made-up names and personal details. They have often found that applications from people with Asian names were less likely to result in being called for interview than applications from those with British sounding names, even when other details, such as exam passes, were the same.

Even when in work, members of minority groups can face discrimination. For example, they may be passed over for promotion.

Black nurses hounded out of 'racist' NHS

For many years the National Health Service relied heavily on black workers, but in 1998 it was reported that the percentage of black staff recruited had fallen in ten years from more than 10 per cent to less than 1 per cent. Black staff face harassment and discrimination from both colleagues and patients. Nearly half of the black nurses interviewed said that racism was so bad that they would leave if they could.

Some sociologists see the problems faced by members of ethnic minorities as the result of being migrant workers. The capitalist economic system needs workers who can move to where work is available; they form a 'reserve army of labour'. In the 1950s and 1960s Britain used its colonies as a source of cheap labour, bringing migrant workers to Britain. When the economic situation changed and there were fewer jobs, these migrant workers were often the first to lose their jobs.

From this point of view, the problems faced by black and Asian people are not to do with race or ethnic differences. Any group of immigrant workers would be facing similar problems.

FIND OUT FOR YOURSELF

One of the best web sites for information on issues affecting black people in Britain is the Black Information Link at http://www.blink.org.

You will find a checklist for what employers can do to avoid racism and racial discrimination at http://www.blink.orh/redrapptool/employment.

ROUND-UP

Members of minority ethnic groups face disadvantages such as lower pay and high rates of unemployment. Some groups do better than others. Class and gender are also important factors.

VOCABULARY

Harassment: being constantly troubled by unwanted attention
Colony: a territory ruled by another country

Age and work

This section looks at two particular age groups, the young and the old, and their situations at work.

In the past children from poor families were expected to work.

Young people under 16

In Britain there are legal restrictions on how many hours under-16-year-olds can work, and what kind of work they can do. This was not always the case. In the Middle Ages and earlier, before there were schools, children were expected to help with the family's work as soon as they were able to.

In the nineteenth century, children worked in a wide variety of jobs. Even at this time, many people saw this as wrong and restrictions on what work children could do were introduced. In 1842 people were horrified by stories of conditions in which children worked in coal-mines, and a new Act prevented children under 10 working in mines. A later act stopped the practice of using little boys as chimney sweeps.

The legal position in Britain today

The Children (Protection at Work) Regulations, 1998

- No child under 13 can work (exceptions can be made for young farmers and actors).

- 13-year-olds can only do certain kinds of light work, such as delivering newspapers.

- Those under 16 can work a maximum of five hours a day on any non-school day (excluding Sundays).

- Under-16s can work a maximum of 25 hours a week; they cannot work for more than four consecutive days; they must have at least two weeks a year free from both school and work.

- Children who work must have a work permit, obtained from schools or education welfare officers.

These restrictions are designed to prevent children's health and education from suffering and to prevent their exploitation as cheap labour. At the same time, it is recognised that children need to begin to learn about the world of work. As well as allowing some part-time work, schools arrange work experience or work shadowing for their pupils.

The restrictions are not well enforced. Children often want to work, and employers gain from being able to pay them low wages, so both sides are willing to break the regulations. Local authorities do not see cracking down on illegal work by children as a high priority, although occasionally shocking cases of abuse do come to light. In 1998 the charity Save the Children estimated that about 80 per cent of the 2 million children under 16 working in Britain were working illegally (*Sociology Update 1999*).

The problem does not only involve paid work. Some children, especially girls, are expected to do domestic labour within the home to the extent that their school work suffers.

Child labour in Britain

It is illegal for anyone under 16 to sell goods on the street and employers can be fined up to £1000. Yet florists employ under-age children to sell flowers on the M25 sliproads and around the Watford area. They are given £2 in the morning to buy food and taken by lorry to sit by roadsides alone. The children are expected to sit underneath polythene sheets in freezing weather. In the evening they are transported back and given £20 for the day's work – about £2 an hour ... If flowers were missing and not paid for, their value was deducted from their wages.

'Under age and underpaid' by Tessa Mayes and Angus Stickler, *Guardian*, 2 March 1994.

Child labour in other countries

In many countries the situation is much worse than in Britain. Many children do difficult and dangerous work, missing out on their education. Sometimes they are supporting families. Some work in workshops manufacturing goods that are later sold as well-known brands in Britain and the west. Some campaigners have organised boycotts of some of the brands involved to try to stop the exploitation of **child labour**.

 FIND OUT FOR YOURSELF

In a small group, research the work members of your class or of another class do. Include those who do not have jobs – they are important too. Find out how many hours people work, when, how long they have been working, what they are paid and so on. Present your findings as tables and charts with a written explanation.

After leaving school

There are no restrictions on work over the age of 16. Increasingly, many students in schools, further and higher education work part time to finance their studies and social lives. Those who do not stay in education often find it hard to get a job; young people have a higher unemployment rate than any other age group. Those who do work, whether part or full time, are often poorly paid.

Older workers

Older workers can face ageism; that is, they can be discriminated against because of their age. For those looking for new jobs in their 40s or 50s, age can count against them. In some industries, people are considered to be 'over the hill' by 50. Skills learned as a young adult may become out of date. Ageism is based on negative stereotypes of older people. Older people are thought of as 'wrinklies', 'codgers' who have 'one foot in the grave'. This attitude is very different from that

which exists in other societies. Many cultures value the experience and wisdom of older people who are looked up to as 'elders'. In modern society, however, the pace of change has been so quick that some of the experiences of older people are seen as irrelevant.

Many workers now retire earlier than the official retirement age of 65 for men and 60 for women. A hundred years ago, before old age pensions, most people did not retire; they simply had to carry on working as long as they could. Now many people can look forward to years of leisure after retirement, especially if they have a second pension. For others, early retirement may be little different from unemployment, with some of the negative features associated with unemployment – poverty, loneliness and a sense of failure.

QUESTIONS

1. What is meant by child labour?

2. Why were the restrictions on children working originally introduced?

3. Describe the negative stereotype of older people as workers.

4. Give one reason why schools arrange work experience placements for their students.

5. Why do you think the laws on children working are so often ignored in Britain? Have different reasons for each of these four groups who are involved: local authorities, employers, parents, children.

ROUND-UP

Both young and old people face particular problems in work. Regulations in Britain protect children from exploitation, but these regulations are often ignored. Older people often face ageism and difficulties in finding new jobs.

VOCABULARY

Consecutive: one after the other
Work experience: a student's placement at a workplace, doing some work but unpaid
Work shadowing: a student's placement involving following one worker and watching what he or she does

Industrial relations

With the exception of self-employment, work involves a relationship between employer or manager and workers. This relationship is often a difficult one, because there is a lot of potential for disagreement. Workers want better pay and conditions, employers want to make higher profits. This section looks at types of conflict that can occur.

Working men defending their rights – or mindless militants wrecking the economy?

Working together?

The attitude of employers and many politicians to **industrial relations** is that everyone, workers and bosses, should work together to make the company or organisation successful. They are partners; if profits fall because of **strikes** or any other reason, then everyone who works there, including the bosses, will suffer; for example, everyone will lose their job if a factory closes down.

In order for both sides to feel they are in partnership in this way, they have to create a situation that is acceptable to both sides. The employers need to create a good working environment, pay reasonably well and look after their workers' welfare; in return, the workers will be expected to work hard and to be flexible when necessary. In practice, because the situation changes constantly, there are often likely to be disagreements and disputes. Employers in many industries meet trade union or other workers' representatives regularly to discuss and try to resolve matters of concern. This is called **collective bargaining**, and happens both in particular workplaces and, in big companies, at regional or national level. When it breaks down, either side may turn to **industrial action**.

Industrial action

Usually the term industrial action makes people think of strikes, but there are other forms of industrial action too. These are the main types of industrial action taken by workers:

- Strikes – workers refuse to work temporarily, until a problem or dispute is settled. Strikes that are backed by trade unions are official strikes, those which are not are unofficial. Sudden unofficial strikes are called wildcat strikes.
- Work to rule – workers continue to work, but to make a protest they stick rigidly to the rules and regulations, for example going home exactly on time even if the work is not finished.
- Sit-in – workers take over a factory or workplace and refuse to leave, usually because the company wants to close it down and make them redundant.
- Informal conflict. There are also many ways workers can express dissatisfaction less obviously:
  - Sabotage – deliberate damage to the machinery or product. Sabotage may appear to be mindless vandalism, but it can be a way of expressing frustration, or of breaking routine.
  - Absenteeism – staying off work, perhaps giving a false excuse, such as being ill. In many jobs being off ill for a short period does not involve any loss of pay and a medical certificate is only required after several days off. Workers may also take long lunch hours, or extended breaks.
  - Negligence – working, but with little care and attention, so that the work or product is shoddy.

An example of industrial sabotage

'When 600 shipyard workers employed on the new Cunarder QE2 finished on schedule they were promptly sacked by John Brown's, the contractors involved. With what looked like a conciliatory gesture they were invited to a party in the ship's luxurious new bar, which was specially opened for the occasion. The men became drunk, damaged several cabins, and smashed the Royal Suite to pieces.'

'Industrial sabotage: motives and meanings' by Laurie Taylor and Paul Walton in *Images of Deviance*, edited by Stanley Cohen, Penguin, 1971.

The men wrecked what they had made. Why do you think they did this?

It is also possible for employers to start industrial action. This is usually a 'lock out', when employers lock the gates or doors and refuse to let the workers into work. Also, many incidents of industrial action can be seen as provoked or sparked off by employers' actions and decisions. For example, if a group of workers strike to keep a factory open, this can be seen as provoked by the employers' decision to close the factory.

Strikes

Strikes attract far more attention than other types of industrial action. The most famous strikes, such as the **General Strike** of 1926 and the miners' strike of 1984–85 are important historical events.

Since 1979, various new laws have made strikes more difficult than they used to be. This has reduced the number of strikes considerably. This does not necessarily mean that workers today are more contented, just that it is harder to express dissatisfaction through strikes.

Laws that limit union power

- Secondary action – going on strike to support workers elsewhere – is illegal.
- Restrictions on picketing. Picketing involves strikers at the entrance to a workplace trying to persuade anyone from going to work while a strike is on, and to prevent strike-breakers from elsewhere being brought in by the employers.
- Balloting. There now has to be a complex voting procedure before a union can call an official strike.
- Strikes have to be about the workers' own pay and conditions; if they are about wider issues, such as politics, they are illegal.

What causes strikes?

Among the main reasons for strikes are:

- workers demanding a pay increase or resisting a pay cut – workers compare their pay to those of workers in similar jobs and consider pay rises elsewhere; if they feel what they are offered is unfair they may consider striking
- workers either demanding an improvement or resisting a change in working conditions that employers have made.

A number of factors influence the number of strikes:

- Jobs which are boring and frustrating are more likely to lead to strikes than those which are interesting and rewarding.
- Workers in some kinds of jobs are very reluctant to strike because by not working they affect people. This applies, for example, to teachers and nurses; however they might feel about what their employers are doing, they do not want to damage children's education or the health of patients.
- Strikes are less common when there is high unemployment. This is because employers can easily take on new workers in place of those on strike. So high unemployment weakens the position of workers and unions.

▶ FIND OUT FOR YOURSELF

Choose one of the following historic strikes and research it using reference books and CD-ROMs such as Microsoft Encarta:

- The General Strike of 1926
- The coal-miners' strike of 1984–85. (In looking up references it may help to know that the miners' leader was Arthur Scargill.)

Present your findings to the rest of the class.

QUESTIONS

1. What is meant by collective bargaining?

2. What is the difference between an official strike and an unofficial strike?

3. Identify and explain three types of informal industrial action.

4. Identify and explain two reasons for strikes.

5. Picketing has been made difficult as a way of reducing the effectiveness of strikes. Why is picketing so important for a successful strike?

ROUND-UP

The relationship between employers and workers always has the potential for disagreement and conflict because the two sides tend to have different interests. Industrial action can take many forms, but strikes, although not common, attract the most attention. Strikes have been made much more difficult by new laws.

VOCABULARY

Conciliatory: intended as a friendly gesture
Militant: someone who is aggressive in supporting a cause

Trade unionism

Trade unions are the main way in which workers organise to defend themselves against exploitation by employers. They are an attempt to put right a very unequal power situation, making sure that workers have some say in their working conditions and levels of pay.

Pride in the union – unity is strength.

Trade unions

Trade unions are organisations of workers set up to win and defend rights at work and improve working conditions. Most trade unions – 74 – belong to the Trades Union Congress (TUC). About one in three of all employees belong to a trade union. Some kinds of work, such as education and health, have higher rates of union membership than others. Union membership is, for example, very low among hotel and restaurant workers, and in farming. Men are slightly more likely to belong to unions than women.

What trade unions do

- Protect their members' rights.
- Help members if they have a problem at work.
- Negotiate with employers for higher pay.
- Negotiate for better conditions such as more holidays and on health and safety issues.
- Campaign on wider issues, such as trying to influence government policies in ways which are in members' interests.
- Increasingly in recent years, they offer members extra services such as loans, cheaper insurance and holidays and so on.

Unions in decline

Trade unions have been in decline since 1979, when the Conservative government of Margaret Thatcher was elected. The government attacked unions with new laws greatly restricting their ability to act on behalf of their members (see Industrial relations on pages 214–15). They were able to do this because politicians and the media blamed trade unions for strikes that were seen as damaging the economy.

The number of people belonging to trade unions fell, from around 13 million in 1979 to around 7 million in 1996 (*Social Trends*) and some smaller unions amalgamated with bigger ones. There was also a big fall in the number of strikes and the number of days of work lost through strikes.

To keep going, trade unions began to offer new services to members, such as financial and legal services. They have also tried to target for recruitment groups who used to have low rates of membership, such as women and the young.

The election of the Labour government in 1997 seemed to slow the decline of the unions. There have been no new restrictions on unions, but no return to the situation before 1979 either.

Craft unions and closed shops

The earliest workers organisations in Britain that were referred to as trade unions were **craft unions** in the nineteenth century. These tried to bring together in one organisation all members of a particular trade or craft, for example printers, or coal-miners.

Craft unions tried to protect their members' rights by preventing outsiders taking the jobs. They negotiated agreements with employers to take on only workers who had the right training, and who were members of or who joined the union – and the unions tried to control the training. This meant that they could in effect decide who got jobs and who didn't, and keep their own status and pay high. This situation is called a **closed shop**.

Closed shops were sometimes used to keep women and ethnic minorities out of some kinds of work.

General unions

Not all unions recruit only people in particular jobs. There are also **general unions**, which began as organisations of unskilled workers but now often include people working in a wide variety of jobs. They try to recruit members in all kinds of work; they are open and inclusive, whereas craft unions were closed and exclusive. The biggest trade union in Britain, the Transport and General Workers Union (TGWU), is a good example of this.

There are also industrial unions, which have members in different kinds of work within one industry, for example the Banking, Insurance and Finance Union (BIFU).

Trade unions and politics

Trade unions have always been closely associated with the Labour Party, which they played a big part in founding. For much of the twentieth century, until Tony Blair's 'New Labour' reforms, the trade unions had a large say in deciding Labour's policies and in electing its leaders.

Taken together, the trade unions and the Labour Party are described as the **Labour movement**. The role of trade unions is industrial, looking after the interests of workers at work; while the Labour Party's role was political, looking after the wider interests of the whole working class. New Labour has moved away from this way of thinking about the party's role, and sees itself much more as representing everyone, not just its traditional working-class supporters.

Professional associations

Organisations of professions often do not call themselves trade unions, but carry out very similar functions for their members. Doctors, for example, through the General Medical Council (GMC) control who can practise as a doctor; for a doctor to be 'struck off' the GMC's register is effectively the end of his or her career.

Professional associations are less likely to strike or take other industrial action then trade unions. They have a different outlook to, for example, factory workers. In some kinds of work, there is a choice between different types of organisation to join. Teachers, for example, can join one of three trade unions or a smaller organisation that sees itself more as a professional association and has a 'no strike' policy, the Professional Association of Teachers (PAT). There are also some small subject-based unions.

▶ FIND OUT FOR YOURSELF

Visit the web site of the TUC, the organisation which brings together over 70 unions and nearly 7 million union members, at http://www.webhost.tuc.org.uk.

Visit the home page of a trade union, and explore it to find out what unions do and what they see as their priorities. Here are some suggestions:

■ UNISON, Britain's biggest union, organising workers in the public sector: http://www.unison.org.uk
■ TGWU: http://www.tgwu.org.uk.

QUESTIONS

1. What is a trade union?
2. Identify and explain two roles of trade unions.
3. Explain the differences between craft unions and general unions
4. What is meant by the Labour movement?
5. How were trade unions affected by changes to the law by the Conservative governments of 1979 to 1997?

ROUND-UP

Trade unions exist to defend the interests of their members in any way related to work. Some unions are based on one craft or industry, others are general. Unions have been in decline for some time but there are some signs that this decline has now been halted.

VOCABULARY

Amalgamated: combined, creating a single new organisation
Struck off: removed from the register of approved people

The future of work

This section looks at two recent developments that have not yet been considered in this chapter, and then looks ahead to what work may be like in the future.

Call centres – a new type of production line?

The future of work

Two recent developments in the world of work are the **long hours culture** and **teleworking**. Both will be considered in some detail because they may be the way that work will develop in the future.

The long hours culture

Compared to other European countries, British workers tend to work long hours, to work at weekends and to have few holidays. For more and more people, the working week extends into weekends and evenings. Computer technology and mobile telephones mean that work can be done in the office or at home, or even on the way to and from work.

The traditional weekend away from work has disappeared for many people. This applies to all kinds of work. Lower paid workers are putting in overtime to earn extra money, and higher paid workers are working to keep up with the demands of their job. Also more people are taking on a second job.

One result of this increase in the amount of work done is that more people complain that they do not have enough time, for their families and for social and leisure activities.

The increase in working time is also related to the extension of hours of business. We now increasingly expect shops, services and facilities to be available at any time. Some supermarkets

open 24 hours a day, seven days a week. Some areas of work, such as finance, depend on what happens in other parts of the world, so people may be working at night to follow developments in the USA or Japan.

This increase in work does not apply to everyone. There are many individuals and families without any paid work. So some families are 'work rich' (for example a professional couple, both working long hours) and others are 'work poor' (for example both unemployed and those dependent on welfare). The difference will also, of course, be one of income and living standards. This pattern may then increase the gap between rich and poor.

Long hours are not new. A hundred years ago, many factory workers worked 12-hour shifts and only had Sundays off. This is now seen as exploitation, and the gradual move towards shorter hours, paid holidays and so on is seen as an improvement. Yet now many people are choosing, or are being pushed into, working long hours.

FIND OUT FOR YOURSELF

Has the 24-hour society arrived? Make a list of shops, garages and any other businesses or services in your area that never close. Use a local directory such as Yellow Pages – watch out for the boxed advertisements that say '24 hours'. To balance this, draw up a list of services not available 24 hours (for example your bus service may stop at night).

Teleworking

In recent years one of the areas in which there has been many new jobs is in telephone **call centres** and data entry services. This shows how developments in computer and information technology have changed, and continue to change, the nature of work. By 1999 there were between 300 000 and 400 000 people working in call centres in Britain (*Sociology Update 2000*). Most call centre workers are women.

Call centres provide customer services and sales for many companies. Some companies have their own call centres, others use firms who provide staff and technology for them. Call centres have become possible because almost everyone now has their own telephone and because people can buy over the telephone using credit and debit cards. Databases of information also mean that call centre workers can quickly access detailed information about callers and customers.

Call centres have been described as the production lines of the twenty-first century. They are like production lines in mid-twentieth century factories in that they are repetitive, require few skills and are not well paid. Call centre operators have few opportunities to use their initiative; they are told exactly what to say and calls are closely monitored. There are few opportunities to talk to other workers.

Call centres are new, but in these ways they seem like an older type of work. Sociologists would point out that production lines were associated with high levels of alienation.

Work in 2020

Here are some suggestions about what work might be like in 2020, according to a 1998 report:

- People will no longer work 40/40 (40 hours a week for 40 years).
- More people will work short term and part time, having contracts with several employers at the same time.
- Information technology will mean that many people will work from home; there will be fewer traditional workplaces like offices and factories.
- Work will be worldwide; the people and companies workers deal with could be anywhere in the world.
- People will have to acquire new knowledge and skills throughout their working lives. This is one of the reasons for the emphasis on vocational education and on 'life long learning'. ('The only certainty is uncertainty' by Lisa Buckingham, *Guardian*, 28 April 1998, based on the report 'Redefining work by the Royal Society for the encouragement of Arts, Manufactures and Commerce'.)

All of these predictions are based on trends that can already be seen. For example, two-thirds of the new jobs created between 1993 and 1998 were not permanent. The overall impression is that workers in the future will need to be more flexible, prepared to have several jobs at the same time and to move quickly to new work, acquiring new skills.

QUESTIONS

1. What is meant by Britain's long hours culture?
2. What are the likely effects of long hours culture on family life?
3. What are the differences between work-rich and work-poor households?
4. In what ways are call centres like production lines?
5. Do you think the changes suggested in the box Work in 2020 will make work better or worse? Give reasons for your answer.

ROUND-UP

The trend towards longer working hours has led to a growing gap between work rich and work poor households. Long hours seem unavoidable but many people resent them. Teleworking, an apparently new type of work, in fact has similarities to earlier production line work. Teleworking and other trends provide clues about what work may be like in the future.

VOCABULARY

Overtime: hours worked extra to the normal day or week, usually paid at a higher rate
Flexible: willing and able to adapt as conditions change

Work – sociology in practice

How we spend our time

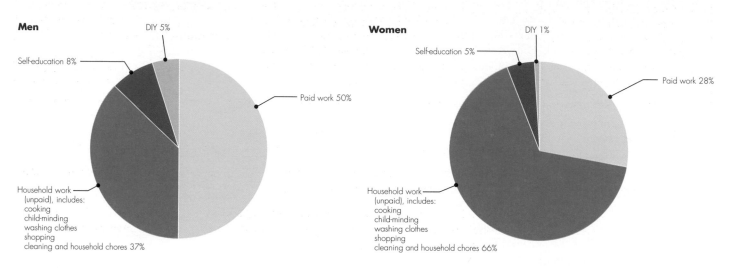

Men

DIY 5%

Self-education 8%

Paid work 50%

Household work (unpaid), includes:
cooking
child-minding
washing clothes
shopping
cleaning and household chores 37%

Women

DIY 1%

Self-education 5%

Paid work 28%

Household work (unpaid), includes:
cooking
child-minding
washing clothes
shopping
cleaning and household chores 66%

Note: the figures above are averages, and will vary according to factors such as age, occupation and number of children. The figures include pensioners.

Office for National Statistics, 1997.

'Every time a person digs the garden or goes to the supermarket or does the washing up, this is work just as surely as agricultural labouring, serving hamburgers or working in an hotel. The big difference is that people are not paid for the first three. This means that in the UK unpaid work is not counted as economic activity.'

Sociology Update 1998.

Questions

1. Look back at the section Work and leisure: terminology (pages 196–7). How do the charts illustrate problems in defining what work is?

2. What differences between men and women do the charts show, and how would you explain them?

3. The charts include work of many kinds – but in what two other ways do we use our time? Explain using examples.

Child labour

FOOTBALLS bearing the Manchester United club crest and a picture of Eric Cantona are being made by child labourers in India working for as little as 6p an hour.

Child labour is regularly used in the production of a wide range of sports goods. Children as young as seven stitch footballs for sale in the U.K.

There may be up to 30 000 children working in India's sports goods industry. Some of the work they do – sewing all day in bad light, hunched over their work – can damage their health. It is even more likely to affect their education.

A Christian Aid report calls for clubs like Manchester United and companies like Adidas to encourage their suppliers to gradually phase out child labour while protecting family incomes.

A consumer boycott would not solve the problem. Many families rely on children to support them. If children cannot do work like this, they are more likely to do more dangerous and degrading work than go to school, which they cannot afford.

Adapted from 'The foul smell of soccer's sweatshop child labour' by Sarah Boseley, *Guardian*, 12 May 1997.

Questions

1 (a) Why is child labour attractive to the children's employers?
(b) Child labour like this was once common in Britain too. Why was it ended?

2 Although the situation here is clearly wrong, it cannot easily be changed without making life more difficult for the children concerned and their families. Why is this?

3 Britain has laws against child labour, yet they are rarely enforced. Why is child labour in India seen as wrong while child labour in Britain is not? Do the different circumstances justify this different attitude?

High and low rates of unemployment

This table shows the percentages of different groups who were unemployed, by the ILO definition.

	High rate of unemployment	Percentage	Low rate of unemployment	Percentage
Age (men)	16–19	21	45–54	6
Area	Merseyside	16	Oxfordshire	4
Educational qualification	None	14	Above A level	4
Ethnicity	Black	21	White	9
Gender	Men	10	Women	6

Social Trends 1996/1997.

Questions

1 Look back at the section on Unemployment (pages 204–5) and study the table. Which groups are most likely to suffer from unemployment and why?

2 Look back at the section on Minority ethnic groups and work (pages 210–11). What disadvantages do minority ethnic groups face at work? Which groups do better than others and why?

3 Why is unemployment lower for women than for men?

Work – important terms

alienation	getting no satisfaction from work
automation	when work is done by robots or other automated machinery
call centres	large offices with workers using telephones for sales and services
child labour	children doing paid work
closed shop	when in order to get a job at a workplace, a person had to belong to a union
collective bargaining	regular negotiation between employers and workers' representatives
communal economy	unpaid voluntary work, for example for a charity
craft unions	a trade union organising workers in one craft or occupation
discrimination	when someone is disadvantaged or treated unfairly
division of labour	the way work is divided, so that people specialise
domestic economy	unpaid work in the home
formal economy	paid work
general strike	when all or nearly all workers strike
general union	a trade union which organises workers in many different occupations
hidden economy	work which is not declared for tax or other official purposes
housewife	a role for women based on staying at home, housework and childcare
housework	domestic chores
industrial action	any action taken by workers against employers
industrial relations	relations between employers and workers (or unions representing workers)
Industrial Revolution	the economic and social changes between about 1750 and 1850 in which modern industry developed
informal economy	work which is not officially recorded
job satisfaction	the extent to which people find their work fulfilling
Labour movement	trade unions, the Labour Party and other smaller groups such as the Co-operative movement, working together
leisure	a freely chosen activity which is unpaid
long hours culture	pressure on workers to work long hours
mass production	producing many identical products, as on a production line
mechanisation	when machines take over work previously done by people
non-work	unavoidable activities which are neither work nor leisure
primary sector	sector of the economy involving collecting or extracting raw materials
redundancy	being laid off, no longer required by an employer
secondary sector	sector of the economy involving processing of raw materials into manufactured goods
service sector	see tertiary sector
strike	stopping work; a form of industrial action
teleworking	working using telephones and information and communications technology
tertiary sector	sector of the economy involving providing services
trade union	an organisation of workers
unemployment	being able to work, but not working

Work – exam-style questions

Source A

The labour force 1995, Great Britain, Spring 1995

Population aged 16 plus:	44.4 million (male 21.5 million, female 22.8)
In employment	25.3 million (male 14.0, female 11.3)
Unemployed	2.4 million (male 1.6, female 0.8)
Economically inactive	16.7 million (male 6.0, female 10.7)
Of those in employment: Full time	19 million (male 12.8 million, female 6.2)
Part time	5.9 million (male 1.0, female 4.9)

Sociology Update 1996, from *Employment Gazette*, October 1995.

Foundation tier

1 What is the meaning of the term unemployed? [2 marks]

2 Women are more likely than men to be working part time. Identify one reason for this. [3 marks]

3 Identify two groups who are more likely to be unemployed than others, and for each explain why this is the case. [4 marks]

4 Identify and explain two reasons why more men are unemployed in Britain than was the case 30 years ago. [5 marks]

5 'Becoming unemployed can have very serious effects on individuals.' Do you agree? Refer in your answer to three possible effects of unemployment. [6 marks]

Higher tier

1 Women are more likely than men to be working part time. Identify one reason for this. [2 marks]

2 Identify two groups who are more likely to be unemployed than others, and for each explain why this is the case. [3 marks]

3 Identify and explain two reasons why more men are unemployed in Britain than was the case 30 years ago. [5 marks]

4 'Becoming unemployed can have very serious effects on individuals.' Do you agree? Refer in your answer to a variety of possible effects of unemployment. [10 marks]

Work – further research

There are revision questions at the Hewett School web site: www.hewett.norfolk.sch.uk/curric/soc.

The main government site on employment is at: www.dfee.gov.uk.

10 Politics

This chapter is about politics in a broad sense – not just party politics. It covers the different ways in which people and groups can exercise power over others. This involves what happens in, for example, schools and workplaces as well as government.

There are different types of political system. Britain today is a democracy, but the exact form this takes is changing quickly. In the last few years we have had reform of the House of Lords and the setting up of new assemblies for Wales and Scotland. There will undoubtedly be more changes in the near future. This chapter should help you make sense of them. This is important, because at the age of 18 you will get the right to vote and the right to take part in politics. The right to vote is a right that has only been achieved through long struggles and much sacrifice, both here and in other countries. It is important that you value the right to vote and use it wisely.

IN THIS CHAPTER YOU WILL LEARN ABOUT:

- power and different types of authority
- different kinds of political systems and political ideologies
- how the British political system works
- the role of parties, pressure groups and new social movements
- voting behaviour, including differences by class, age, gender and ethnic group

CHAPTER CONTENTS

Defining the terms: politics, power, authority

This section discusses the three terms in this part of your course: politics, power and authority.

People with authority: where does authority come from?

Politics

When you hear the word politics, you probably think of the main political parties, politicians, the Houses of **Parliament** and so on. These are important aspects of politics, and you will find a lot more about them later in the chapter.

However, this is in some ways a narrow way of thinking about politics. Politics is not just national. You may also have thought of international politics (for example the European parliament), or regional politics (for example the Scottish and Welsh assemblies), or local politics (for example your local council). Politics is even present in a school, when the governors or the head teacher make decisions, or when there is a school council.

Power

Politics is about **power**. Power is when an individual or group is able to achieve its aims despite opposition from others. So, for example, when the Labour Party won the 1997 general election, it was able to form the government. It could then introduce its own policies despite opposition from the parties it had defeated.

Power is not just about what we normally think of as politics. It is a part of all social situations. If you are in a school, for example, then there are people and groups in the school with more or less power than others. The head teacher and the governors are the most powerful people, followed by teachers, who can make pupils do what they want them to do (usually!) (see Chapter 8 for more on schools).

There are also power relationships in families and in places of work. Traditionally fathers have held power in families. Families like this are called 'patriarchal' (see Chapter 7 on families). Today many families try to spread power more equally; everyone has a say in taking important decisions. In places of work there will be managers and boards of directors who take decisions.

Types of power

The most obvious way of exercising power is by taking a decision that other people have to accept. This is what governments do when they pass a new law, or what teachers do when they decide what work their pupils have to do.

However, some sociologists have argued that power is in fact much more complicated, and that there are two other 'faces of power' as well as decision making.

The first of these is non-decision making. This is when a group has the power to prevent issues from being debated and decisions from being taken. Some things will simply never be discussed at all. So power is not just about taking decisions, but about deciding what kinds of things decisions can be made about.

Behind this is a third, even less visible, face of power. This is when the powerful are able to make other people want what they want them to want. They can do this by propaganda, or by controlling what people know through the mass media.

Coercion and authority

Why is it that some people and groups have power? The sociologist Max Weber suggested that power was based either on **coercion** or **authority**.

Coercion means force. This is when people submit to the power of others because they are forced to and have no choice; they may be threatened with punishment or even death if they do not give in.

Authority is when people do what those in power want because they accept that it is the right thing to do. If someone has authority, we accept that he or she has the right to make decisions and sometimes to tell us what to do. At different times, you probably accept the authority of, among others, parents, teachers, sports referees and umpires and the police. Sometimes people have power through authority over just a part of our lives. For example, you would accept the authority of a doctor to tell you what you needed to do to recover from illness, but not that of a referee!

In practice, it is often not easy to separate coercion and authority. For example, most of the time pupils behave as teachers want them to because they accept that teachers have the right to tell them what to do, and that it will help them to learn. But pupils also behave because they know that the teacher can use coercion by imposing a punishment such as a detention. The coercion a teacher can use is limited; for example, physical punishment is no longer allowed.

Where does authority come from?

Why do some people have authority and others not? Weber suggested that there are three different kinds of authority – three types of reason why people accept being told what to do by others:

- **Traditional authority**. This kind of authority is based on history and tradition; we accept that some people are in authority because this is the way it has been. For example, the royal family have authority based on tradition. Traditional authority can also be based on religious books and values.

- **Legal rational authority**. This is when we accept someone's authority because of the position the individual holds. In the cases of a head teacher, a manager and a referee, we accept that they have the skills and abilities to do their job and we trust them to make the right decisions. If we do disagree with the decisions, we still accept that they have the right to take decisions because of their position.

- **Charismatic authority**. Charisma is a quality some people have of impressing others by seeming special or even unique. We accept their authority because of their personal qualities. Individuals who had or have tremendous charisma include Mahatma Gandhi, Martin Luther King and Nelson Mandela, and religious leaders – and also dictators like Adolf Hitler.

It is in practice hard to separate legal rational authority and charismatic authority. A **prime minister** or president of a country has legal rational authority that comes from having that position, but he or she won an election to get that position probably because he or she possessed some charismatic authority. Some teachers have charismatic authority, and are able to inspire their students, as well as having the legal rational authority that all teachers have because they are teachers.

FIND OUT FOR YOURSELF

With a partner, read though a daily newspaper. As you do so, find as many examples as you can of situations where someone has taken a decision which other people have had to accept, even if they disagree. You may find examples from politics, court cases, sport and so on. This will show you who has power in particular situations.

QUESTIONS

1. What is meant by power?
2. What is the difference between coercion and authority?
3. What are the three types of authority, according to Weber? Give an example of each.
4. Name three people who you think have or had charismatic authority. Give reasons for your answers.
5. Discuss how decision making and non-decision making have affected what your school or college is like.

ROUND-UP

Politics is much wider than party politics. It is about the exercise of power. Power applies in all social situations. Power can be exercised through coercion (force) or authority, when people accept that the powerful have a right to be powerful.

VOCABULARY

Patriarchal: when the man is the head of a family or other institution

Propaganda: information designed to support or damage an organisation or cause

Board of directors: the group of people who run a company or other organisation

Dictatorship and democracy

KEY FOCUS For most of history, people have been ruled over by an individual, such as a king or emperor, or a ruling group. The system of democracy, which means 'government by the people', has only recently become the accepted political system in most parts of the world. Earlier political systems include monarchy and aristocracy.

Democracy in action.

Aristocracy

The term **aristocracy** is usually used today to mean people with inherited titles, such as dukes and earls. Another meaning of the word, however, is a political system in which this group of people hold power.

This was the case in the Middle Ages, in the system known as feudalism. The aristocracy were the feudal lords or barons who had power over everyone in a particular area. Above the aristocracy was the king, to whom the aristocracy owed allegiance.

The aristocracy's power was based on control of land. They had the power to allow peasants to farm; in return, the peasants had to give part of their crop to their lord, and had to be prepared to fight in his army if needed. The lord protected his people from attack by outsiders.

The aristocracy in Britain gradually lost its political power, although it still has enormous wealth in the form of land. The power of the aristocracy and monarchy was replaced by **democracy**.

Dictatorship

In a **dictatorship**, power over a nation is in the hands of one ruler, a dictator, who has complete control. Dictators usually rule by coercion; people obey because they are forced to and threatened with punishment if they do not.

In a dictatorship, the government controls aspects of social life, such as the mass media, the legal system and the police. In a democracy, in contrast, these institutions have some independence from the government.

Dictatorships are able to control almost every aspect of people's lives. Where their control is total, they are called totalitarian. In dictatorships, there are no elections; or if there are, the results will be rigged. There may be only one party, or people may be told who to vote for and threatened with violence if they disobey. Disagreement with the government is not allowed. People who criticise the dictatorship, known as dissidents, face imprisonment, torture and death. There are, however, always dissidents; it is impossible for a dictatorship to get rid of all resistance completely.

Dictators in Europe in the twentieth century included:

- Hitler (in Germany)
- Mussolini (in Italy)
- Franco (in Spain).

The former Soviet Union and other communist countries were also dictatorships that did not allow free elections. Dissidents in the Soviet Union were often sent to labour camps in Siberia, and even put in mental institutions (on the grounds that they must be insane if they disagreed with **communism**). By the end of the twentieth century, however, all western European countries had been democracies for some time. There are still dictatorships in Asia and Africa (although most countries in these continents are democracies).

Example of a military dictatorship – Burma

At the time of writing, an example of a dictatorship is Burma in South East Asia. In 1990, a general election was won by Aung San Suu Kyi and her National League for Democracy. The **military dictatorship**, called SLORC (the State Law and Order Restoration Council) ignored the election result and stayed in power. Suu Kyi was put under house arrest for several years, but Burmese people continue, at great risk, to campaign for democracy.

Dictatorship is often the result of a democratic government being overthrown. The armed forces, because of their possession of arms, sometimes seize power in this way, creating what is called a military dictatorship.

Dictatorships today are put under pressure by other governments to hold elections so that democracy can be restored. Dictators usually argue that they have to remain in power because of special circumstances, that the time is not yet right to hold elections. In this way they can hold on to power.

Democracy

The political system of democracy is based on allowing people a say in decision making. In ancient Athens, all adult male citizens gathered to discuss and vote on important issues. This is called direct democracy. (Notice that women and slaves did not count.)

This cannot work in large societies so instead we have indirect or representative democracy, in which people vote for members of parliament to represent them in discussions and voting. Candidates at general elections belong to political parties, and the party that has the most members of parliament usually forms the government.

These are some of the ways in which British citizens can participate in democratic politics:

- by voting in elections – general elections, elections for the Scottish and Welsh assemblies, European elections, local council elections
- by joining (or even starting) a political party
- by standing as a candidate in an election
- by joining a **pressure group**
- by expressing an opinion to an MP or other elected representative, through writing a letter or attending a surgery
- by expressing an opinion publicly, for example in a letter to a newspaper.

In spite of this, many people feel that they have very little say in decisions made about them.

- Some people do not register to vote.
- Not all those who register do actually vote. At the 1997 general election, only 71 per cent of those registered voted, and the figure is much lower for other kinds of election.

Some people argue that real power in Britain (and other countries) is in fact in the hands of a small group of people, an elite. Britain's top civil servants, judges, army officers and so on tend to have a shared, very privileged background. They remain powerful whoever wins elections, exercising their power through the two less obvious faces of power – non-decision making and control of information. If this is true, Britain's political system is as much an **oligarchy** (rule by a small group) as a democracy.

FIND OUT FOR YOURSELF

There are several excellent books about life in dictatorships. Reading one or more these will help your study of English literature as well as sociology:

- *Animal Farm* by George Orwell
- *1984* by George Orwell
- *Talking in Whispers* by James Watson.

QUESTIONS

1. What is meant by a dictatorship?
2. What is the difference between direct democracy and indirect democracy?
3. Name three dictators in Europe in the twentieth century.
4. Identify and explain three ways in which people can take part in democratic politics in Britain.
5. In what ways is democracy better than other systems such as dictatorship or aristocracy?

ROUND-UP

Dictatorships and democracies are completely different political systems. Britain is a democracy, with frequent elections in which people vote for their representatives. On the other hand, countries such as Burma are dictatorships, where freedom is restricted and the ruling group keeps a tight grip on power.

VOCABULARY

Allegiance: loyalty
Surgery (in politics): when an MP or councillor is available to meet people he or she represents
Dissidents: people who disagree with the government

Left and right: political ideologies

KEY FOCUS Among the most common words you will come across in politics are left and right. This section explains what they mean, and introduces you to the most important political ideologies; that is, sets of political ideas about the way things are and the way they should be.

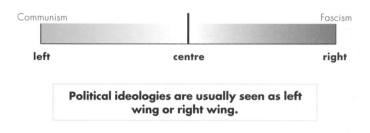

Political ideologies are usually seen as left wing or right wing.

Left and right

When the French king Louis XVI called a meeting in 1789, the aristocracy sat on the king's right and representatives of ordinary people on the left. This is where the terms left wing and right wing in politics came from.

Broadly speaking, the left is in favour of greater equality – of all people being treated equally. The left is opposed to the capitalist economic system because it creates inequality – capitalism allows some people to become much richer than others. The poor are seen as victims of an unjust system. According to the left, governments need to bring in new ways of creating equality.

The right do not favour equality, believing that inequality is natural and right. Those who work hard, who have greater ability and so on deserve to be better off than those who do not. They believe that the poor have only themselves to blame. The capitalist system is seen as good because it creates wealth and prosperity, and allows freedom. According to the right, governments should do very little, simply let the system work.

Communism is the most left-wing set of political ideas, **fascism** the most right-wing. Communism and fascism are explained below.

British political parties are all closer to the centre of the spectrum. The Conservative Party is to the right of centre. Margaret Thatcher's governments of 1979 to 1990 moved the Conservative Party further to the right than it had been before. The Labour Party is traditionally a left-wing party, although many people feel that the Blair government elected in 1997 was more in the centre. The Liberal Democrats are somewhere between the two main parties.

Not everyone feels that discussing politics in terms of left and right is useful:

- Some people argue that the two extremes – communism and fascism – were in some ways similar to each other. Both led to dictatorships, lack of freedom and punishment of dissent. Perhaps the real difference is between the extremes and the centre.

- Left and right disagree strongly on inequality and the role of the state, but on many important issues there are no clear left- and right-wing views. For example, joining the European single currency, or animal rights, might be supported or opposed by either left or right.

- Recently it has been argued that the world, and politics, have changed so much that the terms left and right are no longer helpful. For example, both fascism and communism seem to many people to belong to the past, rather than being relevant today.

The third way?

Politicians including British Prime Minister Tony Blair and former US President Bill Clinton have described their style of politics as a **'third way'**, which is neither left nor right. They say the third way avoids the endless debate between left and right, taking the best of each. The third way has been described as the politics of 'the radical centre'.

It follows the right in valuing private enterprise and encouraging individuals to be responsible for themselves. It follows the left in believing in helping the weak and poor and emphasising communities rather than individuals. Third way ideas have been developed by, among others, the leading British sociologist Anthony Giddens. They have been taken up by the British Labour Party and by similar parties in Europe.

Critics of the third way argue that it is impossible to compromise between left and right in this way.

Political ideologies

Ideologies are sets of ideas based on a particular view of the way things are and the way they should be. Political ideologies provide ideas to believe in a similar way to religion. Here are brief accounts of some of the main ideologies.

Communism

Communism is based on the writings of Karl Marx. It is a reaction against the capitalist economic system. Communists believe that capitalism must be overthrown in a revolution led by the working class. This will create a new type of society, where there is equality and where the means of producing wealth (such as factories and farms) are owned by everyone. The first communist country was the Soviet Union, but communism ended there and throughout eastern Europe in 1989. The only official communist states at the time of writing are China, Vietnam, Laos, North Korea and Cuba.

Fascism

This extreme right-wing **ideology** was successful in Italy under Mussolini, Franco in Spain, Hitler in Germany and elsewhere in Europe in the 1940s. It was strongly anti-communist and anti-democratic. Fascist leaders were dictators who stamped out dissent. Racism and extreme nationalism were usually part of fascism. Germany's fascist party, the Nazis, believed in the superiority of the German people, and their right to dominate or destroy those they regarded as 'lesser races'.

Conservatism

Conservatism is a right-wing ideology, but clearly different from fascism. Conservatives believe in keeping old institutions, and avoiding radical changes, so that society is kept stable. They believe that inequality is necessary and desirable. Societies need a rich, powerful ruling class to govern them. Radical attempts to change society for the better, such as communism, are seen as based on a wrong view of human nature; they are bound to go wrong.

Socialism

Socialism is a left-wing ideology, but less extreme than communism. Its main beliefs are in public ownership of industry and greater equality. Socialism, like communism, is based on advancing the interests of the working class, but through gradual democratic change rather than revolution.

Green ideology

For Greens, the central political issue is how to protect the natural environment from pollution and exploitation by people. Greens believe that the survival of humanity and even of the whole planet is put at risk by our present way of life. While all other political ideologies favour industry as a way of increasing wealth, Greens question whether we can continue to have industries using up natural resources. **Green ideology** is relatively new, and Green parties have so far only achieved limited successes.

c w FIND OUT FOR YOURSELF

In a small group, choose one of the political ideologies listed above. Using reference books, Microsoft Encarta or other sources, research this ideology. Find out about the main beliefs and about important people and events. Present your findings in the form of a large poster for display. (For Green ideology, you may need to look under **environmentalism**.)

QUESTIONS

1 What is meant by an ideology?

2 What is the difference between left wing and right wing?

3 Choose two political ideologies and explain briefly what each stands for.

4 Identify and explain two reasons why some people think that the terms left and right are less important than they used to be?

5 Which of the ideologies do you tend to agree with most? Give reasons for your answer.

ROUND-UP

Left wing and right wing refer to contrasting political positions. Socialism and communism are left-wing ideologies; conservatism and fascism right-wing ideologies. Newer ideologies, such as the Green ideology, are hard to classify in this way. Some people argue that the terms left and right are becoming less useful in understanding politics.

VOCABULARY

Dissent: disagreeing with the government
Revolution: a sudden, dramatic change of political system, often violent

The British political system

KEY FOCUS In the section on Dictatorship and democracy, Britain today was described as a democracy. While this is true, there are also some aspects of British politics that are not democratic. This section looks at the political system in Britain today, at how democratic it is and at how it might change.

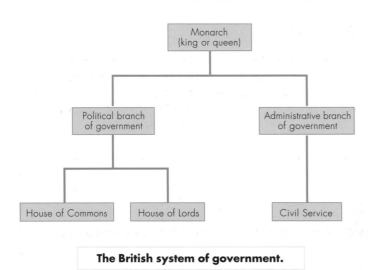

The British system of government.

The right to vote

The extension of the franchise – the right to vote – has been an important part of the development of the British political system. Here are some key dates:

1832	The First Reform Act gave the right to vote to middle-class men – 95 per cent of people could not vote.
1867	The Second Reform Act extended the right to vote to skilled working men – 87 per cent of the population could not vote.
1884	Almost all working men allowed to vote.
1918	Women over 30 given the right to vote.
1928	Women over 21 allowed to vote (same as men).
1970	Everyone over 18 allowed to vote.
1989	British citizens living abroad allowed to vote.

There are still a few groups of people who are not allowed to vote. These include:

- citizens of foreign countries, even if they are permanently resident in Britain
- the insane
- peers (lords)
- those in prison serving sentences of a year or more
- those under 18 – the biggest group not allowed to vote.

Citizenship rights

The right to vote is only one of the rights that citizens expect to have in a democracy. Here are some that most people would agree on:

- individual freedoms – thought, speech and belief
- the right to own property
- the right to be treated equally, and not to be discriminated against.

A further set of rights is about what governments should provide for their citizens. In the early and mid-twentieth century governments provided these through the institutions of the welfare state (see Chapter 13 Poverty and Welfare). Towards the end of the century, some of these rights were reduced as governments cut back the welfare state:

- the right to education
- the right to work
- the right to health care and a healthy life.

The electoral system

Governments are elected at general elections, which must be held at least every five years. At a general election, all registered voters can vote in the **constituency** where they live for a candidate. The main political parties – Conservative, Labour and Liberal Democrat – have candidates in almost all constituencies. One candidate, the one receiving the most votes, is elected as **Member of Parliament** (MP) for each constituency. This is called the **first past the post** system.

Parliament

Parliament has two houses – the House of Commons and the House of Lords.

MPs sit in the House of Commons in Westminster, where they debate issues and vote on bills put forward by the government. If passed, bills have to be signed by the monarch. They then become Acts of Parliament. Although in theory MPs represent their constituencies, on most issues they vote with the party they belong to. MPs occasionally change parties. They do not have to fight a new election if they do so. If an MP dies or resigns in between general elections, there has to be a by-election, when voters in that constituency choose a new MP.

The House of Lords is much less powerful than the Commons but is sometimes able to hold up or change bills.

The party that has a majority of MPs forms the government. The British system tends to produce governments with clear majorities, but occasionally there have been coalitions. This is when two or more parties combine to form the government. Usually this will be because the biggest party does not have a majority over the other parties combined, so needs reliable support.

The Prime Minister is usually the leader of the party with the most MPs, although in theory the king or queen can decide who to appoint. A party can change its leader at any time, so there can be a new Prime Minister without a general election. This happened when John Major took over as leader of the Conservative Party from Margaret Thatcher in 1990.

The Prime Minister has a team of ministers, each responsible for an area of government policy and supported by junior ministers, advisers and civil servants. The most senior ministers form the **Cabinet**, meeting regularly to decide policies.

Other elections

British citizens also elect:

- Members of the European Parliament (MEPs)
- local councillors – British local government is complicated; some areas have one council, others have two (for example a district council and a county council).

Citizens living in Scotland and Wales also vote for members of their regional assemblies.

A democracy?

Here are some ways in which Britain is not fully democratic:

- The head of state – the king or queen – is not elected. In the USA, the head of state is the president, and there is a presidential election every four years.
- The House of Lords is not elected.
- Some countries also have elections for public officials such as judges and magistrates.

Extending democracy

There has been much discussion about political reforms to increase participation in politics. The setting up of the Scottish and Welsh assemblies, the reform of the House of Lords and the direct election of a Mayor of London have been the first

reforms brought in by the Labour government elected in 1997. Future reforms may include:

- regional assemblies for English regions
- changing the first past the post system to a **proportional representation** system, where the number of MPs elected reflects the votes the party received
- more use of referenda, when particular issues are voted on
- making it possible to vote at different times and in different places (for example in supermarkets)
- electing members of the House of Lords.

▶ FIND OUT FOR YOURSELF

Visit the British Parliament's web site. The home page is at http://www.parliament.uk/. There is a section designed for students at http://www.explore.parliament.uk. Try the quest for the mace, and the political puzzle which will test how much you know about how Parliament works.

QUESTIONS

1. What is meant by the franchise?
2. What are the two Houses of Parliament, and who sits in each?
3. Identify and explain two ways in which the British political system is not fully democratic.
4. Identify and explain two reforms that would make the system more democratic.
5. Do you think that 18 is the right age for people to be allowed to vote? Explain your answer.

ROUND-UP

British citizens have rights including the right to vote. Although Britain can be described as a democracy, there are some aspects of the political system that are not fully democratic. Recent reforms have begun significantly to change the system.

VOCABULARY

Magistrate: the official who judges minor cases, in a magistrate's court
Coalition: an alliance between two or more parties

Political parties

KEY FOCUS Political parties in Britain today include Labour, the Conservatives and the Liberal Democrats. They compete against each other in elections to win power.

Year	Party forming government	Prime Minister
1945	Labour	Clement Attlee
1950	Labour	Clement Attlee
1951	Conservative	Winston Churchill
1955	Conservative	Anthony Eden (to 1957) Harold McMillan (from 1957)
1959	Conservative	Harold McMillan (to 1963) Alec Douglas Home (from 1963)
1964	Labour	Harold Wilson
1966	Labour	Harold Wilson
1970	Conservative	Edward Heath
1974 Feb.	Labour	Harold Wilson
1974 Oct.	Labour	Harold Wilson (to 1976) James Callaghan (from 1976)
1979	Conservative	Margaret Thatcher
1983	Conservative	Margaret Thatcher
1987	Conservative	Margaret Thatcher (to 1990) John Major (from 1990)
1992	Conservative	John Major
1997	Labour	Tony Blair
2001	Labour	Tony Blair

General elections, 1945–2001: power has swung between the two main parties.

Parties

Political parties are organisations which put up candidates at elections and which hope to form the government. They have policies on a wide range of issues, such as the economy, education, health, defence and so on. Their policies are published in manifestos that set out for voters what the party will do if elected. If the party is elected, it can claim that it has a mandate to carry out the policies in its manifesto; that is, that voters have given their approval to its policies.

Political parties are membership organisations. Members belong to a constituency party or association, and may also belong to a local branch of the party based on a local government area or ward. Members usually have the chance to:

- take part in choosing candidates (and to put themselves forward as candidates)
- discuss and vote on policies and issues
- campaign for the party, especially at election times (They may deliver leaflets, or ask people how they intend to vote. Those who say they will vote for that party can then be reminded to vote on the day, or even offered a lift to the polling station. This is called canvassing.)
- take part in fund raising activities
- take part in social activities.

The main parties

Labour

At the time of writing, Labour was the party in government. Labour has traditionally been seen as a left-wing party supported by the working class and based on the political ideology of democratic socialism. Its critics, however, have argued that in government it has consistently failed to carry out radical policies (see the section on Left and right on pages 230–31).

The Labour party has always had very close connections to the trade union movement, relying on unions to support it financially. Trade unions still sponsor many Labour MPs. It is also closely connected to other working-class organisations such as the Co-operative movement. Its support has always been strongest in working-class areas, and in cities rather than the countryside.

Labour first won a general election in 1923, but the first Labour government with a clear majority was from 1945 to 1951, led by Prime Minister Clement Attlee. This government introduced the National Health Service and nationalised – took into public control – many industries. Labour was again in power from 1964 to 1970, and from 1974 to 1979. It then had a long period in opposition until its spectacular victory under Tony Blair in 1997.

During the long period of opposition from 1979 to 1997, the Labour Party reformed its organisation. It revised its policies so as to make itself more attractive to voters other than those who had always voted Labour. In recognition of these changes, it is sometimes referred to now as 'New Labour'. Some members – or ex-members – believe that the Labour Party has abandoned its origins.

The Conservative Party

The Conservative Party is on the right wing of British politics and is supported mainly by the middle and upper class. Some working-class people have also always supported it. The Conservatives are the party of big business, supported financially by many companies and wealthy individuals.

The Conservative Party was in power for much of the twentieth century. Since World War II, there have been two very long periods of Conservative rule, from 1951 to 1964 and from 1979 to 1997. The dominant figure in the latter period was Margaret Thatcher, Prime Minister from 1979 to 1990. Mrs Thatcher moved her party away from older Conservative ideas and introduced sweeping changes, including the privatisation – selling off – of most of the industries Labour had nationalised, and the dismantling of the welfare state.

There were, however, very deep divisions within the Conservative Party, and in 1990 Margaret Thatcher was forced to resign. Her successor, John Major, rallied the party to win the 1992 election narrowly. In 1997, however, the Conservatives suffered a humiliating defeat, from which it appeared they would take many years to recover.

The Conservative Party is strongest in England, especially southern England, and outside the big cities.

The Liberal Democrats

The Liberal Democrats are the third party of British politics, some way behind the other two. This was not always the case. The Liberal Party won elections in the past but was replaced by Labour as the main alternative to the Conservatives after World War I.

The present Liberal Democrat Party is the result of a merger between the Liberal Party and the Social Democrat Party, a small party that split off from Labour in the 1980s.

Although the Liberals win quite a few votes in many constituencies, they do not win many seats, often finishing second or third. They would do better under a system that, unlike the first past the post system, gave parties seats in proportion to the number of votes they got nationally.

The Liberal Party is particularly strong in rural areas in Wales and Scotland, and in the south west of England.

Other parties

Other important parties include the Scottish National Party, Plaid Cymru (the Welsh national party) and the Green Party. The British National Party is an extreme right-wing party with racist policies. There are many other parties. Sometimes candidates who do not have a party behind them stand for election as an independent.

FIND OUT FOR YOURSELF

Find out which political parties members of your family support, and why. Ask whether they have supported or voted for a different party in the past, and why.

QUESTIONS

1 What is meant by a political party?

2 Identify and explain two activities that members of political parties can take part in.

3 What are the two main parties in British politics? Write a sentence summarising the political ideology of each.

4 From the table at the beginning of this section, work out (a) how many years Labour has been in power, and how many years the Conservatives have been in power, (b) who was Prime Minister for most years?

5 Why is the Labour Party today sometimes described as New Labour? Do you think this is accurate?

ROUND-UP

The main parties in Britain are Labour and the Conservatives. Parties develop policies, published in manifestos, and put up candidates at elections. Anyone can join a political party as a member, and to be a successful politician it is necessary to belong to a party.

VOCABULARY

Dismantling: taking apart
Manifesto: the published statement of the aims and policies of a party
Canvassing: when parties ask people which party they intend to vote for

Pressure groups

KEY FOCUS

Political parties are not the only organisations that are essential in democratic politics. Pressure groups are another way in which people can get together to have some influence on decision making. This section looks at the different types of pressure groups, how they work and how important they are.

Pressure groups such as Amnesty International are an essential part of democratic politics.

Pressure groups and political parties

Along with political parties, pressure groups are essential to democratic politics. They differ from political parties in these ways:

- Pressure groups try to influence the government but do not want to be the government. They focus on one issue or a related group of issues, such as animal rights.
- Political parties try to get their candidates elected in order to win political power and have policies on a wide range of issues.

There are many pressure groups and they vary considerably from each other. There are several ways of classifying them.

Interest and promotional pressure groups

Interest groups, or sectional pressure groups, represent the interests of a particular group of people. Examples include:

- the AA and the RAC – representing the interests of motorists
- trade unions – representing the interests of workers in particular industries (see the section on Trade unionism on pages 216–17)

- professional associations, such as the British Medical Association (BMA) – representing the interests of their members (doctors).

Protective pressure groups usually aim to recruit as members or supporters everyone who belongs to the group they wish to represent.

Promotional pressure groups represent particular beliefs or points of view. Examples include:

- Amnesty International – campaigning against execution, torture and imprisonment for political beliefs
- Greenpeace – campaigning on environmental issues
- Royal Society for the Protection of Birds (RSPB) – campaigning for bird lovers, and birds.

Anyone can join a promotional pressure group, although of course in practice only those who agree strongly with the beliefs or values will do so.

It is often hard to distinguish between these two types of pressure group. For example, Shelter both campaigns on homelessness and represents the interests of homeless people.

Insider and outsider groups

An alternative way to classify pressure groups is according to how much access they have to politicians and government departments.

Those who are taken seriously, who will be consulted as a matter of course on issues affecting them, are called insider groups. They are considered to be respectable, and their opinions are considered to be sensible and serious.

Outsider groups are those that are not consulted because their aims or their methods are not recognised by the government. For example, on animal rights issues the government might consult the Royal Society for the Prevention of Cruelty to Animals (RSPCA), an insider group, but not the Animal Liberation Front (ALF), which is an outsider group because of its methods, which have included raids on laboratories and attacks on scientists.

Some groups have much greater resources than others. They manage to raise money for their campaigns, and this gives them a greater chance of success than others.

Pressure group methods

What do pressure groups actually do to try to influence government policies?

Here are some of their methods:

- Lobbying government. Insider groups can influence policy through contacts with ministers and civil servants.
- Campaigning. This covers a wide range of activities including public meetings, press conferences, advertising, organising petitions, carrying out research, publishing leaflets and so on.
- Direct actions, protests and demonstrations (and in the case of trade unions, strikes). These may involve actions that can be seen as illegal.

Pressure groups and the law

Sometimes the activities of some outsider groups are against the law. Actions that might involve arrest and prosecution include:

- hunt saboteurs disrupting fox hunting
- animal rights activists raiding laboratories and releasing animals
- protests that disrupt traffic, such as anti-traffic protestors blocking a motorway, or demonstrators against animal exports blocking ports
- destroying fields of genetically modified crops.

Sometimes the actions are such that opponents of the pressure group can accuse it of **terrorism**. It could be said that terrorist organisations are extreme outsider pressure groups, trying to force governments into particular policies through the use of violence. The Irish Republican Army's (IRA) aim was to force the British government to give up control of Northern Ireland. Other supporters of this aim used non-violent, traditional pressure group methods, while the IRA used violence.

How important are pressure groups?

Positive views of pressure groups

- Because we have representative, rather than direct, democracy, pressure groups are a way of involving people more in politics, especially between elections. They are an additional way in which people can make their views known, and so they strengthen democracy.
- Pressure groups are a way in which people can advise and warn the government; for example, groups like Greenpeace have done a lot to increase awareness of environmental problems.

Negative views of pressure groups

- Many people do not get involved in pressure groups, so their voices are not heard.

- There are so many pressure groups that governments waste a lot of time listening to them and trying to reach agreements with them.
- To Marxists, the only significant pressure groups are the powerful insider groups like the bankers and financiers of the City of London. Other groups only provide an illusion of democracy; they cannot bring about real change.

FIND OUT FOR YOURSELF

In a large group, make a list of as many different pressure groups as you can. Start with the ones mentioned on these pages, but try to add more. Then try to sort them out into different types: interest and promotional pressure groups, insider and outsider groups, what they campaign on, what tactics they use.

QUESTIONS

1. Name five pressure groups, and write one sentence for each explaining what it does.

2. What is the difference between interest and promotional pressure groups? Use examples to explain your answer.

3. Identify and explain three ways in which pressure groups try to achieve their aims.

4. What tactics that pressure groups might use run a risk of being seen as against the law. Illustrate your answer by referring to examples.

5. How important are pressure groups to democratic politics? Explain your answer.

ROUND-UP

There are many pressure groups and many kinds of pressure groups. Some represent interest groups while others promote a particular view. They use a wide range of methods including, in a few cases, breaking the law.

VOCABULARY

Lobbying: attempting to influence politicians
Petitions: a document signed by a large number of people asking for action from the government or other authority

New social movements

A third type of political organisation, as well as parties and pressure groups, is new social movements. These are loosely organised, usually without leaders, and they often use direct action tactics such as demonstrations and occupations.

A new kind of direct politics?

Social movements

Social movements are groups that try to influence society by campaigning for or against change.

It is not easy to distinguish pressure groups and political parties from social movements. Pressure groups tend to have hierarchical, formal organisations; that is, they elect leaders and committees, have formal meetings and so on. Political parties are also formal; for example, members have to pay fees and get membership cards. **New social movements** (NSMs) are much looser and open.

New social movements

The movements usually described as NSMs include:

- the environmental and ecological movement
- women's liberation and feminism
- peace and anti-nuclear movement
- gay and lesbian liberation movement
- the animal rights movement.

Within each of these broad movements are a range of different organisations and informal groups of interested people. For example, the environmental movement includes pressure groups like Greenpeace and Friends of the Earth as well as more informal groups such as some local people getting together to protest against a new road or campaign on a green issue. There is also a political party, the Green Party, which is clearly part of a much broader environmental movement. You do not have to belong to Greenpeace or the Green Party to be an environmentalist; some belong to neither, some to one or the other, some to both.

Some NSMs do not have such a broad agenda, and instead focus on a single issue. These are often short-lived movements sparked off by a dramatic event. For example, the murder of schoolchildren at Dunblane led to a movement to change the law on owning guns.

There have always been social movements, but old social movements (OSMs) tended to be more formal and organised, and to focus on work and economic issues. Examples include the movements against slavery and to end the exploitation of children at work, and the trade union movement.

Several of the NSMs 'took off' in the 1960s and 1970s, becoming popular and making politicians and parties consider issues they had tended to ignore before.

Because NSMs are so loose, and because anyone can get involved, there are inevitably many arguments and differences of opinion. These are often about the best way to achieve goals that most people involved agree on. In particular, activists often disagree on how much to trust and work with established pressure groups and political parties.

What makes NSMs different?

- Interested in wide issues related to the quality of life and expressing individuality.
- Not based on class, but usually mainly middle-class support.
- No formal membership.
- No formal structure (no chairperson, secretary, committees, etc.).
- Everyone can take part in decision making and in direct actions.
- Often have a strong sense of being morally right.
- Often the movements are international, because the issues they focus on are international.
- Supporters are often young; NSMs appeal more to young people than traditional parties do.

Young people's politics – the appeal of NSMs as opposed to political parties

> Britain's best known eco-warrior [Swampy] took part in protests against road building and the expansion of Manchester airport. Born in Buckinghamshire, middle class background, left school at 17. Became a hunt saboteur at 17, gave out anti-road leaflets at 18. 'If I wrote a letter to my MP, would I have achieved all this?'
>
> 'A plague on all your houses' by Ruaridh Nicoll, *Guardian*, 29 January 1998.

NSM tactics

NSMs campaign mainly through direct action. This can take many forms. In recent years some of the more spectacular and newsworthy have included:

- road protestors occupying trees and buildings on sites scheduled for clearing
- animal rights protestors breaking into laboratories and releasing animals into the wild
- protestors against exports of live animals blocking the way of lorries into ports
- protestors against genetically modified crops destroying fields of crops
- protests against globalisation, such as those in Seattle and Prague in 2000.

Some protests have a strong element of fun and celebration. They are symbolic, designed to draw attention to issues.

Other tactics are more traditional including:

- handing out leaflets
- signing petitions
- sit-down demonstrations
- getting stories into local and national news
- boycotting a company (not buying its products or services).

The police and other authorities often find it difficult to deal with direct action. A very heavy approach is likely to win support for the protestors, who will these days have video cameras to film any violent or unacceptable behaviour by the police. In planned protests such as those in London on 1 May 2000, the police wanted to negotiate with the organisers, so as to minimise any dangers and inconvenience to the public. The trouble is that with NSMs there are no organisers to negotiate with.

The future of NSMs

Any formal organisations set up within NSMs may have some success, because the authorities like to be able to deal with clearly identified groups who have leaders. This has helped, for example, Greenpeace and Friends of the Earth. However, organisations like these face pressure to become respectable and avoid direct action. If this happens, they may be seen as out of touch. New forms of direct action groups will spring up to replace them.

It seems likely that the number of NSMs and of direct action protests will continue to grow.

IT ▶ FIND OUT FOR YOURSELF

Investigate one example of a long-running campaign based on a boycott. Products made by the company Nestlé have been boycotted because the company has been accused of promoting its baby and infant foods as better than breastfeeding. This has been said to have serious effects on the health of many babies and infants in third world countries. You can find the point of view of the coordinators of the boycott at http://www.babymilkaction.org. You can find the company's point of view at http://www.nestle.com. Use the web site's search engine to find the company's Infant Formula Charter.

QUESTIONS

1. What is meant by a new social movement?

2. Using examples, explain the difference between old social movements and new social movements

3. Give three examples of using direct action which have been big news in recent years.

4. Why do some organisations give up direct action and become more respectable?

5. Why do you think NSMs and direct action seem to have a strong appeal to young people?

ROUND-UP

New social movements are loosely organised groups campaigning on a wide range of issues. They use direct action tactics as well as more traditional tactics. Young people are more likely to be involved in NSMs than in political parties.

VOCABULARY

Hierarchy: an organisation with several levels – leaders at the top, their deputies and assistants on the next level, and so on
Agenda: a list of matters of interest or to be discussed
Boycott: to refuse to have any dealings with

Voting behaviour

KEY FOCUS

Voting is most people's main involvement in politics, although there are many other ways of participating. How people vote can be influenced by many different factors. These include the social characteristics of the voter, and the parties' images and policies.

The right to vote: a right that people have had to fight for.

Participation in politics

There are many different ways in which people can take part in politics. These include:

- standing for election to a local council, regional assembly, national or European government
- joining a political party and campaigning for it
- attending political meetings
- joining a protest or demonstration
- voting in elections
- writing letters to politicians or the media.

Voting

Types of voter

Some people are loyal to one political party, identifying quite strongly with it. They will not change their minds during an election campaign. They can be called loyal voters.

Other people may vote for different parties in different elections. They 'float' from one party to another and are called floating voters.

Tactical voters carefully work out who to vote for to affect the outcome. For example, a Liberal Democrat supporter in a seat which the Liberal Democrats have no hope of winning may vote Labour to make sure the Conservative is defeated.

Other people do not vote at all. In 1997, 29.6 per cent of those registered to vote did not vote. Others were not registered. There are several reasons why people do not vote:

- Apathy – they are not interested in politics and do not feel their vote is important.
- They may not know how to vote, or may not understand what the issues are.
- They may not feel that any of the candidates or parties represent their views.

The number of people voting in an election is called the turnout. The turnout is biggest for general elections, and is often very low for local council elections.

Social characteristics

This section looks at just one of these ways of participating in politics – voting. Different groups of people are more likely to vote than others, and more likely to vote for particular parties. In other words, voting behaviour is related to people's social characteristics.

Class

The Labour Party has traditionally won most of its votes from the working class while the Conservative Party has won most of its votes from the middle class. Both parties try hard to win the support of C2 voters (see pages 58–9); that is, skilled manual workers. It is thought that this category is the one most likely to change from one party to another.

Gender

In most elections women are more likely to vote than men, and usually women are slightly more likely to vote Conservative than men are.

Age

Young people are less likely to vote than older people. When they do vote, they are more likely to vote Labour, whereas retired people are more likely to vote Conservative. There are different opinions about why this should be:

- It could be that young people are more radical and idealistic, and become more conservative as they get older, *or*
- it could be that it is the particular experiences of people who are older now that makes them Conservative. Perhaps those who are middle aged today, who grew up in the freer 1960s and 1970s, will be less conservative when they are older.

Ethnicity

Minority ethnic group members are less likely to vote. Many Afro-Caribbeans are not registered to vote and at the 1997 election there was a campaign to try to get young black people to register and vote. Members of ethnic minority groups are much more likely to vote Labour than Conservative.

Region

The Conservative Party is strongest in the south of England and in rural areas, the Labour Party in the north of England and in Scotland and Wales. These regional differences are partly related to class differences. The Conservatives did not win any seats at all in Scotland in the 1997 election. In Scotland and Wales, however, the nationalist parties challenge Labour, and the Liberal Democrats are strong in some areas such as the south west of England.

Religion

This is not now particularly important in England, Scotland and Wales but elsewhere religion can be a strong influence. In Northern Ireland, for example, Catholics and Protestants tend to vote for different parties.

Political factors

Policies

The parties publish manifestos which tell voters what they intend to do if they win. The policies parties adopt can affect whether people vote for them or not. Parties therefore spend a lot of time finding out what policies would be supported by the people whose votes they want to get.

Party image

Just as important as policies are the general impressions people have of parties. The media play a big part in creating these images through the way they report the news, and the parties themselves try to create positive images.

Leaders

A party's leader is its best known public face. A popular leader with a very positive image can help a party win votes even if its policies are not popular; similarly, an unpopular leader can lose votes.

Political socialisation

People's ideas about politics are shaped by the people and other social influences around them. Parents have a big influence on their children's politics. Children can be socialised into loyalty to a particular party, or to a set of political values.

The impression people get of a party, its leader and its policies is shaped by the mass media. How newspapers, television and radio report on politics is therefore very important.

FIND OUT FOR YOURSELF

Look back to the results of the research you carried out in the section on Political parties (see page 236). Can the people you interviewed then be described as loyal, floating or tactical voters? (They may have been different kinds of voter at different times.)

QUESTIONS

1. List three ways in which people can take part in politics.
2. What is meant by a tactical voter?
3. Identify and explain two reasons why some people do not vote.
4. Which party are members of minority ethnic groups most likely to vote for? Why do you think this is?
5. Three types of political factor are explained above: policies, images and leaders. Which of these do you think is the most important in influencing how people vote? Explain your answer. It may help to think about the two main parties, Labour and Conservative, at the moment.

ROUND-UP

There are different kinds of voters – loyal, floating and tactical voters – as well as those who choose not to vote. There are many influences on how people vote, including their social characteristics (their class, age, ethnicity and so on) and the parties' policies and images.

VOCABULARY

Registered: in order to vote, a person has to be on the register, also called the electoral roll
Idealistic: believing that it is important to try to reach ideals

Class and politics

KEY FOCUS

The two main parties in British politics are strongly associated with classes, although not as strongly as they used to be. The electoral struggle between Conservative and Labour has been seen as a struggle between the middle and upper classes on one hand and the working class on the other.

Margaret Thatcher: Conservative Prime Minister 1979 to 1990; middle class background – father owned a grocer's shop; studied at Oxford University; married a rich businessman.

Tony Benn: Labour MP and former minister; born into the aristocracy; gave up his title to become a Labour MP.

These politicians' class backgrounds were important influences on them.

Class and the main parties

There are two main political parties in Britain, Conservative and Labour, and in terms of the number of people, two main classes, the middle class and the working class (the upper class is important but small). Labour has traditionally been seen as the party of the working class, and the Conservative Party as the party of the middle class. Labour has relied for money and other forms of support on the trade union movement, which is identified with the working class although many middle-class workers now also belong to unions. The Conservative Party relies for its funding on business and industry.

As you have seen, however, there are many other influences on voting. The connection between class and voting is not straightforward. In both main classes there have always been people who voted against expectations.

Working-class Conservatives

For the Conservative Party to win elections, it must win some support from the working class. So the Conservative's most recent victories, in 1979, 1983, 1987 and 1992 depended on working-class voters, especially those from category C2 (skilled manual workers).

Some members of the working class are loyal Conservative voters because they have an attitude of deference; that is, they have an exaggerated respect for the type of people who run the Conservative Party. They see people born into a high social class, going to public schools and so on, as naturally better at running the country.

This attitude is now less common and it is more likely that working-class Conservatives are looking at party policies and deciding they will be better off under a Conservative government. This means they are pragmatic voters. In the 1980s and early 1990s, then, many working-class people voted Conservative because they hoped to benefit from the Conservatives' policies, such as low taxes and selling off council housing.

One sociologist, Frank Parkin, has pointed out that the Conservatives are very much the party of the British establishment. Labour are outsiders, often represented in the media (at least in the past) as dangerous outsiders. Perhaps working-class Conservatives are 'normal', and the unusual behaviour, which we need to try to explain, is why so many people vote Labour.

Middle-class radicals

Just as some working-class people vote Conservative, some middle-class people also break expectations by voting Labour. They are often those who have a higher education and who are working in the public sector – as teachers, social workers and in the health services.

There are a number of possible reasons for this. One is that the same values that led people to work in these kinds of jobs – in public service, helping the community, looking after those who need help, and so on – are closer to Labour values than Conservative ones. Another is that Labour is seen as more likely to support the public sector, through more funding – that may mean pay rises.

Class dealignment

The idea that most of the working class support Labour and most of the middle class support the Conservatives is called **class alignment**. The idea that this is increasingly not the case is called **class dealignment**.

Here are some arguments for class dealignment; that is, that class is not as important as it used to be:

- Fewer voters are loyal voters; more voters are willing to switch parties.
- Class overall is seen by many people as less important than it used to be, so it would not be surprising if it were less important in politics. It is often argued that rising living standards, ownership of consumer goods and so on break down old class barriers.
- Other parties, which are not as obviously based on class, get more votes than they used to in the 1950s and 1960s (Liberal Democrats, nationalists).
- The parties themselves are less interested in class. For example, the Labour Party under Tony Blair tries to show itself as representing the whole country, not just the working class.

However, class is still undoubtedly important in voting behaviour:

- The core support of both main parties is still from their traditional class supporters. Although Labour tries to win the middle class, it still needs its traditional working-class voters to win elections.
- Even during the Conservative-dominated elections of 1979 to 1992, Labour continued to win the support of its core working-class voters.

Class voting at the 1997 general election

AB voters (professional and managerial): 42 per cent voted Conservative, 31 per cent Labour, 21 per cent Liberal Democrat

DE voters (semi-skilled and unskilled manual workers): 21 per cent Conservative, 61 per cent Labour, 13 per cent Liberal Democrat

Overall election result: 31 per cent Conservative, 45 per cent Labour, 17 per cent Liberal Democrat

Politicians

In the past, there was a clear division between the parties in terms of the social background of MPs. Conservative MPs were almost always from privileged backgrounds, and had attended public schools and often Oxford or Cambridge universities. They were from upper middle-class, or even upper-class, backgrounds. Labour MPs were often from working-class backgrounds, and had not had the privileges and education that Conservatives had had.

The gap between the parties has been narrowing for many years. Conservative MPs are less likely than they used to be to have been to public school. Labour MPs are less likely to be from traditional working-class backgrounds, and more likely to have a university education and to have had a professional occupation.

QUESTIONS

1. What is meant by deference?
2. Identify and explain two reasons why a working-class person might vote Conservative.
3. What is meant by class dealignment?
4. Identify and explain two reasons for thinking that class is less important when it comes to voting behaviour than it used to be.
5. How important is class in voting behaviour? Explain your answer.

ROUND-UP

Class has in the past been seen as the most important factor in voting behaviour, with both parties relying on loyal voters from the class they represent. In recent years this view has been challenged as other factors become more important. Class dealignment is the idea that class is less important in deciding which party someone will vote for than it once was.

VOCABULARY

Pragmatic: behaviour that is decided by practical consequences rather than theories or ideas

Gender and politics

KEY FOCUS

This section looks at women as voters and as politicians. Women won the right to vote much later than men. This has held back the involvement of women as politicians. Although Margaret Thatcher made it to the top, politics is still dominated by men.

1997 – a record number of women MPs – but most of the top politicians were still men.

Voting behaviour

1997 general election:
Men – Conservative 31 per cent, Labour 44 per cent, Liberal Democrat 17 per cent, other parties 8 per cent
Women – Conservative 32 per cent, Labour 44 per cent, Liberal Democrat 17 per cent, others 7 per cent

As you can see from the box on voting behaviour, there was very little difference in the way men and women voted in 1997. Usually women are slightly more likely to vote Conservative, but this difference almost disappeared in 1997. This may be because Labour had a much larger number of women candidates than in the past, and so had the image of a 'female friendly' party. Labour also projected itself as strongly supporting the family, and this may have influenced female voters.

There are several reasons why women have been more likely to vote Conservative than Labour:

- Because women in the past were less likely to go out to work, they had less contact with Labour ideas through places of work, trade unions and so on.
- The Conservatives have often had the image of 'the party of the family', and this has appealed to women because the family is so important in their lives.
- It has been argued that because women have the main role of looking after their families, they are less willing to take risks, and feel that the Conservatives are likely to bring greater stability and less change.
- Older voters are more likely to vote Conservative. Because of their greater life expectancy there are more older women than older men. If this is an important factor, the difference in voting is more to do with age than gender.

Women as politicians

Successful women in politics

- Sirimavo Bandaranaike (Sri Lanka): Prime Minister – in 1960 became first elected female prime minister of any country.
- Indira Gandhi (India): Prime Minister for 15 years between 1966 and her assassination in 1984.

The right to vote

For a long time women did not have the same rights to vote as men. The right to vote was won by women after years of struggle that sometimes brought a violent response. Early feminist movements saw the right to vote as an essential step towards equality. The first country to give the right to vote to women was New Zealand in 1893; Britain did not give women the right to vote on the same terms as men until 1928.

At the time of the campaign for the right to vote, many women hoped that women would be able to transform politics, making it more compassionate. On the whole, this has not happened. Politics did not change greatly. Parties continued to be dominated by men, although there were sometimes influential women. For a long time, women were less likely to vote than men even though they had the right to vote. Some of the most successful women politicians have been very right wing, even authoritarian. Margaret Thatcher, for example, was particularly tough and ruthless.

What has happened is that parties and politicians have had to pay more attention to the issues that affect women, so as to win their votes. Such issues include equal rights and equal pay at work, family matters, the care of children, maternity rights and abortion. Parties need to appeal as much to women as to men if they are to win elections.

- Golda Meir (Israel): Prime Minister 1969–74 – a founder of the state of Israel.
- Margaret Thatcher (Britain): Prime Minister 1979–90.
- Corazon Aquino (Philippines): President 1986–92.

Margaret Thatcher was one of the most successful politicians of the late twentieth century, winning three general elections in a row. For a woman to be chosen to lead the Conservative Party in 1976 was very unexpected. She quickly established herself as a very strong leader who did not tolerate disagreement within her party. She did not increase women's involvement in politics. Almost all of the ministers she appointed were men.

The 1997 general election in Britain resulted in the election of double the number of women MPs there had previously been: 18.5 per cent of British MPs were women. There were 101 women MPs representing Labour alone; the previous highest number of women MPs from all parties combined had been 41 in 1987. The increase in the number of women Labour MPs was partly the result of selection processes that increased women's chances of being selected. Labour had seen the under-representation of women as a problem and acted to change the situation. In about 40 safe seats there were women only shortlists from which candidates were chosen. Women in Tony Blair's 1997 cabinet included Mo Mowlem, Margaret Beckett and Harriet Harman. Women though were still very much a minority; four out of five MPs and all the party leaders were men.

The election of so many women MPs in 1997 created several problems. Not least of these is the lack of women's toilets; the House of Commons has been in effect a men's club throughout its history. Women MPs have begun to demand changes in the way that the House of Commons works. For example, most debates and votes are in the afternoons, evenings and sometimes late at night. These hours do not suit women with family responsibilities. Women MPs want the House of Commons reformed so that it does not damage their family lives.

Some of the problems women face in the House of Commons are ones they are already used to. Being active in local politics, and being a candidate in elections, also involves a big commitment of time and money, and the disruption of family life.

Several European countries, such as Sweden, Finland, Denmark and the Netherlands, have a better record than Britain on women's involvement in politics. There are, however, many countries where women have been less successful. The USA, Russia and China have never had a female top politician. In a few countries, especially in the Middle East and Africa, it is still unacceptable for women to be party political leaders.

IT ⚑ FIND OUT FOR YOURSELF

Visit the web site of the Fawcett Society, which campaigns on behalf of women. Find the section of the site that is about women in politics: http://www.gn.apc.org/fawcett.

Find the results of the survey of all women MPs that the Fawcett Society carried out in 1998. Find out why the Fawcett Society is in favour of proportional representation.

QUESTIONS

1. When did women in Britain win the right to vote on the same terms as men?
2. Name two women who have been leaders of their countries.
3. Identify and explain two reasons why women are usually more likely to vote Conservative than men are.
4. Discuss some of the problems faced by women MPs.
5. What kinds of policies can be said to be 'female friendly'; that is, will encourage women to vote for the party with those policies?

ROUND-UP

Women won political rights later than men, and in some ways have not yet caught up. Although Britain has had a female Prime Minister and a growing number of women MPs, politics is still dominated by men. Women have been more likely to be Conservative than men in the past, but this difference may now be disappearing.

VOCABULARY

Authoritarian: in support of strict obedience to authority
Under-representation: Fewer than there should be given the numbers in the population

Ethnicity and politics

KEY FOCUS Britain's ethnic minorities make up about 6 per cent of the population but there are few politicians from minority backgrounds. This section looks at the relationship between minority groups in Britain and voting and political activity.

Paul Boateng, one of a tiny band – Britain's ethnic minority MPs.

Registering to vote

Nearly a quarter of black people in Britain are not registered to vote – a much higher percentage than for the whole population (6 per cent) ('Looking to the Future', *Guardian Education*, 4 February 1997).

For the 1997 general election, there was a campaign called Operation Black Vote to get more black people to register so that they would have the right to vote. Many members of ethnic minorities live in **marginal seats** (that is, ones which are not 'safe' for one party) so their registration and vote could have a big impact. It was hoped that candidates would have to pay more attention to issues relevant to black people. Operation Black Vote worked with a similar campaign, Swing the Vote, which tried to get young people in cities to register.

Voting behaviour

Members of ethnic minorities are much more likely to support and vote Labour than other parties. Black Afro-Caribbean people are even more strongly Labour than the Asian minorities. In 1992 (when Labour lost the election) it is thought that 90 per cent of Afro-Caribbean people voted Labour, and 71 per cent of Asian people.

The Conservatives win more support from Indians than from other minorities. About a fifth of Indian people voted Conservative in 1997 ('Where the black vote goes', *Guardian*, 25 November 1999). This reflects the success of Indian people in business and the professions, and the middle-class status of many of them.

The reason most often given for supporting Labour is that it is the party of the working class. This reflects the fact that members of ethnic minorities are mainly working class (see the section on Minority ethnic groups and work on pages 210–11). Class is as important as ethnicity in influencing voting.

A second important reason, however, is the images of the two parties. Labour is seen as more supportive of ethnic minorities, more 'ethnic minority friendly'. Middle-class members of ethnic minorities are more likely to vote Labour than middle-class white people. Labour is seen as having taken a greater interest in and been more sympathetic to minorities and to the issues that affect them.

The Conservative Party, on the other hand, is struggling to shake off an image of hostility to minorities. The Conservatives are often seen as anti-immigrant and unsympathetic to minorities.

This image has been created by several incidents over many years. In the 1960s a leading Conservative, Enoch Powell, led a racist campaign to deport non-white people. Other Conservatives have made statements that have been taken as racist. For example, before her first victory in 1979, Margaret Thatcher referred to British people feeling swamped by alien culture. A black Conservative candidate, John Taylor, failed to win the supposedly safe seat of Cheltenham in 1992. This suggested that loyal Conservative voters would not vote for a black candidate. These incidents all reinforced the perception that the Conservatives do not represent Britain's minorities. The Conservatives are trying to change their image so that they appear friendlier to minorities.

Feeling left out

Some younger members of minorities are, like other young people, disillusioned with party politics. This partly explains why so many do not register to vote. Before the 1997 election, only 16 per cent of black people under 25 said they intended to vote. Of those who do vote, many vote Labour, but as the best of a bad lot rather than from any positive choice. They feel the political system is racist and has nothing for them. Labour is then less able to rely on the support of minorities than it used to be.

More members of ethnic minorities would vote and be active in politics if there were more candidates from minority groups. Some feel that if the big parties will not accept them and take their concerns seriously, the only answer is to have separate parties.

Diane Abbott, Labour MP

> There are no blacks or Asians in New Labour's inner circle. Mr Blair has to take a much more positive approach. To get more black MPs we need more commitment from the leadership.

> The House of Commons is a club for white middle-class males, and that means others are excluded from it.

Paddy Ashdown, former leader of the Liberal Democrat Party (quoted in 'PM slams ethnic mix in Commons', *Guardian*, 29 May 1996)

Politicians

Britain's first MP from an ethnic minority (other than Jewish people) was Sir Dadabhai Naoroji, elected for the Liberal Party in Finsbury in 1892. In the next 30 years there were two more Asian MPs.

It was not until 60 years later that there were more MPs from ethnic minorities. Over this time, however, there were several successful councillors in local government. In 1987, four ethnic minority MPs were elected:

- Diane Abbott, the first black woman MP, Labour MP for Hackney North and Stoke Newington
- Keith Vaz, a Goan born in Yemen, Labour MP for Leicester East
- Bernie Grant, Labour MP for Tottenham
- Paul Boateng, Labour MP for Brent South.

In the 1997 general election there were 42 major party candidates from ethnic minority backgrounds. Nine were elected. Minorities make up about 6 per cent of the population; since there are 659 MPs, there would need to be about 40 minority MPs to reflect proportions in the population.

Nevertheless, progress has been made, although rather slowly. The Labour government elected in 1997 had two junior ministers from ethnic minorities, Keith Vaz and Paul Boateng. By then there were two Sikh MPs, a Muslim MP, and a second black woman MP, Oona King. In addition, there are many successful local councillors who may be able to make the move into national politics in the future.

C ► FIND OUT FOR YOURSELF

Non-white politicians and public figures in other countries have often been sources of inspiration for black and Asian people in Britain. Use Microsoft Encarta and/or reference books to find out about one of the following:

- Nelson Mandela (South Africa)
- Malcolm X (USA)
- Martin Luther King (USA)
- Mahatma Gandhi (India).

Present your findings to the class.

QUESTIONS

1. Name the two junior ministers from minority ethnic groups in the 1997 Labour government.

2. What is the aim of Operation Black Vote?

3. Identify and explain two reasons why members of most minority ethnic groups are more likely to vote for Labour than for other parties.

4. Why are members of Britain's Indian community more likely to vote Conservative than members of other minorities are?

5. How could political parties encourage more members of minorities to vote and to be active in party politics?

ROUND-UP

Britain's minorities are strong supporters of the Labour Party, with the partial exception of Indian people. This seems to be related to class as much as ethnicity. However, even Labour has few successful politicians from minorities and there is evidence of a feeling that politics tends to ignore minorities.

VOCABULARY

Deport: send to another country
Anti-immigrant: opposed to immigration and hostile to immigrants

The nation-state

KEY FOCUS The world is divided into nation-states; they are the main political units. This section shows how nation-states are a fairly recent development, and how their suitability is sometimes questioned.

1066–1536	The kings of England (who were of Norman, French-speaking origin) ruled from London over England and large parts of France, but not Wales and Scotland. The English kings in practice had little authority over the 'border' areas far from London, such as the far north of England. They ruled a medieval realm, not a nation-state.
1536	The Act of Union joined the kingdom of England with the principality of Wales.
1603	King James VI of Scotland became king of England as well, but Scotland and England continued to be separate kingdoms.
1707	The modern nation-state was created by the Act of Union between England and Scotland. Since then there have been changes involving the status of Ireland. At present, the six counties of Northern Ireland are part of the nation-state that is the United Kingdom. The Republic of Ireland is a separate nation-state.

The road to the British nation-state.

What is a nation-state?

Modern societies are **nation-states**. A nation-state exists when there is a government, which has authority derived from laws, ruling over a territory. Nation-states also:

- tax their citizens
- have a national currency
- have a civil service bureaucracy to run the country
- usually have a permanent army
- have symbols of the nation, such as a national flag and a national anthem.

Nation-states are not, as you might think, natural and normal. The development of nation-states has happened over the last 400 years or so, and some nation-states are very new.

The political units that existed before the nation-states of today were very different in several ways:

- The territory that traditional states ruled over did not have clear boundaries. Today nation-states claim sovereignty over territories with clear-cut borders, and are even willing to go to war to defend this claim.

- In the past the authority of a state over much of its territory was often very weak. The king or government was distant and unimportant to most people, who were subjects. Today people are citizens of nation-states, with rights and duties that go with this status.

- With nation-states came the idea of nationalism – a strong identification with a national community. This is encouraged by national symbols (such as a flag), by a sense of shared tradition, by having teams in international sports events and so on.

The United Kingdom today

The nation-state ruled by the government in London is the United Kingdom of Great Britain and Northern Ireland. It has a complicated history, as you have just read. Its unusual structure shows in sports competitions. In some competitions, such as the Olympic Games, the United Kingdom enters one team. In others, for example football internationals, there are four teams: England, Scotland, Wales and Northern Ireland.

Many people in Scotland and Wales see themselves as more Scottish or Welsh than British. This is because Scotland and Wales have distinctive cultures that make them different from England. In both Scotland and Wales there are nationalist parties that win significant support. In response to this, assemblies have been set up for both Scotland and Wales. The British government has then given up some of its authority over Scotland and Wales. Some people believe that, especially for Scotland, this is the first step towards independent nation-states separate from England.

Nation-states: too big?

The nation-state, as you have seen, belongs to a particular period of history – the last 400 years or so in Europe, and much less in most of the world. Some people argue that the nation-state is no longer the best form of government. It is, they say, both too big and too small; we need smaller and bigger political units.

The idea that the nation-state is too big can be seen in what has happened in Scotland and Wales, where nationalism has grown and new assemblies have been created. Many people there felt that the government in London was too remote and did not represent their interests. In particular, the Conservative governments of 1979 to 1997 were based on support in England, and were far less popular in Scotland and Wales.

There have been demands in other countries for regions to have more control over their own affairs. For example, in France, Bretons in Brittany and Basques near the Spanish border have campaigned for greater freedom from the French government in Paris, while the island of Corsica has an independence movement. The province of Quebec in Canada recently voted narrowly against breaking away from Canada and becoming independent.

Increasingly, groups of people who see themselves as a people with a distinct identity and culture want to rule themselves, rather than be ruled by a government in the remote capital city of a nation-state.

Nation-states: too small?

At the same time, it is clear that nation-states are too small to deal with some of the biggest problems facing the world today. There are global problems that cannot be kept within the borders of a nation-state. Such problems include:

- environmental pollution
- global warming
- the drugs trade
- nuclear power and disposal of nuclear waste
- poverty
- extinction of species of plants and animals
- the arms trade and landmines
- health problems such as Aids.

No nation-state acting alone can deal with any of these problems. To solve them all nation-states need to work together. They already try to do this through international organisations, such as the United Nations, and through treaties and international agreements. Nation-states are not, however, very good at this; they exist to look after their own citizens, so they tend to be selfish. Some people argue that nation-states need to give up some of their powers to much larger political units, representing much larger areas, such as the European Union.

Nation-states then are being squeezed. This can be seen in the case of Britain. The British government is less powerful than it used to be. It has passed some of its power down to smaller units, the Scottish and Welsh assemblies, and some upwards towards a larger unit, the European Union.

▶ **FIND OUT FOR YOURSELF**

It has often been said by opponents of independence for Wales and Scotland that they are too small to be independent. In fact, there are seven tiny 'countries' within Europe that are not nation-states or regions: Andorra, Channel Islands, Monaco, Liechtenstein, San Marino, Isle of Man, and the Vatican. Because they are small, they are often overlooked, but in fact all of them date back to the Middle Ages and are older than the nation-states that surround them. Choose one of these 'microstates' and use reference books and CD-ROMs to research their history, society and politics. Present your findings to the class.

QUESTIONS

1. What is meant by a nation-state?

2. Name three international problems which nation-states find it impossible to solve on their own.

3. Identify and explain two ways in which nation-states are different from the kinds of political units that existed before them.

4. Name two regions of different countries, other than Britain, where there are independence movements.

5. Do you think it is right that in some sports Britain is represented by different teams for England, Wales, Scotland and Ireland or Northern Ireland? Give reasons for your answer.

ROUND-UP

Nation-states like the United Kingdom have only existed in the last few hundred years. Nation-states have governments, pass and enforce laws and raise taxes. Nation-states seem to be too big for people to feel they represent them well, yet too small to deal with the many problems the world faces.

VOCABULARY

Sovereignty: unrestricted power
Realm: a kingdom

Politics – sociology in practice

Operation Black Vote

'OPERATION Black Vote is a non-party political campaign, supported by a broad coalition of mainly black organisations. Its main objectives are:

- to urge black people to register to vote
- to enable the black community to claim its place in British democracy
- to demonstrate a collective community potential that could significantly influence the outcome of many seats at the general election
- to confront politicians with the reality of what it means to be black in Britain, to force them to address the inequality of opportunity faced by black people; and to encourage them

to recognise our unique perspective and positively promote the cultural diversity of British society in the best interests of society as a whole.

… We know the main political parties claim to stand for better black political representation – for a just, multi-racial Britain, different but equal ... But our day to day experiences tell us that talk is cheap. They talk about representation and equality while the United Nations declare the (Conservative) government's Asylum and Immigration Bill racially biased; the Liberal Democrats fail to expel candidates who peddled racist propaganda; and Labour suspend some constituency parties with high Asian membership.

Doing nothing is a choice. An 'up the system' attitude is often seen as a valid form of resistance. The problem is it plays into the hands of those who want to marginalize us – to condemn us as a 'problem'…

Participation is the only choice … Unless we speak out, the political parties will have little incentive to address the institutionalised racism that plagues British society. We must use the democracy we have to demand a better democracy – one that works equally for everyone, regardless of race and colour.'

Adapted from
http://www.gn.apc.org/charter88/campaign/obv/obv, 22 October 2000.

Questions

1 Why, according to this passage, is it important for black British people to use their right to vote?

2 Look at the section Prejudice and discrimination (pages 108–9) to remind you what is meant by institutional racism. Then look at the section in this chapter on Ethnicity and politics (pages 246–7). In what ways can the British political system be seen as racist?

3 What changes could be made in order to create 'a better democracy'?

Buy Nothing Day 2000

'25 November 2000 was Buy Nothing Day. Around the world people took part by not doing any shopping. There has been a Buy Nothing Day since 1992 and it has grown into a big international event celebrating consumer awareness and simple living.

Buy Nothing Day exposes the environmental consequences of consumerism. The rich western countries – only 20 per cent of the world's population – are consuming 80 per cent of the earth's natural resources, causing a disproportionate level of environmental damage.

Who runs it?
You do. It's your day, so get involved! Tell your friends, put up posters and refuse to shop on Buy Nothing Day …

What will I achieve?
It's incredibly challenging to last 24 hours without shopping. You'll feel detoxed from consumerism and realise shopping is less important. For a brief moment, you'll get your life back, that's a big achievement

What is so bad about shopping?
It's not that shopping in itself is so

harmful, it's what we buy. The two areas that we need to concentrate on are the environment and third world poverty. We need to worry about the way our goods are produced. Increasingly large companies use third world labour to produce goods because it's cheap and there aren't the systems to protect workers like there are in the west.'

Adapted from http://www.buynothingday.co.uk, 23 October 2000.

Questions

1 What are the aims of Buy Nothing Day?

2 Look back at the section on New social movements (pages 238–9). In what ways does Buy Nothing Day seem like a new social movement and unlike older kinds of political protest?

3 Look back at the section on The nation-state, especially the part headed Nation-states: too small? (pages 248–9). In what ways is Buy Nothing Day involved with issues which are beyond the ability of nation-states to tackle?

The six points of the People's Charter, 1838

The first important movement to get the right to vote for working people in Britain was the Chartist movement. Below is the charter (from which the Chartists get their name) which they presented to Parliament. At this time only a small number of wealthy men could vote.

1. A VOTE for every man twenty-one years of age, of sound mind, and not undergoing punishment for crime.
2. THE BALLOT – to protect the elector in the exercise of his vote.
3. NO PROPERTY QUALIFICATION for Members of Parliament – thus enabling the constituencies to return the man of their choice, be he rich or poor.
4. PAYMENT OF MEMBERS, thus enabling an honest tradesman, working man or other person, to serve a constituency, when taken from his business to attend to the interests of his country.
5. EQUAL CONSTITUENCIES, securing the same amount of representation for the same number of electors, instead of allowing small constituencies to swamp the votes of large ones.
6. ANNUAL PARLIAMENTS ...

Questions

1 Study the six points of the charter. Then decide which of these points have now been fully met, and which have not. Explain your answers.

2 What objections might a feminist make to this charter?

3 You will have noticed that the Chartists were very concerned about MPs being bribed or paying people to vote for them. This concern may seem dated but there have been several controversies in recent years involving politicians and money. Investigate one of the following cases and explain it to the class:
(a) Jonathan Aitken, Conservative government minister, receiving money from Mohammed al-Fayed, owner of Harrods.
(b) Geoffrey Robinson, a Labour millionaire MP, loaning money to Peter Mandelson, a member of the Labour cabinet, to buy a house.
(c) Bernie Ecclestone, the boss of Formula 1 racing, donating money to the Labour Party.

Politics – important terms

aristocracy	government by a hereditary ruling class
authority	the power or right to rule others
cabinet	the committee that decides government policy, made up of ministers and headed by the Prime Minister
charismatic authority	authority derived from special personal qualities
citizenship	having the rights of a member of a nation-state
class alignment	when people's votes can be predicted from their class position, that is working class voting Labour, middle class voting Conservative
class dealignment	when class alignment no longer applies
coercion	force
communism	a left-wing political ideology, now associated with dictatorship
Conservativism	a right-wing political ideology
constituency	an area represented by an MP
democracy	a political system based on voting
dictatorship	when power is held by one person or a small group, without voting or debate
environmentalism	see Green ideology
fascism	a right-wing political ideology associated with dictatorship
first past the post	the voting system in British general elections, where the candidate with most votes wins
Green ideology	a new political ideology based on environmental issues
ideology	sets of political ideas about the way things are and the way they should be
legal rational authority	authority arising from occupying a particular position
marginal seat	one which could be won by one of two or more parties
Member of Parliament	an elected representative of a constituency, sitting in the House of Commons
military dictatorship	a dictatorship controlled by the armed forces
nation-state	a modern political unit
new social movement	a broad and loose political movement
oligarchy	rule by a small group of people
Parliament	the House of Commons and House of Lords together
political socialisation	the process by which people learn political ideas and beliefs
power	the ability to achieve aims despite opposition
pressure group	a group trying to influence government, usually focusing on one issue or representing a particular interest
Prime Minister	in Britain, the head of the government; usually the leader of the party winning the most seats in a general election
proportional representation	alternatives to the first past the post system, giving seats according to the numbers of votes cast
socialism	a left-wing political ideology
terrorism	attempting to achieve political goals using violence and terror
third way	said to be a new kind of politics avoiding the old division between left and right
traditional authority	authority based on history and tradition

Politics – exam-style questions

Source A

Voting by social class, 1997 general election: percentages of members of social classes voting for each party

	AB	C1	C2	DE
Conservative	42	26	25	21
Labour	31	47	54	61
Liberal Democrat	21	19	14	13

Note: ABC1 = middle class, C2DE = working class

NOP/BBC exit poll, 1 May 1997 in 'Anatomy of a non-landslide' by John Curtice, *Politics Review*, September 1997.

Source B

Why do people vote for a party? A variety of reasons has been suggested. One that seems to has been strong in the past is **political socialisation**. Many people develop a strong emotional bond to a party early in their lives, because of the influence of family or community. This means that they tend to vote for the same party at each election; they are loyal voters. However, many people today do switch votes from one election to the next.

Foundation tier

1. Look at source A and answer these questions:
   (a) What percentage of AB voters voted Conservative? [1 mark]
   (b) What percentage of DE voters voted Labour? [1 mark]
   (c) For which party did most AB voters vote? [1 mark]
   (d) Which was the only class in which Labour did not get more votes than the other parties? [2 marks]
   (e) Name two other political parties that take part in general elections. [2 marks]
   (f) Using the source, explain what is meant by the term class alignment. [2 marks]

2. Look at source B and answer these questions:
   (a) What is meant by a loyal voter? [1 mark]
   (b) What is meant by political socialisation? [2 marks]

3. Identify and explain one other influence on voting other than class position. [2 marks]

4. Identify and give one example of a type of political organisation other than political parties. [2 marks]

5. Why do some working-class voters vote for the Conservative Party? Give two sociological reasons. [4 marks]

Higher tier

1. Look at source A and answer these questions:
   (a) Which was the only class in which Labour did not get more votes than the other parties? [2 marks]
   (b) Name two other political parties that take part in general elections. [2 marks]
   (c) Using the source, explain what is meant by the term class alignment. [2 marks]

2. Look at source B. What is meant by political socialisation? [2 marks]

3. Identify and explain one other influence on voting other than class position. [2 marks]

4. Identify and give one example of a type of political organisation other than political parties. [2 marks]

5. Why do some working-class voters vote for the Conservative Party? Give two sociological reasons. [4 marks]

6. Why do some people who are eligible to vote not vote in general elections? [4 marks]

Politics – further research

The British Politics Page: www.ukpolitics.org.uk.

Try the Hewett School site's suggestion for a project on political parties. Follow the links to Sociology GCSE Year 11: www.hewett.norfolk.sch.uk/curric/soc.

All the political parties and many politicians have their own web sites.

11 Crime

255

KEY TERMS

corporate crime
crime
dark figure of crime
delinquency
deviance
labelling
law
policing
social control
white collar crime

Crime is an aspect of social life that affects us all at some time. Even if you have not been a victim of crime, crime will have influenced what you do, from locking doors to planning how to get home safely at night. The media show us a world full of crime, from real-life crime in the news and programmes like *Crimewatch* to television dramas and films.

There are many aspects of crime that interest sociologists. One is that what counts as a crime does not stay the same, but changes over time. The punishments also change; people are no longer put in the stocks in Britain. Crimes are also different in different countries.

Sociologists are also interested in who commits crime and why. To understand this, we need to distinguish between different kinds of crime, and look at different groups of people (for example women commit far less crime than men). We also need to study statistics on crime, although this involves realising that they are not complete and accurate.

Sociology can help us understand crime and criminals, but it also shows that crime is complicated and that there are no easy answers.

IN THIS CHAPTER YOU WILL LEARN ABOUT:

- how much crime there is and who commits it
- different types of crime
- explanations about why people commit crime
- how crime is dealt with by the police, courts and others
- how crime may change in the future

CHAPTER CONTENTS

Crime and deviance

KEY FOCUS

Crime and deviance refer to the breaking of laws and unwritten rules. What counts as criminal and deviant varies over time and between societies, and depends on the social situation in which the act takes place.

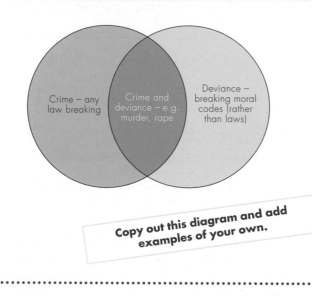

Copy out this diagram and add examples of your own.

The difference between crime and deviance

Most of the time, most people follow the rules and norms of their society; that is, they conform. When they do not conform, sociologists can use different terms according to what they have done:

■ **Crime** means the breaking of rules that have been made into laws by the rulers or government of a society. Different countries have different laws.

■ **Deviance** means behaviour that most or all people disapprove of in the society. Such behaviour will not conform to the society's norms and values. Norms, you will remember are unwritten rules for behaviour and are based on values which define what is thought of as good and right in a society. When behaviour is serious and strongly disapproved, there will probably be a law against it. Different cultures have different norms and values, and so different ideas about what is deviant.

■ **Delinquency** is a term to describe behaviour by young people that is disapproved of. Mostly it is deviant, but sometimes delinquents break laws as well, and so commit crime.

If you read the above carefully, you will realise that not all deviance is crime. Deviance applies to a very wide range of behaviour, and crime is a category within this of behaviour that is so strongly disapproved that there is a law against it.

Is all crime deviant? Logically, it ought to be; but in fact it can be argued that there are some offences which may be crimes under the law, but where most people would not think of the offender as being a criminal or even as 'deviant'. For example, it is against the law to park on double yellow lines, and a magistrate could fine a motorist who does this, but we would not think of the motorist as a criminal.

Sanctions

Crime, deviance and delinquency are punished by **sanctions**. These vary enormously. For crime, the sanctions can range from fine to prison sentences to (though not in Britain today) death. For deviance, the sanctions are likely to be of a much lower order. If someone pushes ahead of you in a queue, you may 'tut', or make a comment, to let the person know you disapprove. In a classroom, when a pupil is misbehaving, a teacher might simply catch the individual's eye, or say his or her name – or send him or her out.

Although we normally think of deviance as something negative, sometimes people do things which are heroic or generous that very few others would do – someone who gives all his or her money to charity, or someone who risks his or her own life to rescue others. These are deviant too, because they are not expected. They may be rewarded rather than sanctioned. Some deviance may be tolerated, rather then rewarded or sanctioned. We often call this eccentricity; people with a reputation for being eccentric are often allowed to do things that others would not get away with.

Social definition of deviance

Whether an act is seen as deviant or not depends on the social situation. Many of the acts that count as deviance would not be deviant in another situation. For example, it is normal not to wear any clothes while taking a bath or shower or when on a nudist beach. It would be deviant to be clothed. Nudity is however deviant in most other situations, and might even be treated as criminal (the crime being 'indecent exposure').

This idea can be extended to history and to other cultures. What is normal in one society may be deviant in another, and what was acceptable in the past may no longer be today.

Historical examples

Attitudes have changed dramatically in Britain over the past 50 years in these (and other) areas:

- women working in what were once 'men's jobs'
- men helping to care for infants by pushing the pram, changing nappies, etc.
- acceptance of births outside marriage, of cohabitation and divorce
- acceptance of homosexuality
- less acceptance of smoking.

FIND OUT FOR YOURSELF

Ask your parents or other older people what other attitudes have changed. Add other examples to the above list.

Cross-cultural examples

If you travel abroad, you will quickly have to get used to the different norms that apply. In Japan, for example, the following would be normal, but might seem strange to you:

- eating with chopsticks
- bowing
- sitting on the floor
- wearing a mask over your mouth when you have a cough or cold
- not wearing outside shoes when indoors.

However, because you are recognised as a foreigner, it may be acceptable for you not to do all the things Japanese people do. So whether an act is seen as deviant or not can depend on who is doing it, as well as in what situation.

These examples demonstrate that whether an act is deviant or not depends not so much on the act as on the social situation in which it happens. Deviance is socially defined.

Crime is also socially defined. What is legal in one country may be illegal in another. Drinking alcohol is socially acceptable (even approved in some situations) in Britain today for adults, but is illegal in Saudi Arabia and other Islamic countries, and was illegal in the USA during Prohibition. Laws constantly change. Older laws may be dropped if they seem irrelevant, while new laws are introduced to cope with new problems or situations.

Rules

As well as laws, which define crime, and norms that are the unwritten rules of everyday life, there are rules. Rules are more explicit than norms, and are often written down. Rules tell people how to behave in many different situations: in schools, hospitals, shops and so on. Clubs and organisations have rules. Rules are all around us. Sometimes they sound more like requests, with no threat of sanctions (on a bus, 'Please do not distract the driver's attention'); at others, they give a clear warning of possible consequences (on a train's alarm cord: 'Penalty for improper use: £25').

FIND OUT FOR YOURSELF

Research the prohibition of alcohol in the USA by looking in Microsoft Encarta, in encyclopaedias or other reference books under 'Prohibition'. Prohibition was from 1920 to 1933. You will find strong links between Prohibition and organised crime such as the Mafia and American gangsters like Al Capone.

QUESTIONS

1. What is the difference between crime and deviance?

2. In Britain today, when and for whom and in what circumstances would the following not be deviant:
   (a) carrying a gun
   (b) driving over the speed limit?

3. Think of examples of acts which are against the law but are unlikely to result in the person committing them being thought of as a criminal.

4. What rules apply in your sociology lessons? Make a list, then mark which of them are written somewhere and which are not. Are these rules different from those in other lessons?

5. Prohibition was an attempt to cut crime (crime was – and is – strongly linked to drinking). Yet Prohibition actually led to a greater amount of crime. Why was this?

ROUND-UP

Crime involves breaking the law; deviance involves breaking norms and expectations. They are punished by sanctions. Crime and deviance are socially defined; that is, whether they are seen as crimes or deviant acts or not depends where and when they happen and who commits them.

VOCABULARY

Eccentricity: behaviour which is thought of as strange or odd, but not unacceptable

Tolerate: to put up with, without showing approval or disapproval

Cohabitation: a couple living together without being married

Measuring crime

KEY FOCUS The Home Office regularly publishes statistics of the number of different types of crime committed. These statistics often make the news headlines, especially if the crime rate is going up. Do they tell us the whole story about crime?

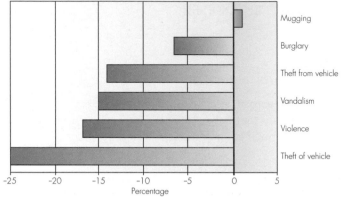

Crime rates: percentage change in crime, 1995–97

British Crime Survey, 1998.

Which crime has increased? Which crime has fallen most?

The Home Office also publishes statistics about people who have been convicted of offences. From this, we know that the majority of convicted criminals are young men of working-class backgrounds, and that black men are over-represented compared to their numbers in the population.

Questioning the figures

The crime figures do not give us the full picture of crime. They are a count only of the number of crimes recorded by the police. How many other crimes are there? And what kind of person commits those crimes? In order for a crime to reach the official statistics and be recorded, two things have to happen:

- The crime has to be reported to the police. This doesn't always happen, and there are many reasons why a crime might not be reported:
  - The victims and/or witnesses may be too frightened of the consequences.
  - They may feel the police will not or cannot do anything.
  - If it is a theft of an uninsured item, they may feel there is no point reporting it because there is no chance of getting it back.
  - They may not want to get the offender into trouble – it might even be a member of their family.

The crime rate

Notifiable offences recorded by the police

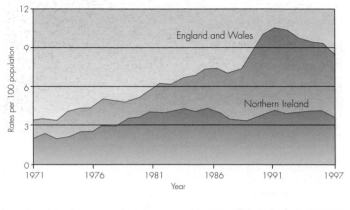

Social Trends Pocketbook 1999.

The crime rate rose steadily from the 1950s, when there were less than half a million crimes recorded each year, to a peak of 5.6 million in 1992. Since then the crime rate has fallen slightly. However, the trends are different for different types of crime.

■ The police have to record the incident as a crime. There may not be enough evidence to do this (for example the wallet reported stolen might have been lost) or the police may decide not to proceed further.

The police influence the figures in other ways. Police forces do not always record crime in the same way. If several houses close together are broken into at the same time, this may be recorded as one crime or as several. Some forces do not record thefts of goods below a certain value, but the set value varies. The police have considerable discretion over how they categorise incidents (for example whether an attack is assault with intent to rob or just assault). The police also have priorities that lead to the uncovering of some crimes but may help conceal others; they concentrate their resources on places where they think trouble is likely, such as inner city areas and 'problem' estates rather than suburbs.

The dark figure

The British Crime Survey is one way in which researchers have attempted to get a more complete picture of crime. By asking a representative sample of people what crimes they have been a victim of (this is called a **victim survey**) the survey hopes to count crimes that were not reported to the police, for whatever reason. These unrecorded crimes have been called **'the dark figure'** – they are like the part of an iceberg below the water, invisible but very important.

The dark figure, according to the British Crime Survey, is several times larger than the recorded crime figure. There are important differences between the reporting rates of different crimes. For example, it seems that a higher proportion of violent offences are being reported. This means that a rise in recorded violent offences might not mean that there are more violent offences, just that more are being reported! On the other hand, burglary and theft seem to have risen more rapidly than the figures for recorded crime suggest.

Even these surveys underestimate crime. Crimes of which companies and organisations, rather than individuals, are victims will not show up in these surveys. Victims of some crimes, such as sexual assaults, may still be unwilling to admit them.

Self-report studies

An alternative way of trying to get a more accurate figure of crime is to ask people what crimes they have committed. This is called a **self-report study**. It runs into the following problems:

■ People may not cooperate.
■ Even if they do, they may not tell the truth.
■ Self-report studies are usually done with teenagers, who are less able to refuse.
■ Self-report studies are usually about delinquency, which includes non-criminal behaviour, rather than crime.

FIND OUT FOR YOURSELF

Here's a self-report study aimed at teenagers for you to try. Answer yes or no to the following:

■ I have travelled on a bus or train without a ticket.
■ I have lied about my age in order to get a lower price or fare, or to get into a place I should not be in.
■ I have taken items from a shop without paying.
■ I have bought goods that I suspected were stolen.
■ I have kept the money when given too much change in a shop.
■ I have kept money I have found in the street.
■ I have ridden a bicycle after dark without lights.
■ I have dropped litter in the street.

All of these, incidentally, are offences, though you might want to argue about how seriously each should be taken. If you were in court, of course, your opinion would count for nothing compared to that of the judge or magistrate!

QUESTIONS

1. What is meant by the 'dark figure' of crime?

2. What is meant by a victim survey?

3. One type of crime that is significantly under-reported is bicycle theft. Think of as many reasons as you can why someone might not report that his or her bicycle had been stolen.

4. Why should the results of self-report studies be treated with caution?

5. Why do sociologists use crime statistics with caution?

ROUND-UP

The crime statistics are a valuable source of information about crime, but we need to bear in mind how they are put together. A fuller picture can be gained from also using victim surveys, which help to reveal the 'dark figure' of crime.

VOCABULARY

Convicted: found guilty by a judge, jury or magistrate
Discretion: some freedom to choose what to do in a particular situation
Categorise: sorting into categories; for example, the police have to decide what offence has been committed

Biological and psychological explanations

KEY FOCUS

There are competing explanations for crime. Sociological explanations, which look at, for example, family background and the social environment, are only one way of looking at crime. Here we look at two alternative ways of looking at crime, the biological and the psychological.

Two of the photos used by Lombroso in his study of criminals – it used to be believed that criminals looked different.

Biological explanations: criminals look different

One of the earliest biological theories of crime was that of an Italian doctor, Cesare Lombroso, in the mid-nineteenth century. After studying criminals in Italian prisons, Lombroso believed that criminals had distinctive physical features. In other words, it was possible to tell who was a criminal by looking at him or her. Some of the physical features he identified were: large jaws, large ears, dark skin, flat nostrils, thick hair, the inability to blush, insensitivity to pain.

He also thought epilepsy was a cause of crime. Criminals, he thought, were throwbacks to an earlier, primitive type of human. He did not claim his theory explained all crime; some criminals were not his primitive types and were just taking advantage of opportunities.

Today, this sort of theory seems very old fashioned. And yet we do have stereotypes of what typical criminals look like. In films, it is sometimes possible to tell the villains by what they look like.

The theory is potentially a very sinister one. After all, if we know who is likely to commit crimes, why not lock them up before they have done anything? It is also linked to racism – did you spot Lombroso's mention of dark skin? While he did

not mean black people, at the time he was writing many Europeans believed that they were the most advanced race and other races, such as black people, were at a lower stage of evolution. So it was thought that non-Europeans were most likely to be criminals.

Modern biological theories are more likely to be concerned with biochemistry or genetics than with what people look like. Imbalances of chemicals and hormones may be one factor that contributes to crime. For example, it has been claimed that convicted criminals have lower levels of a brain chemical called serotonin than other people do.

Genetic explanations of crime claim that individuals can inherit genes that predispose them – make them more likely than others – to commit crimes. The claim is usually made about violent crimes. Scientists today are in the process of mapping all the genes that people have, and believe they will be able to identify genes that, for example, make some people more vulnerable to particular diseases. Can the same be true of crime?

If there are genes for crime, then the individuals with those genes are not responsible, or not wholly responsible, for their actions. They can say, 'It wasn't me – my genes made me do it'. It wouldn't be possible to get criminals to 'go straight' – they just wouldn't be able to. The way to reduce crime might be to stop people with criminal genes having children. This would not be acceptable in a democratic society; it sounds too much like the Nazis' attempts to get rid of everyone they disapproved of.

One big problem with genetic explanations of crime is that crime covers many different acts; what is crime, as we have seen, varies through time and between societies. Even 'violence' can cover domestic violence, pub brawls, civil wars and rape. It seems unlikely that all of these can be explained by one gene. The USA has a lot more murders than European countries. This cannot be because more Americans have genes for violence, because many Americans are descended from Europeans. The answer is more likely to be in the nature of American society today, for example a lot more people there have guns.

If it is true that crime seems to run in some families – that people of several generations in that family commit crimes –

this is not evidence of genes causing crime. It is just as likely that the family environment was responsible. Perhaps older criminals in the family even taught younger members how to be criminal. This would be a sociological explanation using the idea of socialisation.

Psychological explanations: criminals' minds are different

Psychological explanations are in many ways similar to biological explanations, and can be combined with them. They explain crime by the criminal's personality and mental stability.

For example, the psychologist Hans Eysenck believed that there were two basic types of personality, the introvert and the extrovert, which people are born with. Introverts were shy and quiet; extroverts were confident and out going. Eysenck argued that extroverts were more likely to be criminals, because they were more likely to get into situations where they might get into trouble. Put another way, they are harder to socialise, and social control has less of a hold over them.

Other psychological explanations include:

- the theory that crime is often related to mental illnesses such as schizophrenia
- the idea that particular crimes can be explained by psychological disorder; for example, kleptomania, an uncontrollable urge to steal, and pyromania, an uncontrollable urge to set fire to things
- Eysenck's idea of extrovert personalities is around today in a slightly different form, with concern about hyperactivity in children and Attention Deficit Disorder (ADD)
- that some men have uncontrollable sex drives which make them more likely to rape and commit sex crimes.

According to these explanations, criminals are 'sick' (mentally, not physically) and the appropriate response is not punishment but help and treatment. Criminals can be cured if their problems are diagnosed and treated correctly. A shoplifter who is able to convince a judge that he or she is suffering from kleptomania may escape a prison sentence and instead be offered psychiatric help.

Sociologists, not surprisingly, think sociological explanations of crime are more convincing than biological and psychological ones. One of the biggest problems with the biological and psychological explanations is that they tend to suggest that the criminals are not responsible, that they driven by forces beyond their control. Many people would argue that

even if some people are born predisposed to crime, there is nothing inevitable about this. Sociological explanations must then play a big part in explaining crime.

FIND OUT FOR YOURSELF

Read newspaper reports of crime over the next week. Try to find reports that suggest that the crime has a biological or psychological explanation. Present your findings to the class.

QUESTIONS

1. What is meant by a biological explanation of crime?
2. What is meant by a psychological explanation of crime?
3. Kleptomania is the name given to an uncontrollable urge to steal. Why would this be a psychological explanation of some theft?
4. How might a sociologist explain the higher murder rate in the USA compared to Europe?
5. At the time, some people who believed Lombroso's theory argued that the best way to deal with criminals was not imprisonment but transportation to the colonies, such as Australia. Why did they think this?

ROUND-UP

Biology and psychology both offer explanations of crime. They see criminals as individuals who are different from non-criminals in that they have different genes or mental characteristics. Sociologists accept that these factors may play a small part in explaining some crimes, but believe social factors are more important.

VOCABULARY

Sinister: suggesting evil
Diagnose: to find out what is wrong by analysing something carefully
Transportation: being sent to live in a foreign country as a punishment. Two hundred years ago British offenders were often transported to Australia

Sociological explanations of crime and deviance

KEY FOCUS

Sociologists look at social factors rather than biological and psychological factors to explain crime. A wide range of social factors has been suggested, including socialisation, peer groups and subcultures, and lack of opportunities. Other explanations look at the type of society we live in.

Hanging around with the wrong crowd – being socialised into delinquency?

Socialisation, home and family

Socialisation is the process by which we learn to conform to society's norms. One explanation for crime and deviance is that they happen as a result of socialisation going wrong in some way. For example, it has been suggested that for boys in lone-parent families, not having a father around as a role model can lead to anti-social behaviour. The boys, it is said, do not learn to channel their energy into supporting a family.

Longitudinal research has tried to follow what happens to individuals over a long period of time, to see if there is a link between what happens in childhood and what happens later in life. For example, will the child who is hyperactive or cruel to animals be more likely to be criminal in later life? One suggestion has been that some children develop anti-social behaviour very young, for reasons such as:

- poor parenting,
- a troubled family life with arguments, violence and alcohol and drug abuse
- their own low reasoning ability (Farrington in *Oxford Handbook of Criminology*).

'It is clear that problem children tend to grow up into problem adults, and that problem adults tend to produce more problem children' (Farrington in *Oxford Handbook of Criminology*).

Peer groups and subcultures

Another agency of socialisation is the peer group. The explanation here is that the peer group may have norms and values that approve of and encourage delinquent or criminal behaviour. These may take over from the norms and values learned in primary socialisation.

For example, a teenager may join a gang that is involved in delinquency. If the gang has a well-developed set of norms and values which are clearly different from the norms and values of the rest of society, we can call it a **subculture**.

Some possible features of a subculture, and how they might cause delinquent behaviour:

- Little value placed on education – truancy, bad behaviour in school.
- No respect for authority – rudeness to teachers and other adults.
- Dislike of school rules – breaking those rules, or testing the boundaries.
- No respect for public property – vandalism, graffiti spraying.
- Enjoyment of thrills and risk – fights, 'twocking' (taking a car without the owner's permission).

In some areas, a criminal subculture involving adults may exist. Crime may be a way of life in a particular area, such as an inner city. A young person may be introduced by adults to the world of crime early on, in a minor role, and gradually progress to a full criminal career.

FIND OUT FOR YOURSELF

From your own knowledge of rule breaking, is it more likely that a group will break rules than someone on his or her own? Do group members sometimes encourage each other to break rules?

Lack of opportunity

Another set of explanations of crime suggests that it happens most when people are unable to get the things they feel they are entitled to. When there are few jobs or it is impossible to get good qualifications, people may turn to crime to get the rewards, such as money and prestige, that other people are able to achieve by legal means.

This seems to apply most when you might not expect it – when living standards are rising. As you saw in the section on Measuring crime (pages 258–9), crime rose fastest during the period after World War II, when many people were becoming better off. It had not risen much during the depression of the 1930s. This suggests that it is not simply living in poverty that causes crime, but being aware that most other people are doing better than you are. Sociologists call this **'relative deprivation'**.

The nature of society

Marxists and other writers emphasise how society is divided between the rich and poor, the haves and have-nots. For them, crime is the inevitable outcome of a society based on conflict and exploitation. Our economic system, capitalism, is based on:

- materialism – valuing the ownership of material goods more highly than, for example, spiritual values
- consumerism – wanting more and better consumer goods such as cars, clothes, the latest technologies
- competition – companies compete for customers, and as customers we compete with other people, to be better off and own more and better consumer goods.

The media, through advertising and the lifestyles they show us, constantly encourage these values, making us want more and more (even though we may not need it). The system encourages greed and selfishness. It is hardly surprising then that some people turn to crime to get what society is telling them they should want.

According to Marxists, the laws are made and enforced by the ruling class. Since the ruling class has the most property, the law protects property. This can be seen sometimes in very severe punishments for large thefts, such as a bank robbery, while the sentences for violent offences may be lower. Marxists would say this shows that a capitalist society places a higher value on property than on human life. The things that wealthy and powerful people do are treated less severely than the things working-class people do. For example, a company evading tax is seen as much less serious than a person making a false claim for social security – even if the amount the government is worse off by as a result is much greater. In the words of a popular saying, 'There's one law for the rich and another for the rest of us'.

QUESTIONS

1. What is meant by relative deprivation?

2. Identify and explain three features of a subculture which would lead to delinquent behaviour.

3. What sorts of things could be meant by the term poor parenting? Do people always agree on what being a 'good' parent means?

4. Why, according to Marxists, does the law punish large thefts more severely than violent offences?

5. 'Some schools have banned Pokemon trading cards because they have led to arguments and fights in the playground.' Can you explain the craze for collecting Pokemon cards in 2000 using the ideas under the heading The nature of society?

ROUND-UP

Sociological explanations look at a variety of social factors to explain crime and deviance – the family and socialisation, peer groups and subcultures, lack of opportunities and the nature of our society. Each explanation has some usefulness in explaining some types of crime and deviance.

VOCABULARY

Exploitation: taking advantage of someone in a way that is very wrong
Evading: getting out of
Social security: government payments to people who are in need

Labelling

The idea of labelling is a distinctively sociological attempt to explain crime. It looks not so much at what someone has done, but at how others react to it. Some people become labelled as deviant by others; how does this happen and what effects does it have?

Man rated alcoholic sues doctor

A television sales executive who admitted drinking a bottle of wine a day on a business trip sued a company doctor who said he was an alcoholic.

Peter B. claimed that being called an alcoholic had put the 'kiss of death' on his career. He resigned from a £40 000 a year job when he was offered a better job by his employers' rivals. But then he had to take a routine medical, and the doctor decided he drank too much.

Mr B. admitted drinking one or two glasses of wine a day, and that on a business trip to Monte Carlo he had a bottle of wine a day, divided between lunch and dinner.

Mr B.: 'If every employer took the view that this was not acceptable, there would be nobody in the industry.'

Doctor's lawyer, in court: 'The truth of the matter is that it had been discovered that you were drinking far more than was good for you.'

Adapted from the *Guardian*, 12 November 1996.

This man was labelled alcoholic by his doctor and lost his job. But he says he isn't an alcoholic ...

What is labelling?

Labelling is an inevitable part of social life, a way we make sense of what is going on around us. It is rather like stereotyping; we think of someone in terms of one or a few characteristics we have decided are important. For example, a teacher may get labelled by pupils as a 'good' teacher, or a 'soft' one, or as 'strict'.

How does this apply to deviance? Most people commit acts that could be called deviant at some time – yet only a few of them are thought of as being deviants. So some people get labelled, whereas others do not. This can happen in a school, for example. Some pupils get a reputation for being troublemakers, while others who break the rules just as much may not get thought of in this way.

Labels are negotiable

When someone is labelled, they do not have to accept this label. They may say that this is not a description of them – just as the man in the news item above was sure he was not an alcoholic. They may change their behaviour, so that people think that what led to the label was 'out of character', a one-off event that will not be repeated. The labelled person may be able to persuade others to agree with him or her – or he or she may have to accept the label.

FIND OUT FOR YOURSELF

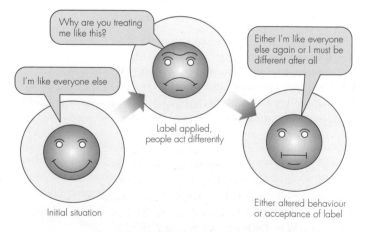

I'm like everyone else

Why are you treating me like this?

Either I'm like everyone else again or I must be different after all

Initial situation

Label applied, people act differently

Either altered behaviour or acceptance of label

Think through how this diagram works by redrawing it to show a particular situation: a girl whose friends start to make comments that she is getting overweight.

Master status

Some particular deviant identities are very strong. If one of these labels 'sticks' to someone, we will change the way we think about that person. We may even look back at things in the past and reinterpret them; what may have seemed innocent or normal at the time may look different once a person has been labelled as, say, 'a sex offender' or a 'thief'. The label has then become the most important thing about the individual, his or her **master status**. Someone labelled in this way is likely to change the way he or she thinks about himself or herself. This is because it is difficult to continue to claim that a label is wrong when everyone around you is convinced it does fit you. For example, people in a mental hospital may be convinced they should not be there at first, but because doctors, staff and other patients all treat them as if they were mentally ill, they may come to feel that they really are.

So not all labels are negotiable. Some 'stick' more than others, and are difficult to shake off. Other labels which are likely to become master statuses include paedophile, homosexual, drug addict and murderer.

Who labels?

We all apply labels as part of everyday life. This may make little difference; a teacher may not even be aware of how he or she is labelled by pupils, and in any case the pupils may have different opinions. However, the agencies of social control are in much stronger positions to apply labels and make them stick. In the case of criminal offences, it is the courts who apply labels by finding someone guilty of an offence, and the police who make this possible by charging them and providing evidence.

Who gets labelled?

Whether someone gets labelled or not depends partly on who he or she is. Behaviour that is tolerated in one person may not be acceptable from another person. Class, gender, age and ethnicity can all be involved in this.

The sociologist Aaron Cicourel did participant observation research with the police in California. He found that the police had a stereotype of what the typical young offender was likely to be like – black, from a working-class area and with an 'attitude' towards authority. Those who fitted this stereotype were far more likely to be arrested and charged than those who did not. A middle-class white boy involved in similar delinquent activity would be warned but not charged, especially if his parents supported him (for example by explaining how he was a good boy really, how disastrous an arrest would be for his education and so on).

This means that wealthier and more powerful members of society are more able to avoid labels than the poorer and less powerful. At this point it is worth looking back at your work on crime statistics – and asking if the higher rates of crime by young working-class men are in fact the outcome of labelling by the police and courts rather than of more criminal activity.

A deviant career?

Being labelled makes it harder to continue with a normal life. People will treat the labelled person in terms of the label – as a drug addict, thief and so on. This can become a self-fulfilling prophecy; that is, the person ends up more strongly committed to the deviance, and may even have a 'deviant career'.

QUESTIONS

1. What is a master status?

2. What is meant by a deviant career?

3. What does saying that labels can be negotiated mean? Explain your answer by referring to the story of the man labelled alcoholic.

4. Using an example, explain what is meant by a self-fulfilling prophecy.

5. How is labelling different from the other sociological explanations of crime (look back at the previous section).

ROUND-UP

Unlike other explanations, labelling theory looks at how people respond to deviance rather than why it happens in the first place. It shows how labelling can change people's image of themselves and how this can lead to more deviance.

VOCABULARY

Alcoholic: someone who cannot stop himself or herself drinking alcohol
Negotiable: open to being negotiated
Reinterpret: to change what you think about something, perhaps because you have new information

Types of crime

So far we have been looking at the kinds of offences most people think about when they think of 'crime'. We now look at some types of crime that tend to be forgotten or not thought of as crime.

An unfortunate accident? Or deliberate illegal dumping of chemicals to save money and make profits?

What is crime?

What do most people think of when crime is mentioned? The answer is probably murder, violent assaults, burglary and robbery. These are the kinds of crime that people feel most afraid of. These, together with car crimes, are also the crimes that dominate the official statistics. They form the basis of crime fiction novels, of television dramas and of factual television programmes such as *Crimewatch*.

There are, however, other types of crime which, when taken into consideration, change this picture of crime. They are often less likely to come to light or to be reported. They are also, by their nature, more likely to be committed by upper-class or middle-class people. This changes the impression given by the statistics, that most crime is by the working class. Perhaps it is

the case that working-class people commit the sorts of crimes that are more likely to lead to arrest and conviction.

White collar crime

There are opportunities to commit crime in most jobs, and so what sociologists call **occupational crime** is common. However, the opportunities vary between jobs, often depending on how much the worker is supervised, and how much contact he or she has with money or valuable goods. Middle-class and professional people often work more on their own and are given greater trust; the crimes they can commit as a result of their jobs are called **white collar crimes**. The scale of occupational crimes varies enormously; individuals working in a supermarket might fiddle small amounts of money or help themselves to food for their own use, while someone working in a large corporation may be able to steal huge amounts.

White collar crimes include:

- embezzlement – stealing money from a company by, for example, falsifying accounts
- fraud – such as claiming to have qualifications you don't have
- fiddling expenses claims
- pilfering – stealing from the company
- tax evasion
- bribery and corruption – offering or receiving money in return for favours.

Occupational crimes, including white collar ones, are often thought of by the people committing them as not really crimes. We even use different words – fiddles, perks and so on – which play down their criminal nature. They are thought of as to some extent acceptable, because 'everyone does it'.

Occupational crimes, when they are discovered, are often dealt with by the company. The offender will be disciplined or demoted or sacked. The police and courts are unlikely to be involved because of the bad publicity the company would get, so many offences do not reach the crime statistics.

Corporate crime

Occupational and white collar crimes involve individuals (or sometimes groups of workers) stealing for themselves.

Corporate crimes are committed in the interests of the company, and often with the knowledge and approval of those running the company. Such crimes can have huge consequences, yet may never come to light. When they are uncovered, the penalty for a company is likely to be a fine, which will be paid from the company's accounts. It is unusual for the directors or chief executives to face trials and prison sentences.

Examples of corporate crime include:

- sale of goods known to be dangerous
- breaking health and safety laws
- polluting the environment and dumping poisonous waste.

All of these are ways companies try to increase their profits, which, in our economic system, is their main purpose. Marxists are particularly interested in corporate crime because they see it as a result of the way the capitalist economic system works.

Victims of corporate crime include the following:

- Consumers – we may be misled by false advertising claims, or buy faulty, dangerous or poor quality goods. We may be overcharged, or wrongly charged (for example a garage may charge for work it has not done). We may eat foods that damage our health, or take medicines that make us more ill.

- Employees – about 500 people a year are killed at work. These are routinely referred to as 'accidents', but it is thought that in the majority of cases health and safety procedures are not being followed. Corporate killing might be a more appropriate term.

- The public – we are all victims of crimes against the environment, or those which result in the government spending a lot of money (which will come from taxes we pay).

With corporate crime it is difficult to decide who is to blame. Court cases are rare, even though the costs in money and lives are huge.

Beyond actions by companies which are clearly crimes there is another, wider area of concern: actions that many people might think should be criminal, but are not. Some companies produce and make profits from products they know will kill people. They claim they are not responsible for what happens, but opinions are beginning to change in some areas. For example, in the USA cigarette manufacturers, who marketed their products as safe when they knew they were not, face court cases brought by their victims.

⬤▷ FIND OUT FOR YOURSELF

Over the next week, either read a newspaper or watch television news programmes. Try to find examples of white collar and corporate crimes. Present your findings to the rest of your class.

Government crime

Although governments make laws, they can break them too. They can also break international treaties and agreements they have signed. In some countries, governments are responsible for torture, imprisoning and executing their opponents and committing atrocities against minorities. These actions may not be criminal by the laws of that country, but will be seen as crimes by the international community.

QUESTIONS

1. What is meant by occupational crime?

2. What occupational crimes are possible for (a) doctors, and (b) supermarket checkout operators?

3. What is the difference between white collar and corporate crime? Use examples to explain your answer.

4. Which three groups of people can be victims of corporate crime? Give an example of a corporate crime affecting each of them.

5. Why are Marxists particularly interested in corporate crime?

ROUND-UP

For most people, 'real crimes' are the types of crime that dominate the media and the official statistics, but there are other types of crime which are widespread but less likely to be reported or to be treated as crime. White collar and corporate crime show that there is crime at all levels in society.

VOCABULARY

Atrocities: wicked or ruthless actions
Demoted: the opposite of promoted; when someone is moved to a lower position in an organisation

Formal and informal social control

KEY FOCUS

How does society make most people conform most of the time? Informal and formal social control agencies constantly remind us of how we should and should not behave, and of the consequences for those who do not conform.

New attempt to ban fox hunting

THE government is considering allowing time for the House of Commons to debate whether fox hunting should be outlawed. The government is against fox hunting but it is a controversial issue which arouses strong feelings. Many people in the countryside support hunting, and say that many jobs would be lost if it were to be banned. On the other side, supporters of animal rights say that fox hunting is cruel. If it is necessary to kill some foxes to keep down numbers, there are more humane ways to do it.

An attempt to create new law, and change the way people act.

Social control

Social control refers to the ways in which society tries to ensure that its members conform to laws, rules and norms; that is, to make sure that they do not commit acts of crime and deviance.

The forms social control take can be divided into the formal and the informal.

Formal social control means the creation of laws and rules and using them to control people's behaviour. The agencies of formal social control include the government, the police, judges and the courts and prisons.

Informal social control means how we are persuaded to conform most of the time through being taught and reminded about what is acceptable and what is not. The agencies of informal social control are also the agencies of socialisation. They include:

- the family
- the education system
- peer groups
- the workplace
- the mass media
- religion.

By teaching what behaviour is not acceptable, and what the sanctions will be, they are agents of social control.

Informal social control works so well that most people behave in acceptable ways most of the time. When informal social control doesn't work, formal social control takes over and deals with the offenders.

Agencies of formal social control

The legislature

This term refers to the branch of government that is responsible for legislating, that is, for making laws. In Britain this is the House of Commons and the House of Lords, which together make up the Houses of Parliament.

In order for a new law to be created, a bill (the term given to a proposal, a law before it becomes law) is brought before Parliament. It is then debated by Members of Parliament (MPs) in the House of Commons, and by members of the House of Lords. The bill may be amended if the House votes for this. After both Houses have passed the bill, it is signed by the monarch and becomes an Act of Parliament and has the force of law.

Many Acts of Parliament do not affect the issues of crime and deviance; they include, for example, decisions about how to spend money and changes to education and the health services. Others, however, create new criminal offences.

An example of this was the Criminal Justice Act 1994 that created several new offences:

- 'Aggravated trespass' – when trespassers intend to disrupt a legal activity, such as fox hunting or building a new road.

- Travellers – it became an offence to camp anywhere after a local authority had asked them to leave.
- Squatting – it became an offence to occupy a house for more than 24 hours after a landlord had obtained an eviction order.
- Raves – it became an offence for a person to refuse to leave the site of an unlicensed outdoor festival or rave. Defining a rave gave the government some difficulty; it did not want to make outdoor opera performances illegal as well! In the end, the Act referred to, 'sounds wholly or predominantly characterised by the emission of a succession of repetitive beats'.

For and against the Criminal Justice Act 1994

For the Act:

> In the last 30 years the balance in the criminal justice system has been tilted too far in favour of the criminal and against the protection of the public. The time has come to put that right.

Michael Howard, Home Secretary,
Conservative Party Conference, 1993

'... crackdown on squatters, "Ravers", "New Age Travellers" and hunt saboteurs' Conservative Party Campaign Guide, 1994

Against the Act:

> This is politically-driven legislation by people who have never been to a rave, don't understand young people and have never met a traveller or squatter. It's a collection of prejudices bundled together with no internal logic.

Andrew Pudephatt, General Secretary of the
civil rights organisation Liberty

The police

The role of the police forces is to enforce the law and to investigate crimes. The police are considered in the next section.

The judiciary

This refers to courts, which try those accused of crimes and convict and sentence those who are found guilty. Most serious cases are dealt with by Crown Courts, with a judge and jury. Minor offences are dealt with by Magistrates Courts, which are presided over by a magistrate. Courts can impose a range of sanctions on those found guilty, including **probation** orders, **community service** orders, fines and imprisonment, according to how serious the offence is.

The penal system

This refers to the people and organisations that deal with offenders. These include prisons and the probation service.

You can find out more about the sentences that can be imposed and the organisations concerned in the section Dealing with offenders (see pages 272–3).

QUESTIONS

1 What is meant by informal social control?

2 Name three agencies of informal social control. For each, write a sentence explaining how this agency might help stop people committing crimes.

3 State two new offences created by the Criminal Justice Act of 1994.

4 What are the four main agencies of formal social control? What are their main purposes?

5 Organisations that have rules also need to have a formal system of enforcing them. In your school or college, are there equivalents to the agencies of formal social control? Who is responsible for what?

ROUND-UP

Social control is enforced informally, by agencies that teach us and remind us how we are expected to behave. It is also enforced formally, through the making and enforcing of laws, and the trial and punishment of alleged offenders.

VOCABULARY

Preside: to be in charge of
Prejudice: making up your mind before you know about something

The police

The police are the most important agency of formal social control. The police are necessary, yet many people have misgivings about their behaviour at times. This section looks briefly at the role of the police and some recent concerns about the police.

Which is the real police officer – or is it both?

History

Small, traditional societies do not have police forces (or prisons or mental hospitals). This is partly because there is likely not to be much crime; informal social control by the community will be very strong. There is little need to resort to formal control and full-time, paid law enforcers.

The police became necessary with the development of modern, industrialised society. The period 1750 to 1850 was one of rapid social change, in which large numbers moved from the countryside to the new industrial cities. The first proper police force in Britain, the Metropolitan Police, was set up in 1829, and by 1850 there were 200 police forces around Britain. Unlike most other industrial countries, Britain does not have a national police force, but regional police forces.

The role of the police

The role of the police is:

- to prevent crime
- to protect life and property
- to arrest offenders and maintain public order.

To enable them to do this, the police have rights that ordinary citizens do not; they can arrest people, tell them to disperse (move on), and use reasonable force if they are not obeyed.

To a Marxist sociologist and to others who see society as deeply divided, the police are one of the ways in which the ruling class maintains its power and wealth. The police are servants of the ruling class. They enforce laws the ruling class has passed, and make sure that the working class do not threaten the system. From this point of view, the creation of police forces was connected to the rise of capitalism rather than of industrialism. The police have been used against working-class and protest movements, as in the General Strike of 1926 and the miners' strike of the mid-1980s.

Even though the police can be seen to be on the side of the powerful, they do also protect the working class against crime. This is why there is a rather ambivalent attitude to the police; many people are rather suspicious of them, disliking the feeling of being watched over, yet they turn to the police when they need them. This ambivalence is reflected also in the difference between the popular image of the smiling village bobby on a bicycle who knows everyone on his or her beat, and the police officer in riot gear crouched behind a shield.

Police work

Although the main duties of the police are solving crime, they spend a lot of time on other work. A police officer is as likely to be in the police station, writing reports and carrying out administrative work as to be on patrol. Traffic patrols and dealing with accidents also take up a lot of time.

The recent small fall in the crime rate has not meant less work for the police. While recorded crime goes down, more incidents are reported. This may be because mobile telephones make it much easier to call the police; several people now usually report road accidents. There are, however, more police to cope with the extra work; the combined police forces of England and Wales now number nearly 100 000.

Most people say they would like to see more police officers on the street, deterring crime by being seen to be around. One of the concerns expressed during the trial in April 2000 of Tony Martin for shooting two burglars on his Norfolk farm was that the police were always too far away to be useful. Some people felt they needed to be able to protect themselves, because in a rural area it would be a long time before the police arrived.

Racism and sexism in the police force

There is much concern that the police do not reflect the community they police. The MacPherson inquiry after the Stephen Lawrence case (in which a young man was murdered by racists who were never brought to justice because the police failed to do their job properly) identified as a major problem the lack of officers from minority ethnic backgrounds in the Metropolitan Police. In 1996, 1.2 per cent of police officers were from minority ethnic groups compared to 5.2 per cent of the economically active population.

There has also been concern that the lower ranks of the police develop a subculture, often called canteen culture, which is very racist, sexist and homophobic (insulting to gay people). Women and black and Asian people in the police are expected to put up with crude abuse and name-calling. If they object, they are accused of not having a sense of humour. This may be changing as the police forces themselves change. High proportions of new recruits now have degrees, and there are plenty of police officers who cannot stand 'canteen culture'.

Bent coppers

The Metropolitan Police was set up in 1829 to replace its earlier equivalent, the Bow Street Runners, because of corruption. Since then British police forces, and the Metropolitan Police in particular, have frequently had problems with corruption. Police officers can fail in their duties in many ways, for example:

- by accepting bribes
- by keeping or selling stolen and confiscated goods
- by running protection rackets
- by assaulting suspects.

Investigations of corruption often resulted in officers leaving the force but very few trials and convictions. In the early 1970s nearly 500 officers had to resign from the Metropolitan Police after one investigation but there were only 13 prison sentences (one problem in this case was that the number two in the investigation turned out to be one of the most corrupt officers).

The police now take corruption very seriously and recognise it

as a continuing problem that cannot be completely eliminated. There is even a hot line for officers to pass on anonymous information about their colleagues (*Guardian*, 16 September 1998).

Despite these problems, Britain's police forces compare favourably to many other countries where wages and status are low so that officers resort to making money illegally. Nor do Britain's police face allegations of being 'trigger-happy' as often as the US police who carry guns most of the time.

FIND OUT FOR YOURSELF

Invite a police officer into school to discuss the role of the police with you. Ask your teacher to help you arrange this.

QUESTIONS

1. When was the first proper police force in Britain set up and what was it called?
2. What is meant by a police canteen culture?
3. Identify three types of crime that police officers might commit.
4. Explain the Marxist view of the role of the police.
5. Do you think the British police should carry guns all the time? Give reasons for your answer.

ROUND-UP

The main agency of formal social control in modern industrial societies is the police. To Marxists, the police are servants of the capitalist ruling class. Problems identified in the British police in recent years include the shortage of women and ethnic minorities, racism, sexism and corruption.

VOCABULARY

Ambivalent: divided between two different opinions
Administrative work: office work, such as filling in forms and writing reports
Homophobia: prejudice against gay people (homosexuals)

Dealing with offenders

KEY FOCUS

This section looks at what happens to people who have been found guilty of criminal offences. There is a range of punishments available in Britain, from taking no action to long terms of imprisonment. Other punishments have been used in the past and in other countries.

Punishment in the past.

Sentences

These are the choices a court has when someone is found guilty of an offence:

- Absolute discharge – the person is guilty but no action is taken against him or her.
- Conditional discharge – no action is taken, but if the person commits another offence he or she will be sentenced for both the new crime and the first one.
- Fine – the offender has to pay a sum of money. A fine is the punishment for about three-quarters of all those found guilty.
- Probation order – an offender who is on probation is supervised by a probation officer for between six months and three years. This means the offender is being checked up on regularly, and also that he or she gets help to stop him or her offending again.
- Community service order – the offender has to do work which is helpful to the community without being paid. Sentences are for between 40 and 240 hours.
- Combination order – this is a combination of probation and community service.
- Prison – this is reserved for the most serious offences.

IT C FIND OUT FOR YOURSELF

Research probation by visiting the web site of the Home

Office's Probation Unit, which is responsible for the probation service at http://www.homeoffice.gov.uk/cpd/probu.

The penal system

This refers to both the prison and probation services. Their role is to deal with people who have been found guilty of offences. The penal system has several purposes:

- To punish individuals who have been found guilty.
- To reform offenders, to try to ensure that they will not commit further crimes. To achieve this, prisons may offer training and education, teaching skills so that offenders will have a chance to get a job and 'go straight'.
- To deter – the punishment acts as a warning to others of what they can expect if they break the law. The media play a part in this by reporting what sentences offenders have been given.

FIND OUT FOR YOURSELF

In a small group, look through newspapers for reports of court cases. Make a note of what the offence was, what the verdict was and what punishment, if any, the court imposed. Also see if any reasons are given for the punishment.

In a national paper, you will probably only find reports of serious crimes, unless someone famous is involved. Look in a local paper for reports of less serious offences.

Prisons

Prisoners used to be badly treated, for example by being beaten. This is no longer the case in Britain today. Prison is, however, a major punishment. Prisoners:

- lose their freedom
- have no proper income
- are not allowed the company of their families and friends (except at set visiting times)
- are not allowed sexual relationships
- cannot wear their own clothing
- cannot use their own personal items
- are often in overcrowded and unpleasant conditions
- are told what to do most of the time.

There are different types of prison. Prisoners are sent to different prisons depending on how serious their offences are and whether they are likely to be a danger to others. Open prisons allow prisoners considerably more freedom than maximum security prisons.

In Britain 125 out of every 100 000 people are in prison. This is a very low rate compared to Russia and the USA, but is the second highest in western Europe. British courts are more likely to give prison sentences, and to give long prison sentences. In recent years there have not been enough places in prison for the number of people receiving prison sentences.

Prisoners have to learn how to live in prison. They have to go through a form of secondary socialisation, learning not just the prison rules but also the norms of prison life. Prison is so different from the world outside that many prisoners find it very difficult to adjust when they are eventually released. These problems may make it more likely that they will reoffend.

> *Comparing prison and probation*
> Cost per month of an offender on probation: £183
> Cost per month of a prisoner: £2070 (Digest 4: Information on the Criminal Justice System in England and Wales, Home Office, 2001)
>
> The best way of measuring how successful punishments are is whether the offender commits more crimes. There is little difference between probation and prison: offenders are equally likely to reoffend.

Other cultures

Different kinds of punishment have been used in different societies today and in the past. Some of those from history include:

- the stocks
- whipping
- branding with hot irons
- hanging.

Most punishments in the past were carried out in public, and often attracted large crowds. Prisons were rarely used to punish people until about 200 years ago.

In other penal systems in the past, revenge has also been important. In some cultures, for example, the victim (or relatives, in the case of a murder) may be allowed to carry out the punishment themselves.

The death penalty

The most severe punishment of all is no longer applied in Britain. It is widely seen as barbaric and an offence against human rights. Many people though do say they would like the death penalty brought back, usually for particular offences such as terrorism or murdering a police officer.

Many states in the USA have executed prisoners, usually murderers, in recent years. The methods of execution, depending on the state, are electrocution, gassing, lethal injection or firing squad. However, opposition to the death penalty is growing. There is particular concern that so many executed prisoners are black men.

There is very little evidence that the death penalty works. It may satisfy a need some people have for revenge, but it does not stop murders or other serious offences.

QUESTIONS

1. List three different types of sentences that a court can give.
2. List three different types of sentences that British courts cannot give today.
3. What is the cost per year of keeping an offender in prison?
4. Identify and explain three purposes that the penal system has.
5. Do you think that it would be a good idea to send fewer people to prison and put them on probation or give them community service instead? Give reasons for your answer.

ROUND-UP

Several different kinds of punishment are available when dealing with offenders. Prisons are only for the most serious cases; most offenders are fined. Probation seems to work as well as prison in preventing people from reoffending.

VOCABULARY

Supervised: watched over
Verdict: the decision made by a court
Reoffend: to commit more offences
Revenge: getting your own back for something done to you

Gender and crime

KEY FOCUS

Girls and women commit far less crime than boys and men. Rather than ignoring them when we study crime because of this, it is worth asking why this is. To understand crime we need to recognise that most criminals are men. Yet in recent years women have been committing more crime.

Offenders found guilty of or cautioned for indictable offences, by gender, type of offence and age, England and Wales, 1997 (rates per 10 000 population)

| | 10–15 years | | 16–24 years | | 25–34 years | | 35+ years | | All aged 10+ years (000s) | |
	Males	Females	Males	Females	Males	Females	Males	Females	Males	Females
Theft and handling stolen goods	124	58	216	70	85	30	18	7	149	52
Drug offences	12	1	158	17	63	9	8	1	86	10
Violence against the person	30	11	71	11	32	5	7	1	50	9
Burglary	43	3	71	3	18	1	2	–	39	2
Criminal damage	11	1	18	2	7	1	1	–	12	1
Robbery	6	1	11	1	2	–	–	–	6	1
Sexual offences	3	–	4	–	3	–	2	–	6	–
Other indictable offences	11	3	101	18	59	12	11	2	72	13
All indictable offences	240	80	651	122	269	57	50	11	420	88

Social Trends Pocketbook 1999.

Why do women commit less crime than men?

How much crime?

The table shows that, according to official statistics, men commit far more crime than women. Overall, nearly five times as many men as women were found guilty or **cautioned**. Theft and handling goods is the most common offence for both men and women; however, there were three times as many men as women committing these offences.

Some women do of course commit crime, and in recent years several female criminals have become notorious. Most famous of all is probably, Myra Hindley, who was, with Ian Brady, one of the Moors Murderers in the 1960s.

Why do women commit less crime?

- Socialisation. Boys and girls are socialised differently. Girls are expected to be more passive, while boys are encouraged to be more active and also to be tough and able to fight

when necessary. These differences may make it more likely that boys will get into trouble with the police later.

- Opportunity. Females often have less opportunity to commit crime than men. As children and teenagers, girls are usually more closely supervised; parents will want to know where they are, what they are doing and when they will be home. Boys are often given (or take) more freedom. Later, women are usually responsible for looking after children. This also restricts opportunities for crime.

Do the statistics underestimate female crime?

The statistics only record crimes reported to the police and recorded as crimes. It may be that the types of crime women do commit are less likely to be reported; perhaps woman are better at concealing the evidence.

Self-report studies with teenagers do tend to show that the gap between boys and girls offending is much smaller than the official statistics suggest. However, such studies are usually about delinquent rather than specifically criminal behaviour, and it is never certain whether respondents are being truthful.

Are women committing more crime than in the past?

The number of offences by women has been rising faster than the rise in crimes in general. It seems that women are committing more offences than used to be the case. Explanations for this can be developed from the reasons given above for women's lower rates of crime:

■ Changing socialisation – the socialisation of girls today includes the importance of being assertive and resourceful, rather than always relying on a male. The media have played a part in this, for example through role models such as the Spice Girls.

■ Greater opportunity – women now have similar opportunities than men, including opportunities to commit crime. They go out to work more, and go out more at night.

Women in the criminal justice system

There are over 2000 women in prison in Britain, a big increase over the last 20 years. The vast majority are in prison for non-violent offences, often for not paying fines so that they had money to look after their children.

Are women treated more leniently by the police and courts? The idea that they do has been called the **chivalry factor**, taking up the idea, strong in the past in British culture, that men should protect women. The suggestion is that the police are more likely to caution rather than charge women, and that the courts are likely to impose lighter sentences, particularly if the woman has or is expecting children (it is not usually considered relevant if a man on trial has children).

An alternative theory says that, for some offences, women are actually treated more harshly. This happens when the offence involves neglect or abuse of children. Because we see caring for children as a woman's natural role, it seems unnatural and outrageous when this does not happen.

Women as victims

There are crimes of which women are much more likely than men to be victims. These include rape, sexual assault and domestic violence. These are all offences that are believed to be seriously underestimated in official statistics because the victims do not always report them.

Feminists and others have argued that the criminal justice system has not taken these offences seriously enough in the past. The police and courts have treated insensitively women who have been raped. In court women have been questioned about their sex lives and even been cross-examined by the rapist.

Women are afraid of being victims of these crimes, and this can affect their lives. For example, they may avoid going out, especially alone, at night or to certain areas. While these are sensible precautions, most assaults and rapes are not by strangers but by people the victim already knows.

A ▶ W FIND OUT FOR YOURSELF

Work in a small group. Find out by asking other students if it is true that girls are more closely watched over by their parents? Do parents expect girls to tell them where they are going, to be home at a certain time and so on? Do they do the same with boys? Produce a questionnaire with these or similar questions. Present your findings in the form of tables or charts showing numbers giving particular answers.

QUESTIONS

1 Look at the table at the beginning of the section. For each of the eight types of offences listed, work out an approximate ratio (to the nearest whole number) of offences by males to offences by females (all ages together).

2 Work out the percentage of all indictable offences committed by women.

3 Identify and explain two reasons why women commit less crime than men.

4 Do you agree that girls and women have less opportunity than men to commit crime? Answer by referring to different types of crime.

5 Do you think women will commit a higher proportion of crimes in the future? Give reasons for your answer.

ROUND-UP

Women commit far less crime than men, and when they do they commit different types of offences. Women are treated differently to men in the criminal justice system. The amount of female crime has been growing.

VOCABULARY

Indictable: when someone is formally charged with a serious offence
Insensitively: without being sensitive to others' feelings
Leniently: not punishing as severely

Age and crime: juvenile delinquents

KEY FOCUS Many young people get into trouble with the police and other authorities. Those who are constantly in trouble are called juvenile delinquents. Some are involved in crime as well as anti-social behaviour. Most do not become criminals when they are adults.

People being worried about juvenile delinquents is nothing new.

Are the statistics accurate?

Self-report studies and other research tend to confirm that young people commit a lot of offences, though usually fairly minor ones (see page 274). However, there are some reasons for doubting that this is the whole picture:

■ Teenagers are under quite close social control, watched over both by parents and at school by teachers. The police also see them as potential troublemakers. So it may be that offences they commit are highly likely to be noticed.

■ On the other hand, crime by older people may be under-recorded; they are more likely to be in occupations where white collar crime, which we know to be under-recorded, is possible.

HINTS AND TIPS

Self-report studies are explained on page 259. White collar crime is explained on page 266.

What is delinquency?

Delinquency refers to the undesirable, anti-social behaviour of young people. It may include some crime, but it also covers deviant behaviour that is not criminal, such as defying authority, truanting from school and so on. It can cover staying out late, swearing, outrageous dress or tattoos and body piercing. For girls, sexual activity under the age of 16 may be a cause for concern.

The phrase often used is juvenile delinquent, and the word juvenile is as vague as delinquency. In Britain children under 10 cannot be charged with criminal offences, and it is unusual for those under 14 to be charged unless there is clear evidence of intent. After 17 young people are treated as adults.

Delinquency in the past

It seems that it has always been the case that older people complain about the behaviour of young people, and say that it isn't like it was when they were young. In the 1840s people complained about gangs of 'street Arabs'; then it was 'hooligans' in the 1890s and all sorts of groups – Teddy Boys, skinheads, punks and so on – in the second half of the twentieth century.

> 'The report on the Moss Side disturbances in 1981 said, "… the means used to manifest violent feelings have, beyond doubt, become uglier … At one time to kick in the head somebody lying on the ground was regarded as un-British, as was the use of a knife in a fight." The awkward fact, however, is that a hundred years ago when the notorious Scuttlers kicked and hacked their way to territorial supremacy against rival gangs, the citizens of Manchester were saying exactly the same thing.'
>
> *Hooligan* by Geoffrey Pearson, Macmillan, 1983.

Explanations of delinquency:

Some of the factors linked to delinquency are:

■ family problems such as breakdown of the parents' marriage
■ failure at school
■ use of alcohol and drugs.

Peer groups and subcultures

Peer groups are particularly important for teenagers. Peer groups may encourage delinquent behaviour. Sometimes the peer group may have clear norms and values that indicate the existence of a subculture.

The sociologist Albert Cohen suggested that delinquency was caused by the **'status frustration'** boys who were failing at school felt. They needed the approval of others and a feeling of success, but could not get this at school where they were labelled as failures. Their reaction was to turn the school's values upside down. Their subculture was based on rudeness, disobedience and breaking the rules. They could win status in the eyes of their peers by breaking the rules, and at the same time get some revenge.

While Cohen argued that there were delinquent subcultures, others do not think that delinquents have different values to everyone else. The values that get people into trouble – such as being tough, or a taste for risk and adventure – are widespread, at least among boys and men. There are perfectly legal ways to express these values – sport and outdoor activities, for example. Where delinquents are different is that they express these values in the wrong way, at the wrong time.

The sociologist David Matza suggested that everyone has two sets of values:

- conventional values, which most people keep to most of the time
- subterranean values, such as aggression, greed and sexuality.

Everyone shares the subterranean values, but we can only express them at certain times and in certain places. Delinquents are people who follow subterranean values in the wrong places and the wrong times. They 'drift' into trouble – and usually out again.

Social control

It has been argued that social control is weaker over teenagers than over other age groups. Adults usually have responsibilities that limit the scope they have to commit crime. They have to look after children and have to pay for a house, a car and so on. Teenagers are not tied down in these ways; they do not usually have to earn a living or support and care for others.

What can be done about delinquency?

In a sense, juvenile delinquency sorts itself out – young people grow up. But this may not be until after they have done considerable damage, both to themselves, by messing up their education and even getting a criminal record, and to the victims of their anti-social behaviour.

As well as the measures taken against crime in general, the government has been looking at new measures:

- Curfews – young children not to be out without an adult after a set time.
- Parental responsibility – encouraging parents to intervene more to try to prevent delinquency. Part of this

may be to make parents pay compensation to victims of their children's crimes.
- Providing activities to keep young people occupied such as after-school clubs.
- Reducing exclusions from school – on the grounds that being allowed to stay on allows someone to move away from trouble by being able to study and perhaps get qualifications.

C ▶ FIND OUT FOR YOURSELF

How are young offenders dealt with? The authorities try to avoid sending young people away to institutions, so what do they do? Find out by looking up reference books or CD-ROMs (for example look up 'juvenile crime' in Microsoft Encarta). Present your findings in the form of a poster.

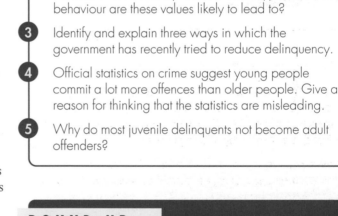

QUESTIONS

1. What is meant by delinquency?

2. Identify two of the main values of the anti-school subculture described by Cohen. What types of behaviour are these values likely to lead to?

3. Identify and explain three ways in which the government has recently tried to reduce delinquency.

4. Official statistics on crime suggest young people commit a lot more offences than older people. Give a reason for thinking that the statistics are misleading.

5. Why do most juvenile delinquents not become adult offenders?

ROUND-UP

Young people commit more crime than older people. Anti-social behaviour by young people is called juvenile delinquency. There are differences of opinion about whether delinquents have different values – a separate subculture – or whether they share the same values as everyone else.

VOCABULARY

Conventional: normal
Exclusion: when someone is not allowed to attend school as punishment

Minority ethnic groups and crime

KEY FOCUS This section looks at British black and Asian people both as offenders and as victims of crime. The situation is different for different minority groups. Black people are over represented in crime statistics. Members of minority groups are also often victims of racial harassment and violence.

Challenging stereotypes – both the uniformed officer and the plain clothes detective are chasing a criminal who is out of the picture.

Afro-Caribbean people and crime

Afro-Caribbean people are about seven times as likely as white and Asian people to be in prison. There are two possible explanations for this:

- that Afro-Caribbean people do commit substantially more crime
- that the criminal justice system is racist and works against them, for example by giving harsher sentences.

In fact, these two explanations can both be true; if Afro-Caribbean people do commit more crime this can be in response to an unjust, racist system.

Afro-Caribbean people tend to live in inner city areas where

opportunities are limited. They do not do as well at school on average as white children, and suffer high rates of unemployment, partly as a result of discrimination. Crime then may be a way of surviving in difficult circumstances.

The relationship between Afro-Caribbean people and the police has been a source of concern for many years. The police have tended to accept the evidence of the official statistics, that black people are more likely to be involved in crime. They have policed areas such as Brixton in London sometimes in a very heavy-handed way. Young blacks are seven times as likely to be stopped and searched than white people. There are few black police officers. Sometimes the police feel like invaders in enemy territory while the local population feel they are victimised and harassed. The result is to increase the number of young Afro-Caribbean people getting into trouble.

Asian people and crime

The proportion of British Asian people in prison is roughly the same as their proportion in the population. Compared to Afro-Caribbean people, there has been less concern about Asian people. They are seen as more law-abiding as a result of:

- greater economic success (though this applies much more to Indian people than to Pakistani or Bangladeshi people)
- stronger family and community ties providing effective social control
- a distinct culture which provides a feeling of belonging and an alternative source of status
- the strength of religious belief.

In the past few years, there have been predictions that crime by young British Asian people will grow. This is partly because there will be more Asians of the age at which people commit most offences. Like Afro-Caribbean people, British Asian people have been victims of discrimination and racism.

Many young Asian people feel growing anger at what they see as police indifference to the harassment and violence they face, and organise into gangs in self-defence. Riots in Bradford in 1995 also helped break down the stereotype of Asian people as passive victims of violence.

The criminal justice system

There is evidence that the criminal justice system treats ethnic groups differently, both as offenders and victims. Black people are more likely to be charged rather than cautioned, and to get tougher sentences for the same offences, than whites. On the other hand, crimes of racial harassment, violence and even murder, of which minorities are victims, are often not properly investigated.

Racial harassment and violence

Although the police keep records of racially motivated incidents, it is difficult to be sure how many there are. This is because the racial motive is not always clear, and because the police themselves are often reluctant to admit that race is involved.

In 1999 the Joseph Rowntree Foundation found that harassment is part of daily life for many black and Asian people, and that the authorities are reluctant to take it seriously. Victims (often women) described how they had to accept daily abuse, and find ways to cope, such as keeping children indoors and never going out alone. The constant abuse has serious effects on mental and physical health (*Guardian*, 21 June 1999).

In 1997 a report by Human Rights Watch said that Britain had one of the highest rates of racially motivated crime in Europe; it estimated 32 500 assaults and 26 000 acts of vandalism a year. The report documented 14 racist murders between 1991 and 1994 (including that of Stephen Lawrence) as well as severe beatings and people forced to leave their homes. The report also expressed shock at the number of incidents of police brutality, including unlawful killings, against members of minorities (*Observer*, 11 May 1997).

The Stephen Lawrence case

In April 1993, a black teenager, Stephen Lawrence, was stabbed to death at a bus stop in London by a gang of white youths who were heard to use racist abuse. Despite there being many witnesses, some of whom gave them names, the police failed to investigate the murder fully. Because of the persistence of his parents, who refused to give up, the case became a national scandal, especially when the identities of the killers became known and they could not be prosecuted.

The eventual inquiry found the police had mishandled the case, and described the Metropolitan Police as institutionally racist. It recommended urgent measures to increase the number of police from minorities and to improve awareness of race issues.

⯈ FIND OUT FOR YOURSELF

Find out more about the Stephen Lawrence case at http://www.blink.org.uk/campaign/stevelaw.

The case of Michael Menson

Three men set musician Michael Menson, who as REBEL MC had hit singles in the early 1990s, on fire. He lived for 16 days and described what had happened, but the police believed he had committed suicide. As in the Lawrence case, his family refused to give up and the killers were eventually brought to justice.

> The things [the police] failed to do were so wilful and so blatant that it just has to be wilfully deciding not to take appropriate action. We … felt that by not investigating it the police were almost sending a message to these people that, 'that's fine, you go and burn a black man in the street to death and nothing is going to be done about it'.

Dr Essie Menson, Michael Menson's sister (quoted in *Guardian Weekly*, 6 January 2000)

QUESTIONS

1 What is meant by racial harassment?

2 How many racial assaults are there in Britain in a year, according to Human Rights Watch?

3 Identify and explain two reasons that have been suggested for the lower crime rates among British Asian people.

4 What are the two possible explanations for the high rates of Afro-Caribbean people in prison?

5 What could police forces do to try to be less racist? You may find it helpful to look back at the section on the police.

ROUND-UP

Britain's minority ethnic groups have very different experiences of crime and justice in Britain than the white majority. Both Afro-Caribbean and Asian people are victims of racial harassment and violence, while Afro-Caribbean people also commit a high percentage of crime relative to their numbers in the population.

VOCABULARY

Heavy-handed: harsh
Indifference: not caring

The future of crime and social control

This section looks at some recent developments in crime and social control, and looks into the future.

The future of crime control?

New crimes

The nature of crime, and the ways that society deals with it, have begun to change.

Changes in technology bring about the possibility of new types of crimes, and for old crimes on a greater scale. The clearest example of this is computer crime. This term covers a range of offences, including:

- hacking (breaking into closed information systems)
- piracy of computer software
- stealing credit card details
- posting illegal material on the Internet (though what is illegal is different in different countries, and no country owns the Internet).

Drug traffickers, money launderers and terrorists all use the Internet.

Computer crime

In a robbery attempt in 1995, a Russian criminal sat in a flat in Saint Petersburg and hacked into the headquarters of Citibank in New York, thousands of miles away. Some $10 million had been moved before the hacker was detected ('The age of the digital sleuth' by Martin Kettle and Owen Bowcott, *Guardian*, 12 December 1997).

Nick Leeson, an employee of Barings Bank in Singapore, established secret accounts and built up a massive fortune. A mistake turned this into a loss of £830 million and bankrupted Barings. His crime was made possible by the development of banking and trading through computers and electronic communications.

Computers and other new technology can also make it easier for the police to keep records. For example, they can easily look up records on many people who might be suspects for a particular crime.

Older forms of social control change

The old system of formal social control was based on police forces and prisons that were publicly funded and controlled by the government. This has begun to change:

- The police are no longer responsible for all policing. This was always the case to some extent, but more and more organisations now employ private security guards. High streets are still patrolled by the police, but shopping malls are private spaces controlled by what are in effect private police forces.

- Prisons are expanding and growing in nearly all countries. Britain now has the second largest prison population in Europe, with numbers increasing by 50 per cent in the 1990s. This has led to problems in housing all those given prison sentences by the courts. In 1997, the government even resorted to using a prison ship. Prisons are increasingly run by private security companies, such as the Wackenhut Corrections Corporation which in 1999 ran 52 prisons in the USA, Australia and Britain ('Analysing private prisons' by Chris Reed, *Guardian*, 7 April 1999).

Both policing and prisons are being privatised – and turned into profit making industries rather than public services.

New technology, new social control

Technological developments have made possible much greater social control through surveillance.

Closed-circuit television (CCTV) is now all around us – in shops, on roads, in streets. It makes possible surveillance around the clock, every day, and provides evidence for use in trials.

There are also new technologies for identifying people. Shops can already use electronic files that will identify known shoplifters as soon as they enter the shop. It is likely that soon individuals will be identified by their unique iris (eye) patterns or even their voices. Passports and credit cards may become unnecessary.

These developments have implications for civil liberties. We have lost our privacy (you cannot avoid being on CCTV) and we will find it hard to control what information all sorts of companies and organisations keep about us. We may also find it hard to correct any wrong information they hold.

A mugging in 2015?

AS Meg opens her car door she is pushed. She turns and sees a woman wearing a balaclava and gloves so as not to leave DNA clues. The woman sticks chewing gum on the carcam's lens. The thief has two minutes: the carcam has sent a signal to Meg's home computer and her private security company. These will locate her position and inform the police.

Next the woman sprays cheap scent so the police cannot use her body scent to track her down. Then the woman uses a device to transfer credits from Meg's smart card on to an anonymous cash card (there has been no cash since 2009). But then she hears a siren. She drops the smart card – she can't take it because it contains a tracking device. She runs off.

Meg smiles, knowing that her smart card has infected the thief's cash card with a virus which will have wiped out any credits.

Adapted from 'Welcome to the crimes of the future' by Alan Travis, *Guardian*, 25 March 2000.

Globalisation

Crime is increasingly not confined to individual countries. To deal with crime, police forces need to cooperate with other police forces. This has happened for many years through Interpol. Some international aspects of crime are:

- the drugs trade – there is a limit to what the British police force can achieve in controlling heroin and cocaine use when these drugs are part of huge multinational industries run by criminal organisations
- terrorism, espionage and arms dealing

- the international trade in people – smuggling of refugees into Europe
- crimes involving the Internet and global electronic communication (see new crimes above).

Recent events that highlight how crime has been globalised include:

- the trial in the Netherlands in 2000 of two Libyans for blowing up a US aeroplane with passengers from many countries over Britain (the Lockerbie incident)
- the attempt by Spain to extradite from Britain the former dictator of Chile, General Pinochet.

FIND OUT FOR YOURSELF

How many closed circuit television cameras do you walk or drive past, or see in shops and elsewhere? Watch out for them and keep a count. This should show you the extent to which we are all under surveillance.

QUESTIONS

1. What is meant by the term surveillance?
2. Identify and explain three types of computer crime.
3. Identify and explain three ways in which some crime is now global.
4. In your experience, does closed circuit television deter crime and delinquency? Give reasons for your answer.
5. Write a paragraph agreeing or disagreeing with the statement, 'Privatising the police and prisons can help reduce crime'.

ROUND-UP

Current developments include the growth of surveillance and the privatisation of formal social control agencies such as the police and prisons. Crime is increasingly globalised, and the rapid expansion of the Internet and electronic communications changes old crimes and creates new ones.

VOCABULARY

Iris: the coloured part of the eye; everyone's irises are unique
Extradite: when a criminal or suspect is sent back to the country where he or she is wanted from another country
Civil liberties: the rights we expect to have as citizens

Crime – sociology in practice

Who offends?

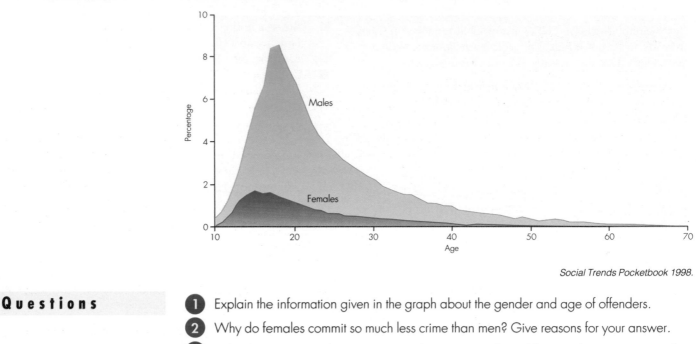

Offenders as a percentage of the population, by gender and age, 1996

Males

Females

Social Trends Pocketbook 1998.

Questions

1. Explain the information given in the graph about the gender and age of offenders.

2. Why do females commit so much less crime than men? Give reasons for your answer.

3. Why do young people commit so much more crime than older people? Give reasons for your answer.

4. In what ways might a sociologist question the accuracy of statistics such as these?

Mafia trains teenage killers

THE Mafia has set up a school for teenage killers in the Sicilian countryside, where pupils as young as 11 are taught to shoot, assemble weapons and ride pillion on motor-scooters.

The existence of the school emerged from an investigation into four murders in three days in the southern Sicilian fishing port of Gela ...

'In this city there is a crime school that is an alternative to compulsory state education,' Mr Tinebra (chief public prosecutor of Caltanisetta) said. 'Instead of going to school, many boys go into the countryside where there are people who teach them to shoot and turn them into killing machines.'

A 17 year old Mafia member told magistrates, 'The first time I was barely

11 years old. We fired, aiming at plants or tree trunks, and then they taught me how to assemble and disassemble the weapons.'

Adapted from 'Mafia sets up crime academy to train child assassins' by Philip Willan, *Guardian Weekly*, 19 August 1999.

Questions

1. Look back at the section Sociological explanations of crime and deviance (pages 262–3). What evidence is there in the passage above about the importance of socialisation in causing crime?

2. Look back at the paragraphs headed Peer groups and subcultures on page 262. How can the idea of subcultures explain what is described in the passage above?

The Mafia is an example of organised crime. Find out more about the Mafia by researching encyclopaedias or other reference books. The Sicilian Mafia is also known as *Cosa Nostra* ('our affair').

4 You could also try to find out about other crime organisations: the Triads of Hong Kong; the Yakuza of Japan; the Yardies of Jamaica; drug cartels in Colombia and elsewhere.

White collar crimes

'THE police are turning a blind eye to multi-million pound "white collar" fraud crimes and concentrating instead on catching the poor.

Law enforcers and politicians ignore white collar crimes because they see them as victimless and because the offenders are wealthy. White collar crimes include corporate crime, fraud, embezzlement and "fiddling" at work.

Scandals such as the cases involving Nick Leeson and Barings Bank (£865 million), Bank of Credit and Commerce International (between £12 billion and £15 billion), Robert Maxwell and Barlow Clowes indicate the vast sums involved, yet only a tiny number of people are brought to justice. People involved in cheating the Department of Social Security are far more likely to end up in court, although the amounts of money involved are tiny in comparison.

Year ending April 1995:
A crime of the rich: £66 billion unpaid tax – 357 prosecutions
A crime of the poor: Department of Social Security mounted 9546 fraud cases, mostly involving small sums of money. Estimated saving £650 million'

Adapted from 'Poverty, Crime and Punishment' by Dee Cook, Child Poverty Action Group, 1997.

Questions

1 Look back at the section Types of crime (pages 266–7). In what ways are white collar and corporate crimes treated differently from other crimes?

2 Carry out research into other cases of fraud, corporate crime and white collar crime that have come to light since this report.

3 Look back at the paragraphs headed The nature of society on page 263. This is about how Marxists see crime. The passage argues that the rich and the poor are treated differently. Explain how this supports the Marxist view of crime.

Crime – important terms

caution	when someone who has committed an offence is given a formal warning
chivalry factor	when men treat women more favourably
community service	being made to do unpaid work for the community as a punishment
computer crime	any crimes involving computers and information and communications technology
corporate crime	crimes committed by companies and business organisations
crime	actions which are against the law
dark figure (of crime)	crimes which are not reported or recorded and so do not appear in the statistics
delinquency	offences and anti-social behaviour by young people
deviance	actions which break norms and rules
label	a name applied to someone
master status	when a label becomes seen as the only or most important thing about a person
occupational crime	crimes which are related to the jobs people have
probation	when offenders are placed under the supervision of probation officers as an alternative to sending them to prison
relative deprivation	when people feel they are not well off compared to others
sanctions	any of the ways people can be punished for breaking norms
self-report study	when people are asked what offences they have committed
status frustration	(Albert Cohen) when working-class boys cannot win status and approval from parents and teachers so do things which some of their peers admire
subculture	when a group of people has a set of norms and values different from everyone else
victim survey	a method of research in which people are asked what crimes they have been victims of
white collar crime	crimes committed by people in middle-class jobs (businesses, offices and so on) which are related to their jobs

Crime – exam-style questions

Source A

Average sentence length in months for adults sentenced at Crown Courts in England and Wales (selected offences only)

	Men	Women
Robbery	54	28
Sexual offences	40	12
Criminal damage	34	41
Drug offences	33	30
Violence against the person	24	22
Burglary	22	19
All offences	24	20

Social Trends Pocketbook 1999, Home Office.

Foundation tier

1 Look at source A. What was the average sentence in months for men found guilty of violence against the person? [2 marks]

2 Look at source A. For which offence did women receive longer sentences on average than men? [3 marks]

3 State two punishments, other than prison sentences, which can be given by the courts. [4 marks]

4 State two reasons why female criminals are treated differently from male criminals. [5 marks]

5 Using sociological knowledge, explain why women commit less crime than men. [6 marks]

Higher tier

1 Look at source A. For which offence did women receive longer sentences on average than men? [2 marks]

2 State two punishments, other than prison sentences, which can be given by the courts. [3 marks]

3 State two reasons why female criminals are treated differently from male criminals. [5 marks]

4 Using sociological knowledge, discuss the reasons that have been put forward to explain why women commit less crime than men. [10 marks]

Crime – further research

The best site for crime statistics (not just British ones) is: www.crime.org.

You can reach the home site of any British police force from: www.police.uk.

The Howard League for Penal Reform campaigns for changes in the way offenders are dealt with: http://web.ukonline.co.uk/howardleague.

The Nashville, USA, police have a site at which by answering a few questions you can find out how much at risk of being a victim of crime you are: www.nashville.net/~police/risk.

On a specialised area of deviant and criminal behaviour try: www.streetgangs.com.

12 Media

The mass media surround us. In any one day, you probably spend several hours using or consuming the media in some way – watching television, listening to music, reading magazines, surfing the Internet. Much of this was unimaginable not all that long ago. This shows just how much the media have changed our lives, and changed society, so that studying them is an essential part of sociology. Some sociologists say that we now live in a media-saturated world, even that the media have taken over from the real world. Do you know the people in *Coronation Street* or *Albert Square* better than your own neighbours?

IN THIS CHAPTER YOU WILL LEARN ABOUT:

- different forms of media, such as the press and broadcasting
- the history of the media and recent changes
- how the media can be censored or can be biased
- what effects the media might have on people
- how different groups of people, such as women and minority ethnic groups, are represented in the media

CHAPTER CONTENTS

What are the mass media?

To begin this chapter, we consider what exactly we mean by the mass media. This involves looking at the history of the media, and at what media there are today and how much people use them.

There have always been ways to spread the news. Today, the news reaches more people more quickly.

Media

A medium is any way of communicating. It connects two people or groups of people – those sending out a message and those receiving it. The plural of medium is media.

Mass

The word mass in mass media refers to very large groups of people being involved in the communication. For example, a popular television programme may be watched by millions of people – they are the mass. On the other hand, if you telephone a friend, the communication involves only the two of you, so the telephone, although it is a medium, is not being

used as a mass medium here. With mass media there is also usually a large number of people involved in making the media product – look at the length of the credits at the end of a film!

The word mass suggests very large groups of people who are similar to each other. So the word is misleading. The mass is in fact made up of many different groups who make different choices about which media they use and how often. Sometimes the mass media have very small **audiences**.

Mass media

The main mass media today and which we look at most in this chapter are:

- television
- radio
- newspapers
- magazines
- cinema
- recorded music.

These are not the only mass media. What else could you add to this list?

Sometimes it is helpful to distinguish between media technology and media products. For example, a video recorder is a piece of media technology which allows you to watch two different types of media product, pre-recorded video cassettes and television programmes you have recorded. Advertising can take several different forms that reach us through different technology – television, radio, billboards, magazines and so on.

QUESTION

Would you count the following as mass media? Why or why not?

- Books
- A play in a theatre
- The Internet
- E-mail
- Closed-circuit television

History of the mass media

Modern mass media can be said to have begun with the invention of the printing press with moveable type in the fifteenth century. This made possible pamphlets, books and later newspapers. Earlier books had been handwritten.

By the end of the nineteenth century, many more people were literate and there was great demand for newspapers and other publications. There then followed a series of advances in communications and technology: telephones and telegraphs, photography, film, sound recording, radio and then television. These transformed social life and were soon an inescapable part of our culture and our main sources of information and entertainment.

Since about 1980 there has been further rapid development in the mass media. New media include satellite and cable communications, **digital television**, computers, video games and the Internet. Increasingly, media are hard to separate from each other. You can access the Internet by computer, telephone or television; you can watch a film on your television or computer, using a television channel, a video or a DVD.

FIND OUT FOR YOURSELF

In Britain today the media are unavoidable. Test this by making a list of all the times you have encountered the media since you got up this morning – listening to the radio, watching television, reading a paper or even a cereal packet, seeing advertising. Some sociologists of the media say we live in a media-saturated world.

While the media have fundamentally changed the way we live, it is important to realise that the media have not affected everyone in the same way. It takes many years for a newly introduced technology to reach everyone, usually because of the cost. It will be years, if ever, before everyone in Britain uses a computer or the Internet or has a digital television. Looking beyond the developed world, the media play a smaller part in many people's lives. There are still people in poorer countries who have never used a telephone – a piece of media technology that is now 150 years old.

Economic influences

The technological developments outlined above did not just happen. For a particular technology (for example television) to be used, it has first to be developed by a company or government, and then people have to be persuaded that the product is worth buying. In the case of television, it is not enough to have a television set – you want there to be programmes to watch as well! So as well as factories making television sets and shops selling them, you need a broadcasting system and production companies making programmes.

The growth of the mass media has been powered by economics. The media are owned and controlled by large companies whose motive (reason for existence) is to make profits. New media technologies will only be developed if companies feel there is a profit to be made. Sometimes a big gamble is involved; the new technology may lose money for years before it finally reaches enough people to become profitable.

This happened with **satellite television** in Britain in the late 1980s and 1990s. At first, very few people bought dishes and receivers. The television company Sky ran at a loss for several years. By buying rights to films and major sporting events (so that viewers without a dish and receiver could not see them), it gradually won more customers and eventually became very profitable.

QUESTIONS

1. What is meant by mass media?

2. When can modern mass media be said to have begun?

3. Explain what is meant by the term new media, giving three examples.

4. The most recent development in television is digital. Set-top boxes are being given away (although customers then have to pay subscriptions). Explain why, although the companies will lose money at first, this might pay off in the long run.

5. Some writers say that we are now entering a second media age. What do you think is meant by this?

ROUND-UP

After centuries of slow growth of print media, the mass media really took off early in the twentieth century. The twentieth century was the age of broadcasting. Today, we are entering a new phase of media expansion with new technologies. The media dominate our social world.

VOCABULARY

Literate: able to read and write
Inescapable: it is not possible to get away from them
Transform: to change completely

Newspapers

KEY FOCUS

Despite the rise of new media, newspapers continue to be very important in Britain. Here we look at the history and current situation of the press, at different types of newspapers and how they operate as businesses.

Different newspapers for different types of reader.

Tabloids and broadsheets

Britain has 11 national daily newspapers, as well as Sunday newspapers and evening and regional and local newspapers. The press is owned by companies.

It is usual to divide these 11 newspapers into two groups by their size and format, into tabloids and broadsheets. In fact, there are two distinct types of tabloids, which can be described as mid-market and popular tabloids. The differences are not only in paper size; they are also in type of reader, the way news is reported and in the kinds of advertising they carry.

National daily newspapers

- Broadsheets – *The Times, Daily Telegraph, Guardian, Independent, Financial Times*
- Mid-market tabloids – *Daily Mail, Daily Express*
- Popular tabloids – *Sun, Mirror, Star, Daily Record*

Most of these newspapers also have a Sunday equivalent, published by the same company. Sometimes this is obvious – the *Sunday Express*, the *Mail on Sunday* and so on. Sometimes it is less so; the *Observer* is the Sunday paper of the Guardian Media Group and the *News of the World* is published by News

International, which also publishes the *Sun. The People* is published by the Mirror Group, which also has the *Sunday Mirror*.

Readership

Each group of newspapers has different readers. More than half of all readers of broadsheets are in professional and middle-class occupations, but only between 20 and 30 per cent of mid-market tabloid readers and less than 10 per cent of popular tabloid readers. This affects the content of each newspaper, and also the kinds of advertising they carry. Broadsheet newspapers carry advertisements for luxury goods because advertisers know that broadsheet readers, unlike tabloid readers, are likely to be able to afford them.

W C **FIND OUT FOR YOURSELF**

Work in a small group. Choose a mixture of tabloids, mid-market tabloids and broadsheets. Each person should have one newspaper to study. Look at:

- how much space there is for particular types of news and articles, for example sport, financial news, foreign news, television, show business gossip
- what kinds of advertisements there are
- the way the news is reported.

What differences between different types of newspaper can you find? Present your findings to the class.

QUESTION

Which of the following would you be more likely to find in a broadsheet, which in a tabloid, and which might be in either?

- Horoscope
- Foreign news
- National Lottery winning numbers
- Stock exchange news
- Advertisement for a new model of car
- Cryptic crossword
- Strip cartoons

Now check your answers by studying some newspapers.

Competition

Competition between newspapers is within these groups. For example, when in the newspaper price wars of the 1990s, the cover price of *The Times* was cut so much that it sometimes ran at a loss, the aim was to win readers away from rival broadsheets, especially the *Independent*. The price cuts would have little or no effect on tabloid sales.

Sales of national daily newspapers

Sun	3.6 million
Daily Mail	2.4 million
Mirror	2.3 million
Daily Express	1.1 million
Daily Telegraph	1.0 million
The Times	0.7 million
Daily Star	0.5 million
Financial Times	0.5 million
Guardian	0.4 million
Independent	0.2 million
Scotsman	0.1 million

Newspapers have two main sources of profits. One, obviously, is from sales of newspapers, but this is less important than sale of space in the paper to advertisers. Broadsheets are able to charge more for advertisements because they are known to reach readers with money to spend. The importance of advertising can be seen in the existence of 'free' local papers that depend totally on advertising to make a profit. They attract advertisers by being known to reach large numbers of readers. Usually they guarantee to deliver to every house in an area.

The success of newspapers is measured in two ways:

- by the number of copies sold
- by the total number of readers (because each copy can be read by several people) – this is important in attracting advertisers.

Other newspapers

There are also:

- regional daily newspapers such as the *Western Mail* and *Liverpool Daily Post*
- local evening newspapers
- local weekly newspapers
- local 'free' newspapers (usually weekly)
- newspapers for particular kinds of reader or with specific content, for example *The Voice* is a weekly newspaper aimed at black people.

FIND OUT FOR YOURSELF

What are the local and regional newspapers where you live? Visit a large newsagent and see what is on sale.

Historical perspective

There are fewer newspapers than there used to be, and therefore less choice for readers. Fewer newspapers are sold, but the decline is a slow one. About 14 million papers are sold every day; this has fallen from about 16 million 20 years ago. It will be a long time at this rate before newspapers lose their importance. Newspaper companies do, however, feel the pressure of competition from other media. For example, many newspapers now have Internet sites.

IT ▶ FIND OUT FOR YOURSELF

Visit the web site of a British broadsheet newspaper, such as the *Independent* – www.independent.co.uk. Now visit a web site of a newspaper from another country. Compare what stories are the main news that day. Here are some suggestions to try:

- *Sydney Morning Herald* (Australia) – www.smh.com.au
- *New York Times* (USA) – www.nytimes.com
- *Irish Times* (Ireland) – www.ireland.com
- *Frankfurter Allgemeine Zeitung* (English edition) (Germany) – www.faz.com

QUESTIONS

1. Name three broadsheet national daily newspapers.
2. Approximately how many daily newspapers are sold each day?
3. What is the biggest selling daily newspaper? How many copies a day does it sell?
4. Why do broadsheet newspapers not need to sell as many copies as tabloids in order to make a profit?
5. Design the perfect tabloid front page. Think carefully and make up news stories that are about famous people, gossip, scandals and so on.

ROUND-UP

The press is controlled by a small number of companies whose purpose is to make profits. There is competition, but only between newspapers aiming for the same kind of readers. Newspapers need to have readers in order to attract advertisers.

VOCABULARY

Financial: to do with money
Horoscope: the stars – predicting the future
Cryptic crossword: one where the answers are hidden in clues that might have several meanings

Broadcasting

The media were transformed in the twentieth century by the development of broadcasting, first of radio and then of television. Broadcasting has a very different history to the press; in particular, this section looks at the importance of public service broadcasting.

Distinctively British – an authoritative and respected voice.

QUESTION

Match the BBC radio station to the content it provides:

Radio 1   sport and talk
Radio 2   classical music
Radio 3   light music
Radio 4   current affairs, entertainment and drama
Radio 5 Live   pop music

FIND OUT FOR YOURSELF

What local radio stations can you receive? Make a list and note whether they are commercial or BBC stations.

Radio

Although most people use the radio now to listen to radio stations, that was not its main use in the early days. Radio was first used by armies and by ships for communicating from one point to another. Later the telephone became the main medium for one-to-one communication.

For a long time almost all radio listened to in Britain was broadcast from the BBC. From one radio station at first, the BBC gradually grew to four stations – Radios 1, 2, 3 and 4 – by 1967. Before Radio 1 started in 1967, many young people listened to illegal 'pirate' radio stations, such as Radio Caroline, which broadcast pop music from ships at sea.

Early broadcasts were on long wave or medium wave. VHF (FM) greatly improved sound quality. Short-wave radio is used mainly for sending signals very long distances; the BBC World Service, which can be heard all over the world, is broadcast mainly on short wave.

There followed a big expansion of radio with:

■ BBC local radio
■ · local commercial radio (with advertisements)
■ national commercial stations such as Talk Radio and Classic FM
■ Radio 5 (now Radio Five Live).

Television

Television has become the most successful medium of all. More than 99 per cent of homes have a set, and about two-thirds have more than one set. On average people in Britain watch about 25 hours a week.

The **British Broadcasting Corporation** (BBC) is a publicly owned body, funded by the television licence fee. It exists to provide a service to British people, not to make a profit for shareholders (it doesn't have any). The BBC is guided by the principles of **public service broadcasting** – to produce high quality programmes for the whole nation.

The first BBC television broadcast was in 1936. Very few people had television sets then; a television cost as much as a car. The area television could reach gradually grew until it covered all of Britain, but television remained a luxury for the few. The biggest growth was for BBC TV coverage of the coronation of Queen Elizabeth II in 1953. Lots of people bought televisions for this, and people crammed into the front rooms of those who had TV sets to watch the ceremony. The BBC's monopoly ended in 1955 with the creation of Independent Television (ITV), funded by advertising but also closely regulated by the government. Since then there have been a whole series of changes – BBC2 in 1964, colour, Channel 4 and then multi-channel television with satellite, **cable** and digital.

Key dates in British television history

1936	First BBC television broadcast – to only about 400 TV sets, all in the London area
1938	5000 TV sets – but then the service closes as war approaches
1953	Coronation – big growth in ownership of TV sets
1955	ITV starts
1964	Launch of BBC2
1967	Colour television
1970	Change from 405 line VHF service to 625 line UHF
1981	Channel 4 starts
1984	First commercial satellite television service, Sky Channel
1997	Channel 5 starts

Public service broadcasting

Public service broadcasting has been very strong in Britain. The BBC has been seen as 'the voice of Britain'. Public service broadcasting has established firmly the idea that, after paying the licence fee, television should be free. The attempts by companies trying to introduce 'pay-TV' to replace 'free-TV' therefore face a big problem. The majority of viewers at the moment (2001) do not have multi-channel and subscription services. There is still a strong feeling that big public events, such as the FA Cup Final, must be shown on BBC or ITV so that they are accessible to everyone.

Viewing figures – top five television programmes, 1999

Programme	Audience (millions)	Transmission date
1 Coronation Street	19.82	7 March
2 Who Wants to be a Millionaire	19.21	7 March
3 Coronation Street	19.03	4 January
4 Coronation Street	18.22	13 January
5 Heartbeat	17.01	23 February

Royal Television Society, 2000.

Viewing figures

The success of television programmes and companies is measured by viewing figures. The Broadcasting Audience Research Board (BARB) uses a panel of about 4500 homes, a cross-section of the population. There are set-top meters and family members register when they are watching by using a handset. The main terrestrial channels compete for higher viewing figures than their rivals. There is particular rivalry between BBC and ITV; this can be seen in the careful scheduling of programmes to attract viewers away from the other channel at particular times.

IT ▶ FIND OUT FOR YOURSELF

Find out more about the BBC by visiting its web site: www.bbc.co.uk/info. Follow links to find out about the BBC's Charter, what happens to the licence fee viewers pay, the BBC's plans for the future and much more. You can find out more about the history of BBC radio and television, and listen to some clips of old broadcasts at www.bbc.co.uk/thenandnow.

QUESTIONS

1. Name two national commercial radio stations.
2. What is meant by public service broadcasting?
3. What are the differences between the BBC and new television companies such as Sky? Think of (a) who the programmes can be seen by, and (b) what each organisation's purpose is.
4. Compare radio to television. Which stations are the equivalent of BBC TV channels? Which are the equivalent of ITV (think of those that carry adverts)?

ROUND-UP

The BBC, funded by a licence fee, maintains the tradition of public service broadcasting in Britain. 'Free' TV is increasingly being challenged by the commercial television companies.

VOCABULARY

Monopoly: a company has a monopoly in the market if it has no real rivals
Regulated: controlled
Accessible: available

Who owns the mass media?

KEY FOCUS

In this section you will learn about patterns of ownership of the mass media, in particular newspapers and television. The mass media today are owned by a small number of very powerful corporations. The wealth and power of these corporations has helped them drive smaller companies out of business.

Murdoch tries to buy Manchester United

RUPERT Murdoch has made a £624 million bid to buy Manchester United football club. Murdoch's BSkyB satellite television company already has the rights to screen Premiership football matches, but now wants to take over the top club as well.

Manchester United already has its own television channel – MUTV – and Murdoch wants to make sure that this and other club-owned channels do not eat into the popularity and income of BSkyB. The move is sure to be opposed strongly by the clubs fans.

Should satellite, cable and digital companies be able to buy rights to screen major sporting events, so that they are available only to those willing to pay?

The media giants

The mass media are owned by a fairly small number of giant corporations. Among the largest in the world, operating in many countries but based in the USA are Disney, Time Warner and News Corporation.

HINTS AND TIPS

When watching television or a film, watch the credits at the end closely for references to these companies.

These corporations usually have interests in several media; for example, they may make films, own television channels and publish books. They are cross-media corporations rather than specialists in one medium.

British companies also often have interests in several media, but because the patterns of ownership are so different, newspapers and television will be considered separately here.

Newspapers

Rupert Murdoch's company News International, which owns the *Sun*, the *News of the World*, *The Times* and the *Sunday Times*, sells 35 per cent of the national newspapers sold in Britain. Just five companies produce 96 per cent of all national newspapers.

The number of national newspapers in Britain has stayed roughly the same for many years. In the 1980s many people thought that new technology and working practices would make it possible to produce newspapers more cheaply, and that there would be more newspapers.

Several new papers were launched in the 1980s, but only one of them, the *Independent*, has survived, and it has an uncertain future. Another new paper, *Today*, was the first full-colour newspaper, but it closed in 1995, having been bought by News International. The new papers failed because the older established papers had advantages and competed aggressively.

The larger companies have advantages because they can afford to spend more to increase future profits, and can sometimes be subsidised by other parts of the company.

Some of the tactics used to try to sell more copies and squeeze competitors have been:

■ reducing the cover price; at times, News International's titles sold for less than the cost of producing them – a large company can afford this, especially if subsidised by profits from other parts of the company, but a small newcomer cannot

- increasing the number of pages and having more supplements – this increases production costs
- use of colour and more use of pictures
- stories, preferably exclusive, that meet people's interest in scandal and gossip about celebrities.

Television

Unlike newspapers, the television industry is not yet dominated entirely by privately owned corporations. The biggest company is the BBC, a public body, independent of direct government control and funded by the television licence fee. The BBC has traditionally provided all its services free to licence holders. ITV, which is funded by the advertising it broadcasts, also provides free programmes.

For many years BBC and ITV dominated television in Britain. Although their channels are still the most popular, there are now many more channels provided by cable, satellite and digital companies. To receive these, viewers usually need to buy special equipment (a dish or decoder) and then to pay a subscription. For some programmes, such as a new film or a major sporting event, they may have to pay a further charge. These newer television providers therefore make money from both advertisers, **pay per view**, from subscriptions and other charges.

Where TV gets its money

BBC – television licence fee
ITV – advertisers
Satellite, cable and digital – advertisers and subscriptions and pay-per-view charges

Satellite television, provided by Rupert Murdoch's Sky, has grown in recent years through acquiring the rights to show popular films and big sporting events, which have been sold to the highest bidder. People who do not subscribe have lost the right to watch events they once took for granted, such as Premiership football matches.

The rise of satellite, cable and digital shows how market forces are now important in the world of television. The BBC's competitors believe that the licence fee gives the BBC an unfair advantage. The BBC argues that its unique position enables it to provide high quality programming less influenced by commercial pressures.

FIND OUT FOR YOURSELF

Do research on what media are owned by Rupert Murdoch. Look in encyclopaedias or reference books under Murdoch or under News International and News Corporation.

Does it matter who owns the media?

No, it doesn't:
The media have to provide what the public wants. If they don't, they will lose audiences or readers and money. There are newspapers and programmes (and now channels) to cater for all interests and to reflect a range of opinions. We can choose what to buy and watch, and we can complain if we don't like something. This is called the pluralist view.

Yes, it does:
Giant corporations who are only interested in profits run all the media. They are not interested in quality, or in promoting debate on important issues, only in money. If the biggest are able to drive their competitors out of business, they will be able to charge what they like, and will concentrate on programmes which are quick and cheap to make.

QUESTIONS

1. Name three giant media corporations.
2. Identify and explain two tactics newspapers have used to try to win more readers.
3. What is the difference between the way BBC and ITV are funded?
4. List the arguments that can be put forward for and against pay per view for an important sports event.
5. In 1999, Rupert Murdoch tried to buy Manchester United football club.
   (a) Why do you think he did this?
   (b) Why did many fans try (successfully) to stop him?

ROUND-UP

The media, both globally and in Britain, are in the hands of a small number of companies which compete fiercely against each other. Television is different from the press in having a public service, the BBC, which is partly protected from market forces.

VOCABULARY

Subsidised: receive help in the form of money
Cross-media corporations: those with interests in several media
Market forces: the free market allows competition between companies

Researching the media

KEY FOCUS

All of the methods discussed in Chapter 2 Research methods can be used in studying the media – surveys, interviews, participant observation, and so on. There are also two methods that are specifically concerned with the media – content analysis and semiology.

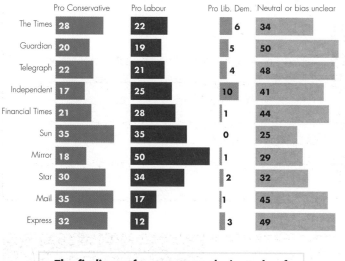

Newspapers: percentage of stories which are clearly positive about each main party

	Pro Conservative	Pro Labour	Pro Lib. Dem.	Neutral or bias unclear
The Times	28	22	6	34
Guardian	20	19	5	50
Telegraph	22	21	4	48
Independent	17	25	10	41
Financial Times	21	28	1	44
Sun	35	35	0	25
Mirror	18	50	1	29
Star	30	34	2	32
Mail	35	17	1	45
Express	32	12	3	49

The findings of a content analysis study of newspaper coverage of the 1997 general election campaign.

HINTS AND TIPS

If you want to do research on the media for your coursework project, this section should give you ideas and help you go about it in the right way.

Content analysis

Content analysis is a method that produces quantitative results. It involves counting the number of times a word, or idea, or image appears in the media. In studying newspapers and magazines, column inches (or column centimetres) or words are counted. In studying films and television, time on screen is usually counted. In studying films and television a video with a pause button is essential!

These are some typical research projects by content analysis:

- Counting the number of column inches in different newspapers given to a particular news item. The researcher would also of course note on which pages the

coverage occurred, how much prominence it was given, whether there were photographs to accompany it and so on.

- Counting the number of times particular words were used in reporting an item. This is important because different words have different meanings and affect how we think about something. An example is given below.

- Counting the number of times certain types of people, such as people with disabilities, appear on a television programme or channel, and the way in which they are shown (as needing a lot of help, or as independent, for example).

Example: The Falklands War

The Glasgow Media Group recorded all national television news bulletins during the Falklands War in 1982. One aspect of the research was a close study of the words used. They found that in reporting deaths of British servicemen when HMS *Sheffield* was sunk, both BBC and ITV used 'hard' words such as 'killed'. When they reported the sinking of the Argentine ship *Belgrano*, 'killed' was not used and instead 'soft' terms were used, those that might be used to report deaths in a natural disaster – 'loss of life', 'casualties' and so on. The effect was to hide British responsibility for the deaths on the *Belgrano*, but to make it clear that Argentina was responsible for the deaths on HMS *Sheffield*. Reporting of HMS *Sheffield* also emphasised the grief felt by survivors; there was nothing similar in reporting on the *Belgrano*.

This might be what you would expect in wartime, especially after you read the section on censorship in wartime later (see page 306). The point here is that careful research by content analysis provides evidence for the claim that, in this case at least, patriotism was seen as more important than balanced reporting.

HINTS AND TIPS

Quantitative means involving numbers.
Qualitative means involving description.
Find out more in Chapter 2 Research Methods.

Semiology

Semiology is also a study of the content of the media, but it is qualitative. Semiology means the study of signs. Signs as used here mean both images and words. Semiology looks at the meanings that signs used in the media have. These meanings are on two levels, which are in practice difficult to keep apart:

- **Denotation** – the simple meaning of a sign. The three letters DOG are a sign for a particular animal (though there is no reason they should be, and different languages refer to what we call dogs by different words).

- **Connotation** – the cultural meaning of a sign, which can vary. DOG may 'connote' danger if it is a warning notice on a gate, or it may mean a human's best friend, or even (in some countries) a menu outside a restaurant. What is meant by connotation becomes clearer if we consider colours. Red can mean danger, blood, heat, passion (a red rose has a different meaning to another colour rose). White means cleanliness, purity and innocence (hence a white wedding dress). Black means evil. In some old Western films, black and white are used as very clear signs – the sheriff has a white hat, the outlaw a black one. This is a particularly obvious example of something semiologists say is built into all images.

Semiology can be used to study any kind of visual image in the mass media, including:

- photographs in magazines and newspapers
- advertising in magazines and newspapers
- film posters
- images from television and film.

Any image used in the mass media will carry a particular meaning. For example, a newspaper editor may want to include a photograph of a famous person to accompany a news story. The editor will have available several photographs, and will choose the one that best suits the meaning that is required. A photograph of the person smiling will give a very different impression to one of the person frowning.

Semiology should not be seen as an alternative to content analysis; the two can be combined. Semiology is more open to individual interpretation than content analysis. One of semiology's points is that connotations are not fixed, although advertisers may try to 'anchor' a particular interpretation through the words they use to accompany an image. This means that different researchers may interpret – decode – the same image differently.

FIND OUT FOR YOURSELF

Choose an advertisement (it's best to find one in colour) from any magazine or newspaper and attempt a semiological analysis of it.

QUESTIONS

1. What is meant by content analysis?
2. What are the two levels of meaning that signs have?
3. What are the connotations of (a) blue, (b) green, and (c) yellow? (Try to find several for each colour.)
4. Why is content analysis described as producing quantitative results?
5. What are the differences between content analysis and semiology?

ROUND-UP

The mass media can be studied using two methods not found in other areas of sociology: content analysis, which produces quantitative data, and semiological analysis, which involves a qualitative interpretation.

VOCABULARY

Patriotism: love for your country
Decode: to turn a hidden message into ordinary language

The news

We rely on the media to tell us what is going on in the world. This section looks at how the media decide what news is, and how they present it to us.

Why the news is important

News tells us what is going on in the world. It helps us to make decisions about what we believe in and what we feel is important. It enables us to take part as informed citizens in a democratic society. Most people rely on television, radio and newspapers for news (as well as family and friends). There are, however, serious concerns about news. Are we always told the truth? Is the news **biased**, so that we only get part of the story? Is the news **'dumbed down'**, so that we hear what has happened but cannot understand why? Why do some stories make the news while others don't?

How is news selected?

Stories reach newspapers and television news studios continuously. Out of a huge number of possible stories, the news organisation must select which to use and which to reject. How does this happen?

Journalists, **editors** and other people working in the news act as **gatekeepers**; they allow some stories through, and reject others. To get into the newspaper or bulletin, a story will need to be passed by a series of gatekeepers. It could get dropped at the last minute if something important happens.

Gatekeepers ask, is this story newsworthy? Some factors which affect whether a story is seen as newsworthy or not:

- Has it just happened (news should be new!)?
- Is it dramatic, perhaps with conflict or argument?
- Does it involve personalities, celebrities, or ordinary people readers and viewers can identify with?
- Can it be presented in a way that most readers or viewers will understand?
- If it is foreign news, does it involve British people or British interests?
- Are there pictures or video footage available?

These are called **news values**.

Agenda setting

Agenda setting is the idea that in selecting what is news, the media decide what we will talk about and be interested in. There are huge variations in how apparently similar cases are treated. One murder trial, such as that of Louise Woodward, the British nanny tried in the USA for murder of the baby she was looking after, became a major story while other murder trials of British people abroad pass almost unnoticed. The media decided that this case was very newsworthy.

Behind the scenes, it may not be the media who are the main agenda setters. The government, for example, can manipulate what is in the news by choosing when to release news and by the **'spin'** it puts on the news.

Time and space

In selecting the news, the media work under constraints of time and space.

A newspaper has to be printed at a certain time to reach retailers later that morning. News that happens at night is a problem. When Princess Diana was killed early on a Sunday morning, it was too late to be included in most Sunday newspapers, while Monday's papers had to find new angles because almost everyone had heard the news from television, radio or friends on the Sunday.

Newspapers are produced to a set format; a certain amount of space for sport, for financial news, for foreign news and so on. This gives only a limited amount of flexibility. There will be a set amount of news of a particular type, even if not much that is newsworthy has happened. Television and radio bulletins also have a fixed number of minutes to fill. Bulletins can be extended if a major news event happens, but they are never cancelled (though they may be shorter than usual on bank holidays). Sometimes you can spot 'slow news days' when top stories would on other days not have had much coverage at all!

Whom do we trust?

Percentages agreeing with the view that 'the reporting is exactly in line or approximately in line with what really happened': television – 85 per cent; radio – 79 per cent; newspapers – 48 per cent (*Sociology Update 1998*).

Why do people trust television more than other media?

The answer probably lies in the public service broadcasting tradition (see the section on Broadcasting (pages 292–3)). The BBC has considerable prestige and we have come to expect its news to be truthful and unbiased. ITV and other television channels have tried to reach the same standards as the BBC. The immediate appeal of images, with a reporter 'on the spot', gives us a feeling of seeing what is really going on.

Why do people have less trust in newspapers?

Newspapers are known to be run by profit-motivated companies. We suspect they (at least the tabloids) will sensationalise or even make up stories to win readers. We know newspapers take sides with political parties.

Foreign news

One of the main news values is that foreign news is more newsworthy if it involves British people or British interests. The English language is also important; it helps if someone being interviewed can speak English rather than a translator or subtitles being needed.

FOR three weeks (Mozambique) laboured under the worst floods in living memory. No one outside took much notice … Britain gave some money to cope with the medical emergency. The United Nations sent a team to investigate. But it was only when the television cameras arrived, and viewers across Europe and the United States got a glimpse of what it is to have your house washed away while you climb the nearest tree, that the crisis was taken seriously … Some time in the next few years, another calamity will befall another African country. And the victims had better hope that it is a slow news week on CNN.

'Yet another disaster that needed TV's endorsement'
by Chris McGreal, *Guardian Weekly*,
9 March 2000.

Much foreign news in Britain comes from the USA and from western Europe. There is much less news from other parts of the world. Here another news value comes in – disasters, wars, and so on are usually news. Much of the news about poorer countries involves their problems. Good news is not news. Because images are needed, a disaster may not be reported until a camera crew arrives. This happened with the Mozambique floods in 2000.

▶ C FIND OUT FOR YOURSELF

Look at the front page of a newspaper, or the first five stories on a television or radio news bulletin. For each story decide why this story was seen as newsworthy. Use the list of important news values but do not limit yourself to this. Present your findings to the class.

QUESTIONS

1. Give two reasons why the news is important.

2. Give a reason why people believe television news is more accurate than news in newspapers.

3. What is meant by news values? Give three examples.

4. What is meant by saying that 'in selecting the news, the media work under constraints of time and space'? Use examples to explain your answer.

5. What do you think Chris McGreal means by '… the victims had better hope that it is a slow news week on CNN'.?

ROUND-UP

The news is presented to us as an accurate reflection of reality. In fact, it is made by people working for news organisations, who take decisions about what to report and how to report it. Even a major disaster may be ignored, but when it is reported the media have the ability to motivate people to help.

VOCABULARY

Constraints: things that restrict what you can do
Newsworthy: interesting enough to be reported in the news
Sensationalise: to make something more shocking

Effects of the media (1)

KEY FOCUS

The media are all around us, but how much do they influence us. This section looks at how theories about media effects have developed, from early assumptions that the media had powerful, immediate effects to a greater interest in different audiences and how effects might be long term.

A radio play of *The War of the Worlds* in 1938 was so realistic that many people believed there really was an invasion from Mars.

The hypodermic syringe theory

When the new mass media of the early twentieth century appeared, they seemed amazingly powerful. The earliest theory about effects of the media assumed that they had very powerful effects. According to this hypodermic syringe theory, the media worked like drugs injected into a body. To advertisers, it seemed that all they had to do was get their message to people and they would sell more. To dictators, the mass media seemed to provide a way of brainwashing people through **propaganda**. Hitler's Nazis broadcast their views to German people through radios with loudspeakers on lampposts. Stalin had a train with a film projector, screen and seating travelling around the Soviet Union showing communist propaganda.

This early theory now seems very simplistic. This is partly because today we are much more used to the media and how

they work. We think, or like to think, that we know how advertisers exaggerate and that we would see through propaganda. We recognise that although the media can have important effects, these are much less immediate and take the form of gradual shaping of opinion over a long period.

Audiences

The **hypodermic syringe theory** treated audiences as unthinking and passively taking in media messages. In fact, audiences interpret, make sense of and respond to the media; they are active not passive.

Audiences make use of the media. The theory which stresses this is called the uses and gratifications approach. As individuals we have needs that the media can meet, so we use the media as and when we want them. Notice that this puts the audience very much in control, unlike the hypodermic syringe theory. For example, individuals might watch television because they want specific information (will it rain tomorrow?), or for entertainment when they want to relax, or for company if they feel lonely.

Audiences are also made up of different types of people, who may have different reactions to the same programme. How we react to a media product may depend on our age, sex, ethnic group and class background, as well as our individual likes and dislikes. We 'read' the media in different ways. Often, there is a 'reading' which we are intended to follow, but we do not have to. For example, a film may intend you to identify with the hero, but you may feel more sympathy for the character intended to be the villain. The pop star Madonna in her early career was seen as a sex object by many men while feminists approved of her widening the range of behaviour traditionally allowed to women. They bought her music for very different reasons.

Cultural effects

Another theory is that the media have significant but long-term effects. For example, some feminists have argued that from early childhood we continuously take in messages and images from the media about what boys and girls, men and women are like and how they should behave. Because of the content of the media, many people have grown up believing that, for example, 'a woman's place is in the home'. We will have access to alternative ideas from our own lives, and even from the media themselves sometimes, but the overall effect is a slow shaping of what we think of as natural and normal.

Similar ideas have been used by the Glasgow Media Group in a series of studies of the news. They have shown how, for example, when strikes are reported, the emphasis is always on how this affects the public. Strikers are given very little opportunity to explain why they are on strike. The effect of this biased reporting is to leave people, at least those not directly involved, with the impression that strikers are always in the wrong.

Moral panics

One particular effect the media can have was described by Stanley Cohen in his research on mods and rockers. Cohen showed how, on a 'slow news weekend', the news media seized on some minor incidents involving young people in seaside resorts. The exaggerated and sensationalised reports led to what he called a **'moral panic'**. There were demands for a crackdown, for harsh sentences and for more police on the streets. Members of the public boarded up their windows in fear of another invasion by the teenagers. Cohen shows that there was in fact more trouble because the media predicted it, and even encouraged it. The teenagers involved were **'folk devils'**, who came to stand for everything that some older people thought was wrong with 'young people today'.

Moral panics occur regularly, although they do not always involve a folk devil. Watch out for (the examples are taken from reporting of the mods and rockers):

- exaggeration – 'Day of terror by scooter groups' (few of the young people had scooters)
- inflated language – 'riot', 'orgy of destruction'
- prediction
- symbolisation – words and styles became symbols, for example a fur-lined anorak came to mean that the wearer was a mod
- demands for tough action by the government, police and courts.

The mods and rockers became **scapegoats** for a lot of unconnected worries that people had about how Britain was changing at the time. Moral panics in the last few years have included the drug ecstasy, football hooligans and asylum seekers.

QUESTIONS

1. Explain what is meant by the hypodermic syringe idea of media effects.

2. Explain what is meant by the uses and gratifications model of media effects.

3. Identify and explain two ways in which audiences might use the mass media.

4. Choose any two television programmes or films and show how they might be interpreted very differently by different groups of people.

5. Explain what is meant by a moral panic, referring to at least two examples.

ROUND-UP

The hypodermic syringe theory suggested that the media have direct effects on audiences. The uses and gratifications approach shows how audiences can be in control. But the media can have important effects, both through the shaping of ideas and opinions over a long period and in creating moral panics.

VOCABULARY

Propaganda: information designed to help or damage a cause or organisation
Simplistic: oversimplifying something complex
Scapegoats: people who are wrongly blamed for something

Effects of the media (2)

KEY FOCUS We have already looked at the effects of the media in general terms; we now look at one particular aspect, the claim that violence in the media can lead to violence in real life.

Clinton attacks violence in films

Horror videos inspired students who killed friend who teased them

Natural Born Killers cited in two French murder cases

Calls for Sky to cancel showing of Chucky film

A great deal of panic – but not much evidence.

The moral panic

In 1993, two 11-year-old boys from Liverpool were found guilty of murdering a 2-year-old boy, James Bulger. The way the murder was carried out was said to be similar to scenes in a horror film available on video, *Child's Play 3*. The judge suggested in his summing up that watching horror videos had influenced the murderers.

The result was a moral panic about violence in films and videos. The *Sun* ran a campaign under the headline, 'For the sake of ALL our kids ... BURN YOUR VIDEO NASTY'. The media and politicians called for more **censorship**, saying that watching violence was an obvious cause of the rise in crime by young people. In fact, the police officers in the Bulger murder investigation said that neither *Child's Play 3*, nor videos in general, had caused the murder. The media ignored this, and the moral panic continued.

Since then, films that have been criticised for being too violent have included *Reservoir Dogs*, *Natural Born Killers* and *Fight Club*. In the USA, it has been claimed that media violence has contributed to the number of shootings in schools. President Clinton said that by the age of 18 the average American had watched 40 000 murders and 200 000 acts of violence on screen.

What is violence?

This is not as easy a question as it might seem. The media show different kinds of violence – some of which you might argue do not count as violence:

- in the news and documentaries, real footage of wars and dead bodies
- in cartoons like *Tom and Jerry*
- in sports such as boxing.

Fictional violence in films and dramas varies enormously too. Sometimes it is treated in an almost humorous or unrealistic way. In the *Rambo* films, the main character shoots hundreds of enemies, but there is no blood and no grieving relatives. Realistic violence, such as domestic violence in a soap opera, may be much more disturbing, because it is closer to what we know can really happen.

How do we react?

The overwhelming majority of people who see violence on screen will have no thought of copying it in any way. We may even be repelled by what we see. News coverage of a war may encourage us to contribute to the relief effort; showing what has really happened may be necessary to help the victims.

However, it is possible that we may become used to violence – **desensitised** to it. Perhaps because we have seen a lot of violence on screen, real-life violence will come to seem less shocking. We may even take in the message that violence is the only or best solution to some problems, especially if heroes we are intended to identify with use violence.

Research on audiences, however, has shown that audiences, including quite young children, understand the nature of television and other media. We know the difference between what is real and what is not.

Research

There have been many attempts to try to prove a link between watching violence on screen and violent behaviour. All of these attempts have faced several problems, including deciding what we mean by violence. Another problem is trying to separate screen violence from all the other factors that might have influenced someone to act in a violent way. After all, there are many other factors that have been linked to violent behaviour – being rejected by parents, failure at school, etc.

Laboratory research involves showing people screen violence, and then seeing if their behaviour immediately afterwards is violent. This involves trying to prove a version of the hypodermic syringe theory (see the previous section). Bandura and his colleagues did this with a group of young children. The children who had been shown violent behaviour did behave more violently than those who had not – but the violence involved hitting a doll. Not only is this not the same as violence against a person or creature, but it is possible the children may just have been trying to please the researchers.

Other research has looked at whether people convicted of violent offences watch more violent television than others do. Research in 1994 by the Policy Studies Institute found that young offenders did not have significantly different viewing habits from non-offenders. Both offenders and non-offenders liked *Eastenders* and *Brookside*, and their favourite film was *Terminator 2* – which was not one of the films mentioned in the arguments as being too violent. Offenders did like *The Bill* more than non-offenders, but the researchers felt this was because they saw it as more relevant to their lives.

Conclusion

Overall, the evidence is unclear. While many people feel that common sense suggests that some people – but only vulnerable people, not themselves – must be influenced, research has not found any clear links. What we can say is that the media play only a limited role, if any. After all, life was very violent before there were any mass media! The media make a convenient scapegoat. It is easier to blame a handful of films than to tackle the underlying causes of violence.

FIND OUT FOR YOURSELF

Over the next week, keep a record of all the television programmes you watch. Beside each one write any incidents of violence. At the end of the week, try to work out how much violence you saw. You could try to do it in the way President Clinton did – work out how many murders or violent deaths you saw.

Do you think the controls on what is shown on television, such as the 9 pm **watershed** and cutting of scenes from films, made a difference to your viewing?

QUESTIONS

1. Which horror video did newspapers say influenced the boys who murdered James Bulger?

2. According to President Clinton, how many murders on screen has the average American 18-year-old seen?

3. Look back at the features of moral panics described in the last section (page 301). In what ways does the moral panic over violent films fit this description?

4. Identify and give examples of three different types of violence that are shown on television.

5. In the film *Pulp Fiction*, a man is shot accidentally in a car, with blood and brains spattered everywhere. This is accompanied by light-hearted dialogue between the others in the car. What are the possible reactions of people to violence they have seen on screen? List as many as possible. Which of these are the most likely to happen?

ROUND-UP

What links there are, if any, between screen violence and real-life violence, remain a highly controversial issue. The media may influence some people occasionally, but other factors are likely to be much more significant. The media – certain films in particular – have been scapegoats in a long running moral panic.

VOCABULARY

Repelled: to keep away from something because it is disgusting
Desensitised: to stop being sensitive to
Scapegoat: someone who takes the blame when others are at fault

Advertising

Advertising is found throughout the mass media. While some argue that it is necessary for the economy and useful for us as consumers, others argue that it is misleading and harmful.

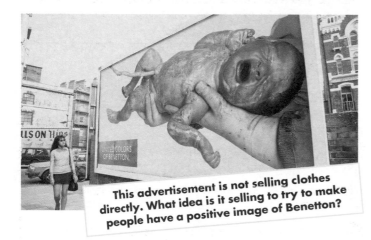

This advertisement is not selling clothes directly. What idea is it selling to try to make people have a positive image of Benetton?

Information or exploitation?

Advertising is found in virtually all mass media, with the exception of BBC television and radio – and even the BBC advertises its own programmes and products.

Advertising is an important source of income for almost all media companies. For newspapers, for example, it is at least as important as the money from sales of the newspaper. In fact, it could be said that newspapers contain news only to get readers so that they can sell advertising space. This is shown by local free newspapers that depend entirely on advertising.

Advertisements have come a long way. From early advertisements that gave readers and viewers information in a straightforward, supposedly factual way, they have now become clever, ironic and playful. Sometimes they seem to have little relation to the product they are supposedly selling. This can be because the advertisers are not allowed to say anything about a product such as cigarettes. But, for example, the clothing company Benetton has used striking photographic images that seem to have little to do with selling clothes. Advertisements like these are attempts to make us associate a brand or product with positive ideas and values.

Advertising and the media today

In 1997, £13.4 billion was spent on advertising in Britain, nearly £5 per week for every person. Advertising is a huge industry. As well as using established media, such as newspapers, radio and television, advertisers have their own specialist media – billboards, bus shelters, the sides of buses and taxis and so on. Television advertising attracts a lot of attention because of its high production values. Television advertisements are often as good as the programmes around them – witty, entertaining, using top actors and other celebrities, either on screen or doing voice-overs. However, the biggest advertising sector is still print – magazines, newspapers and directories like Yellow Pages.

Advertising has grown in importance in the last 20 years or so. It became central in politics with the Conservative Party's 'Labour isn't working' poster advertisement, which played a big part in winning the 1979 election. Earlier political advertising had not attacked opponents so directly; now it has become normal.

Advertisers are in a position to exercise considerable influence over the content of the media. If they do not like a particular programme or publication, advertisers can threaten to withdraw their business. It is hard to be sure how often this happens, as cases rarely become public knowledge.

Opinions on advertising vary enormously. The case for and against advertising, as argued by its supporters and those who question it, is given below.

The case for advertising

Advertising gives us information about new or improved products and services, allowing us to choose to buy products we would not otherwise know about. They give us a wider range of choices.

Advertising increases consumption, that is, it encourages people to spend money. Greater demand for products allows companies to expand and create more jobs for people, using the greater profits they are making. Advertising therefore helps the economy to grow, and is good for all of us.

The case against advertising

Advertising often contains negative or offensive images. Some advertisements use **stereotypes** of women, minority ethnic groups or other minorities.

Advertising can encourage people to want things they cannot have. Advertisements are full of images of luxury, of beautiful people living lives of leisure and wealth. Such advertisements are insulting in a society which still has poverty and homelessness, and in a world where money should be spent on improving everyone's lives rather than encouraging the better off to buy things they don't need.

The things that advertisements encourage us to want are often useless or even harmful. There are very few advertisements for fresh fruit and vegetables, which are an essential part of a healthy diet, but a lot for packaged foods that are full of additives, sugars and fats and are unhealthy. There's a lot more money to be made from the latter! We are encouraged to throw out something that may be perfectly good and replace it with something we do not really need. Some products that are advertised as good are directly harmful, to our health or to the environment. Advertisements often make misleading claims and exaggerate.

Advertisements aimed at children are particularly exploitative. Young children may not understand what advertisements are and accept messages at face value. Children are encouraged to want to have all sorts of toys, sweets and foods which their parents may not be able to afford or may not want them to have. Some children's programmes are really long advertisements, whose main purpose is to sell toys or other products. Young people are also vulnerable; for example, teenagers may take in from fashion advertisements the message that being very thin is attractive, and may damage their health through trying to lose too much weight too quickly.

The influence of advertising

The early hypodermic syringe theory of media effects (see the previous section) gave advertisers hope of enormously increased sales. It seemed all they had to do was advertise their product, and sales would go up. Of course, this didn't happen, yet companies continue to spend vast amounts of money on advertising. Advertising continues to grow. New types of advertising include sponsorship of television programmes and sports teams, and product placement in films. Is it money well spent?

The evidence is unclear. When advertising of products such as cigarettes and alcohol has been banned in some media, it seems to have little effect on sales. Clearly there are things that people will buy whether they are advertised or not. Advertising may have more impact when it comes to competition between brands.

One of the problems with the hypodermic syringe theory is that the audience is seen as passive. In fact, audiences do not simply accept advertising messages at face value. We know that advertisements are trying to make us buy something, so we are sceptical. We may even watch and be entertained by a clever advertisement, but never have any thought of buying the product.

FIND OUT FOR YOURSELF

Advertising is all around us even in ways you may not realise. Test this for yourself by carrying out these two small pieces of research:

- As you watch television over the next week, keep a record of programmes that are sponsored by an advertiser. At the time of writing, for example, *Coronation Street* is sponsored by the confectionery manufacturer Cadbury's.
- As you watch a new or recent film, keep a record of all the times that a named product appears. For example, one of the characters may drink a can of Coca Cola. Coca Cola will have paid for this; it is a form of advertising called product placement.

QUESTIONS

1. Name three different mass media that have advertisements.
2. How much was spent on advertising in Britain in 1997?
3. What is meant by product placement?
4. Which children's programmes could be thought of as long advertisements? Do you think this kind of advertising is wrong? Explain your answer.

ROUND-UP

Advertising is a large industry and an important aspect of the mass media. It is not clear how much influence advertising has on audiences, although advertisers continue to spend a lot of money on advertising. As audiences we are aware of how advertisers try to manipulate us. There are however concerns that some people, such as young children, are vulnerable to misleading claims and harmful images.

VOCABULARY

Ironic: using words to mean the opposite of what they usually mean
Exploitative: taking advantage of somebody
Sponsorship: when someone provides money for a particular purpose.

Freedom, censorship and bias

KEY FOCUS The media are controlled and influenced in many ways by government and by other powerful forces. Some information is censored; some is reported in an unbalanced or biased way.

- Abba – 'Waterloo'
- Blondie – 'Atomic'
- Boomtown Rats – 'I Don't Like Mondays'
- Eric Clapton – 'I Shot the Sheriff'
- Desmond Dekker – 'Israelites'
- Roberta Flack – 'Killing Me Softly With His Song'
- John Lennon – 'Give Peace a Chance'
- Paper Lace – 'Billy Don't Be a Hero'
- Bruce Springsteen – 'I'm on Fire'
- Stevie Wonder – 'Heaven Help Us All' (*New Statesman*, April 1991).

These songs were banned by the BBC during the Gulf War. Try to listen to them and work out why.

Government control

In all modern societies governments try to control and influence the media to some extent. The media, however, tend to see their job as reporting of the whole truth, as defenders of the freedom of speech. In Britain, though not in many other countries, the press has always been in private ownership. Broadcasting, however, has been closely controlled by the government. The BBC, a public corporation, is in theory free from government control, but it relies on a licence fee set by the government. The government also appoints the BBC's board of governors and controls the allocation of ITV franchises.

Censorship

In Britain there are several legal restrictions on what can be reported:

- The D-notice system means that editors and producers have to seek advice from the armed forces before they can publish information about military intelligence, weapons systems and other defence matters.
- The Official Secrets Act covers a range of types of information about which nothing can be published. Most such information is eventually made public years later – the Thirty Years Rule.

- Anyone who publishes insulting or damaging material about a person can be sued for libel by that person.

We also have restrictions on sex, violence and swearing in the media. Films and videos are subject to (slightly different) **certification** aimed at ensuring that they are only watched by people of appropriate ages. **Terrestrial television** has a 'watershed' which restricts screening of material seen as inappropriate for children before 9 pm. Films on television, even after the watershed, may be cut, although this is often to make them fit the available time rather than because of content.

The most significant kind of censorship may be by producers and other media workers themselves. In making a film, for example, they will know what audience they are aiming for and what film certificate they need to reach that audience. The script will be tailored to meet these needs. To get a '12' certificate, for example, certain swear words will not be used. This is called self-censorship.

Censorship in wartime

Censorship applies particularly during wartime, when governments see it as essential not to make public any information that the enemy could use. The armed forces will restrict the media's access to areas where there has been fighting, carefully controlling what they are allowed to see and know. Even when the media have information about casualties and defeats, they are unlikely to use it because of a sense of loyalty to 'our side'. This goes against the media's normal peacetime view of itself as providing truthful information.

Control of the media in wartime

For government control:
- Information could help the enemy.
- News of casualties and defeats could damage morale, both of the troops and of the public at home.
- By supporting our side, the media can help end the fighting quickly and avoid further casualties. The truth can wait.

Against government control:

■ The public have a right to know what is going on.

■ The media should try to be objective in order to report the truth.

■ The media should be independent of the armed forces, and should not only report what they are allowed to by the armed forces.

Politics and the media

Politicians of all parties constantly try to use and manipulate the media. They can do this directly, for example, through posters advocating their policies and through party political broadcasts. They also try to ensure their views are heard on television, in the press and so on.

Politicians from all parties have claimed that the media is biased against them. Both BBC and ITV have been accused at different times of being pro-Labour or pro-Conservative. The accusations are usually that the other party is given more time to put across its views, or that its views are reported more favourably. Television and radio are obliged to aim for 'due impartiality', to be objective and impartial; in this case, it means giving equal time and prominence to all parties.

Newspapers are much more likely to support a particular party. For many years the press was overwhelmingly Conservative, and the *Sun* in particular ran fiercely anti-Labour campaigns that may have influenced how people voted. At the 1997 election, however, some traditionally Conservative papers were less enthusiastic about their party and Labour got more favourable coverage. Labour won with a huge majority. Possible explanations for this include the following:

■ Conservative papers knew that their readers were likely to vote Labour this time, so reported Labour more favourably so as not to lose readers.

■ People who normally voted Conservative were influenced by the papers they read, and did not vote Conservative this time.

■ The papers, seeing opinion poll findings, may have decided to back the likely winners in the hope of favourable treatment when Labour was in power.

Other groups with an interest in politics have become much more skilled in using the media. The environmental campaigning group Greenpeace in particular has been able to get a lot of coverage through staging protest in a 'newsworthy' way, ensuring that striking images and video footage are easily available.

The wider picture

Due impartiality has its limits; it only applies to what is generally agreed and accepted. For example, the British media have consistently condemned the IRA, describing its members as 'terrorists' (rather than, for example, 'freedom fighters') and the deaths it causes as 'murders'. This fits with the way the majority of British people saw what was going on, but for supporters of the IRA this would be biased reporting – though perhaps what you would expect from the other side in a war.

More broadly, some writers, such as the leading investigative journalist John Pilger, argue that the bias is much deeper than supporting one party rather than another. The media, they say, consistently fail to question many features of our society, such as the way our economic system, capitalism, allows some people to become extremely wealthy while others live in poverty. Questioning the nature of the whole system is simply not allowed. A lot of information is not news.

QUESTIONS

1. What is meant by 'due impartiality'?

2. Does due impartiality apply in wartime? Why, or why not?

3. Describe two kinds of legal restriction on reporting in Britain.

4. Write a paragraph in support of the claim, 'The media cannot be impartial and unbiased'.

ROUND-UP

The mass media see themselves as objective, independent sources of balanced information, serving the public in a neutral way. However, they are subject to restrictions and censorship, and censor themselves. The media can be biased in what they choose to report and how they report it.

VOCABULARY

Morale: confidence and optimism
Advocating: arguing in favour of
Opinion polls: research which asks a small group of people in order to find out what the larger group they belong to thinks

Gender and the media

KEY FOCUS This section and the following two sections look at the relationship between different groups and the media. Here we consider women and men, in three ways: their work in the media, how they are shown in the media and how they consume the media.

BBC sports personality and presenter, Sue Barker, is just one of many women found throughout the media today – but are women treated the same as men?

Gender and working in the media

Like most areas of employment, the media have always been dominated by men. More women now work in the media, but few reach the highest paid and most important positions.

Some parts of the media are easier for women to get into than others. In newspapers, political news and current affairs have traditionally been seen as men's areas while women are more likely to be working on features and lifestyle articles. Some women have succeeded in breaking into men's traditional areas; for example, Kate Adie of the BBC and Catherine Amanpour of CNN have been very successful war reporters.

In films and television dramas, men tend to get the 'star billing' and to be paid more than female actors. Women's careers as actors depend more than men's on their looks. Beyond a certain age, even with plastic surgery to preserve youthful looks, female actors find that there are fewer starring roles available. This is less of a problem for men; a star like Sean Connery can still find leading roles in his 60s – and the female 'love interest' for him will be much younger than he is.

There have been attempts to set up feminist media as an alternative to the mainstream, male-dominated media. Women have also succeeded in recent years in bringing feminist ideas and women's issues into mainstream media.

Representations of gender

Stereotypes are narrow, fixed ideas about what certain types of people are like. Women, men, minority ethnic groups, people with disabilities and other groups are often shown as stereotypes.

Women tend to be shown in a limited number of stereotypical roles in films and television, for example, as dumb sexy blondes, as contented housewives, or as ruthless career women. The situation has improved in recent years, with a number of films and dramas showing women taking the lead (as with the Sigourney Weaver's Ripley character in the *Alien* film series, stronger and more resourceful than the men) or in new areas of work (as detectives, forensic scientists, football managers, ambassadors and so on). Some films show women in new and unconventional ways and address issues that concern women. However, older stereotypes are still in use, and older programmes, full of images that seem old-fashioned now, are continuously recycled as repeats. The effects of sexist stereotyping will be around for a long time.

Gender stereotypes are also evident in advertising. Men are more likely to be shown as having jobs, or as having higher paid jobs, and are more likely to be shown in a setting other than the home. Women are still often shown at home, as housewives and mothers. Men and women are still associated with different products. Voice-overs (the 'commentary' to an advertisement, with the person not shown) are usually male; advertisers believe male voices carry greater authority so we are more likely to buy the product.

Do stereotypical representations matter?

Stereotypes clearly exist, although sometimes these days they are deliberately turned upside down. Do they have any effect?

One view is that if we are exposed often enough over many years to these stereotypes, we will come to 'internalise' them, to accept them as true. A boy exposed to these stereotypes may grow up believing them, and may one day be in a job where he can discriminate against women. A girl may grow up believing that men only find certain kinds of women attractive. To find her ideal mate (which the media have told her she should do) she should slavishly imitate a particular image of women; for example, she might pretend to be less clever than she is.

Against this view, it should be remembered that the media are only one source of information and ideas. We do not unthinkingly take in what we see, and these days we are much more aware of stereotyping and sexism in the media.

HINTS AND TIPS

There are many opportunities to test out the ideas on these pages in your own viewing and reading. Here are some suggestions:

■ Compare the kinds of magazines teenage girls and teenage boys buy and read.
■ Compare the way men and women are shown in soap operas and police dramas. Is it men or women who are strong characters taking the lead, or weak characters who are dishonest and unreliable?
■ Do the media treat men's and women's sport differently?
■ Are the advertisements in men's and women's magazines for different products?
■ What is seen as appropriate for the women's section of newspapers?

Any of these could be the beginning of a coursework project.

Gender and audiences

Many media products are clearly aimed at one sex rather than the other. There are women's magazines, from *Sugar* to *Cosmopolitan* to *Woman's Own*, and men's magazines like *Loaded* and *GQ*. Other special interest magazines sell much more to one sex rather than the other (not many women buy angling magazines, for example). Newspapers tend to be aimed at male readers. Some even have special pages for women – which must mean that the rest of the paper is for men! The exception is the *Daily Mail*, which has consciously (and successfully) tried to attract women.

On television, soap operas and costume dramas have a particular appeal to women. Men prefer documentaries, sport and action adventures. The sociologist David Morley found other interesting differences about television watching:

■ Men almost always decide which programme is on.
■ Men prefer to view attentively, in silence, while women combine watching with conversation and tasks like ironing.

■ Men carefully plan their viewing, women tend not to do so as much (*Family Television*, Routledge, 1986).

 FIND OUT FOR YOURSELF

In a small group, draw up a questionnaire which you could give out to students in your year asking about what happens in their families. You can ask about the things Morley found out about but try to add related ideas of your own. Present your findings as charts and tables.

Males use computers more than women, at least outside places of work. Computer and video games are marketed much more with boys in mind than girls. The hero of 'Tomb Raider', Lara Croft, is a powerful, assertive – and physically attractive – female character. Is she there to attract girls to play these games – or because boys enjoy looking at her?

QUESTIONS

1 What is meant by a stereotype?

2 Why are male actors often able to continue having starring roles at a later age than female actors?

3 Identify three stereotypical roles for women in films and television. Can you find an example of a character that fits each of these?

4 Does it matter if the media show men and women in stereotypical ways? Write a paragraph to justify your answers.

5 Try to design an advertisement (for any product you like) that is not sexist and does not contain stereotypes.

ROUND-UP

The media have traditionally been dominated by men. Women have been restricted to unimportant jobs and shown in degrading and stereotypical ways. This has played a part in keeping alive sexist ideas. The media can, however, also play a part in breaking down these old assumptions.

VOCABULARY

Slavishly: like a slave, only able to do as told
Assumptions: things that are taken for granted and not questioned
Degrading: reducing the status

Minority ethnic groups and the media

KEY FOCUS Minority ethnic groups have had a substantial presence in Britain for many years. This section looks at members of ethnic minorities as workers in media industries and as audiences, and at how minorities have been represented in the media

Trevor MacDonald, Britain's top newsreader, is from a minority ethnic group.

Working in the media

Black and Asian people are very much in the minority in the mass media. A survey in 1996 found that, with the exception of newsreaders, children's and educational programmes, television was almost a no-go area for minorities. The researchers were particularly surprised that black faces were absent as presenters in areas in which it is usually assumed minorities had been successful, pop music and sport.

Newsreading is the area where non-whites have been most successful. Trevor McDonald, Moira Stewart and others are household names, and Martin Bashir is one of the best known reporters following his interviews of Princess Diana and Louise Woodward. Some have also been successful behind the scenes, for example Tony Dennis, producer of *Cracker* and *Band of Gold*, and film director Sam Mendes. Things are also changing in comedy; for a long time, Lenny Henry was the only well-known black comedian, but now shows like *Goodness Gracious*

Me and *The Real McCoy* provide platforms for non-white comedians. Imported American television and films also provide examples of black stars: Oprah Winfrey, Bill Cosby, Will Smith and so on.

Representations

As with women, minority ethnic groups have often in the past and still today been shown in stereotyped and offensive ways. Common stereotypes of non-white people in the past included:

- the dangerous savage (native Americans in most westerns, for example)
- the noble savage (native Americans in *Dances with Wolves*)
- the entertainer (based on the idea of black people having 'natural rhythm')
- the devious villain (often from the Far East).

Today, non-white people are often portrayed as problems, for example young black men are often the criminals and drug dealers in police dramas. Storylines involving black people tend to emphasise conflicts, problems and cultural differences. Non-white people are shown when the theme is racism or racial conflict, but shown far less often as ordinary people living ordinary lives.

More recently, there has been concern about how often Arabs are shown as terrorists and other types of villains in American films. Arab-Americans are worried that films like *The Siege* caricature Muslims and imply that normal Islamic religious practice is associated with terrorism ('Arabs in US vent fury at film about Islamist terror', *Guardian*, 7 November 1998).

Soap operas do sometimes have characters from minority ethnic groups, because this reflects the population of the types of areas they are set in. However, these characters are not often developed as fully as white characters and do not last long. The characters whose lives are followed for years by soaps tend to be white. When *Eastenders* began, a Turkish family running a café were among the main characters, but they were soon dropped and plots followed other, white, families such as the Fowlers and the Beales instead.

In the news, minority ethnic groups have been treated as problems in two main ways:

- The 'numbers game'. The media have focused on the

number of immigrants to Britain. They have often implied that there is a threat to British values and suggested that members of ethnic minorities are 'outsiders' who do not really belong. In 1999 and 2000 this idea re-emerged in the racist moral panic about refugees and asylum seekers.

■ Crimes and rioting. In the 1970s the crime of mugging was reported as if young black men only committed it. This created a new stereotype and a moral panic. Senior police officers and politicians tried to 'crack down' on muggers and in doing so created bad feelings between the police and black communities. In the 1980s the media reported riots as 'black riots' even when white people were involved as well. The media took racially motivated crimes against black people less seriously.

Hostility to foreigners – **xenophobia** – can also be found in the British media. Coverage of international football by the tabloids, for example when England plays Germany, often resorts to crude and insulting stereotypes with references to World War II.

In advertising, non-whites have usually simply been absent. However, in the 1980s multicultural adverts became fashionable. This partly reflected the need of companies to appeal to consumers around the world. However, while advertisements like this can be seen as anti-racist in promoting racial harmony, they also remind us of racial stereotypes and the physical differences they are based on.

The effect of representations

As with representation of gender, we need to consider whether these stereotypes and negative representations matter. Moral panics have affected people's lives and have contributed to discrimination and prejudice. On the other hand, positive representations can help to break down barriers.

FIND OUT FOR YOURSELF

In a small group, carry out a content analysis of members of ethnic minority groups on television. Divide responsibility for watching programmes or channels within the group. Decide how you are going to record your findings. Present your findings to your class.

Minorities as audiences

On television, there have been programmes, usually on BBC2 and Channel 4, aimed at specific minorities. These usually specialised in reporting news and current affairs items of particular interest to the minorities. While this can be seen as positive – catering for a need – it also meant that mainstream current affairs programmes could pay less attention to such stories. This division between white and non-white programming is still evident sometimes, for example in comedy programmes.

As we have seen, different audiences respond differently to programmes. As part of her research on young British Asians in London, Marie Gillespie studied the appeal of *Neighbours*. *Neighbours* features mainly white Australian middle-class families. Perhaps surprisingly, young Asian people identified very strongly with *Neighbours*, because their community also was based on family life and gossip.

FIND OUT FOR YOURSELF

Watch programmes from several television drama series. Make a note of appearances of black characters and how they are shown (for example as criminals). Then consider whether you have found evidence of ethnic stereotyping.

QUESTIONS

1. Name three successful black or Asian people in the British media, and what they are famous for.

2. What is meant by xenophobia?

3. What are the two main ways in which the media have reported minority ethnic groups?

4. Why do you think there are few long running characters from minority ethnic groups in British soap operas?

5. Should news items of particular interest to minority ethnic groups be on the main news bulletins, or in specialised late night programmes? Give reasons for your answer.

ROUND-UP

Minority ethnic groups have found it difficult to break into media industries. In the news they have been portrayed as problems, even when they are the victims; in films and television drama they have tended to have minor parts and to be shown in stereotypical ways.

VOCABULARY

Muslim: a follower of the religion Islam
Refugees: people escaping from hardship or persecution
Asylum seekers: people who on arriving in a country ask for special permission to stay, in order to escape persecution

Age, class and the media

This section looks at young and old people and the media, and class and the media.

Turning toddlers into TV addicts?

Children, young people and the media

Young people as audiences

According to a survey by Livingstone and Bovill, British children spend about five hours a day using the media. About half of this is spent watching television. About two-thirds of young people aged 6 to 17 have a television in their bedroom; the image of a family watching together is now out of date. However, children often watch with friends so viewing is not completely a solitary activity.

These figures are higher than for other European countries. French and German children watch an hour less a day and few have their own television. The main reason seems to be that British parents feel that playing outdoors unsupervised is far more dangerous than it was for them when they were children. If children are at home watching television, at least they know they are safe.

As children watch more, they have become more media literate. Even very young children can recognise heroes and villains, predict plots and understand the purpose of advertisements. To reflect this the programmes have changed in style. No longer are programmes like *Blue Peter* presented by aunt and uncle figures.

Since children watch so much, there is not surprisingly adult concern about what they watch. Parents strongly approve of the 9 pm watershed, according to Livingstone and Bovill. They feel unable to control children's viewing themselves, but trust the television channels to regulate the content.

There is no evidence that young people spend a lot of time watching violent films. They prefer factual programmes, dramas and soap operas, and music channels.

BBC programming for pre-school children is dominated by two daily series, *Teletubbies* and, for childen growing out of them, the *Tweenies*.

Two views of the Tweenies

'The message is clear. Boys are no good and girls are dominant. The girls' love of pink and their obsession with clothes is totally ridiculous, as is the slant on the little black boy. In effect, what they are saying is that he is an outsider who is good at football and can just about be relied on to hoof a bit. They appear to be falling into several traps all at once.' Lucy Pilkington, journalist

'The BBC strongly denies that the characters were pandering to racial or gender stereotypes. "We were very keen to have a proper multicultural picture without stereotyping, that's why the characters are one step away from reality. Milo isn't black, he's purple."' Ray Thompson, who commissioned the series

'Tweenies follow Tinky Winky's footsteps', *Guardian*, 29 July 1999.

Another concern about children and television is about merchandising. There are millions of Teletubby and Tweenie dolls in the shops, and other products. With some children's television, it can seem that the programmes are just long commercials to get children, via their parents, to buy the merchandising. High quality programmes, such as the best cartoons, are expensive to produce and would not get made if it were not for the profits from the spin-off merchandising.

A W FIND OUT FOR YOURSELF

In a small group, devise a questionnaire to find out about younger children's use of the media (for example whether they have their own television, how much they read magazines, how often they go to the cinema). Decide on the age group you will question (for example a younger year group in your school). Include charts and tables in your presentation of your findings.

Representations of children

One common stereotype of children is as helpless, vulnerable and innocent. In the past, in advertisements, they often also had large round eyes and chubby cheeks, and gazed adoringly at their parents. They were usually blonde and white too.

However, children are now shown in a wide range of ways. In some films and programmes, children are shown as having greater wisdom and sense than adults. Examples of this include *The Simpsons* and *Home Alone*. Such representations of course have a strong appeal to children.

Despite the assumptions we tend to make about childhood innocence, there are times when we have to think differently about children. Like people of any age, children are capable of brutal and criminal acts. Within one newspaper and bulletin, it is possible to find stories that show children as innocent victims and others which worry about children becoming more delinquent and badly behaved.

Representations of older people

Negative stereotypes of older people are common; they are 'old biddies', 'old codgers', 'wrinklies' who have 'one foot in the grave'. Do the media help to create and perpetuate these stereotypes?

While there are negative images, especially in comedy and cartoons, there are also many positive ones. This partly reflects the need for the media to reach older audiences. Older people make up a large and growing proportion of the population, so the media have to appeal to them.

There is one fairly new and positive stereotype of old age – the rebel who fights against bureaucracy and against the ways society expects old people to behave. This stereotype can be found in the television sitcoms *One Foot in the Grave* and *Waiting for God*.

Class and the media

In the study by Livingstone and Bovill, there were considerable differences between working-class and middle-class children. Working-class children were far more likely to have a television in their bedroom, middle-class children to have a computer. Computers are still considerably more expensive than, for example, televisions and videos, so some families cannot afford them. Almost everyone has access to television, radio and newspapers although there are class differences in which channels and programmes are watched.

Representations of class

Class is more difficult to pin down than gender, ethnicity and age. It is however a theme that runs through much of the British media. British soap operas (though not American ones) are usually about working-class communities, as are some situation comedies. *The Royle Family* attempted a realistic portrayal of a northern working-class family, avoiding stereotypes about crime, drugs and constant arguments.

QUESTIONS

1. Name one British soap that shows a working-class community.

2. Why do British children spend more time using the media than children in other countries?

3. Look at the box giving two opinions about the Tweenies. Which argument do you find more convincing, and why?

4. Find other examples of films or television programmes in which children are shown as being more sensible, intelligent and strong than adults.

5. Is it right to advertise toys, snack foods and so on on children's television? Give reasons for your answer.

ROUND-UP

The media are very important in British children's lives, and children are now media literate at a young age. Children are often, but not always, shown very positively in the media, as are older people. Class is also an important aspect to consider in both use of the media and representations in the media.

VOCABULARY

Bureaucracy: petty rules and the officials who enforce them

Merchandising: things for sale which are linked to the popularity of, for example, a football club or pop group

Realistic: true to life

The future of the mass media

The media keep changing. Reading this chapter, you will have become aware of some current trends. In this section we take a closer look at what seems to be happening at the moment, and what this might mean in the future.

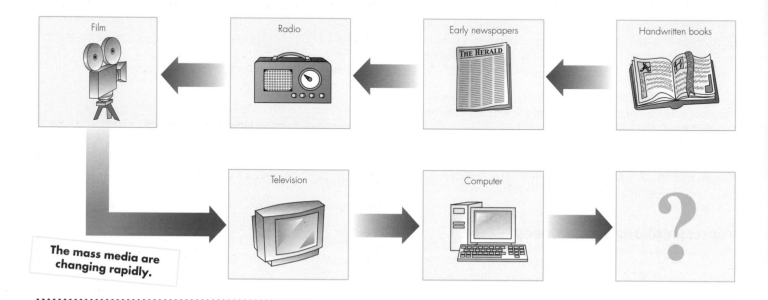

The mass media are changing rapidly.

Convergence

One of the most striking ways – at least to older people – that the media are changing is that it is becoming harder to keep different media separate. For example, until very recently, the only way to access the Internet was using a computer. Now the Internet can be accessed by television and by the latest mobile telephones (WAP phones). Newspapers are available on line on the Internet as well as in the traditional print version. We can listen to broadcast music on television and on the Internet as well as on radio, as we always used to. We can listen to pre-recorded music on mini discs, on CDs, cassettes and vinyl. Some media seem to be converging (joining up) with each other so that it's hard to tell them apart.

It is still unclear how far this **convergence** will go. As you have seen in this chapter, take up of new technology is often slow. Governments can play a big part in this. Digital television will receive a huge boost if the government eventually decides to 'switch off' analogue television so that there is only digital television. Giving everyone free access to the Internet is another possibility. It will be a long time before the majority of the population can make full use of new media (and by then, there will of course be newer possibilities). But it may be that we are seeing the beginnings of one single medium, the Internet, replacing all the others.

What will happen to the older media? Will print newspapers become a thing of the past as people get news (tailored to their particular interests) delivered online? While we cannot be sure, we can say that earlier predictions about new media replacing old were wrong. Television did not replace newspapers, books or radio, though some people at the time expected this. Nor did television kill off cinema, as again people expected at the time. In fact, television helped the cinema, because television companies bought the rights to screen films after they had been shown in cinemas.

Intertextuality

A trend related to the convergence of the media is that more and more the media are about other media. This is called **intertextuality**. Some examples are:

■ magazines about soap operas

■ television programmes about cinema films or about the Internet

■ some television series (like *The Simpsons*) which are full of references to other television programmes, films and other media.

FIND OUT FOR YOURSELF

Successful ideas often move quickly from one medium to another. Find at least one example of each of these:

- a book that was made into a film
- a film that was turned into a television series
- a song that was used on a film soundtrack
- a film about television
- a television series that has its own magazine or comic
- a film that became a stage play or musical, or vice versa.

Globalisation

Another striking feature of the mass media today is how they reach around the world:

- You can watch television channels in many languages on cable and satellite.
- In our big cities you can buy newspapers from all around the world.
- On holiday or travelling abroad, you can find (if you want to) British newspapers and watch or listen to the BBC's world services.
- In an Internet café on the other side of the world, you can access your e-mail and all the sites you would if you were at home.
- In most countries, you can watch television programmes from many countries. Sometimes the links are unexpected, for example Brazilian soap operas are very popular in Russia.

Some media products are now aimed at a global audience rather than national audiences. The BBC makes programmes (such as *Teletubbies* and the *Tweenies*, discussed earlier) in the hope and expectation of selling them to television companies around the world. Recently, a Japanese cartoon series, *Pokemon*, has been, after some changing of names and so on, a huge success in Britain and the USA. Some Hollywood films, to ensure they appeal all around the world, emphasise how we all belong to the same species – against threats such as dinosaurs, aliens and meteors.

As with convergence, it is important to end on a note of caution. Whole areas of the world and large groups of people are being left out of media **globalisation**. There are no huge profits to be made in Africa, or from the poor in other parts of the world. In many countries a lot of adults are illiterate, so they cannot read newspapers, magazines and books. The technology of other media, such as radio sets and televisions and computers, are beyond what many people can afford.

Interactivity

The traditional mass media were based on one-way communication. For almost everyone, newspapers, radio, television and film were part of their lives but also separate,

produced far away. Ordinary people had little opportunity to shape the media, except writing letters to newspapers and radio phone-ins. This began to change a little when video cameras became affordable; people could send in their clips to be shown on television. The media became increasingly **interactive**. With word processing and photocopying, small organisations and individuals became able to produce publications that looked professional.

The Internet changes this again. Anyone with a computer and the necessary software (which is easy to get hold of and use) can publish their own Internet pages – and many do. Suddenly, a 'publication' produced by an individual may be read by anyone anywhere. We can all be producers as well as consumers of media. Whether anyone will ever find and look at your web page is another matter!

QUESTIONS

1. Name three ways in which the Internet can be accessed.

2. What is meant by convergence? Explain using an example.

3. What is meant by intertextuality? Explain using an example.

4. What opportunities are there for ordinary people to contribute to or be heard on the media? Think of as many examples as you can.

5. In what ways is the Internet different from all the media we have had until now?

ROUND-UP

The media have changed constantly, and the speed of change has been increasing. With the Internet and digital television and other media, we seem to be entering a new media age. But it is important not to exaggerate what is happening; many people around the world are shut out of the world of new media.

VOCABULARY

Illiterate: unable to read or write
WAP phones: the latest generation of mobile telephones, which can be used to access some web pages and other Internet services

Media – sociology in practice

Media effects: the case of St Helena

ST Helena is a remote island in the South Atlantic. Until 1995 there was no television service for the small population.

The introduction of television provided an opportunity to study the effects of television on the island's children. Researchers could compare how the children behaved before they had ever watched television with how they behaved afterwards. This was a unique opportunity to conduct what is called a natural experiment.

Previous research had suggested a link between television viewing and violent behaviour, but this did not happen in St Helena. Researchers filmed children at play during school breaks. They found no increase in hitting, punching, pinching or fighting. This was in spite of the facts that there is slightly more violence on the cable channel beamed to St Helena than on British terrestrial television, and that St Helena has no 'watershed'.

The head of the research, Tony Charlton, said, 'St Helena has given us a unique opportunity to look at children's behaviour both before as well as after the introduction of television in a real-life setting … What we are seeing is that violence is not a direct cause of violent behaviour in young people. A healthy family, school and community environment are far more important influences in shaping behaviour.' The people of St Helena have a strong sense of community that helps prevent anti-social behaviour.

Adapted from 'Island's youth pass TV test' by Kamal Ahmed, *Guardian*, 21 July 1997.

Questions

1 What is meant by the:
(a) watershed
(b) natural experiment?

2 According to the researchers, television viewing is only one influence on the way young people behave. What other influences are there?

3 Why do you think children on St Helena have not become more violent since television was introduced?

4 Look back at the section Effects of the media (2) (pages 302–3). Write a 500-word essay, 'Can violence on television make children anti-social?'.

Not just Mickey Mouse

Disney is one of the five largest global media giants. Here are just some of its holdings:

- several major film, video and television production studios, including Disney and Buena Vista
- theme parks and resorts
- 550 retail stores and many associated products
- ABC television and radio networks in the USA
- ten American television stations and 21 radio stations
- the global cable television channels Disney, ESPN and ESPN 2 (ESPN dominates international televised sport, broadcasting in 21 languages to over 165 countries)
- seven American daily newspapers
- three record labels
- three magazine publishing companies
- shares in television companies around the world, including Eurosport.

Questions

1. How does the information about Disney above illustrate what you have learned about ownership of the media (see the section Who owns the mass media? (pages 294–5) and globalisation in The future of the mass media (pages 314–15))?

2. Find out more about Disney by visiting the web site www.disney.com. Using the site guide, visit 'Entertainment' to find out more about the range of interests Disney has. Visit 'Inside the company' (again using the site guide on the home page) to find out more about how Disney operates as a business.

3. Using your own knowledge of Disney films and other media products, and looking back at the section Gender and the media (pages 308–9), write an essay discussing representation of women in Disney media products

Get a life – turn off your TV set

White Dot is an anti-television campaign group. It encourages people to give up the habit of a lifetime and reject the 'plastic box'.

IT'S called television! And all you have to do is turn it off! It's that simple. You are going to be amazed at what happens next. Give up your TV and you are doubling your free time! It's a whole extra ten years of your life …

All those things that television promised you: excitement, sex, friendship, understanding – it lied. A plastic box can't give you any of those …

Someday people will look back on television as the dangerous experiment on human guinea pigs that it really is. Your descendants won't have anything to do with it … They'll be shocked at what you did with your time – disgusted. White Dot is just trying to hasten that day. Real life is a craze that's going to sweep the nation.

The average time people spend watching TV is four hours a day – one day a week, doing nothing but sitting and staring. Some people devote that much time to God. What are you worshipping? Add it up. If you were on your death-bed and someone could give you back those missing ten years to be with people you loved, would you take up their offer? Or would you say, 'No thanks, I'm glad I spent that time watching TV.'?

To help you decide, use the handy chart below. Assuming that you live to be 80 (most people don't) it can tell you how long you have left and how much of that time you'll spend watching television.

This 'handy chart' tells you how many of your remaining years will be spent glued to the box:

Your age	0	10	20	30	40	50	60	70
Years left	80	70	60	50	40	30	20	10
TV years	13.3	11.7	10	8.3	8.2	5	3.3	1.7

'Get a life – turn off your TV set', *Guardian Editor*, 25 July 1998.

Questions

1. What is White Dot trying to achieve, and why?

2. Why do you think there is a campaign against television, but not against newspapers?

3. Do people spend too much time consuming mass media? Give reasons for your answer.

Media – important terms

agenda setting	how the media decide which issues are important and which are not
audience	the people a medium reaches, its consumers (not just listeners)
bias	favouring one side rather than another
British Broadcasting Corporation (BBC)	Britain's public service broadcasting organisation
broadcasting	sent from a central point to a mass audience, like radio and television
cable television	television programming delivered by fibre optic cables laid underground
censorship	cutting out words or scenes, usually because they are considered dangerous or offensive
certification	films and videos receive certificates according to the audiences they are thought suitable for
connotation	in semiology, the associations a sign has
content analysis	quantitative study of media content
convergence	the way in which different media seem to be becoming the same
denotation	in semiology, the surface meaning of a sign
desensitised	when people stop being sensitive to something (for example violence)
digital television	a relatively new way of delivering programming, with high quality pictures
dumbed down	the media are said to challenge their audiences less intellectually
editor	a person who can decide on media content, able to act as a gatekeeper
folk devils	a group of people represented by the media during a moral panic as wrong or bad
gatekeeper	a person whose job involves allowing some items into the news and stopping others
globalisation	the media are present, and media companies operate, all over the world
hypodermic syringe theory	the theory that the media have immediate, dramatic effects
interactivity	when people can create their own media or influence the content of the media
intertextuality	when media refer to other media
moral panic	when a group of people or their activities are reported in an exaggerated way by the media, with calls for tough action against them
news values	how newsworthy a news item is is decided by news values
pay per view	when viewers pay an extra charge to watch one programme
press	the newspaper industry
propaganda	deliberate attempts to influence what people think and do
public service broadcasting	broadcasting regulated by the state, non-commercial
satellite television	programming delivered by satellites in orbit around the earth
scapegoat	a person or group blamed for something another person has done
semiology	the study of signs; a qualitative way of studying the media
spin	when politicians or others try to influence what we make of news and events
stereotype	an exaggerated and misleading representation
terrestrial television	programming delivered from a transmitter on the ground
watershed	a time before which programming is censored
xenophobia	irrational fear or hatred of foreigners

Media – exam-style questions

Source A

The media are agencies of socialisation. There has been concern that if there are stereotypes in the media, children may think that this is the way things really are, or the way things should be. For example, if women are represented always as housewives and mothers, children (both boys and girls) may believe that this is the way things should be.

Foundation tier

1 What is meant by an agency of socialisation? [2 marks]

2 Study the photo in source A. State two ways in which it shows a woman in a stereotyped manner. [3 marks]

3 Using sociological knowledge, give one reason why women have often been shown in a stereotyped manner in the mass media. [4 marks]

4 State two other types of stereotype (other than gender) that can be found in the mass media. Explain your answers by using one example of each. [5 marks]

5 Do you agree that children can be influenced by gender stereotypes in the media? Give two sociological reasons for your answer. [6 marks]

Higher tier

1 Study the photo in source A. State two ways in which it shows a woman in a stereotyped manner. [2 marks]

2 Using sociological knowledge, give one reason why women have often been shown in a stereotyped manner in the mass media. [3 marks]

3 State two other types of stereotype (other than gender) that can be found in the mass media. Explain your answers by using one example of each. [5 marks]

4 Do you agree that children can be influenced by gender stereotypes in the media? Give sociological reasons for your answer. [10 marks]

Media – further research

There are two excellent large sites of material on the mass media, although most of the content is aimed at students at A level and higher:

- www.aber.ac.uk/media/Functions/medmenu
- www.leeds.ac.uk/ics/theory.

The *Guardian* newspaper has a media supplement on Mondays, and a web site section at: www.mediaguardian.co.uk.

13 Poverty and Welfare

321

KEY TERMS

absolute poverty
community care
culture of poverty
cycle of deprivation
means testing
poverty trap
relative poverty
underclass
universalism
welfare state

Millions of people in Britain live in poverty. As you will see, there has been some progress towards reducing poverty. Fewer people now go without the essentials of life than used to be the case. But poverty does not keep still; those who do not have what most people in a society expect are also poor.

The main way that governments have tried to provide for their citizens is through the welfare state. This has become very expensive, and some people argue that it has not been successful. Governments now face difficult choices about how to spend the money available (they are reluctant to put up taxes to bring in more money, because they think they will lose votes). Increasingly, we have to pay for things that used to be free or for which there were basic charges. Older people in particular often feel angry about this; they paid taxes when they were working, expecting more help in old age than they are now getting.

The terms poverty and welfare cover a series of questions that go to the heart of what we want society to be like. For example, should we (through the government) look after vulnerable groups, such as the elderly and those with disabilities – or is it up to people to look after themselves?

IN THIS CHAPTER YOU WILL LEARN ABOUT:

■ the extent of poverty in Britain today
■ different descriptions and definitions of poverty
■ the origins and development of the welfare state
■ how voluntary groups and the private sector also contribute to welfare
■ the likely future of welfare

CHAPTER CONTENTS

Who are the poor?

KEY FOCUS Some groups of people are more likely to be poor than others. This section looks at each of these and the particular reasons why they are vulnerable to poverty.

Some poverty is very visible – but much of it is harder to see.

People in poverty

People who live in **poverty** are likely to belong to one or more of the following groups:

- lone parents and their children
- the unemployed, especially the long-term unemployed
- the low paid or without skills and qualifications
- the chronically ill or disabled
- those who are dependent on social security **benefits** as their only income
- asylum seekers – people applying to stay here to escape from persecution in another country. They receive only a very small allowance, mainly in the form of supermarket vouchers which cannot be exchanged for cash.

There are of course plenty of people in these categories who are not poor. For example, members of the royal family could be described as lone parents or unemployed! Rather, these groups are more at risk of being in poverty than others. If they are poor, they are less likely to move quickly out of poverty.

In addition, poverty is related to social characteristics that you have come across throughout this book: class, ethnicity, gender and age.

Ethnicity

People from minority ethnic groups are more likely to have a low income than the white majority. The groups most disadvantaged in this way are Pakistanis and Bangladeshis. Poverty among minority ethnic groups is linked to:

- lack of qualifications and skills
- high rates of unemployment
- low pay when employed
- living in deprived social environments – areas with poor housing, failing schools and so on.

Ethnic minorities have been used as a source of cheap labour. Many came here as immigrants in the 1950s and 1960s to take low paid, unskilled work, but hoping that their children would be able to build on these beginnings. However, for many this was prevented by racism and discrimination.

For Pakistani, Bangladeshi and some other minorities there are restrictions on the kind of work women can do outside the home because of cultural traditions. While some women work at home, this kind of work is often very low paid. At a time when more and more households depend on more than one person working, some Asian families rely on a single breadwinner who is unlikely to be in a well-paid job.

Members of some ethnic minorities suffer from greater poverty because of unwillingness to claim benefits. It is seen as shameful to claim benefits, so some try to survive without.

Women

Women are more likely to be poorer than men, for the following reasons:

- Women live longer, so there are more women pensioners than men. Fewer of them have occupational **pensions** to add to their state pensions. Savings may be used up.
- Women are more likely than men to be lone parents. It is difficult to combine bringing up young children with paid work; even when the children are old enough to go to school, a lone mother has either to find part-time work with suitable hours of work or pay a childminder.
- Women who work earn less on average than men. They are more likely to be in temporary, casual or part-time work.
- Women have to take on the care of children, ageing parents or sick or disabled relatives more often than men.

Older women living on their own and lone mothers make up two of the largest groups living in poverty.

Some married women who do not work experience a kind of hidden poverty. Their husband may earn an adequate wage, but only give his wife a small amount for running the household. So, for example, she may go without herself to make sure the children are fed and clothed. A woman may be poor in a household with an income above the poverty line, or she may be more deeply in poverty than the rest of her family.

Age

Children

The largest group of people in poverty in Britain today are children. Many but not all are being brought up by one parent. Bringing up children has become very expensive; the arrival of a baby can push a household into poverty. Many parents struggle to provide what their children need, for education and for socialising with friends.

Research published in 1997 by the Joseph Rowntree Foundation classified one in ten children as 'poor'. This was based on going without at least three things most children could take for granted, such as three meals and fruit every day, a bed of their own and new shoes that fit. One in 30 children were said to be 'severely poor' because they went without five or more of these things.

The survey also found that one in 20 mothers sometimes went without food to ensure their children ate enough. Most of these were lone mothers. The researchers argued that in setting benefit levels the government has underestimated what it costs to bring up children ('Poor parents go without to feed their children', *Guardian*, 18 July 1997).

There has been concern that children growing up in poor families learn how to be poor. They do not expect to do well at school or work. This raises the possibility of poverty being passed down from one generation to another.

The elderly

The state old age pension has for many years not been increased at the same rate as prices have gone up, so it is worth much less than it used to be. Pensioners who do not also have an additional pension or substantial savings are at risk of poverty. This applies particularly to women, who are less likely to have an occupational pension because they have not worked continuously.

The Conservative governments of Thatcher and Major encouraged more people to start private pensions. However, there are many retired people now who did not have private pensions because they trusted the government to keep state pensions at a reasonable level. So at the moment we have large numbers of people on inadequate pensions.

People with disabilities

A further group that needs to be considered here is people with disabilities. Not only does a disability make it harder to find work, but there may be extra costs arising from the disability, for example needing to have the house adapted in some way. One of the most controversial changes made by John Major's Conservative government of 1992 to 1997 was to introduce tighter testing procedures so that many people lost the rights disabled people have to certain benefits.

▶ FIND OUT FOR YOURSELF

Look again at the discussion of the Joseph Rowntree Foundation's research under the heading Children. In a small group draw up a list of ten things which most children take for granted and which not having could be taken as an indicator of poverty. Then put these in order. Be prepared to say why you made your decisions to the class.

QUESTIONS

1. Identify two groups of people who are at risk of living in poverty.

2. Identify and explain two reasons why members of ethnic minority groups are more likely to be living in poverty than the majority group.

3. Identify and explain two reasons why women are more likely to be living in poverty than men.

4. Identify three events that could push an individual or family into poverty.

5. How can poverty be passed on from one generation to the next?

ROUND-UP

Some groups are more likely to be in poverty than others: members of ethnic minorities, women, children and the elderly and people with disabilities. There is particular concern at the moment about lone parents and their children.

VOCABULARY

Pension: a regular payment made to people over a certain age. State pensions are paid by the government; some people also receive an occupational pension, paid by a former employer, or a personal pension from a fund into which they have made payments over many years

Measuring poverty

KEY FOCUS

What is meant by poverty? On one level, it is not having the necessities of life, yet on another level it can mean missing out on what people around you expect; for example, parents may feel poor if they cannot afford Christmas presents for their children. This section looks at different definitions of poverty.

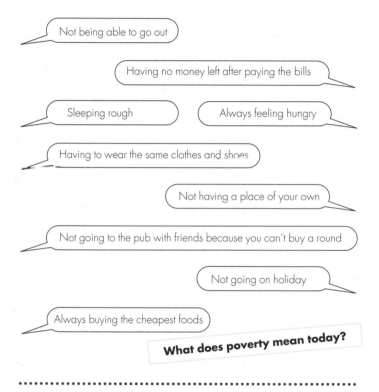

Not being able to go out

Having no money left after paying the bills

Sleeping rough

Always feeling hungry

Having to wear the same clothes and shoes

Not having a place of your own

Not going to the pub with friends because you can't buy a round

Not going on holiday

Always buying the cheapest foods

What does poverty mean today?

Absolute poverty

This is when people do not have the basic necessities of life. The necessities are:

- food
- clean water
- shelter (somewhere to live)
- heating
- clothes.

People who live in **absolute poverty** do not have enough income to buy the minimum they need to survive.

Although it seems straightforward, this definition has some problems. Not everyone has the same needs; a healthy adult may be able to survive in conditions where a child or elderly person could not. How much is needed, for example, of food? – enough to prevent hunger, or a healthy diet containing fresh fruit, vegetables and so on? And what about people who can afford to eat well, but choose an unhealthy diet?

Relative poverty

This idea was developed because of problems with the idea of absolute poverty. **Relative poverty** is when someone is poor compared to others in their society. People in Britain today who are poor are not often in absolute poverty – they are unlikely to be at risk of starving to death – but in relative poverty, because they do not have other things that people take for granted. For example, they may not have a refrigerator, telephone or television.

A standard of living that means poverty in Britain might not mean poverty in another country. In some poorer countries, very few people have fridges, telephones or televisions, to use the examples above. Poverty from this point of view is relative to others in the same society.

There is no agreement about exactly what people in relative poverty miss out on. In any case, this will change all the time, as standards of living in the society change. In the early 1960s, the majority did not have cars, televisions or holidays abroad. Yet all of these might be considered necessities today.

In Britain, one very important study of poverty, by the sociologist Peter Townsend in the late 1970s, used 12 items as indications of poverty. The items are Townsend's decisions about what most people wanted and expected at the time:

- No holiday away from home in the last 12 months.
- Has not had a relative or friend to visit for a meal or snack in last four weeks (adults).
- Has not been out to a relative or friend for a meal or snack in last four weeks (adults).
- Has not had a friend to play or for tea in last four weeks (children under 15).
- Did not have a party on last birthday (children).
- Has not had an afternoon or evening out for entertainment in last two weeks.
- Does not have fresh meat (including meals out) as many as four times a week.
- Has had one or more days in last two weeks without a hot meal.
- Has not had a cooked breakfast most days of the week.
- Household does not have a refrigerator.
- Household does not usually have a Sunday joint (three out of four times).

■ Household does not have sole use (that is, has to share) of these four amenities: a flushing toilet, a sink or washbasin with cold water, a fixed bath or shower and a cooker.

The official definition of relative poverty used in Britain today is half the national average income.

Subjective poverty

Both of the above ways of defining poverty can be used by a sociologist or other outsider to measure whether someone is poor. However, we also need to consider the feelings and opinion of the people studied. It is important whether or not they feel they are poor; this is known as **subjective poverty**.

Some people might fall below the level of income which defines poverty, but not feel themselves poor, particularly if others around them are in the same situation.

Environmental poverty

The three definitions so far have looked at the situation of individuals and families. There is another aspect of poverty: **environmental poverty** – the quality of life that comes from living in a particular social environment Among the things that might make a low income more bearable are:

■ being near to good health care (doctors' surgeries, hospitals)
■ being near to good schools
■ clean air, no pollution, no heavy traffic
■ being near parks and open spaces
■ being near public transport, such as buses and train stations
■ being near to shops.

All of these help raise the quality of life and avoid stress and hardship. They cannot compensate completely for a low income, but they can make an enormous difference. They help people take a full part in the life of the community they live in, even if they are not well off.

Measuring poverty

How much poverty there is depends on how you define it. When a Conservative minister claimed in 1996 that there was no poverty in Britain, he meant that there was no absolute

poverty. When research reports and news articles say a certain percentage of people live in poverty, they will be referring to relative poverty. Remember though that they will have used their own definition of what relative poverty is. Townsend, whose research was referred to above, defined relative poverty in such a way that he was bound to find that lots of people lived in poverty. Always ask, what does the writer mean by poverty?

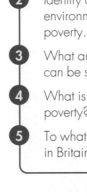 **FIND OUT FOR YOURSELF**

Design a questionnaire to find out what people think are the essential things needed for a 'normal' life. Decide who to give your questionnaire to and then carry out the questionnaire. Analyse your findings. To what extent do your respondents agree with Townsend?

Researching poverty

KEY FOCUS This section looks at a few of the major research projects that have studied poverty in Britain, and the different ways in which they have defined and described poverty.

Seebohm Rowntree – finding out about poverty.

Absolute poverty

Some of the earliest studies of poverty in Britain were by Seebohm Rowntree. He researched poverty in York in 1899, and again in 1936 and in 1950. He used an absolute definition of poverty. He worked out a shopping list that would meet the basic necessities of life, then worked out how much it would cost. This cost was his poverty line; those whose income was less than this were in poverty, those whose income was above it were not.

Rowntree's list of necessities was just that. It excluded all 'luxuries', such as newspapers or children's pocket money, or the father's beer and tobacco. Where families had an income that put them above the poverty line, but spent the money on

'luxuries' (any non-essential items), Rowntree described them as being in secondary rather than primary poverty.

This was, of course, a very harsh definition of poverty. Rowntree was assuming that people would spend their money in the most efficient way. Yet in 1899, Rowntree found a third of his respondents below the poverty line. This number fell in his later research, to 1.5 per cent in 1950. Rowntree believed that poverty was disappearing. What was happening was that absolute poverty was disappearing – but relative poverty was not.

Rowntree's basic approach was used by governments to calculate the level of National Assistance payments, and later Supplementary Benefit and Income Support.

Relative poverty

One of the researchers on relative poverty was Townsend, whose list of 12 indicators of poverty you read about in the previous section. Townsend used a wide definition of poverty, and found evidence of widespread poverty in the 1960s and 1970s. Notice that Townsend had moved the study of poverty away from how much income people had (although he did use this) towards their quality of life.

A further step was taken by Mack and Lansley's study of *Breadline Britain* in 1983, which was also a television series. Whereas Townsend had drawn up his own list of indicators of poverty, Mack and Lansley asked people what they thought were essentials. Most people agreed on these: things like heating, an indoor toilet, beds for everyone, carpets and refrigerators were seen as necessities. Mack and Lansley also tried to find out when people did not have a necessity through choice. You may have noticed that Townsend's indicators included having a joint of meat on Sundays: this would make all vegetarians poor! And today, unlike at the time of Townsend's research, few people have a cooked breakfast. This is a matter of choice (related to changing lifestyle) rather than indicating poverty.

Mack and Lansley defined households as being in poverty if they were without three or more of the things that most people thought of as necessities. They found that about 14 per cent of the population were poor – a lower figure than Townsend's.

They repeated the research seven years later. There had been some changes in what people considered necessities, reflecting changing expectations. For example, the percentage who thought having a refrigerator was a necessity had gone up from 77 per cent to 92 per cent; on the other hand, fewer people thought that having a week's holiday away from home each year was essential.

In 1990 the number in poverty had risen from seven and a half million to 11 million. This indicated that poverty was still a huge problem.

Subjective poverty

In the 1960s, after nearly 20 years or so of the **golden age welfare state**, it was widely believed and hoped that poverty had been ended. In fact, it had just become less noticeable. Coates and Silburn showed this in a dramatic way in their book *Poverty: The Forgotten Englishmen*. They concentrated on how poverty was experienced by the people they studied, who lived in an area of Nottingham called St Ann's. They found many people living in desperation on low wages and inadequate benefits.

Their book attacks the idea that the poor are to blame for their poverty. They showed that the poor did not waste their money on drinking and betting. They showed that poverty had become less visible than in the 1930s, but was still present. Children were no longer in rags, but a close look would reveal that the shiny shoes were too small or too big, and the clothes were always second-hand. Poor people did sometimes have what others might consider luxuries, such as refrigerators, but they had been bought cheaply when old and broken, and mended to keep them going a little longer.

There has been little qualitative research into the experience of poverty more recently. Researchers find it hard to get funding. Poverty is a topic most people would rather not think about too much.

What it's like to be poor

'The doctor told him (the woman's husband, who has stomach ulcers) he needs fish and chicken regularly but we can't afford it ... We seem to live off chips and potatoes ... We only have a cooked meal three times a week to cut down on gas.'

'It is a very depressing thought to think that we might have to spend maybe the next five years on Social Security. It is very disheartening, depressing thought, to bring your new baby into the world, because when I had him, do you know one of my first thoughts was "Isn't he beautiful ... oh, I'm so happy, oh God, how am I going to manage to bring him up and keep him fed and clothed decently?" That sums it up for me.'

Hardship Britain by R. Cohen *et al.*, Child Poverty Action Group, 1992.

HINTS AND TIPS

Qualitative research (different from quantitative research) is explained in Chapter 2 Research Methods.

QUESTIONS

1. What type of poverty was being researched by (a) Rowntree, and (b) Mack and Lansley?

2. How many people were living in poverty in Britain in 1990, according to Mack and Lansley?

3. Why had poverty been underestimated, according to Coates and Silburn?

4. Do you agree with Rowntree that, for a father, a newspaper, cigarettes and pocket money to give to his children, are luxuries? Give reasons for your answer.

5. 'You can't be poor if you've got a television.' Do you agree? Explain your answer.

ROUND-UP

Early research on poverty, such as Rowntree's, concentrated on absolute poverty, defined as income below a very low level. Later researchers looked at relative poverty and began to consider quality of life as well as income. Qualitative research on the subjective meaning of poverty gives insights into what it is like to be poor.

VOCABULARY

Golden age welfare state: the period of the fully developed welfare state, from the late 1940s to the 1970s (see sections on the welfare state)

Poverty line: a level of income below which people are said to be in poverty

Explaining poverty: cultural explanations

KEY FOCUS Why does poverty exist, and why has it proved so hard to reduce it or get rid of it? This section looks at one set of answers that have been suggested to these questions: those that argue that the poor are poor because of cultural differences.

The poor are still with us – why has poverty survived?

Why is there still poverty?

'The poor are always with us,' goes a popular saying. This does seem to be true, if we use a relative definition of poverty. This is despite the activities of campaigners and reformers, the determination of those who created the **welfare state** and the dedication and hard work of many people in both the state and **voluntary sectors**. Why is poverty a problem that is so hard to solve?

Sociologists have explained poverty in several different ways. These can be divided broadly into:

■ those who see the people who are in poverty as the problem
■ those who see them as victims of an unjust or failing system.

The first are described as cultural explanations, because they argue that the poor have a different culture – different values and ways of behaving – from the rest of society. The second set of explanations, considered in the next section, are called structural explanations.

The culture of poverty

This is the idea that poor people have a particular culture that tends to keep them in poverty. This culture has values that

may help to make life bearable and actually stop the poor escaping from poverty. These values include the following:

■ Immediate gratification – the attitude that you should enjoy life now. If you have a bit of money, spend it. The social security system encourages this; if you have savings above a certain limit, you lose your benefit, so it makes sense not to save.

■ Fatalism – the attitude that you cannot do anything to improve your situation. You just have to accept the way things are.

Children in poor families are, according to this theory, socialised into these values. So at school, for example, they are more interested in having a good time than learning (immediate gratification) and do not believe it is worth working to get qualifications and a job (fatalism). Their parents will not be very interested in education and will not encourage them to do well. The result is that they end up in the same situation as their parents.

The cycle of deprivation

Cycle of deprivation

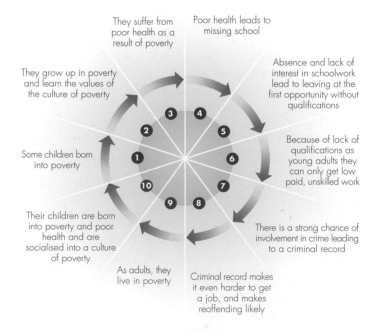

They suffer from poor health as a result of poverty

Poor health leads to missing school

They grow up in poverty and learn the values of the culture of poverty

Absence and lack of interest in schoolwork lead to leaving at the first opportunity without qualifications

Some children born into poverty

Because of lack of qualifications as young adults they can only get low paid, unskilled work

Their children are born into poverty and poor health and are socialised into a culture of poverty

There is a strong chance of involvement in crime leading to a criminal record

As adults, they live in poverty

Criminal record makes it even harder to get a job, and makes reoffending likely

The **cycle of deprivation** shows how poverty can be passed from one generation to the next. The **culture of poverty** is passed from adults to children. They learn to be fatalistic and to seek immediate gratification. They learn not to value schoolwork, and not to expect much from life.

For both of the above explanations, what needs to be done is to break the cycle that passes on poverty from one generation to the next. The children of the poor need to be socialised into the same values as the rest of society.

The New Right and the underclass

This third explanation draws on both the culture of poverty and cycle of deprivation ideas. For example, Charles Murray, a sociologist whose views have been described as New Right, argues that an **underclass** has been created in Britain. An underclass is a group at the bottom of society and cut off from society. The underclass is said to have been created by the welfare state, because welfare encourages **dependency**. People are no longer willing to work and behave like respectable citizens because they know the state will look after them. The welfare state itself has created the culture that keeps poverty going. The values and behaviour of the underclass are seen as being like a disease contaminating society.

New Right thinkers are particularly concerned about the growing number of lone mothers. They argue that boy children brought up without father figures will be unable to be good fathers themselves. They will run away from the responsibility, and will not have the steady jobs that make it possible to be a breadwinner and support a family. Instead, young men become involved in petty crime and drugs. Their sons in turn will not learn to do what a man should do, according to the New Right: work to support a family.

To the New Right, the solution is to cut back the welfare state dramatically, or even end it altogether. For example, if teenage girls deliberately get pregnant in order to get housing and benefits, there should be no housing or benefits – the girls would not get pregnant in the first place if they knew life would be very tough for them.

Problems with cultural explanations

One problem with all three of these explanations is that there is no clear evidence that the poor do have a different culture or values. When they do behave differently, this is a logical response to their situation (for example, spending rather than saving because you lose your benefits if you have savings).

You may have noticed that the New Right strongly condemns the poor. To some, this is blaming people for a situation that is not their fault and beyond their control. The New Right is a strongly moral position that judges others harshly.

FIND OUT FOR YOURSELF

Design a poster presenting the idea of the cycle of deprivation in a striking and visual way. Show how the cycle could be broken.

QUESTIONS

1 What is meant by the cycle of deprivation?

2 Describe two values that are associated with the culture of poverty.

3 What is meant by dependency on welfare?

4 Explain the views of New Right thinkers like Murray. Why do some people disagree with these views?

5 What could be done to break the cycle of poverty?

ROUND-UP

There are different explanations for poverty. These can be divided into cultural and structural explanations. Cultural explanations include the linked ideas of the culture of poverty, the cycle of deprivation and a culturally distinct underclass.

VOCABULARY

Fatalism: a belief that nothing you can do can change your situation

Immediate gratification: wanting to enjoy something now rather than waiting till later, for example spending money rather than saving it

Petty crime: less serious crime, such as vandalism and stealing items of little value

Explaining poverty: structural explanations

KEY FOCUS A second set of explanations of poverty moves away from looking at the poor and their culture to looking at the kind of society that we live in and how it might generate poverty.

Once in poverty, it is very difficult to get out.

- Some of the rules have the effect of keeping people in poverty, for example losing benefits if you study.

- Many people do not claim what they are entitled to. This may be because they do not know what they are entitled to; the system is very hard to understand and leaflets explaining benefits are often hard to follow. Or they may feel a sense of shame if they claim. The process of applying and claiming can be humiliating.

- A lot of the welfare state's resources go to people who don't need them. For example, many people who could afford to pay for health care are treated under the National Health Service. All families with children receive child benefit. If resources were targeted at the people who really need them, it is argued, poverty could be reduced.

These are all criticisms of the welfare state that have some justification. Behind them is support for the idea of a welfare state, but a feeling that the form it took did not work well enough. The answer would be to strengthen the welfare state by providing it with much greater resources, and to reform it so that it concentrated on helping the poor.

Structural explanations

Supporters of structural explanations of poverty reject the cultural explanations you looked at in the previous section. They tend to see the cultural explanations as based on mistaken ideas (such as that the poor have different values) and prejudice (against single parents, for example). Instead they try to explain the existence and survival of poverty by looking at society, not just at the poor. It is possible to see two explanations.

The failure of the welfare state

This is the view that we still have a lot of poverty because the welfare state has failed. There are a number of arguments here:

- Social security benefits are not high enough. Many of those who depend on benefits are in poverty, so the benefits need to be higher to lift them out of poverty. Governments have contributed to poverty by failing to set benefits at a high enough level.

The structure of society

Another view is that poverty is inevitable in the kind of society we live in. We live in a society in which there are classes. The poor are those at the very bottom of the class system, but somebody has to be at the bottom. Since the nature of our capitalist society is to allow some people to be better off than others, those at the bottom will be poor relative to them. Poverty is a result of having an unequal society.

This view is interpreted in very different ways by different sociologists. For functionalists, this situation is acceptable, even the best situation. Relative poverty is a sort of side effect of rewarding those who have talent and work hard. It is unfortunate, but necessary for society to work.

For Marxists, on the other hand, we live in a capitalist society that allows some people to become very rich by making profits out of the work of others. The system is unjust, based on exploitation. It is inevitable in this kind of society that some people will be poor compared to others. Poverty can even be useful to the capitalist system; it helps to keep wages down and profits the rich make up. Perhaps the welfare state was never seriously intended to get rid of poverty completely, just to keep the working class contented enough not to start a revolution.

For Marxists, to get rid of poverty the capitalist system needs to be replaced with a fairer system based on equality. This would get rid of both absolute and relative poverty. The Marxist solution is not even a remote possibility at the moment.

The underclass

The idea of the underclass, which you came across in the last section, is also used in some structural explanations. Here it no longer has the meaning of immorality and a threat to society which the New Right use of it has. Rather, it is used as a simple description of those who are at the bottom of the class system and cannot easily escape.

Among the groups that have been said to be likely to belong to the underclass are:

- elderly people living on the state pension
- lone parents and their children
- young people without skills and qualifications
- the long-term unemployed
- some minority ethnic groups.

The underclass is not simply the lowest level of society; it is cut off from society so that people in the underclass cannot get back into mainstream society. People in the underclass are trapped there; they cannot easily escape from their poverty. Surviving on a low income is so time consuming that it becomes impossible to break out.

The poverty trap

This leads to another term used in explanations of poverty – the **poverty trap**. This is the idea that once in poverty it is hard to escape. For example, someone on a low wage who got a pay rise might lose their entitlement to means-tested benefits, and be no better off.

It is also expensive to be poor. For example, if you have only a limited amount of money each week you need to buy small amounts of foods and essentials. You cannot afford to buy in bulk, although larger packs and quantities work out cheaper. Poor people also shop at their local small shop; the supermarket may be an expensive bus ride away (if there are any buses). The local shop will be more expensive but may be willing to sell small quantities.

Problems with structural explanations

The structural explanations are more convincing to many people than the cultural explanations. Perhaps the biggest problem with structural explanations is that they make poverty seem inevitable. It would be easy to give up trying to do anything about it.

In fact, there is evidence that small-scale local projects can make a big difference. So too can ideas that take a new approach to old problems. The magazine *The Big Issue*, sold by homeless people, was a brilliant idea: it gave homeless people the chance to earn money, to be part of a supportive team and to take the first steps back to a normal life. At the same time it made the public more aware of the problems of homelessness.

FIND OUT FOR YOURSELF

Try to buy a copy of *The Big Issue*. It is sold on the street in cities by homeless people. Read what it says about why the magazine exists. You will probably find that some of the articles are relevant to your study of sociology.

QUESTIONS

1. What is meant by a structural explanation of poverty?

2. Identify and explain two ways in which the welfare state has been said to be failing to solve the problem of poverty.

3. Identify three groups who are at risk of belonging to the underclass.

4. What is meant by the poverty trap? Use an example to explain your answer.

5. Compare and contrast the Marxist and functionalist views of poverty.

ROUND-UP

Structural explanations of poverty argue that poverty arises from the way society or aspects of it are organised; it is not the fault of the poor themselves. Such explanations make poverty seem an almost impossible problem to solve, because such big changes are needed. However, initiatives like *The Big Issue* can make a difference.

VOCABULARY

Prejudice: an opinion which is not based on thought or on considering evidence
Immorality: behaviour that breaks moral rules and is seen as wrong

The creation of the welfare state

KEY FOCUS   A welfare state takes responsibility for the security and well-being of its citizens. This section looks at the development of the welfare state in Britain up to 1951, showing how it gradually extended to cover more people, adopting the principle of universality.

TACKLING THE FIRST GIANT

The welfare state as a crusade – slaying the giants.

The welfare state

The basic principle of the welfare state is that a community should look after everyone who is part of it. Those who are well off should contribute part of what they have to provide for those in need. In a welfare state, this is organised by the government through taxation and welfare benefits.

Its earliest beginnings

The very beginnings of the welfare state can be seen in the **Poor Law** of the late sixteenth century when Elizabeth I was queen. Wandering beggars who roved the countryside looking for work and food were seen as a problem, The Poor Law made ratepayers in parishes look after the sick, disabled and aged, and provide work for those who were poor but could work. This provided some basic security for the poor.

The nineteenth century

The Industrial Revolution of the late eighteenth century changed Britain. By the nineteenth century large numbers of people were living in the new, rapidly growing, industrial towns and cities, having moved there from country areas. They were the new working class. Wages were low,

unemployment was high and there was a lot of poverty and hardship. Governments were worried that this could lead to protests and even to a revolution such as there had been in France in 1789.

In 1834 a new Poor Law was passed. This created **workhouses**, where the poor were made to do hard work in return for very basic essentials. It was assumed that being poor was a result of individual failings; for example, that the unemployed were lazy and could find work if they wanted to. Conditions in workhouses were deliberately made so bad that anyone working even in the worst job outside the workhouse would be better off. The sick, the disabled and the old endured the same awful conditions as the unemployed. People lived in dread of having to move into the workhouse.

HINTS AND TIPS

See page 328 for a picture of life in a workhouse.

Early twentieth century

Throughout the nineteenth century, governments had begun to take on more responsibilities for looking after people. For example, new laws had prevented women and children from being exploited in some kinds of work, such as mining, and primary schools had been introduced.

The following were important steps towards the welfare state, introduced by Liberal governments:

- 1908 – Old Age Pensions Act. This was not for everyone; people who had been found guilty of drunkenness or any crime, who had not worked continuously, who had received poor relief or who could support themselves did not get pensions.
- 1911 – National Insurance Act. Workers, employers and government paid contributions into a fund from which workers who were sick or, in some kinds of work, unemployed, could receive money.

These provisions were gradually extended to almost everyone. But in the late 1920s a severe economic depression began and large numbers of people needed help. The system was not designed to cope with this. A new payment – 'the dole' – was introduced for those whose insurance had run out. The dole was means tested; that is, the family had to have little or no savings or income in order to get it. This proved very controversial. For example, if a child of an unemployed man managed to earn a little money through odd jobs, this amount would be deducted from the man's dole.

The Beveridge Report: slaying the giants

During World War II, a committee chaired by Sir William Beveridge produced a report calling for a fully developed welfare state (1942). This became enormously popular both at home and among troops fighting abroad. The Beveridge Report provided a vision of what Britain would be like after the war. Beveridge's ideas were put into effect by the Labour government of 1945 to 1951.

After defeating Hitler, said Beveridge, the next task was to defeat 'five giants on the road to social reconstruction and progress':

- Want (poverty) – new National Insurance Acts extended old age pensions, unemployment and sickness benefit to everyone. There was a needs test to make sure claims were genuine, but this was less harsh than the old means test.
- Disease – a National Health Service, completely free (including prescriptions) was introduced, covering doctors, opticians, dentists and so on.
- Ignorance – free secondary education for all.
- Squalor (for example living in slums) – slums were demolished. The government took over responsibility for ensuring that everyone had a home they could afford, building large numbers of council houses for rent.
- Idleness (unemployment) – the government committed itself to the goal of full employment; that is, that everyone who wanted to work should be able to.

From the cradle to the grave

The new welfare state built on foundations laid earlier but was a huge step forward. It was based not on helping only the poorest, but on providing security for everyone, 'from the cradle to the grave'. It was universal – that is, everyone was entitled to it. The principle of **universality** was a big change from the previous system of **means testing**. For example, every family in the country was entitled to a weekly cash payment for every child after the first under the Family Allowance Act of 1945.

▶ FIND OUT FOR YOURSELF

Find out how much the welfare state has changed. Interview an older person, such as one of your grandparents, about health, education and welfare when he or she was young. Decide on the kinds of questions you want to ask before the interview. Make sure you find out the time period the person you interview is telling you about. Make a note of what you find out and present your findings to the rest of the class.

QUESTIONS

1. What was a workhouse?
2. What were the five giants that the welfare state was intended to destroy?
3. Choose any three of these 'giants' and describe what was done to try to end them.
4. Explain the difference between means testing and universal benefits.
5. 'The welfare state was intended to support everyone, not just the poor.' Do you agree? Give reasons for your answer.

ROUND-UP

The origins of the welfare state can be traced back hundreds of years. At first support was only for the very poor, but gradually the scope of the welfare state was extended. The Beveridge Report, which led to the modern welfare state, established the principle of universalism.

VOCABULARY

Squalor: dirty and disgusting conditions
Ratepayers: rates were an old system of local taxes. Ratepayers owned their houses

The welfare state today

KEY FOCUS   This section continues the story of the British welfare state, from the 'golden age' of the 1950s and 1960s through the changes introduced by the Conservative governments of 1979 to 1997.

In the 1980s the Conservatives under Margaret Thatcher introduced major reforms of the welfare state.

The golden age

The new laws, benefits and organisations set up by the Labour government of 1945 to 1951 brought in what has been called the 'golden age' of the welfare state. During this period, both parties agreed on the basic structure of the welfare state. When they were in power in the 1950s, the Conservatives did not try to change fundamentally the system set up by Labour. ... e some changes, including the introduction of ... charges for those who could afford to pay. This ... away from the idea of universalism. The costs of ... state were met through high taxes.

The welfare state under attack

In the 1970s, the welfare state was criticised from different points of view. These were some of the charges made against it:

- That it had become too expensive, that the country could no longer afford to be so generous. The growing expense was partly due to the changing population. For example, when old age pensions had been introduced most people had died soon after retirement, but as more people lived longer, the cost to the government of paying pensions went up. At first, it had been thought that the National Health Service would be able to get rid of most illness, so that costs would fall. In fact, health service spending grew. So the welfare state turned out to be more expensive than anticipated.

- That this growing expense was partly the result of inefficiency, for example with money going to people who did not really need it. This was a criticism of the principle of universality. It was argued that the welfare state would be cheaper and more efficient if it only supported those who really needed help.

- That many people claiming benefits were '**scroungers**'; that is, they did not need the money, were lying about their situation (for example claiming to be unemployed when they were working), or were choosing to be unemployed when they could be working. This idea was largely created by the mass media, especially tabloid newspapers, which put stories about 'social security fraud' on the front pages.

- Related to this, the idea that the welfare state encouraged people to rely on the state, not on themselves; that it took away people's initiative, making them passive and helpless. This is called a culture of dependency.

The end of the golden age

From 1979 onwards, the Conservatives made significant changes to the welfare state that undermined some of its main features:

- A move away from universality, from everyone having the right to certain benefits. For example, charges were introduced for sight tests; free sight tests became means tested rather than universal. Universal benefits such as unemployment benefit were reduced so that more people had to rely on selective, means-tested benefits. It was argued that this would make the system more efficient and free resources so that they could be used to help those who really needed help

- **Privatisation**. Many services which had been run by local authorities were privatised, for example meals in schools and hospitals, and collecting rubbish. Again the argument was that this would increase efficiency. Private health care was encouraged. Those who could pay were, for example, able to get an operation before those who could not. Charges were brought in for some medical services, such as some inoculations for travel abroad. Dentists were encouraged to move into private practice, and in some areas it became difficult to get dental treatment on the National Health Service. Another form of privatisation was the sale of council houses at prices well below their value. Privatisation creates a two-tier system: there will be those who can afford to pay for the best, and those who cannot who have to rely on whatever is provided for them.

- **Community care.** Many care homes, such as mental hospitals and hospitals for the elderly, were closed down and the people living there returned to the community where relatives, voluntary organisations and local councils were expected to look after them. This reduced costs but there were fears that some people would not be properly looked after.

- Competition. This was introduced in the health service. For example, doctors were encouraged to 'shop around' hospitals to find the best deals for their patients. The idea was that hospitals in competition with each other for business would improve their services. Hospitals had to become like businesses.

The government tried to cut down the amount spent on the welfare state. Benefits rose very slowly, not as fast as prices, and more people were prevented from claiming benefits. The result was a reduced welfare state where there had been a move backwards towards means testing and away from universality.

The welfare state under New Labour

Following its election in 1997, the Labour government did not attempt to reverse these changes. While Labour believes in the welfare state, it has accepted that there can be no return to the golden age.

The main welfare provision that Labour introduced is called '**Welfare to Work** – a **New Deal**'. The aim of this is to help groups, especially the young but also lone parents and the long-term unemployed, who at present often rely on welfare,

to find work and support themselves. This will help people to become self-reliant, and also, it is hoped, eventually reduce the amount the government has to spend on social security. Overall, Labour's approach seems to be to find a 'third way' between the golden age welfare state (now too expensive) and the Conservative changes (seen as creating inequality and injustice).

To make work more attractive than claiming benefits, a national minimum wage has been introduced. Although this is lower than many had hoped, it immediately lifted some low paid workers out of poverty.

The welfare state no longer provides care from the cradle to the grave. Most of its universal provisions are for children and the elderly; those who can are expected to look after themselves – by taking out health insurance, having a private pension, owning their own home rather than renting a council house, and so on.

QUESTIONS

1. When was the golden age welfare state?

2. What is meant by privatisation?

3. Identify and explain two criticisms which were made of the welfare state.

4. Identify and explain three ways in which the Conservative governments of 1979 to 1997 changed the welfare state.

5. What have been the policies of the Labour government elected in 1997 to the welfare state?

ROUND-UP

The golden age welfare state brought in by Labour after World War II was hard to maintain as costs went up and the economic situation declined. In the 1980s the Conservatives shifted away from universal provisions and towards encouraging people to rely on themselves, not on the welfare state.

VOCABULARY

Prescription charges: charges for medicines prescribed by doctors and dentists

Inefficiency: wasting money and resources

The welfare state: success or failure?

KEY FOCUS

You have learned about the history of the welfare state and recent changes to it, but what has it achieved? This section looks at the ways it has improved people's lives, but also at ways in which it has failed which, to some people, means it was a mistake.

The old slums are gone – but problems remain.

Has the welfare state succeeded?

There are several different arguments about how effective the welfare state has been:

■ The welfare state has been successful in improving living standards and eliminating absolute poverty.
■ The welfare state has not been successful; there is still a ...overty and inequality.
...a of the welfare state was misguided. It wastes ...people should rely more on themselves, not the

Successes

Looking back to the five giants that Beveridge's plan set out as problems to be tackled, the welfare state has undoubtedly made great progress:

■ Want (poverty) – while there is still considerable relative poverty, the welfare state acts as a safety net, providing a basic income for those who without it would need to beg or live on charity.
■ Disease – there has been an increase in good health, with longer life expectancy and fewer infant deaths.
■ Education – everyone is educated up to the age of 16 so that most young people leave schools with qualifications. Most now stay in education beyond 16; there are many more places in colleges and universities for people who want more education
■ Squalor – old slums have been demolished, although some of the tower blocks built to replace them have turned out to be just as unattractive as places to live.
■ Unemployment – although unemployment is high compared to the golden age of the welfare state, the state provides training opportunities to help people into work.

Failings

In each of the five areas, things are better than they were before World War II. Nevertheless, Beveridge and the other pioneers of the welfare state might well be disappointed, even shocked, by some aspects of life today:

■ people sleeping rough or in hostels because they are homeless
■ people begging on the streets of cities
■ the way we have come to accept high rates of unemployment as inevitable
■ people needing to 'top up' welfare payments because they are inadequate; for example, state old age pensions will provide only a very basic income so people need a second pension as well
■ the extent of relative poverty – people going without things that others take for granted, especially the number of children living in poverty
■ hospital waiting lists
■ some services being so expensive that some people cannot afford them, for example going to the dentist

- some young people still leaving school without qualifications or prospects
- people who slip through the safety net now that welfare relies on the voluntary sector.

Poverty, homelessness and unemployment in particular can be seen as giants that have not yet been destroyed.

Behind this list of failings are two underlying problems:

- The welfare state has been accused of helping those who do not need help, at the expense of those who do. The principle of universality (everyone having the same entitlements, however well off they are) means that, for example, even rich people receive child benefit and free health care (unless they choose private health care). Middle-class people have benefited more than working-class people from some aspects of the welfare state. In education, for example, it is middle-class children who gain qualifications and stay in education in greater numbers. Those who leave early without qualifications are those from disadvantaged backgrounds – exactly the people the welfare state was supposed to help. In health, middle-class people who know the system and their rights can often get better care than working-class people.
- Some groups of people are far more likely to suffer from a range of disadvantages than other groups. The welfare state has not eliminated inequality; it has not ensured that everyone is treated equally. For example, members of minority ethnic groups are more likely than the rest of the population to leave school without qualifications, to be unemployed and to be living in poverty.

For some people, the welfare state has failed in these ways because it has not been adequately funded. If social problems are to be tackled effectively, funding needs to be increased.

For others, the welfare state has actually created some of these problems. It has gone too far, and needs to be reformed and reduced.

Dependency culture

The welfare state, it is argued, encouraged people to be passive, not to do anything themselves to improve their situation. For example, there was little point in looking for a job, or training to get qualifications, if you received unemployment benefit because the benefit was nearly as much as you could hope to get paid for doing a job.

Related to this is the idea that the welfare state undermined family values. In the past, one of the roles of the family was to provide help to its members in times of need. Under the welfare state, people could rely on the government instead. So some people see the welfare state as contributing to what they see as the decline of the traditional nuclear family – the increase in divorce, in lone-parent families and so on (see Chapter 7 Families).

The solution, from this point of view, is to greatly reduce or even completely end the welfare state, so that individuals and families are completely responsible for themselves. Only a very small number of people should need help from the state.

Scapegoating

The whole idea of the welfare state has been criticised by right-wing politicians and by sections of the media. One idea they have used is that people who use the welfare state, such as social security claimants, are 'scroungers', taking 'taxpayers' money' when they do not need it. The long-term unemployed were assumed to be lazy, unwilling to work. Those who were off work sick were assumed to be malingering, exaggerating their symptoms. Teenage girls, it was said, deliberately got pregnant so they would be given council housing. These groups were blamed for their situation.

QUESTIONS

1. What is meant by benefit fraud?
2. State three aspects of life today which demonstrate ways in which the welfare state has not succeeded.
3. Identify and explain the two problems underlying the shortcomings of the welfare state.
4. What is meant by arguing that the welfare state has created dependency?
5. Which of the five giants do you think we have made most progress in overcoming? Give reasons for your answer.

ROUND-UP

The welfare state has led to many improvements in the quality of life and has provided a safety net for many vulnerable people, yet it has failed to get rid of poverty and inequality. Some people argue that it needs more money if it is to work, others that it creates as many problems as it solves.

VOCABULARY

Eliminated: got rid of
Undermined: weakened
Malingering: pretending to be ill or exaggerating illness

Welfare beyond the state

KEY FOCUS   Alongside the welfare state there are other forms of care and help: informal care by relatives, the work of charities, and profit-making businesses. All of these have become more important in recent years.

Feeling sorry's not enough

HELP the AGED
help the frail

Help the Aged, 32 Dover Street, London W1A 2AP.

Campaigning on behalf of the elderly poor.

Beyond the welfare state

As well as the welfare state, there have always been other forms of care and help for those who need it. Today these are:

- **informal voluntary care** by relatives or members of the community
- the voluntary sector – charities and similar groups
- the **private sector** – businesses providing services for which people have to pay.

These have always existed. Charities were important before the welfare state; for example, Doctor Barnardo founded homes for orphans, and Victorian philanthropists (people who believe in doing charitable work) tried to help the poor and needy. The end of the golden age welfare state meant that forms of help provided by individuals, charities and businesses became more important than ever before.

Informal voluntary care

This is care provided by family members or others. Many people have always cared for, for example, the elderly, disabled and mentally ill. They take care of their personal needs,

feeding and cleaning them, looking after their homes, doing shopping and other errands and so on. Exactly what is done depends both on what the person cared for needs and what the carer can do. Many vulnerable people would be unable to live outside institutions and hospitals without this kind of support.

It is usually but not always women who do this kind of care work. Many carers feel lonely and unable to get even temporary relief from the hard work of caring. Some are elderly, looking after children or spouses with disabilities, and worried about what will happen if they die. This kind of situation causes stress and ill health.

The voluntary sector

Charities do a range of kinds of work:

- They offer help directly to people who need it.
- They raise public awareness of groups with particular needs, for example suffering from a particular illness or disability.
- They offer help to welfare state institutions, for example hospitals or schools.

Volunteers who give up some of their time to charity work may help people directly (usually only after having been given training) or may help to raise funds for the charity, for example by helping in a shop. Charities need funds to keep going. As well as the work they do, most employ full-time staff and need to be able to pay them. Charities raise money from the public through shops and donations, through grants from government bodies and the National Lottery, and sometimes by charging for their services.

There are not always charities for all groups who need them. For example, while there are charities for sufferers from more common diseases and disabilities, there may not be any for less common problems. Where there are charities for particular groups, they will have a very good understanding of the needs of the group.

Not all organisations in the voluntary sector are charities. Some are campaigning pressure groups, for example the Child Poverty Action Group (CPAG). Charities are not allowed to be political, but because CPAG is not a charity it can criticise the government and push for more resources for children in poverty.

There are also self-help groups who get together to improve their situation. The activities of such organisations help to balance the tendency of some charities to portray the people they work for as passive victims.

Examples of voluntary organisations

Age Concern
Barnardo's
Child Poverty Action Group
The Samaritans
Scope
Mencap
Shelter
Gingerbread

The private sector

Since the changes to the welfare state brought in by the Conservative governments between 1979 and 1997, there has been a big growth in the private sector of businesses providing services and charging for them. Sometimes people pay the company directly; sometimes a local authority, hospital or other organisation will contract a company to provide a service. There are private nursing homes, hospitals, schools, nurseries and residential homes

Residential and community care

In the past, many people with physical and mental disabilities were housed in institutions called **asylums** or, in popular slang, 'loony bins'. They were shut off from the outside world, with little possibility of release.

Most of these asylums have now been closed down as part of the move to 'community care'. In practice, community care means care by relatives, usually with some support from the local authority, social workers or other professionals. As you have seen, many relatives struggle to look after those who need care.

The move to community care was very controversial. There was much wrong with asylums, which in many ways resembled prison. Stories are still emerging about the abuse of vulnerable people that can happen in institutions. On the other hand, many people felt the government was more interested in saving money than helping. There were also fears that some of those released into the community would be dangerous, to themselves and others. This is true only of a very small minority.

The future

It seems likely that informal and formal voluntary care and private care will continue to grow. There will be a growing number of elderly people who will need care and services; the state will almost certainly be unwilling or unable to provide all of this. At the moment, it is estimated that about one in six adults provide informal care for others. This proportion will grow. But not everyone has relatives and friends able and willing to help, and not everyone who needs help is recognised as such. One of the problems will be ensuring that no one falls through the net.

▶ FIND OUT FOR YOURSELF

Choose one of the organisations mentioned in this section or a similar local or national group. By visiting the organisation's web site or by writing or telephoning for information, find out more about what it does. Present your findings to the rest of the class.

QUESTIONS

1. What is meant by informal voluntary care?
2. Name a campaigning pressure group which is not a charity.
3. Identify and explain three kinds of work that charities do.
4. Why was the introduction of community care controversial?
5. Why is it likely that voluntary care will grow in the future?

ROUND-UP

Gaps in welfare state provision have always been filled by informal and formal voluntary care and by the private sector. These have greatly increased in importance in the last ten years or so as the welfare state has been cut back. One particular policy, care in the community, has increased the number of people caring for relatives, friends or neighbours.

VOCABULARY

Spouse: a person's partner in marriage
Donation: gift
Philanthropist: someone who believes in being charitable

Social security and welfare today

KEY FOCUS This section looks at how much is spent on social security and how, and where the money comes from, comparing Britain with other countries. It also looks briefly at new developments following the election of Labour in 1997, and at how welfare spending might change in the future.

Social security benefits per week for the over-25s, 1998

Jobseeker's allowance	£50.35
Incapacity benefit	£64.70
Family credit	£48.80–£59.60
Income support: Single person Couple Lone parent (plus allowances for dependent children)	£50.35 £79.00 £50.35 £17.30–£30.30 per child
Retirement pension: Single person Married couple	£64.70 £103.40

Sociology Update 1999.

How much are you entitled to? The information isn't always easy to get or to understand.

The cost of social security

The figures in the table above show you how much people getting the main social security benefits received in 1998. These amounts are usually increased by very small amounts each year; you should try to find out what the up-to-date figures are.

The total cost of social security in 1997–98 was about £100 billion. This is about one-third of total government spending. This figure does not include spending on health and social services and on education, which are also parts of the welfare state. The money that the government spends on social security comes from taxes. There are two main types of taxes: income tax which people pay from their wages or salary, and indirect taxes such as value added tax (VAT) which are paid on goods and services. While usually only those in work pay income tax, everyone, including the poor and social security claimants, pays VAT through things that they buy.

Taxes are not popular and political parties often promise to reduce taxes in order to get votes. If the welfare state were to be expanded so that it tackled poverty and hardship more effectively, taxes would have to be increased. Political parties would be concerned that they would lose votes.

Those who defend the high amount spent on social security argue:

■ that nearly everyone pays money into the system, in order to receive help when they need it – it is an insurance system, not a free hand-out

■ that the price is worth paying on compassionate grounds; in any civilised society, there should not be great hardship or great inequalities – we should look after each other

■ that the price is also worth paying on selfish grounds. The cost of not having a welfare state would be social breakdown and a fall in the quality of everyone's life. There would be high rates of crime and violent protests.

Type of social security benefit

These are the main types of benefit:

■ Contributory benefits – people pay towards these throughout their working lives (through National Insurance and other contributions) and draw on them as they need them. They include sick pay, incapacity allowance, retirement pensions.

■ Means-tested benefits – people only receive these if their income and savings are below a certain level. They include income support, jobseeker's allowance, family credit, housing benefit.

■ Non-contributory benefits – these are paid without means testing to people in particular groups, such as those caring for disabled people or bringing up children, regardless of income and savings. They include child benefit, one-parent benefit, invalid care allowance.

Nearly everyone will be eligible for some kind of benefit at some point in his or her life. More than half of all families are receiving some kind of benefit at any time.

Comparing Britain and other countries

Many people see the high cost of the welfare state as a big problem. It is a huge amount of money; however, the amount

Britain spends is not very high compared to some other countries. Britain's spending is not particularly high or low, as the table below shows.

Spending on social security

Country	Percentage of gross domestic product*
Japan	5.5
USA	7.5
Britain	13.0
Germany	15.0
France	18.5
Sweden	22.0

* The total the country earns

New strategies: social exclusion and 'Welfare to Work'

The Labour government elected in 1997 said that one of its priorities was to tackle **social exclusion**. This term is difficult to define, but it uses the idea of environmental poverty; that is, that poverty is about the low quality of life in particular areas as well as the situation of individuals and families. Social exclusion is about the ways that people are cut off from the mainstream of life in the rest of society. It covers, among other things, failure at school, drug abuse, poor health and poor housing. The government intends to tackle these and other problems through new initiatives.

Central to the attack on social exclusion is 'Welfare to Work'. This means that receiving welfare will be increasingly a step up into work, only temporary. Work is seen as the key to getting people to be independent and support themselves. Policies will include tackling obstacles that stop people getting into work (such as the lack of childcare for lone parents, or the lack of advice available).

Future costs

Because people live longer, there will be more retired people in the future. At the same time, because of the lower birth rate and the lower number of children most women now have, there will be fewer people of working age.

At the moment, the welfare system works by those who are in work paying taxes that are used to pay benefits, including pensions. When the workers retire, they will be supported by the next generation. This has been called the **contract between generations**. Will it break down when there are fewer people working and more people needing support?

The media have spread alarm about this, with talk of a 'time bomb', suggesting that at some time in the early twenty-first century Britain will no longer be able to pay for the pensions and health and other services that older people need. Although it is true that a high proportion of spending goes to the elderly, this idea is exaggerated. At the moment, it looks as though Britain will have to spend a slightly higher percentage of its gross domestic product.

PS W C ▶ FIND OUT FOR YOURSELF

Work in a small group. Choose one of the following groups of people: unemployed people, lone parents, people with disabilities. Now try to find out what benefits and welfare payments your group might be able to claim. There are several possible ways to do this. Post Offices and Benefit Offices have leaflets, as do Citizens' Advice Bureaux. You could also visit web sites. Present your findings to the class. Include your thoughts on how easy it would be for your group to find out about what they are entitled to.

QUESTIONS

1 What percentage of government spending, approximately, is on social security?

2 What are the two main types of tax?

3 What is meant by the contract between generations?

4 What are the three main types of benefit? For each, write a one-sentence description and give one example.

5 What is social exclusion and how is the government tackling it?

ROUND-UP

Britain spends a huge amount of money on social security, but not a high amount compared to some other countries. The Labour government elected in 1997 has brought in new strategies on welfare, aimed at attacking social exclusion. Welfare spending may need to rise slightly in the future because of changes in the age structure of the population.

VOCABULARY

Expanded: made bigger
Initiatives: new policies

Poverty and welfare – sociology in practice

Poverty – comparing Britain and other countries

'Poverty affects a larger proportion of people in Britain than it does in other industrialised countries. This was the conclusion drawn by the west's leading economic think tank, the Organisation for Economic Co-operation and Development (OECD), in a report published at the end of 1999. The report investigated relative poverty in industrialised countries during the years 1991–96. It found that, at any point in time during the six years of the study, there were on average 20 per cent of the British population living below the poverty line.'

Population affected by poverty each year

Country	Percentage
Netherlands	6.1
Sweden	7.4
Germany	10.0
USA	14.0
UK	20.0

Sociology Update 2000

Questions

1. Look back at the section on Measuring poverty (pages 324–5). What is meant by relative poverty? What other ways of measuring poverty are there?

2. There are at least two ways of explaining the data shown in the table. Expand on each of the following arguments:
   (a) A New Right sociologist would argue that continuing poverty is a result of the welfare state making people dependent on welfare …
   (b) An alternative view is that the welfare state has been undermined by changes in the ten years or so before these figures were compiled …
   The sections on Explaining poverty: cultural explanations (pages 328–9) and Explaining poverty: structural explanations (pages 330–31) will help you.

3. What measures have been brought in since the research shown in the table which might reduce the numbers in poverty in Britain? You will find information in the sections The welfare state today (pages 334–5) and Social security and welfare today (pages 340–41).

Beveridge and after

Beveridge tells how to banish want

SIR William Beveridge's Report, aimed at abolishing Want in Britain, is published today.

He calls his Plan for Social Security a revolution under which 'every citizen willing to serve according to his powers has at all times an income sufficient to meet his responsibilities.'

Here are his chief proposals:

All social insurance – unemployment, health, pensions – lumped into one weekly contribution for all citizens without income limit – from duke to dustman.

These payments, in the case of employees, would be:

Men 4s. 3d. Employer 3s. 3d. Women 3s. 6d. Employer 2s. 6d.

Cradle to the grave benefits for all, including:

Free medical, dental, eyesight and hospital treatment.

Children's allowances of 8s. a week each, after the first child.

Increases in unemployment benefit (40s. for a couple) and abolition of the means test; industrial pension in place of workmen's compensation.

A charter for housewives, including marriage grant up to £10; maternity grant of £4 (and 36s. for 13 weeks for a paid worker); widow's benefit; separation and divorce provision; free domestic help in time of sickness.

Old age pensions rising to 40s. for a married couple on retirement.

Daily Mirror, 2 December 1942.

Questions

1 To what extent has the welfare state succeeded in abolishing Want? What has prevented complete success?

2 Consider the references to men and women in the article. Do you think that discrimination by sex was built into these plans? Explain your answer.

3 If a government were elected which was committed to abolishing poverty today, what might its 'chief proposals' be? Write your answer in the form of a front page article for a modern newspaper.

Poverty around the world

According to the United Nations, the number of people living in poverty worldwide rose to more than 1.3 billion by the mid-1990s – nearly one in five of the world's population.

ACCORDING to the United Nations, the 225 richest people in the world have a combined wealth of more than $1 trillion – equal to the annual income of 47% of the earth's population. The three richest people – Microsoft's Bill Gates, the Walton family of Wal-mart Stores and legendary investor Warren Buffett – have assets that are greater than the combined gross domestic product of the 48 least developed countries.

'It is estimated that the additional cost of achieving and maintaining universal access to basic education for all, basic health care for all, reproductive health care for all women, adequate food for all and safe water and sanitation for all is roughly $40 billion a year,' the United Nations said.

This is less than 4% of the combined wealth of the 225 richest people.

Among the 4.4 billion people in developing countries, almost three fifths lack basic sanitation, one third have no safe drinking water, one quarter have inadequate housing, while one fifth are undernourished and the same proportion have no access to modern health services.

Adapted from 'The rich and poor grow further apart' by Larry Elliott and Victoria Brittain, *Guardian*, 9 September 1998.

Questions

1 What kind of poverty is being discussed in the final paragraph? Explain why you have chosen your answer.

2 What would you add to the list of the essentials of life listed in the final paragraph?

3 Find out more about poverty worldwide and attempts to tackle it by visiting http://www.oneworld.org/guides/poverty/index. Present your findings in the form of a poster for wall display.

Poverty and welfare – important terms

absolute poverty	not having the essentials of life
asylums	institutions in which the mentally ill and others used to be confined
benefits	payments to support those in need
Beveridge Report	the report in 1942 which led to the setting up of the welfare state
community care	when people are looked after in the community rather than in institutions
contract between generations	money from taxes paid by people of working age goes to support those who are older; in return, the workers expect to be looked after in their old age
culture of poverty	the theory that it is the norms and values of poor people that keep them poor
cycle of deprivation	how poverty can be passed from one generation to the next
dependency (on welfare)	relying on welfare so that the will to support oneself is lost
environmental poverty	not living in a physical and social environment which meets expected standards
golden age welfare state	the time when the welfare state, based on universalism, was strongest – roughly 1945 to 1976
informal voluntary care	provided by family members, friends or neighbours
means testing	when eligibility for benefits depends on financial situation
New Deal	originally used in the USA in the 1930s, now a description of the policies of the Labour government elected in 1997
pensions	state, company or private payments to old people
Poor Law	the earliest laws in Britain dealing with poverty
poverty	being poor, but there are different interpretations about what this means
poverty trap	being unable to get out of poverty, particularly when getting a job does not mean extra income because benefits are lost
privatisation	services previously provided by the public sector are provided by companies whose aim is profit
private sector	companies providing services which they charge either the government or the receivers or both for
relative poverty	when someone is poor in terms of the values and standards of society at that time
scapegoat	when someone is blamed for something that is not his or her fault, distracting attention away from the real cause
scrounger	a term of abuse for someone who claims more benefit than he or she is entitled to. Sometimes used, wrongly, for any claimant
social exclusion	a form of relative and environmental poverty that shuts people out of what most people in society expect
social security	a system of providing financial support for those in need
subjective poverty	when people feel poor
underclass	a group at the bottom of society and cut off from it
universality	when welfare benefits are available to all, regardless of their wealth and income
voluntary sector	provides help and services without charge, for example charities
welfare state	the network of government organisations that look after the health and welfare of the population
Welfare to Work	a set of policies of the 1997 Labour government, designed to reduce dependency on welfare by making work easier to get
workhouse	before the welfare state, an institution where the poor, elderly, disabled and others received basic subsistence

Poverty and welfare – exam style questions

Source A

'Around seven in ten families received some sort of social security benefit in 1995–96. Some benefits, like child benefits, are universally available. Virtually all families with dependent children receive child benefit. Some benefits, such as the state retirement pension, depend upon the individual's record of contributions to the National Insurance Fund, including those by their employer on their behalf ... A high proportion of lone-parent families also receive income-related benefits, such as housing benefit, council tax benefit and income support.'

Social Trends Pocketbook 1998.

Source B

The largest group of people living in poverty in Britain today is children. According to recent research, one in ten children live in poverty. Many of these live with only one parent. They were said to be in poverty because they went without at least three things that most children could take for granted, such as three meals a day, a bed of their own and new shoes that fit.

Foundation tier

1 Look at source A and answer these questions:
   (a) What percentage of families received some sort of social security benefit in 1995–96? [1 mark]
   (b) Name one benefit that is universally available. [1 mark]
   (c) Name one income-related benefit. [1 mark]
   (d) What does the state retirement pension depend on? [2 marks]
   (e) Identify two groups who may receive social security benefits. [2 marks]
   (f) What is meant by an income-related benefit? [2 marks]

2 Look at source B and answer these questions:
   (a) What percentage of children live in poverty in Britain today, according to the research referred to here? [1 mark]
   (b) Is this source referring to absolute poverty or relative poverty? Give a reason for your answer. [2 marks]

3 Identify two groups (other than children in lone-parent families) who are likely to live in poverty. [2 marks]

4 What is meant by universality, when referring to social security benefits? [2 marks]

5 'There is no absolute poverty in Britain today.' Do you agree? Use sociological knowledge and give two reasons. [4 marks]

Higher tier

1 Look at source A and answer these questions:
   (a) What does the state retirement pension depend on? [2 marks]
   (b) Identify two groups who may receive social security benefits. [2 marks]
   (c) What is meant by an income-related benefit? [2 marks]

2 Look at source B. Is this source referring to absolute poverty or relative poverty? Give a reason for your answer. [2 marks]

3 Identify two groups (other than children in lone-parent families) who are likely to live in poverty. [2 marks]

4 What is meant by universality, when referring to social security benefits? [2 marks]

5 'There is no absolute poverty in Britain today.' Do you agree? Use sociological knowledge and give two reasons. [4 marks]

6 Britain spends an enormous amount on social security. In what ways can it be argued that this is money well spent? [4 marks]

Poverty and welfare – further research

The Joseph Rowntree Foundation has summaries of research findings at: www.jrf.org.uk.

Oxfam works against poverty in Britain, as well as in poorer countries: www.Oxfam.org.uk.

14 Population and Development

The collection of data on how many people there are, how long they live, where they live and so on is an interest shared by governments and social scientists. Social scientists who research population are called demographers. They use a variety of measures – birth rate, death rate, life expectancy, and so on, and you need to learn what these mean. These terms can be used to help understand not only the population of Britain, but that of the world. Here we reach a vital question – are there, or will there soon be, too many people?

We then look briefly at poverty and inequality at the global level, and at how aid, trade and debt affect progress towards development.

People don't stay in one place. They migrate, seeking a better life elsewhere. The idea of migration provides a link to the idea of urbanisation – people moving to towns and cities, looking for 'streets paved with gold'. Cities around the world continue to grow and now contain most of the world's poor people.

IN THIS CHAPTER YOU WILL LEARN ABOUT:

- the measures used in the study of populations
- how the British and world populations have changed over time
- world poverty and inequality
- how people move within and between countries – migration
- life in cities and in the countryside

CHAPTER CONTENTS

Studying population

KEY FOCUS This section introduces the subject of demography and looks at how the British and world populations have grown over the past 200 years and are expected to continue to rise.

People: how many? Where? Why? – the kinds of questions demographers ask.

Demography

The study of population is called **demography** and the social scientists working in this field are demographers. They are particularly interested in how the size and composition of populations changes over time. So they study the rates of birth, death, marriage and **migration** (people moving from one place to another). They also look at other factors that might affect the size and composition of the population, such as food supply and climate.

The study of demography is very important because it helps governments to plan ahead. Studies of population provide vital information about how many schools we will need, or how much new housing we need.

The British population

In 1999 the British population was estimated to be 59 236 500.

The population has been growing continuously since the Industrial Revolution of the mid-eighteenth century. Although the Industrial Revolution caused much hardship and misery at first, there were gradual improvements in many areas of life that led to more people living longer.

As you can see from the table of population increase, after a

rapid growth in population in the nineteenth century, the twentieth century had a slower population growth. This slowing down of population growth is expected to continue.

The annual rate of growth (how much the population increases each year) is expected to fall from 0.3 per cent to 0.2 per cent by 2021.

Population increase in the UK, 1600–1951

Year	Number of people
1600	3 million
1800	6 million
1851 Census	22 million
1901 Census	38 million
1951 Census	50 million

World population

Since 1750, the world's population has increased from an estimated 0.8 billion to 6 billion. Most of this population growth was in the twentieth century.

World population, 1950–2020 (millions)

	1950	1960	1970	1980	1990	2000*	2010*	2020*
Asia	1402	1702	2147	2641	3184	3689	4161	4591
Europe	547	605	656	693	722	729	722	709
Africa	224	282	364	476	629	820	1052	1317
Latin America and Caribbean	166	217	284	359	438	515	589	658
Northern America	172	204	232	255	282	309	332	358
Oceania	13	16	19	23	26	30	34	39
World	2524	3027	3702	4447	5282	6091	6891	7672

*projection

Social Trends Pocketbook 1999.

QUESTIONS

Look at the table of world population.

1 In which continent do most people live?

2 Work out approximately (to the nearest whole number) how many times bigger each continent's population was in 2000 than it was in 1950. Which continent has had the biggest rate of increase? Which has had the smallest?

3 Which continent's population is expected to fall by 2020?

Reasons for population growth

The Industrial Revolution affected population in two main ways:

- The division of labour. Industrial production led to more specialised work divided between different firms and individuals. This increased the efficiency with which the things that people need could be produced – food, clothes, houses and so on. It became possible to support a growing population.
- The growth of cities. Cities were where the growing population could live and work. Cities are the focus of the three sections later in this chapter.

The demographic reason for population growth was a fall in the **death rate**.

Death rate: the number of people per 1000 population who die in a year

Year	Deaths per 1000
1770	32
1870	20
1920	10
2000	10

As you can see from the table, the high death rate fell during and after the Industrial Revolution and eventually stabilised in the twentieth century. There was a dramatic fall especially in the infant death rate or infant mortality rate, that is, the number of infants dying.

Infant mortality rate: the number of infants dying per 1000 per year

Year	Deaths per 1000
1770	200
1870	100
2000	6

Once, parents knew that there was a strong possibility a child would not survive to adulthood. Today, it is unusual and considered tragic for a child to die.

Why did the death rate fall?

- Better diet. This is particularly important for children. Children who did not have an adequate diet were far more likely to die from common infectious diseases such as scarlet fever.
- Better sanitation. Governments began to spend money on running water, sewers and drainage and rubbish disposal. Until then many people's environment had been extremely unhealthy by today's standards. Piped water and flush toilets led to a big fall in diseases which are encouraged by poor hygiene, such as cholera and typhoid.
- Better medical care. Advances in medical knowledge helped people to live longer. Women were less likely to die in pregnancy and childbirth. People were more likely to survive surgery and to be given effective medicines. By the twentieth century, children were being inoculated against some diseases that had once been big killers.
- The welfare state. Help available from the state and from voluntary organisations has provided a safety net against some of the worst deprivations.

QUESTIONS

1 What is meant by demography?

2 Why was the division of labour an important factor contributing to population growth during the Industrial Revolution?

3 Identify and explain three reasons why the death rate fell during and after the Industrial Revolution.

4 Why do women live longer than men on average?

5 Is it possible that life expectancy will continue to increase? Give reasons for your answer. (This is not discussed in the text, but it might help if you think about why life expectancy has increased.)

ROUND-UP

Demography is important in providing information for those planning social provisions. The world and British populations rose dramatically after the Industrial Revolution as the death rate fell. The British population increase is now slow but world population is expected to continue to rise significantly.

VOCABULARY

Inoculation: a way of giving immunity to a disease
Transformation: a dramatic change

Birth and fertility rates

KEY FOCUS   Another key statistic used by demographers as well as the death rate is the birth rate. This section looks at how demographers study birth and fertility.

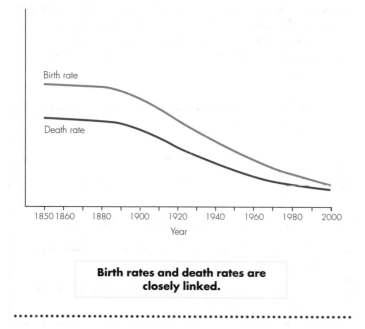

Birth rates and death rates are closely linked.

The fall in birth rate

The **birth rate** is the number of live births per 1000 of the population in a year. The **fertility rate** is a very similar measure that counts the number of live births per 1000 women of childbearing age (15 to 44). Britain had a high birth and fertility rate of between 30 and 40 until about 1870. Then, as the death rate, especially for children (see previous section) fell quickly, so did the birth rate. It is now about 12.

The birth and fertility rates seem to be closely related to the death rate. At one time, many children did not survive to adulthood – if a couple had six children, only three or four might survive. This was important because the parents would rely on their children to look after them, as they got older. As it became normal for most children to survive, it was no longer necessary to have as many children in order to have the same number reach adulthood. A little later, the development of the welfare state meant that people could expect some help from the government in old age. It was no longer necessary to have children as a kind of insurance, to make sure you would be looked after.

This was only possible because of better birth control. The discovery of the vulcanisation of rubber in the late nineteenth century, which made rubber more elastic and strong, led to

the rubber condom (which was used to prevent the spread of diseases as well as for birth control). Other contraceptives such as the diaphragm and the cap became available around the same time (although the one which gave women greatest control over their own fertility, the contraceptive pill, was not available until the 1960s). Many people objected to these new methods, and many still relied on the older ways of stopping conception – abstaining from sex, getting married later in life, illegal abortion and withdrawal before ejaculation. In any case, however, the outcome was falls in the birth and fertility rates.

Variations in the birth rate

The birth rate has fluctuated – moved up and down – since the early twentieth century. In particular, there were increases – against the general downward trend – just after World Wars I and II (1914–18; 1939–45). These did not last long. After World War I, there were many women who were unable to get married and have children because women outnumbered men (due to deaths in the war). There was also considerable unemployment, so some people put off marriage in the hope of being better able to afford it later.

There was another increase in the birth rate between around 1954 and 1964. This is sometimes called the **baby boom**. It seems to have been the result of many women deciding to have children at that time. As the economic situation improved with recovery from the war, many older women who had put off starting a family had babies. At the same time, younger women started families earlier; it was no longer as important to work for several years after marriage to save money. So a lot of births were crammed into a short period. The baby boom was followed by a lower birth rate for the next ten years or so.

Once there has been a baby boom, there will be another one, on a slightly smaller scale, around twenty-five years later. This is simply because there will be more women than usual reaching the ages when most women have children. Understanding these trends is very important for planning schools, for example how many teachers and classrooms will be needed.

The number of single mothers does not seem to be related to the birth rate. While it is true that there are more lone parents (see the section on Lone-parent families in Chapter 7), this does not mean a rise in the number of children, just that more parents are choosing to (or having to) bring up their children alone.

Other statistics

Related sets of statistics which demographers produce and analyse, include the following:

- The average number of children a woman has. Many people think the average is 2.4 children, after the TV sitcom of that name. In fact, the figure has been falling steadily and is now around 1.75 children.
- The average age at which women start to have children. This has been rising steadily; more women put off having their first child until they are in their late twenties or even older. Reasons for this are:
  - that it has become much safer to have children later in life
  - that problems with the baby or mother's health can be detected more quickly
  - that more women want to progress in their careers before taking time off work to have a family.

The rise in life expectancy also means that those who become parents at what would once have seemed to be a late stage in life (say, in their forties) can still expect to see their children grow up.

- The percentage of women who do not have children at all, whether through choice or infertility. The choice is made possible by birth control. The contraceptive pill is important because it puts the woman in control; she does not have to trust the man to use contraception. It is now possible for women to have active sex lives without having children. The choice is also connected to women's greater independence and commitment to careers. The percentage of women who have not had children by the age of 45 is around 20 per cent; for those ten years older it was around 12 per cent.

- The number of abortions. Abortion became legal in 1967, and the number of abortions increased after then to around 150 000 a year. Before abortion was legalised it was often done in secret in dangerously unsanitary conditions by unskilled people, and could result in the death of the mother. Although abortion remains controversial because of arguments about exactly when a foetus becomes a baby, it is now an option available to women through the health service.

Life expectancy

At the same time as the death rate fell, **life expectancy** went up. This means that on average people lived longer.

Life expectancy at birth

Year	Men	Women
1901	45.5	49
1961	67.8	73.6
1993	73.6	78.9

Women's life expectancy has always been several years higher than men's. Boys and men have a higher risk of dying young in accidents, war and so on. A much higher proportion of people reach old age, and even advanced old age, than used to be the case.

QUESTIONS

1. What is meant by the birth rate?
2. What is the relationship between the death rate and the birth rate?
3. Why was there a 'baby boom' in the late 1950s?
4. Why has the average age at which women have their first child been rising?
5. How did the contraceptive pill affect women's choices about sex and family?

ROUND-UP

The birth rate and fertility rate were once very high but fell at the same time as the death rate fell in the late nineteenth century. They have fluctuated since then but the overall trend has been downward. There is now concern about the low level of births.

VOCABULARY

Vulcanisation: a way of treating rubber to make it more elastic and strong
Contraception: ways of preventing pregnancy
Abortion: ending a pregnancy by removing the foetus

Britain's changing population

KEY FOCUS

This section looks at some of the ways the population of Britain is changing: the changing proportions of people of different ages, of different backgrounds and where they live.

Population by gender and age, UK, 1997

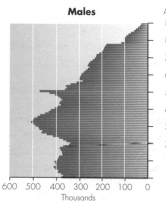
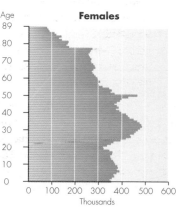

Social Trends Pocketbook 1999.

Can you spot the baby boom?

Gender and age

How long people can expect to live is still increasing.

Women still live longer than men on average. Although slightly more boys than girls are born, they are less likely to survive into old age. This means that among older people, women outnumber men.

Look at the chart of population by gender and age above. Identify the approximate ages at the time of this chart of the 'baby boom' generation. This will be where there is a 'peak' in the pyramid.

There is an earlier, smaller peak among people born just after World War II. This helped create the later peak because there were more women of child-bearing age. On the other hand, there were a low number of births in the middle and late 1970s, so that, at the time of writing this book, there are a smaller number of people in their mid- twenties.

Age

As you study the chart of population aged 65 and over, it is important to remember that the number of people alive is related to the number born. So as the 'baby boom' generation

Population aged 65 and over

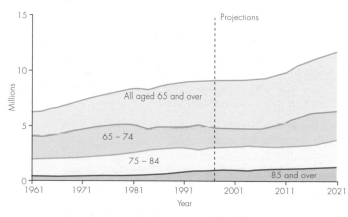

Social Trends Pocketbook 1998.

reaches retirement age, the number of people aged 65 and over will increase steeply.

From the chart, when, approximately, will this be?

We have already seen that the birth rate fell as the death rate fell in the late nineteenth century. At the moment, both are fairly steady, but there has been concern that the number of births may fall so far that the population begins to fall. If more women choose to have fewer children (and probably later in life) or none at all, then the number of babies born may be less than the number of people dying. This has been called the **birth dearth**.

The United Nations has predicted that by 2050 the British population will have started to fall, though only slightly. Other European countries, because of the ages of their populations, face a more serious situation. Looking even further ahead, the United Nations says that the population of Europe could fall by a half in a hundred years.

This situation is serious because of its consequences for social structures:

- A smaller population would have a much higher proportion of older people, who use the welfare state more than others. Fewer people would be working and paying taxes at the same time as governments needed more money to spend on welfare.
- Fewer people means fewer customers for services and goods. This could weaken the economy and lead to a recession.

In practice, it is unlikely that the United Nations' predictions will become reality. This is because they are projections based on what is happening at the moment. It is likely that governments will intervene to change the situation. There are two ways to do this:

■ By encouraging people to have more children.
■ By encouraging **immigration**.

Region

There are significant differences in population structures between different parts of Britain.

The map shows that although overall 21 per cent of the population were aged under 16, they were not evenly distributed around Britain. The highest percentage was 28 per cent, in the western parts of Northern Ireland, while the lowest percentages were in Edinburgh, Dorset and the Isle of Wight.

This is only one example of regional differences. Other differences include:

■ **Population density** – the number of people per square mile. The highest population density is in the south east of England.
■ Older people. Areas such as the south coast of England

have higher percentages of older people because they are attractive areas to retire to. However, they also require younger people to provide the services retired people require.

■ Family types – for example, there are more single parent households in the north of England.
■ Some cities, such as Sheffield, have high numbers of young adults because they have large universities and colleges.
■ Coastal and holiday areas have a higher population in the summer because they attract tourists, and also people working in the tourism industry.
■ Some areas are experiencing depopulation, that is, the population is falling. These are usually countryside areas where there are fewer jobs than in the past. Young people move away to look for work, leaving an ageing population.

There are some clear differences between the north and south of England. These differences show in other ways, such as the types of jobs available. This has led some people to suggest that there is a North-South divide. There are also significant related regional differences in poverty, unemployment, wage rates, cost of living and house prices.

Percentage of people aged under 16 by area, UK, 1997

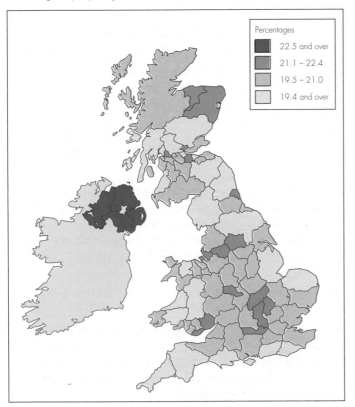

Percentages

■	22.5 and over
■	21.1 – 22.4
■	19.5 – 21.0
□	19.4 and over

Social Trends Pocketbook 1999.

QUESTIONS

1 What is meant by the birth dearth?

2 What is meant by depopulation?

3 Identify and explain two ways in which governments could respond to a falling population.

4 Identify and explain three ways in which population structure can vary between regions.

5 Do you think there is a North-South divide in England? Use the information here and your own knowledge.

ROUND-UP

Britain's population structure can be considered in terms of gender, age, region and other differences.

VOCABULARY

Tax allowance: an amount of income which is free of tax
Recession: a fall in economic activity and prosperity
Dearth: a severe shortage

The Census

KEY FOCUS

The Census is the biggest demographic survey, attempting to gather information about everyone in Britain every ten years. This section looks at how this huge operation works and what the information is used for.

count me in
Census2001

The Census – our main source of demographic information.

The Census

The **Census** is a social survey carried out every ten years in Britain. It provides a wealth of demographic information. It is the main source of information on how many people there are, where they live, the work they do and so on. Because it is carried out regularly, changes over time can be tracked.

Many other countries also have censuses. When you read that a country has a population of so many million people, this will almost always be the result of a census.

In Britain there has been a census every ten years since 1801.The only exception to this was 1941, during World War II; this was because it was thought that the information gathered by the Census would be useful to the enemy. Before 1801 there were several 'one-off' censuses. The best known of these is the Domesday Book in 1086, when William I, having conquered England, ordered a detailed survey of land and property so that he knew about the kingdom he now ruled.

Over the years the Census has developed and changed. Since 1841 every household must fill in a form on a certain day (always a Sunday, since this is when most people are at home). Since 1961 computers have been used to analyse the results. It is still often several years before the full reports can be published. Although people's names and addresses have to go on the forms, the results do not contain information about any individuals or families. The forms are kept locked up for 100 years.

The 2001 Census

The most recent Census, the twentieth full Census, was in 2001. At the time of writing, no results were available. Teams of temporary workers called enumerators delivered leaflets to every household several weeks before the day. Each enumerator was responsible for about 200 households. Then they delivered Census forms to every household several days before Census day, and tried to ensure that homeless people received them too. Forms were available in several languages. The enumerators collected them afterwards, and the forms were sent off for processing. Details of every person staying in that household on that day had to be entered on the Census form. It is against the law not to fill in a Census form.

The 1991 Census

The most recent Census for which full results are available cost about £135 million – 115,000 enumerators were employed, as well as about 1800 temporary staff at the centre in Titchfield, Hampshire, where the completed forms were processed.

In 1991 new questions were asked for the first time about people's ethnic origins and about long-term illnesses. Previously it had been thought that ethnicity was too controversial a topic to ask about.

The 1991 Census missed out more people than ever before. The Census is meant to be a complete count of everyone in the country, but it is thought, using information from other surveys and sources, that about 2 million people were missed out. Some people have always tried to avoid the Census because they are suspicious about what the information might be used for. In the past, men thought they might be conscripted into the army, or have to pay more tax.

There were two main reasons why the 1991 Census missed so many people:

- The poll tax, or community charge. At the time of the 1991 Census many people were trying to avoid paying this controversial tax. People who had managed to avoid being put on the poll tax register reasoned that if they filled in a Census form, their details would be passed on to the poll tax authorities. They therefore avoided filling in a Census form despite the possibility of being taken to court and fined if they were caught. The poll tax was later abolished and replaced by the council tax, which does not use a list of individuals and so is less controversial.

- Homelessness. As a result of government policies in the 1980s, there had been a big increase in the number of people who were homeless. While enumerators made efforts to find people in shelters and hostels, and even in places where homeless people were known to be, they inevitably missed out some of those sleeping rough. Only 2700 people were found sleeping rough, with none at all in Birmingham or Cardiff. The real figure was probably much higher.

What the Census is used for

Census results, and information from other demographic research, can help the government and civil service plan ahead. They help governments plan how much money to give to local authorities:

- Education. If the government knows how many babies were born in a certain year, it knows how many school places will be needed, and how many teachers. It may need to increase or cut the number of places for people training to be teachers.
- Health. The government can train the required number of doctors, nurses and other health workers, and provide the type and quality of care needed.

- Housing. Local authorities can plan for groups with particular needs, such as the elderly and people with disabilities. Demand for more homes in the private sector can also be predicted.
- Transport. Information can be gathered on how people travel; how many have cars, how they travel to work and so on. This can help planning of public transport and new roads.

FIND OUT FOR YOURSELF

Your nearest big library will have the most recent Census findings about your area. Go to look at these and see what other kinds of information the Census gathers. Alternatively, your school library or geography department may have some summaries of information from the Census.

QUESTIONS

1. How often is the Census carried out?
2. Why is the Census done on a Sunday?
3. Identify and explain two reasons why the 1991 Census missed out quite a lot of people.
4. What are the Census results used for?
5. Why are the Census forms (rather than the findings based on them) kept locked up for 100 years?

ROUND-UP

The census is the most important survey producing demographic information. This expensive yet vital operation helps government plan policies. In 1991 about 2 million people were missed out because of the poll tax and homelessness.

VOCABULARY

Enumerator: temporary Census worker, delivering and collecting the forms

Conscription: when people are made to join the armed forces

Too many people?

KEY FOCUS   Is it true that the increase in world population is a threat to the survival of everyone? Will there soon be overpopulation – too many people, all needing to be fed and all using up the world's resources?

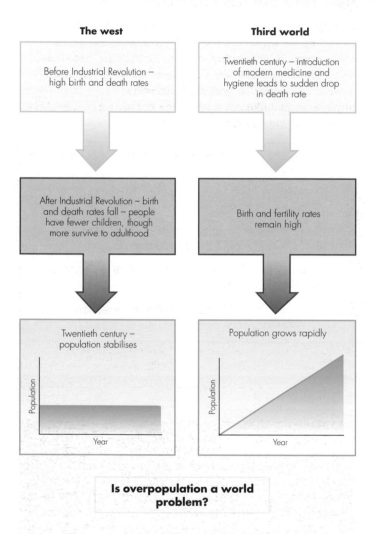

The west

Before Industrial Revolution – high birth and death rates

After Industrial Revolution – birth and death rates fall – people have fewer children, though more survive to adulthood

Twentieth century – population stabilises

Population / Year

Third world

Twentieth century – introduction of modern medicine and hygiene leads to sudden drop in death rate

Birth and fertility rates remain high

Population grows rapidly

Population / Year

Is overpopulation a world problem?

Overpopulation

The idea of **overpopulation** is that there are too many people; that if there were fewer people living standards could be higher. This idea can be applied to individual third world countries, such as India, but also to the world as a whole, because of third world populations.

Populations are now only growing very slightly in most developed countries; in some they are starting to fall a little. There is no overpopulation in Europe, North America and Japan.

The countries where population is still growing fast are the developing countries of the third world. Overpopulation is most noticeable in the cities, where birth rates and migration from the countryside combine to produce high and quickly growing populations.

Why are there so many people?

The difference between the west and the third world is that in the west birth rates and death rates are now low, while in the third world the death rate has fallen while the birth rate has not (see the diagram). It may be that the high population growth in the third world is the result of a 'time lag'. Third world countries are still at the lower death rate, high birth rate stage. Birth rates have already started to fall, but not to western levels. People will have fewer children as standards of living rise. In particular, research has shown that girls who are educated, have jobs outside the home and live in towns will have small families.

At the moment, however, many third world countries have a very different age structure from western countries. There are far more young people, and less old people, as a proportion of the population than in the west. This creates difficulties. Children need to be supported, and they need to be educated. But many countries cannot afford even primary education for all their children, and many children work or scratch a living on the street in the cities. The high number of young people is likely to mean more births.

Traditional attitudes

One reason the birth and fertility rates remain high is traditional attitudes:

- It is still often seen as good to have many children. Children can work on family farms, and support their parents in old age.
- Families are often patriarchal, that is, run by the man. Even if a woman wants fewer children her husband may overrule her.
- Some religions not only approve of large families but also disapprove of contraception. The Catholic Church, which has great influence in Latin America and other parts of the world, opposes contraception and abortion.

Malthus and the population time bomb

Two hundred years ago Thomas Malthus suggested that population increased much faster than food production. This meant that populations were bound to reach a point when they could not feed themselves:

Population grows geometrically: 1, 2, 4, 8, 16, 32
Food production grows arithmetically: 1, 2, 3, 4, 5, 6

This would mean starvation and disease (which would reduce the population to a sustainable level). Malthus, who was a clergyman, said that people should put off getting married, and then not have sex until they could support children.

Was Malthus right? Even at the time, many people disagreed with him. Since then, there have been advances in agriculture, such as using pesticides and fertilisers, that mean we can grow more food. So perhaps food production can keep up with population.

The problem is inequality

The world does in fact grow enough food to feed everyone – but many people starve. The problem is one of inequality. The rich have far more than they need; they can even afford to throw food away, or feed it to pets. The poor do not even get enough to stay healthy on. If food (and the money to buy it) could somehow be distributed equally there would be no problem.

From this point of view Malthus was wrong about the relationship between population growth and hunger. He thought population growth caused hunger. In fact, they are both caused by inequality. Poor people have more children because they are poor; it is the best insurance against being even poorer. Abolish poverty, and people wouldn't need as many children. In developed countries, it is expensive to have children.

Western lifestyle

Could everyone though have the same standards of living as in the west? The answer is probably not – for environmental reasons. People in rich countries consume enormous amounts of the world's resources through their lifestyle – driving cars, eating meat and so on – and leave huge amounts of waste. If the whole world lived as we do, reserves of oil and minerals would run out, global warming would speed up and wildlife habitats would be taken over for farms and cities.

So – how many people?

How many people can the world support at a sustainable level? The answer is we don't know. It would help enormously if the west cut its consumption and changed the technology it uses. In the meantime, many third world countries, supported by the United Nations, do what they can to control population growth. Better education, health, family planning and women's rights are the way forward. The world's population will continue to grow, but perhaps the growth can be kept to a manageable level.

IT ⚑ FIND OUT FOR YOURSELF

Population Concern is an independent international charity based in Britain which works with partner organisations throughout the developing world to improve access to sexual and reproductive health services and information. Find out more about its work by visiting its web site http://www.populationconcern.org.uk. There are useful links to other sites on population.

QUESTIONS

1. What is overpopulation?

2. Identify and explain two ways in which traditional attitudes encourage population growth.

3. Explain why Malthus believed food production could never match population growth.

4. What can third world governments do to reduce population growth?

5. In what ways could western countries change their lifestyles to use resources more efficiently?

ROUND-UP

From Malthus on, many people have predicted that unchecked population growth will lead to disaster. The best way to control population growth is by educating girls and by them having control over their fertility. The world does have enough food for the 6 billion people alive today, but the unequal distribution of wealth means that many go hungry.

VOCABULARY

Abolish: get rid of
Sustainable: able to be kept at a steady level

Migration

KEY FOCUS The overall population of a nation and its composition is affected by migration as well as by birth and death rates. This section considers migration, especially in and out of Britain and why this has been a controversial issue.

In search of a better life?

Migration

People move into and out of the United Kingdom all the time. At times, more people enter than leave (immigration); at others, more people leave than enter (**emigration**). These movements have a significant effect on the population of a country and so are of concern to demographers.

It is very difficult to measure migration accurately because it is hard to separate it from short-term visits. Someone may go to another country for a short visit, then decide to stay; or may intend to move permanently but later decide to go home. For official statistics an immigrant is someone who enters a country intending to live there for a year or more, and who has not lived in that country in the past year. This definition therefore includes as immigrants people working on short-term contracts and students, all of whom would probably return home after a few years. When they do go home, they will be immigrants into their own countries according to this definition.

Net migration

Net migration figures give us the total number of people leaving in proportion to the total number entering.

There was a net outflow of people from Britain to other countries from 1900 to 1930, and again in the 1960s and 1970s. This means that more people were emigrating than immigrating. There was a net inflow from about 1930 to 1960, made up first of refugees from Nazi persecution in

Europe and later of immigrants from the West Indies and the Indian subcontinent. There has been a net inflow again since around 1980, averaging around 36 000 people a year. Over the whole century, there was a net outflow, so migration did not increase Britain's population.

Reasons for migration

Average annual international migration, by main reason for migration, UK, 1991–95 (thousands)

	Inflow	Outflow	Balance
Work-related	45	64	−19
Accompany/join partner	75	58	17
Formal study	49	11	38
Other	45	44	1
No reason stated	24	35	−11
All reasons	239	213	26

Social Trends Pocketbook 1998.

There are various reasons why people choose to move in or out of a country. The most common reasons given are shown in the table above. However, as you can see, many migrants do not give any reason.

Sociologists usually look for reasons for migration in terms of **push and pull** factors.

Push factors: reasons for leaving one country

- Lack of opportunities (for work or education)
- To escape from a low standard of living
- To escape from persecution or hostility

Pull factors: reasons for entering a particular country

- Better work and educational opportunities
- Higher standard of living
- Freedom from persecution

People who are escaping persecution can apply for asylum – special permission to be allowed into a country – and are called asylum seekers. This is not a new phenomenon; Britain has accepted people escaping persecution abroad for centuries.

New Commonwealth migrants

When politicians and the media talk about immigration, they usually mean by people from the Caribbean, Asia and Africa; and in recent years, perhaps also eastern Europe. They forget that this is only a part of the bigger picture; many people from Europe, North America and elsewhere also migrate to Britain. The word immigration can then conceal what is really meant, which is race.

During the 1950s and 1960s, Britain encouraged the immigration into Britain of working age people from what became known as the New Commonwealth. In practice this meant mainly the West Indies and the Indian subcontinent. The Old Commonwealth referred to the parts of the British Commonwealth that had been dominions and had high white populations (the result of earlier migration) – Australia, Canada and New Zealand.

Immigration from the Old Commonwealth was not controversial; that from the New Commonwealth was. The underlying reason was racist. White people were welcome, black people were not. New laws prevented people from the New Commonwealth immigrating unless they had close relatives settled here.

HINTS AND TIPS

You can find further information about Britain's ethnic minorities and their histories in Chapter 5 Ethnicity.

The future of migration

In the last ten years it has become much harder for people from poorer countries to migrate to richer countries, but easier for people from rich countries to move around. For example, citizens of the European Union (EU) countries, including Britain, can move to other EU countries very easily. Moving within Europe is easy, but it is very hard to get in. Europe's policy of keeping out people from poor countries has been called Fortress Europe.

Demographers have shown that rich countries will face problems arising from the falling birth rate and the growing proportion of elderly people. More workers will be needed – and they are not being born in sufficient numbers. The problem is more marked in countries such as Italy, Germany and Spain than in Britain. It is possible that Fortress Europe will have to dismantle the legal barriers that keep immigrants out. This will be to avoid the problems of underpopulation rather than because of more liberal attitudes.

▶ FIND OUT FOR YOURSELF

There have been many migrations in history. (The Bible describes several migrations that were probably real historical events.)

Choose one of the following, or any other migration of a large group that you know of, and investigate it using reference books, CD-ROMs and other resources such as the Internet:

- The Atlantic slave trade, which moved many black African people to America.
- The creation of the state of Israel; Jewish people from around the world moved there.
- Migration of Europeans to colonies in America, Asia, Africa and Oceania.

Design a poster to display your findings.

QUESTIONS

1. What is migration?
2. Has migration increased or decreased Britain's population over the last one hundred years? Explain your answer.
3. What is meant by push and pull factors. Explain using examples.
4. What is meant by Fortress Europe?
5. 'When people talk about immigration, they tend to forget about white immigrants.' Do you agree? Give reasons for your answer.

ROUND-UP

Migration is the movement of people between countries. It is hard to measure. People move for many reasons, which can be thought of in terms of push and pull factors. Over the last century, there has been a net outflow of people from Britain. Immigration has been a controversial political issue, but may be the best solution to emerging problems of underpopulation.

VOCABULARY

Net migration: the difference between the number emigrating and the number immigrating. There can be a net outflow (more people emigrating) or a net inflow (more people immigrating)
Dismantle: take apart
Dominions: the parts of the British Empire that were allowed to largely govern themselves, such as Australia, New Zealand and Canada

World poverty and development

KEY FOCUS One of the most striking features of the world today is also one of its most pressing problems. There is a huge gulf between rich countries and poorer countries. This section and the next examine some of the aspects of this situation.

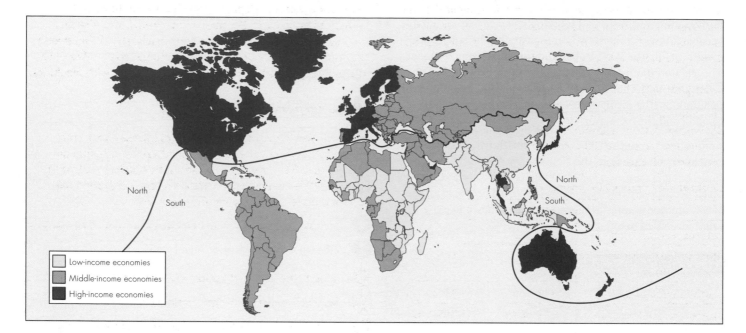

Inequality between countries.

Sociology in Focus by Taylor *et al*, Causeway 1995; based on
World Development Report 1994, World Bank

Rich world, poor world

There is considerable inequality within most countries. In the USA, for example, Bill Gates of Microsoft has a personal fortune which amounts to more than is owned by the 106 million poorest Americans (*Human Development Report*, United Nations, 1998). Even in poorer countries, there will be some rich people.

There is considerable inequality also between countries. The world is divided into a rich, developed world and a poor developing world. Until recently, many people hoped that poorer countries would catch up, but progress has been disappointing and slow in many countries.

This is not just a matter of relative poverty, with everybody becoming better off but those at the top doing so more quickly. In some parts of the world, especially in Africa, living standards are actually lower than in the recent past on some indicators (see the chapter 13 on Poverty and Welfare for an explanation of relative and absolute poverty).

Third world – or South?

There are several ways of grouping the countries of the world. One is to describe the poorer countries as the **third world**. This goes back to the Cold War, when the world was divided politically into two hostile blocks, centred on the USA and the Soviet Union. The USA and its western allies were the first world, the Soviet Union and its communist allies the second world. The rest of the world – often used as a battleground by the two blocks – was the third world.

Now that the Soviet Union no longer exists, it makes sense to see the world simply as two worlds. One easy way of doing this is to use a map of the world – because on the whole the rich world can be called the North and the poor world the South.

The terms minority world (for developed countries) and **majority world** (for the rest) draw attention to the fact that the majority of people live in the poorer countries, and that only a privileged minority live in the richer countries.

■   Rich world: North America, Europe, Japan, Australia and

New Zealand. Economically developed. Previously countries with empires and colonies, or 'lands of white settlement' – settled by Europeans with the indigenous people exploited or even exterminated.

■ Poor world: South and Central America, the Caribbean, Africa, most of Asia. Economically less developed. Previously colonies of the rich world. High illiteracy, poor diets, deaths from preventable diseases. High percentage of population farming. Little diversity of industry.

Not all countries fit easily into this way of looking at the world. There are many countries in the middle, and some countries have been developing quickly, especially the so-called Asian tigers such as South Korea and Singapore.

Comparing rich and poor

The countries chosen here represent the extremes – they are at the top and bottom respectively of the *United Nations Human Development Report*, which ranks countries according to their level of **development**.

Comparing levels of development

	Canada	**Sierra Leone**
Life expectancy at birth	79 years	37 years
Infant mortality rate (per 1000)	6	164
Adult literacy rate	97%	31%
Gross national product per head	US$19 020	US$200

Human Development Report 2000, United Nations.

Measuring development

Economic growth can be measured easily; the usual way of measuring a country's economy is by working out its gross national product, that is, the total wealth a country produces in a year. However, this does not always tell us much about the quality of life. How unequally is the wealth distributed? And how much of it is spent on public goods and services, such as health and education?

The United Nations Human Development Index (HDI) measures not only the economy of countries but also life expectancy, education and the distribution of income. The UN also publishes a Gender-related Development Index which takes into account inequality between the sexes.

Sustainable development

Westerners spend $37 billion a year on pet food and perfumes. The UN says that would provide education, food, health care, water and sanitation for all those now deprived of the basics – with $9 billion to spare.

Guardian, 9 September 1996.

Many people argue that it is not possible for all poorer countries to follow the same path of industrial development as the rich countries did. Development was partly based on colonising other countries and exploiting their resources – which poorer countries today cannot do. Another reason is that the cost in damage to the environment is too high. Industrial development means using up natural resources that may not be replaceable (such as rain forests) and creating pollution.

Instead countries need to try to achieve **sustainable development**: development which does not have high environmental costs. For poorer countries, it can also mean not using the latest, most expensive machinery. What poorer countries tend to have is large populations, so it makes sense to give people work rather than replacing them with machines.

IT ▶ FIND OUT FOR YOURSELF

You will find an enormous amount of information at the *Human Development Report* web site. To start with, find out where the United Kingdom stands in the tables based on the Human Development Index (HDI) and the Gender-related Development Index: www.undp.org/hdro.

QUESTIONS

1. What percentage of people in Sierra Leone are literate?
2. What is meant by the term majority world?
3. Why is it unsatisfactory to measure development only by economic factors?
4. What factors does the Human Development Index measure to reach its assessment of how developed a country is?
5. What is meant by sustainable development and why is it important?

ROUND-UP

The world's countries are very unequal; some are rich, others poor. Development can be measured by many different factors, but it is important not to look only at economic growth and to look also at factors related to the quality of life for all.

VOCABULARY

Indigenous: native
Exterminated: wiped out

Aid and debt

KEY FOCUS   This section continues the investigation of world poverty, by looking at attempts to reduce poverty through different types of aid, at the debt crisis and at the fair trade movement.

Zimbabwe in Africa, between 1990 and 1996:

- Health and education spending were cut by a third.
- The infant mortality rate doubled.
- Unemployment went up 50 per cent.
- Wages of those who had jobs fell by a third.

The impact of the debt crisis.

Aid

Aid is help given by the rich countries to the poorer ones. It can take the form of money, goods or services. Often it is in the form of loans, which will one day have to be repaid, rather than grants.

Aid can be:

- given directly by one country to another – bilateral aid
- given through international organisations such the European Union or the World Bank – multilateral aid
- given by voluntary agencies which raise money mainly through appeals to the public.

The first two types of aid listed above are given by governments.

Voluntary agencies

Among the best known voluntary agencies in Britain which send aid are:

- Oxfam
- Christian Aid
- Action Aid
- Comic Relief
- Voluntary Service Overseas – sends people to do voluntary work.

Most agencies also campaign, raising awareness in rich countries of these issues and trying to influence government policies. (See the section on Pressure Groups in Chapter 10 Politics for more information.)

Does aid help?

The United Nations recommends that rich countries give a minimum of 0.7 per cent of their gross domestic product (GDP) as aid. Almost all give far less.

Aid has been given for many years, yet the problem of world poverty remains unsolved. What has gone wrong?

The view of governments and most agencies is that aid is important and does help; things would be even worse without aid. However, the agencies also say that some aid is inappropriate or inefficient. Aid needs to be targeted at the people who need it most. Too much aid has actually been harmful. Too many aid projects:

- are too large
- need highly paid foreign experts (rather than providing jobs for local people)
- are based on a lack of understanding of local conditions
- ignore the wishes of local people
- are damaging to the environment.

Aid by governments is not purely charity – it is often influenced by self-interest. A lot of aid has gone to countries that are better off than the poorest:

- It goes to those countries with whom the donor country has historical links; for example, much British aid goes to Commonwealth countries, most of which were once British colonies.
- It goes to those countries which the donor country sees as a valuable trading partner.
- It goes to those countries whose political system and government the donor country approves of.

Among the countries receiving a large amount of aid are China, Egypt, Indonesia and Israel. None of these are among the world's poorest countries.

Some writers believe that aid is so harmful that poor countries would actually be better off without it:

- Aid creates dependency – New Right thinkers see aid much as they see social security and welfare in their own countries (see Chapter 13 Poverty and Welfare). Aid can take away people's will to look after themselves, making them lazy. The New Right blames world poverty today not on the history of colonialism but on the inefficiency of southern governments, who are seen as wasting money and not trying to help their people.

- Aid is imperialism – Marxist and other thinkers see aid as a way in which rich countries keep control of the poorer ones, and prevent them developing. Aid from this point of view wasn't ever intended to end poverty – it's a sort of confidence trick that keeps things as they are.

The debt crisis

Many poorer countries owe a lot of money to richer countries. This is because in the past, especially the 1970s and 1980s, western banks had a large amount of money – and banks can only make money by loaning it for investment. Money was lent to poorer countries at high interest rates. The global economy then began to work against many poorer countries – the prices of exports like coffee fell – and they found it hard to keep up the interest payments, leading to a **debt crisis**.

It became clear that paying interest would keep many countries poor far into the future. The organisation Jubilee 2000 began to campaign for the cancellation of debts. Western governments gradually agreed to some debts being written off, but insisted on imposing strict conditions about economic policies on governments of the debtor countries. These strict conditions often involve a fall in living standards for many people; the government may be told to cut its health and education spending to 'balance the books'.

The result has been social unrest in many countries. One of the best-known examples is the Zapatista uprising in Mexico.

The debt crisis hurts everyone

The writer Susan George has argued that the debt crisis has affected rich countries too – we experience what she calls the 'debt boomerang':

- Environment – poorer countries are forced to exploit their natural resources quickly and cheaply, for example by cutting down rain forests. The result is global warming and loss of animal and plant species.
- Drugs – some poorer countries can only make money through one export to the rich world, that is illegal drugs.
- Immigration – many people flee from poverty, trying to enter the rich world.
- Unemployment – jobs are lost in rich countries when countries in debt cannot afford to import the goods we produce.

Everyone agrees that most of the debts are unpayable but the negotiations over how much debt to wipe off, for which countries and when have been going on for a long time with only slow progress.

Fair trade

Free trade – the way the economic system normally works – is supposed to help poor people and poor countries. However, the producers in southern countries receive very little of the price their product eventually sells for in a western shop or supermarket.

A way of helping southern producers which has been growing quickly in recent years is the **fair trade** movement. Fair trade involves a long-term partnership between producers and organisations in the rich world. They work together to improve the livelihood of producers and to make western consumers aware of what happens. Fairly traded products (usually coffee, tea, chocolate, cocoa, honey and bananas) are now available in many shops and supermarkets.

FIND OUT FOR YOURSELF

Find out more about fair trade by watching out for fairly traded products in the shops. They can usually be identified by clear labelling. Often there is a brief explanation on the packaging about how you are helping by buying the product.

QUESTIONS

1. Name three voluntary organisations working in the field of world poverty.

2. What is the difference between bilateral and multilateral aid?

3. Identify and explain three ways in which rich countries are affected by the 'debt boomerang'.

4. Does aid help the South? Give reasons for your answer.

5. In what ways can ordinary people in a rich country like Britain help end world poverty?

ROUND-UP

The poverty of the Third World is improved little, if at all, by the present situation with regard to aid, debt and trade. Within each of these three areas, however, there are movements for and signs of change.

VOCABULARY

Donor: the person giving
Interest rates: the rate at which charges are made for borrowed money

Living in cities

KEY FOCUS Today, about three-quarters of the British population lives in towns and cities of more than 20 000 people. Living among large numbers of other people is a common experience. This has not, however, been the case throughout most of history.

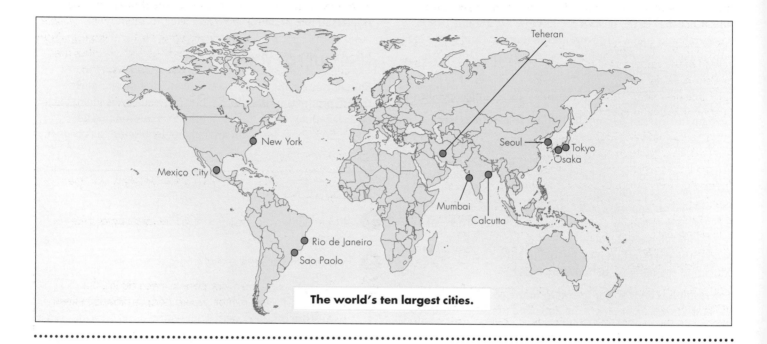

The world's ten largest cities.

History of cities

The earliest people were hunter-gatherers, on the move continuously in search of water and food. When farming began, people were able to settle down in one place. They needed to protect themselves and their food from people who had not turned to farming and who saw them as an easy supply of food. They built walls or fences around their homes and fields. This was the beginning of towns and cities. Settlements were usually near rivers so that water could be obtained easily.

The earliest cities date from between 3000 and 4000 BCE. Some of the great cities of the ancient world were Thebes and Memphis (in Egypt), Babylon and Nineveh (in Mesopotamia), Carthage, Jerusalem, Athens and Rome. Before the modern period, there were also great cities in Africa, America, China and India.

Cities made it possible to have a division of labour; that is, not everyone had to be a farmer or engaged in producing food in some way. With cities came merchants and traders, priests, professional warriors, government officials and even artists, musicians and so on.

Urbanisation

Starting just before the Industrial Revolution of the mid-eighteenth century, there was a big increase in the numbers of people living in towns and cities. Large numbers of people migrated from the countryside to the rapidly growing towns where there was work in factories. This meant that the proportion of the population living in towns and cities increased considerably. This process is called **urbanisation**.

The urbanisation of England and Wales

Year	Percentage of population living in towns with over 10 000 inhabitants
1801	33
1851	50
1901	80

Urban Growth and Change in Britain by P. Lawless and F. Brown, HarperRow, 1986.

The size of the cities was also a new development. In the early eighteenth century, the five biggest cities apart from London – Bristol, Exeter, Newcastle, Norwich and York – all had populations of less than 20 000. Yet in the early eighteenth century huge cities grew rapidly from what had once been villages: Manchester, Liverpool and Birmingham. By 1850, Liverpool had nearly 400 000 people, Manchester more than 300 000.

These three great cities grew as a result of industrialisation. Their factories and industries provided jobs that people moved from the countryside to take. Those who had moved there outnumbered people who were native to the cities.

Other cities and towns grew as a result of related changes. The spread of the railways led to the growth of railway towns such as Crewe, Derby and Swindon. Seaside resorts grew to cater for the huge new populations in the cities; for example, people in Liverpool and Manchester could go on day trips to Blackpool.

London was different in that it already had a population much larger than anywhere else in Britain. It had been a trading, financial and artistic centre for many years before the Industrial Revolution. Urbanisation had therefore happened much earlier in London than elsewhere in Britain. But it too grew rapidly at the time the new cities were growing: from 1 million people in 1800 to more than 6 million in 1900. This growth was largely a result of London's position as the capital of the British Empire, which during this time expanded rapidly.

Life in the new cities was difficult and unpleasant for many people. The growth of the cities was not planned. Many people lived in cramped and dirty conditions, without running water or sewers, paved roads or street lighting. Improvements to **urban** life such as parks came later. There was a lot of poverty and high death rates. Cities, however, provided opportunities that the country could not, and many lived in hope of gradually improving their lot.

The government and the higher classes were worried by the new city populations. They feared unrest, riots and even revolution (France had had a revolution in 1789). Cities brought people together and made it possible for them to campaign with others to change their situation. Thus cities played a part in the growth of trade unions and of political movements like socialism.

Urbanisation in less developed countries

Cities have also grown enormously in poorer countries in Asia, Africa and Central and South America. Some cities have grown from settlements that were present before colonisation; others were created during the colonial period as ports or as industrial or administrative centres. In some countries one city is far larger than all others. Often parts of a city are modern and well planned, while other parts are 'shanty towns', built by the people living there from whatever materials they can find.

The movement of people from country areas to cities continues around the world. For many, cities still seem to offer 'streets paved with gold' – a chance to make a living and perhaps achieve something. They also offer contact with the global culture of the modern world – international brands of soft drinks, fast food and fashion; music, films and so on.

The growth of cities in less developed countries has been much faster than the developed world's earlier urbanisation. It has also been said that third world cities tend to drain people and resources from their hinterlands (the **rural** areas around them) and provide little in return. Many – often most – people cannot find jobs and survive by begging and scavenging. From this, some people have concluded that third world cities are too big, and have described this as **overurbanisation**.

QUESTIONS

1. What is urbanisation?

2. Name three British cities that grew rapidly during the Industrial Revolution.

3. Which British city was already very large before the Industrial Revolution?

4. What are shanty towns?

5. Although conditions were poor in cities during the Industrial Revolution, many more people moved to them than left. Why was this?

ROUND-UP

Cities have existed for thousands of years. At the time of the Industrial Revolution Britain experienced urbanisation, an increase in the proportion of the population living in cities. Conditions were poor at first, but slowly improved. Urbanisation in less developed countries is sometimes seen as overurbanisation.

VOCABULARY

Division of labour: when work is organised in a way that allows people to specialise

Colonisation: the taking over of a country by another country, turning it into a colony

Hinterland: the area around a city that depends on it and supplies it

City life today

Until the second half of the twentieth century cities in Britain had been growing. This began to change; more people chose to live outside cities. This section looks at the trends for people to move to the country, to suburbs and to new towns, and at how cities have responded to this.

London's docklands transformed – for better or worse?

Deurbanisation

In the last 30 years or so, people have been moving away from British towns and cities and to the countryside and suburbs. Larger cities such as Liverpool have been losing population and some smaller towns and villages have been growing as people move in. The growth of the suburbs – housing areas around the outskirts of cities – is called **suburbanisation**. The movement away from cities is called **deurbanisation** or counter-urbanisation.

It is not just people who move out of cities, it is also jobs. In the past, businesses were often in city centres, in what was called the **central business district**. Many moved out, however, to new business parks and investment areas outside the city. Shops have also moved out, to out-of-town shopping centres and 'retail villages'.

Suburbs

The first suburbs were for the middle classes, so that they did not have to live near to the working classes in city centres. By the twentieth century, however, many workers also lived in suburbs, commuting to their work using the newly developing public transport of buses, trams and trains.

Suburbs were often seen as pleasant places to live, with larger houses with gardens, less noise and bustle than inner cities and so on. Later, however, many people associated them with dullness and conformity; they seemed to be too safe compared to the vibrant life of the cities.

New towns

New towns have been built and people from cities encouraged to move there. One of the largest new towns is Milton Keynes in Buckinghamshire, which covers what were once several small villages. Other new towns include Runcorn, Washington, Stevenage, Telford, Irvine, Bracknell and Basildon.

Because new towns are carefully planned and built, they are very different in design from towns that have grown in a piecemeal fashion over hundreds of years. New towns often try to incorporate some of what are seen as the good points of country life; for example, there will be lots of parks and green areas. One particular early type of new town, the **garden city** (such as Welwyn Garden City and Letchworth), tried to combine the best of both city and country in carefully planned communities where working-class and middle-class people would mix and get on.

Reasons for deurbanisation

Why have people been moving out of cities?

- It has become much easier to commute to work. Many people used to live in towns and cities because they had to be near to their work. Owning a car makes it possible to live many miles away from work. Some people are also able to work from home.
- Cities, especially inner cities, are associated with social problems, for example crime and pollution.
- The countryside, on the other hand, is associated with a more relaxed lifestyle, belonging to a community and so on.

Whether cities and countryside are really like this is considered in the next section; the important thing here is that many people do believe that country life is better. Those who want to escape the inner city but stay close to the conveniences of the city may move to the suburbs.

Gentrification

As the workers who used to live in inner cities close to their workplaces moved out, the inner cities changed. Often middle-class people moved in, after property developers had improved the housing or built new housing. With the new middle-class owner-occupiers came restaurants, boutiques, delicatessens and other new shops and services aimed at the middle class. The whole feel of such areas changed dramatically. The price of houses often shot up as they became very desirable places to live for people with enough money. Local people might move out as the areas became too expensive for them to live in. Areas of London that have been gentrified include the Docklands, Islington and Hampstead.

A middle-class takeover of a previously working-class area is called **gentrification**.

Regeneration

Governments and local government have tried to keep cities alive as people and jobs have been lost. They have tried to revive inner-city areas through **regeneration**, moving away from the old reliance on industry. Instead, cities increasingly turn to the following:

- Cultural attractions – tourists and other visitors are encouraged to come. Cities advertise themselves, promoting their old buildings, museums, galleries and shops. Sometimes they 'theme' themselves, as, for example, a 'city of culture'. New service sector jobs are created.
- New city centre shopping areas, such as shopping malls – trying to attract shoppers back from the out-of-town developments that were built as cities declined.
- Sport can play a role in regenerating some cities. Sheffield's hosting of the World Student Games in 1992 was intended to bring new jobs and facilities. Manchester's unsuccessful attempts to host the Olympic Games have been part of plans to revive the city.

The Docklands

The docks area of the East End of London used to be the home of thousands of dock workers and their families. In the 1960s the dock industry declined and the use of containers meant fewer workers were needed; the area decayed The docklands area was rebuilt completely in the late 1980s and early 1990s, with new offices and residences. Did this regenerate the area?

- Those that say 'Yes' point to the creation of new jobs and new housing and offices.
- Those that say 'No' point out that local people could not afford the new housing and that the new jobs were white collar ones for which local people often did not have the qualifications.

So the Docklands was a controversial development. It required huge amounts of government spending, but arguably did little to help local people.

There were similar controversial dockland developments in Liverpool and at Leith in Edinburgh.

FIND OUT FOR YOURSELF

Imagine that you live in an area that is beginning to become gentrified. What are the possible advantages and disadvantages for you and your community? Draw up a list of the arguments.

QUESTIONS

1. What is gentrification?
2. What is deurbanisation?
3. How is a new town different from an 'old' town?
4. Why did middle-class people in the nineteenth century find the idea of living in the suburbs attractive?
5. Identify and explain two ways in which cities that have lost their old industries can be revived.

ROUND-UP

Since the 1960s many cities have experienced deurbanisation as people and jobs have been lost to the countryside, suburbs and new towns. There have been attempts to regenerate cities and city centres but these have often been controversial. Some old working-class areas have been gentrified as more prosperous people have moved in and taken over, pushing up the price of housing.

VOCABULARY

Commuting: travelling regularly between home and work
Conformity: being the same as everyone else
Containers: vast boxes to carry cargo. From the 1960s cargo was moved in large containers; this reduced the number of dock workers needed

City and country life

KEY FOCUS

By bringing large numbers of people together, the city created a new way of life. This urban way of life has often been contrasted with country life, which is seen as much better. In fact, there are both positive and negative aspects to both city and country life.

Living in the country – what's the reality?

City life

Many writers have argued that the growth of cities created a new kind of social life. Previously people had lived in small communities where everyone knew each other. City life was said to be different because:

- most social interaction is between people who do not know each other and will probably never meet again – people have contact with others only in one role (as a bus driver, or shop assistant and so on), and for short periods
- people live close to many others, and to people they do not know
- people from a wide variety of backgrounds live close together, for example from different classes and ethnic groups.

These ideas can be taken further. For example, it can be argued that there is more crime in cities because of the nature of city life; people can lose themselves in the crowd, steal from strangers and so on. In a small rural community, there would only be a few suspects for any crime; in a city, there might be thousands.

It has also been suggested that city life gives people a wide

choice of lifestyle, whereas in a small community the opinions of family and local people restrict this choice. People can reinvent themselves and adopt new images and identities.

Country life

Writers who take the above view of city life often contrast cities with the countryside. The country is seen in a romantic way as everything the city is not. The country is seen as crime free and problem free; people know each other and look after each other; life is slower but more rewarding. This is a very popular view. It can be seen in paintings and books, and even in packaging and merchandising. A picture of a country cottage, for example, may be used to sell many different products.

Is it really like that?

The city

These views of both city and country life, while they have some truth in them, are also exaggerated.

There are communities in cities. While it is possible to lose yourself in the crowd, many people living in cities feel they belong to a community. This situation is shown in soap operas like *Eastenders* and *Coronation Street*. The term **urban village** has been used to describe communities that happen to be in cities, but in other respects are like villages. There may be recognisable social centres (a pub, for example), local clubs and associations and so on that create a sense of belonging. People may live in a huge city, yet belong to a small part of it.

The country

Country life is not nearly as ideal as it is sometimes shown to be. Rural areas were always sharply divided by class: there were landowners, tenant farmers (who did not own the land they farmed) and farm workers.

These are some of the problems of country life:

- A shortage of jobs, especially for young people, who may have to leave home to find work.
- A lack of services and amenities. It may be a long way to the nearest school, post office, bank, library, doctor and so on. Many village shops have closed and services have been lost in recent years.
- Little public transport. There are fewer buses, so it has become almost essential to have a car. Yet some people cannot afford cars, and some – the young and the old – may not be able to drive anyway.
- Many jobs, such as those on farms, are low paid.
- People may feel lonely and isolated.
- Young people may feel bored and frustrated, and this may lead to delinquency and petty crime. The countryside is not free of vandalism or more serious crime.

The countryside has also been changed by deurbanisation. In many areas people who used to live in cities have moved in, often commuting to work in the city. They are attracted by the myth of country life. In fact, their arrival can make problems worse. There can be tension between locals and 'incomers'. The new arrivals may cause resentment by not taking part in community life, or they may do so in a way that annoys locals, by trying to change things quickly.

Sometimes houses are bought by outsiders for use only at weekends or as holiday homes. This means there are fewer homes for local people, and those that are available are more expensive, because the increased demand has pushed up the price. Young adults may not be able to find anywhere to live. The population during the week will be smaller, so local shops and businesses will find it even harder to keep going.

Ownership of second homes can contribute to the decline of a village community. The problems are even worse when the second homeowners are clearly different from the locals; in parts of Wales there has been great resentment about English people buying second homes. The Welsh language is strongest in rural areas, so the arrival of English speakers can seem to threaten language and culture.

Shared problems

The reality then is that both city and country life have similar problems: unemployment, low pay, poverty, even social isolation (it is as easy to be lonely in a city as in the countryside). Both city and country too have social divisions between groups with different interests, for example based on class and status. The problems are sometimes less visible in the countryside, but they are still there.

▶ FIND OUT FOR YOURSELF

'The myth of country life.' Explore what is meant by this. Collect as many examples as you can find of country life being shown as free of problems, with happy, friendly village communities. You could start with: television series, advertising (including labels), paintings, etc. Make a note also of any examples you come across of this stereotype being broken. Present your findings to the class.

QUESTIONS

1. What is an urban village?
2. Identify two ways in which, according to some writers, city life is different from life in smaller communities.
3. Identify and explain three problems in rural areas.
4. What problems are found in both urban and rural areas?
5. What could be done to improve life in rural areas? Give reasons for your suggestions.

ROUND-UP

City life has often been seen in negative ways, and contrasted with country life which is seen as better. These contrasts are exaggerated. In both city and country communities there are social tensions and inequalities as well as more positive aspects of life. Communities can exist in both city and country.

VOCABULARY

Romantic: imaginary and idealistic
Merchandising: how goods are displayed

Population and development – sociology in practice

People pressure

'THE global population doubled between 1950 and 1987 and is now 6 billion. It took over 100 years for the world population to double from 1.25 billion to 2.5 billion, but only 37 years for the next doubling. World population rises by about 87 million people a year.

Is there a population time bomb? Will the world be able to support an ever growing population – or will there be growing problems of famine and war as we fight over limited resources?

In fact there is a hopeful trend. World population growth began to slow down in the 1990s. The cause was a decline in fertility. In 1950 women worldwide had an average of 5 children. By 1995, the average was 2.9 children. If this continues, the population of many countries will stabilise in the next century. Europe's population is stable and expected to decline. China's population should stabilise within 40 years. But some countries with high population growth will face the dilemma of how to satisfy the basic needs of their populations.'

Adapted from *The A to Z of World Development*
by Andy Crump, New Internationalist
Publications, 1998.

Questions

 Describe the trends in world population growth outlined above.

Look back at the section on Birth and fertility rates (pages 350–51). Many experts now think that educating women and helping them to help themselves is the key to controlling population growth. Why do you think this is?

The passage implies that stable, and even falling, populations would be a good thing from a global point of view. Why might governments concerned only about their own population take a different view?

Country life

Item 1

LIFE is better in countryside Britain, according to a new government study, 'Population Trends 91'. Rural dwellers have advantages over urban dwellers – they have better jobs and health, bigger houses and more cars. One in three households is headed by somebody with a professional or managerial job, compared with fewer than one in four of city households.

Despite popular ideas about invasions by 'townies', the numbers living in the country have not gone up much. There is still plenty of green space.

The study includes no comparisons of incomes and services, which might cast a different light on rural life. The figures for rural areas also include people for whom their country home is a second home.

Adapted from 'Life is better in countryside Britain'
by David Brindle, *Guardian*,
20 March 1998.

Item 2

VILLAGE life is grinding to a halt as scores of shops, post offices, pubs, banks and building societies close, according to research by the National Federation of Women's Institutes. Rural life is also being damaged by shortages of police, public transport and cheap housing. Twenty-five per cent of villages had no primary school, 71 per cent had no regular police presence, 30 per cent had no village shop and 24 per cent no post office. The threat to village shops was increasing as there were more supermarkets within driving distance.

Adapted from 'Village life grinds to a halt as banks, shops and buses vanish'
by James Meikle, *Guardian*,
6 July 1999.

Questions

1 Look back at the section City and country life (pages 368–9). Look at item 1 above. What other advantages to rural life can you add?

2 Look at items 1 and 2. What kinds of people have a better quality of life in the countryside? Who is affected most by the changes described in item 2?

3 How different is city life from country life?

A greying population?

> 'N 1999 some 40 per cent of the UK population were aged 50 and over. By 2020 this figure will have risen to 50 per cent. In twenty years time, one half of all British people will be over 50 years old.'
>
> Office for National Statistics, 1999.

Questions

1 Look back at the sections Studying population (pages 348–9) and Birth and fertility rates (pages 350–51). Why has the proportion of the population over 50 grown? (Hint: you need to consider the fall in the birth rate as well as rising life expectancy.)

2 What social and economic problems might result from a continuing rise in the proportion of the population over 50? What reasons are there for thinking that the proportion will stop rising?

3 How is the age structure of Britain different from the age structures of many third world countries?

Population and development – important terms

aid	help or assistance, usually financial
baby boom	an increase in the number of babies born
birth dearth	the recent fall in number of babies born in some countries
birth rate	the number of babies born per 1000 population in a year
census	a government survey of everyone living in a country
central business district	central area of a city with businesses, shops, etc.
death rate	the number of deaths per 1000 population in a year
debt crisis	the present situation in which many poorer countries owe money they will never be able to repay
demography	the study of population
development	the process of developing from a poor country to a rich one
deurbanisation	people moving away from cities
emigration	migration out of a country
fair trade	a new form of trade which involves ensuring that producers are adequately rewarded
fertility rate	the number of live births per 1000 women of childbearing age
garden city	a planned new city, with a lot of open spaces
gentrification	when the middle class takes over an old working-class residential area
immigration	migration into a country
infant mortality rate	the number of infants dying per 1000 population in a year
life expectancy	the number of years a person will live on average
majority world	a fairly new term for poorer countries, drawing attention to the fact that the majority (about 80 per cent) of the world's population live in these countries: Africa, Asia, Latin America and the Caribbean and parts of Oceania
migration	movement in or out of a country for a long period
net migration	the difference between the numbers immigrating and emigrating
new towns	a town planned as a complete unit
overpopulation	a population higher than can be supported
overurbanisation	when cities grow too big to support their population
population density	the number of people living in an area
push and pull	factors that influence migration
regeneration	bringing new life to a run-down area of a city, such as docks
South	a term for the poorer two-thirds of the world; see majority world
rural	relating to the country
suburbanisation	people moving to the suburbs (outer fringe of a city)
sustainable development	development which can continue without exhausting natural resources
third world	a term for the poorer two-thirds of the world; see majority world
urban	relating to towns and cities
urban village	a community like a village, but within a city
urbanisation	the process by which a growing proportion of the population live in cities

Population and development – exam style questions

Source A

Population of the United Kingdom, in thousands, 1961–96

	1961	1971	1981	1991	1996
England	43 561	46 412	46 821	48 208	49 089
Wales	2 635	2 740	2 813	2 921	2 989
Scotland	5 184	5 236	5 180	5 107	5 128
Northern Ireland	1 427	1 540	1 538	1 601	1 663
UK (total)	52 807	55 928	56 352	57 807	58 801

Sociology Update 1999, based on Office for National Statistics, General Register Office for Scotland, Northern Ireland Statistics and Research Agency.

The total population has been affected by the birth rate, the death rate, migration and longevity (increased life expectancy).

Source B

The majority of British people now live in towns and cities. This is the result of urbanisation. During the Industrial Revolution, many people left the countryside, where there were few jobs and opportunities. Cities seemed to promise a better life, with jobs in the new factories. Migration from rural to urban areas was thus the result of push and pull factors.

Foundation tier

1 Look at source A and answer these questions:
   (a) Which region of the United Kingdom had the smallest population in 1996? [1 mark]
   (b) In which region did the population fall between 1961 and 1996? [1 mark]
   (c) In which year was the total population of the United Kingdom highest? [1 mark]
   (d) What is meant by birth rate? [2 marks]
   (e) What is meant by migration? [2 marks]
   (f) What is meant by increased life expectancy? [2 marks]

2 Look at source B and answer these questions:
   (a) During which period of history was there a lot of migration from the countryside to cities? [1 mark]
   (b) Identify one 'push' factor that encouraged people to leave the countryside, and one 'pull' factor that attracted them to cities. [2 marks]
   (c) What is meant by the term urbanisation? [2 marks]

3 Identify two reasons for increased longevity (greater life expectancy). [2 marks]

4 Identify and explain two social problems in rural areas in Britain today. [4 marks]

Higher tier

1 Look at source A and answer these questions:
   (a) What is meant by birth rate? [2 marks]
   (b) What is meant by migration? [2 marks]
   (c) What is meant by increased life expectancy? [2 marks]

2 Look at source B and answer these questions:
   (a) Identify one 'push' factor that encouraged people to leave the countryside, and one 'pull' factor that attracted them to cities. [2 marks]
   (b) What is meant by the term urbanisation? [2 marks]

3 Identify two reasons for increased longevity (greater life expectancy). [2 marks]

4 Identify and explain two social problems in rural areas in Britain today. [4 marks]

5 Using sociological knowledge, discuss the ways in which rural life is similar to city life. [4 marks]

Population and development – further research

The American census site is at: www.census.gov.

You can find out all about censuses around the world at: www.censusatschool.ntu.ac.uk/files/GlobalCensus.doc.

There are several excellent sites for information on development: www.oneworld.org.

CAFOD, a Catholic development agency, has schools and young people's sections at: www.cafod.org.uk.

The *New Internationalist* magazine has a wealth of information on global issues at: www.newint.org.

Religion is a cultural universal; that is, some form of belief with associated rituals is found in every society. Religions play a leading role in much of the world's history. A large part of the sociology of religion is about whether this will continue, because some sociologists believe that religion is becoming less important, and may even die out.

As you will see, Britain is one country in which religion does seem to have become less important, or at least to have changed a lot. Yet, in most of the world religion remains a vital force. It is part of many of the conflicts going on, and part of how many discontented groups express their demands for change. There are few signs that the new century will be any different. Religion cannot be ignored – whether you yourself have any religious beliefs or not.

KEY TERMS

church
civil religion
cult
denomination
fundamentalism
New Age
New Religious Movements
religiosity
sect
secularisation

IN THIS CHAPTER YOU WILL LEARN ABOUT:

- how religion can be defined and measured
- he different types of religious organisations
- how religion is related to gender, age, class and ethnicity
- the debate about whether society is becoming less religious and more secular
- recent developments such as the rise of New Age beliefs and of fundamentalism

CHAPTER CONTENTS

What is religion?

KEY FOCUS   This section considers what it is we are studying when we study religion. This is more difficult than you might think. Sociologists do not always agree on what religion is or what purposes it serves.

Important ceremonies in life are almost always religious.

What religion is

A religion:

- has a set of beliefs about the nature of the world and the universe
- has a set of practices or rituals for its adherents (believers) to follow
- gives explanations for why things happen
- guides people on how to behave in particular situations
- usually involves belief in a god or in supernatural powers.

It is very difficult to say what religion is. Some sociologists define religion by saying that it is to do with the **sacred**. Something is sacred if it is considered extraordinary and set apart from the rest of the world. This means that people feel a sense of awe when they see them. All sorts of things can be sacred to different people: places, objects, even animals and people. Most religions have places of worship, such as churches, temples and mosques, which are regarded as sacred.

The opposite of sacred is **profane** or secular. Profane things are part of the everyday world and there is nothing special about them.

The idea of sacredness, then, means that something which might seem quite ordinary becomes extraordinary in the eyes of followers of a religion. Because people believe something is sacred, they act differently. Religion is therefore about beliefs

and behaviour. The beliefs and behaviour are shared with other people; they create communities.

Religion is also about the big questions of the nature of life, death and the universe. Faced with these questions, many people turn to religious explanations.

Institutional and personal religion

- Institutional religion is the religion of an organisation such as a **church**, its practices and rituals.
- Personal religion is the religion of an individual, usually based on an institutional religion but often today also drawing on other religious ideas, and adapted to the needs and situation of an individual.

Thinking about religion in this way means that we recognise that, for example, not everyone who belongs to a church believes the same things or practises his or her religion in the same way. It is also possible to be religious yet not belong to a church.

What religion does

Functionalism: the positive side of religion

Another way of thinking about religion is to start with a different question. Instead of asking what religion is, we can ask what it does. This approach is taken by functionalist sociologists.

The functions of religion:

- Religion can give meaning and purpose to life, and provide answers to some of the questions that trouble people. It can explain why something has happened. If someone dies, for example, it can be said that god has taken that person to live in the next world. This makes it easier for people to accept death, and easier for them to carry on with their lives. The main points of transition in our lives – birth, marriage and death – are still often marked by religious observances.
- Religion provides a way of socialising young people into the norms and values of their culture. These have an extra force because they are seen as coming from a god.
- Religion links people together in communities. It gives

them a sense of belonging, creating social solidarity. Everyone will share the same values. This helps society to function well.

The New Right

New Right thinkers argue that there has been a sharp decline in morals and behaviour in recent years. They contrast the situation today with the past – and argue that we need to return to strong religious values if we are to return to a more stable society. So, for example, New Right thinkers argue for teaching of religious beliefs and values in schools, to teach children right from wrong.

Marxism: the negative side of religion

Marxists, like functionalists, are interested in what religion does. They find this more interesting than the actual content of religion – what people believe in. So they tend to see all religions as similar because all religions play a similar role in society.

For Marxists, the role of religion is to help preserve the social order, in which a small ruling class oppresses and exploits a large working class. Religion teaches the poor that they should not protest about their situation. Instead, they should accept it as god's will that they are poor while others are rich. If they are good (which means not protesting) they are told they will get their reward after they die, for example by going to heaven. Religion acts like a drug, stopping people realising that the society they live in is based on injustice and exploitation. As Marx put it, 'Religion is the opium of the people'. Marx recognised though that religion helped people make sense of and survive in an unjust world.

Marxists find evidence for this view of religion in the teachings and practices of the main religions.

Christianity

The hymn 'All Things Bright and Beautiful' contains the lines (not often sung these days):

'The rich man in his castle, the poor man at his gate God made them high and lowly, and ordered their estate.'

Hinduism

Hindus believe that they are born into a caste (a level in society) according to how they have behaved in previous lives (see Chapter 3, page 55). This suits the high caste of priests, because the other castes assumed that those souls reborn into priestly families deserve this honour.

Feminists often have a similar negative view of religious organisations, seeing religions as playing a part in keeping women in a lower position in society. You can read more about this in the section on Gender and religion (pages 390–91).

FIND OUT FOR YOURSELF

Explore further the idea of the sacred. Choose one of the religions below (preferably one you do not know much about) and then use encyclopaedias, CD-ROMs and any other sources of information you have to compile a list of the people, places, dates and things that are considered sacred by followers of this religion:

- Islam
- Hinduism
- Buddhism
- Judaism.

QUESTIONS

1. Explain the difference between 'sacred' and 'profane'.
2. Name three things or places that are considered sacred by Christians.
3. Identify and explain two functions of religion that have been suggested by functionalists.
4. Why is religion particularly important at times such as birth, marriage and death?
5. What did Marx mean by 'religion is the opium of the people'?

ROUND-UP

Religious ideas can be seen as based on separating the world into sacred and profane (or secular) things. The sacred is the focus of religious feelings. Functionalists see religion as having positive functions, while Marxists and feminists see religion as an agency of social control, used to justify the way things are.

VOCABULARY

Awe: a sense of overwhelming wonder
Opium: an addictive drug extracted from poppies

The world's main religions

There are thousands of religions. Many are very small, and have only a few followers in one area. The largest religions are sometimes referred to as world religions. They are described here only very briefly; you should consult other books to learn more about them.

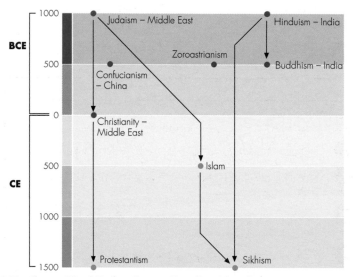

Note: The terms BC and AD refer to Christianity. To step beyond this and adopt a wider view, the terms BCE (Before Christian Era) and CE (Christian Era) are used here.

The origins of the world's main religions.

Christianity

Christianity is the most widespread religion, with about 1.9 billion followers – a third of humanity. There are Christians all around the world, but many are in Europe and the Americas.

Christianity began in the Middle East as a **sect** based on a **charismatic** leader, Jesus. It is based on Judaism, and shares a holy book (the Old Testament of the Bible) with Judaism. Christians were at first persecuted under the Roman Empire, but Christianity later became the official religion of the Empire. Christianity is a **monotheistic** religion; that is, it says there is only one god. The earlier Roman religion which it replaced was **polytheistic**, believing in many different gods.

Christianity split first into the Roman Catholic Church, based in Rome, and the Orthodox church, based in what is now Istanbul in Turkey. Later, the Protestant Reformation led to the formation of many smaller Christian churches or **denominations**. There are now many different forms of Christianity.

Islam

There are over a billion followers of Islam, who are known as Muslims, in the world. Most are in the Middle East and North Africa, but there are also many in parts of Asia and in West Africa.

Islam's holy book is the Qu'ran, the word of god as given to the prophet Mohammed, who lived in the sixth century. The city of Mecca in Saudi Arabia, where Mohammed was born, is the centre of Islam, and all Muslims have to make a pilgrimage to Mecca at least once.

Like Christianity, Islam is a monotheistic religion. Unlike Christianity, its main prophet is not a divine figure. Like Christianity, Islam is divided into several different forms, the best known of which are the Sunni and Shia branches of Islam.

Hinduism

Hinduism is older than Christianity and Islam, going back about 2500 years. It is the main religion of India, but it is also found wherever Indian people have settled. There are about 775 million Hindus.

There are many Hindu legends and stories, but no holy book that can be compared directly to the Bible or Qu'ran. There are many Hindu gods and goddesses. Some see these gods as different embodiments of a single spirit.

It is important for Hindus to follow rituals, especially those associated with the caste system. Some of these are private, such as cleansing after contact with someone from a lower caste; others are public, such as the Kumbh Mela every 12 years, when about 15 million pilgrims bathe in the Ganges – the largest gathering of people in the world.

Hinduism is a good example of a religion which is used to support and justify a particular form of stratification and inequality – the caste system. Position in society is accepted as the consequence of behaviour in previous incarnations (lives).

Judaism

Judaism, the religion of the Jews, is much smaller and the oldest of the world's religions dating back over 5000 years. Judaism has between 14 and 15 million followers. The state of Israel was founded as a homeland for Jewish people. It is the only country in the world where the majority are Jewish, but there are important minorities in many countries, including Britain. Jewish people have often faced persecution in countries they settled in. This persecution reached its strongest point in World War II, when the Nazi dictator Hitler and his regime in Germany were responsible for the deaths of about six million Jewish people.

Judaism shares the monotheistic god of Christianity and Islam, but rejects both Jesus and Mohammed as prophets. The Old Testament is one of Judaism's holy books, along with the Talmud, a collection of commentaries and interpretations.

Jews do not seek to convert followers of other religions. Their religion is based on correctly following god's will and behaving correctly, rather than on belief.

Buddhism

Buddhism, like Hinduism, is from India. There are about 330 million Buddhists, the vast majority in Asia.

Siddhartha Gautama, the founder of Buddhism, lived about 2500 years ago and devoted his life to seeking spiritual enlightenment. Buddhists today try to follow his example, following moral rules which include abstaining from the pleasures of the material world. Wealth, for example, can prevent people achieving spiritual enlightenment.

Buddhists do not worship a god although they respect other religions; rather Buddhism is about following a way of life which can lead to nirvana, a state of oneness with creation. Like Christianity it is inspired by the life and example of one man.

Living without religion

Throughout history there have been many people who have not accepted religion. People who do not believe there is a god are called atheists. Those who are not sure whether there is a god or not are called agnostics. Atheism and agnosticism are not belief systems; they do not say anything about how to live.

Many people in Britain today do not have fixed religious ideas but nevertheless have clear ideas about how to live; that is, a set of morals. A common moral system which does not involve religious belief is humanism. Humanists believe in using science, reason and experience to make sense of life, and in being kind and generous – 'treat others as you would want them to treat you'.

FIND OUT FOR YOURSELF

Several religions have not been mentioned here because of lack of space. Working with a small group, choose one of the religions below to research further, using whatever resources you can find. Present your findings in the form of a poster for wall display.

- Confucianism
- Daoism
- Zoroastrianism
- Jainism
- Shinto
- Sikhism
- Bahai.

QUESTIONS

1 Which religion has the most followers in the world?
2 Which of the religions discussed here is the oldest?
3 Explain how the beliefs of Hinduism can be used to justify inequality.
4 What is the difference between an atheist and an agnostic?
5 What are the similarities and differences between Christianity and Islam?

ROUND-UP

The main world religions are Christianity, Islam, Hinduism and Buddhism. Judaism is often added to this list because of its significance in laying the basis for Christianity and Islam. There are also many other religions. There have always been many people who do not accept religion, but this does not mean they do not follow a moral code.

VOCABULARY

Charismatic: having charisma, a special quality that inspires people
Pilgrimage: a special journey to a sacred place
Embodiment: giving a bodily form to a spirit or idea

Measuring religion

KEY FOCUS It is often said that society is less religious than was the case in the past. To assess this claim, a sociologist would want to have a way of measuring how religious people are. This section explains how this can be done, and some of the problems involved.

QUESTIONNAIRE
Do you have a religious faith?

Finding out about religious belief.

Religiosity

Religiosity means how religious people are. Sociologists use various ways of measuring religiosity. Religiosity is difficult to measure. Sociologists can carry out research to find out:

■ how many people attend churches or other places of worship
■ how many people belong to a religious organisation
■ how many people say that they are religious or believe in a god or gods.

Church attendance

One way of measuring religious practice is to find out how many people attend a church or other place of worship. The table below gives the results from the *British Social Attitudes Survey* in 1997 on this question.

Percentage of people attending religious services or meetings, 1997

	Males	Females
Once a week or more	10	15
Less often but at least once a month	7	11
Less often but at least once a year	16	20
Less often than once a year	3	5
Never or practically never	63	48

Social Trends Pocketbook 1999.

However, there are people who may have religious beliefs, even belong to an organisation, but who do not attend a church or other place of worship.

When churches count how many people attend, they usually do this on Sunday mornings. This runs the risk of leaving out people who attend at other times.

Church membership

Different organisations have different ways of measuring their membership, and therefore figures on membership need to be treated with caution. The Church of England includes anyone who has been baptised, whether or not as adults they practise their religion or not. So large Christian churches tend to have large memberships on paper, but this does not tell us much about religious belief and practice. Smaller religious organisations often require much more commitment (for example attending a meeting every week) in order for someone to be counted as a member.

Membership figures for the main religions in Britain, 1995

Christian:	
Roman Catholic	1 915 000
Church of England	1 785 000
Presbyterian	1 100 000
Methodist	401 000
Other religions:	
Muslim	580 000
Sikh	350 000
Hindu	155 000
Jewish	94 000

Social Trends 29, 1999.

Measurement problems

Some of the problems involved in measuring religion have already been mentioned. There are other questions that anyone doing this kind of research needs to consider:

■ Many people seem only to go to church or feel a need for religion at times of rites of passage – births, marriages and deaths. Others go to church only at Christmas or for other important festivals.

■ People may go to church, yet not have religious beliefs. Children and young people, for example, may only go to church because their families insist. In the past, there was little choice about attending church, and it was, then and now, also a social occasion and a way of being involved in a local community.

■ People may believe, yet never or rarely go to church. They may worship alone, with families or with others at home. They are not necessarily less religious because they choose to do this.

■ People may accept religious teachings without believing in a god. For example, someone may believe that Christian teaching about, for example, being kind and generous, even to strangers, provides a good code for living, yet not be a Christian.

■ Questions need to be asked in ways that do not leave out people who are not Christian. That is why it is important, for example, to talk about places of worship rather than just churches. Churches are Christian places of worship, and there are many other types of place of worship, such as mosques, temples and synagogues, in Britain today.

Measuring religious belief

Another way of studying religion is to ask people about their beliefs. The main problem here for researchers is to decide what religious beliefs are, and to ask in a sensitive way. But the answers that researchers get will depend on how they ask. Here are some questions that researchers could ask in a questionnaire or interview:

■ Do you believe in God? In a spirit or lifeforce? In heaven? In hell?
■ Do you believe that things in the Bible are true?
■ Do you believe in life after death? In reincarnation?
■ Is God important in your life?
■ Do you think of yourself as a religious person?

Research of this kind shows that there are many people who have some kind of religious feelings but who are not members of an organisation or church attenders. Many people believe but do not belong. When questions are asked about beliefs which can be seen as on the fringes of religion – about faith-healing, witches, UFOs and so on – the numbers are even higher.

Measuring religion in society

Finally, it is important to consider the place of religion in a wider social context. Some of the questions that might be asked here, as a way of measuring how religious society is, include the following:

■ How well respected and important in a local community are priests?
■ Are the views of religious leaders listened to by politicians and other decision makers?
■ How many schools are run by religious groups?
■ How important is religion in schools (both as a subject in the curriculum, and in collective worship)?

PS ▶ FIND OUT FOR YOURSELF

You have been set the task of finding out how religious members of your class are. You have decided to do this by using a questionnaire. Work out a suitable list of questions to ask.

QUESTIONS

1. What is meant by religiosity?
2. Which is the largest non-Christian religion in Britain?
3. Identify and explain two reasons why church attendance is not necessarily a good measure of religiosity.
4. Identify and explain two reasons why church membership is not necessarily a good measure of religiosity.
5. Should people who go to church only once or twice a year be counted as practising Christians? Explain your answer.

ROUND-UP

Religiosity is a difficult thing to measure. Sociologists can collect data on church attendance, church membership and how religious people say they are, but all of these involve problems in deciding what to ask and how to ask it.

VOCABULARY

Mosque: a Muslim place of worship
Synagogue: a Jewish place of worship
Reincarnation: the belief that after death the soul can be reborn in another body

Churches and sects

Sociologists who study religious organisations say that there are basically four different types of organisation. Not all religious organisations fit easily into these categories, but they provide a useful way of thinking about religious organisations.

The four types of religious organisations are churches, sects, denominations and cults. This section looks at churches and sects, and the next section looks at denominations and cults.

The Amish – a sect with beliefs and practices that make it different from mainstream American society.

Churches

The word church, as it is commonly used, has two different meanings. It can mean a particular building that people worship in, or it can mean an organisation. It is the second meaning that is used here.

Churches as organisations are big. They usually have many followers or members, often in several different countries. It is often difficult to tell who is a member and who is not, because churches do not make many special demands on people. For example, many people in England are counted as members of the Church of England because they have been baptised or because their parents were members. They may not though have made any decision themselves to be a member. Even those who say they are members may only go to church very occasionally.

Churches are accepted as an essential part of society. The head of a church, for example, will be highly respected and may even have considerable influence on political decisions.

Churches have a professional clergy; their priests are specially trained and work, usually full time, for the church. Churches are hierarchies; there are people at different levels of power and authority. In the Roman Catholic Church, for example, the Pope is the head, but below him are cardinals, and then other ranks including priests. The church's requirements are much stricter for a priest or other employee than for members; for example, a priest may be expected not to have any sexual relationships.

Churches claim that their teachings are true and are the only true teachings. This has been described as claiming 'a monopoly on the truth'.

An example of a church: the Roman Catholic Church

The Roman Catholic Church is the largest church in the world, with about a billion members around the world. It is the largest church within Christianity. In England and Wales there are about five and a half million Catholics.

The Roman Catholic Church has a hierarchical structure. At the top is the Pope, also known as the Bishop of Rome, the leader of the church, based in the Vatican City in Rome. Below him are cardinals (the Pope's advisers) and bishops, priests and deacons, and then **lay** members. Catholics have to obey not only the Bible but also the instructions of the Pope. They are told not to use artificial means of contraception, and see abortion as a sin.

The Roman Catholic Church has often been deeply involved in politics and public affairs. In many countries Catholics have formed political parties. The Roman Catholic Church has throughout its history tried to convert non-Catholics. Missionaries went from Europe to all parts of the world and there are many still working in South America, Africa and Asia.

Despite its enormous power on a global scale, Catholics have at times been discriminated against and even persecuted in some countries where Catholicism was not the main religion.

Sects

Compared to churches, sects are small. In many ways they are the opposites of churches. The one thing they have in common with churches, which makes sects and churches different from denominations and cults, is that they claim a monopoly on the truth.

Members of sects have to commit themselves strongly to the sect (unlike members of churches). They will have made a conscious decision to be members and to devote a lot of their time and energy to the sect.

Sects often do not get on with the society around them. Their beliefs make them different, and they may be treated with hostility by non-members.

Because sects are small they cannot have a full-time professional clergy. This means that most members of a sect can treat each other as equals; there is no hierarchy.

An example of a sect: the Amish

The Amish are a Christian sect with about 175 000 members who live in several parts of the USA, notably Pennsylvania and Ohio. Their founder, Jakob Ammon, told his followers to live lives as separate as possible from the rest of the world. The Amish keep to the Puritan way of life their ancestors had several hundred years ago when they first arrived in what is now the USA. They wear old-fashioned clothing which marks them out as different. They reject almost all modern technology. For example, they do not use radios and television, telephones or even zips. They use horses and carts, rather than tractors and cars.

The Amish do not set out to convert new members, because this would increase their contact with the outside world.

The Amish are sometimes seen in a romantic and idealistic way by people who feel that things were better in 'the good old days'. They have even become a tourist attraction. It is, however, not possible to keep a completely unchanging life style. The Amish have begun to use their image to make and sell craft goods such as furniture, dolls and jewellery.

Because the Amish are a sect, there are strong pressures on the members to keep to this way of life. Of course, many young people feel pulled away from their community by modern American life. The Amish allow young people some freedom to experience modern life. Many young people eventually decide to continue the Amish lifestyle.

FIND OUT FOR YOURSELF

The film *Witness*, starring Harrison Ford, is a thriller set in an Amish community. Find a video of this film and watch it to learn more about the Amish.

Comparing churches and sects

	Churches	Sects
Claim monopoly on truth	Yes	Yes
Size	Very big	Small
Hierarchical organisation	Yes	No
Professional clergy	Yes	No
Involvement in public affairs	Yes	No
Members have to be committed	To some extent	Yes

QUESTIONS

1. Who is the leader of the Roman Catholic Church?
2. What is the one similarity between churches and sects?
3. Identify and explain three facts which make the Roman Catholic Church a good example of a church.
4. Identify and explain three facts which make the Amish a good example of a sect.
5. Why is it difficult for a sect to keep its beliefs and practices over a very long period of time?

ROUND-UP

Religious organisations are churches and sects. Both claim a monopoly on the truth, but are otherwise very different. The Roman Catholic Church is a good example of a church, while the Amish are a good example of a sect.

VOCABULARY

Hierarchy: the way something is organised into several ranks
Puritan: a Protestant who kept to a very simple way of life
Lay members; laity: members of a church who are not clergy (priests)

Denominations and cults

KEY FOCUS

In the previous section it was explained that there are four types of religious organisations. This section looks at the two types of religious organisation which were not described in that section: denominations and cults.

An ouija board: communicating with spirits – a form of religious belief that has a cult following.

Denominations

Denominations are similar to churches, but are smaller and less powerful. They are often called churches, and like churches they are seen as respectable, but when looked at closely they can be seen to be different.

Their priests are often working only part time and may not be paid. They do not claim a monopoly on the truth (look back to the last section for a reminder of what this means). They see it as difficult to claim to have all the answers when there are so many different religious beliefs. So they tolerate other religions. A member of a denomination does not think that someone who belongs to a different denomination or church is bound to go to hell. They will even work with outsiders in social reform movements or as missionaries.

An example of a denomination: Methodism

Methodism is a Christian denomination which began with the teachings of a Church of England clergyman, John Wesley, in the eighteenth century. Methodism is a non-conformist denomination; that is, it does not conform to strict observance of the teachings of the Church of England and the Book of Common Prayer. Other non-conformist Christian groups in Britain include the Baptists, the Quakers and the Salvation Army.

Wesley's ideas were based on Puritanism and on everyone finding their own spiritual salvation. Wesley's ideas stressed belonging to a religious community and helping each other. Methodism was attractive to members of the working class,

because the Church of England was associated with the rich landowners. Methodism became associated with social movements: with trade unionism and other working-class organisations in Britain, and with the movement in the USA to abolish slavery. It also has strong rules against drinking alcohol.

There are now about 400 000 Methodists in Britain; the numbers have been falling for a long time. There are also Methodists in other countries, especially the USA.

While Methodism can be described today as a denomination, in its early years it was more like a sect, requiring strong commitment from its members. This shows how religions change over time: a sect split off from a church and developed into a denomination.

Cults

The term **cult** as used by most sociologists has a rather different meaning from the use of the word by the media. Most of what the media call cults – small groups of devoted followers of a leader, with little contact with the outside world – are what sociologists call sects.

Cult here means something much looser and freer and covers a wide range of beliefs. Like denominations, cults do not lay claim to a monopoly of the truth. Belonging to a cult can even be combined with belonging to a denomination. This is because belonging to a cult need not mean very much: it can just mean being interested in a set of ideas and following them up in some way. For example, someone who is interested in spiritualism – the belief that we can communicate with the spirits of the dead – may go along to a few meetings, perhaps even attend a séance, but then lose interest. People drift in and out of cults, with no long-term commitment to them. It is therefore very difficult to measure how large cults are.

People also differ a lot in how committed they are to a cult. In the case of astrology – the belief that the stars and other heavenly bodies determine our lives – people who learn how to read astrological charts are more committed than someone who just read the stars in a magazine.

Cults have little or no organisation, no hierarchy and no professional clergy. How much individuals get involved is up to them. Cults are often seen as strange or deviant, but not usually in a way that is unacceptable.

An example of a cult: spiritualism

The idea of communicating with the dead can be found all around the world. Modern spiritualism, however, can be traced to the mid-nineteenth century when several people claimed to be in touch with a spirit world. This sparked off considerable interest and a lot of scientific research. At its most developed, spiritualism can be like a denomination – there are spiritualist churches, for example. But it is like a cult in that many people express, but soon lose, interest.

Spiritualists believe that some gifted individuals, called mediums, can communicate with spirits. This communication usually takes place at a special meeting called a séance. A number of people join hands around a table while the medium tries to summon a spirit. The medium may use an ouija board or planchette. The spirit may speak, or move objects, or make rapping sounds.

Comparing denominations and cults

	Denominations	**Cults**
Claim monopoly on truth	No	No
Size	Quite big	Variable
Hierarchical organisation	Yes	No
Professional clergy	Yes	No
Involvement in public affairs	Yes	No
Members have to be committed	To some extent	Yes

Making sense of religious organisations

You have now studied all four types of religious organisations. A way of understanding the difference between them was suggested by the sociologist Roy Wallis. He looked at how organisations were seen by their members or believers, and noted that churches and sects see themselves as having a monopoly on the truth whereas denominations and cults do not. He then looked at how the organisations are seen by wider society and noted that churches and denominations are seen as respectable whereas sects and cults are not.

The difference between churches, denominations, sects and cults

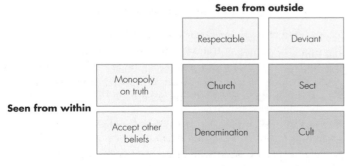

Based on Wallis (1976).

Learn about other examples of the types of religious organisations. Work in a small group, and use any resources you can find: the library, CD-ROMs, the Internet and your school's religious studies teachers. Here are some suggestions:

- church: Church of England, Islam
- sect: Christian Science, the Salvation Army
- denomination: Baptist movement
- cult: astrology.

Show how the organisation you have found out about fits the type of religious organisation. Present your findings to the rest of the class.

QUESTIONS

1. Who was the founder of Methodism?

2. What one characteristic do denominations and cults share?

3. Identify and explain three facts about Methodism which make it a good example of a denomination.

4. Identify and explain three facts about spiritualism which make it a good example of a cult.

5. Explain how Methodism illustrates how religious organisations develop.

ROUND-UP

Two other types of religious organisation, apart from churches and sects, are denominations and cults. Both accept or tolerate other beliefs; they do not claim a monopoly on the truth. Methodism is a good example of a denomination, while spiritualism is a good example of a cult.

VOCABULARY

Social reform movements: any movement attempting to improve social conditions, for example by helping the poor

Ouija board: a board with the letters of the alphabet on. People taking part in the séance hold a pointer or glass, which, it is claimed, spirits move to spell out messages

Planchette: a heart shaped board on which, it is claimed, spirits can write messages

New Religious Movements

From about the 1970s, sociologists noticed that there were New Religious Movements (NRMs) that did not fit easily into the four types of organisation you have studied in the previous two sections (churches, denominations, sects and cults).

A Unification Church mass wedding – evidence of the strength of one New Religious Movement.

The rise of new groups and beliefs

The classification of religious organisations into churches, denominations, sects and cults works well for western organisations that have been around for some time. There are many groups however who do not fit neatly into these categories. The 1960s and 1970s in particular saw the rise of many new groups and beliefs. Some of these are close to being sects and cults, but the term **New Religious Movements** (NRMs) is now widely used by sociologists to describe these and later groups.

Some NRMs are based on eastern religions such as Hinduism and Buddhism. These became popular in the 1960s. They include Transcendental Meditation (TM), Krishna Consciousness and Rajneeshism.

Often eastern religious ideas are combined with western ones to create a new hybrid. A new religion formed from two or more earlier sets of beliefs is called a **syncretic** religion. Examples include the Unification Church (also known as the Moonies) which combines Christianity and Buddhism.

Other NRMs are based on ideas from psychoanalysis and are about improving the self. Some of these do not claim to be religions, but are similar to religions in some ways, such as often having a strong leader. Examples include Scientology, Primal Therapy and Rebirthing.

Conversion or coercion?

Some NRMs (usually of the kind referred to in the mass media as cults) have been accused of forcing people to join by brainwashing them; that is, somehow depriving them of their free will. This has made stronger the tendency to see such groups as bizarre and dangerous. There have been extreme cases, where members of a group have committed suicide together, but these are far from typical.

When someone joins an NRM, there can be a big change in their personality and behaviour. This will probably puzzle family and friends (if the person stays in touch with them – and if they don't, this too will be a cause of concern). In fact, however, people would not join NRMs unless they felt they were being offered something important. Some NRMs are aggressive in the way they try to persuade people, but people join for reasons which seem good to them.

Eileen Barker, a sociologist, spent several years studying the Unification Church, or Moonies, who had been accused of brainwashing young people into joining. Barker concluded that the Moonies did present their movement in a positive way to newcomers, and gradually increased the demands they made, but this was not brainwashing. People could leave whenever they wanted to.

Young people and NRMs

NRMs seem to have a strong attraction to young people. As more people stay in education after 16 and take time before settling into a career, there is a longer period when young adults are not fully independent. This is a time when young people are most likely to join an NRM. Parents may well be upset by this, as it seems to disrupt family life and they may find it difficult to understand the reasons.

Because NRMs vary so much, it is difficult to generalise; people join different groups for different reasons. Some of the reasons young adults give for joining NRMs include:

- as a gesture of independence, showing that they have personalities and beliefs of their own
- as self-development, in the hope of realising their potential
- to find answers to big questions about death, injustice, suffering and so on

- to give expression to spiritual and social values
- for companionship.

Some young adults who join NRMs are homeless or are in trouble in some way. Others, however, are starting promising careers and see membership of the NRM as a way of furthering their career.

There are a huge range of beliefs available today, from which people can 'pick and mix' their own religion or their own values. Many people dip into a wide range of ideas about religion, spirituality and self-development. Some find what they are looking for in one set of ideas, and decide to join an NRM. Before joining they need to find out all they can about the NRM.

In and out

NRMs have a very high turnover of members; people are unlikely to stay members for more than a few years. Often people will have joined the NRM as a solution to a problem which is now resolved; their lives have moved on, and so they move on too.

Types of NRM

The sociologist Roy Wallis suggested that NRMs could be classified according to their attitude to the outside world.

Some NRMs encourage their followers to cut themselves off from the world, mixing only with other members. They are hostile to the outside world, and in return are often treated with suspicion and hostility. This is similar to what tends to happen to sects. Wallis called these world-rejecting NRMs. Examples include the Children of God and the Branch-Davidian movement, led by David Koresh, who claimed to be the messiah. The Branch-Davidian headquarters in Waco, Texas, was besieged by the police in 1993, and many members died in a fire at the end of the siege.

Other NRMs allow their followers to be fully involved in the world. These NRMs claim to help people achieve the ends that are generally approved of by society: to work hard and be successful in work and in personal life. Wallis called these world-affirming NRMs. Examples include Transcendental Meditation and Scientology. For example, the film actor John Travolta claims that he was able to relaunch his floundering acting career through practising Scientology.

Finally, there are NRMs which are rather like denominations in that they accept a variety of beliefs and see religion as largely a personal matter. Members can continue with their everyday lives, keeping religion largely separate. Wallis called these world-accommodating NRMs. An example is Pentecostalism.

FIND OUT FOR YOURSELF

Investigate one of the NRMs referred to on these pages. The easiest to find out about will probably be Scientology or the Unification Church (Moonies). Use your school library, CD-ROMs, the Internet and any other available sources of information. Present your findings in the form of a poster suitable for wall display.

QUESTIONS

1. What does NRM stand for?

2. What is meant by a syncretic religion?

3. Name the three types of NRM suggested by Wallis and give one example of each.

4. Identify and explain two reasons why NRMs are particularly attractive to young adults?

5. Why do most members of NRMs not stay members for a long time?

ROUND-UP

As well as the four types of religious organisations, there are many new religious movements. These can be described as world-rejecting, world-affirming or world-accommodating. People join for many reasons, and they are particularly attractive to young people.

VOCABULARY

Hybrid: of mixed origin, a cross between two different types

Psychoanalysis: a way of studying the mind and mental problems, based on revealing the unconscious mind

Self-development: developing or improving your abilities and your position

The New Age

KEY FOCUS This section looks at a recent development, the growth of New Age beliefs. These cover a wide range of ideas, which are not always strictly religious but which involve spirituality or the supernatural.

Spirituality for sale on the high street.

New Age beliefs and ideas

Astrology	Paganism
The Celestine Prophecy	Pendulum Dowsing
Channelling	Psychosynthesis
Crystals	Shamanism
Earth Mysteries	Sufism
Feng Shui	Tarot Cards
Herbalism	Qabalah
Homoeopathic medicine	UFOs and alien abduction
I Ching	Zen Buddhism
Meditation	

New interest in angels, in legends of King Arthur, in Ancient Egypt, in the truth or otherwise in biblical stories such as Noah's Ark and the flood

Involvement and commitment

NAMs do not have members; they are not organised in a way that makes membership possible. Rather, people come across the ideas through books, magazines, tapes and sometimes public talks at which practitioners present their ideas. For most people, involvement in New Age beliefs involves no more than some reading, dipping into some of the many ideas on offer. If they put the ideas into practice, this rarely involves any significant changes in lifestyle. Someone might, for example, rearrange their furniture after reading a book on Feng Shui. For some people, though, the encounter with New Age beliefs may be similar to the experience of being converted to a traditional religion. A small number of people do devote themselves to New Age beliefs, some making a living from them or adopting an alternative lifestyle.

There is such a range of beliefs on offer that rather than talk about movements it may be more appropriate to think of the New Age as a vast pool of ideas into which people can dip.

NAMs tend to attract people who are middle class and educated. They also attract women more than men.

The spread of New Age ideas

The growth of the New Age can be seen by considering the number of books published on New Age themes and the

The New Age

As you have seen, the 1960s and 1970s gave rise to many New Religious Movements (NRMs). Closely related, and dating from a slightly later period, is the rise of **New Age** Movements (NAMs):

■ NRMs are usually closer to the definition of sects (see pages 382–3).

■ NAMs are usually closer to the definition of cults (see pages 384–5).

The New Age refers to a very wide range of beliefs and practices. Some of these are related to older religious beliefs, or traditions within older religions; others are occult beliefs that have a long history. Some are borrowed from eastern religions or are based on ancient myths. What makes them new is that they have been given a new popularity by the surge of interest in such ideas in the 1980s and 1990s.

number of television programmes. Books by New Age writers such as Deepak Chopra and Wayne Dyer are best sellers. Many of the large publishing companies have specialist imprints for their New Age books.

Many television programmes and films tap into New Age beliefs. An obvious, hugely successful example from the 1990s was *The X Files*; there were also many factual programmes exploring New Age ideas. Several Hollywood films of the 1990s were based on ideas such as the existence of angels, life after death, reincarnation and magic.

New Age beliefs are also part of the world of business. Many shopping malls and high streets have shops specialising in the New Age. Bookshops have sections for New Age books.

New Age themes

It is possible to distinguish several themes that run through all or most New Age ideas. The sociologist Steve Bruce (*Religion in Modern Britain*, Oxford University Press, 1995) suggests that there are three New Age themes:

- New science. New Age ideas are usually hostile to or sceptical about modern science. Often this is because the ideas clash directly with science; for example, the belief that magic works. Sometimes New Agers claim that science will one day prove what they believe. New Agers look for other sources of proof than science. They assume that anything from a pre-modern culture is superior to something modern. This has led to great interest in, for example, Native American ways.

- New ecology. New Age ideas are often associated with a concern for the natural world and the environment. Part of the hostility towards science comes from believing that the world has been damaged by our scientific, industrial lifestyle. New Age beliefs see the earth as a living being, Gaia (named after a Greek goddess). Gaia is seen as needing to be protected from people.

- New psychology and spirituality. New Age beliefs place a strong emphasis on the self and the spirit. The self can be made perfect, they claim, and we have immortal souls

Why the New Age?

New Age beliefs became strong in the 1980s at a time when individuality and choice were important ideas. There is greater tolerance of different ideas and less pressure to conform to a single version of one religion such as Christianity. Religions and cultures from all around the world and throughout history have become available, so that people can now 'pick and mix' ideas and create their own personal religion.

FIND OUT FOR YOURSELF

Investigate the extent and reach of New Age ideas by visiting a local bookshop. Find the New Age section (you may need to ask an assistant as it may go under another heading). Count the number of books available on different New Age ideas, including any not mentioned here.

QUESTIONS

1. Name three ideas or beliefs that can be described as New Age.

2. Name two television series which are based on New Age ideas.

3. Identify and explain two ways in which NAMs are cults.

4. Identify and explain the three themes of New Age beliefs suggested by Bruce.

5. What arguments would be used by those who are against New Age ideas?

ROUND-UP

Since the 1980s there has been a big growth in interest in New Age beliefs. These are often like cults, requiring little commitment. People can dip into a wide range of ideas. Three themes can be identified in NAMs: new science, new ecology and new psychology and spirituality.

VOCABULARY

Spirituality: concerned with spiritual rather than material matters

Imprint: a publishing company may have several imprints – labels for groups of different books, for example Penguin Books' New Age titles are Arkana Books

Materialism: interest in money and possessions rather than moral values and ideals

Gender and religion

KEY FOCUS

Most religions are male-dominated; the founder, key figures and leaders are almost always men. Yet women are more religious than men. This section looks at the relationship between gender and religion.

In 1991, 65 per cent of those regularly attending church were women – yet all of those conducting the services were men

What is the relationship between gender and religion?

Gods and goddesses

Most religions involve worship of gods who are definitely men. Goddesses are found all around the world in many religions, but they are usually part of a pantheon of gods and are not the most important gods. Some are very feminine, gentle and loving, or are simply the wives of the important gods. Others are very warlike and destructive. It has been said that goddesses reflect the full range of female roles and attributes.

Important goddesses

Ancient Greek mythology:
Athena (goddess of wisdom), Aphrodite (goddess of love), Hera (sister and wife of Zeus, king of the gods)

Hinduism:
Devi (the mother goddess), Durga, Kali, Sarasvati, Lakshmi (docile wife of the god Vishnu)

Paganism (a term applied to the religions that existed in Europe before Christianity):
The Great Goddess, known by different names in different areas; Gaia, the earth mother

Despite the importance of these female gods, the main gods and prophets in the world religions are all male.

Christianity

There are many female characters in the Bible, but most of the main characters are men. The story of Adam and Eve, the first man and woman, says that Eve was created after Adam, and from one of his ribs. Mary, the mother of Jesus, is prayed to and treated almost like a divine figure in Roman Catholicism, but she is not part of the Holy Trinity.

Women have always made up the majority of church attenders and members of Christian churches. The main way women have expressed strong religious conviction has been to become nuns, but there were always more monks and monasteries than nuns and convents in the past.

Women have always been prevented from being priests in established churches. The smaller radical sects were the first to allow women to become priests. It was not until 1992 that the Church of England allowed women to be ordained. This was very controversial, and some male priests left the church in protest. The Roman Catholic Church continues to prevent women becoming priests, on the grounds that none of Jesus's disciples were women, and prefers women to keep to the traditional roles of wife and mother.

Women have then made some progress towards equality in recent years. This is part of the movement towards greater equality in society generally. It can also be seen as a response by churches to the fall in the number of members; ordaining women may be a way of attracting new members or keeping those who might otherwise leave.

Some smaller organisations such as sects have allowed women to play a greater role. Sects appeal to underprivileged groups, often offering them salvation. As women are underprivileged in most societies, sects have a strong appeal to women. As sects grow and become more respectable, however, they tend to backtrack from sexual equality.

Islam

Like Christianity, Islam is a very male-dominated religion. The Qu'ran, like the Bible, can be interpreted in many different ways, and it has been used at times to justify a very distinct role for women. Women in some countries are kept separate from men, and do not go out in public unless chaperoned and wearing the veil. The most extreme form of this at the moment is Afghanistan under the government of the Taliban, where females are not allowed to go to school or to work outside the home. In other countries women have considerably more freedom.

Many Muslim women do not feel that such restrictions are necessarily bad. Wearing the veil, for example, gives freedom from unwanted attention from men and makes it possible to take part in public life. It is also an expression of the requirement for hijab, or modesty, which applies both to men and women.

The feminist view of religion

Feminists see established religions as a form of social control over women. Women learn from religious stories, beliefs and practices that their place in the world is different from and lesser than men's place. Religions (not just Christianity) reflect the values of society, and these values are patriarchal.

Some feminists argue that in pre-history people worshipped a female god, not a male one. They point out that the earth is usually seen as female ('mother earth'), and that females are more associated with creating and sustaining life than males. At some point in history, then, this early worship of an earth mother was replaced by male-centred religions. Witches are sometimes seen as carrying on this ancient religion, and suffering persecution by men who saw witchcraft as simply evil.

Women and religion: an example

Mary Baker Eddy was the founder of Christian Science. An American woman living in the nineteenth century, she taught that Jesus's miracles were the normal operation of God's laws. Through prayer Christians could channel these laws and could heal the sick. Christian Science grew into a denomination with, at its height, several thousand churches, mainly in the USA but in other countries too.

IT ▶ FIND OUT FOR YOURSELF

The real lives of nuns are rather different from what is shown in films like *Sister Act*. Visit the web site of the convent at Dysart in Scotland to find out more about nuns today: http://www.fortunecity.com/victorian/cloisters/32/index.htm.

QUESTIONS

1 Name two goddesses from different religions.

2 Give two restrictions which are placed on women in some Islamic countries.

3 Identify and explain two facts which feminists could use to justify the claim that religions are patriarchal.

4 Name a religious organisation founded by a woman, and give the woman's name.

5 Why do sects attract women who want to play a leading role in a religion?

ROUND-UP

Women make up the majority of those who practise and believe in religions, yet they have been kept from playing a major role in all of the major world religions, which are dominated by men. Women have begun to make some progress towards equality in religion, for example by becoming ordained as Anglican priests.

VOCABULARY

Attributes: qualities
Pantheon: all the gods of a religion
Chaperoned: someone who accompanies and watches over an unmarried woman, usually an older woman or a male relative

Religion in Britain today

KEY FOCUS This section looks briefly at age and class of church members and attenders. It then looks at how religion in Britain has been changed by the growth of world religions brought here by immigrants, and at the religiosity of minority ethnic groups.

THE EAST LONDON MOSQUE

Islam – a growing presence in Britain.

Age and religion

Churchgoers in each age group, 1998

Age	Percentage attending church
Under 15	19
15–19	6
20–29	9
30–44	17
45–64	24
65 and over	25

UKCH Religious Trends.

One of the reasons for the high church attendance by those over 65 is that there are significantly more women in this age

group (because men have a lower life expectancy) and we know that women are more likely to be churchgoers.

Class and religion

Middle-class people are more likely to attend church than working-class people, and more likely to be active church members.

Sects have tended to attract people who are at the bottom end of society. They often attract the poor by promising a dramatic reversal in which god will turn against the rich – 'the world turned upside down'. Early Methodism, for example (see the section on Denominations and cults, page 384) attracted many working-class followers. There have, however, also been sects which have attracted people mainly from the middle class.

Ethnicity and religion

Since World War II, Britain has become a much more ethnically and culturally diverse country. This cultural diversity includes religion. Immigrants to Britain have brought with them their own religious beliefs and practices.

British Asians and religion

Islam

British Muslims have their origins in many countries. Most people whose family origins are in Pakistan and Bangladesh are Muslim, but there are also Muslims from Arab countries, from East Africa, India, Iran and Cyprus. About half of all British Muslims live in or around London, and most of the rest in Birmingham, Manchester and South Yorkshire. It is difficult to assess how many Muslims there are in Britain. Most estimates include everyone who belongs to a Muslim family, regardless of the beliefs and practices of individuals.

Hinduism

British Hindus have their origins in India, although many came to Britain from East Africa. They are though from all different parts of India, and therefore have different languages and cultures. They are also divided by caste. There are well over 100 Hindu temples in Britain.

Sikhism

Most British Sikhs come from the Punjab, rule of which is disputed by India and Pakistan. Most live in London and other large cities. There are about 180 gurdwaras in Britain.

All these religions have grown considerably in size and importance in Britain over the last 30 years. Members of Asian minority ethnic groups are much more likely than white British people to identify themselves as followers of a religion. Keeping strongly to religion can be a way of defending a culture (for example language and style of dress). Many Asian immigrants felt when they arrived that Britain was a secular country in which moral values were weak, and have tried to pass on strong religious beliefs to their children to counter this. For recently arrived immigrants, religion can provide a sense of belonging and of community while finding your way in a different country.

Afro-Caribbeans and religion

Britain's Afro-Caribbean population is mainly Christian and Protestant. During the early years of immigration, they often met prejudice in British churches and, partly as a result of this, many black Christians belong to churches which are exclusively black. The largest group of churches are Pentecostalist ones.

Pentecostalism

About 80 per cent of those who belong to a church are Pentecostalists. Pentecostal services involve lively singing and dancing, and sharing of experiences. Worshippers often 'speak in tongues', claiming to be possessed by the holy spirit. The style of worship is said to be derived from African culture.

Other minority ethnic groups

Jews

Judaism is the oldest immigrant religion in Britain, and the only one which is in decline. There have been Jewish people in Britain since the Middle Ages, but changing times and the emigration of some Jews to Israel means that there are fewer practising Jews. A number of younger Jews no longer attend synagogue or follow Jewish rituals.

Irish

The Irish are probably the largest ethnic minority in Britain. Irish people are more likely than white British people to identify themselves as religious, and they are overwhelmingly Roman Catholic.

This chart shows the levels of religiosity among ethnic groups in Britain.

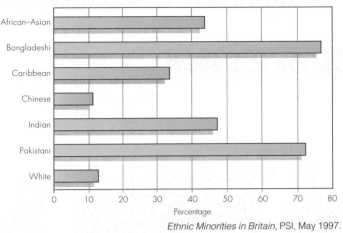

Percentage of people agreeing with the statement 'Religion is very important to how I live my life'

Ethnic Minorities in Britain, PSI, May 1997.

QUESTIONS

1 Which age group is the least likely to attend church?

2 Which is the largest non-Christian religion in Britain?

3 Which is the only religion of an ethnic minority group to have declined in recent years?

4 Identify and explain one reason why an immigrant group might keep strongly to its religious beliefs and practices.

5 Look at the chart on the importance of religion. What do these figures tell us about the level of religiosity of white and minority ethnic groups?

ROUND-UP

Older and middle-class people are more likely to be church members and regular attenders than younger and working-class people. Several religions brought to Britain by immigrants from Asia are now important, and are growing at a time when traditional Christianity is in decline. Levels of religiosity are much higher among minority ethnic groups than among the white majority.

VOCABULARY

Gurdwara: a Sikh place of worship
Speaking in tongues: also called gift of tongues; speaking, often unintelligibly, under the influence of strong religious feeling

Secularisation: religion in decline?

KEY FOCUS

Is religion in decline? Are we less religious than we used to be? The process of religious decline is called secularisation. Some sociologists believe that secularisation has been taking place for many years, while others are not convinced. This section looks at some of the evidence for and against secularisation.

A sign of the times?

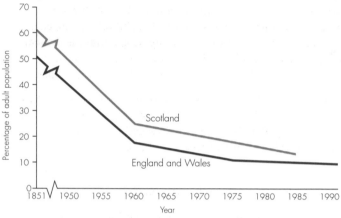

Adult church attendance in Britain, 1851–1989

Knowledge and the Social Sciences: Theory, Method and Practice edited by David Goldblatt, Routledge, 2000.

What is secularisation?

Secularisation involves the following:

- People no longer need religious or supernatural explanations; science now provides answers.
- Religion has become a matter of personal and private choice.
- Churches and other religious organisations are no longer as important in social and political life as they used to be.
- Churches and other religious institutions have become more concerned with, for example, charity and helping the poor, rather than religious issues.

Measuring secularisation

Church attendance

This is the biggest area of concern for religious leaders. The numbers of people attending Christian churches in Britain has been falling for many years. At the same time there are fewer churches; some have been converted into housing or offices, or have been demolished. Sunday has become a day on which people do the same sorts of things they do on other days; they can work, or go shopping, or watch or take part in sports. Sunday is no longer a day reserved for rest and for worship.

The chart shows that church attendance has fallen considerably, and continues to fall. However, this need not necessarily mean secularisation. It might mean instead that people are just as religious as in the past, but now choose to worship in private and at home.

It should also be remembered that church attendance does not necessarily measure commitment to religion. In the past it was an offence not to attend church without a very good reason.

Religious belief

Belief is much more difficult to measure than attendance. The results of research tend to depend very much on exactly what questions are asked. The majority of British people believe in some kind of supernatural power. The number who believe in a personal god (such as the gods of Christianity and the other main religions) has fallen, but some people instead now say they believe in some kind of spirit or life force.

Science versus religion

In the past, many people explained the world around them in terms which today seem to be superstitions. In the Middle Ages, for example, there was widespread belief not only in a god but also in spirits, witches, devils and other supernatural

The evidence: for and against secularisation

	For secularisation	Against secularisation
Church attendance	Falling ...	...but not in non-Christian religions and NRMs
In the past	Religion was very important ...	... but people may have attended church without believing
Religious belief	Fewer believe ...	...but many practise religion at home
Rise of science	Reveals religion as superstition	Science cannot explain everything
NRMs	Not really important	Show that religion is still important

forces. Then the growth of science began to produce explanations for events which meant that people no longer needed to turn to superstitions and the supernatural. For example, Charles Darwin's theory of evolution, developed in the nineteenth century, proved to many people that the biblical story of creation could not be literally true. Many people expected that science would eventually make religion unnecessary.

However, for many people science is not a complete substitute for religion. We have not all become atheists. Many scientists believe in a god. Beliefs not only in a god but in the supernatural continue to be widely held.

New religions and New Religious Movements

Those who argue that secularisation has taken place tend to concentrate on the traditional Christian churches. Once other religions and religious movements are taken into account, the picture changes. However, it should be remembered that while new religions may be growing they involve smaller numbers than the older churches.

- Organisations in decline (as measured by membership) – Roman Catholic, Church of England, Presbyterian, Methodist, Baptist, Jewish.
- Organisations which are growing – Mormons, Jehovah's Witnesses, Islam, Sikhism, Hinduism.

Members of the organisations which are growing tend to be more strongly committed to their religion than members of those which are in decline. Moreover, the declining organisations tend to have an older membership and fewer young members, suggesting that their decline is unlikely to be reversed in the near future.

Writers who argue that secularisation is happening see the growth of New Religious Movements (NRMs) as evidence of the decline of religion. NRMs are a symptom of the change from a society with one main religion to one where there is an enormous choice. They point out that many NRMs do not require a strong commitment from followers, and that people tend only to belong for short periods. Most NRMs do not act, as churches once did, as the centre of communities.

Those who are not convinced that secularisation is happening, on the other hand, see NRMs as evidence of religion adapting

and surviving in changing circumstances. They are real religions, and cannot be easily dismissed.

FIND OUT FOR YOURSELF

Was the reaction to the death of Princess Diana on 31 August 1997 an indication that religion is still strong? Judge for yourself by researching how people reacted. Visit your school library to look for resources, or use the Internet. BBC and ITN reports from the time are available online.

QUESTIONS

1. Write one sentence explaining what is meant by secularisation.

2. State three things people can do on Sundays which are not connected with religion.

3. Give one reason why falling church attendance does not necessarily prove that secularisation is happening.

4. Give one example of a belief in the supernatural which remains strong despite not being acceptable to science.

5. Has Britain become more secular? Write a 500-word answer showing evidence that would be used by those who agree and those who do not.

ROUND-UP

Secularisation is difficult to prove or disprove. It is possible to use strong evidence on both sides. What is certain is that religious beliefs and practices have changed and are continuing to change, so that we have to reconsider what we mean by religion and by secularisation.

VOCABULARY

Converted: turned into
Demolished: knocked down

Religion around the world

KEY FOCUS

This sections puts into a global perspective some of what you have learned about religion in Britain. It considers the rise of fundamentalism in some countries, and the different style and strength of religion in the USA.

...SO SEND ALL YOUR MONEY TO ME, THE REVEREND...

Televangelism – a new way of reaching the masses ... and raising money.

Secularisation? The global picture

In the last section, we considered the evidence for and against secularisation, focusing on Britain. When we look at religion globally, the picture is rather different. Britain and some other western societies do seem to have seen a decline in the importance of religion, at least for some sections of their populations. This is not true, however, for most of the world – and not for the USA or for one particular part of Britain, Northern Ireland. Britain, with its falling church attendance and absence of religion from public life, is more the exception than the rule.

Religion on the rise

There are some countries where religion is becoming stronger:

- Countries where Islam has become stronger in recent years – Afghanistan, Iran, Algeria, Nigeria.
- India – a strongly Hindu political party is in power.
- Russia – since the end of communism in 1989, there has been a huge revival of the Orthodox Church.
- China – the Falun Gong sect claims to have about 100 million members, nearly twice as many as the Communist Party.

Fundamentalism

Some of the religious revivals of recent years can be described as fundamentalist. Religious **fundamentalism** is when followers of a religion insist on the absolute truth of their sacred books (for example the Bible in Christianity and the Qu'ran in Islam). Fundamentalism is very conservative; it puts forward traditional ideas and does not allow them to be questioned. Fundamentalists see other versions of their religions as too tolerant and open to change. They reject any possibility of understanding or working with followers of other religions. There is, to them, only one true faith, and all who do not believe are to be despised or pitied.

Characteristics of fundamentalism

- Sacred books seen as literally true.
- Intolerant of other religions and of science – only the sacred book is true.
- Believe in a personal experience of god – for example in the Christian fundamentalist idea of being 'born again'.
- Right-wing beliefs such as opposition to equality for women and homosexuals.

Why fundamentalism?

Fundamentalism emerges in response to problems. It has a strong appeal in countries where many people live in poverty and feel threatened by change. It provides something to hang on to and reasserts traditional values.

The USA

Church membership is much higher in the USA than in Britain. About half the American population attend church at least once a month and about two-thirds claim to be members of a church (*Sociology* by J. Fulcher and J. Scott, Oxford University Press, 1999); 95 per cent say they believe in a god. Many Americans believe in the literal truth of the Bible. Many believe the creation myth in the Bible rather than the scientific theories of evolution.

Civil religion

The sociologist Robert Bellah argued that above all the religions in the United States and linking them together was a **civil religion**. In this the religious content has been reduced to a level almost everyone can agree on.

This civil religion, argued Bellah, is present in American patriotism, in the singing of the national anthem, in the pledging of allegiance to the flag and so on. These everyday rituals carry out one of the main functions of religion identified by functionalists (see the section What is religion? on pages 376–7). The United States is very multicultural, with people from many different backgrounds, so a single church cannot bring everyone together. Instead the civil religion of Americanism is broad enough to give everyone, whatever their religion, a sense of belonging. Americanism, like a religion, has its own saints, its sacred places, its ceremonies and myths about its heroic figures.

Americanism

The following have become sacred in America's civil religion:

- 'Saints' – Washington, Lincoln, Kennedy, Davy Crockett.
- 'Sacred Places' – the Statue of Liberty, the Lincoln Memorial.
- 'Ceremonies' – the Fourth of July, Memorial Day.
- 'Myths about heroes' – the Battle of the Alamo; the wagon trains opening up the frontier.

FIND OUT FOR YOURSELF

Is there a civil religion in Britain? If so, is it as strong as Americanism? What are its saints, sacred places, ceremonies and myths about its heroes? If you live in Wales or Scotland, see if you can work out what would make up a Welsh or Scottish civil religion.

Televangelism

In the USA, religious television channels have become important. They are usually built around a charismatic preacher whose version of Christianity is evangelical or fundamentalist. Several preachers have used television to establish what can be called '**electronic churches**', reaching their followers through television rather than the traditional means of church meetings. This is called **televangelism**. It is strongly associated with right-wing politics.

About 5 per cent of the American population watch such channels regularly, and many more tune in occasionally. Programmes include appeals for donations, and some churches and preachers have been able to raise many millions of dollars in this way. There have, however, been several cases of fraud and of adultery which discredited some televangelists.

Until recently, there have been few openings for televangelists in Europe. As the number of available television channels expands, there is likely to be scope for televangelism. One religious channel which already exists is the God Christian Channel. Its aim is to make 'real Christians' out of Catholics, Anglicans and Methodists. This indicates its fundamentalist position.

Despite their use of television, evangelical and fundamentalist Christians in the USA see most of the mass media as destroying moral values. The following is an extract from a film guide on a US web site for Christians.

- '*Star Wars: The Phantom Menace*: New Age pagan world view with strong, moral elements, many mystic teachings and some occult elements where characters have magical powers, including ESP, mind control and foretelling the future without the power of the Holy Spirit. *CAUTION*
- *South Park: Bigger, Longer and Uncut*: Anti-Christian, anti-God, anti-morality, intentionally immoral with the most vile content in the history of mainstream movie making; 340 counted obscenities ... rebellion, theft, lying, cheating and a surplusage of other depraved content. This is a blasphemous, evil movie. *EVIL*'

Crosswalk.com at http://movieguide.crosswalk.com, quoted in *Guardian Editor*, 23 July 1999.

QUESTIONS

1. What is meant by a civil religion?
2. What is meant by televangelism?
3. Identify and explain two characteristics of religious fundamentalism.
4. Do you think televangelism would be successful in Britain? Give reasons for your answer.
5. Religion in Britain is weaker than in most other countries. Do you agree? Give reasons for your answer.

ROUND-UP

Across much of the world, religion is as strong and as important as ever. Fundamentalism has grown in some countries recently, in reaction against social change. The USA is strongly religious and fundamentalist Christianity is strong, helped by televangelism.

VOCABULARY

Profanities: swearing by using religious terms (such as god) inappropriately

Religion and social change

This section looks at the roles religion can play in preventing or making possible social change, at religion in conflicts around the world and at how religion has at times been used by poor and oppressed peoples to express their grievances.

Religion lies at the heart of many conflicts.

Religion and conflict

Religion plays a part in many of the wars and conflicts around the world:

- Middle East – Jerusalem is a holy city for Jews, Christians and Muslims. It is controlled by Israel, the Jewish nation state, and this is a continuing source of conflict between Israelis and Muslims in neighbouring countries. Nearly a thousand years ago, there was a series of wars – the Crusades – in which Christian invaders from Europe tried to take Jerusalem from the Muslims.
- Northern Ireland – at present there is an unstable peace after nearly 30 years of war. The two sides are divided by religion as well as by political differences. The Catholic community favours being part of the Irish Republic while the Protestant community wants to stay part of Britain.
- Former Yugoslavia – in the series of wars in the 1990s that followed the disintegration of the nation state of Yugoslavia, Christians and Muslims were often on different sides.

Religion prevents conflict

Look back at functionalism, Marxism and religion in the first section in this chapter (see What is religion?, pages 376–7). You will see that these theories agree that religion tends to prevent social change, although they disagree about whether this is a good thing or not.

For functionalists, religion provides a common set of values which makes everyone feel they belong to a community. This leads to a stable society which need only change gradually.

For Marxists, religion is a form of social control by which the working class is kept in its place by the ruling class. The working class accepts the way things are, and does not revolt – so religion again leads to stability. But this is seen by Marxists as wrong because the working class is being fooled. To use a Marxist term, the working class is in a state of false consciousness.

The two other theoretical approaches introduced in the first section also see religion as making societies stable and preventing change. The New Right sees religion as a force that can hold back the moral degeneration of societies. Feminists see religion as a form of social control by which men prevent women achieving a more equal society.

Religion causes change

Some sociologists, however, point to examples from history where religion has clearly played a part in social change. Sometimes, of course, the rise of a religion is itself an important part of social change. Christianity began as a small sect persecuted by the authorities of the time (the Roman Empire), spreading revolutionary ideas. Eventually, the Roman Empire itself became Christian, and Christianity became a large and respectable church, rather than a sect.

This example suggests that religion can be used by poor and oppressed people. Religion can provide comfort, and the strength to carry on against great odds. Slaves in the USA adopted the Christianity of the slave owners, yet adapted it to their needs and their culture, adding music and dance from West Africa. Biblical stories about the return to the promised land gave hope and strength to many. They found that the religion of the slave owners could be turned against them to argue for the abolition of slavery.

Religion also played a big part in the campaign to end the apartheid system in South Africa, and in bringing about the end of communism in Poland.

Around the world, many religious people are involved in campaigns to improve the conditions of the world's poor. Some charities and agencies are openly religious (for example Christian Aid), while those that are not often draw a lot of their support from religious people.

Liberation theology

In the 1960s and 1970s a number of Catholic priests in South America took a stand against poverty. Young, idealistic priests working in poor communities felt it was their duty to protest, to side with the poor against their oppressors. They justified their actions by referring to the Bible, and to what they said Jesus would have done in their situation. They saw Jesus as a revolutionary person fighting slavery and injustice. They said that oppression was wrong, according to Christian values, and that it could be prevented. It was therefore their duty as Christians to take a stand – and even, some said, to fight.

This was a radical reinterpretation of Christianity, one which was strongly influenced by Marxist ideas. It is known as **liberation theology**. Some priests went as far as to support or even fight with revolutionary guerrillas. Some lost their lives; a famous example is Bishop Oscar Romero, archbishop of San Salvador, murdered in his cathedral because he spoke out against the government of El Salvador.

At the same time, as some priests were standing up for the poor (and risking their lives), the hierarchy of the church opposed them and supported the governments which the revolutionaries wanted to overthrow. Pope John Paul II condemned liberation theology. This illustrates the two-sided nature of religion: it can be used to support and justify the way things are, yet it can also be used to support and justify radical attempts to change the system.

Weber: religion and social change

A different view of the relationship between religion and social change was put forward by the German sociologist Max Weber. Weber studied how religion influenced the development of our present economic system. He concluded that religious ideas, even held by a fairly small group, could have far-reaching effects.

Weber studied a Puritan sect known as the Calvinists, followers of John Calvin in the seventeenth century. Earlier Christians who had been successful in business had spent their money, for example on large houses and luxuries. One particular belief of the Calvinists led them to behave differently.

This belief was predestination, that, even before someone was born, God had decided 0whether they were to be saved or damned. The only way people could find out what their fate was by how successful they were in their work. Calvinism approved of hard work and a simple life style. The result was that the values of Calvinists were, by chance, those that helped them succeed in business. Calvinists were the first capitalists, investing their profits in their business instead of spending them. They made our capitalist economic system possible – quite unintentionally. Weber called Calvinist ideas the Protestant ethic, and said that they fitted the spirit of capitalism.

QUESTIONS

1 What is meant by liberation theology?

2 Name one region of the world where religion is a source of conflict. Explain your choice.

3 Give two examples from history of the use of religion by poor or oppressed people.

4 What are the similarities and differences between the functionalist and Marxist views of religion and social change?

5 Why, according to Weber, did Calvinism help create the capitalist economic system?

ROUND-UP

Religion sometimes is a conservative force, preventing change, yet it can also be the cause of far-reaching social changes. It can be used by the poor and oppressed to give voice to their grievances, and it motivates the more fortunate to help others.

VOCABULARY

Disintegration: the breaking up into smaller parts
Abolition: putting an end to
Guerrillas: volunteer fighters against a stronger regular army

Religion – sociology in practice

Christmas – for all?

NEARLY 3 million Britons of other faiths face a dilemma at Christmas. Muslim, Hindu, Sikh and Jewish families are surrounded by carol-singing, Christmas decoration, Santa Claus and the Nativity. If they let their children take part, will they become confused about their own faith? For Jews and Muslims, the idea that God could take a human form (Jesus in Christianity) is totally unacceptable. Should they try to protect their children from the festivities?

Dilip Kadodwala (a Hindu, with two sons aged eight and six): 'Hindus … see Christ as another incarnation of God to show us the right path. I try to inculcate in my children a sense of the family of religions and that they are not all at odds with each other … We will give the boys presents but we try to encourage them to see them as New Year presents because I want them to remember the religious message of Christmas … and to be a bit sceptical about all the materialism. We also talk about Mother Christmas to get away from some of the patriarchy. That is less problematic in the Hindu pantheon which has female gods.'

'Christmas comes once a year – to all',
Guardian,
23 December 1996.

Questions

1. Look back at the section on Religion in Britain today (pages 392–3) for information on the religions of minority ethnic groups. What dilemmas face non-Christian families at Christmas time in Britain and why?

2. Look back at the section on Gender and religion (pages 390–91). For Mr Kadodwala, one of the strengths of Hinduism is that it has female gods. In what ways can Christianity be seen as a patriarchal religion?

3. Has Christmas become too materialistic and less religious? Design a questionnaire and find out from members of your sociology class what they think.

Rastafarianism

Rastafarianism was brought to the world's attention by the reggae music of Bob Marley. It dates back, however, to Jamaica in the 1920s. It is based on the Old Testament, seeing black people as like the Israelites in exile. Rastafarianism teaches that black people have to return to Africa if they are to be saved from exploitation and poverty. Jamaica (to which Africans were taken as slaves) and countries like Britain represent 'Babylon', places of evil from which the chosen people must flee and return to the promised land. Rastafarianism has a distinctive style, with hair worn in long dreadlocks and use of the colour combination of red, gold, green and black. Its approval of marihuana use brings it into conflict with authority.

Rastafarianism has been very attractive to Afro-Caribbean men in Britain and elsewhere. It mixes religion and politics, and can be a way of expressing resistance towards white authority and racism.

Questions

1. Rastafarianism is a sect. Look back at the section on Churches and sects (pages 382–3). What typical characteristics of a sect does Rastafarianism show?

2. Look back at the section on What is religion? (pages 376–7), and particularly at the Marxist view of religion. In what ways does Rastafarianism suggest that religion need not always be 'the opium of the people'?

3. Find and listen to reggae music which has Rastafarian lyrics, for example by Bob Marley and the Wailers, Burning Spear, Culture, Third World and Steel Pulse. Collect from the lyrics quotations which express Rastafarian ideas.

Religion on television

Until 1993, both BBC1 and ITV were required to transmit religious programmes at the same time on Sunday evenings. These were *Songs of Praise* on BBC1 and *Stars on Sunday* and *Highway* on ITV. Total viewing figures were around 14 million, about what would be expected for prime-time slots. The audiences tended to be mainly churchgoers, with women and older people over represented.

In 1993 this requirement was ended, although both channels still have to have some religious content. As a result religious programmes have much less airtime.

Questions

1 Look back to the section on Secularisation (pages 394–5). How can the information above be seen as evidence in the debate about secularisation?

2 Why are churchgoers more likely to be older and to be women? Is this pattern the same for all religions in Britain?

3 How much religious programming is there on television now? Look at the section on Content analysis in Chapter 12 (pages 296–7). Carry out a content analysis of religious programming on all terrestrial channels on a Sunday, using television listings for that day. After you have done this, consider whether, given the numbers of people who attend church and who have religious beliefs, followers of religions are adequately provided for on television.

Religion – important terms

charismatic	describes someone who has a powerful personality, able to inspire others, typical of some religious leaders
church	a large, structured religious organisation
civil religion	a set of beliefs and rituals with little religious content, but fulfilling the function of religion by bringing together all citizens of a country
cult	a small, loose religious grouping
denomination	a fairly large structured organisation which does not claim a monopoly on the truth
electronic church	an organisation in which the leader reaches his or her followers largely by television (or the Internet)
fundamentalism	the return to a purer and stricter form of a religion
lay	not of the church
liberation theology	the belief that Christianity must involve opposing exploitation and oppression
monotheistic	a type of religion in which there is only one god
New Age	beliefs in a wide range of spiritual and supernatural ideas
New Religious Movements	new organisations, usually like sects
polytheistic	a type of religion in which there are many gods
profane	to do with daily, non-sacred life
religiosity	the measure of how religious someone is
sacred	to do with religion and the gods
sect	a small organisation with strong beliefs, usually keeping itself separate from the world
secularisation	the process of a society becoming less religious
syncretic	a new religion which combines elements of two or more older religions
televangelism	preaching by television, associated with right-wing evangelical Christianity in the USA

Religion – exam-style questions

Source A

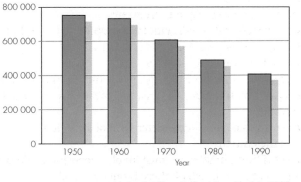

Methodist decline

Methodist Church; Sociology Update 1997.

The Methodist church's membership is declining faster than that of any other Christian denomination.

Lower tier

1 How many people belonged to the Methodist church in 1990?   [2 marks]

2 What is the name given by sociologists to the decline in importance of religion?   [3 marks]

3 What is meant by a denomination? Use an example to illustrate your answer.   [4 marks]

4 Using sociological knowledge, give two reasons why the membership of Christian churches and denominations has been falling.   [5 marks]

5 Do you agree that religion is in decline? Give two sociological reasons for your answer.   [6 marks]

Higher tier

1 What is the name given by sociologists to the decline in importance of religion?   [2 marks]

2 What is meant by a denomination? Use an example to illustrate your answer.   [3 marks]

3 Using sociological knowledge, give two reasons why the membership of Christian churches and denominations has been falling.   [5 marks]

4 Is religion in decline? Consider the evidence both for and against.   [10 marks]

Religion – further research

The BBC site has a religion section: www.bbc.co.uk/religion. As well as news on religion, there is a section on the main religions in Britain.

Index